ENTERTAINMENT MARKETING & COMMUNICATION

ENTERTAINMENT MARKETING & COMMUNICATION

Selling Branded Performance, People, and Places

Shay Sayre

California State University—Fullerton

PEARSON
Prentice Hall

Upper Saddle River, New Jersey,   07458

Library of Congress Cataloging-in-Publication Data

Sayre, Shay.
  Entertainment marketing & communication : selling branded performance, people, and places / Shay Sayre.
    p. cm.
  ISBN 0-13-198622-8 (13: 978-0-13-198622-0) 1. Leisure industry—United States—Marketing. 2. Performing arts—United States—Marketing. 3. Entertainment events—United States—Marketing. 4. Amusements—United States—Marketing. 5. Tourism—United States—Marketing. 6. Recreation—United States—Marketing. 7. Consumer behavior—United States. 8. Communication in marketing—United States. I. Title. II. Title: Entertainment marketing and communication.
  GV188.3.U6S29 2008
  790.2—dc22

                                                                                    2007024980

Editor in Chief: David Parker
Product Development Manager: Ashley Santora
Project Manager: Melissa Pellerano
Editorial Assistant: Christine Ietto
Marketing Manager: Jodi Bassett
Senior Managing Editor: Judy Leale
Permissions Coordinator: Charles Morris
Operations Specialist: Arnold Vila
Cover Design: Bruce Kenselaar
Cover Photo: Getty Images, Inc.
Director, Image Resource Center: Melinda Patelli
Manager, Rights and Permissions: Zina Arabia
Manager, Visual Research: Beth Brenzel
Manager, Cover Visual Research & Permissions: Karen Sanatar
Image Permission Coordinator: Kathy Gavilanes
Composition: ICC Macmillan Inc.
Full-Service Project Management: ICC Macmillan Inc.
Printer/Binder: R.R. Donnelley/Harrisonburg
Typeface: Times 10/12

Credits and acknowledgments borrowed from other sources and reproduced, with permission, in this textbook appear on the appropriate page within the text.

Pearson Education LTD.
Pearson Education Singapore, Pte. Ltd
Pearson Education, Canada, Ltd
Pearson Education–Japan

Pearson Education Australia PTY, Limited
Pearson Education North Asia Ltd
Pearson Educación de Mexico, S.A. de C.V.
Pearson Education Malaysia, Pte. Ltd.

10 9 8 7 6 5 4 3 2 1
ISBN-13: 978-0-13-198622-0
ISBN-10: 0-13-198622-8

This book is dedicated to my children Aubyn and Ryan, my grandson Sage, my mom, and my husband Dennis.

Brief Contents

Table of Contents

Preface

Entertainment Marketing & Communication: Selling Branded Performance, People, and Places is the first textbook to focus specifically on entertainment marketing. We all love to be entertained, and entertainment is pervasive in our lives. As the communication world expands, our ability to receive and engage in entertainment experiences is continually improved. Because experience is sold as a commodity, marketing is key to selling tickets for those experiences. With this text, students of marketing and communication can now share the secrets and benefit from the insights of today's entertainment professionals. It is a ticket to marketing success.

The goal of *Entertainment Marketing & Communication* is to invite you in, to allow you, the student or the practitioner, to really experience and adapt the principles of marketing and communication theory to the entertainment industry. This book provides not only a wealth of content, but it also offers a clear and up-to-date framework for you to use in *applying marketing principles to the entertainment world*.

Structure and Organization

This book's *marketing communications framework* is grounded in four key perspectives:

1. **Theoretical or principles perspective:** Theories underlie the study of communication, and marketing principles serve as models for developing new and interactive techniques.

2. **Behavioral perspective:** Principles of consumer behavior and audience motivation provide real understanding of why and how people use entertainment.

3. **Implementation perspective:** Planning and strategy development are tools of marketing and communication that enable students to directly apply their knowledge.

4. **Evaluative perspective:** The message only gets across completely through real-life examples. Five case studies provide great opportunities to analyze and critique what is really happening today in entertainment marketing.

Entertainment Marketing & Communication also integrates the perspectives of and important insights from two related fields:

1. **Communications:** This area of study recognizes the critical need to develop persuasive and effective communication among audiences, consumers, and employees.

2. **Interactive technology:** This field plays a vital role for both marketing and communicating about entertainment.

The text is divided into five parts, each focusing on key areas of entertainment marketing.

Part 1: The Entertainment Industry provides a contextual introduction by characterizing today's *experience culture.*

Part 2: Entertainment Audiences and Audience Research guides you through the theory and practice of specific methods and looks at approaches to audience segmentation and research.

Part 3: Applying Marketing and Communications Principles to the Entertainment Industry focuses on branding, integrated communications, promotion, and campaign planning.

Part 4: Industry Applications covers marketing applications for five areas: live performance and events, destinations and tourist services, attractions and themed spaces, mediated entertainment, and stars and celebrities.

Part 5: Case Studies from the Real World of Experiential Entertainment presents five detailed cases related directly to the applications presented in Part 4. They include marketing for a performance venue, a luxury resort brand, a theme park, a film brand, and a celebrity.

▪▪▪ Chapter Highlights

Specialized features in each chapter build a learning framework for practitioners and students of marketing and communication:

- *Focus on ...* features highlight and expand upon specific areas of chapter content.
- *Focus on Ethics* allows readers to see both sides of an ethical issue generated within the realm of entertainment marketing.
- *Focus on Careers* presents profiles of men and women who hold entry and mid-level positions in the entertainment industry.
- *A Closer Look* provides in-depth exploration of a real-world situation brought to light in the chapter.
- *Now Try This,* at the end of each chapter, promotes better understanding of content by engaging readers in interactive and experiential activities.
- *Questions: Let's Review* provide a platform for verbal debate and student engagement.

▪▪▪ Faculty Resources

Instructors can access a variety of print, media, and presentation resources through www.prenhall.com/sayre.

▪▪▪ Acknowledgments

My thinking and writing about entertainment has been shaped in important ways by my colleagues in the Department of Communications at California State University–Fullerton, who developed one of the first entertainment majors in the country. I want especially to acknowledge Fred Zandpour, Coral Ohl, Cynthia King, and Mary Joyce.

Consulting to and working in the promotion industry provided me with an indispensable source of insight and learning. I am grateful for my experience with Young & Rubicam Advertising and Gail Stoorza Public Relations, where I served as an account executive for entertainment-based clients.

I commend Development Editor Trish Nealon and Editorial Project Manager Melissa Pellerano for their encouragement. And finally, I thank the reviewers who provided guidance and direction throughout the text development process.

About the Author

Shay Sayre has experience promoting many aspects of the entertainment and tourism business, beginning with McGraw-Hill publishing in New York City, where she produced promotional materials for trade books. Sayre has acted as an account executive at Young & Rubicam Advertising, promoting films for clients such as Paramount Pictures, and representing 3M's product division. As an account planner for a public relations agency in San Diego, Sayre handled promotions for a celebrity tennis resort and the city's convention and business bureau. She directed marketing for the San Diego Symphony and promotions for PSA Airlines before receiving her Ph.D. from the University of San Diego.

Since 1986, Sayre has been a professor with the California State University System at San Francisco, San Jose, and Fullerton. She has taught graduate courses for Emerson College in Brussels; for Queensland University of Technology in Brisbane, Australia; and for Fullerton's M.A. degree program in Hong Kong.

Her previous books include *Entertainment and Society: Audience, Trends & Impacts* (Sage, 2003), *Qualitative Methods for Marketplace Research* (Sage, 2001), and *Campaign Planner for Integrated Brand Communications* (Thompson/South-Western, 2006). Professor Sayre also has published in prestigious academic journals, including the *Journal of Advertising; Consumption, Markets, Culture;* and *Advances in Consumer Research,* and has presented papers at marketing conferences worldwide.

Introduction

Marketing an Experience

We live in an entertainment society. Today, our experiences are as important as our possessions, and activities occupy our attention. Our very identities are linked with what we choose to experience. Our challenge as marketers is to promote entertainment experiences to audiences whose options and tastes vary widely. Not a product, not a service, real-time entertainment is an *involved experience.* One can locate it, buy tickets for it, travel to it, and participate in it.

Marketers are responsible for attracting audiences. Entertainment marketing communications tell audiences not just how to access entertainment, but also how to experience it. To attract, develop, and maintain entertainment consumers, communication must motivate people to attend events presented at *specific venues.* Ticket sales, subscriptions, or booked travel are marketers' goals. We never lose sight of the reality that entertainment is a business with an accountable bottom line.

The entertainment industry is divided into live and mediated forms. Live entertainment includes sports, music, gaming, tourism, hospitality, and recreation. Mediated entertainment, or entertainment presented through media, includes print, broadcast, film, and Internet experiences.

To present a manageable analysis of these experiences, they must be defined; boundaries must be drawn to distinguish them from other marketed entities. To do this, we focus on aspects of entertainment performed in or at specific venues and for which tickets are sold. Our job is to sell experiences and the places audiences go to enjoy them—theaters, stadiums, resorts, museums, festival grounds, concert halls, amusement parks, comedy clubs, casinos, and even malls.

How Did We Get Here?

From a historical perspective, nonmediated entertainment has been around since the beginning of human culture. Music, sports, and gaming were the first forms of entertainment developed for public amusement. Theater, music and dance performance, and gaming are outgrowths of ancient rituals that have metamorphosed into billion-dollar industries.

Games and sports originated as forms of play. Cave paintings indicate that early *homo sapiens* played games of sport long before the Olympic games were developed.

Chariot races took place in ancient Greece long before horse racing became a popular waging activity in the United States. Spectator sports remain one of the world's most popular categories of games and are a billion dollar industry today.

Games are based on a mathematical theory that helps us understand rules and strategy. Gaming today accounts for billions of dollars in business revenues. Technology has taken games and sports beyond their original forms, providing us with the ability to accurately calculate probability and chance, to play games online, and to witness sports events in the comfort of our homes.

Music developed and entertained early. Leisure activity began as a way to reduce the drudgery of farming and labor. Songs were sung in fields to music produced with primitive instruments such as drums and bone whistles. Musical festivities are recorded as early as Neolithic times. Musical instruments were first known to be produced in about 5000 B.C, in Asia Minor, where they were played to entertain lords and warriors. Today, many of us play and/or enjoy instruments that have added acoustics to traditional structures. As we download songs onto our iPods by the thousands or attend mega-concerts given by our favorite performers, we may still whistle while we work.

Theater was formalized in ancient Greece. Theater, one of the greatest contributions to leisure-time entertainment, was first performed in outdoor amphitheaters for thousands of Greeks. Dramatic festivals were so popular in Athens that business was suspended and prisoners were allowed to attend stage performances. Live theater still flourishes, but many plays are adapted for the large screen, which has moved from movie theaters to in-home theaters via DVD technology.

Today, entertainment is an outgrowth of leisure time. So, how did we arrive at our current condition, in which our entertainment experiences mirror our identities? The more time people have to spend away from work, the more sophisticated entertainment becomes. We will see how the ancient human need to entertain and be entertained has combined with the outgrowth of leisure time to develop the entertainment industry.

▪▪▪ Approaching Entertainment as an Area of Study

This book presents the principles and practices for developing marketing strategies, mediated communications, and promotional messages for the entertainment industry. It creates a single comprehensive source for the entertainment marketing discipline. Its topics are based on the activities that consumers spend on and enjoy, and that have existed for some time. Perhaps most important, however, this book covers in-depth activities that have not been the focus of other entertainment marketing resources.

Any author who is writing a textbook for a relatively new field faces a major challenge, and that is *choosing a vernacular of expression.* In this case, so many words exist for *entertainment* that it becomes almost a catch-all for everything we do in life outside work and responsibilities. Experience-based entertainment seems to rule out pure viewing, but there is no question that couch potatoes receive gratification from the watching experience. Words for marketing, promotion, integration, and communications all have application for entertainment but in ways that differ from other products and services.

So, to get a handle on this problem, we have segmented the entertainment industry into five manageable units. These *experiential genres* are segments of the entertainment industry that require *active participation by an audience.* Participation in all activities within these experiential genres requires payment for access or entry, such as purchasing tickets or subscriptions. (Television is somewhat of an exception, both because participation is not so active and tickets are not purchased, although cable subscription is payment for access.) Although they appear in various chapters, sports, music, print media, radio, and video games are not treated here in any depth because these topics are amply covered in other texts.

This text approaches entertainment marketing by defining these five experiential genres and their subsets. The genres and subsets are not always mutually exclusive; for instance, resorts are often located at theme parks, and there is an overlap between Hollywood and film. However, for our purposes here, the text adheres to the typology presented below.

Experiential Genre Typology

Live Performance	Destinations & Tourist Services	Venues & Themed Spaces	Mediated Entertainment	Stars & Celebrities
Concerts	Resorts	Malls	Film	Star System
Drama, Comedy	Cruise Ships	Parks	Television	Fame
Circus, Dance	Destinations	Casinos	Internet	Celebrity
Opera	Tours	Museums	Radio	Fans

■■■ How *Entertainment Marketing* Is Organized

This book is divided into five parts that include fifteen chapters and five case studies. The text flows naturally from an industry introduction into an audience-based focus. Then general marketing aspects are applied to the industry, which prepares the reader to approach specific strategies for each of the five entertainment genre. Cases from each genre give students an opportunity to test their understanding of the text by applying solutions to real-life problems. This general-to-specific approach allows students to build and expand their understanding of how entertainment differs from other types of marketing practices.

In *Part One,* we introduce the concepts of leisure and play, two elements essential for facilitating the emergence of experiential consumption. Mergers and conversions occupy their own chapter to set the stage for how industry structures change. Our definition of entertainment as it relates to a marketing mission accompanies discussion of the special characteristics of entertainment marketing and how it differs from product and most service marketing. We emphasize the importance of venues for entertainment experiences, subscription and ticket sales, donations and purchase pricing strategies, online delivery systems, and the nature of *servicecapes.* Entertainment industry ethics are introduced here as well.

Part Two is dedicated to the characterization of entertainment audiences and audience research. We define audiences and explore the nature of people who watch, cheer on, and participate in real-time entertainment. Audiences are profiled by their involvement and motivations, and are segmented by benefit, lifestyle, and demographics. We meet the people, whom we call *prosumers,* who bring new behavior to entertainment consumption. The role of niche marketing and global lifestyle segments are discussed next, followed by methods of studying and measuring audience behavior. We detail qualitative and quantitative research methods and their role for understanding entertainment consumers. Audience and media measurement factors are evaluated for their usefulness in campaign evaluation. Tools for analyzing Internet audiences are also included here.

Part Three provides the nuts and bolts of marketing and integrated communications. We revisit the 5Ps and 4Cs of entertainment as they apply to experiential marketing and branding. The concept of integrated and convergent marketing and promotional communication is expanded upon, including brand positioning and brand objectives. We conclude by explaining how to use market research for planning strategies and provide some "how-tos" for developing a comprehensive integrated marketing communications (IMC) campaign, including evaluation methods such as exit polling, attendance measures, and revenue indicators.

In *Part Four,* each of the experience genres is discussed at length. Marketing live performances—what's on stage and what's on tour—begins the section. Then, principles of resort, casino, and cruise ship promotion are presented, including how to attract guests and patrons, deliver travel services, and promote destination cities and countries. Next, we explore the marketing of attractions and discuss the role of *theming.* Mediated entertainment, specifically movies and television program promotion, is included next for its importance to the industry. Finally, we look at the role of stars and celebrities as brands and their importance for box office draw.

To help you apply the concepts presented in this text, *Part Five* features case studies that correspond to the five entertainment genres covered in Part Four. Examples are drawn from original campaigns developed for a performance center, luxury destination, amusement park, film brand, and entertainment celebrity.

In our postscript, we speculate about the nature of future audiences of entertainment and how technology will continue to change entertainment delivery. You will find Web resources throughout the text to help with your research and marketing problems.

Each chapter begins with a set of objectives in question form; discussions are supplemented with illustrations, tables, and *Focus on . . .* and *A Closer Look* features. Summary points, things to do, questions for discussion, and additional readings also enhance chapter presentations.

▪ ▪ ▪ The Result

After completing this text, you should have a thorough understanding of how to identify and attract audiences, promote experiences, and generate revenues for real-time entertainment and its performance venues. Our hope is that this text provides you with useful marketing direction, a sense of excitement about the industry, and fodder for further discussion with fellow students. Your generation will determine just where the future of entertainment lies. By grounding yourself in the principles and ethics of the business as presented here, you should have a good start at making a difference in the industry and business of entertainment.

CHAPTER 1

And Leisure Begot Entertainment

[Leisure] is better than occupation and is its end;
and therefore the question must be asked,
What ought we to do when at leisure?
— ARISTOTLE

Chapter Objectives

After reading this chapter, you should be able to answer the following questions:

- *What is* entertainment marketing?
- How is marketing entertainment *different* from marketing products and services?
- How does the concept of *play* figure into entertainment marketing?
- How does today's entertainment *environment* work?
- What *codes of ethics* exist in today's entertainment industry?

Let the Excitement Begin!

The average American spends more money on entertainment than on gasoline, household furnishings, and clothing, and spends nearly the same amount on entertainment as on dining out.[1] Among affluent consumers, more money is spent on entertainment than on health care, utilities, clothing, and food eaten at home together. People west of the Mississippi River spend about 20 percent more on entertainment than the national average.

What are the best entertainment buys? On a dollar-to-minutes-of-enjoyment basis, video games are a good value, at about 12.5 cents a minute (or fractions of a penny for those who can play "Half Life" their entire lives). The worst value in this sense is live opera: A middling seat in the New York Metropolitan Opera House to experience *Aida* costs about 37 cents a minute. The best value might be a seat at a Loews Cineplex to see *Harry Potter and the Goblet of Fire,* which costs a viewer only 7 cents a minute.[2]

People do not make entertainment decisions based on costs alone, however. Many variables are at play. The point is this: with such huge amounts of money being spent on entertainment, marketers must meet the competitive challenge to bring both afford-able and enjoyable options to global audiences.

But the way we think about entertainment products—movies, music, TV programs, video games, or words (books, magazines)—must now be regarded as composite bits of information that can be produced and processed and distributed as a series of digits that represent sounds and pictures and texts. Why? Because, today, technological development provides a common tool for all marketing efforts generated to promote entertainment products.

▮▮▮ This Is Entertainment Marketing

We begin with a look at the foundations of entertainment experiences before they metamorphosed into today's box office draws. At the heart of entertainment is the concept of *leisure*. The historical concepts of *performance* and *game playing* are also crucial to understanding the meaning of leisure in contemporary life. Derived from the Latin word *licere,* which means to be free, leisure has been described as a variety of state-of-mind characteristics. For Aristotle, the term implied both availability of time and an absence of occupation; in fact, he believed that absence of occupation is what leads to happiness.

In a historical framework, once people could satisfy their basic survival needs, something resembling leisure time was time left over. Leisure activity began as a way to reduce the drudgery of farming and labor. Factory workers in the industrial age escaped the dreariness of assembly lines by playing card games during their breaks.

More formal entertainment traces its beginnings to performance and games of skill. Whether these activities were practiced as religious, mystical, or cultural rituals, they developed into the theater, games, and sporting events we enjoy today. Street per-formers advanced to acting on stage; stone-kicking became a game with rules and fans; migration evolved into travel and tourism.

Today, the term **leisure** is broadly used to designate time not spent at work in a profession or an occupation in pursuit of compensation, or in taking care of children and the household. Free time is no longer a time reserved for contemplation, nor is it the purview of an elite society. To the contrary, contemporary leisure is time used for going places and doing things. All sorts of consumption activities containing significant elements of amusement and diversion are now considered to be **entertainment**. Thus, **entertainment marketing** simply consists of the techniques and strategies developed to sell tickets to (or otherwise elicit payment for) activities that amuse and involve us.

Leisure Becomes Big Business

An attraction to entertainment is based in human needs that have evolved with time. People who pursue leisure activities are consumers in the entertainment industry, and entertainment consumers expect what they purchase to produce a pleasurable and sat-isfying experience. So, marketers must address psychological and emotional factors as well as physical and mental ones. Available time has become a primary commodity in our attention-based economy, so the demand for leisure is affected by the cost of time to produce and consume entertainment products. As such, the cost of time and

Tickets provide access to multiple forms of entertainment experiences.

consumption-time intensity (or "bang for the buck") are significant factors for consumers who select among entertainment alternatives.

Since the Industrial Revolution more than a century ago, leisure time in the United States has steadily increased. Although the average work week has not changed dramatically over the last several decades, packaging the time set aside for leisure has naturally evolved from standardized hours toward more long holiday weekends and extra vacation days rather than toward reducing the hours worked every week. As a result, personal consumption expenditures for entertainment are likely to be intense and compressed into smaller components instead of being evenly spaced throughout the year.

Another factor in the growing demand for entertainment is the three broad demographic shifts that have occurred in the past decade. These show (1) the emergence of a technologically savvy teenage audience, (2) an increase in the entertainment demands of 18–34 year olds, (3) and a continuation of spending on leisure among baby boomers (35–64). Aggregate spending on entertainment is concentrated in the middle-age groups, whose income is peaking at the same time leisure may be relatively scarce.

Statistics support the fact that today entertainment and leisure are big business. According to the *Fortune* 500 list of largest industries in 2006,[3] entertainment ranked 48th, with 1.8 percent revenue growth, and ranked 11th in profit growth since 2001 (20.6 percent). As the 17th most profitable industry, entertainment's return on revenues yielded an 8.4 percent profit revenue. Disney, News Corporation, CBS, and Viacom were listed as the largest entertainment media companies in this category. Hotels, resorts, and casinos ranked 14th largest, with revenue growth of 14.4 percent and a five-year profit growth of 9 percent (ranked 30th). The category yielded a 6.8 return on revenues, with Hilton as the largest company.

At the wholesale level, entertainment markets are now generating annual revenues exceeding $100 billion. Entertainment has consistently been one of the largest net export categories for the United States.[4] A notable trend of the 1980s was the association many consumers made between their identities and the brands and products they owned. In the twenty-first century, it is consuming experiences—*we are what we do and where we go to do it*—that may underlie consumer identity.

Exhibit 1.1 outlines historical milestones in the development of live and mediated entertainment into the business of entertainment as we know it today.

Leisure Triad

The way we pass our free time takes various forms, and each category of leisure addresses a particular need or function. We engage in three types of leisure activity: amusement, entertainment, and recreation; all of them are experiential.

Amusement consists of diversions such as games and the satisfaction derived from playing them. This chapter presents an overview of games and gambling because they play an important role in generating revenues around the world.

▪ ▪ ▪ **EXHIBIT 1.1 Entertainment Industry Milestones[1]**

Decade	Event
1930s	FM radio invented Federal Communications Commission formed to regulate broadcast content TV service begins with three networks
1940s	First computer developed for business use 331/3 rpm* vinyl recordings introduced First CATV system installed for residential use
1950s	Disneyland opens in Anaheim, California First satellite launched by Soviets for communications purposes
1960s	Sports Broadcasting Act passed by Congress FM popularized, AM relegated to news, talk
1970s	Disney World opens in Orlando, Florida Microprocessors introduced to facilitate smaller computers HBO begins satellite program distribution First home video game released for distribution Atlantic City legalizes casinos and gambling begins First VCR appears for Betamax formatted films CNN begins broadcasting 24 hour news
1980s	Compact discs introduced for personal use Mirage opens in Las Vegas, strip redevelopment grows
1990s	News Corporation distributes global TV programming Internet popularized; search engines develop Telecom deregulation permits new ownership potential Digital video discs popularized for film and music
2000s	Merging of advertising and entertainment functions Audience-produced content (blogs) invade the Internet Theming characterizes malls, restaurants, hotels, and parks Technology changes the way people communicate, enjoy entertainment, and control content

*revolutions per minute; 78 rpm and 45 rpm single-song records preceded the "long-playing" 331/3 rpm multiple-song record.

Entertainment refers to live and mediated performance experiences such as a concert, dance, or drama, including the pleasure received from viewing comedy or magic.

Recreation consists of activities or experiences carried on within leisure time, either for personal satisfaction or creative enrichment. The recreation industry developed as recreation activities for adults expanded and because more and more people seek a break from a cycle of boredom and fatigue. In later chapters, we will focus on marketing recreation destinations, such as the luxury resorts and spas consumers visit for health and relaxation, as well as the ways consumers experience travel and tourism.

Terminology

Although the leisure triad is used in some industry categorization, a better way to view the entertainment industry is as being content-based. Entertainment *content* comes to audiences in three distinct ways: as *live performance* (theater, musical concerts), as *interactive experience* (recreation, amusement parks, travel, gaming), and as *media* (movies, TV). For the purposes of this book, the term *experience* will characterize all forms of entertainment content. To market experiences, then, is to understand all the components of how audiences perceive experiences, and how experiences are promoted and measured.

How We Experience Entertainment

We experience entertainment in a variety of ways based on our participation and what we derive from the experience. The four realms of entertainment experience are: passive, educational, escapist, and esthetic. *Passive entertainment* occurs when people simply absorb an experience through their senses without much participation; this occurs when viewing a performance, listening to music, or reading. *Educational entertainment* requires the active engagement of the person's mind, the type of involvement that occurs with problem solving. By creating experiences that straddle the realms of education and entertainment, guests absorb the events unfolding before them while actively participating in them. *Escapist entertainment* experiences involve much greater immersion than other types of entertainment or educational experiences. Escapist

The aesthetics of a Parisian café.

entertainment is intended to provide a respite from real life in venues such as theme parks, casinos, and virtual reality games. In *esthetic entertainment,* audiences immerse themselves in a cultural experience with a visual component of the moment, such as standing at the rim of the Grand Canyon, visiting an art gallery or museum, or sitting in a Parisian café observing passers-by.[5]

As prologue to our discussion of marketing experiences, we need an overview of the theoretical principles that drive the entertainment industry and motivate its audiences. First, let's look at how entertainment marketing differs from marketing products and other services.

▪▪▪ What Makes Entertainment Marketing Unique

In a world where a plethora of media and distractions compete for our attention, that attention becomes a scarce resource. For some, obtaining attention is a way of obtaining positional wealth—publicity. Celebrities, for example, gain their status from entourages of fans who form around them, giving continual attention to celebrities' every move. An entertainer must get an audience's full attention to elicit positive responses, such as applause, good reviews and word of mouth, and, ultimately, the motivation to purchase more tickets.

Social needs and changing demographics require us to refocus on how we market entertainment experiences. To obtain audiences' attention, marketers must deal with the temporal aspects of entertainment brands, mainly *perishability* and *intangibility*.

Experiences Are Perishable

Changes in trends and tastes by entertainment consumers are continual. What's in this season is out the next. Because entertainment is a luxury, not a necessity, and because it must be available to audiences when they want it (not a minute sooner or later), entertainment providers are in a perennial contest to keep themselves alive. A product's shelf life lasts as long as audiences buy tickets. After that, the product is gone. Think of entertainment content as fruit that ripens, then rots. Once it is rotten, not one pays to own it!

Combining the best director, top acting talent, and fantastic set design does not, for instance, guarantee a Broadway success. Even after months of production and, in some cases, expenditures of millions of dollars, there are no guarantees that audiences will show up if a play receives bad reviews after its first performance. Similarly, if a film isn't a box office buster during its first weekend of release, distribution is reduced and the movie disappears from sight. The crucial time-bound aspect of entertainment is its **perishability**. As with fruit, experiences are time-sensitive, and they diminish in importance as time passes.

Experiences Are Intangible

We buy souvenirs of experience-based entertainment, but we cannot take home the experience itself. It is in our memory, not in our shopping bag. We may purchase a book, but the experience of reading is nonetheless mental. Although the book jacket and graphics may seduce us into buying the book, the experiential pleasure of that book lies in its verbal consumption.

Experiences are not investments, such as gold or art, and they are not consumables, such as shampoo. Experiences are **intangible**—of the moment and with ever-changing content. Products, on the other hand, have utilitarian or intrinsic value and have a presence. Likewise, services are performed for a price—dry-cleaning businesses clean your clothes, and insurance agencies protect your car. But neither products nor services are experienced in the same way that entertainment is. And that is what entertainment marketers sell—a piece of time requiring attention from participants.

Promoting intangible entertainment content and experiences is an entertainment marketer's biggest challenge. The value of the experience is predicated on an audience member's willingness to pay for the opportunity to turn his or her attention toward indulgence in a performance or activity. When was the last time you paid for an experience? If you think about the reasons for your purchase, you will begin to understand the role of marketing in motivating consumers to purchase an intangible.

Time Is Attention

Demand for leisure is affected in a complicated way by the cost of time to both produce and consume entertainment products. For instance, reading a book uses more time per dollar of goods (you can spend hours reading for free) than frequenting a nightclub (usually with a cover charge); in other words, it is less expensive for the consumer to read than to party. But partying may be more fun! The cost of time and the consumption-time intensity of experience are significant factors when selecting from among entertainment alternatives.[6]

Like money, attention has *instrumental value* because it can get you other things that you might want. It also has *terminal value* because many people want it for its own sake. We value both the attention we give and the attention we receive. Valuable as it is, however, attention cannot be bought. This is where entertainment comes in—it puts information into a form that can earn attention. Great ads or musical lyrics take plain, brown-paper-bag information and put it in a gift box.

Pleasure providers must capture the attention of audiences and entertainment consumers in order to get them to the venue, destination, or box office. Consumers receive a steady infusion of mediated messages, but most consumers block out such promotional "white noise" by refusing to pay attention to it. A primary function of entertainment marketing is finding ways to attract and hold audience attention in the presence of too much media stimulation from hyperreal communication.

One of the most attention-intensive modern-day activities is surfing the Web. The number of people communicating through the Web—and trying to get attention through it—is continuously rising. The growth in the Web's capacity to send multimedia or virtual reality signals allows marketers to capture user attention through these means.[7]

Societal Needs Matter

With the demands of family and work taking a huge toll on people's time and energy, many forms of entertainment seek to provide relief from the stress of everyday life. We begin our day with a workout at the gym, we catch a glimpse of the morning newspaper, we play CDs on the way to work, we listen to a radio talk show on the way home, we use e-mail to contact friends, we play a few online games, we eat in a themed restaurant, we shop in a mega mall, we rent a DVD, we see a movie or TV show, and we read a mystery novel before falling asleep. Every activity outside of our jobs is a form of entertainment.

Although we cannot avoid or escape encounters with entertainment, we are selective about which forms to use, how often we use them, and how much we are willing to spend on them. Marketing can be used to help direct this selectivity—to persuade audiences to watch, listen to, and buy tickets to the specific experiences that meet their needs.

▬▬▬ Play Theory and Entertainment Marketing

As leisure time proliferates, marketers concentrate on expanding the *notion of play*. According to Huizinga,[8] in *Homo Ludens,* play existed even before culture itself, accompanying and nourishing culture from the beginning of civilization. Huizinga asserts that all the great archetypal activities in human society are permeated with play. To characterize play as a cultural function that separates it from the context of ordinary life, he defined its main characteristics as follows.

Play Is Different from Other Types of Experiences

Play differs from other experiences because it

1. is a *voluntary* activity—no one forces us to play.
2. is set *apart from reality*—it is an interlude in the day that provides temporary satisfaction.
3. is *limited* in terms of its locality and duration—it has a beginning and an end.
4. is controlled or governed by *rules.*
5. has a sense of persistent *social community*—sports fans are such a community.
6. promotes a sense of symbolic *secrecy*—it is different from everyday life.
7. is a *sacred and profound* activity—it involves rituals, ceremony, and a venue for symbolic representation.

Some aspects of contemporary play assume different characteristics than those set forth by Huizinga. For instance, as an *extra-mundane activity* (activity outside the parameters of the ordinary), play was thought to provide people with the rewards that they could not find in work or in the consumption of the ordinary world. Yet, today, much of our consumption of the ordinary world is filled with all forms of entertainment and play.

Contemporary play is an outgrowth of a devotion to pleasure, known as *hedonism*. Influenced by the Romantic doctrine of the nineteenth century, which valued individualism, power, and sensitivity, hedonistic consumption designates a conceptual framework of leisure activity; in other words, it is a force behind the will to consume a great deal of pleasurable things. Hedonism is expressed in activities that are self-indulgent as well as pleasurable, such as game playing and shopping. As a facet of cultural movement, hedonism is a shaping force behind our individual pursuits of pure pleasure and immediate gratification.

Play Theory: A Strong Distinction between Leisure and Work

Play, viewed as an outgrowth of leisure time activities, gets its definition from the Latin word *ludenic,* which refers to games, recreation, contests, theater, and liturgical presentations. According to William Stephenson,[9] the spirit of play is essential to the development of culture—stagecraft, military exercises, debate, politics, and marriage conventions are all cultural aspects grounded in play.

The pleasure of finding the biggest wave and riding it home.

Making a strong distinction between leisure and work, **play theory** suggests that work deals with reality and production, while play provides self-satisfaction. This theory explains that play is pleasure, and pleasure is a concept at various levels:

- physiological pleasure (a massage soothes the body)
- pleasure of associations with objects and the relationship between self and things (riding a favorite bicycle or playing with a special golf club)
- pleasure from objects themselves (film- or star-licensed possessions)
- pleasure through communications (discussing a film with friends)

According to the theory, everything not work is pleasure. As a society devoting more time to leisure and play, we are dependent on marketers to help us sort out the play options for our out-of-work activity.

Playing Games

In today's culture, play takes on new meaning. Much of today's entertainment centers on games and gambling. The lure of winning is enough to interest consumers; it is the marketer's job to pull them into a particular gambling venue—a casino. We focus on gaming and gambling because they are important to understanding audience motivations for engaging in this popular form of chance-based entertainment.

Gaming is a term used to reference both games of competition and games of chance. From playing hide-and-seek as children to buying lottery tickets as adults, games entertain us throughout our lives. Games of competition require skill, such as achieving chess-mate, scoring a goal, or overtaking an opponent. Gambling activity, on the other hand, is based primarily on chance—no skill is involved in rolling dice or playing slot machines. Chess is a game; bingo is gambling. Cards can be either: played without wagers, they are a game; when betting is involved, they become gambling.

Taking a Chance

In gambling, players bet something of value on the outcome of a game or an uncertain event whose result may be determined by chance. They risk money in the hopes of winning the game or contest. Gambling activities range in complexity from a coin toss to betting on cards in poker. Outcomes may be determined solely by chance (craps and roulette) or by a combination of strategy and chance (poker). Gamblers may participate while betting on the outcome, or they may be restricted from participation in the cases of lotteries and sports.

Gambling has a negative image, so to change this image, the gambling industry now calls itself the *gaming* industry. A $60 billion industry, gaming has entered the coveted and lucrative mainstream of American entertainment. Merrill Lynch predicts that online gaming (consisting of more than 53,000 sites in 2004), will reach $125 billion in 2015. Online players in the United States number 5.3 million. Asia, with the world's biggest growth potential, claims 4 million online players. Houses of gaming have become full-fledged entertainment venues in their own right and have strong client potential for entertainment marketers. Gaming is but one entertainment experience, and is covered more thoroughly in Chapter 13. Other types of experiences are the main focus of this text.

Marketing Performance, Interaction, and Media Experiences

The entertainment industry is too broad to allow for all-inclusive treatment, but we can categorize many of the experiences it offers. So, we concentrate on five entertainment experience genres that require planning, communication, and promotion—campaign development—to ensure revenue generation: (1) live performances, (2) destinations and places, (3) attractions and themed venues, (4) mediated entertainment, and (5) celebrities and stars. Let's take a look at the experiential nature of each entertainment genre.

Enjoying Live Performances

Dance, opera, musical concerts, theater, and the circus are included in the experiential genre in which live people perform for live audiences. Often combining media with action, concert promoters are taking their performances to new venues and new dimensions. Sports also are performed live. In marketing local, regional, national, or global performances, reliance on reviews or star power is not enough to

Cirque du Soleil performs *Ka* in Las Vegas.

fill the house. Audience research and expectation delivery are key to developing an effective promotion strategy for this oldest type of entertainment, which is most often performed in a specific venue. Chapter 12 further discusses marketing live performances and events.

Experiencing Destinations and Places

The places we visit to engage in serious relaxing are part of an exploding tourist industry. Tourism has long been an important aspect of human geography and is vital to some economies. Marketing destinations is a primary way that some local economies survive. From small villages promoting arts (Laguna Beach, California) to the most popular city on earth (Paris), localities recognize the value in developing a recognizable brand that lures visitors and creates revenue. Laguna Beach markets itself as the home of the "Pageant of the Masters," a performance presenting the world's masterpieces using human figures. Local artists display their work in nearby Festival of Arts, Sawdust Festival, and Art Affair. During the summer, thousands flock to the city to gaze on and purchase art. Combined with its surf and sand attractions, Laguna Beach's art attracts regional visitors by engaging in co-promotions with hotels, restaurants, and galleries, and by providing an interactive Web site.

Australia capitalized on its exposure in the film *Crocodile Dundee* to promote coming "down under" with the 2002 promotion slogan, "Put a shrimp on the bar-b." The country's tourist industry ran an American television network campaign that created awareness and interest for American tourists, many of whom booked Qantas Airlines flights to Sydney for a glimpse of the famous Opera House—which, not coincidentally, also was featured in the country's advertising campaign. Chapter 13 is dedicated to marketing tourist destinations and services.

Hong Kong ad directed at American tourists.

▪▪▪▪▪▪▪▪▪ BOX 1-1 ▪▪▪▪▪▪▪▪▪

Focus on Venues

MUSEUMS AS MOVIE STARS

Museums are often pieces of art in their own right, such as New York's Guggenheim, which features a spiral gallery designed by Frank Lloyd Wright (pictured above). This and other museums have provided backdrops for movie scenes, such as *Rocky* (Sylvester Stallone runs up the stairs of the Philadelphia Museum of Art), *Batman* (Jack Nicholson's Joker runs wild in the Metropolitan Museum of Art in New York), and *A League of Their Own* (Tom Hanks' team visits the Baseball Hall of Fame in Cooperstown, New York). *What films have you seen that feature museums as props?*

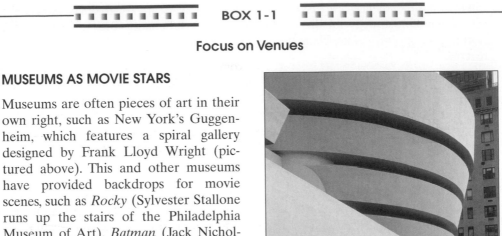

Experiencing Attractions and Themed Venues

For many leisure consumers, it's not just what you do, it's where you do it. *Venues* are places—buildings, ships, and cultural centers—where entertainment takes place. Performing arts centers, casinos, spas, resorts and cruise ships, museums, theaters, cinemas, and theme parks all house entertainment experiences. As private enterprise continues to invest in architectural innovation, performance venues are becoming destinations of their own.

As performance competition grows, producers looked to venues to provide a competitive edge over other forms of entertainment. Each event is associated with a physical home or venue specially designed and equipped to maximize audience enjoyment. Rome's Coliseum, Stratford-on-Avon's Globe Theater, and Sydney's Opera House are some of the world's most famous performance venues.

In order to pay for venues, marketers must identify the target market, develop appropriate messages to send them, and implement a successful promotional plan to lure patrons, donors, and guests to these venues in great numbers. Chapter 8 expands on venue marketing, and Chapter 12 features marketing attractions and themed spaces.

Mediated Entertainment

Television and movie marketing requires special skills and strategies to convince potential audience members that the viewing experience is worth their time and money.

Unseen mass audiences in dark theaters watching movies—or, even more so, at home viewing television—are more difficult to identify and reach than other audience types.

Television

Both network and cable stations must promote their programming to attract either advertisers or subscribers. Cable has been able to direct its programming to special audience segments (sports fans, avid enthusiasts) by positioning their brand appeal accordingly. Networks, on the other hand, are struggling to promote news, reality, and sitcom programming to mass audiences. The changing nature of television technology requires a whole new approach to marketing mediated experiences.

Movies

Major studios rely on trailers, distribution, and product placement to promote blockbuster films. Independent studios and filmmakers, on the other hand, commonly make do with film festival exposure and Internet buzz to gain attention and recognition. In spite of enormous budgets and global distribution, every so often a *sleeper* (unpromoted) film sneaks into theaters to earn large box office draws. Promotional techniques for new releases require creative merchandising and brand associations in order to reduce the margin between ticket revenues and production and marketing costs.

Celebrities and Stars

We love to love people we consider special or important, and in today's society, that often means those who look good and dress well on the screen and as captured in photographs. Many performances succeed because of the star power they offer audiences. **Celebrities** are people who become well known through media exposure or their outstanding accomplishments. Some accidental celebrities (those who earn fame unintentionally) capitalize on their temporary status to develop a new business or product (Monica Lewinsky, for example, who started her own fashion design company) that relies on their name brand for success. Celebrity is notoriety; stars are made. Hollywood crafts stars by employing publicists, agents, and image artists. Stars are engineered and become a brand in themselves. Magazines, fan clubs, paparazzi, and celebrity-watch television keep the private lives and loves of stars in front of the public, creating a separate and extremely lucrative star industry.

Johnny Depp is consistently voted as one of Hollywood's most popular stars.

▮▮▮ The Entertainment Industry Environment

Entertainment is an industry that depends not only on getting to market before a trend has passed (or on creating the trend in the first place), but also on great marketing efforts to create big box office receipts. Major advertising agencies that represent the entertainment industry handle large budgets, work within intense time frames, and are repeatedly faced with decisions that can make or break their clients. Large clients, in turn, offer mega-million-dollar media budgets that keep agencies competitive. Other factors that cause volatility and cannibalization in the industry are its moguls and mergers: Ever unsteady, the shifting sands of ownership and direction create unsettled environments in which entertainment experiences are created and distributed. This volatility further contributes to convergence (merger), which blurs the distinction between advertising and entertainment marketing—advertising drives entertainment and entertainment features advertised brands.

Global Advertising Agencies

Advertising agencies represent the largest entertainment companies, vying for huge media budgets that drive marketing programs. As of April 2006, the biggest players and their clients are presented in Exhibit 1.2.

Cannibalism

A dynamic and changing industry, entertainment entities change ownership regularly, often through unfriendly takeovers. Some of the biggest fish in entertainment shape, control—and often capture through acquisition—the development and delivery of what we experience. Five of the biggest fish in the entertainment tank are Barry Diller, Rupert Murdoch, Robert Iger, Judy McGrath, and Leslie Moonves. The following *Focus on* box profiles the current big entertainment moguls.

Industry Economics

According to a top-ranked entertainment industry analyst,[10] the industry frequently observes the following eight economic characteristics:[11]

1. In a steady growth phase, profits from a very few highly popular products are generally required to offset losses from many mediocrities. This is especially evident in movies and network television productions.

▮▮▮ **EXHIBIT 1.2   Major Entertainment Advertising Agencies**

Agency	*Entertainment Client(s)*
McCann Erickson	Columbia Pictures
DDB Worldwide	Universal Studios & Theme Parks
Western Media	Disney Studios
Grey Advertising	Warner Bros. Studios, WB Network, *Entertainment Weekly, People Magazine*
TWBA	ABC TV Network
Young & Rubicam	Showtime, Viacom, Blockbuster Video, Sony Electronics Game
Saatchi & Saatchi	News Corp

▮▮▮▮▮▮▮▮▮▮▮   BOX 1-2   ▮▮▮▮▮▮▮▮▮▮▮

Focus on the "Big Guys"

ENTERTAINMENT MOGULS

Old Boys

Barry Diller came up through the ranks at ABC Television Network. His knowledge of pricing in licensing movies to networks was behind his purchase of most of Paramount's movies. He eventually assumed that studio's presidency. Later, snapped up by media giant Rupert Murdoch, Diller became one of the highest paid executives at Murdoch's company, News Corp. When Murdoch turned down his request for an equity position, Diller left News Corp and put together IAC/InterActiveCorp, which has amassed a sprawling Internet and retail empire that includes Ticketmaster, television shopping network HSN, online dating service Match.com, and search engine Ask Jeeves Inc. Diller's most recent project is a $100 million, 10-story glass tower in Manhattan designed by architect Frank Gehry.

Rupert Murdoch, age 75 in 2006, is capitalizing on the technology that is shifting power away from the established and media elite and toward the people. With the $580 million purchase of MySpace, the News Corp chief is betting he can transform a free social network into a colossal marketing machine. News Corp's $23.8 billion constellation includes movie studios (20th Century Fox, Searchlight), TV networks (Fox, FX), magazine publishing companies (*TV Guide, Weekly Standard*), newspapers (*New York Post, UK Times*), and satellites (SKYE, DirecTV). A billion Internet users are looking for news, sports, and entertainment; another billion are on mobile phones. Murdoch knows there are a lot more people making news

and entertainment choices now than ever before, and he is out there to capitalize on those choices.

Robert Iger became CEO of Disney on December 30, 2005, and immediately agreed to let Apple sell ABC's television shows over the Internet. Iger is bullish on broadband Internet, wireless phone networks and video-on-demand that reach viewers through TV-enabled cell phones, videogame players, digital video recorders, and the iPod. Under his leadership, Disney projects double-digit earnings growth for its cash cow 10 TV stations and 64 radio stations. Iger acquired Pixar Animation Studios as a companion to the Disney's businesses—movies, television, theme parks, and consumer products—to generate revenue for all the divisions around the world. In 2006, a Disney branded cell phone network for families was introduced, along with ABC News Now, a 24-hour Internet news channel distributed by AOL, Comcast, and SBC Yahoo.

New Guy and a Gal[12]

Judy McGrath turned MTV into a cultural phenomenon, with 400 million viewers in 164 countries. The former women's magazine writer oversees the MTV Networks empire that includes 100 MTV networks globally, Nickelodeon, VH1, TV Land, Comedy Central, Spike TV, CMT, Nick at Nite, the new LOGO channel serving gay and lesbian consumers, MTV2, The N, and MTV and Nickelodeon Films, as well as the company's online and digital businesses. On McGrath's watch as chief executive officer, the channels have broken new ground, not just in reality television, but

(Continued)

also in the areas of entertainment biopics and animated comedies.

Leslie Moonves, former president of Warner Bros. Television, joined CBS in 1995 and proceeded to break the Peacock network's (NBC's) hold on Thursday night with shows such as *Survivor* and *CSI*. His new missions are creating mini-*CSI* episodes for viewing as short clips on cell phones, Google Video, and CBS.com, and producing a soap opera available only by cell phone. CBS, a public company with $14.5 billion in revenue in 2005, has slightly increased its total prime-time viewers over the past 11 seasons and has the largest number of total television viewership of the "big four" networks (CBS, NBC, ABC, and Fox). Moonves is a masterful seller of advertis-

ing time; he has increased ad revenue more than 6 percent over the previous season. Under his direction, CBS paid $325 million for CSTV, a college-sport cable network that operates athletic Web sites for 250 colleges and universities. When not touting his wireless strategy to investors, Moonves is approving lead actors for all new shows.

As you might conclude from the close ties among and between these players, the entertainment industry continuum reaches beyond Hollywood. What were once simply movie studios have become entertainment conglomerates that have synergized into one huge interwoven web of entertainment marketing and revenue.

2. The unique features of entertainment products must continuously be brought to the attention of potential audiences, causing marketing expenditures per unit to be proportionally large. As life cycles of entertainment products are brief, marketing typically adds at least 50 percent to the cost of the average major feature film release.

3. Because almost every dollar of revenue first goes toward recouping direct costs, ancillary markets provide disproportionately large returns. For instance, films derive more than half their revenues from exposures on cable and home video rather than from initial theatrical release; spin-offs are sources of significant additional income. Price discrimination effects are readily observed in ticket pricing for cultural events, and sequencing films through various exhibition windows, from screen to DVD to television.

4. Capital costs are relatively high, erecting a formidable barrier to entry by new competitors. Most industry segments thus come to be ruled by large companies with relatively easy access to large pools of capital. These tendencies can be seen in gaming, theme park, cable, film, movies, and broadcasting industries.

5. The cost of production is independent of the number of consumers. And although delivered to consumers in the form of private goods (DVDs), many entertainment products and services (movies, TV programs) have public good characteristics.

6. Many products and services are not standardized, resulting in considerable freedom for entrepreneurs to originate plays, operas, and ballets. When the production is live performance, however, it is difficult to enhance productivity, and the costs of creating and marketing these entertainment products tends to rise at above-average rates.

7. Technology makes it easier and less expensive to manufacture, distribute, and receive entertainment products and services. The result is more varied and more affordable mass-market entertainment.

8. New delivery methods are continually evolving, but new entertainment mediums tend *not* to render older ones extinct, as new deliver methods also are continually evolving. For instance, rapidly increasing Internet use has not kept people from reading books, newspapers, and magazines, although daily newspaper subscriptions are declining.

The economics of each industry segment vary; they are treated separately in Part Three of this text.

Entertainment Ethics

For the entertainment industry (as for most industries), ethics provide guidelines or tools for making choices. Not "good" or "right" choices, necessarily, but choices based on moral criteria, whatever they may be in a particular case.

Ethical Dilemmas

Areas where ethical issues arise and where laws may exist to protect victims include these situations and cases:

- **News.**   According to many entertainment journalists, a reporter in Hollywood is only as good as his or her Rolodex is large. To stay well connected and land the big interviews, entertainment journalists have to balance what the actor/agent/publicist/studio wants with the "real" story. The system is quid pro quo—if reporters do a story for the agency/client, they get to interview a sought-after star in return. Compromise may involve unethical practices.

- **Film reviews.**   Settlement of a class action lawsuit against Columbia Pictures gave anyone who saw *Hollow Man, Vertical Limit, A Knight's Tale, The Animal,* or *The Patriot* a payment of $5. Why? Reviewer David Manning's quotes filled print and TV ads with praise for those movies while other reviewers trashed them. The problem was that Manning didn't exist; Colombia Pictures made him up.[13]

- **Radio.**   New York State Attorney General Eliot Spitzer took Sony to task over the practice of paying off disc jockeys to give favorable airplay to Sony tunes—a practice that will now cost Sony $10 million. Sony BMG Music engaged in all kinds of material flattery in order to secure playtime for certain songs. The process was so well oiled that Sony had fixed payola rates for music play. One Sony memo indicated that some stations could bill Sony for $1,000 if they played a song at least 75 times. In one instance, Sony bought 250 "spins" of a Good Charlotte song for $17,000.[14]

- **Agencies.**   For the past decade, the entertainment industry has been concerned about a small but growing problem of unethical talent, modeling, and background agencies. Some of these agencies claim to be part of the legitimate industry but are really in business to defraud thousands of people every year out of millions of dollars. To protect against such frauds, the entertainment industry developed a code of ethics for such agencies to define their roles and set standards for them.

- **Television.**   To deflect parental concerns about questionable program content, the National Association of Radio and Television Broadcasters (NARTB) developed a code of self-regulation for the television industry. The code contributed to the larger process of determining the parameters of "responsible" programming, or what is appropriate for family viewing in the domestic environment. Ethical issues surface with regard to differences in the definitions of "responsible" programming and "appropriate" programming.

Codes of Ethics

Entertainment corporations' codes of ethics vary somewhat but contain similar areas of concern, especially with regard to conflict of interest and confidentiality. Exhibit 1.3

▪▪▪ **EXHIBIT 1.3** Codes of Ethics

COMPANY POLICY ON ETHICS

A. Conflicts of Interest

The primary principle underlying the Company's conflicts of interest policies is that associates, and officers in particular, must never permit their personal interests to conflict or appear to conflict with the interests of the Company or its customers.

1. Receipt of Bribes, Commissions, Honorariums, Loans, Gifts, Gratuities, and Entertainment

The company does not permit or condone bribes, kickbacks, improper commissions, honorariums, loans, gifts, gratuities or any other illegal, secret, or improper payments, transfers or receipts. No associate may accept a gift from or give a gift to any customer or prospective customer of the Company.

2. Fair Competition

Under no circumstances should associates enter into arrangements with the Company's competitors affecting pricing or marketing arrangements. Such arrangements are illegal under federal and state antitrust laws.

3. Conduct with Competitors

In all contacts with competitors, whether at trade/business association meetings or in other venues, do not discuss pricing policy, contract terms, costs, inventories, marketing and product plans, market surveys and studies, production plans and capabilities; and, of course, any other proprietary or confidential information.

Discussion of these subjects or collaboration on them with competitors can be illegal. If a competitor raises any of them, even lightly or with apparent innocence, you should object, stop the conversation immediately, and tell the competitor that under no circumstances will you discuss these matters.

B. Confidentiality

Officers and associates must not divulge any non-public information regarding the Company to any outsider except for a legitimate business purpose and with the express understanding that the information is confidential and is to be used solely for the limited business purpose for which it was given and received. This information may include, but is not limited to: salary and personnel information, customer lists, budgets and forecasts, and marketing and sales plans and all employment opportunities offered.

Source: www.ethicsweb.ca/codes/.

contains excerpts from one code as an example of the wording and content of such codes.

Although codes of ethics are not legally binding or punishable by law, ethical misdemeanors can results in the loss of one's job or reputation. To avoid punitive reprimands or penalties, you should think seriously before taking part in compromising situations. Ask yourself questions about your duty and intentions: Am I doing the right thing? Am I proceeding with good will? Are my dignity and respect maintained? If you can answer "yes" to these questions, chances are you have made an appropriate choice.

FINALLY: LET'S SUM UP ▪▪▪▪▪▪▪

The entertainment industry operates with an economic landscape whose foundations are hours at work, productivity trends, expected utility functions, demographics, and other factors that affect the amounts of time and money we spend on leisure-related services. In the United States, spending of disposable income on entertainment has risen to more than 10 percent— very big business, indeed. When measured in dollar value terms, entertainment has consistently been one of the largest net export categories for this country.[15] Are you ready to enter the business? When you finish this book, you will be.

GOT IT? LET'S REVIEW ▪▪▪▪▪▪▪

- Entertainment marketing is the process of promoting amusements, leisure, and recreation to potential and current audiences and travelers.
- Entertainment marketing differs from marketing products because experiences are perishable, intangible, and based on time as a scarce resource.
- The seven characteristics of play set it apart from other types of experiences; contemporary play is an outgrowth of hedonistic consumption.

- Five entertainment experience genres include live performance, destinations/ places, attraction and venues, media, and celebrity/stars.
- Four men and one woman control most of the entertainment industry and are considered powerful moguls by marketers and corporations alike.
- Ethical issues are important considerations when marketing in the entertainment industry.

NOW TRY THIS: LET'S APPLY WHAT WE'VE LEARNED ▪▪▪▪▪▪▪

1. Trace a film studio (e.g., Paramount, MGM, 20th Century Fox) from its inception to its place in today's corporate conglomerate structure. How does the studio's evolution reflect the nature of today's entertainment industry structure?
2. Four classifications of play are: *agon* (competition), *alea* (chance), *mimicry* (simulation), and *ilinx* (vertigo). Go online and find out which games and forms of entertainment fit into each classification.

3. Exhibit 1.1 lists entertainment milestones for their technological and political significance. Which companies (Microsoft, Sony, AOL, etc.) should be included in this exhibit for their contribution to entertainment development?
4. Go online and find out who the other important entertainment moguls are this year. What other women have taken their places among the entertainment moguls?

QUESTIONS: LET'S REVIEW ▪▪▪▪▪▪

1. How have the changes in the way we experience leisure time been reflected in the significant growth of the entertainment industry?
2. What are the major characteristics of marketing all forms of entertainment experiences?
3. What is the role of venues in marketing entertainment performances?
4. What role do ethics and codes of ethics play in entertainment marketing?
5. How have mergers and moguls affected the entertainment industry in the last year?

MORE TO READ ▪▪▪▪▪▪

C. S. Aron. *Working at Play: A History of Vacations in the United States*. London: Oxford University Press, 1999.

A. N. Greco, ed. *The Media and Entertainment Industries*. San Francisco: Allyn & Bacon, 2000).

B. J. Pine and J. H. Gilmore. *The Experience Economy: Work Is Theater & Every Business Is a Stage*. Cambridge, MA: Harvard Business School Press, 1999.

S. Sayre and C. King. *Entertainment and Society: Audiences, Trends and Impacts*. Thousand Oaks, CA: Sage Publications, 2003.

M. J. Wolf. *The Entertainment Economy*. New York: Times Books/Random House, 1999.

D. Zillmann and P. Vorderer, eds. *Media Entertainment: The Psychology of Its Appeal*. San Francisco: Lawrence Erlbaum, 2000.

NOTES ▪▪▪▪▪▪

1. Bureau of Labor Statistics, 2005.
2. Damon Darlin, "Your Money," *New York Times,* Nov. 19, 2005.
3. *Fortune,* April 17, 2006.
4. U.S. Department of Commerce.
5. B. J. Pine and J. H. Gilmore, *The Experience Economy: Work Is Theater & Every Business Is a Stage* (Harvard Business School Press, 1999), pp. 30–35.
6. Harold L. Vogel, *Entertainment Industry Economics* (Cambridge, UK: Cambridge University Press, 2001), p. 5.
7. Michael Goldhaber, "The Attention Economy and the Net" (1998), firstmonday.org/issues/goldhaber, accessed Aug. 2005.
8. J. Huizinga, *Homo Ludens* (Boston: Beacon Press, 1950).
9. W. Stephenson, *The Play Theory of Mass Communication* (New Brunswick, NJ: Transaction Books, 1988).
10. Vogel, pp. 352–354.
11. Vogel.
12. *Fortune.*
13. John Horn, "The Reviewer Who Wasn't There; Sony Resorts to Some Questionable Marketing Practices to Promote New Movies," *Newsweek* Web Exclusive, June 2, 2001.
14. arstechnica.com/news.ars/post/20050803-5165.html.
15. Vogel, p. 31.

CHAPTER 2

Our Merged, Merged World

You've no idea what a difference it makes,
mixing things with other things.
—LEWIS CARROLL

Chapter Objectives

After reading this chapter, you should be able to answer the following questions:

- What is the impact of *technology* and the *Internet* on the entertainment industry?
- What role does *globalization* play for the industry's marketing practices?
- How has convergence between entertainment and advertising come about and how does it determine the way the industry functions?

As young people watch films on their phones and download music into their MP3 players, marketers realize that audiences must be reached where they live—and that is where they interact with media and messages. So, advertisers develop branded games, branded films, and branded contests to entertain these potential consumers. At the same time, the entertainment industry accepts brand placements in films, books, and broadcasts to generate revenue. This synergistic relationship is crucial for the success of both advertisers and entertainment. Starting at the corporate level, technology is the driving factor in this joint venture that oversees the fusion of entertainment and promotion. This chapter presents an overview of the current technological and global environment that fuses advertising and entertainment marketing.

Entertainment Technology

Technology, digitalization, and Internet access have strongly affected every aspect of the entertainment industry. We can point to four major shifts in the nature of entertainment that have developed since we entered the digital age in the mid-1990s:

- First, our entertainment has evolved from mass entertainment, which is developed for a common denominator, to *personal entertainment,* in which consumers use media tools and content for personal expression. Rather than sitting with a group in a dark theater, audience members now preview films online or engage in interactive games.

• Second, content has changed from being prepackaged, or simply created for you, to being *self-generated:* you create it yourself. Audiences can now create their own game scenarios, author blogs, publish online fiction, and develop new episodes of old television series.

• Third, experiences have switched from being episodic, with a definite beginning and end, to *persistent,* meaning that entertainment is ongoing and has no clear starting and stopping point. Our phones ring to melodies by Beethoven or the Beatles, live billboards enhance our transportation, in-seat movie screens amuse us while we fly, and iPods allow us to conduct our lives to music.

• Finally, entertainment has shifted from being a virtual, or separate, experience to being an *embedded* experience, in which digital information, images, music, and even experiences are fused with objects in the physical world. Cell phone movies are an example of embedded information.

The impact of digitalization is most apparent over the Internet, in the nature of games, and how we communicate across borders. This section expands on those changes.

Connecting Online

The Internet provides audiences at home and at work with immediate, continuing access to global information and entertainment. Audiences have taken the Internet on the road; technologies that enable widespread mobile Internet access include long-lasting portable energy sources, low-power flexible displays, Wi-Fi and Bluetooth wireless communications, and global positioning systems (GPS). **Blogs**, or Internet commentary (whose name grew out of the term "Web logs"), and strong search engines such as Google allow audiences to communicate and to connect in ways that both inform and entertain.

Blogs act as promotion and feedback for entertainment providers. For example, in the music industry, these online "conversations" are acting as incubators for new musical talent and can be fertile testing grounds for music labels. A label manager at Vice Records[1] was hesitant to promote a new album by then-unknown Norwegian pop star Annie until he saw the positive word of mouth she was receiving in blogs. Blogs also empower audiences; as bloggers, people can influence content and how products are developed and promoted.

Google, AOL, and Yahoo search engines provide access to entertainment and simultaneously promote events and venues. Advertising revenues enhance users' ability to access both information and products. Google's brand has become a verb, as in "I googled the applicant for the job," "google this disease," and so forth. And with the addition of ScholarGoogle and ImageGoogle, even academics get to have fun searching the Web.

Expanding Internet Usage

Worldwide adoption of Internet technology has connected everyone to everyone else. As of 2005, Asia—with only 9 percent of the world's population—has the highest percentage of Internet users globally, while Africa and the Middle East have experienced

▪ ▪ ▪ **EXHIBIT 2.1**   World Internet Usage and Population Statistics

World Regions	Population	Population % of World	Internet Usage	Usage Growth % 2000–2005	% Population Penetration	World % Users
Africa	896,721,874	14.0	23,867,500	428.7	2.7	2.5
Asia	3,622,994,130	55.4	327,066,713	186.1	9.0	34.2
Europe	731,018,523	11.4	273,262,955	165.1	37.4	28.5
Middle East	260,814,179	4.1	21,422,500	305.4	8.2	2.2
North America	328,387,059	5.1	223,779,183	107.0	68.1	23.4
Latin America	546,723,509	8.5	70,699,084	291.3	12.9	7.4
Oceana/Australia	33,443,448	0.5	17,655,737	131.7	52.8	1.8
WORLD TOTAL	6,620,102,722	100	957,753,672	165.3	14.9	100

Data provided by www.internetworldstats.com.

the most increased usage over the past five years. Exhibit 2.1 provides a glance at recent data to confirm a continually expanding user base worldwide.

Game Technology Fosters Creative Interaction

Because the cost of producing a video game is 1/20th of the cost of producing a film, revenues from game sales outpace the return on investment (ROI) of blockbuster films. Interactivity is the reason. For example, the fictional, puzzle-solving game known as *The Beast* represents a new genre of alternate-reality games sweeping the marketplace.

Games have a grassroots role in entertainment media experimentation. So far, game playing has had enough of an impact to generate a few new social and cultural practices. For example, it has changed the way some children and adolescents relate to each other—two boys can sit in the same room playing GameBoy without so much as a word to each other and still be communicating. Games have become part of mainstream culture. We play them on handheld devices, on PCs, on mobile phones, on TV sets, on portable game machines, and in arcades. A $20 billion a year industry, video games have captured 60 percent of Americans averaging age twenty-eight, 43 percent of whom are female. There are Nintendo gaming consoles in more than 600,000 hotel rooms and 50,000 airline seats.

Time Warner's venture GameTap, which offers computer users with broadband connections an opportunity to play hundreds of games on demand, links it with game producers including Activision, Atari, Midway, Namco, Sega, and UbiSoft. Sold by Turner Broadcasting System division of Time Warner, GameTap

Games on demand.

▪▪▪▪▪▪▪▪▪▪   BOX 2-1   ▪▪▪▪▪▪▪▪▪▪

Focus on Ethics

GRAND THEFT AUTO

Parents whose kids spend hours playing video games are worried about the games' influence on children's behavior. Here, we consider the ethics of exposing violent and sexual content to minors without providing censorship capabilities.

Overview

The first installment of the Grand Theft Auto (GTA) video game series released in 1997 gained success from its allegedly controversial game play. Throughout the series, players take on the role of criminals and are free to roam through a large city committing various illicit acts, including stealing cars; shooting and running over pedestrians; taking drugs; and having sex with prostitutes. The game series, considered by scholars to encourage violence and degrade women, has received considerable commercial success; it was ranked the top-selling game in the United States in 2001 and had sold 35 million copies by 2005. Two factors believed to compromise gamers are violence and sexual content.

Violence

According to the Institute for Global Ethics, the key issue concerning the Grand Theft Auto series is its hyperviolence. Computer and video games have been scrutinized by the mass media for encouraging violent and aggressive behavior, particularly in children and teenagers, and the Grand Theft Auto series' contribution to this trend was evidenced by the moral panic its release evoked in parents. Violence against police officers and women are central themes in the series, and it has been suggested that the series promotes such actions in real life. One real-life example is of an American teenager who stole a car and then shot three people, two of whom were police officers. The teen had played hundreds of hours of Grand Theft

(Continued)

Auto, and his actions are thought to have been inspired by the series and to resemble a scene from one of the games.

Some scholars argue against this notion, claiming that the complexity of a video game such as Grand Theft Auto is actually beneficial for our brains because it challenges our thinking. They further suggest that game violence contextualizes the actions within the game space and the options given in the game are restricted to the game itself, not to reality. Other studies on exposure to violence,[2] however, suggest that playing violent video games increases aggressive behavior. A review of the video-game research literature reveals that violent video games can increase aggressive behavior in children and young adults. Research also reveals that exposure to violent video games increases physiological arousal and aggression-related thoughts and feelings among both boys and girls. Playing violent video games also decreases pro-social behavior.

Sexual Content

Scenarios relating to sexual activities are prominent in the series, particularly in Grand Theft Auto "3" and "San Andreas." In "3," it is possible for a player's character to pick up a female prostitute, have sex with her, and then kill her to take back the money paid to her. However, actions of this nature are done by the player's choice, and the consequences of these activities are punishable by the police within the game.

A "Hot Coffee" game modification, when installed with "San Andreas," unlocks several mini-games that prompt players to have the game's hero engage in X-rated acts. Rockstar Games, the company behind the series, was reprimanded by the Entertainment Software Rating Board (ESRB) for including this content code in the game without reporting it to the ESRB.

In their defense, game players argue that the material attainable for viewing is not controversial because the sexual content is so overtly ridiculous that it should be seen as comedy within the context of the game.

What do you think?

1. Compare the scholar's argument about violence with the actions of the teenage car thief. Which view do you endorse? Why?

2. What should be the role of a ratings board? Should penalties that include fines rather than mere reprimands be enforced?

SOURCE: Developed by students in New Media Technologies of the Creative Industries Faculty, Queensland University of Technology, Brisbane, Australia.

▪▪▪▪▪▪▪▪▪

lets subscribers download and install software from its Web site, which also features free original content, such as video clips and e-mail cards. The appetite for gaming is further evidenced by the inclusion of products and brands in games from Daimler-Chrysler, Kraft Foods, and Orbitz and the decision by filmmaker Steven Spielberg to develop games with Electronic Arts game company.[3] Although this text does not focus on technology marketing per se, we must acknowledge the competitive role games play when we market entertainment experiences.

Content Development and Technology

In our global era, necessary focus has been given to the future of digital, satellite, and Internet radio as a means of increasing the flow of information and culture across

geographic boundaries. At the same time, however, radio remains primarily a local experience. Though broadcasting itself can be argued to be a social innovation rather then a technological one, there are two reasons for the continued interest in radio: low-cost and ease of production, access, and broadcast. Also, opportunities for listening are increasing, both online and through unlicensed or independent micro-radio stations. Another important factor in radio's ongoing popularity is the audience's emotional and cultural relationship with it. At its best, radio is about the intimacy between the speaker's or singer's voice and the listener.

Marketers are slicing radio audiences into ever-narrowing niches of gamers, surfers, and iPoders. Providing additional evidence of media convergence, Infinity Broadcasting's Clear Channel and Sirius have pod media on radio, while ABC and NBC produce their own version of a daily headline download, and Scripps-Howard and *Business Week* deliver audio versions of their print products.

Podcasting, the practice of downloading and playing live and recorded video through an iPod or other MP3 player, is almost a rebellion against the blandness of commercial radio. It offers audiences more power to raise their voices as a global audience. Podcasting is inexpensive and has a lot of creative potential, because it combines aspects of TiVo and blogging with the dimension of audio. Podcasting is a logical progression in grassroots media. There were twice as many podcasters as commercial radio stations in 2005,[4] each with its unique voice and available through an iTunes download. Podcasting is a way to circumvent imposed programming as delivered by corporate-owned stations. Forrester Research, a company tracking podcast audiences, predicts that by the end of the decade, 12 million people will be listening to podcasts as part of their media diet.[5] Audience members create their own podcasts and become pod stars or Internet radio deejays or talk-show hosts. Radio may not be dead, but it will have to devise new ways to compete with consumer-controlled media or market itself as more than syndicated programming. Stations have another option: They can join the movement to become podcast friendly, as did public radio station WNYC, which increased its listeners by 40,000 per week through podcasting.

▪▪▪ Global Effects

A multidisciplinary technology revolution is changing the world. The fast pace of technological development and breakthroughs makes foresight difficult, but the technology revolution seems globally significant and is quite likely taking place across all dimensions of life: social, economic, political, and personal. The revolution of information availability and utility will continue to profoundly affect the world in all these dimensions. Competition for technology development leadership will depend on

▪▪▪▪▪▪▪▪▪ BOX 2-2 ▪▪▪▪▪▪▪▪▪

A Closer Look at Nonprofit

NPR: THE 800-POUND PODCASTER

With dynamics similar to those of the Public Broadcasting System, National Public Radio (NPR) has been a trendsetter by embracing new technology. That was certainly the case in the 1990s when the network began to archive its programs and provide streaming-audio Web casts of some of its features, such as "All Things Considered." The network has also embraced high-definition radio. As of 2005, NPR is a trendsetter in the podcasting realm—not because it provides downloadable MP3 files, but because it may have a proven way to make money with them.

Online Economics

According to VP Ken Stern, NPR has an existing on-air sponsorship model that has been transported to the podcasting world. This model features 90 seconds of on-air sponsorships per hour. Ten-second "Gateway" sponsorships (which introduce the program as "brought to you by") and interior sponsorships within the podcasts (brands mentioned within the program) are NPR's standard, on-air model. The targeted reach (number of listeners) and frequency (number of delivery times) of the podcast listeners offers NPR sponsors some influence over an audience with a great deal of disposable income. This tactic of *aggregating* podcast listeners has not escaped the notice of commercial broadcasters. For example, Infinity Broadcasting's nine all-news mornings are now supplemented by individual podcast pages, and each station offers a selection of downloadable files on its Web site. Podcast pioneer Adam Curry's own fledgling venture, PodShow, is attempting to aggregate podcast listeners, too. PodShow recently secured some venture-capital financing.

Ultimately, though, the reality is that NPR's brand presence on the Web is formidable when compared with the presence of single commercial radio stations—even one as important as Infinity news's WINS in New York. According to Nielsen//NetRatings, WINS generated 3.2 million Web page views during

(Continued)

September 2005. That number represents the overall total for page views; it does not break out unique visitors or provide any other specific data.

By comparison, NPR's own Web site generated nearly seven times that total—20.3 million Web page views—during the same month, with help from its member stations. As of October 2005, there were 52 separate stations and networks providing a total of 174 different podcasts, all available at NPR's Web site. Bolstered by new growth, NPR has developed strong online sales activity and is expected to quadruple its revenues from online in 2006, which includes podcasting and all the other aspects of NPR's Internet presence.

An important aspect of the organizing process is culling content from the enormous number of individual podcasts that are available globally. Stern says he expects NPR to begin curating its own Web site podcasts and to allow listeners to comment on the content in some fashion.

What do you think?

1. Can technological innovations save radio from becoming obsolete?

2. In your opinion, what role will satellite radio play in NPR's future?

SOURCE: Tony Sanders for *Radio Monitor,* Oct. 28, 2005.

future regional economic arrangement (e.g., the European Union), international intellectual property rights and protections, the character of future multinational corporations, and the role and amount of public and private sector research and development investments.

Current trends in the technological sector include competition among regional economic alliances increased support for a global intellectual property protection regime and a desire for the equitable division of responsibilities for research and development (R&D) funding responsibilities. Such legal and economic factors have a direct impact on how we develop, market, and use entertainment products and experiences.

As a result, global marketing strategies must mix the right proportion of standardized and customized content and branding. The choices involve sending a single content or brand to a global market, localizing content and keeping the brand global, or localizing both brand and content. Disney has chosen to keep a global brand, image, and content structure while localizing messages and customizing secondary considerations, such as food and park layout. Cirque du Soleil, on the other hand, presents standardized global performances marketed locally. By strategically balancing configurations of a global/local message with standardized/customized content, entertainment marketers can maximize box office revenues. Chapter 3 discusses the cultural impact of globalization on entertainment content.

Television is the best medium for disseminating global messages without changing content: U.S. soap operas and dramas reach global audiences (often with subtitle additions). Theme park formats can remain similar across borders, but local foods are often incorporated into the content. Films and cruise ships, using standard content, localize their advertising messages. Theater, on the other hand, often customizes its programming and advertising messages with local appeal. Exhibit 2.2 diagrams the global-local relationship between standardized content (same for everyone) and content customized for a local region.

▪▪▪▪ **EXHIBIT 2.2** Approaching Global Entertainment

```
                          Standardized Content
                                  ^
Global                 TV         ^     Film, Cruise ships      Local
message —————————————————————————^—————————————————————————— message
                                  ^
                                  ^
            Theme parks           ^          Theater
                                  ^
                          Customized Content
```

Transnationals: Media Corporations and Entertainment Flows

Nationally based media and entertainment companies with overseas operations in two or more countries are called **transnational media corporations (TNMC)**. Exhibit 2.3 presents the major TNMC players. Highly global in its approach to business, a TNMC operates in preferred markets with an obvious preference and familiarity toward its home market. News Corp, for example, generates 76 percent of its total revenues inside the U.S. and Canada, followed by its markets in Europe (16 percent) and Australasia (8 percent). Similarly, Viacom generates an estimated 84 percent of its revenues inside the U.S. and Canada. The remaining 16 percent of Viacom's global revenues are generated largely from Paramount Pictures and the company's Music TV international subsidiaries and joint partnerships.[6]

Global markets are a natural result of transnational business taking place between economies that will mutually benefit from doing business with each other. Driven by

▪▪▪▪ **EXHIBIT 2.3** Transnational Media Corporations

Company	*World Hdq.*	*Principal Business Operation*
Bertlesmann AG	Germany	Book & record clubs, book publishing, magazines, music and film entertainment
NBC Universal	USA	TV & film entertainment, cable programming, theme parks
News Corp Ltd.	Australia/USA	Newspapers, magazines, TV & film entertainment, direct broadcast satellite
Sony	Japan	Consumer electronics, videogame consoles & software, music and film entertainment
Time-Warner	USA	Cable programming, magazines, publishing, music & film entertainment, Internet service provision
Viacom	USA	TV & film entertainment, cable programming, broadcast TV, publishing, videocassette & DVD rental/sales
Walt Disney	USA	Theme parks, film entertainment, broadcasting, cable programming, consumer merchandise

trends in deregulation and privatization, high-speed technology has helped create new market integration, such as the telecommunications business that is currently booming in India.

Privatization has increased the volume of programs purchased from commercial sources and increased competition for software products among potential program buyers—which, in turn, has affected the international TV and film markets. The TNMC and the concept of global brands are becoming realities in terms of news, sports, and music entertainment. Significantly, burgeoning TNMCs and coproduction ventures are going to foster a programming philosophy based on the assumption that the world can be broken down according to cultural continents, i.e., areas where cultural factors are similar. This means that the next generation of global TV viewers is likely to be people who can simultaneously appreciate world MTV and still have a decided preference for locally originated drama or sporting event.

▪▪▪ Convergence: A Symbiotic Relationship

According to Scott Donaton, the editor of *Advertising Age,* the world's largest media publication, the entertainment marketing industry is encountering a **Madison and Vine** dynamic that is transforming the way in which media, music, and advertising industries merge to reach their markets. (Madison Avenue in New York is synonymous with advertising, while the intersection of Hollywood and Vine streets in Los Angeles is the symbolic corner of the entertainment industry.)

Mix, Match, and Mold

Convergence comes in a variety of shapes and forms, but six common themes prevail. Stated as rules, they may serve as guidelines for developing a "Madison and Vine" approach to entertainment marketing.

1. Reject the status quo—change is an economic necessity.
2. Collaborate—deals happen when movie studios, TV networks, ad agencies, marketing firms, and PR agencies work together.
3. Demand accountability—the bottom line gives credibility to return on investment.
4. Stay flexible—adapt branded entertainment models or evolve them into new forms.
5. Let go—market control must yield to audience collaboration with content producers.
6. Respect the audience—marketing is changing from intrusion to invitation, from dumbing-down content to respecting the consumer's intelligence.

One example of convergence was the 2003 Victoria Secret Holiday Fashion Show in New York City, which featured lingerie-clad runway models wearing angels' wings; performances by Sting, Mary J. Blige, and Eve; and an after-show party at which Donald Trump rubbed elbows with P. Diddy.[7] The live show was filmed for broadcast on network TV. Developed to target the sought-after young male demographic, the first annual show drew millions of dollars in free publicity, including the front page of the *Wall Street Journal.* Cloaked as entertainment, was this runway extravaganza simply an hour-long commercial for the Victoria Secret retail chain? The answer is your call.

Reality television is a second example of convergence, one in which entertainment-advertiser alliances are created as sponsors take part in program content. Without

Contestants in the reality-television show *Survivor*

product sponsors, shows such as *Survivor* could not afford to produce single-run programming (*single-run* refers to shows that can be aired only once; reruns are not an option for "reality TV"). Wal-Mart, seeking to improve its image, has sponsored an educational reality show called *The Scholar,* which features intellectual rather than physical challenges for participants.

A third convergence example is BMW's production of a 10-minute commercial designed to show off the capabilities of the X5 sport utility vehicle, part of the company's series of eight celebrity-studded product films. Assembling acting and directing stars from Hollywood, the Fallon Ad Agency, which produced the commercials, broke the rules by giving the commercials' directors total control of creative content. The BMW films became such an Internet phenomenon that the company had to add servers to meet the demand for downloads. The year of the films' releases and for the two years following it, BMW sold a record number of vehicles, beating its own record for three consecutive years. Finally, the series was introduced into the permanent collection of the Museum of Modern Art. So are the films art? Entertainment? Advertising? We contend they are all three—a cool convergence of branding and entertainment. A fourth example of convergence taps into the music culture, where poor CD sales and strong competition were killing production companies in the early 2000s. The solution? Put brands and logos into the CDs design or lyrics, or use music as background for product advertising. While music tie-ins are more valuable to new artists than established

Sony uses experiential marketing in the San Francisco Metreon venue.

ones, Mitsubishi's commercial music became a popular Internet download. Sting's single "Desert Rose" was a commercial for both Jaguar and his music. Chapter 3 presents important strategies and tactics that capitalize on the convergence of advertising and entertainment.

Experiential Marketing

The convergence notion expands further when manufacturers become creators of experiences to connect consumers with their brands. **Experiential marketing** consists of messages designed to increase a consumer's purchase intention for a product or service through the fusion of activity with brands. Instead of selling skis from a rack, sport retailers construct sawdust ski slopes where consumers may experience the brand before they buy it. Cuisinart invites shoppers to cook with its kitchen products during classes or special events as part of their experiential marketing program.

During national research conducted in 2005 by the Jack Morton Company, 2,574 consumers in the top 25 U.S. markets completed surveys about their consumption experiences.[8] Here are the key findings:

- Experiential marketing drives purchase consideration across age, gender, and ethnicity.
- Seventy percent of consumers say participating in experiential marketing would increase purchase consideration.
- Sixty-six percent say experiential marketing is extremely influential on brand opinion.
- Seven in ten consumers said participating in a live experience would make them more receptive to the brand's marketing.

Implications for entertainment marketers are extensive: fusing entertainment content with products and brands creates excitement about both entities.

The Role of the "Big" Agency

The *Red Book* contains more than 2,500 advertising agencies, yet only a few big agencies control most of the entertainment providers, corporations, and franchises. In 2005, more than $40 billion was spent in measured media buys for the entertainment industry. Necessary to support blockbuster films and new TV network and cable program launches, entertainment advertising budgets continue to increase, making both types of properties attractive and profitable clients. Most of the major agencies use outside firms to supply research, data, direct marketing, trailers, media planning and buying, public relations, and Internet and lobbying activities and functions, yet they maintain control over concepts. In addition to the global giants, small and mid-sized agencies provide creative projects for entertainment companies.

Although not all entertainment companies are turning to a single agency for worldwide promotions, an increasing number are lining up their brands with just a few international agencies—a strategy called **alignment fever**. This trend has spelled success for global agency networks; the top 10 agencies' combined share of global advertising spending has doubled in the past decade.

As advertising agencies have opened up units specializing in entertainment, Hollywood talent agencies have created units specializing in marketing, as have industry lawyers. Product placement firms have reinvented themselves as strategic integration specialists. Former studio, agency, network, talent, and marketing executives became backers of specialty companies servicing the entertainment industry. Such consortiums are joining to identify appropriate measurement tools to determine their return on investment.

With lucrative sponsorship, licensing, and product placement deals (see chapters 8 and 15), many clients are forming marketing partnerships with advertising and promotion agencies to develop special applications for branding. And agency billing practices are changing methods of compensation from a percentage of media buys to a share of the profits. Such a practice makes accountability more important and means that agencies become partners rather than service providers. The convergence of marketing with entertainment entities is creating unique partnerships, and in some cases building bridges to connect these very different businesses in a win-win situation. A list of agencies and their clients is presented in Exhibit 2.4.

Stealth Marketing[9]

Stealth marketing, or undercover marketing, is a subset of *guerrilla marketing* (a war or battle strategy), in which consumers do not realize they are being marketed to. For

▪ ▪ ▪ **EXHIBIT 2.4**   **Major Advertising Agencies Representing the Entertainment Industry**

Agency	Client Company
McCann Erickson	Columbia Pictures
Western Media, Division of Interpublic	Disney Studios
Grey Advertising	Warner Bros. Studios, WB Network, *Entertainment Weekly, People Magazine*
TWBA, Division of Omnicom	ABC TV Network
Young & Rubicam, Div of WPP	Showtime, Viacom, Blockbuster Video, Sony Electronics Game
Saatchi & Saatchi	News Corp

example, a marketing company pays actors to use a certain product visibly and convincingly in locations where target consumers congregate. While there, the actors talk up the product to people they meet at that location, even handing out samples if it is economically feasible. The actors often are able to sell consumers on the product they are touting without those consumers even noticing it.

When targeting consumers known to be consistent Internet users, undercover marketers have taken a significant interest in using Internet chat rooms and forums as a "location" for guerrilla marketing. In these settings, people tend to perceive everyone as peers, the semi-anonymity reduces the risk of being found out, and one marketer can personally influence a large number of people.

Whatever the risks, undercover marketing requires only a small investment for a large potential payoff. It remains a cheap and effective means of generating buzz, especially in markets such as tobacco and alcohol where media-savvy target consumers have become increasingly resistant or inaccessible to other forms of advertising.

Agencies Use Entertainment to Market Themselves

Competition for clients is tough among ad agencies, and some agencies call attention to themselves by breaking traditional client-generating strategies. For instance, to help win some beer accounts, WPP Group's JWT staged an elaborate stunt at the National Beer Wholesalers Convention in Las Vegas. The agency hired a group of actors to perform three days of street theater at the convention to promote a fictitious beverage called beerka. A "wedding" was held to "marry" beer and vodka to produce beerka. Dressed in wedding attire, the actors spent five hours at the Las Vegas airport on the convention's first day holding signs welcoming the beerka wedding party. Later, they circulated around Ballys, where the wholesalers' convention was held, handing out wedding invitations to beer executives. When attention waned, actors staged a fight on the convention floor. Conventioneers who wanted to find out more were directed to a Web site. After the convention, JWT sent wedding DVDs to 40 beer executives who had attended the convention. Why? To create a buzz about their agency.

Rather than settle for a buzz, Donny Deutsch, the president of ad agency Deutsch Inc. used the entertainment industry to position himself as the voice of the ad business to "give his agency a brand presence in the industry."[10] Deutsch is a media guy: his show on CNBC, "The Big Idea with Donny Deutsch," and his book, *Often Wrong, Never in Doubt,* have brought attention to himself and the agency. Purchased by Interpublic Group in 2000, Deutsch Inc. has not fared as well from Donny's publicity as Donny himself; the agency lost nine accounts including Bank of America, Mitsubishi, and Revlon with total billings of $849 million. Donny Deutsch continues to entertain, but neither his clients nor his boss are amused.

Industry Consolidation

Along with the convergence of technology, advertising, and entertainment, acquisitions proliferate. In the 1990s, Sony expanded its technology business by acquiring companies that produce film and TV, and it developed its own movie media entity, Sony Productions. Apple entered the music distribution business after developing the iPod in 2001. Disney branched out beyond parks and resorts by purchasing a sports network, a film production company (Pixar Animation), and a television network; forming

▪▪▪▪▪▪▪▪▪   BOX 2-3   ▪▪▪▪▪▪▪▪▪▪

Focus on Careers

PROFILE OF A PR INTERN

As a **public relations intern**, Pauline Perenack works in the television industry for "Boyd Coddington's Hot Rods and Collectibles," one of the features of a reality show called *American Hot Rod*. On the show, a car is built from scratch as the cameras roll, and Perenack works on location with crews from the Discovery Channel as they film each week's segment, filling a variety of assignments.

Part of Perenack's job is writing press releases about upcoming car unveilings and attending to members of the media who cover the show. She also acts as the contact person for media organizations that want interviews or to develop feature stories on the show or its stars. With access to one of the most well-known hot-rod shops in the country, Perenack watches cars being built in preparation for being taken apart and rebuilt as part of the reality show, which is taped at a later date. "Meeting people from around the world is the most stimulating part of the position," says Perenack.

After graduating from the University of Calgary in 2004 with a major in communications, Perenack began interning to gain experience in television. "Internships allow you to angle your career toward a particular position, or simply walk away if you find it's not the industry for you. Making contacts to use later on to find a job is another advantage of being an intern. Or, you can take a job with the sponsor of your internship. After eight months here, my boss offered me a permanent position."

In Her Words

Challenge

Making the right connections is the biggest public relations task. After my boss, Boyd, was asked to come for an appearance and overnight stay on board the *U.S.S. Nimitz*, I heard him on the phone refusing to appear if his wife, Jo, couldn't come along. Since it was against ship policy to have married people travel together, I knew we were in trouble. Boyd just won't travel without Jo! During the few weeks that followed the invitation, I worked hard to develop a positive connection with the ship's public affairs officer. He finally understood the situation and arranged for them both to spend the night aboard the ship, even though they had to have separate quarters!

Frustration

The most frustrating experience I had involved a misunderstanding that occurred when I got the task of answering some of the hundreds of e-mails that come into the shop every day. In response to what I

(Continued)

interpreted to be an inquiry from a French man about purchasing one of the show's cars, I said they were not for sale. In fact, the inquiry was about having a car of his own customized as part of the show. My confusion created the loss of an important client as well as ill will between myself and my boss. What I learned was that tact and verification work better than a knee-jerk response based on assumption. Always make certain you check for accuracy.

an Internet group; and developing games based on its *Pirates of the Caribbean* movie franchise. Beverage giant Seagram is now in the theme park and movie business. The gaming software market, while still somewhat fragmented, is consolidating as well. Electronic Arts holds the biggest share (20.8 percent) of the market, which is more than double the share of its close competitors Activision (8.3 percent) and Nintendo (7.7 percent).[11]

As large companies continue to gobble up media and entertainment properties, power shifts and empires rise and fall. A few conglomerations run not only the Hollywood studios, but also the giant media companies that own the studios. They created a new version of Hollywood, but they failed to master the corporate intrigues that would

Macy's Thanksgiving Day Parade, a sponsorship event.

▪▪▪**EXHIBIT 2.5**   Moguls and Monopolies

President	Corporation	Holdings	Countries
Robert Iger	Disney	Parks, Resorts ESPN, ABC Disney Channel	China, Japan, Europe Latin America 182 nations
C. M. Armstrong	AT&T	Liberty Media Media stocks	South Africa, Asia cable
Michael Linton	Sony	film production TV Sony Entertain.	Europe, Asia 5 continents Latin America, Asia, Europe
Jack Welch	GE	NBC, CNBC	Europe, Asia
Rupert Murdoch Peter Chernin	News Corporation	TV 20th Century Fox	U.S., Asia, L.A.
Edgar Bronfman	Seagram	Universal Music Group Universal Studio Parks TV channels	Global Asia Europe, Asia
Gerald Levin	AOL/Time Warner	200 subsidiaries CNN International HBO	200 nations Europe, Latin America, Asia
Barry Meyer Bob Pittman Sumner Redstone Tom Preston Brad Grey	Viacom	Warner Brothers AOL Nickelodeon MTV Paramount Pictures Blockbuster CBS	worldwide
Thomas Middelhoff	Bertelsmann	TV, radio BMG music Random House	Europe Asia, South Africa, Brazil
Brian Roberts	Comcast	cable TV, phone E! TV, Style, Golf, Outdoor Life networks	23 states U.S.
J. Messlert	Vivendi Universal	Universal Music Canal+ TV Vivendi Universal Games	Global France Global

enable them to rule not just the studio lot, but also the business world beyond. This generation of creative moguls, instead of making Hollywood the center of the universe, gave us a world that is now governed by the wants and needs of 17-year-old boys on any given Saturday night.[12] At this writing, the scorecard in Exhibit 2.5 recaps who owns what and where.

The conglomerates listed above continue to amass, consolidate, and cross-pollinate their interests in publishing, broadcasting, cable programming, movie and TV production, distribution, theme parks, lodging, and real estate. Mergers such as the deal

:ween Disney and Apple to provide ABC TV shows on its iTunes store for playing
the video iPod, and the agreement between Apple and Pixar Animation Studios to
:ribute short animated features are two examples of cross-industry efforts at content development and distribution.

Ties That Bind Advertising and Entertainment

Tie-ins are a way to connect an event or product with another event or product, so that both brands benefit from the association. For marketers aiming at the lucrative children's audience, few opportunities are more valuable than the Macy's Thanksgiving Day Parade. More than 50 million viewers watch the three-hour parade on network television, while 2.5 million people line the parade route to watch the event in person.[13] The parade is a launching pad for promotional campaigns, including product tie-ins involving movies, TV shows, and merchandise.

In 2005, a huge Chicken Little balloon was used to remind viewers of the movie, which opened in theaters the same month. Similarly, a Scooby-Doo balloon matched plush toys available at Macy's stores nationwide, and a float featuring characters from *Hi Hi Puffy Ami Yumi* coincided with the Cartoon Network's promotional campaign for the show. In the 2004 parade, a balloon appearance of SpongeBob SquarePants was timed to coincide with the release of the feature-length movie that year; Sponge Bob fans went wild.

A float sponsored by Pillsbury, called the Holiday Lovin' Oven, carried the Doughboy character and the season winner of the *American Idol* contest. And Garfield was back to promote his new 2006 film release. Unapologetic commercialism determined most of the event's cast of characters, although a few oldies, such as Mr. Potato Head, licensed from Hasbro by the U.S. Potato Board to promote potato nutrition, were included.

FINALLY: LET'S SUM UP ▪▪▪▪▪▪▪

A global audience population, digital technology, and the desire of multinational conglomerates for revenue streams have joined to generate a pervasive synergy that allows entertainment to be everywhere. Combine technology's reach with businesses' global push and you have messages woven into every aspect of audiences' lives. The danger, of course, is that the more pervasive the messages, the less consumers are likely to react and respond to them. The need for authenticity pushes audiences toward stimuli that deliver a more creative answer to their needs. Your job as marketer is to entice audiences into venues where they may delight in the sights and sounds of an entertainment experience.

GOT IT? LET'S REVIEW ▪▪▪▪▪▪▪

- Technology has made entertainment in the digital age a personal, self-generated, persistent, and embedded element of our society.
- Global intellectual property protection impacts the use and development of entertainment experiences worldwide.

- The convergence of advertising and entertainment, known as the Madison and Vine syndrome, necessitates the marriage of the industries.
- Multinational media corporations are segmenting the globe into cultural continents for program content delivery.

Now Try This: Let's Apply What We've Learned ▪▪▪▪▪▪▪

1. Using the Internet, check out the newest forms of reality games. Develop a franchising idea to carry these games into the workplace.
2. Check out the Web sites for three of the companies featured in Exhibit 2.2. Which site does the best job of capturing your attention? Which elements are most useful for developing entertaining interaction?
3. Go to the WPP Web site and check which companies are now under the parent company. What does this monopoly suggest for the future of branded entertainment?
4. Investigate Disney's marketing for their Hong Kong theme park. How does it differ from the way Disney markets its parks in the U.S., France, and Japan?

Questions: Let's Review ▪▪▪▪▪▪▪

1. What other examples of the Madison and Vine syndrome (the merging of advertising and entertainment) can you identify as useful for marketing experiences?
2. How does "experiential marketing" differ from marketing experiences?
3. How has digitalization changed the focus of entertainment for providers of children's television and gaming?
4. What is the role of the big agency for entertainment marketing?

More Stuff to Read ▪▪▪▪▪▪▪

Marieke de Mooij. *Global Marketing and Advertising: Understanding Cultural Paradoxes.* Thousand Oaks, CA: Sage, 1998.

Scott Donaton. *Madison & Vine. Why the Entertainment and Advertising Industries Must Converge to Survive.* New York: McGraw-Hill, 2004.

Mike Enlow. *Online Stealth Marketing.* eBooks2006.com, 2006.

Yahya Kamalipour. *Global Communication.* Australia: Wadsworth, 2002.

Notes ▪▪▪▪▪▪▪

1. Brian Montopoli, "Little Known Brands Get Lift Through Word-of-Blog," *New York Times,* June 6, 2005.
2. C. A. Anderson and B. J. Bushman, "Effects of violent video games on aggressive behavior, aggressive cognition, aggressive affect, physiological arousal, and prosocial behavior: A meta-analytic review of the scientific literature," Iowa State University, Department of Psychology, 2001.
3. Stuart Elliott, *New York Times,* Oct. 17, 2005.
4. P. Lewis, "Invasion of the Podcast People," *Fortune,* July 25, 2005, p. 204.
5. "Big Media Wants a Piece of Your Pod," *New York Times* online, July 4, 2005.
6. Richard Gershon, "The Transnationals: Media Corporations, International TV Trade and Entertainment Flows," in Ann Cooper-Chen, ed., *Global Entertainment Media* (Lawrence Erlbaum, 2005).
7. Brian Steinberg, "Madison Avenue Is Getting the Beat," "Advertising" column, *Wall Street Journal,* June 23, 2005.
8. Liz Bigham, from a Jack Morton Worldwide (division of Interpublic), corporate promotion piece; Bigham describes the survey and its findings.
9. As defined by http://en.wikipedia.org/wiki/Stealth_marketing.
10. Devin Leonard, "Media Bubble" column, *Fortune,* Oct. 31, 2005, p. 46.
11. Geoff Keighley, "Could This Be The Next Disney?," *Business 2.0,* January 2003.
12. "In Hollywood, All Players but No Power," *New York Times,* Aug. 8, 2005.
13. Julie Bosman, "Advertising" column, *New York Times,* Nov. 23, 2005.

3

Characterizing Our Experience Culture

Culture has always been driven by the marketplace.
It's just that today the marketplace, having invaded every
nook and cranny of our lives, is completely supplanting culture;
the marketplace has become our culture.
—TOM ROBBINS[1]

Chapter Objectives

After reading this chapter, you should be able to answer the following questions:

■ What makes entertainment an *experience industry?*
■ How does *service marketing* differ from entertainment marketing?
■ How does entertainment marketing address *timing* and *attention?*
■ What *convergence strategies* work for marketing both experiences and brands?
■ How does *audience fragmentation* underlie the marketing challenge?
■ What *global paradigm* can be used for understanding cultural differences?

Chapter 2 showed us how merging technologies and corporations affect the way audiences receive entertainment. This chapter grounds our understanding of how entertainment marketing differs from product and service marketing. As a way to delineate the unique characteristics of entertainment marketing, we look at aspects of services marketing and of entertainment marketing as they converge in the hospitality industry. We also discuss the cultural dimensions of entertainment marketing and the volatile characteristics of today's fragmented entertainment audiences.

Entertainment Is an Experience Industry

Entertainment is an experience industry. So, is it a service industry as well? Entertainment as a commodity involves service *only* when its core product is *customer service* satisfaction, which is an essential component of operating resorts, lodging, spas, and

▮▮▮ **EXHIBIT 3.1**   **The Experience Realms**

		Absorption		
	Entertainment		*Educational*	
Passive				**Active**
Participation		*		**Participation**
	Esthetics		*Escapist*	
		Immersion		

Source: The Experience Economy, 1999, p. 30.

performance venues. Such experiential venues must have a service culture that differentiates them from the competition; they must become the *provider of choice* for visitors.

According to a Marriott executive, "If a company takes care of its employees, they will take care of its guests." The hospitality industry's philosophy focuses on attracting and retaining quality employees. In this industry, customer expectations are higher because of the service comparisons they can make within industry segments such as restaurants and lodging. Venues such as concerts, theme parks, and museums also adhere to this customer service philosophy.

In *The Experience Economy,* authors[2] Joseph Pine and James Gilmore present a view of staged experiences as *experience realms* of engagement, organized by type and level of involvement. Exhibit 3.1 diagrams this experiential view. Four levels of audience participation—passive and active (horizontal axis) and absorption and immersion (vertical axis)—describe connections that unite customers within an event or performance. Coupled with these dimensions are four realms of a single experience—entertainment, education, escape, and estheticism. These realms are mutually compatible domains that often commingle to form uniquely personal encounters. The *entertainment* realm contains the type of passive absorption experience that is provided by mediated and staged performances. Absorbing activity that gradually unfolds, such as what visitors experience in museums, falls into the *educational* realm. Audiences may participate in the *escapist* realm by actively participating in immersive environments, such as theme parks, casinos, and Internet chat rooms. Although passive, immersion in art or visual delights carries audiences into an *esthetic* realm. Marketers can use this realms model to understand the relationship between an experience and its target audience.

Marketers may enhance the "realness" of a particular experience by blurring the boundaries between realms to promote an immersive venue of entertainment experiences. Ontario Mills shopping center in Southern California was designed to merge aspects of all four realms. First, it provided businesses that offer both staged entertainment and escapist experiences—a 37-screen movie house, an arcade/restaurant, and Spielberg's Gameworks. Then, it laid out these businesses on distinctive streetscapes with neighborhoods to provide esthetic and educational experiences. The result is a cumulative adventure that transcends shopping by itself. By marketing all levels of an attraction—educational, escapist, esthetic, and entertainment—a generic space becomes a mnemonic place that creates memories and fosters play. As we will see in later chapters, successfully staged marketing events involve more than just offering an experience; success is contingent on the qualities inherent in successful service businesses that accompany entertainment experiences. So in many instances, service and entertainment marketing intersect. They are, however, different entities, as the next section illustrates.

▪▪▪ Distinguishing among Product, Service, and Entertainment Marketing

All forms of entertainment rely to some degree on service elements. And although some entertainment content is considered product, experiences are not products, services, or commodities. By comparing the dimensions of products with those of entertainment, we can identify the challenges presented to experience marketers. Exhibit 3.2 outlines the differences between and the implications of marketing products and experiences.

▪▪▪ **EXHIBIT 3.2** Products vs. Entertainment[1]

Products	*Experiences*	*Implications*
Tangible	Intangible	Entertainment cannot be inventoried Pricing is difficult
Standardized	Context-dependent	Audience satisfaction depends on delivery and many uncontrollable factors
Production and consumption separate	Simultaneous production and consumption	Audiences participate in transaction Audience members affect each other Employees affect audience satisfaction Mass production difficult Experience cannot be returned or resold
Nonperishable	Perishable	Hard to synchronize supply & demand with experience Entertainment cannot be returned or resold

Because entertainment is delivered as an *action*—a performance, experience, or event—it cannot be felt, seen, tasted, or touched in the same way as a tangible product can be. Entertainment is *intangible.* As such, it presents marketing challenges, because the demand for this intangible entity fluctuates. Seasonality, tour schedules, film releases, and performance dates often drive experience promotions. Also, because entertainment is an experience, not a tangible product, and the actual cost of a "unit of experience" is hard to determine and to price.

McDonald's standardizes it hamburgers and its fries, but entertainers rarely present the same performance twice (every version is different), and no vacation, theme park visit, or shopping spree is experienced the same way as another. Consumer satisfaction is context-dependent and predicated on how the experience is delivered as much as the content of the performance. A rude usher can ruin a ballet for an audience member. No two participants have the same expectations or standards for experiences; and often the experience is dependent on the actions or behavior of other audience members. Therefore, ensuring consistent experience delivery quality is quite challenging for marketers.

Products are produced or manufactured, then sold and consumed; experiences are sold first, then produced and consumed simultaneously. A theme park can provide an experience only after the ticket has been purchased; the production satisfaction comes from audience interaction with the production and consumption experience. The Danish developers of LegoLand theme park began with a product—children's building blocks—and morphed that product into an experience in which participants travel around the park to view cities and environments made entirely of Legos. Workstations provide kids with an opportunity to construct Lego creations on their own or with friends and parents. And, of course, everyone is encouraged to purchase Legos to take home.

Experience providers and audience members interact with one another as entertainment is literally consumed, and a better-quality entertainment experience is the result. The real-time nature of entertainment means that marketers can customize offerings for individual audience segments by changing venues and content to fit audience needs.

The major distinctions among products, services, and experiences are summarized and elaborated in Exhibit 3.3. Unlike products, **services** are intangible activities

---

▮▮▮ **EXHIBIT 3.3**   Economic Distinctions among Products, Services, and Experiences

Offering	*Products*	*Services*	*Experiences*
Economic function	Make	Deliver	Stage
Nature of offering	Tangible	Intangible	Memorable
Key attribute	Standardized	Customized	Personal
Method of supply	Inventoried after production	Delivered on demand	Revealed over a duration
Seller	Manufacturer	Provider	Stager
Buyer	User	Client	Guest
Factors of demand	Features	Benefits	Sensations

Source: Pine and Gilmore, *The Experience Economy,* 1999, p. 6.

customized to the individual request of known clients. Services accomplish specific tasks, and products supply the means. Most advanced countries have shifted to service economies in which consumers prefer to purchase services rather than commodities. However, whenever a company uses services as the stage and products as props to engage a consumer, it sells experiences.

Some distinctions among products, services, and entertainment are less obvious than others. What is the distinction between intangible and memorable, for instance? *Intangible* means that service is bestowed, not built, and can be delivered well or poorly. *Memorable* means that an experience stands out among others for its unique qualities. Services are customized to the needs of a consumer group, while experiences are ours alone. While subtle, these distinctions are what render experiences as the most pleasurable form of leisure-time entertainment for participants—the better the service, the more enjoyable the experience.

Entertainment experiences cannot be saved, stored, resold, or returned. If you miss the play, it moves on to another location or performance venue. Marketers cannot inventory *perishable* experiences—events that exist in real time. They can only use past research to predict box office receipts. Thus, forecasting and planning for capacity venue utilization are challenging decision areas for entertainment marketers.

The GAPS Model of Service Quality[3]

In many instances, services contribute to experience satisfaction. Tourist services—resorts, spas, and certain other venues—package experiences around products and services that, while perishable, have a sustainable foundation. These services measure success in terms of audience satisfaction. A key model developed to help experience providers assess their satisfaction strategy is based on closing the gaps that exist between *audience expectations* and *audience perceptions*. **Expectations** are standards or reference points the audience member brings to the experience, and **perceptions** are subjective assessments of the actual experience. Sources of expectations come from marketing factors, such as pricing, advertising, and promotion, and from personal experience, such as needs, competitive offerings, and world-of-mouth communication.

The GAPS model of service quality suggests that four *gaps* that negatively affect service may occur within a providing organization. The four provider gaps are based on the organization's lack of effectiveness with these factors: (1) not knowing what customers expect, (2) not selecting the right experience designs and standards, (3) not delivering experience designs and standards, and (4) not matching performance to promises. A GAPS audit evaluates the difference between consumers' expectations and perceptions.

Provider gaps occur most often in hotels that are considered places to experience entertainment and live performance. Las Vegas hotels, themed and infused with museum exhibits, live shows, gambling, and shopping, must measure their own performance to distinguish themselves from the plethora of competition.

Measuring Service Quality at the Venetian Hotel

In order to dramatize how the GAPS model is applied to a resort experience, we will look at one client's particular experience at the Las Vegas Venetian Hotel. Built by Steve Wynn, the Venetian has enjoyed high occupancy and positive publicity in the recent past.

When selecting a hotel for a family reunion with her mother, sister, and daughter, our client had high expectations that were predicated on several sources: a Travel Channel show on Las Vegas, an article in the Sunday *New York Times* Travel section, the hotel's Web site, and positive word-of-mouth from a friend who said the Venetian was "her favorite place in all of Las Vegas." Complete with an indoor/outdoor canal, gondola rides, and canal-side restaurants, the Venetian received reviewers' praise for its enjoyable Madame Tussauds wax museum and its distinguished Guggenheim art exhibits.

When booking, our client asked for a handicapped suite to accommodate her mother, who is in a wheelchair, and beds for three adults. She was assured there would be adequate handicap accessories in the suite, two king-sized beds, and a pull-out sofa. She reserved five days and nights in the hotel at $425 per night.

The group's experience-based perceptions of the services they should have received did not meet their expectations. Here is how the GAPS model can be applied to characterize the hotel's deficiencies as our client and her family experienced them.

Gap 1: Not Knowing Consumer Expectations

Our client had four expectations of service that the hotel did not meet: (1) handicapped accommodations to code, (2) safe harbor for a garaged car, (3) careful loading and unloading of luggage, and (4) remuneration for any damage caused by hotel employees. The Venetian did not meet our client's expectations according to these GAPS factors of analysis:

1. *Inadequate marketing research orientation to understand how to respond to consumer needs.*
   - The Council on Aging has specific guidelines for providing handicapped lodging, and these were obviously ignored. Our client had to order a special toilet seat and make arrangements for a wheelchair that would fit around large beds.
   - Hotel valet parkers took our client's SUV into the hotel parking garage; when retrieved, it had a dented front fender and soiled seats for which no one took responsibility.
   - The valet allowed a package to fall off the luggage cart and smash to the cement; he laughed as he picked up the parcel and put it into the trunk of the client's car.

2. *Lack of interaction between management and patrons.*
   - Requests to management for remuneration were either ignored or passed to another department.
   - Letters to the operations manager of the hotel went unanswered.

3. *Lack of market segmentation.*
   - Because a large percentage of Las Vegas visitors are handicapped or have disabilities, a hotel serving this demographic should focus on the segment's needs.

4. *Inadequate service recovery.*

- Management did not acknowledge the problems that occurred or the client's dissatisfaction and failed to provide a remedy.
- After days of endless dialogue following the unhappy visit, our client received a letter informing her that damage reports must be filed before leaving the hotel premises.
- Our client did not receive compensation for the damage to her car or reimbursement for a glass platter that was dropped and broken by the valet as he loaded the car for departure.

Gap 2: Not Having the Right Experience Designs and Standards

Our client's expectations for high-quality service design may be due the following standard deficiencies as characterized by these factors of the GAPS model:

1. *Absence of customer-driven standards.*

- More than half the vacationing population is older than 60 years of age, yet the Venetian has not made adequate changes in their hotel design configurations to accommodate this population.
- Slot machines have fixed chairs, prohibiting use by wheelchair-bound patrons.

2. *Servicescape design doesn't meet customer needs.*

- Unsecured parking structure.

Gap 3: Not Delivering on Experience Designs and Standards

Our client's expectations of careful employees and responsive management may be a result of this GAPS factor:

1. *Deficiencies in human resource policies.*

- Hiring of incompetent staff.
- Inadequate training of personnel.
- Lack of published service standards.

Gap 4: Not Matching Performance and Promises

Our client's expectations for quality performance could have resulted from these GAPS factors:

1. *Absence of strong internal marketing program.*

- Employees had a different agenda from that of the hotel management.

2. *Lack of adequate education for customers.*

- No signage or literature stating a policy that damages incurred on the premises must be reported before leaving that premises.

3. *Overpromising.*

- Advertising and personal selling overstated the hotel's ability to provide necessary equipment for handicapped, safety for garaged vehicles, and care for guest belongings.

The GAPS model provides an understanding of the nature and extent of the gap between customer expectations and perceptions of experience. The model stresses the

▮▮▮ **EXHIBIT 3.4   SERVQUAL Instrument for Measuring Quality**

KEY ELEMENTS OF ENTERTAINMENT SERVICES MARKETING

Access: approachability and ease of contact with venue or destination
Example: *Locating a stadium near a freeway off-ramp*

Communication: two-way conversations; listening to audience feedback
Example: *Conducting exit interviews and implementing changes suggested*

Competence: skills and knowledge to provide advertised experience
Example: *Superior visuals and acoustics for staging an opera*

Courtesy: respect for audiences by experience providers
Example: *Helpful ushers, pleasant tour guides*

Credibility: provide honesty and reputation
Example: *Make refunds available for dissatisfaction or missed performance*

Reliability: ability to perform promised experience on a consistent basis
Example: *Last visit provides the same pleasure as the first*

Responsiveness: immediate adaptation to audience preference changes
Example: *Expand the number of box seats to meet demand*

Security: freedom from danger and risk in a venue or at a destination
Example: *Regular maintenance of park rides*

Tangibles: appearance of physical facilities, personnel, visual materials
Example: *Interior ambiance creates a sensual experience*

Understanding consumers: know their lifestyle considerations
Example: *Aging population requires more elevators, wheelchair access*

Source: SERVQUAL, Delivering Quality Service, 1990.

importance of the providing organization's need to focus on the audience and to use knowledge about the audience to drive business strategy. Another measurement tool developed to assess quality, the SERVQUAL instrument, is profiled in Exhibit 3.4.

▮▮▮ Time and Attention

Once we acknowledge the importance of advertising entertainment, we must look to what makes promoting entertainment so different from promoting products. The cultural industries—recording, arts, television, radio—commodify, package, and market experiences as opposed to physical products or services. Their stock and trade is selling short-term access to simulated worlds and altered states of consciousness. Unlike products with tangible qualities, entertainment brands rely heavily on intangible assets—not bricks and mortar—in order to generate future net cash flows.

The *intangible assets* of experience-based brands are franchises, licenses, royalties, goodwill, copyrights, trademarks, and the brand or logo itself. Customer relationships, employee skills, and management strategies drive profits in the entertainment business. The value of entertainment enterprises depends first and foremost on the marketing and communication used to create excitement around and generate revenue from those enterprises.

Using a network-based approach to organization, the Hollywood culture is the prototype for capitalist systems. In other words, it depends on forming relationships for raising capital. The entertainment industry, which deals with the risks accompanying perishable and intangible products, must find a quick audience for each unique experience in order to recoup its investment. In this climate, transnational companies stay on top by controlling finance and distribution channels, while pushing the burdens of ownership and management of physical assets onto smaller entities.

Marketing's role is that of impresario of cultural productions. Marketers help entertainment producers create elaborate fantasies from the bits and pieces of contemporary culture and sell them as live experiences. Our job is to find new themes for eliciting human response. The unique aspects of entertainment marketing are overviewed here with the caveat that each plays a major role in how promotions are executed in the entertainment industry. *Immediacy* and *attention* are key business elements in entertainment marketing.

Timing Is Crucial for Branded Entertainment Promotion

Purchasing products is primarily a need-based activity; when you are out of toothpaste, you go buy more. With entertainment, however, need is not the driving factor. No one needs to hear a concert or see a play. So, marketers promoting entertainment must create desire in order to stimulate purchase activity.

Because entertainment is available 24/7, marketers must know when and to whom a promotional message should be directed. Many entertainment experiences are time-sensitive—a concert plays for only one night, a play for only several weeks. Therefore, the marketer's actions of planting the seed and creating desire in consumers are time-sensitive as well. Once the concert or play has gone, no amount of awareness or desire can affect past sales.

Immediacy Is Key

The opening weekend of a movie makes or breaks the film, so promotional messages must begin as "teasers" even before the film is complete. Trailers, licensed products, and product tie-ins must be conceived and implemented well in advance of release. True, the film has an afterlife on DVD and rental, but the brand changes from hype to holdover.

Audiences are used to having a plethora of entertainment options available whenever they want them. When consumers decide to act on a desire to see a concert, they consult reviews, schedules, and past brand associations. Each of those influences must be positive to close a sale, in other words, to convince the consumer to purchase a ticket. In order to make a sale, marketers must manage messages and monitor impressions for maximum exposure. Audiences who cannot find the information they need to make an entertainment choice will select another option. And once the selection opportunity passes, it is gone.

To entice audiences, try the *Sayre 3T technique:* tickle, transfer, and trap. *Tickle* audiences with excitement or suspense well in advance of the event. *Transfer* that tickle into the desire to attend with product tie-ins, celebrity endorsements, and clever promotions. Then, *trap* the audience by offering an easy and immediate way for them to purchase tickets. With multiple, successful completions, your branded experience has a good chance of becoming a hit.

The Attention Principle

With so many technological options available to us today, information is no longer a scarce resource—attention is. In the workplace, computer screens juggle messages, text documents, PowerPoint presentations, spreadsheets, and Web browsers all at once, forcing people to multitask and become masters of dealing with continual interruption. This condition of *continuous partial attention*[4] allows workers to connect with each other and the world. Like workers, consumers are subject to thought interruptions, and consumers selectively choose which messages receive attention. Therefore, before marketing can be effective, it must grab a consumer's attention. And attention, as a scarce resource, is a valuable commodity—an attention economy is based on getting the "ear" of an audience first, before a message can be transmitted. Whether you are promoting a play or a casino, you must gain the interest of your audience so that they will pay attention to your marketing message. Messages directed at entertainment promotion must either educate or motivate, and they must convince consumers that your activity or venue is worth their attention. This is not easy in a world where every other brand promoter is trying equally as hard to capture your consumer's attention with a competitive message. Once marketers get consumers' attention, we must create awareness about an event, celebrity, destination, or venue. Without knowledge about the when and where of entertainment activities, audiences cannot attend. A primary function of entertainment marketing is getting news of the event into the consumer's *evoked set* of experiential brands. An **evoked set** is all the experiential brands and activities known to an individual audience member that are used when making purchase decisions. Unless information reaches the target segment, audience choices are severely limited. Reaching audiences effectively requires riding the *trend wave*. What interested audiences yesterday may not interest them today.

Holding audiences' attention is another marketing challenge. While audiences will pay for entertainment, and even pay well, entertainment providers—those who produce the plays, build the venues, and the play the music—often find it difficult to make a profit from the sales of that content alone. Similarly, concert venues and theaters often do not make a profit from ticket sales alone. Instead, they may make their money through concession sales—the drinks, popcorn, and T-shirts you buy while you are there. Thus, while corporations may not be able to buy audience attention directly, they do so indirectly, by covering the costs of the entertainment "bait" that will capture consumer attention for them.

Weaving products and services into experience is one form of convergence. When we think about marketing experience, however, another form of convergence occurs: the marriage of advertising and entertainment. This union, which has grown increasingly strong in the last couple of decades, is not likely to dissolve in the near future. In fact, the symbiotic relationship between product and entertainment promotion is bound by economic cement that probably will hold the entities together for a long time. Once acknowledged, convergence must be approached strategically and viewed as a powerful marketing tool.

▪▪▪▪▪▪▪▪▪▪▪   BOX 3-1   ▪▪▪▪▪▪▪▪▪▪

A Closer Look at Ethics

ALTERNATIVE REALITY BRANDING

To introduce Audi's 2006 A3 model, the McKinney & Silver advertising agency used a variety of untried methods to suck the public into its innovative "Heist" campaign. Like alternative-reality gaming, the unorthodox campaign blended actual events with the imaginings of game creators by combining real events with fiction; online video, including a cyberspace play; blogs; conventional print and TV ads; and journalism. A unique form of branded entertainment, the campaign skated across multiple media platforms and live events to attract young consumers who had all but turned their backs on 30-second spots and static Internet banners or print ads. The campaign was so unusual and contained so many risky elements, that Audi employed a lawyer to be part of the ad team full time.

Based on a fictional drama, the campaign began with a staged car theft at a New York City dealership and continued when handbills, which indicated that information about the theft was being sought, were posted at the International Auto Show. The stunt was augmented by ads placed in major magazines and on blogs, and by streaming videos featuring fictional characters purporting to have "witnessed" aspects of the theft.

The story was moved forward in part by means of a cyberspace play. One of the play's characters was a computer hacker who is a partner in a company that recovers lost and stolen art. This character learns that a notorious art thief has stolen an A3 from a Manhattan dealership—and the stolen car happens to contain his computer files. He tracks the car to a New Jersey chop shop and steals it back from the thieves. Back in real life, the

(Continued)

dealership from which the car was "stolen" was turned into a "real-life" crime scene, complete with police tape, a smashed glass door, and security officers standing guard.

In the meantime, fake ads that looked like ads for real companies specializing in art recovery were placed in *Wired, Esquire,* the *Robb Report,* and *USA Today.* Actors advanced the plot by creating c-mails, online "security films," and blogs that the characters used to communicate within the story. These story augmentations were followed by more than 125,000 people who tapped into various Web sites created by Audi. Fans even launched their own Web sites, such as Smirkbox.com and Argn.com, which enabled devotees to follow the action.

Actors hired for the play showed up in character at major music festivals to stage fights, thefts, or escapes, and appeared in Los Angeles at the E3 Expo of the interactive media industry. The online play leaked into real life at Coachella, the Indio, California, music festival, when the in-character actors were barraged by gamers, who forced the online video producer to change the script to incorporate some fans into the story. The TV ads for Audi's A3 were directly tied into the game: The ads asked viewers to report any information of the stolen car's location on Audiusa.com/a3 Web site; print ads were tagged with the same plea.

The target audience—college-educated men 25–34, earning more than $125,000 a year—thought the "Heist" campaign was cool, proving that buzz marketing, designed to create word of mouth, can surpass traditional media campaigns by maintaining consumer brand interest.

What do you think?

1. Some consumers thought this was a "bad marketing idea" because it made light of a robbery. Is Audi treading on ethical "thin ice" here?

2. What dangers can develop from creating fictional action within a real setting?

SOURCE: David Kelly, *Business Week,* May 16, 2005.

▪▪▪ Convergence Marketing Strategies

Chapter 2 introduced the notion of convergence between different business genres, which provides the backdrop for entertainment marketing. This chapter expands that concept by discussing convergence strategies that are essential for entertainment marketing. One of the dangers of convergence is that first, experiential marketing content will be developed with a specific advertiser in mind, and that only after this content has been created will thought be given to seeking an audience. Success in entertainment marketing resides in creative quality that serves both the advertiser and the audience. In order to capitalize on convergence, marketers must develop strategies that lead to providing audiences with quality content. The first step in achieving this goal is for entertainment producers and distributors to collaborate with advertising agencies.

Advertising's Role

The role of advertising in entertainment cannot be underestimated—advertising is essential for success. This is why so many conglomerates own both entertainment and advertising companies: Marrying these businesses is essential to success. Advertising and entertainment convergence takes place in a variety of configurations, including theater advertising and product placement. We bring this point up again to preface the subsequent explanation about the specific ways marketers use entertainment to promote brands, and how brands, in turn, rely on entertainment to sell themselves. First, we discuss media and entertainment's use of advertising to promote products, then we focus on how products are used to promote entertainment.

Media, entertainment, and stars are paired to promote branded products through:

1. "advergames" that combine games and marketing content served up on the Internet. (Mitsubishi's driving game)
2. "advertainment" that pairs stars with branded products. (Rolling Stone featured on a calendar with GM's Chevy; Takashi Murakami's art on designer handbags)
3. integration of product messages into scripted sitcoms and soaps and unscripted talk and reality show television programming. ("So I grabbed a bottle of Bud Lite and climbed into my Beemer")
4. product placement in film and TV shows, video games, and novels. (Hummer driven by *CSI Miami* star)
5. product advertising on TV, DVDs, and the Internet, and in theaters and magazines. (Aflack's talking duck; animated pop-up ads; Coke spots in theater ads for the movie *First Look*)
6. service advertising in printed inserts. (AIG Insurance company put a small book of poems into *New Yorker Magazine*)
7. blogs created to promote products. (Volvo blogs hype the safety of their cars)
8. music tie-ins. (Sinatra and Elvis music used to promote Las Vegas hotels)

One example of the fusion between advertising and entertainment was produced by New York City-based Screenvision in the form of a "pre-show" presented on more than 1,000 digital screens via satellite at Loews, Pacific, and Crown theaters. The October 2005 pre-show program, which was part of an in-cinema advertising campaign, featured a branded entertainment deal with sponsor Samsung Wireless. The pre-show promoted a "Scream Your Way to Hollywood" sweepstakes: a contest for the

Hummer stars in *CSI Miami.*

best recorded scream. The contest winner and a guest were sent to a Hollywood movie premiere. These campaigns are part of a number of tactics that have become increasingly attractive to marketers over the last few years, especially for the 18 to 34 demographic. According to the Cinema Advertising Council, industry revenue rose 23 percent, to $438 million, in 2004.

Leo Burnett USA, the ad agency known for creating Tony the Tiger, has integrated rock stars and artists into its company. In 2005, Burnett began an "artists in residence" program to bring guest musicians, songwriters, and producers into the Chicago agency's headquarters to meet with staffers on a quarterly basis. The hope is that ground-level collaboration can help ad agencies more easily use pop music in advertising messages by cutting through some of the red tape and financial obstacles that surround the use of such songs. (Led Zeppelin's song "Rock and Roll" was used to sell Cadillac, and Apple's iPod Shuffle advertised to the beat of Caesars' "Jerk It Out.") Based on the fact that songs can sell ads and ads can sell songs, the agency-artist alliance is further evidence of the inevitable convergence of advertising and entertainment.[5]

Products are used to promote mediated and live entertainment through:

- licensed merchandise. (Warner Brothers' characters and Yankee clothing)
- advertiser-funded programs. (GE sponsors public broadcasting shows)
- bottle caps and can tops with premiums. (Dr. Pepper tops redeemed for prizes)
- supermarket discount coupons. (half-off the LegoLand gate fee)

Many online games that once were embedded in advertisements now have Web sites of their own. Research shows that computer users spend an average of 3.5 minutes playing each game, and that users e-mail game recommendations to a total of 1.8 million friends a year. Game Web sites include elements of mainstream advertising campaigns and interactive capabilities that include game show hosts and player messaging. Capitalizing on the growing interest among computer users in so-called casual gaming, **advergaming** encourages consumers to engage in a branded experience—to spend time voluntarily with an ad. Orbitz travel company, for instance, offers Sink the Putt and Swing for the Fences on its site (orbitzgames.com), and the company is integrating travel-related games, such as Run for Your Flight and Pick Your Path, with action-oriented and puzzle games. Like other companies, Orbitz wants to convince people that their brand is the way to win at the travel game. A risk with advergaming, however, is that sponsors may become better known for games than for their products or services.

The advertising and entertainment industries' convergent and symbiotic relationship is accompanied by a fusion of TV and the Internet, and advertisers are confident that the Web is reinvigorating the endangered commercial. Such fusion means that viewers don't skip ads because they can't: The ads are digitally integrated into the shows themselves. Known as Internet Protocol TV (IPTV), this process is transforming advertising as we know it by placing ads in the context of shows rather than in commercial breaks.[6]

IPTV technology transforms video content into digital files and makes TV a two-way experience in which viewers chat on their screens or use their cell phones to remotely program the DVRs. In addition to using video-game product placements and text messages on cell phones, advertisers are looking to the Internet to provide the

BOX 3-2

Focus on Music and Culture

BRANDS AND SONGS

In 2004, 40 percent of the *Billboard* Top 20 hits mentioned at least one brand. According to American Brandstand, Cadillac was mentioned in more songs than any other brand, having earned 70 mentions. Hennessy had 69 mentions, Mercedes 63, Rolls Royce 62, and Gucci 49.

Cadillac is probably the best example of how a traditional brand can keep aware of youth culture without trying to exploit it. The company's recent success has been partly due to a healthy respect for hip-hop culture, which they understand without seeking to exploit.

The following lyrics evidence Cadillac's primacy in pop culture:

"I got plenty of room if you think you wanna roll/See this is what they make CADILLAC trucks for/Let's go to a place you ain't never been"
—"Shorty Wanna Ride," by Young Buck

"So, so, come on, come on/Don't get swung on, swung on/It's the knick-knack-patty-whack still riding CADILLACS/Family off the streets, made my homies put the baggies back."
—"Get Back," by Ludacris

But my love is bigger than a Honda
It's bigger than a Subaru.
Hey man there's only one thing
And one car that will do.
Anyway, we don't have to drive it.
Honey we can park it out in back
And have a party in your pink Cadillac.
—"Pink Cadillac," by Bruce Springsteen

SOURCE: AmericanBrandstand.com, 2005.

▪▪▪▪▪▪▪▪▪▪▪   **BOX 3-3**   ▪▪▪▪▪▪▪▪▪▪

Focus on Advergaming

USING DIGITAL MEDIA TO PROMOTE A CAR AS AN INTERNET GAME

After a steep decline in sales, Mitsubishi Motors North America launched a digital game promoting the company's new Eclipse model. The "Thrill Ride Challenge" game is a virtual timed driving race on one of six roads located around the world. Promoted on Yahoo and a variety of Web sites, including ESPN, Yahoo Autos, Edmunds, KellyBlueBook, AOL Autos, MSN, MP3, Gamespot, and iFilm, the game premiered in June 2005, when visitors to Yahoo were greeted by an Eclipse driving across the screen. Game participants with the best game time each week won a Mitsubishi flat-screen TV or an Apple iPod.

SOURCE: Jean Halliday, AdAge.com, June 9, 2005.

▪▪▪▪▪▪▪▪▪

---

same targeting and measurement capabilities from IPTV that they get from the mass Internet because IPTV is a point-to-point service—not a broadcast—every TV can potentially receive a different advertisement based on which shows the viewer has watched and other demographic information. The interaction goes even further: if you want to travel to a place featured on your TV, just click to make reservations.

Currently, on-demand Web entertainment gives its providers an opportunity to reduce costs for viewers, but those viewers must have a high tolerance for watching ads, because on-demand entertainment is beset by them. For instance, the *New York Times* is free online, but once on the site, readers must endure a plethora of advertising. You accept the ads, you get free stuff, which could actually make TV free again. *Forbes Magazine*'s reporter Sam Whitmore predicts that by 2010, advertising conglomerates WPP, Omnicom, and IPG will produce 80 percent of what American watches.[7] In other words, advertisers will produce content rather than commercials. Chapters 8 and 11 present more extensive examples of promotional convergence tools as they are used in an entertainment-integrated marketing campaign.

▪▪▪ The Changing Landscape of the Audience

Similar to marketing products and services, experiential marketing has to contend with ongoing changes in how consumers are categorized, reached, and measured. Some especially crucial changes involve audience products, audience fragmentation, and new audience group configurations. These are discussed briefly here.

Audience as Product[8]

Consumers, mass media organizations, and audience measurement firms together produce the **audience product** that is central to the audience marketplace. The process of producing and selling the audience product begins with audience consumption of media products, as shown in Exhibit 3.5 on the next page.

▪ ▪ ▪ **EXHIBIT 3.5 The Audience Marketplace**

	Audience measurement firms	<	<	<
				^
	>	predicted measured actual	>	Advertisers
Sample of consumers >	^	audience audience audience		v
	V	**The Audience Product**		
	Media organizations	<	<	<

Source: Philip Napoli, *Audience Economics,* 2003.

Consumer interaction with mass media firms (here, *media* means any form of consumable information or entertainment) takes place as media consumption choice; consumers' interaction with audience measurement firms takes place as their consumption habits are monitored. Audience consumption habits are measured using a small sample of consumers whose behaviors are generalized to the population as a whole. Both media and measurement firms are essential to the process: Without media firms, no audience exists to be measured; without measurement firms, no audience data exist to sell to advertisers.

Because they purchase audiences (in advertising rates) before they are actually produced, advertising's demand for audiences has a tremendous influence on the structure and behavior of media organizations *by shaping the content media provide to consumers.* Advertisers' demand for certain types of audiences dictates that media create product that caters to the types of audiences valued most highly by advertisers. Audience measurement firms also are influenced by advertisers' demand for specific types of data about media audiences—techniques are altered to best serve the clients who purchase the data. A reciprocal influence relationship bonds media organizations with measurement firms. Media organizations are major clients of measurement firms. When the industry demands better approaches to measuring media, they too influence the nature of measurement. Conversely, when measurement firms introduce a new method—such as People Meters, which monitor consumers' television-watching habits—the resulting changes in how audiences are measured produce a different profile of the television audience and change the competitive dynamics of media organizations participating in the audience marketplace.

Audience transactions begin with **predicted audiences** (from previous viewing data), which are particularly difficult to characterize because they are continually changing. A marketer predicts the audience segment most likely to view or attend a given event. The shelf life of a predicted audience is exceptionally short, lasting for the period in which a media product is consumed. The marketing challenge inherent in the audience product is that, while media audiences must be sold before the product has been distributed and consumed, the size and composition of a media product's audience cannot be determined until after the product has been consumed, when buying or selling that audience is no longer possible. Buyers and sellers in the audience marketplace devote a great deal of time and effort to forecasting audiences and maximizing the degree to which these forecasts correspond to the subsequent measurement data.

Predicted audience data represent **measured audiences**, the starting point for audience transactions among buyers and sellers. The data that define a measured audience are used to determine the estimated size and composition of the audience reached to determine how much an advertiser spent to reach a particular size and type of audience. The mix of advertising content and basis of dollar allocation result from measured audience data. Measured audiences are the central economic currency in the audience marketplace.

Because measurements are uncertain, the **actual audience** represents the invisible deal in the marketplace—the unknowable measurement. Its ambiguity renders the actual audience a highly contestable component of the audience product. In spite of that fact, buyers and sellers generally treat measured audiences as accurate representations of actual audiences. The nature of an audience product, however, is increasingly difficult to commodify because of its global fragmentation.

Audience Fragmentation

No longer can advertising reach a mass of people at a single time. Audiences have split into thousands of separate lifestyle zones, requiring a whole new approach to message delivery. The proliferation of media choices has fragmented audiences, making it harder and harder to reach them through traditional means. The fragmentation of the old mass markets into mass-market *groups* both creates a budgetary advantage and allows for more target-specific marketing plans. In addition, the global marketplace offers more opportunities to market to more audiences in different ways.

The popular and high-culture entertainment genres have merged in the last few years, and a result of this merging is that audiences no longer fit into traditional demographic classifications. Attend a Grateful Dead concert and witness an audience made up of many generations of fans, including dedicated "Deadheads'" and their children. Kids attend operas and grandparents love outdoor concerts. These days, not only do audiences attend a wide range of entertainment experiences, they are continually changing their performance priorities.

Regardless of what type of entertainment an audience attends, that attendance requires disposable income. Today, the largest disposable incomes belong to baby boomers. The first wave of this generation is now entering its 60s, has free time and patronizes a widely diverse set of entertainment venues and experiences. As marketers, our only option to approaching such a fragmented group of potential audiences is to *segment* the audience. Approaching audience segments, or niches, rather than a huge mass audience, allows us to focus a specific message to a relatively small group of folks. Because people attend entertainment for different reasons, marketers must be able to present the benefits of a single experience to the segment that best fits the benefit.

A cross section of audience members from a recent orchestral performance at the new Disney Center in Los Angeles illustrates the diverse range of motivations for attending such an event: a woman in her 50s liked the musical program; a man in his 60s favored the conductor; a 30-something woman came to experience the architectural venue; 20-something parents brought their kids as a way to introduce music into their lives; and a teenage girl enjoyed the opportunity to dress up for a special occasion.

Audience Group Configuration

As we noted above, audiences no longer act as a single entity; they now form according to individual preferences. An understanding of each audience segment's motives provides marketers with valuable insight into what a performance means to people and, in turn, how to appeal to those people. The choices are varied: A marketer can appeal to parents with messages directed toward integrating music into the family experience and the child's cultural development; appeal to adults with a combination of venue-artist-program messages; appeal to music lovers by providing attendance incentives. As marketers, it is our job to discover audience's individual preferences and then craft messages that appeal directly to a particular audience segment or niche.

Think of the process as promoting a 24-slice pizza, each slice of which has a different topping. Sure, it's a pizza, but one piece doesn't please all. In order to sell every slice, we must market that pizza 24 different ways. We can begin by grouping consumers according to eaters and non-eaters, and then extolling the category benefits of convenience and family adaptability to non-eaters. Next, we can focus on product benefits, such as fat content and crust thickness, for eaters, then direct our attention toward grouping consumers by preferred features, such as meat, vegetable options, cheese type, and combinations. Finally, we can target party packagers for the economy of slice-based distribution. The promotional combinations are endless—hooray for mass specialization.

▪▪▪ Cultural Dimensions and Global Paradigms

Although entertainment is considered to be universal, cultural considerations play a major role in experiential content that crosses ethnic and language borders. Differences among cultures also require that marketing media, messages, and promotional tools are appropriate for use in the targeted country or audience group. Geert Hofstede[9] identified five dimensions that may be used for looking at how well or how poorly content and marketing messages will translate to other cultures: long-term orientation, power distance, individualism/collectivism, masculine/feminine, and uncertainty avoidance. Here is a brief overview of those dimensions and their application to marketing entertainment.

Long-Term Orientation

This dimension focuses on the degree to which a society embraces long-term devotion to traditional, forward-thinking values. A low orientation indicates the country does not reinforce the concept of tradition (parts of the U.S., for instance); a high orientation indicates the country prescribes to the values of long-term commitments and respect for tradition (e.g., Japan).

Entertainment example: A film about samurai, a Japanese martial service tradition that may be unclear to many Western audiences, should be marketed by incorporating messages about the significance of honor and ritual.

Power Distance

The degree of equality between people in a country's society is this dimension's focus. A low distance means the society de-emphasizes the difference between citizen's power and wealth (e.g., China); a high distance means that inequalities of power and wealth have been allowed to grow within the society (e.g., India).

Entertainment example: Branded marketing and product tie-ins are much more effective in countries where wealth and status are represented by exclusive brands (Western nations and Japan) and avoided where social status is not measured by possessions (Africa and the Middle East).

Individualism/Collectivism

This dimension illuminates the degree to which a particular society reinforces individual or collective achievement and interpersonal relationships. A high rank suggests that individuality and individual rights are paramount within the society (e.g., the U.S.); a low rank typifies societies with a more collective nature, characterized by close ties between individuals (e.g., Japan).

Entertainment example: Western films are easily marketed to German audiences who appreciate the notion of individualism, but more difficult to market in parts of Asia where family and groups are revered.

Masculinity/Femininity

This dimension indicates how much a society reinforces the traditional masculine role model of achievement, control, and power. A high level of masculinity indicates the country residents experiences significant gender differences (e.g., Mexico, Iran); high femininity in a country's population reflects dominant values of caring for others and quality of life; feminine cultures treat the sexes equally (e.g., Sweden, Russia).

Entertainment example: Macho marketing succeeds in places where men make most decisions, including those about entertainment (Latino-based cultures), but is rebuked in countries where females have an equal or primary role in selecting entertainment (U.S. and European cultures).

Uncertainty Avoidance

This dimension measures a society's level of tolerance for uncertainty and ambiguity in unstructured situations. A low rank means the country's population has less concern about ambiguity and uncertainty and has more tolerance for a variety of opinions (e.g., France); a high rank means the country has a low tolerance for uncertainty and ambiguity in their everyday encounters (e.g., Germany).

Entertainment example: Marketing entertainment to Germans requires stating explicit times, dates, and profiles, whereas French audiences are more captivated by ambiguous visual communications.

In short, entertainment marketers must familiarize themselves with cultural nuances when promoting media and live performances on a global level. Advertising agencies always maintain local agencies with native speakers to service clients in specific countries in the most informed manner possible. Because we are no longer only nationally focused, marketing messages and promotions must reflect a thorough understanding of cultural differences if they are to achieve profitable box office receipts.

FINALLY: LET'S SUM UP ▪▪▪▪▪▪▪

Experiential marketers must develop expertise in bundling—promoting winning combinations of products and services into memorable experiences. Obstacles to overcome when promoting experiences include tangibility and perishability. Marketers must gain the attention of audiences for immediate buying responses if box office receipts are to be profitable. And marketers must be good shots—target practice is essential for reaching audience segments with a message that incites buying behavior across borders and across cultures.

GOT IT? LET'S REVIEW ▪▪▪▪▪▪▪

- The experience industry must deal with issues and aspects of tangibility, context, production/consumption, and perishability.
- Immediacy (timing) and awareness are key elements in marketing entertainment experiences.
- Services, measured with the GAPS model, are different from experiences in the nature of their functions, offering, attributes, method of supply, and factors of demand.
- Product placement, games, media-integrated messages, and blogs are among the most popular convergence strategies for blending brands with entertainment.
- Attention principle says that everyone is vying for your time, and our attention economy is based on getting the "ear" of an audience to tell them something.
- Hofstede's five cultural dimensions are valuable for developing marketing communications that cross ethnic and national borders.

NOW TRY THIS: LET'S APPLY WHAT WE'VE LEARNED ▪▪▪▪▪▪▪

1. Go online and identify at least two marriages or convergences between advertisers and entertainment companies. Then, check to see whether the product and entertainment genres are owned by the same conglomerate. What can you conclude from your investigation?
2. Using the SERVQUAL instrument, rate a branded hotel you have visited on the key elements of entertainment marketing. What improvements can you suggest?
3. Analyze two experiences you have had as each relates to the customer gap; what were your expectations and perceptions of each experience and how did the difference between the two influence your satisfaction with each experience?
4. Using Hofstede's cultural dimensions, profile a country you have never been to and determine how that country's dimensions differs from those of the U.S. What marketing accommodations would be necessary to promote a concert in that country?

QUESTIONS: LET'S REVIEW ▪▪▪▪▪▪▪

1. Discuss the ways in which marketers incorporate products and services into both mediated and live experiences (TV and travel, for instance).
2. How could you use the GAPS model to improve consumers' perceptions of an older theme park, such as Six Flags, that has failed to keep up with the competition's promotional efforts?
3. How would you convert interruptions into opportunities for capturing a consumer's attention?
4. What aspects of a feminine culture would help you to promote a rock concert?
5. How would buying a 30-second spot on the Super Bowl to announce a new Nintendo game be ambushed by audience fragmentation?

MORE STUFF TO READ ▪▪▪▪▪▪▪

Joseph Pine and James Gilmore. *The Experience Economy: Work Is Theater and Every Business Is a Stage.* Boston: Harvard Business School Press, 1999.

Jeremy Rifkin. *The Age of Access: The New Culture of Hypercapitalism Where All of Life Is a Paid-for Experience.* New York: Tarcher/Putnam, 2000.

Michael Wolf. *The Entertainment Economy: How Mega-Media Forces Are Transforming Our Lives.* New York: Random House, 1999.

Valarie Z. Zeithaml, Mary Jo Bitner, and Dwayne D. Gremler. *Services Marketing: Integrating Customer Focus across the Firm,* 4th ed. New York: McGraw-Hill, 2006.

NOTES ▪▪▪▪▪▪▪

1. *Fierce Invalids Home from Hot Climates* (New York: Bantam Books, p. 194).
2. B. Joseph Pine II and James H. Gilmore. *The Experience Economy: Work Is Theatre and Every Business Is a Stage* (HBS Press, 1999), chap. 2.
3. V. A. Zeithaml, A. Parasuraman, and L. L. Berry, *Delivering Quality Service: Balancing Customer Perceptions and Expectations* (Free Press, 1990).
4. Clive Thompson, reporting a phrase coined by software executive Linda Stone, *New York Times,* Oct. 16, 2005.
5. *Ibid.*, p. 61.
6. Stephanie Mehta, "How the Web Will Save the Commercial," *Fortune,* Aug. 8, 2005.
7. S. Whitmore, "The Era of the Mixmaster," Forbes.com, August 3, 2005.
8. A concept developed by Philip Napoli in *Audience Economics* (Columbia University Press, 2003).
9. G. H. Hofstede, *Cultures and Organizations: Software of the Mind* (McGraw-Hill, 1991).

CHAPTER 4

Venue Economics and Servicescapes

If it wasn't a business,
they would have called it show-show.
—WOODY ALLEN

Chapter Objectives

After reading this chapter, you should be able to answer these questions:

- What distinguishes the various types of entertainment *venues?*
- When does a venue become a *servicescape?*
- What are the main *economic considerations* in marketing experience venues?
- What *financial elements* underlie calculation of a venue's bottom line?

The expansion of the entertainment business follows the growth of leisure time and disposable income. Entertainment is consistently one of the largest net export categories in the U.S. economy. Real expansion has resulted from technological development, which in turn has changed the way we think of entertainment products. Performances and experiences are processed in the human brain as feelings and emotions. Media content entertainment business—movies, music, TV shows, video games, and words—now function as composite bits of information that can be produced and processed and distributed as a series of digits. Entertainment has three distinct types of content: performance, experiential, and media-dependent.

Performance content is developed around music, dance, and theater (or combinations of those elements, such as opera) for presentation by bands, quartets and orchestras, or theatrical and production companies. Performances are presented in specific venues in single locations or by touring. Once completed, the specific live rendition cannot be repeated in exactly the same way, as costumes, performers, conductors, and set designs may be altered or changed. Even venue acoustics may render similar performances differently.

Experiential content occurs in or at attractions, resorts, spas, casinos, theme parks, and travel destinations. As with performance content, it cannot be packaged for duplication. Each visit to a branded theme park creates a new adventure; museums change their exhibitions regularly; and destinations capitalize on seasonal elements for their unique urban, rural, or seaside offerings. Many arts organizations are nonprofit, requiring subsidization from government and private foundation grants and patron contributions.

Experiential content, which includes gaming and wagering activity, attractions that charge gate fees (such as exhibits and parks), and destinations, are dependent on tourism boards for promotion and local and global businesses for visitor accommodations.

Media-dependent content is considered **property,** a tangible item that is created, sold to a studio, and produced for distribution. The output is the basis for branded products sold in a variety of formats (DVD, Internet, cable, on-demand purchase, and so on). Although audiences experience media-dependent content in real time (at the time of viewing), tangible duplications of copyrighted property can also be purchased for repeat viewing, gifting, or archiving.

Media-based content involves "deals" for financing, producing, distributing and marketing, and advertising. Each function requires raising and investing money, assessing and insuring production costs and risks, and planning and executing marketing and advertising campaigns. Media content is provided in a variety of distribution centers rather than a single venue, except for cinemas, and as such is featured in a later chapter.

This chapter focuses on the various types of venues and dimensions used for offering performance- and experience-based content, including commercial service venues. It also examines criteria for venue aesthetics, explores price setting and pricing strategies, and gives an overview of distribution strategies. We also give you a heads up on the types of piracy invading the content marketplace.

▪▪▪ Entertainment Venues

Much of the entertainment offered to audiences is performed in a specific place or space. Performance and experience places are profiled here for their importance to entertainment marketing.

Performance Venues

These are places where stage activities or media are housed and offered to audiences.

Theaters, Performing Arts Centers, and Cinemas

Before the invasion of movie multiplexes, theaters functioned to house live performances. Plays, musicals, dance, and orchestral concerts still perform in elaborate centers catering to the entire live performance experience. Many venues are specially designed to be used for specific entertainment, such as the Magic Castle in Los Angeles, where magic is performed. Outdoor amphitheaters, such as Tanglewood in Massachusetts, and parks, such as Ravinia in the Chicago area, are warm-weather venues. Communities take pride in their arts centers, and thus they pay careful attention to the centers' design and brand image.

Some may think of theater as Broadway—essentially the theater district in New York City. Off-Broadway and other commercial theaters, however, provide entertainment for millions of audiences annually. In addition, nonprofit or regional/repertory theaters funded by subscriptions, grants, and contributions also vie for audiences.

Symphony halls are grand in stature and saturated with ritual. Today, some 1,600 orchestras play in the United States, the most famous in Boston, Chicago, Cleveland, Los Angeles, New York, and Philadelphia. Popular music and jazz concerts are often performed in venues usually operated as stadiums or sports arenas.

Only four major opera companies perform in the United States: the Metropolitan, San Francisco, Chicago Lyric, and New York City operas; smaller companies in Los Angeles and Houston are becoming prominent opera providers. Dance companies include New York City Ballet and the American Ballet Theater, in New York, and San Francisco Ballet, as well as a dozen important modern dance groups.

The circus is still a major form of entertainment in Europe and Asia, although it has fallen out of favor in North America. Venues range from tents to arenas rented for traveling performances by established troupes. A hybrid of performance genres, Canada's Cirque du Soleil originally offered regional tent performances, but grew into five different extravaganzas performed in Las Vegas venues; tented versions are still written for global appearances, however.

Cinemas—media-dependent experiences—are franchised conglomerates that control film distribution and duration. Only a handful of independent cinemas operate today, and many require fund-raising and donation solicitation to keep the venue healthy for audiences who prefer viewing off-Hollywood, or independent, productions. Chapter 14 features marketing for media-based content.

Experience Venues

Experience venues are places where audience members become actively engaged with the activity that is offered or provided.

Casinos

Casinos are legalized establishments where commercial gambling operators make their profits by regularly occupying advantage positions against players. Concentrated in various pockets around the world, casinos locate in areas where governments have enacted relaxed legal restrictions to derive tax revenues from gambling and control cheating.

Casinos typically offer card games such as poker, baccarat, and blackjack. Many also have slot machines and roulette, as well as wagering on sports events. Casino operators are not in the business of providing online gambling, although they maintain Web sites for marketing and reservation systems.

Locations worldwide are fast incorporating gambling into their national economies. In developing countries such as Slovenia, casinos are positioned adjacent to Italian border towns and cater to Italian gamblers by accepting lire and using Italian-language dealers. International destinations such as Macao near Hong Kong, Isla De Margarita off the Venezuelan coast, and Bermuda tempt tourists from around the world to gambling tables. Casinos have the potential to lure travelers and bring tourism to areas devoid of natural wonders, historical monuments, or recreational resorts. Chapter 14 has more information on marketing casinos.

"Rock climbing at REI allows for experiential marketing."

Spas, Luxury Resorts, and Cruise Ships

The Golden Door Spa, the Montage Resort, and Princess Cruise Lines are examples of venues where people go for vacations. Spas focus on health and well-being, while resorts combine recreation, food, and lodging, and cruise lines pack all forms of entertainment aboard ship. Each venue type has grown exponentially over the past five years, and there is no end in sight. Canyon Ranch, a stand-alone spa in Arizona, has packaged its products for use in hotel-based spas such as the Venetian in Las Vegas. Other resorts are building their own spas to provide guests with treatments and products that complement their brand image and contribute to profit revenues. Chapter 12 expands on tourist destinations and services.

Cruises are packaging trips for a variety of markets: seniors, couples, gays, families with children, singles, and every other demographic configuration possible. While on board, travelers may gamble, dine, swim, and engage in a variety of physical and intellectual pursuits. Conventions and business meetings are held on board ships chartered specially for large corporations and trade organizations.

Spa, resort, and cruise experiences all require branding, packaging, and promoting, making venue marketing a necessary element for selling vacation concepts.

Museums

From places that used to be considered storage rooms for the stuffy and dead, museums are reinventing themselves into competitive entertainment venues. Within the past

10 years, rapid expansion of the Guggenheim Museum franchises in Venice, Vegas, Berlin, Bilbao, Paris, Berlin, and Geelong (Australia) has spirited other museums into the content-development business. An alliance between the Hermitage Museum in Russia and MoMA in New York created an independent for-profit e-business to curate international exhibitions drawn from both collections.

The integration of ancient artifacts and modern aesthetics renders museums attractive to postmodern audiences who combine past with present. Museums generate revenue by hosting parties, charity events, and fashion shows among their antiquities. Recognizing the necessity to compete with all other entertainment product offerings, museums are turning to marketers for creative packaging and innovative promotions.

Theme Parks

Theme parks entertain families—they are considered safe place to experience fun. Given this public perception, park management and marketing teams work together to maintain the trust and patronage of visitors. Employee training, crisis management, and environmental design are key elements for successful park maintenance. Disney has an entire marketing staff to oversee quality control and ensure consistency among all park services. Chapter 14 expands on the marketing of themed spaces.

Zoos

In San Diego, the Zoological Society sells memberships for its animal habitats: the zoo and wild animal park. Packages for tours, seniors, and kids help lure visitors to experience the zoo's gorillas and the park's wild lions in their natural habitats. A recent marketing strategy that earned the zoo national recognition included late-night television appearances of some of the zoo's personnel showing unusual pets.

Arenas and Stadiums

Special activity venues are built to house hockey teams (Ducks Arena) and football teams (Shea Stadium), but these venues often are sites for performances as well, such as concerts and touring family shows. Often built at a huge cost, these venues must market themselves to lure performances that create gate revenues.

The verdict is still out as to whether we consider events such as rodeos and drag races live performances or sporting events. Either way, they are performed in arena and stadium venues across the country and need to be branded, positioned, and promoted to compete with other competitive forms of entertainment.

▪▪▪ Venue as Servicescape

A hybrid of performance and experience venues, marketplaces, and consumption sites are built environments called **servicescapes,** a term proposed by consumer researcher John Sherry.[1] Window shoppers and serious buyers wander around these spaces, which are much more than just shopping malls, seeking myriad delights. Shopping is no longer a mere transaction, it is a transformation. The themed *purchase performance* transforms audiences into visitors to other centuries and other countries. A servicescape retailer's mission is to produce the enjoyment of a tactile and visual shopping experience. Whether housed within a mall offering different experiences or uniquely placed for individual discovery, retail has entered the entertainment age.

Shopping Centers and Retail Superstores

Mall of America, the largest shopping center in the U.S., combines retail with kids' camps, live entertainment, hotels, restaurants, gardens, and rides and games to create a complete consumption experience. Smaller centers rely on a consortium of shops to provide an advertising budget, sponsor events, and provide community activities during off hours.

Designed for display and branding more than consumption, *super retailing* has become a specialty of designers such as Armani, who bought an entire block in Hong Kong to offer shops with Armani everything, including fresh flowers. Here, the store is the marketing, and the marketing happens in the store. Retail marketing is discussed later in this chapter and in Chapter 13.

Malls and Shopping Experiences

Urban arcades of the nineteenth century stimulated both the growing consumer culture and development of a consumer self by providing a fantasy-driven landscape of shopping. These arcades were the early version of our shopping malls and gallerias.

Being in the mall is a distinct experience that is shaped significantly by its architectural and aesthetic elements.[2] Malls have become, by default, the dominant public space of advanced capitalism. Various approaches to strategic retailing illustrate the ways brands are staking out their own identity in the marketplace. One approach is creating *flagship* stores, which provide prime city spaces to promote the brand's image. The flagship's antithesis is a series of neighborhood outlets that address local experiential needs. *Stand alone retail* presence is accomplished in a self-contained space and maintains an independent image. *Identity venues* choose from among formats such as factory outlet, theme store, or various hybrids to communicate their brand strategies.

Flagship Stores as Retailing Business Cards

As walk-in 3-D advertising, flagship stores must be co-financed by advertising budgets; as landmarks for the city, they are often featured in travel guides, lifestyle magazines, and TV shows. Flagship store formats fall into one of three categories: *sacred,* such as Nike's awe-inspiring, museum-like edifice; *lifestyle-oriented,* such as Crate & Barrel, where you can find everything for your yuppie home; and *mega,* such as Costco, where you can pick up everything from peanuts to pots and pans. All types of flagship venues are likely to provide visitors with experiential retailing that is both entertaining and image-generating.

The four-story Abercrombie & Fitch flagship on New York's Fifth Avenue is a sprawling nightclub of a place with muscled young men standing guard at the front entrance, their smiles entreating passersby to look. At their backs, the front windows are mysteriously shuttered. Inside, the lighting is moody, and the music thumps at such high volume that you have to shout to be heard. A central staircase with subtly lit frosted-glass-block flooring is a dramatic sculptural counterpoint to the darkness.[3] A central staircase with lighted steps stands out from the darker shopping areas around it. Like Diesel, another store targeting young adults, the flagship sells sweaters, T-shirts, and jeans.

Alessi concept store features a product as landmark.

Concept Stores

Concept stores are in the business of making merchandising fun. By turning lifestyle gadgets into a recurring theme, concept stores display goods as games that are to be experienced.

Sony Metreon, a four-story experience in San Francisco, provides customers with a hundred ways to amuse themselves with Sony products—interactive games, music, television, and video gadgets are everywhere. Sharper Image uses its gadgets to attract attention through innovation. Alessi dramatically displays designer goods by changing the viewing angle—everything from watches to lemon squeezers is at eye level.

Using an ***affect phenomenon*** where shoppers know exactly what they are looking at, concept retailers use shop-in-shop areas as walk-on stages that turn shopping areas into entertainment districts. Flexible display units and stylized carrier bags are a few elements that render an aesthetic avant-garde to concept shops.

Destination Malls

In the spirit of Minnesota's Mall of America, regional shopping centers are increasing their impact as tourist destinations. South Coast Plaza in Orange County, California, for instance, recently became trademarked as the "ultimate shopping resort." The designation gives Plaza a marketing edge to draw both retailers and consumers to its location. Among the largest revenue generating malls in the U.S., South Coast Plaza is surrounded by a performing arts center, parks, hotels, and commercial and residential complexes. A desired destination for Asian shoppers, the mall caters to chartered groups by providing transportation from four adjacent airports, including LAX, the primary Los Angeles airport.

▪▪▪ Space and Place: Venue Design and Management

Frank Gehry's Experience Music Project in Seattle

Research on the effects of environment and atmosphere concludes that careful and creative management of service venues contributes to achieving marketing goals. By observing audiences as they move about entertainment venues, researchers can determine the benefits and delights of consumption at every level.

Location-Based Entertainment

In order to leverage brand equity, create product outlets, and increase brand awareness, investors from retail, restaurant, real-estate development, and entertainment industries are combining entertainment experience with location-based products. For

▪▪▪▪▪▪▪▪▪ **BOX 4-1** ▪▪▪▪▪▪▪▪▪▪

Focus on Servicescapes

WAL-MART AND STARBUCKS AS ENTERTAINMENT VENUES

Wal-Mart stores hold exclusive concerts on Wal-Mart TV on **Soundcheck**, which features half-hour concerts and artist interviews on TV monitors throughout Wal-Mart stores. Each month, Wal-Mart features a band playing four to six songs; shoppers also can watch those songs' videos and download the songs at Walmart.com.

Wal-Mart's 3,000 stores run a 30- to 40-minute performance on Wal-Mart TV every few weeks on Friday nights. Leading up to each concert, stores run two- to three-minute sneak previews on TVs in the home electronics departments. Then, the concerts and interviews are available free at Walmart.com; fans can download songs from performances for 88 cents each.

The series began with a five-song set from punk band Yellowcard and another five songs from rock band Switchfoot. Concerts by country singer Miranda Lambert and R&B band Ne-Yo coincided with new CD releases.

Procter & Gamble's new Gillette Fusion razor cosponsors Soundcheck as part of a media deal between the brand and Wal-Mart.com. Similarly, Starbucks Corp. has staked claims in the music business, movies, and even formed a partnership with the William Morris Agency to emphasize music, film, and book projects that it can promote and distribute from its stores. The effort is a bid to enhance the overall entertainment experience for its millions of dedicated coffee drinkers.

Starbucks touted its national footprint of stores, the passion and trust from its huge and diverse customer base, and its proven track record with word-of-mouth marketing as drivers for the significant interest it has seen — and expects to see — as a partner to music labels and film studios.

Starbucks promoted the film *Akeelah and the Bee* in a marketing and profit-sharing campaign. The film was co-presented by Lionsgate, 2929 Entertainment, and Starbucks Entertainment. Promotions in 5,500 Starbucks locations in the U.S. and Canada included branded cup sleeves, word games on store chalkboards, and features on its Wi-Fi home page and Hear Music Channel on XM Satellite Radio. DVD sales followed.

The coffee retailer has offered a number of music options, from the *Genius Loves Company* collection by Grammy-winning artist Ray Charles to albums by Bob Dylan, Herbie Hancock, and new artist Sonya Kitchell, whose first album, was co-released and marketed by Starbucks. In 2005, Starbucks sold more than 3.5 million CDs, including the Charles compilation.

(Continued)

What do you think?

1. What other retailers might enhance their brands by joining the entertainment business?

2. How does an online delivery system expand the venue beyond its physical location?

3. Should live performances be incorporated into retail locations to enhance the shopping experience? Why?

SOURCE: promomagazine.com/entertainmentmarketing/news.

instance, Sega partnered with MCA Universal and DreamWorks SKG to create Game-Works, a concept that combines food and entertainment with a high-end range of games and simulation, packaged in a venue with a highly themed environment designed to look like the inside of an old factory. Often anchored by cineplexes, urban entertainment centers such as Irvine Spectrum Center, a huge (at 1.1 million sq. ft.) retail and entertainment complex in Irvine, California, optimize the chances for repeat visits by offering clustered experiential venues in a single location. **Co-opetition** is a term coined to describe these joint ventures, where companies working together can optimize opportunities in local and global locations.

Experience Venue Guidelines

According to the author of **Brand Lands**, experiences are designed using strict guidelines. They must (1) be high exposure landmarks, (2) provide places for visitors to explore and move about freely, (3) develop experiences along a specific conceptual line, and (4) contain a core attraction.[4] Those guidelines are explained here.

- *Landmarks* are physical symbols that help guide audiences to a particular location. They may be on storefronts (a yacht model above a nautical gear store), in building interiors (REI's climbing wall), or be decorative items or replicas (Outback Steak House's Australian artifacts).
- *Malls* are places that encourage strolling so visitors may discover merchandise and items of interest in their own time. To stimulate strolling, retailers create and emphasize hubs, such as lavish bouquets in hotel lobbies or dramatic staircases. Every venue should have a clean, dramatic entrance.
- *Conceptual (or concept) lines* provide direction and suspense. Creative design of a venue's atmosphere puts audiences almost inside a brand's image. Image contrast has become a successful concept, such as the now-familiar café in the midst of your local **bookstore**. Authentic **theming** tells a story that can be used to transport visitors into an imaginary world. Designed **theming** casts one element in a starring role, such as a sushi bar aquarium.
- *Core attractions* are a type of walk-in advertising that encourages browsing in retail spaces. A wine tower in a bar, for example, produces a "wow" effect. Neon signage creates a "show" effect that renders Times Square unique.

Design and Aesthetics

We are visual, tactile creatures, and the look and feel of things tap deep human instincts. **Aesthetics** is our sense of beauty as we experience it through our senses. Aesthetics is one of the factors behind why you buy one item and not another, and why you choose to patronize one venue over another. Entertainment relies on the immediate perceptual and emotional effects of aesthetics to entice and maintain audiences. According to industrial designer Hartmut Esslinger, *form follows emotion*.[5] **Everywhere** is now designed, and whoever determines the look and feel controls a great deal of economic value. Also, because our entire physical **landscape** has improved, people generally have become more critical, as an audience, of the aesthetics of our physical spaces.

The aesthetic **approach** was born when manufacturers began to realize the importance of extending advertising into products and experiences themselves. Because functional ideas are so quickly copied, global competition has mandated prioritizing aesthetic over functional design. When used with consumers in mind, aesthetic design can help to differentiate otherwise similar venues and cut through clutter to communicate quality differences. One of the most important dimensions of entertainment satisfaction is reliability; the failure to deliver a promised experience dependably is a direct function of failure in service delivery system and design.

Architectural Theming

Architectural elements and design contribute to the ultimate shopping, eating, and gambling experiences. In pseudo-authentic backdrops, visitors understand the signs and symbols used to communicate a specific location, era, or ethnicity.

Flagship stores are the new environment in which shoppers experience style and ambience. Anthropologie shops, which sell clothing and home fashion items, use cast-iron columns and beams, brick walls, and other relics of loft architecture to form a theme and signal a **lifestyle**.

Replica construction, as it might be called, enables retailers, restaurateurs, and hoteliers to create fantasy ambiance for their visitors. Rainforest Café delivers exotic drinks to patrons who sit in bamboo chairs among jungle greenery listening to bird calls. Gamblers in Las Vegas may choose from among a variety of global cityscapes in which to enjoy their gaming. An extensive discussion of the role of theming for experiential marketing is covered in Chapter 13.

Room-in-Room Principle

Originally conceived for trade shows, room-in-room retail configurations allow different spaces to grow out of the floor of restaurants and shopping areas. Inside, these mini-venues are presented in different true-to-life *taste worlds.* Room-in-room spaces express a particular lifestyle by incorporating warm woods and other luxurious materials into the areas. A modular framework unifies the overall appearance by tying together the open room-in-room architecture with seemingly floating ceiling structures.

Furniture for Watching

In order to create the pleasure of watching what goes on around you, furniture designers have put wheels and swivels on seating in experiential environments. Casinos, restaurants, and performance centers are realizing the value of ""seated freedom," a design that creates a sense of community among audience members. People-watching in malls, airports, and parks may prolong the time the audience spends in a single location, enabling marketers to deliver promotional messages in specific, high-traffic locations.

Convenience and Safety

Even though form should follow fun, form must also adhere to function (architects Louis Sullivan and Frank Lloyd Wright were early proponents of this notion). Venues must provide accessible parking, clean restrooms, and safe environments for audiences, visitors, and consumers. Attached parking garages bring people to venues even in hostile weather.

▪▪▪ Entertainment Venue Economics

As Publilius Syrus said in the first century BCE, *Everything is worth what its purchaser will pay for it.* The problems marketers must solve are, what is a performance worth and what should be charged for it? Then, how much should be spent to promote it so audiences will pay what we ask?

Entertainment products and services have universal appeal, cutting across cultural and national boundaries, and incremental revenues derived from international sources have an important effect on profitability. Profitability, in turn, begins by setting the right price.

■■■■■■■■■ BOX 4-2 ■■■■■■■■■

Focus on Careers

PROFILE OF A VENUE MARKETER

As a **marketing coordinator** for the Dodge Theater and U.S. Airways Center in Phoenix, Kent Walls is responsible for promoting and managing concerts, shows, and sporting events. Kent reports to the Vice President of Marketing and Advertising for the venue that is home to Phoenix's professional sports teams.

A large part of Kent's time is spent developing cross promotions with downtown businesses. He creates PR campaigns that include writing and distributing press releases to state media for both venues, and he edits the venue's Web site. Kent must develop and maintain favorable relationships with local television networks, radio stations, newspapers, artists' management, and promoters.

Kent loves his job, but he acknowledges that the hours he must keep and the intensity levels he must maintain can be tough. "Long hours are part of the industry, and you learn to adapt," he says.

After he graduated with a degree in marketing from Arizona State University, Kent interned for the Arizona Diamondbacks in game operations and marketing. After doing some part-time work with *CBS Arizona Entertainment Weekly* as production coordinator, Kent signed on to his current position. One of his most exciting experiences was acting as a script assistant for *ABC Good Morning America*'s 2006 Oscar coverage, an opportunity he "couldn't resist."

IN HIS WORDS . . .

Accomplishment of Note

The lack of a professional PR **staff** provided an opportunity for me to make an impact within the organization. In the last year, I have focused on building relationships with the local media and establishing a solid base for this very important aspect of marketing within the entertainment industry. The more you can offer clients in terms of marketing and PR services, the more likely they are to return to your venue, which results in increased revenue. I have received compliments from several national promoters commenting on how impressed they are with our venue's emphasis on public relations.

Pitfall to Avoid

A few months into starting my position, my first disaster happened. I was working a Green Day concert, handling all the local television camera crews who were taping coverage of the show. I thought I knew the set-up from previous shows regarding any technical issues. I did not double-check to make sure I had all the answers once everyone was in position. I ended up scrambling for answers to [the] crew's questions just five minutes before Green Day went on stage. I learned that, in this position, one can never assume anything. From now on, I'll always be completely informed on technical issues *before* the media crews show up.

Steps in Price Setting

For entertainment performances, pricing decisions are made as information becomes available about costs, competitors, and consumer demand. Seven steps are suggested to determine appropriate pricing.[6]

1. As with every other marketing aspect of entertainment, pricing decisions begin by *setting pricing objectives*. Profit, sales, and status-quo goals are among the most frequently used objectives. *Profit maximization* is a difficult objective because it requires knowledge of demand and is difficult to predict. Some venues prefer to seek a satisfactory profit or fair rate of return; profit goals are expressed as *target rate of return*. Increasing market share and increasing profit are also pricing objectives. In times of flux, venues may choose to maintain status-quo pricing but exercise aggressive marketing efforts in one area of the 4 **Ps**.

2. The next step in pricing is *estimating demand*. Elasticity of demand reflects the speed at which demand changes in response to price changes. Movie houses that have discounted matinee fares have experienced an increased daytime traffic among seniors. Because elasticity is influenced by the number of alternatives available, theaters must compete with one another to achieve attractive pricing incentives.

3. *Calculating costs* involves considering demand, but costs to provide the entertainment experience are equally important. Monetary costs include fixed, variable, and incremental costs. *Fixed costs*—overhead costs such as rent, interest, and taxes—do not vary with output; they are incurred even if no performances are held. *Variable costs* are the expenses associated with each production; they increase or decrease with the amount of output as labor and technological upgrades. Managers often employ a breakeven analysis to determine what prices might be charged to cover the cost of production. *Incremental costs* are those involved with selling one more seat. The cost of selling an empty seat just before a performance starts is close to zero, so the incremental revenue of each empty seat sold is, in effect, the price of the seat. This is the economic justification for offering day-of-performance discounts, student rush tickets, and other promotions that sell otherwise unsold seats at a deep discount.

4. *Analyzing competitors' prices* is another important step in calculating price. The fact that oligopolies (markets controlled by a few corporations) and monopolies (a market controlled by one company, such as Time Warner) exist can makes direct price competition a moot point. One way to avoid price competition is to differentiate the venue from other venues. Because markets are becoming increasingly subject to global competition, however, entertainment franchises cannot expect consumers to pay higher prices in the long run.

5. *Selecting a pricing policy* involves determining whether to offer a single price or different prices, and whether to price at, below, or above market. One-price policies treat all audience members equally, which is not an industry practice. Variable pricing allows for differences based on single or group purchases, audience member age, time and day of performance or activity, and seat location. Pricing options are elaborated on in the pricing strategy section.

6. *Determining price-setting methods* is not a large factor for entertainment venues, but some methods allow airlines, for instance, to offer lower prices at off-peak hours, or theaters to offer last-minute discounts on remaining seats. Marketers

may conduct break even analyses to determine what will happen to profits at various price levels.

7. *Deciding on a final price* is the final step. The list price is quoted to buyers, but typically a variety of discounts are made for wholesaler or retailer cooperation. *Trade discounts* are offered in return for services performed. *Quantity discounts* are made to stimulate larger purchases to consolidators for buying in volume. Airlines, hotels, and theme parks with lower demand during off-seasons offer *seasonal discounts.*

Actual and Perceived Costs to Audience Members

The price of the ticket is only one of the costs an audience member incurs in order to attend a performance or to subscribe to a series of performances. The actual and perceived costs of a proposed exchange can be defined as the sum of all opportunity costs (what the person alternatively could be spending the money on) as well as any expected negative outcomes, such as difficulties in parking, child care, uncomfortable seats, inadequate restroom facilities, or lengthy transportation.

Perceived value represents the margin of difference between the producer value and what an audience member feels the offering is worth regardless of its production cost, and this value varies by audience segment. Some people are willing to pay high prices for self-actualizing experiences delivered with the certainty of planning ahead; others see value in waiting for last-minute pricing for the discount.

Choosing a Ticket Pricing Strategy

A broad variety of strategies are available for planning. Here, we examine two major strategies: competitive and discriminatory pricing options.[7]

With a **competitive pricing strategy,** the presenting organization is likely to account for the cost of engaging artists or performing groups. This is called *going-rate* or *imitative pricing.* Many managers feel that conforming to a going price is the least disruptive of industry harmony that pays the house first. **Discriminatory pricing** occurs when an organization sells a performance at two or more prices that do not reflect a proportional difference in cost. This practice of **price discrimination** can go a long way toward maximizing audience size and revenue. Several options exist in this strategy:

- *Consumer segment pricing* charges audience groups different prices to acknowledge differences in their willingness or ability to pay. Senior and student discounts are examples of segment pricing. Group sales are another form of segment pricing, because discounts are given to groups purchasing a block of tickets for a single performance. Gift certificates and subscriptions are offered at a special price to encourage current patrons to draw in friends and family.
- *Performance pricing* is applied to performances featuring star or celebrities. Operas starring Luciano Pavarotti, for instance, cost more to produce than the same program performed by an unknown singer.
- *Image pricing* is based on the fact that some audiences will pay a higher price to see a performance in an outstanding venue, pay premiums to attend an opening night gala for its excitement, or incur higher prices for hit or long-run performances.
- *Location and time pricing* places orchestra and box seats at higher prices than those on the main floor, or sets evening or weekend prices higher than tickets for

Disney concert center in Los Angeles uses image pricing to offer visitors more perceived value.

matinee or weeknight performances. Timing also includes the time of purchase: subscribers and early birds pay less for their tickets, while last-minute buyers enjoy even better discounts during "public rush" offerings.

Other factors to consider in developing strategies are the role of scalpers and discount ticket booths, as well as other opportunities for surplus maximization and conditions for price discrimination.

When the experience is highly valued, *ticket scalpers* buy in advance and sell outside venues to audience members who are willing to pay a premium; no additional revenues are generated for the organization with these transactions. *Half-price ticket booths* discriminate in favor of people who are willing to wait in line for hours to save money.

Certain conditions create *opportunities for surplus maximization.* Tickets can be priced at higher levels for opening night performances, special events, celebrations, and holiday performances. Outdoor venues that present concerts in an open area may offer higher prices for audiences who prefer pavilion seating to lawn viewing or listening.

If **price discrimination**—selling a performance at two or more prices that do not reflect a proportional difference in cost as described above—is to work, certain conditions must exist. First, the market must be segmentable, and the segments must show different intensities of demand. Second, members of lower price segments must not be able to resell to a higher price segment. Third, the cost of segmenting and policing the market must not exceed the extra revenue derived from price discrimination. Finally, the practice must not cause consumer resentment or be illegal.

Choosing a Ticket Distribution Strategy

For most audience members, the nature and ease of access to tickets is central to their purchase decisions. Options such as sales through the organization's own box office, centralized ticket agencies, Internet booking, and alternative community outlets all offer distinct sets of benefits.

The venue box office provides a key link to consumers, but is time-consuming at performance time and may be inconvenient for some audience members to access at any time. Centralized ticket agencies (Ticketmaster and other intermediary agencies) save a venue or organization from having to staff a ticketing office. The downside is that these agencies do not share audience names, addresses, or purchasing behavior data with performance provides; venues sacrifice valuable marketing information for efficient distribution.

Internet booking brings convenient purchase and seat selection to audience members. Most systems also provide the option to print tickets, allowing audiences to avoid will-call pickups prior to the performance. *Automated ticket machines,* similar to those in airports, are available in many urban locations to streamline purchase activity.

Most performance venues and event marketers consign with wholesalers and *consolidators* for a percentage of ticket prices. Tickets to events, destinations, and performances are sold online through Web sites such as TicketsPlus, CheapFlights, and Expedia. Another option is the resale ticket market.

StubHub, an open marketplace dedicated to tickets, allows fans to buy and sell tickets to sporting, concert, theater, and other live entertainment events. Connecting sellers and buyers through a secure ticket fulfillment service, StubHub's partners include sports teams in the NFL, NBA, and NHL; media companies such as AOL and Knight Ridder; and leading artists such as Britney Spears, Coldplay, and Alanis Morissette. Audience members use credit cards to purchase e-tickets and can print them at home.

Again, performance content and experiences are delivered to audiences, but the goods sold to audiences are in the form of tickets and subscriptions. Two other forms of goods that are available in venues and help extend the bottom line are franchising and licensing.

Franchising

To extend brand profits and exposure, entertainment enterprises engage in a variety of partnerships, the most profitable of which are licensing and franchising. **Licensing** gives manufacturers the right to put your brand on their products; **franchising** means paying for the brand's name and concept and running the business independently of the larger company.

Franchising entertainment brands involves the integration of media with licensing and merchandising. Business format franchising resulted from parent companies realizing that their intangible assets—the concepts and brand names—are of far greater value than the franchisees' tangible assets—plant, facilities, an so on. The idea is to mass-produce concepts rather than merely products, making franchising the most important form of business organization in the twenty-first century. In every region of the world, the franchising phenomenon is replacing traditional, independently owned, single businesses. The franchising relationship's operating premise pulls the commercial agenda away from broadly distributed ownership of independent business and toward a regime made up of wholly dependent lessees sharing access to networks of powerful suppliers. Such organization shifts the scheme of sellers and buyers into a *system of suppliers and users* in which intangible assets count for more than physical ones. According to Jeremy Rifkin of the Foundation of Economic Trends, this metamorphosis from ownership to access is now a reality.[8]

Through franchising, the culture of media entertainment is being infused with new modes of authorship, production, marketing, and consumption that are characterized by Internet fan clubs, online producer-consumer affiliations, and real-world legal controversies over the proprietary ownership of digital bits of information. Entertainment franchises are more prolific these days than hamburgers. With burgeoning franchises, entertainment companies have begun to delve deeper into marketing strategies that enable them to connect with their customers across their whole range of properties and communications divisions. Chapter 14 has more on franchising as an entertainment marketing tactic and brand extender.

▪▪▪ Financials and the Bottom Line

Entertainment marketers have valuable decision-making tools at their disposal for calculating the bottom line. The **balance sheet** shows the company's assets, liabilities, and net worth at a single point in time. Profit-and-loss statements, or **operating statements,** present a summary of sales and expenses over a specific period of time and serve as a major tool for analyzing a company's financial performance.

Operating statements for entertainment-related companies have six main calculations:

- *Gross sales*—total revenue received during a specific time period
- *Net sales*—revenues retained after subtracting the amount paid to customers for tickets returned
- *Cost of tickets sold*—expenses for retailers or wholesalers, labor, venue operation, and maintenance
- *Gross margin*—obtained by subtracting the cost of tickets sold from the net sales
- *Operating expenses*—costs incurred during the statement period, including marketing expenses and performers' fees
- *Net income before taxes*—calculated by subtracting total operating expenses from gross margin; the bottom line

Performance Ratios

Operating statements also provide data for figuring important **analytical ratios**, which are points of information that enable marketers to evaluate a company's performance by comparing it with their performance in previous operating periods or against performances of competing companies. Gross margin ratio, operating expense ratio, and net profit ratio are a marketer's most valuable calculations.

- *Operation ratio* is the percentage of net sales. It is obtained by dividing each item on the operating statement by the amount of net sales.

- *Gross margin ratio* is the percentage of net sales dollars available to cover operating expenses and to provide a profit after paying for the cost of tickets sold. The higher the gross margin, the more dollars left for expenses and profit.

$$\frac{\text{Gross margin}}{\text{Net sales}} = \text{Gross margin \%}$$

- *Operating expense ratio* is the percentage of each net sales dollar needed to cover operating expenses. If high, salary, commission or advertising expenditures may be excessive.

$$\frac{\text{Total operating expenses}}{\text{Net sales}} = \text{Expense \%}$$

- *Net profit ratio* is the percentage of each net sales dollar that is left after all expenses have been paid, but before payment of federal and state income taxes.

$$\frac{\text{Net income before taxes}}{\text{Net sales}} = \text{Net profit \%}$$

Return on Investment (ROI)

Return on investment (ROI) is an analytical ratio that compares profits with the amount of investment needed to sell tickets. Investment is a company's total assets (venue, land, equipment), minus the liabilities. ROI shows how well a company or venue has used its assets to generate ticket sales and make a profit. Marketers use both the balance sheet and operating statement to calculate the ROI. The formula for calculating the ROI is:

$$\text{ROI} = \frac{\text{Net profit}}{\text{Net sales}} \times \frac{\text{Net sales}}{\text{Investment}}$$

In order to be effective, marketing efforts should include an analysis of operating statements and balance sheets to determine performance in relation to industry averages.

Determining Promotion Budgets

Although setting budgets and allocating funds is always a challenge, marketers can rely on a few practical methods of achieving these goals.

Percent of Future Sales

By evaluating past sales and future goals, budgets can be determined as a percentage of anticipated revenues. If a 5-percent increase is expected in performance box office sales, then the same increase should be given to last season's budget. For destinations, increases in inbound traffic form the basis of calculation. Shopping malls typically have a promotion consortium through which each retailer contributes a percentage of its expected sales for combined advertising and public relations efforts.

Competitive Comparison

Using trade association studies of industry averages, venues and performance companies may opt to meet their competition's promotion budget. This competitive comparison method is not as useful for services as for products, because no venue or performance has specific competitors. Genre competitive spending—say in regional theater—may provide indications of what audiences are willing to pay, but figures vary by demographic, performance type, and season.

Objective Task Method

The objective task method is the most practical way of budgeting for entertainment, because it is tied to future objectives rather than predicted or competitor sales. Once promotion objectives are set, the tasks necessary to reach those objectives and their costs are calculated for each aspect of the promotion mix. Creating brand awareness is the most expensive objective, because the most frequent objective task, achieving desired media reach and frequency, is expensive. Measuring attitude changes tied to experiential branding, while not inexpensive, is a more direct and measurable objective than media messages. The task of connecting audiences to brands through positive experiences involves a variety of options, including sponsorship and event marketing, each of which can be a more economically efficient objective task than media buying.

Piracy

Every year, the motion picture industry loses in excess of $4 billion in potential worldwide revenue from piracy. Because piracy undermines the revenues needed to launch marketing programs and produce content, it has a related impact on marketing efforts. Piracy takes many forms, depending on the medium. The most prevalent examples are:[9]

- *Optical disc piracy* involves laser discs, video compact discs, and DVDs, which are inexpensive to reproduce and have a fast turnaround time.
- *Internet piracy* is the use of copyrighted movies for sale, trade, lease, distribution, uploading for transmission, transmission, or public performance of a movie online without consent.
- *Downloadable media,* digital files that allow movies to be compressed and uploaded for direct download onto computers over the Internet, can be pirated.
- *Hard goods,* copies of movies in any non-downloadable media format, may be stolen for illegal sale, distribution, and/or trading.
- *Streaming media* may be illegally delivered to online users in real time.
- *Circumvention devices* allow someone to secure copyrighted content by going around protection devices such as encrypted software.
- *Camcording,* the use of video cameras to record movies from theater screens, is a form of pirating.
- *Screeners* are illegal copies made from advance copies used for screening and marketing purposes.
- *Back-to-back copying* is the connection of two VCRs to copy an original video onto a blank cassette.
- *Theatrical print theft* entails stealing film to make illegal copies.
- *Signal theft* is illegal tapping into cable TV systems or satellite signals.
- *Broadcast piracy* involves over-the-air broadcasts of bootleg videos of a film.
- *Public performance theft* is showing a tape or film to customers without permission.
- *Parallel importation* is importing goods authorized for distribution but imported without authority of copyright owners.

FINALLY: LET'S SUM UP ▪▪▪▪▪▪▪

Bringing audiences to an attractive venue and pricing experiences correctly are important keys to successful entertainment marketing. Pricing strategies must respect objectives to maximize bottom line profits. Promotion budgets are determined by behavioral and communication objec-tives set for the performance, experience or media venues. And although piracy is responsible for undermining ROI, clever marketing strate-gies act as an insurance policy for entertainment businesses and franchises.

GOT IT? LET'S REVIEW ▪▪▪▪▪▪▪

- *Performance content* is developed around music, dance, and theater for presentation by bands, orchestras, and other musical groups, or theatrical and production companies; *experiential content* occurs in or at attractions (resorts, spas, casinos, theme parks) and through travel destinations; *media content* is property that is created, sold to a studio, and produced for distribution.
- Servicescapes provide *purchase performance* that can imaginatively transform audiences into visitors to other centuries or countries; flagship stores, concept stores, and destination malls drive shopping experiences in unique ways.
- Setting pricing objectives, estimating demand, calculating costs, analyzing competitors' prices, selecting a pricing policy, determining price-setting methods, and deciding on a final price are the essential components of a pricing strategy.
- Promotion budgets may be determined by percent of future sales, competitive comparison, or the objective task method.

NOW TRY THIS: LET'S APPLY WHAT WE'VE LEARNED ▪▪▪▪▪▪▪

1. Check out frontrowtickets.com and ticketmaster.com online and compare each Internet booking service's pricing and ease of purchase for the Broadway show or local concert of your choice. Now go directly to the box office where the event takes place. How does their ticketing procedures com-pare to the ones you found with ticket bro-kers? Which do you prefer?
2. Find the Web site for a mall in your area. What attributes of an ideal servicescape does the mall offer? What can you suggest to improve the shopping experience for this venue?
3. To sample a venue experience, visit the Web site of any museum designed by Frank Gehry (Guggenheim in Bilbao, Spain; Seat-tle's Experience Music Project). Alterna-tively, research a hotel designed by Philippe Starck (Clift Hotel in San Francisco, Man-darin Hotel restaurant in Hong Kong). How does the architecture add distinction to these spaces?

QUESTIONS: LET'S REVIEW ▪▪▪▪▪▪▪

1. Compare performance and experience con-tent for their dependence on venues. Which type of content is more difficult to market? Why?
2. Discuss the various aspects of venue aes-thetics and give examples of each from your home city or state. Explain which is most attractive and why.
3. Which of the three methods for figuring bot-tom line profits is most effective for theme parks? For concert venues? For destination cities?
4. What are the pros and cons of determining promotional budgets using the comparison method?
5. Which types of piracy are most difficult to control? What policing mechanisms can you suggest for international piracy?

MORE STUFF TO READ ▪▪▪▪▪▪▪

Christian Mikunda. *Brand Lands, Hot Spots & Cool Spaces.* Kogan Page, 2004.

Virginia Postrel. *The Substance of Style.* Perennial, 2003.

Bernd Schmitt and Alex Simonson. *Marketing Aesthetics: The Strategic Management of Brands, Identity and Image.* Free Press, 1997.

John Sherry (ed.). *ServiceScapes: The Concept of Place in Contemporary Markets.* NTC Business Books, 1999.

NOTES ▪▪▪▪▪▪▪

1. John Sherry (ed.). *ServiceScapes.* NTC Books, 1998.
2. *Ibid.*
3. John Lei for the *New York Times,* Dec. 9, 2005.
4. Christian Mikunda. Introduction, *Brand Lands, Hot Spots & Cool Spaces.* Kogan Page, 2004.
5. Virginia Postrel. *The Substance of Style.* Perennial, 2003, p. 10.
6. See David Rachman. *Marketing Today,* 3rd ed. Dryden, 1994, chap. 12.
7. For more details, see Philip Kotler and Joanne Scheff (1989). *Standing Room Only: Strategies for Marketing the Performing Arts.* Boston, MA: Harvard Business School Press, chap. 9.
8. Jeremy Rifkin. *The Age of Access.* New York: Tarcher/Putnam, 2000, p. 72.
9. Al Lieberman. *The Entertainment Marketing Revolution.* FT-Prentice Hall, 2002, pp. 304–307.

CHAPTER 5

Audience Culture and Subculture

He always hurries to the main event and
whisks his audience into the middle of things
as though they already knew.
—HORACE

Chapter Objectives

After reading this chapter, you should be able to answer the following questions:

- Who is the *entertainment audience* and how are they motivated?
- What *attitudes* do audiences hold toward entertainment?
- How do *involvement levels* impact entertainment purchases and how are they measured?
- Why are audience *perceptions and satisfactions* important for marketing?
- What are *fan subcultures* and why are they profitable niche markets?
- What factors distinguish fan subcultures from *cults?*

Without audiences, there would be no entertainment industry. Every performance, game, destination, and venue is dependent on the people who patronize these activities and places. To successfully market entertainment, we must understand the needs and motivations of our audiences, spectators, and fans. This chapter is devoted to describing audiences, presenting their motivations, and determining their level of involvement. Only through an understanding of what brings people to an activity or place and why they come back can we effectively market to them.

▪▪▪ Who's in the Audience?

We think of entertainment audiences as *people who come together in one place to give attention to live performance, gaming, or viewing a spectacle.* Audiences have been characterized from a variety of perspectives according to where they watch, what they

83

watch, and with whom they watch. Venues, programming or content format, and membership all determine how groups form.

For instance, concertgoers may attend every event at the new Disney Performance Center simply because they enjoy the enthralling environment of the building. Or, the most recent Cirque du Soleil performance may attract those who appreciate acrobatic innovation. Some people attend an event for social reasons connected with business, others because in some way it is the "place to be seen," while still others enjoy going with a group of fellow season ticket holders.

Audience formation is most often characterized in terms of mass media—people who watch a particular form of mediated entertainment. Audiences of mass media are important primarily because media institutions are in the business of delivering audiences to advertisers through the vehicle of *ratings*. Entertainment marketers, however, also are interested in delivering and promoting experiences to groups of live entertainment consumers, and this involves *generating box office revenues* rather than delivering high ratings. (For our purposes, we exclude sport audiences from our discussion because they are covered extensively in other books.[1])

Unlike a media audience, whose members are masses of viewers dispersed across a multitude of settings, participants in a live entertainment audience are commonly associated with a particular venue or location where the entertainment takes place. The audience is a consumption community, and marketers are focused on the revenue that can be generated from that community members' attendance. Increasingly, the dominant meaning of the term *audience* has practical significance and clear market value. Audience members form groups because of a merging of common interests. Rather than being defined traditionally according to their socio-economic background, new audiences function as *taste cultures*. **Taste cultures** are dependent on entertainment products—outcomes of form, style, presentation, or genre that match the lifestyle of an audience segment. Rap music can be called a taste culture, gaining its identity from the music, fashion, and lifestyle of the genre. Within every taste culture, three types of audiences predominate. They are labeled as spectators, participants, and fans.

Passive audience members as *spectators* are caught up on the awe of performance, a temporary but not deeply involving activity. Spectators at an orchestral concert applaud and perhaps involve themselves in the performance ritual of attendance, but their interaction with the performance's content and the performers remains minimal.

Active audience members as *participants* represent a group likely to be playful or personally committed in one way or another to the entertainment activity. Members actively engage in the activity (blackjack players in a casino), performance (as actors in an interactive play, such as *Tony and Tina Get Married*), or spectacle (dancers in the rituals of the Burning Man Festival). These active audience members are also characterized by what they do during an experience. Participant labels include: *attendee* (of a concert), *visitor* (to a museum, national park), *shopper* (buying at a themed mall), and *guest* (staying at a themed hotel), which are synonyms for audience members that marketers encounter.

Members of the most active audiences in various taste cultures are categorized as *fans;* fans enthusiastically support particular music or genre subcultures, as described in detail later in the chapter. Because of their brand loyalty, fans are a highly sought-after target market.

Audience and Identity

A person's self-concept is his or her perception of identity. Crucial for gaining a sense of self are role models, material objects (i.e., collections), and one's own ideas, beliefs, and values. Psychologists recognize both the *I-self,* who is the information processor, and the *me-self,* who is the person we see in the mirror. For the I-self, one's own decisions are preeminent; for the me-self, the opinions of others are most important. Collections and physical attachments considered to be part of the self are what Russell Belk calls the *extended self.*[2] Audiences may construct their identity from all these forms of self, and marketers' understanding of each part is essential for effective communications.

Identity construction is about projecting a sense of one's self through an engagement that draws the attention of others.[3] In other words, it is the process of making oneself known. Using a model known as the *spectacle/performance paradigm,* Abercrombie and Longhurst advocate a notion of identity in which being a member of an audience is intimately bound up with a construction of the person.[4] If this sounds confusing, the simplest way to phrase this idea is, "You are what you attend." Critical to the meaning of audience membership is the concept of *performance,* an interactive relationship developed between performer and audience. According to these authors, performance occurs at four levels of audience types: *simple, mass, diffused,* and *postmodern.* All levels have significance for marketers because they provide insight into purchase motivations.

Simple Audiences

Marketing to simple audiences is usually accomplished locally through a particular venue or location. **Simple audience** members attend concerts, plays, festivals, carnivals, and sports and religious events; all of these events are live and most have a substantial ceremonial quality about them. *Ceremony* implies a certain physical and social distance between performers and audiences. *Convention* demands high attention and a condensed experience from simple audiences who congregate in specialized venues. Identity levels vary for this group, whose members are our primary entertainment consumers.

Mass Audiences

Marketing to mass audiences involves a mediated advertising strategy. Unlike simple audiences, **mass audiences** are invisible because they are entertained at home or in movie houses. Events aimed at mass audiences do not involve special venues and are characterized by indirect communication with less ceremony and little performance interaction. Attention for mass audiences is low, as they move in and out of attention. Because we are a media-saturated society, we cannot help being part of the constant presence of mass communication.

Diffused Audiences

Marketers to this group must embrace the notion that everyone is an audience all the time. **Diffused audiences** are a factor of our "performative society where human transactions are complexly structured through the growing use of performative modes and frames."[5] This means that people involved in everyday events come to see themselves as performers—as tourists, for instance, as we view spectacles, others view us as spectacles.

The postmodern Burning Man Festival in Arizona combines ancient ritual with modern rave.

(Don't you notice other people photographing the same monuments and streetscapes at which you are clicking away?) So in this sense, we constantly play a role and all social life is considered performance. Shakespeare said it first in *As You Like It:* "All the world is a stage and all the men and women merely players." The diffused audience becomes an imagined community, bounded only by the common role of performers in an imaginary life play.

Postmodern Audiences

Many of today's audience members identify with a *postmodern self,* a concept of identity that is continuously in flux.[6] Postmodernism is the confluence of past and present, new and old in the context of mass media and advanced technology. Look at the buildings of Frank Gehry, an architect whose postmodern style mixes materials and combines structures from the Renaissance and from outer space, to get a better understanding of the postmodern aesthetic. With regard to marketing, a postmodern self allows each consumer to construct his or her own identity from a catalog of cultural options. Marketers must match today's technologically savvy, postmodern audience with a variety of technologically savvy, postmodern marketing strategies!

Characteristic of postmodern entertainment are role-playing games and activities, such as participating in computer-generated games, Renaissance fairs, or an annual rendezvous of Mountain Men. An entertainment culture provides many opportunities to experiment with personal identity; tours of national monuments, participation in community festivals, or attending ethnic or national holidays can all serve this end. Postmodern audience members know they can select from a variety of (at least temporarily) identity-constructing options. As such, they allow marketers the flexibility of promotional diversity.

Marketers prefer simple and postmodern audiences because they provide significant sources of revenue. We should not, however, factor out the competitive role of media for getting the attention of audiences as global consumers of entertainment. And in spite of the prevalence of an entertainment economy, the plethora of competing entertainment options requires marketers to motivate consumer purchases of their experiences over those of the competition.

▪▪▪ What Motivates Audiences?

The foundation of any entertainment marketing effort is an understanding of why audiences attend entertainment events. Motives are reasons for carrying out a particular behavior; consumers are motivated by a desire to satisfy their needs. While there are many definitions of need, marketers define need as a *perceived lack.* Merely lacking something does not create a need, but a consumer's realization that he or she lacks something means that the need is acknowledged. Once people feel the unease produced by an unfilled need, a series of events take place in the consumer's mind; the theory has it that these events lead to purchases that fulfill the needs. Needs are classified as either *utilitarian,* which are functional needs such as relaxation, and *hedonic needs,* which involve the pleasing and aesthetic aspects of experience. A common utilitarian entertainment need might be stress relief; the hedonic entertainment need is most often enjoyment.

A *want* is a specific satisfier for a need. We might need to relax, but we want to attend a concert so we can relax. Motivation is the force that makes a person respond to a need. Audience purchase motivations, while similar to other types of consumer purchase motivations, have special applications to entertainment consumption. Here we discuss both emotional and physical motivators that are performance purchase determinants.

The Psychology of Motivation

Everybody has needs. Recognizing this fact, psychologist Abraham Maslow developed a model that illustrates how people progress from physiological necessities to objects of desire to satisfy their self-esteem. Maslow's Hierarchy of Needs is shown as Exhibit 5.1. Marketers use this pyramid-shaped model to understand motivation that is driven by particular needs at particular times.[7]

Maslow identified human needs as physiological, safety, social, esteem, and self-actualization. The first four needs are "deficit-driven," meaning that each must be fulfilled before one can go on to meet the need on the next level. Looked at from an entertainment marketing perspective, entertainment experiences fulfill social needs through group activity, and fulfill esteem needs by providing special experiences to reward loyal patrons. The final need, self-actualization, is a level of maturity at which a person is beyond striving for basic needs and can "be all they can be." Self-actualized audience members represent an important market for performing arts attendance because of their philanthropic utility—they donate money and attend performances.

Two motives specifically are associated with purchasing entertainment experiences: diversion and stress relief.

• *Diversion* is accomplished by getting away from work or the drudgery of everyday life. Diversion happens when people attend special events, visit parks and amusements, or travel.

▪▪▪ **EXHIBIT 5.1   Maslow's Hierarchy of Needs**

- *Stress relief* comes from letting go of pressures through relaxation and the use of leisure time for sensory pleasures.

Adapting Maslow's hierarchy to suit promotional purposes, entertainment marketers have identified significant emotion-based audience motivations: achievement, power, novelty, affiliation, and self-esteem.

- *Achievement* is one of the most studied motivations. Defined as the drive to experience emotion in connection with evaluated performance,[8] achievement can be individually oriented or socially oriented, where the goal is to meet the expectations of significant others. Winning at Black Jack may gain praise from family members for the player. Individuals may strive to attend all the concerts of a certain performer to achieve their personal achievement goals.

- *Power* is defined as the drive to have control or influence over another person, a group, or the world at large.[9] An aspect of this motive—to create excitement—is situation dependent. One method for achieving power is to collect prestigious possessions or symbols of power. A purse from Cher's closet is worn for social status; an autographed photo of Prince is displayed to indicate star proximity.

- *Novelty* is a motive common to people living in cultures that stress independence and uniqueness. The need to perceive oneself as different from others is strong in Western cultures, and differentiation can be accomplished by experiential participation. Having climbed Mt. Everest or attended an Elton John concert at the Acropolis in Greece are novel experiences that position the participant as unique.

- *Affiliation* is the drive for association with other people. In order to overcome feelings of detachment that a mediated society often foster, audience members connect with each other through fan communities and groups of people who enjoy similar entertainment activities.

- *Self-esteem* in this context is the need to maintain a positive image of oneself. High self-esteem occurs through association with popular entertainment genres, attendance at gala events, winning at craps, or navigating a foreign city. Some audience members want to be associated with what's happening, what's hip and what's hot to improve their self-image.

Risk and Uncertainty

Entertainment consumers must negotiate a balance between risk and uncertainty. Audiences naturally want to minimize risk, which involves not only the possible loss of the money spent on the ticket, but also consequential losses, such as physical injury from active participation. Audience members are faced with a greater degree of uncertainty when purchasing entertainment because it is intangible and variable, and there are no guaranteed performance outcomes. A possible response to consumer dissatisfaction with a performance is to refund the cost of the ticket. With consequential loss from injury, venues must avoid lawsuits by ensuring that risks are explained beforehand, placing disclaimers in contracts, and carrying liability insurance.

Another risk is audience misunderstanding about the nature of the entertainment content. This risk is understood as *cognitive dissonance,* a theory that involves post-decision regret—having made the wrong choice. After spending $250 on opera tickets, an audience member may question her judgment and feel discomfort about her purchase decision, especially as her partner is not an opera lover and agreed to accompany her only out of kindness. She has two options—vowing never to repeat the choice or seeking information to confirm the high value of her action (such as "opera offers a new experience to my partner; the critics raved about this performance"). Appropriate advertising and publicity may serve to dissipate such dissonance for audience members, especially as television commercials and reviewer comments.

With regard to developing future audiences for the performing arts, the debate focuses on core audiences, potential audiences, and nonaudiences. *Core audiences* are more likely to take risks on attending unproven shows, where as *potential audiences* and *nonaudiences* wait for proven stage success before they commit to attending an event. Unlike the retail business, the performing arts "product" is not conceived in response to a consumer demand and therefore enjoys a different relationship with its audience. A full house is not just about the economics—artists need audiences to see their work, and a "feel-good" factor exists for everyone in the venue when shows do well. Audiences loyal to a specific performance or venue may take the risk of attending a show even if an incoming troupe has received poor reviews.

Venues as Physical Motivators

Physical motivators are often stimulated by the performance venue itself. Beautiful, multi-use performing arts centers and museums are being built around the country by corporations interested in revenue enhancements and by cities vying for tourists. Venue attractiveness factors range from location to architecture and aesthetics. Variables such as newness, access, comfort, cleanliness, food, and souvenir offerings determine the venue's popularity. According to research, the more favorable the audience's attitude toward the venue, the higher goes the attendance rate.

Location determinants include the general atmosphere—*entertainmentscape*—of the venue. Audiences want easy access to public transportation, or on-site parking with access situated near freeway ramps. They expect to find adjacent restaurants where they can dine before or after events; and they want safe, friendly environments. Facility aesthetics, both interior and exterior, contribute to a venue's desirability. Architectural distinction enhances attractiveness; interior comfort (seating, layout, lounge areas, access options, décor, lighting, and so on) is vital for audiences' satisfaction and enjoyment. Such amenities, while they do not guarantee return visits, enhance the prospect of sell-out performances.

Internet Audience Motivators

Internet users are highly involved with a heavily interactive medium that is not tied to a venue. According to a study of usage motivations for commercial Web sites,[10] five factors motivate audiences to go online: search factor, cognitive factor, uniqueness factor, sociability factor, and entertainment factor. Each is briefly described here.

• *Search factor*—enjoyment from locating the latest informational updates, shopping sites, and travel/hospitality resources; Google.com and cragislist.org are the most frequently used search sites.

• *Cognitive factor*—motivation lies in Web-based learning and information seeking; check out adrants.com, for example, to keep up on Madison Avenue's ups and downs.

• *Uniqueness factor*—a "what's new and exciting" appeal, including new programs and software; paidcontent.org tracks the latest developments for delivering entertainment; endgaget.com is for gadget lovers; Slashdot.org is a favorite blog covering tech issues.

• *Social factor*—satisfaction through blogging, chat room participation, and even dating; myspace.com is a popular portal for networking.

• *Entertainment factor*—fun through games, poker, and movies found online; e-Bay.com bidding is also a source of entertainment for many Web surfers.

Virtual communities are constructed as places for audiences to be "alternative people," or just to feel like they could be someone else for a few hours. Myspace.com, founded in 2003, listed 36 million users after only two years. By 2005, when Rupert Murdoch acquired the parent company for $580 million, it was the fourth-ranked Web domain in page views worldwide. Myspace contains all five motivation factors, giving audiences hours of engagement.

▪▪▪ What's Inside the Audience?

Once we understand audience needs and purchase motivations, we must address another important strategic level of audience behavior—members' attitudes toward the entertainment experience. Audience attitudes are functions of the purchase process: they can be formed, changed, and measured.

Forming and Changing Audience Attitudes

Attitudes are evaluations of a performance, venue, or activity that express some degree of favor or disfavor; attitudes are context dependent. Motivations to attend performances are often the result of a positive attitude toward an entertainment genre. For instance, asked whether or not you enjoyed your trip to Disneyland, you might include a variety of aspects in your answer. Your enjoyment might be season-based, or it may depend on the people who joined you. Enjoyment-based feelings are nested within cultural and social contexts.

According to the functional theory of attitudes,[11] five factors contribute to forming opinions about entertainment: knowledge about the activity, usefulness of attending, personal values, ego, and social adjustment. Attitudes help us organize and simplify experiences, help us act in our own self-interest, provide a way to express personal values, provide defense against threats to self-concept, and facilitate social relationships.

Of the many theories about attitudes, the *theory of planned behavior* is most applicable to understanding entertainment audiences. This theory recognizes that an audience member's perception of how easy or difficult it is to attend a performance, visit a venue, or engage in an activity underlies his or her motivation to attend. Because many entertainment decisions are made impulsively, it is important for marketers to develop a positive attitude among consumers about the ease of attending an experience or performance.

Audience members use simple strategies for making decisions about attending: strategies of brand preference (for the place, performer, or program), genre familiarity (the more one knows about opera, the more likely it is one will attend), country of origin (cultural and geographic derivation of the performance), and price-related considerations (cost of attending). Before determining the value of an event, audience members anchor their judgments on an initial impression then adjust their attitudes with additional information. Entertainment consumers collect information and weigh the alternatives before making an attendance decision. The ultimate decision is based on the largest net benefit in terms of the exchange resources at issue—what they get for their money. The more expensive the ticket price, the stronger the attempt to select an option they are least likely to regret. Will they be sorry they paid $75 for a seat in the balcony to attend a symphony? Or will the overall experience be well worth it?

Marketing message content is important for forming or changing audience attitudes. Information is key to audience understanding, and providing consumers with a strong knowledge base allows them to form positive attitudes about attending performances. Only after creating favorable consumer attitudes or changing negative attitudes to positive ones can entertainment marketers expect to deliver effective motivational messages. The more we educate audiences, the more they will understand; understanding yields positive attitudes; the more positive the attitude, the more likely consumers are to buy tickets.

Audiences as Consumers

Audiences consume entertainment experiences. In the entertainment buying process, three basic functions occur: buying, paying, and consuming. The *buyer* makes the ticket purchase, the *payer* finances it, and the *consumer* is the one who has the experience; sometimes one person fulfills multiple roles. By understanding the allocation of these roles, marketers can create different buying/paying/consuming scenarios. Exhibit 5.2 presents examples of the possible relationships between participants in the buying process.

The implication of these roles suggests that the buyer's decisions appear to be related to when he or she is reimbursed, both to the degree to which the buyer takes into consideration the payer's preferences versus his or her own preferences, and to situational variables such as the system of reimbursement.

▪▪▪ EXHIBIT 5.2   Audience Buying Roles

Differentiation of Function	Buyer's Role	Payer's Role	Consumer's Role
All three held by same person	◄----------------------------- individual buyer -----------------------------►		
Each of the three held by specific person	teenager	parent	grandparent
One person is payer and buyer; another is consumer		• family buyer • gift purchaser	• family consumers • gift receiver
	◄-----------------------------	• intermediate ----► purchaser	• invited guest
		• host	
One person is buyer and consumer; other is payer	• buyer-consumer of free or paid services	• supplier of free services	• buyer-consumer
		• reimburser	• invited person
	• invited person	• host	
One person is buyer; other is payer and consumer	mandated ◄-------------	mandatory ----------------------------------►	

Source: Bon and Press, in Lambkin, Foxall, Van Raaif, and Hielbrunn, eds., *European Perspectives on Consumer Behavior,* 1998, p. 120.

Here is a sample scenario: suppose a teenager wants to take his grandmother to a performance of *The Lion King* for her birthday. If the parents are paying for the tickets but not buying them or attending the show, the teenager probably will select seats in the orchestra section without regard to price. If the parents are both buyers and payers, they may select the mezzanine for grandma so she can have a better view from above. On the other hand, if the teenager is buying, paying, and attending the performance, he may opt for the cheapest balcony seats. You can see why marketers care who buys, who pays, and who attends. Each function requires a different marketing message to motivate a decision.

This approach is useful for a segmented marketing approach and has applications for various venues, activities, and travel destinations where buying, paying, and consuming roles are not always carried out by the same person.

Tying in Audience Research

Although research is covered in depth in Chapter 6, here we address it as it relates to understanding audience identification, needs, wants, and satisfactions. Three challenges drive efforts to develop reliable audience research:

1. *Closing the gap between what people say they do and what they do in practice.* To eliminate the do/say gap, researchers have used audience stories to develop ethnographic techniques to understand audience behavior. Ethnographers use observations and in-depth interviews to gather data for comparison between members and across segments. Marketers have used the shopping stories of head-of-household women to focus communication messages on the concerns and problems articulated in the stories.

Advertising to children on the Internet.

2. *Interpreting the relationship between the experience and an audience member—i.e., examining the process as it relates to various forms of media and genre.* Variations in audience experiences have led to segmenting audiences for purposes of addressing specific needs through marketing communication. In addition, audience research has grappled with questions of demography—the distribution of meanings and practices across a diverse population. For instance, we try to answer the question, "How do various audience segments react to performance conversions?" One example is adapting the *Phantom of the Opera* stage play to film. Different groups have different reactions to the same question. Hence, how people feel before, during, and after a performance reveals their symbolic, emotional, and cognitive engagement with the experience.

3. *Determining the effects of entertainment/media on audiences.* Although effects research (research of media's impact on audiences) has never proven a connection between content and behavior, researchers continue to probe the relationship between entertainment content and audience actions. The impact of advertising on young children is a hot topic in effects research and ultimately determines what promotional messages can be delivered to children within the context of programming to that segment.

Laddering Technique

An effective method for developing motivational communication messages is through a research technique called **laddering**. Entertainment audiences buy experiences for various reasons; laddering provides market researchers with a means of digging beneath the surface of the buying decision to uncover layers of consumer meanings that reveal audience motivations for purchasing those experiences.

Focus group facility houses clients and participants in entertainment research.

A researcher begins by posing a question to an entertainment consumer, such as, "Assume you wanted to surprise a friend with tickets to a musical performance. What factors do you consider when you are deciding what concert to attend?" During this part of the interview, the respondent narrows the list of important factors to the two that are considered most important. This is where the laddering process begins: The interviewer keeps asking *Why*? (Why is that important; what does the factor give you? Why? Why? Why?) until the informant exhausts his or her ability to respond further. Hopefully, this process yields a particular value (e.g., affiliation, status, excitement, convenience) that is important to audience members for making the decision about which concert tickets to purchase. By using a small sample of respondents, researchers can uncover important values that can direct marketing strategy development. If a senior segment values convenience when attending concerts, for instance, marketing messages must emphasize adjacent restaurants and on-site parking. A successful laddering interview identifies major points for developing effective communication vehicle content.

Research always forms the basis for making marketing decisions. Theme park managers, for instance, commission research on a continuing basis in order to understand engagement levels and to sustain close relationships with visitors. Each year, Disney park management conducts more than 200 different external surveys and dozens of focus groups to track satisfaction and demographic profiles of its visitors. When its research revealed high levels of frustration with long lines, Disney initiated and marketed the FastPass, which permits visitors to bypass lines at rides and attractions.

▪▪▪ Keys to Audience Involvement and Participation

Motivation for consumers of entertainment is designed to foster an involved and participatory experience. When personal needs, values, or self-concept are stimulated in a positive way, consumer involvement is activated. Products, brands, ads, media, and activities are all objects of consumer involvement. Participation levels are useful for developing appropriate marketing messages.

Characterizing by Involvement Levels

Audience involvement in selecting entertainment choices can be cognitive (thinking), affective (feeling), enduring (long-term), or situational (time-specific). All four aspects of involvement help consuming audiences make decisions about entertainment brand, product, and activity consumption. Marketers distinguish entertainment purchases by their level of involvement.

Low-Involvement Audience Members

Low-involvement purchases involve a small financial commitment and bear insignificant consequence for making the wrong choice. If a listener pays a $15 cover charge to hear a jazz group that turns out to be unsatisfactory, the listener has not compromised a great deal of money or time in the bad decision. Decisions about paying for a movie or a cover charge are low-involvement, easily made decisions.

High-Involvement Audience Members

High-involvement purchases require higher levels of decision making and financial commitment. A $200 opera ticket or a $6,000 trip to India are considered high-involvement expenditures that involve informational sources for comparing options before making a decision. Here, consumers spend considerable time researching options prior to making their final purchasing commitment. With entertainment, consumers purchase experience through admission costs or ticket prices, and depend on reviews, buzz, and ratings to help evaluate the alternatives. Purchasing entertainment experiences involves substantial financial and emotional involvement for audience members, which can be characterized around loyalty toward a brand or genre. Four highly involved audience groups are loyalists, information seekers, routine buyers, and brand switchers.

• *Loyalists* are music fans who try to always attend concerts by specific artists, or travelers who regularly patronize a particular airline or hotel brand, or theme park attendees who subscribe to season passes. They are a prime marketing segment in every experiential brand and genre category.

• *Information seekers* love a particular genre, say jazz, but are not loyal to a specific jazz artist or jazz band. This niche segment is ideal for targeting genre-specific marketing messages.

• *Routine buyers* don't necessarily attend every genre-specific performance, say of popular music, but are very likely to attend concerts by a favorite artist, such as Elton John. Performer-based brand marketing works well with this segment.

• *Brand switchers* attend whatever their mood dictates—genre and brand are insignificant factors in determining their choices. This group is the hardest to identify and target, so price promotions are useful motivational tactics here.

As a marketer, you must consider involvement levels when developing marketing objectives, in order to craft an appropriate message for each group. By targeting audiences based more on involvement levels than on usage, entertainment marketers are better able to understand consumer motivations.

Audience Involvement Scale

High Visibility, a book dedicated to celebrity marketing, identifies eight levels of audience involvement.[12] We discuss these briefly for their relevance to understanding how audiences identify and bond with famous people in every experiential genre.

- *Invisible* consumers confine their interest in celebrities to locally prominent folks, such as a popular minister or city council member.

- *Watchers* have a passive celebrity consumption pattern—they observe, but don't chase, famous people.

- *Seekers* are more likely to want more intentional contact with celebrities by attending performances. The largest group, seekers spend the most money, so they are the most desirable audience for the celebrity industry.

- *Collectors* attend events and purchase souvenirs and memorabilia.

- *Fans* are distinguished by their need for interaction with celebrities.

- *Insiders* are groupies who seek to achieve the ultimate form of identification by becoming celebrities' friends.

- *Entourage* members are those who move inside celebrity circles; they have authorized positions in their support systems. Team doctors and star lawyers are among the entourage group; some have a special connection by virtue of their social or professional status.

- *Ensnared* members have the most intense relationship with celebrities; they lack discretion and have the potential to become obsessed fans.

Participation Levels and Marketing Messages

Three involvement levels help marketers understand entertainment consumption and, in turn, determine appropriate message strategies. Audiences are labeled as passive spectators, focused experiencers, or absorbed identifiers. For each level, we determine which message strategy is the most appropriate for use in marketing communication. Message strategies determine whether communication is developed to educate, to promote, or to inform. By understanding audience participation segments, marketers obtain clues to audience dispositions or reasons for being part of an audience, so they may craft effective messages. Message development and strategies are expanded on in Chapter 9.

Passive Spectators

Watching and listening are visual and auditory activities that routinely accompany audience participation. Because they have become routine, however, these senses often dull the level of active involvement in an entertainment activity. Passive audience members are merely receptors, having minimal focus on and identification with the activity they are experiencing. This barely there syndrome characterizes *passive spectators*. These folks occupy seats at a play, but forget the plot a week later. They ride a Ferris wheel, but on reflection, cannot distinguish one amusement park from another. They are present at concerts, but their thoughts are elsewhere. Passive spectators attend because someone takes them along, or because they have free tickets, or perhaps because they are duty-bound to show up. They are light users of entertainment products.

For these folks, the *message strategy must educate*. Information about the creator of a play, the nuances of a particular park, or the uniqueness of a musical genre contribute to enjoyment. By providing knowledge such as this, marketers produce a more informed audience. Opera performances have become more user-friendly by presenting crawling translations (subtitles) of the singing; pre-concert lectures by a conductor enable first-time concertgoers to become acquainted with composers and their music. Informational messages must occupy advertising copy and promotional materials directed at passive audiences.

The objective of using information is to convert passive spectators to active audiences through a continuing message strategy of education. Studies have shown that children who grow up with parents who patronize the arts, or who were introduced to the arts as part of their elementary education, are much more likely to attend performances as adults than people who had no previous contact with the arts. For people who have not been introduced to the arts as children, marketers must provide them with information and promotional opportunities for developing appreciation for a particular entertainment genre.

Focused Experiencers

The more audiences understand what is being performed, the more likely they are to engage in cheering, applauding, and standing ovations during and after a performance. We call members of this educated audience *focused experiencers* for their active attention to the performance. This group is composed of knowledgeable, appreciative entertainment consumers who attend because they enjoy performance. They engage themselves in the moment, they purchase souvenirs, and they help create a buzz around the activity or experience. Consumption levels range from moderate to heavy usage of entertainment activities.

Passive spectators or active audience?

Members of this segment can be loyal to the genre, to the brand, or to the venue—maybe even all three. But they are discriminating, and they consider their choices carefully; brand switching is common. They operate within a specific budget, plan ahead, and actively seek activities they want to attend. In a study undertaken to determine how men and women select their entertainment options within a specific budget, researchers learned that women select for their families or partners, while men choose activities for themselves, stretching their entertainment budget to include a variety of options.[13] Gender-based marketing is used to connect specific entertainment genres with their most likely purchasers.

The *message strategy for this group is promotional.* Communications must contain critical reviews, audience testimonials, and bold assertions that attract the attention of potential audiences. Although they are actively engaged once they arrived, getting focused experiencers to reserve tickets requires a competitive approach to marketing. Incentives can be used for this segment as well, adding an additional reason to select your entertainment over someone else's offering.

Absorbed Identifiers

When entertainment consumers poses a high level of identification with a particular group, genre, place, or activity, they are members of the group labeled *absorbed identifiers.* Their motivation for attending is self-evident—identity by association. They not only love what they do, but they also actively engage in the activity and often join in the production of that activity.

Brand loyalty is common among this segment. They follow a specific band or type of music, get season passes to parks, have memberships at museums, hold subscription to performance seasons, fly the same airline, or stay in the same casino repeatedly. They respond to loyalty programs designed to reward patronage, and can be counted on to devote a significant amount of time and financial resources to their entertainment passion. We consider them heavy users of entertainment.

Absorbed identifiers are experts when it comes to knowing about their passion. They subscribe to related publications, may join an online community, and often provide word-of-mouth promotion for their favorite events and performers. They enjoy being part of performances at a greater level than simple applause—they immerse themselves in the event to the greatest extent possible for an audience member.

Message strategy for this group is informational; communication should be frequent and special. They should receive advance notices of performances, get special subscription rates, enjoy restricted lounge areas, and benefit from complementary services. This segment of revenue-generating consumers is the bread and butter of the entertainment industry, and they must be treated accordingly. Our marketing objective is to keep these consumers attending, playing, or participating. Members of this segment often become avid fans, and as such slip into another dimension of active consumption.

By way of summary, refer to Exhibit 5.3 for a comparison of involvement group characteristics.

Consumer Experience Model

To help marketers further understand how audiences experience entertainment, models are often used as a guide for strategy development.[14] The consumer experience model

▪▪▪ **EXHIBIT 5.3 Audience Participation Groups**

	Audience Involvement Characteristics				
Group	*Loyalty Level*	*Involvement Level*	*Usage Objective*	*Action*	*Message Strategy*
Passive Spectators	none	low	light	convert to active	educational
Focused Experiencers	switchers	medium to high	moderate to heavy	reserve tickets	promotional
Absorbed Identifiers	loyal	high	heavy	keep attending	informational

uses audience experiences to develop a consumer-oriented marketing strategy. The strategy is built on two main aspects—perception and satisfaction—and their specific components.

1. The set of perception, judgment, and choice processes used in making a consumption decision has four components:
    *   Psychological component of information processing and choice (motivation)
    *   Economic component of consumption experience and its evaluation (cost/value)
    *   Consumer knowledge component (information)
    *   Market information component (promotional message)
2. The consumer's satisfaction with consumption experience itself is its own value.

An audience member's internal knowledge base and external information provided by marketers are combined with consumer perceptions and consumer satisfactions to develop event preferences—thus, perception and satisfaction are important elements of the repurchase cycle. This model is predicated on interaction—what consumers take from the marketplace they also give back in future ticket revenues and favorable recommendations. One's internal knowledge base is important, as the consumption cycle is repeated and audience experience grows.

Consumer perceptions are both analytic and synthetic; information is selected out, then synthesized into a world-picture using elements from memory. Audience perceptions are based on three factors: selectivity, expectations, and past experience.

*   *Selectivity* depends on how much is going on in the environment, and on the person's interest and motivation regarding the entertainment genre. The more entertainment activities available, the more selective the consumer becomes.
*   *Expectations* of quality play a huge part in perception; with expectations of high quality or high ticket prices, audience members may select evidence that supports their view and ignore evidence that does not. The more costly the ticket, the higher the audience's expectations.
*   *Past experience* with a venue, a destination, or content genre also helps consumers make judgments about experience quality. A favorable experience usually results in repeat behavior, while a negative experience likely will terminate the user's desire to attend again.

▪▪▪ **EXHIBIT 5.4** Disney's Consumer Orbit

> Attract visitor > respond to visitor inquiries > book tickets >
> track visitors' experiential enjoyment > monitor visitor referrals > use
> promotions to book more tickets

An example of one customer experience model is Walt Disney World's *consumer orbit.* Disney uses this progression scenario to improve visitor experiences and to identify opportunities for repurchase:[15] The consumer orbit is circular (as the name implies) and describes a holistic plan for recruiting and retaining park visitors. These steps involve using marketing to attract visitors and act on their questions through Internet responses to facilitate purchase; making the booking process pleasant and efficient; ensuring visitor enjoyment by controlling and monitoring visitor/employee interactions; and encouraging visitor referrals with promotions and discounts for repeat visitors.

The heart of the consumption experience is the visitor's enjoyment of all components of the Disney parks. Satisfaction measurement systems are used to monitor and improve the customer's experience. The consumer orbit relies on market information provided by satisfied visitors to increase opportunities for continuing the repurchase cycle.

Measuring Attitudes and Involvement

Audience motivational research is accomplished with qualitative methods as just described. Involvement levels of consumption experiences are measured using quantitative techniques. Researchers use semantic differential scales to measure involvement on a continuum; the most common instrument is called the Revised Personal Involvement Inventory (RPII), shown in Exhibit 5.5. Both cognitive (thinking and processing) and emotional items can be measured using a five-point scale.

Measuring Attitudes

Audience enjoyment is a result not only of the audience's involvement, but also of their attitudes. *The theory of reasoned action* says that consumers consciously evaluate the consequences of alternative behaviors, then choose the one that will lead to the most favorable consequences. The theory assumes that consumers perform a logical evaluation procedure for making decisions about purchasing tickets or attending performances. Measuring attitudes is of interest to marketers because attitudes play a major role in consumer purchasing behavior.

Marketers use the Fishbein and Rosenberg models of attitude measurement to develop survey instruments. Rosenberg's model[16] has two main components: perceived instrumentality and value importance. *Perceived instrumentality* is the capacity of the performance to attain the value in question, i.e., the usefulness of the experience. *Value importance* is the amount of satisfaction derived from attaining a particular value or achieving the expected result from the experience. Taken together, these components are good predictors of behavior that is illustrative of attitude.

The Fishbein model[17] focuses on the consumer rather than on the experience. For Fishbein, attitudes can be predicted from beliefs and evaluations; this is not compatible

▪▪▪ **EXHIBIT 5.5   Personal Involvement Inventory**

RPII for Obtaining Museum Audience Opinions

Think about the Museum of Modern Art's gift shop and rate your opinions using the following scale:

Cognitive items

Important	____	____	____	____	____	Unimportant
Relevant	____	____	____	____	____	Irrelevant
Means a lot	____	____	____	____	____	Means nothing to me
Valuable	____	____		____	____	Worthless
Needed	1	2	3	4	5	Not needed

Emotional items

Interesting	____	____	____	____	____	Uninteresting
Exciting	____	____	____	____	____	Unexciting
Appealing	____	____	____	____	____	Unappealing
Fascinating	____	____	____	____	____	Mundane
Involving	____	____	____	____	____	Not involving
Needed	1	2	3	4	5	Not needed

Source: J. Zaichkowsky, "The Personal Involvement Inventory: Reduction, Revision and Application to Advertising," *Journal of Advertising* 23 (4, 1994), 59–70.

with Rosenberg's model. In Fishbein's view, the consumer's belief in the experience replaces the perceived instrumentality aspect. If we combine the two models, we are able to determine three distinct aspects of attitude:

- Perceived instrumentality ("I think the Beatles are the most harmonious band ever recorded")
- Evaluative aspect or affect ("I like harmony")
- Value importance ("Harmony is very important to me")

Note that the second two are not the same; you can like something without it being very important to you. Marketers prize audiences with high involvement levels and positive attitudes toward entertainment experiences; we know them as fans.

▪▪▪ The Fan Subculture

Fans are a marketer's delight because they are the most involved segment of audience members. If, as suggested above, audience membership is closely tied to the construction of personal identity, then fan activity helps us define ourselves. A form of skilled audience, the fan audience is composed of highly prized members of the consuming public. Usually followers of a specific taste culture, fans are avid followers of musical groups, sports teams, celebrities, and mediated genres.

On the extreme end, fan behavior can be pathological, for instance, when an intense fantasy relationship with a celebrity figure results in inappropriate, even dangerous, actions, or when a member of a crowd shouting at a rock star or sports team becomes frenzied or violent. More common, however, fans who are heavy users of a

BOX 5-1

Focus on Ethics

BIGOTRY AS ENTERTAINMENT

Andrew Dice Clay was a standup comedian whose humor was described by one critic as "So gross that it cannot really be repeated in any detail in mass circulation magazines or newspapers, even for the purpose of calling attention to its hatefulness." Another critic called his humor simply "raunchy language and derogation of women."

But CBS was eager to produce a sitcom that would capture an audience of late bloomers, so it cast Clay as a postal worker, devoted father, and loving husband on *Bless This House* for the fall season of 1995. The network gambled that women could be persuaded to watch despite Clay's reputation, which he himself dismissed as just a character, just a joke, not a real guy. As an indication that the real Clay was indeed the show's star, the network dropped "Dice" from his name—Dice has gone Nice, reported the critics.

When the show fizzled in mid-season, Clay recanted his earlier "it's not the real me" line and signed on with HBO for a humor special called *Assume the Position.* HBO, then cable's most successful network, sent its promoters to work. They developed stories focused around the notion that Clay was just as raw, rowdy, and raunchy as ever in an uncensored all-new hour of his trademark adults-only humor.

In response to the changing personas, a *Chicago Tribune* TV critic wrote:

Are there no women, Jews, or people of conscience in the HBO chain of command? Does the channel really believe that "controversy" is a positive value, that income generation is its own justification? And the more Clay revisits his "ranting and raving" past, the less likely it is that anyone could possibly try to rehabilitate his career one more time. Isn't it?

What do you think?

1. If humor by nature asks that normality be dismissed and incredulity embraced, is it above moral considerations?

2. Did Saturday Night Live commit a 'moral injustice' by providing Clay with a legitimate arena as one performer suggested?

3. By banning Clay for life from its station for using the F word during a Music Video Awards night, did MTV help or hurt Clay's "raunchy" reputation?

4. Should "shock-comics" be accorded the rights of free speech or should they hold to a stronger moral obligation for civility?

5. What might happen, and what ethical waves might be created, when promotion shifts from focusing on audiences who want to be there to focusing on an audience that may include children and unsuspecting people, such as TV audiences who are offended by sexism and racism?

SOURCE: P. Patterson and L. Wilkins, *Media Ethic: Issues & Cases,* McGraw-Hill, 2005, p. 293.

Signing autographs for fans.

genre simply organize around stars or media images and engage in a variety of socially acceptable communal activities. Enthusiasm, which involves reciprocity and forms of exchange, is almost always linked with fan activity. Fan identity and activity, and cults, are the focus of this section.

Fan Identity

Recall our discussion of performance and identity at the beginning of the chapter. Unlike many audience members whose identity emanates from the I-self, much of what unites fans is their collective identity—basically, fans are a grouping of me-selves. Fans make meanings of social identity and social experience from the resources of the fan cultural commodity—their extended selves.

Madonna fans have dressed like the star, for example, to construct an empowered identity for themselves in their social circles. Such temporary attachments can be ultimately transformed into the star's identity. Fans' identification with "their" star evolves from devotion to adoration to worship, and it focuses on the construction of the star's image. **Images** are mediated constructions resulting from publicity and exposure. This means that the connection between escapism and identification is built from aspiration and inspiration. When the boundary between self and star is less than fully separate, the fan fantasizes about becoming the star and sharing the star's emotions. In this situation, the fan transforms reality into star identification. Pretending in this way can even involve taking on the identity of the star in blatant imitation. At the point of physical transformation that involves copying and imitating, fans become part of a cult community.

Fans who dress in tie-dyed shirts and attend Dead Head concerts are bound together by their symbolic allegiance to the music and culture of this rock band that originated in the 1960s and performed throughout the 1990s. Fans such as these have become interpretive communities that are sought after by marketers for their patronage and support. Describing the concept of the musical *scene,* Barry Shank said:

> Spectators become fans, fans become musicians, musicians are always already fans, all constructing the non-objects of identification through their performances as subjects of enunciation becoming and disseminating the subject-in-process of the signifying practice of rock'n'roll music.[18]

Because identity formation and reformation is an important aspect of contemporary life, fan activities may be increasingly important in the consumption of entertainment preferences as a form of identity construction. Where and with whom a fan is seen may determine the nature of entertainment preferences. According to philosopher Jean-Paul Sartre, identity formation consists of doing, having, and being. Using this model, entertainment-marketing messages directed to fans must emphasize the unique experience of attending entertainment activities (doing), the necessity of buying branded memorabilia (having), and the exaltation of associating with the scene or event (being). By addressing every aspect of fan identity construction, marketers meet the association-based needs of fans and cultists.

Fan Activity

Fans are most often the objects of marketing attention; they are ideal consumers because their habits can be highly predicted by the culture industry. Although fans do not know each other or have similar backgrounds or shared demographics, they do share their interest in the object of their "fanship."

Fan activity is an intertextual affair featuring consumption of both textual materials and media technologies. In other words, fans derive their sense of reality from a variety of printed and electronic media. Fan activity is characterized by:

1. emotional proximity and critical distance in which the fans act
2. critical and interpretive practices they use
3. consumer activism
4. production of alternative texts (other ways of communicating or producing stories and star encounters or original material based on a person, program, or film)
5. creation of an alternative social community.[19]

Fans of television science fiction, especially shows such as *Star Trek,* exhibit these traits: Trekkies go to conventions, dress up as Mr. Spock and Captain Kirk, write and perform celestial songs, produce music videos, and gather in virtual fan clubs over the Internet. After the television show was cancelled, *Star Trek* fans demanded and thus spawned four more television series, ten feature films, countless television specials, and hundreds of conventions—and all without the Internet! Today, entertainment virtual communities are the water cooler of the new millennium. Check out some examples of the creative efforts of Star Trek brand enthusiasts at www.theforce.net.ezproxyme.fullerton.edu/theater/.

Promoters of the *Phantom of the Opera* film relied heavily on the enthusiasm of *Phantom* buffs to build momentum ahead of the film's opening. Warner Brothers took out early advertising spots in *Playbill* and *Performance* magazines hoping to entice theatergoers. They courted fans online—where legions of them have long maintained *Phantom* sites and chat boards—with an official movie site that was up for months before the movie's release and offered a message board, preview clips, and songs from the film. With a strategy of a limited release, producers hoped to snare more fans per showing and boost the movie's per-screen average gross.

Virtual communities are symbolic communities that seek like fans with whom they interact. Each fan community is structured into a social hierarchy.[20] Moderators of message boards or creators of Web sites devoted to the show or celebrity are at the top of the hierarchy. The next level includes the community members who have been around the longest, and the lowest level is composed of the newer members. The existence of this hierarchy is what allows a virtual community to be analyzed according to social structures being formed by and through human interactions.

Fan sites not only help to establish communities, they also provide sources for fan-based entertainment. Echo Station, a *Star Wars* fan site, sells costumes, art, miniatures and collectibles, games, and books. Fans can enjoy humorous new episodes, editorials, interviews, reviews, and convention news; they can work crossword puzzles, send postcards, and enter trivia contests all from this site.

One element of a fan community is fan appropriation of product content and text. Fans are not only consumers, but also producers. They are proactive and they participate in cultural production of Webzines, stories, and other artifacts—they are producers of the very texts they love to consume. For instance, Web sites based on the film *The Matrix* are becoming structures to reproduce and maintain the community. As the film's fan community grew and shared producer-type activities, the actual producers of *The Matrix* saw a solid consumer base that was primed for its sequels. Fan communities are ready-made sources for ticket revenues.

According to Stephen Brown, "[Fan commodities] are imbued with evocative patina of the past . . . many products, whose life cycles have long since run their course, have been successfully raised from the dead . . . such are the tie-in products from re-runs of old television series."[21] Also called "symbolic capital," fan memorabilia has a cognitive foundation that rests on knowledge and recognition (fame, prestige).[22]

Collecting is the acquisition of objects and experiences that derive meaning from the act of colleting and the collection itself. Once items become part of a collection, they no longer serve their intended function; they become objects of personal significance. For instance, the 152 cookie jars collected by Andy Warhol were not used to store cookies, they were objects of fascination for him; the collection eventually sold for $247,830. There exists a market for media tie-in memorabilia or collectibles—an excellent example of the "dialectic of value," or fluctuation of worth, as objects move in and out of the commodity state. E-Bay offers commodities that should be defined as "exchange-value" merchandise—stuff with monetary value. But because of fans' desire to own merchandise that is often no longer being manufactured, they become use-valuations, or stuff that converts to personal worth.[23] Elvis memorabilia, for example, have become speculative investments as hedges against inflation because they cannot be duplicated.

In order to understand the motivations and collecting behavior of fan communities, researchers study these groups as subcultures. Subcultures exist among musical genre enthusiasts (Strait Edgers), bands (Dead Heads), brand users (Harley Davidson riders), and star worshippers (Michael Jackson fans). Ethnographic research techniques similar to those used by anthropologists help marketers understand fan subcultures so they might tailor appropriate promotional messages to these unique audience segments.

Fan Intensity Ladder

A tool called a **fan intensity ladder** illustrates the hierarchy of flow from one level of celebrity involvement to another; thus, it can be used to develop marketing strategy.[24] For instance, TV and radio stations pull their audiences up the ladder with promotions, contests, and reality programming to generate revenue by developing watchers into seekers, collectors, and fans.

Promoters and publicists in the celebrity industry seek to have their celebrities featured in magazines, interviewed on television, chosen as a spokesperson for a cause, or selected to endorse a product in a commercial. They also create celebrity Web sites (celebrityalmanac.com, celebrityweb.com, celebritysighting.com) that provide fans with access to the latest information about celebrities' activities, love lives, and upcoming appearances.

The Cult Audience

Cults are advanced subcultures whose highly organized members exhibit explicit attachment to celebrities and stars. Elvis fans are cultists who worship the star by attending annual birthday celebrations at Graceland and organizing look-alike contests in Las Vegas. Elvis's death shifted his status from being a capitalist-controlled commodity to being a fan-controlled icon; in death he became a truly popular medium—a vehicle through which people tell stories about their past and present-day lives.[25]

Actor Mickey Rourke had a fan cult in France in the early 1980s, as reflected by this kiosk ad for his early film *Angel Heart* in Paris.

▪▪▪▪▪▪▪▪▪▪▪   **BOX 5-2**   ▪▪▪▪▪▪▪▪▪▪▪

A Closer Look at Fan Communities

THE STRAIGHT EDGE SUBCULTURE

Music has become a powerful social influence, and many subcultures have developed as a response to societal events that confuse or dismay them. One such group, the Straight Edge movement, began as a subcreation of the punk rock music scene and has become a global phenomenon.

Straight Edge is a group, scene, and subculture very much like any other; it provides identity for members through self-expression, lyrics, tattoos, signs, symbols, and ideology. One symbol is the letter X, which resulted from attending punk rock concerts where alcohol was served. Establishments drew a large black X on the tops of the hands of adolescents to signify their under-age status to servers. Over time, "X" emerged as a symbol of solidarity among those rockers who chose not to drink. Today, the X is displayed in numerous forms, such as on clothing, on hands, and in band logos. The symbol identifies the community and gives concert-goers a sense of belonging and identity. Members also form their identity through tattoos and piercing, which serve as symbols of their devotion to the edge. By transforming their lives into artwork, Edgers become living symbols of their own identity. According to one 22-year-old Edger from Southern California, his piercings help remind him that he is in control of his own life at all times, and they "help keep things in proper order."

Straight Edgers describe their culture as a way of life, a longing for uniqueness, and a strong desire to be heard. Straight Edge is about enthusiasm of beliefs, integrity, and individual involvement rather than natural talents or inherent traits. Members live a clean lifestyle without drugs, smoking, and sex; many are vegans or vegetarians. Web site* explains that Straight Edge is not an Internet phenomenon; it is hardcore, and it is about music, fellowship, and being drug free. Members agree: the prevailing theme for this lifestyle is that the death, dying, and destruction of integrity in this

(Continued)

world have forced a need for positivism. Adolescents enter the scene to escape realities and harshness of the world and reject forms of addiction as an avenue of escape. Their philosophy is depicted in H2O's 2002 song, "All We Want:"

And that's all we want

Is to be wanted

No one told

And the kids are going crazy now

While we're screaming for attention

No one told

That's all we want.

As the song ("As the Line Between Machinery and Humanity Blurs," written by a Straight Edge band Atreyu) states, this youth culture doesn't want to be controlled, baby-sat, or mediated by television; it has grown tired of the cold mechanical nature and idealistic images of today's media.

Marketing to these teens begins with research conducted to understand what drives and motivates them to participate. Next, it entails providing awareness about concerts, such as the Ozzfest tour where Straight Edge metal bands prevailed, in media they choose. Small, grassroots, or garage labels organize the work of promoting, selling, and publicizing their own releases. Straight Edgers themselves typically run independent hardcore music labels; they call these labels DYI, or "do it yourself." These vehicles provide the only acceptable way, in Straight Edgers' opinion, to produce CDs and make them available to the hardcore scene. Victory Records, Indecision Records, and Equal Vision Records are the three largest and most influential independent labels of the past decade.

All DIY record labels use fanzines to advertise and get the word out; they consist of band interviews, CD reviews, and record label advertisements. Content includes topics such as music, philosophy, attitudes, vegetarian recipes, and animal-rights. Distributed to local record stores and concert venues, these zines are advertising supported and free to readers. *Maximum Rock & Roll,* a printed extension of a punk radio show, focuses on scene reports and advertisements for record companies. Such fanzines are important for transmitting the Straight Edge culture to its audience.

Internet based Webzines also are popular, allowing bands to directly communicate with their audience with publicity and venue concert listings. The site www.revhq.com provides an extensive catalog of Straight Edge CDs and mail-order merchandise.

What do you think?

1. How does Sartre's notion of identity apply to this subculture?

2. Would you describe the Straight Edgers as a cult or a fan community? Why?

SOURCE: Michelle Weber, graduate student, California State University, Fullerton, 2005.

▪▪▪▪▪▪▪▪▪

Cult geographies[26] are places of sacredness and "para-spatial" interactions in which special meaning is ascribed to a location. When fans valorize cultural places such as Graceland, these spaces transform cult fans into interpretive communities where private sentiments and attachments are shared. Although cult members are desirable as active consumers, cults are the final phase of fan communities where excess may tarnish the image, place, or the object of their adoration.

Fans and cultists are skilled entertainment consumers who typically possess technical, analytical, and interpretive expertise. Cult members are knowledgeable about the technology of performances they favor or games they follow; they have genre-specific analytical skills; and they can interpret performance, games, and spectacle by comparing them with others of like kind. Fan interactions enable fuller and more reasoned judgments of entertainment activities, venues, and performers. Yet, make no mistake, fans communities would not exist without the entrepreneurial complicity of sections of the entertainment industry; fan clubs are dependent on their own commercial significance. Unlike entertainment consumers who are increasingly followers in their tastes, fans and cultists tend to take leadership roles in promoting and supporting particular stars and musical groups. They buy tickets and branded merchandise in bulk, and they produce new artifacts for consumption by other fan members.

Sometimes fans' aggressive enthusiasm poses problems for entertainers, venue managers, and promoters. Mob mentalities may form and converge on performers. Even extreme behaviors such as star stalking may result from intense fan-based enthusiasm. One fan subculture known for its occasional aggressive enthusiasm, Straight Edgers are popular with younger audiences, as shown in the Closer Look section.

▪▪▪ Who Knows What's Next?

Will audiences of the future be much more participatory than voyeuristic? Are they likely to commit themselves to the active experience and abandon viewing one-way mass media? Madison Avenue certainly wants answers to these and other questions about audience behavior. Hoping to get a better handle on fast-changing audience habits, Interpublic Group's PR unit formed an alliance with trend-spotting guru Faith Popcorn; WPP Group hired a trend forecaster as well. These newly formed unions reflect the increasing interest within the advertising and marketing industries in identifying trends as rapid changes in technology make audience behavior hard to predict. Called futurists, Popcorn and others keep tabs on emerging trends, relying on experts from a variety of industries and extensive consumer interviews. According to marketing consultant Al Ries, "If you want to predict the future, you have to study the past."[27] One problem with looking to the past, however, is that it did not have technological advances like the kind we are experiencing in the first part of the second millennium.

No entertainment genre is immune to advances that may render the updates in this book outdated or even archaic. Nevertheless, we present the most recent trends in each aspect of entertainment marketing in this text's Postscript section. As you read each of the succeeding chapters, try to determine what changes are likely, then check your thoughts against the Postscript to see whether the experts think as you think—or whether their ideas are already obsolete.

FINALLY: LET'S SUM UP ▪▪▪▪▪▪▪

This chapter explains why audience interests, motivations, and levels of involvement are important to entertainment marketers. Audiences are developed, nurtured, and rewarded; they can be both fickle in their loyalty and zealous in their support. In order to prepare adequately, marketers must begin every planning and strategy session with current audience-based research—for as goes the audience, so goes the industry.

GOT IT? LET'S REVIEW ▪▪▪▪▪▪▪

- Audiences are classified as simple, mass, and diffused; all levels of audience involvement impact each member's personal identity.
- Stress release and diversion are two of the strongest emotional motivators for entertainment audiences; physical motivators reside in venue aesthetics.
- According to the functional theory of attitudes, five functions contribute to forming opinions: knowledge, utility, value-expression, ego-defense, and social adjustment.
- Three challenges have driven the search for methodological rigor in audience research: (1) the gap between what people say they do and what they do in practice; (2) the relation between experience and audience member; and (3) the question of entertainment/media consequences or effects.
- Audiences may be classified, segmented, and measured by their levels of involvement.
- Fans and fan subcultures are audiences who have a strong emotional identification with particular media, stars, or performance genres.

NOW TRY THIS: LET'S APPLY WHAT WE'VE LEARNED ▪▪▪▪▪▪▪

1. Think about an event you attended recently. How would you characterize your participation level? What involvement segment best describes you? Before attending the event, what was your attitude about the performance genre? Did attending the event change your attitude? How would you rate the venue using the variables discussed in this chapter?

2. Go to your Internet browser home page and click "entertainment." What kind of messages do you find there? At which loyalty segment are they directed? What improvement can you suggest to make the messages more focused toward knowledgeable audience members?

3. Go to an Internet fan site for a particular celebrity or musical group you enjoy. What types of memorabilia are available for sale? How is the fan community developed (chat rooms, discussion boards, conventions, etc.)? Describe the texts (songs, videos) produced by fan members. Would you characterize this fan group as a cult? Why or why not?

4. Using the RPII, survey 10 people about their rational and emotional reactions to a particular band or popular music style. What did you learn about their involvement with the band or style? What message strategy would you use to motivate those with low involvement to attend a performance?

QUESTIONS: LET'S REVIEW ▪▪▪▪▪▪▪

1. Discuss the main motivators for audiences to attend a performance, engage in an activity or visit a venue.
2. What message strategies would you suggest to develop a positive attitude among light users of an entertainment venue such as a local museum or performing arts center?
3. If attendance has dwindled at your theater in the past year, what measures would you take to analyze the reasons for this decline? Once identified, what actions might you take to correct the problems? What messages would you send to your data-base of past patrons?
4. Under what circumstances would you use the laddering technique to determine consumer motivations for selecting a particular casino? Who would you interview? How would you use the results of the research?
5. How would you characterize audiences of the next generation?

MORE TO STUFF READS ▪▪▪▪▪▪▪

N. Abercrombie and B. Longhurst. *Audiences.* Thousand Oaks, CA: Sage Publications, 1998.

B. Avrich. *Selling the Sizzle: The Magic and Logic of Entertainment Marketing.* London: Maxworks Publishing, 2002.

J. Blythe. *The Essence of Consumer Behavior.* London: Prentice Hall, 1997.

M. D. Johnson. *Customer Orientation and Market Action.* Upper Saddle River, NJ: Prentice Hall, 1998).

P. M. Napoli. *Audience Economics: Media Institutions and the Audience Marketplace.* New York: Columbia University Press, 2003.

S. Ratneshwar, D. G. Mick, and C. Huffman, eds. *The Why of Consumption: Contemporary Perspectives on Consumer Motives, Goals and Desires.* Toronto, CA: Routledge, 2000.

S. Sayre and C. King. *Entertainment and Society: Audiences, Trends and Impacts.* Thousand Oaks, CA: Sage Publications, 2003.

NOTES ▪▪▪▪▪▪▪

1. *Ibid.*
2. E. Arnould, L. Price, and G. Zinkhan. *Consumers.* (New York: McGraw-Hill/Irwin, 2004).
3. Andy Ruddock. *Understanding Audiences.* (Thousand Oaks, CA: Sage Publications, 2001), p. 169.
4. N. Abercrombie and B. Longhurst. *Audiences.* (Thousand Oaks, CA: Sage Publications, 1998), p. 37.
5. B. Kershaw, "Framing the Audience for Theater," in R. Keat, N. Whitely and N. Abercrombie (eds.). *The Authority of the Consumer.* (New York: Routledge, 1994), p. 167.
6. C. Thompson and E. Hirschman, "Understanding the Socialized Body," *Journal of Consumer Research* 22 (1995), 139–53.
7. Abraham Maslow, "Hierarchy of Needs," in *Motivation and Personality,* 2nd ed. (New York: Harper & Row, 1954).
8. D. McClelland. *The Achievement Motive.* (Appleton-Century-Crofts Inc., 1953), p. 79.
9. D. Winter. *The Power Motive.* (New York: Free Press, 1973).
10. T. A. Stafford and M. Stafford, "Identifying Motivations for the Use of Commercial Web Sites," *Information Resource Management Journal* 14 (2001), 22–31.
11. G. Maio and J. Olson, "Relationships between Values, Attitudes and Behavioral Intentions: The Moderating Role of Attitude Function," *Journal of Experimental Social Psychology* 31 (1995), 266–85.
12. *Ibid.*
13. Study conducted as part of a graduate research project at California State University–Fullerton, spring semester 2004.
14. *Ibid.*
15. V. Oberle, "Operationalizing the Voice of the Customer in Disney's Educational Strategies."

Paper delivered to the American Marketing Association's 5th Congress, 1995.

16. M. J. Rosenberg. *Attitude, Organization and Change.* (New Haven, CT: Yale University Press, 1960).

17. M. Fishbein, "An Overview of the Attitude Construct," in G. B. Hafer (ed.), *A Look Back, A Look Ahead.* (American Marketing Association, 1980).

18. B. Shank. *Dissonant Identities: The Rock'n'Roll Scene in Austin, Texas.* (Wesleyan University Press, 1994), p. 131.

19. H. Jenkins. *Textual Poachers: Television Fans and Participatory Culture.* (New York: Routledge, 1992), p. 278.

20. For a thorough description of culture hierarchy, see M. Hills, *Fan Cultures.* (New York: Routledge, 2002).

21 S. Brown. *Postmodern Marketing.* (New York: Routledge, 1995), pp. 116–118.

22. Based on a theory presented in P. Bordieu, *Language and Symbolic Power.* (Polity Press, 1991).

23. See the discussion on Appadurai's theory in M. Hill (ibid., 2002), p. 35.

24. *Ibid.*

25. G. Rodman. *Elvis After Elvis: The Posthumous Career of a Living Legend.* (New York: Routledge, 1996), p. 13.

26. D. Horton and R. R. Wohl, "Mass Communication and Para-Social Interaction," *Psychiatry* 19 (1956), 215–29.

27. Suzanne Vranica, *Wall Street Journal,* Nov. 11, 2005.

CHAPTER 6

Segmenting Entertainment Audiences

Do unto others as you would have them do unto you.
Their tastes may not be the same.
— GEORGE BERNARD SHAW

Chapter Objectives

After reading this chapter, you should be able to answer these questions:

- What are the *criteria* for developing audience segments?
- How do *demographic, geodeomographic, and psychographic* segments apply to marketing U.S.-based entertainment?
- How do *global lifestyle segments* affect target audience marketing across borders?
- How are *global demographics* used to promote entertainment performances, attractions, and destinations?
- What *audience segments* are applicable for marketing entertainment to all types of audiences?
- How important are *aesthetics* to audiences of enertainment activities?

As we saw in the last chapter, audiences vary in motivation, attitude, and involvement levels. This chapter describes the way we segment audiences for regional, national, and global targeting. We characterize typical lifestyle segments and the branded product constellations with which they identify. Global demographic segments are explained, and we define several segments that are applicable to all audience types.

▰▰▰ Segmenting Entertainment Audiences

Audience segmentation enables marketing managers to divide total markets into component parts in order to target and deal with them more effctively and more profitably. From among the many **segmentation** possibilities, marketers must determine which approach works best for their client's needs. Although there are many ways to segment entertainment audiences, all segmentation schemes should possess these characteristics:[1]

• *Mutual exclusivity.* Each segment should be conceptually separate from all other segments.

• *Exhaustiveness.* Every potential target member must be placed in a viable segment with other like members until everyone has an appropriate group.

• *Measurability.* In order to make appropriate targeting decisions and track strategy effectiveness, the segment's size, purchasing power, and profile should be readily measurable.

• *Substaintiality.* Each segment should have a large enough potential membership to be worth pursuing.

• *Actionability.* The degree to which the segments can be effectively reached and served through some form of communication.

The Importance of Audience Segmentation

As more and more audiences choose to express their individuality rather than fit into mass markets, segmentaton takes on growing significance. The more people preceive themselves as different, the greater is the competition among entertainment producers to increase each's share of the same market, and the greater is the need for segmentation.

For visitor attractions, the basic product is essentially the same for all audiences. There are always different ways, however, to promote the same essential product to subgroups around a segment's identified needs. For instance, the use of museums for functions and events outside normal hours is one form of such segmentation. Segment identification also is crucial for message development and delivery. Each group of audience members attends events for different reasons, as detailed in Chapter 3. Precise segmentation enables copy writers to select and create effective group-specific informational and/or motivational messages.

Specific benefits of market segmentation:[2]

• provides valuable insight into the design of products and services to more accurately reflect market demand.

• gives direction in pinpointing advertising messages.

• yields substantial cost savings from more accurate service design and promotional message placement.

• enables marketers to focus on various aspects of the competition's strengths and weaknesses by reducing marketplace variables.

• fosters the production of more informed strategic marketing plans and assists in the investigation of changing and developing markets.

▪▪▪▪▪▪▪▪▪▪   BOX 6-1   ▪▪▪▪▪▪▪▪▪

Focus on Niche Marketing

SELLING SMALL-BUDGET FILMS TO MILLENNIALS

As the independent film industry is forced to compete with Hollywood studio cinema, it faces the challenge of reaching its intended audience(s). Filmmaker and director Benjamin Morgan successfully targeted a teen audience by using new media to market his film on kids and graffiti, *Quality of Life.*

Although the U.S. box office gross for corporate studios was approximately $758 billion in 2005, independent's grossed a mere $1.05 billion. To market a small-budget film about graffiti artists in San Francisco, Morgan targeted a younger crowd with which the movie's theme would resonate—the so-called "millennial" generation, those born between 1985 and 1994, with an age range of 12 to 21. Millennials, who do not have college degrees and make under $30,000 per year, are a typical audience but are nonetheless very willing to spend their entertainment dollars on independent films.

Using nontraditional methods such as instant messaging technology and notices on Craigslist and MySpace to attract actors, investors, and viewers, Morgan was able to tap into a technologically savvy, urban, and hip audience that constitutes the newcomers to independent films. For the *Quality of Life* filmmakers, authenticity was the key to telling the story of two graffiti writers to both a millennial audience that would understand the film and to a larger audience.

Morgan continued, "The whole idea of *Quality of Life* crimes is so offensive. It's like the suburbanization of the urban space. Literally, a whitewash over real problems" (Morgan, p. 28).

Referring to their movie as an "ultra-indie" film because of its extremely low budget, filmmakers used unorthodox fund-raising methods, such as selling screen credits for $100, writing a book about the process (to give other ersatz filmmakers a how-to-guide to filmmaking), and holding graffiti art shows in which they split the proceeds with the artists. Audience members were alerted to the film by everything from Web sites, to newspapers to postcards. The audience was also reached through a Web site that celebrates street art and graffiti (www.woostercollective.com) to promote their film.

Morgan's book, *Putting the Pieces Together: A Behind-the-Scenes Look at the Making of* Quality of Life, provided valuable insight into independent filmmaking and served as a primary promotion vehicle.

According to *Quality of Life* producer and writer Brant Smith, festivals are key to promoting independent films:

Well, I mean, for those of you who don't know, the Berlin film festival is literally one of the top four festivals in the world. Up there with Sundance and Toronto and Cannes, so, getting into Berlin, I compare it with ending up with the silver metal at the Olympics. 'Cause not only did our film go to Berlin, we actually ended up winning an award there, which is huge. So, on the one hand, it was really good because we were able to get a little more money, and get more people interested making it happen, 'cause otherwise, nobody's going to care about our movie. It gave us validation. That's what the festivals do, is they give you validation.

(Continued)

Industry data suggest we are seeing a younger audience for independent films, but the *Quality of Life* filmmakers said they still had to contend with the older filmmaking gatekeepers at the international film festivals. Smith theorized that they didn't get into most film festivals because producers don't understand the youth market.

According to industry experts, increasingly, more independent movies are adopting models of grassroots marketing. Unable to compete with the multimillion-dollar advertising budgets for studio blockbusters, small movies are instead targeting localized niche audiences as a way to gain traction. That platform allows a film to open small and then potentially build momentum through word of mouth. Marketers attempting to reach potential independent film audience members can utilize Internet sites already available to independent film fans, including the Netflix site and the Fandango sites, which celebrates street art and graffiti.

What do you think?

1. Urban millennials were thought to be an ideal niche market for these San Francisco filmmakers. Given the prominence of graffiti in cities, how would this film translate to rural youth audiences?

2. How else might Smith and Morgan reach their audiences with a small budget?

3. Was publishing a "how-to" book a good promotional strategy? Why?

SOURCE: Graduate student case study, California State University–Fullerton, May 16, 2006.

▮▮▮▮▮▮▮▮▮

The first step in strategy devleopment for marketing entertainment and venues is determining the most appropriate group or groups to target. There are three options.

1. *Undifferentiated marketing* uses the shotgun approach, ignoring differences between segments and offering a single marketing mix to the entire market. Rarely used by entertainment marketers, this strategy is best applied to products with global similarities in usage.

2. Experential promoters prefer *differentiated marketing,* which targets multiple segments, each with a different incentive and message.

3. *Niche marketing,* which targets small groups of like audience members, works with companies such as Bang & Olufsen, which sell high-end stereo products to audiophiles, or the Lincoln Center, which promotes Wagner to opera buffs. This strategy concentrates all promotional media on a single segment to maximize impressions and impact. The band the Greatful Dead also used this approach. According to the late frontman, Jerry Garcia, "You don't merely want to be considered just the best of the best, you want to be considered the only ones who do what you do."[3]

Entertainment marketers most often use a differentiated approach, targeting groups of audience members most likely to attend performances or buy tickets to attractions. Occasionally, niche marketing is used when a definitive, finite audience group's potential yield justifies the marketing expenditure to reach them. Movie promoters use niche marketing to target Screen Actors Guild members prior to the Oscars, asking them to vote for a specific film, actor(s), or director.

▪▪▪ Regional/National Segmenting Applications

Traditional U.S. market segmenting practices adhere to five general categories: psychographic, geodemographic, demographic and cohort, behavioral, and benefit segments. The most popular and frequently utilized segment by marketers and advertisers is psychographics, or lifestyle segmenting. This discussion centers around regional and national segments, then focuses on global audience segments according to their importance for entertainment marketing. Because cultures differ, some segment structures are only applicable to a single national or local geographic region. We will discuss demographic, geodemographic, and psychographic segmentation for their importance to entertainment marketing.

Demographic Segmentation

Every piece of information on your driver's license reveals a demographic segment of interest to marketers. Some demographic segments, such those based on age and gender, have special needs and are marketed to because their lifestyles have unique requirements. As a group, *mature adults,* for instance, may enjoy visits to entertainment venues more when venue designers and staffs pay attention to services such as providing for dietary needs, providing ambulatory assistance, or making visual and auditory adjustments in programming. In fact, such services may even make visits possible. Because many members of this segment have unlimited resources of time and money to devote to entertainment and tourism activities, this segment is sought after and catered to by marketers of events, performances, and tours.

Global teens.

Three American consumer demographic groups—American baby boomers, Generation Y, and global teens—are changing the way U.S. entertainment is marketed.

Baby Boomers

The American *baby boomer* segment, ages 50–58, total around 78 million consumers, 25 million of whom are now over the age of 50. Representing 27.5 percent of the entire U.S. population, the boomer demographic has an estimated annual spending power of $1 trillion.

Our largest group and biggest spenders, baby boomers are doling out huge amounts of cash to amuse themselves. As boomers grow older, retire, and are freed from work, they become ever more engaged in all forms of activities, morphing free time into "all the time." With considerable financial resources at their disposal, 75 million boomers are eager for advice on what to do with their money. As entertainment marketers, we must be willing and eager to help them make spending decisions by providing interesting and unusual entertainment experiences.

Heavy purchasers of vacations and vacation homes, boomers are also big travelers.[4] Taking advantage of this traveling demographic, the Hong Kong Tourist Authority runs an annual large-scale contest with 50Plus.com to increase awareness of Hong Kong as a travel destination and build a database of mature travelers interested in receiving ongoing information. A promotional campaign that centered on a Hong Kong trip giveaway for two featured hundreds of thousands of banner and button impressions, travel e-mail newsletter mailings, and featured destination sponsorship in newspaper travel sections. The contest generated thousands of entries, indicating that members of the 50-plus segment—the most powerful consumer travel demographic—are very interested in researching travel and interacting online. The promotion confirmed findings of research studies that concluded that the 50-plus age group loves contests, free offers, and incentives.[5]

The heads of virtually every major film studio, record company, and TV network—all boomers—have contributed to shaping the culture in ways that differ from those of their predecessors. Boomers came of age in the 1960s and 1970s, a period of good economic conditions that provided young boomers with a blank canvas for pursuing what seemed like unlimited opportunities. To understand how to market to baby boomers, marketers must understand the large role the concept of *self* plays in the lives of this generation. The sheer numbers of people who experienced childhood at the same time has created a collective memory that encourages nostalgia.

Boomers were the first generation to be raised with television as a continual background presence. They are characterized as independent learners who quickly grasped the goal of self-improvement. Often described as the "me generation," boomers still relate to the music that underscored their "growing up" years, music by bands such as the Doors and the Beatles. Boomers' spending power may be self-made, inherited from trust funds, or enriched by generous retirement plans, but whatever its origins, this power continues to render boomers a highly desirable and responsive market segment. And as they move into middle and older age, boomers are taking their entertainment habits with them.

They key word to marketing entertainment to this segment is *benefit*—like other segments, boomers want a sense of value from their experiences. One of the best

Baby boomers grew up with the Beatles.

attention-getting devices for boomers is packaging nostalgia. War protests, open relationships, and recreational drug use are often parodied in all forms of entertainment, while music used in advertising to boomers is designed to give them a soundtrack from their lives. Films, books, and vintage clothing allow boomers to touch the past. Marketing for the baby boomer segment should connect eras by including images of a rich past, positive images of today, and visions of what can be.

Aging baby boomers, or *empty nesters*, are early retirees who have both the financial resources and leisure time to take advantage of entertainment activities. Using geographic databases, marketers are able to pinpoint these affluent consumers and target them with communications that provide performance schedule information and incentives for purchase.

Generation Y

Another important segment for entertainment marketers is Generation Y, which consists of young adults with big numbers and big bucks. These "echo boomers" represent both challenges and exciting opportunities for entertainment marketers. "Ys" are more difficult to qualify as audience members than boomers in part because of their diversity in race and family profile and because they are dependent on the income or estimated net worth of a parent or head of household. On the other hand, they are the most computer-literate, media-savvy younger generation in history.[6] Their medium of choice is the Internet, and they enjoy logo-imprinted clothing and accessories from their favorite films, shows, and brands—in other words, although difficult to qualify, they are ripe for entertainment promotion. Entertainment marketing strategy for Ys can be developed, in part, based on the group's branding needs and its propensity for rebellion.

Teenagers

The teen market's prevailing use of technology—they disperse information through "word of mouse"—and teens tendency to share things online make this group elusive

▪▪▪▪▪▪▪▪▪ **BOX 6-2** ▪▪▪▪▪▪▪▪▪

Focus on Demographic Segmenting

TARGETING YOUNG ADULTS

The book *He's Just Not That Into You: The No-Excuses Truth to Understanding Guys* is billed as a frank relationship guide for the 18–35 crowd. Inspired by the TV program *Sex and the City,* the title hit the No. 1 spot on Amazon.com Inc.'s Web site during its last season. Similarly, according to the *New York Times'* October 2005 book list, *America (The Book),* a political satire by Comedy Central cable network's Jon Stewart, host of the talk-show program *The Daily Show,* became the country's No. 1 nonfiction best-seller. Realizing that television is a cultural marker for young audiences, marketers acknowledge that selling books to this audience must reference TV, because their target readers are addicted to at least one reality TV show, own an iPod, and love TiVo.

To market Stewart's book, Time Warner Books actively cross-promoted with Viacom's Comedy Central and drew so many 20-something fans to a book signing at a Borders bookstore in New York that the store sold out of its copies of *America.* Warner Books also bought ads in 28 college newspapers and offered book giveaways on 25 radio stations nationwide (including campus stations interviews) that attract young male listeners.

Publishers seeking this demographic are using the Internet more aggressively and targeting more esoteric Web sites, such as dailycandy.com. Online games and contests work better than buying pop-up ads, according to the director of online marketing for Time Warner Book Group. For instance, to reach young readers interested in poker playing, books on the subject are promoted through poker parties, promoted on Bravo's *Celebrity Poker Showdown,* and advertised on pokerpages.com. Booksellers also reach this segment by choosing other topics popular with teens, such as Japanese graphic novels and videogame-strategy books, which also have been profitable, and by teaming with nontraditional retail outlets frequented by the segment, such as Urban Outfitters.

What do you think?

1. What other place-based promotions might work with 18- to 35-year-olds?

2. How has the college demographic changed in the past five years? What does this mean for advertisers?

SOURCE: Jeffrey Trachtenberg, *Wall Street Journal,* Oct. 5, 2005.

▪▪▪▪▪▪▪▪▪

and challenging to reach with traditional marketing strategies. Despite this, teens strongly influence at least two markets: Teens' intense interest in music keeps electronic innovations alive, and the fact that movies are one of the few activities teens can do outside the home makes them a prime audience for film marketing. Teens' real strength as a marketing segment, however, is in their global power, which is discussed later in this chapter.

Geodemographic Segmentation

The geographic aspect of market segmentation has been enhanced in recent years by computerized mapping techniques based on satellite technology that are linked with customer databases provided by census and market research survey data. These tools are capable of targeting individual buyers and households with great precision.

Geodemographic segmentation has value for direct marketing and local media selection for entertainment promotional messages. By combining geographic location with other demographic information, researchers have developed analysis techniques that spans a wide range of marketing and site-location applications, including neighborhood description, customer and prospect analysis, facility planning, advertising, direct mail, and multichannel marketing. The chief advantages of neighborhood segmentation are the inherent simplicity of the technique and its ability to synthesize vast amounts of data into manageable pieces. Examples of the most commonly used mapping techniques follow.

One system, Prizm lifestyle segmentation, enables marketers to target audiences on a regional level. This system describes every U.S. neighborhood by 62 clusters based on census data, consumer surveys, and other research methods. Clusters highlight audiences in terms of buying habits and media patterns. Venue and region-based entertainment marketers can access data for particular zip codes by lifestyle segment. Developed by the Claritas company of San Diego, California, Prizm software (zip codes) can help marketers develop prospect lists for direct mail campaigns or suggest appropriate media for targeting advertising messages. For instance, zip codes of affluent neighborhoods can be targeted with promotions for lifestyle-based entertainment and travel. Wilderness Safari Company uses this method to distribute adventure-based vacation catalogs to boomer-occupied zip codes in metropolitan areas.

The UK's ACCORN (A Concise Classification of Residential Neighborhoods), which provides an analysis of census data to supplement survey research, is a British equivalent of Prizm. Neighborhood classification ranges from the least prosperous areas to the most prosperous and include striver, aspirer, settler, riser, expander, and thriver categories. U.S. MOSAIC 2005 is the latest in a series of neighborhood classifications built by Experian and Applied Geographic Solutions (AGS). MOSAIC 2005's international lifestyle segmentation research spans more than 20 years and nearly 20 countries.

Psychographic Segments

Psychographics are based on lifestyles, which imply a pattern of behavior that reflects and is reflected by the consumption of product clusters or combos. These clusters are groups of specific brands, products, or consumption activities that relate to one another.

We measure lifestyle through psychographics that link individual psychological factors to characteristic patterns of consumer behavior, enabling us to identify and profile a market segment. Preferred over simple demographic information, psychographic segments provide information about the *why* of audience preferences. Behavioral characteristics of lifestyles that can be quantified are consumer *activities, interests,* and *opinions.*

Psychographic segmentation is quantified through extensive item batteries that cover activities, interests and opinions (AIO-studies), and lifestyle surveys. VALS,

▪▪▪ **EXHIBIT 6.1 VALS**™

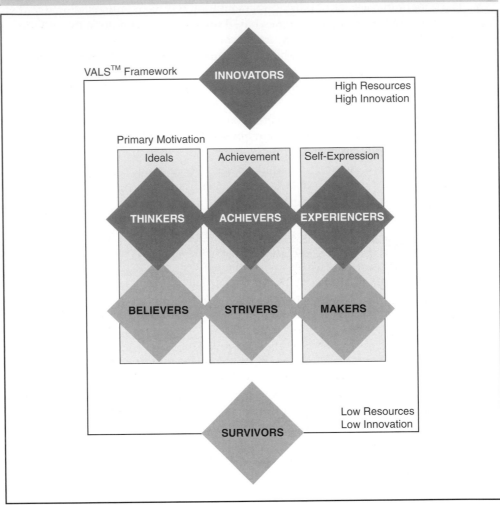

Source: www.sric-bi.com/VALS

developed by SRI Consulting Business Intelligence, is the the most common U.S. classification system based on values and lifestyles.

VALS classifies people into segments based on their control of resources and three aspects of their basic motivational self-orientation: ideals, achievement, and self-expression, as shown in Exhibit 6.1.

One model of lifestyle grouping, developed by Stanley Plog[7] for the tourism market, classifies the U.S. population according to psychographic types along a continuum from psychocentric to allocentric traits. *Psychocentric,* or self-centered, travelers tend to be self-inhibited and nonadventuresome. They like familiar places, avoid risk-taking, prefer guided tours, don't speak other languages, prefer standard hotel accommodations, and buy souvenirs to record their visits. The interest patterns of *allocentrics,* on the other hand, focus on varied activities. These travelers try new places, enjoy a sense of discovery, have high activity levels, enjoy meeting people from all cultures, seek little-known hotels and restaurants, and travel to a variety of destinations. By understanding the wants and needs of such diverse travelers, marketers can direct specific promotions at particular segments. For instance, senior segments respond to cruise ship marketing that addresses the psychocentric needs of that market by containing messages assuring cruisers of low-risk, inclusive, English-speaking vacations. Promotions that include rock climbing, shore activities, and multicultural cuisine are designed to attract more active allocentric cruisers, who tend to be younger and more physically fit.

In total, four market segment classifications, including the two just discussed, have application for experience-based entertainment. These classifications' correlative motivations are described below:

- *Psychocentric consumer* motivations involve ego enhancement and a quest for status; this is the group most likely to visit amusement parks.
- *Mid-centric consumer* motivations include health and shopping; this group enjoys national and state parks, health spas, and malls.
- *Near-allocentric consumer* motivations include trying new lifestyles; this group prefers sports, theater tours, and special entertainment.
- *Allocentric consumer* motivations include learning and a sense of power and freedom; this group frequents gambling casinos and resort hotels.

Lifestyle segmenting for entertainment centers on experiential activities; marketers must figure out which product goes with which segments (creating service assortments) for a particular lifestyle to maximize opportunities for promotional contact. *Product combos* have implications for media preferences and merchandise that might be marketed in conjunction with particular activities or at specific venues. Combining Budweiser duffle bags with baseball audiences is one example. By pairing educational programs with adventure travel, Eddie Bauer provided, through its sponsorship, product assortments that complement both lifestyle segments. As indicators of consumer preferences, however, combos are somewhat insensitive to geographic location, education, and occupation. Exhibit 6.2 presents product combos grouped around specific entertainment experiences.

▮ ▮ ▮ **EXHIBIT 6.2   Product Combos Oriented Around Performance Preferences**

Opera	*Gambling*	*Lotto Playing*	*Adventure Travel*	*Rock Music*
Armani suit	Dockers	Levis jeans	LL Bean	Big Dog sweat shirt
Jaguar	Corvette	Ford pickup	Subaru	VW van
French wine	Jack Daniels	Bud	Evian	Miller
Rolex	Seiko	Timex	Swiss Army	Swatch
New Yorker	*Sports Illustrated*	*People*	*Outdoor*	*Entertainment Weekly*
American Express card	Old Spice	Marlboro	Timberland shoes	iPod

■■■■■■■■■ BOX 6-3 ■■■■■■■■■

Focus on American Tourist Lifestyles

SEGMENTS OF TRAVEL CONSUMERS

Travel market researchers have identified types of travelers and given them appropriate names to designate their lifestyle preferences. Among them are:

Galloping Groupies: This group consists of couples and singles who make reservations to travel with tour groups. They account for 52 percent of all reservations, preferring to leave everything to the experts. Groupies carry cameras, like to shop, and never wander into unfamiliar territory without their guide. Sturdy walking shoes, telephoto lenses, and currency changers accompany them everywhere. Tour expenditure segments, which last from one to three weeks, record the highest amount of spending per capita.

Rough Riders: These consumers are singles or pairs of adventuresome travelers seeking excitement and thrills. They plan their own trips to climb mountains, white-water raft, trek in the wilderness, or scuba dive. These folks camp out or stay in remote lodgings. They prefer cutting-edge activities in exotic locations, and inspiration fuels their enjoyment. Their adventures last from ten days to six weeks, but spending is limited to advance purchases of supplies and gear.

Eco-Lovers: Eco-lovers are older adults who want to experience nature without harming it. Whale watching is one type of eco-tourism in this emerging sector of tourism. Eco-tours promote photographic safaris to the Galapagos Islands, Alaska, and Africa. Often buying packages or travel in pre-arranged small groups, eco-travelers have abundant leisure time and a desire to spend their money on animal gazing.

Histrionics: This group consists of mature couples or adult family groups who want to trace their ethnic origins or wish to experience a different culture. They visit museums and historical monuments, learn the language, and eat local cuisine. Education is complemented by mementos purchased to record the group's discoveries. Histrionics' travels range from day trips to multi-week migrations during which they contribute to the coffers of cultural venues.

Cruisers: These consumers are couples on honeymoon, families, singles on the loose, or retired adults in search of luxury without the hassle of moving locations. Cruise ships provide an all-inclusive opportunity for gourmet dining, live entertainment, and outdoor activities. This growth segment spends top dollar on their trips that last from three days to six months.

Ties That Binders: Families and family members who travel to visit their relatives make up this segment, which constitutes 66 percent of all travel. These visitors prefer to travel by car, stay with relatives, and drive straight through when possible. Some take planes or trains, but rely on friends and relatives to provide the lodging. They spend less on travel than any other segment.

What do you think?

1. How might these segments be used to market a destination?

2. Why do marketers use typologies to segment populations?

■■■■■■■■

Cohort Segmentation

Age cohorts are groups of people who grew up in the same time period, who age together, and who are influenced by events occurring during their formative years. **Cohort analysis** is a useful tool for anticipating trends because it looks at how specific groups, such as baby boomers, will influence the entertainment marketplace. Given this aging cohort's free time, disposable income, and desire for adventure, travel and tourism revenues will continue to grow. And because boomers listened to the Beatles and Bob Dylan as teenagers, their appetites for listening to rock and popular music is not expected to decline—revealing a continuing trend for 60s music. Venues such as Cleveland's Rock 'n' Roll Hall of Fame and Seattle's Experience Music Project serve this audience cohort's quest for the music of their past. Analyses of cohort lifestyles are the basis for trend prediction, which results in meeting cohort entertainment needs.

The 60+ audience groups is one of the most valuable segments for entertainment marketers. Under-60 boomers have 77 million members of their generation cohort, presenting a formidable challenge for marketers. For older audience groups and mature markets, segmenting by lifestyles is more effective than simply looking at cognitive age (how we see ourselves, which is usually 10 years younger than our actual age) because people age so differently. Mature audience segment often require special access, more intermissions, and brighter lighting. Advertising for cruise lines and learning tours features older models to reflect the lifestyle of this aging target segment.

Generational influences—life stage, formative experiences, and current condition—are indicators of the values, preferences, and marketplace behaviors of consuming audiences. *Life stage* refers to where one is in life physically or psychologically; *formative experiences* are shared traits that define and differentiate generations; and *current conditions* are events that affect what people buy. The phrase, "you are

Life-stage audience.

who you are because of where you were when" may describe the power of generational influences.

The *Yankelovich Report on Generational Marketing*[8] looks at the power of the most significant generations, mature audiences, boomers, and GenX; these broad groupings reflect MONITOR data that provide the most accurate view of developing trends and best explain ongoing events in the marketplace. Developed in 1971 and repeated annually, MONITOR remains the longest running and most complete continuous tracking study of American values, lifestyles, and buying motivations. The study tracks changing social climate and translates that data for marketers. The report illustrates how generational factors provide a framework for understanding the entertainment marketplace.

▪▪▪ Global Lifestyle Segments

Global market segmentation is the process of dividing the world market into distinct subsets of customers who have similar needs. Criteria for global market segmentation are based on the same criteria as national segments; demographic and psychographic criteria are the most relevant marketing segments for global consideration.

Global Demographic Segmentation

Although not a significant determinant of global marketing, demographics may illuminate specific trends among a specific age group that span nationalities and international boundaries. One such segment is the teen market. Youth marketing has been a focus of Asian marketing for quite a while, because in the West, youth is such a high-value market.

Teens

Thirty-two million strong, the worldwide teen market (12- to 17-year-olds) is diverse, vibrant, and growing—and a crucial force to be reckoned with. Their beliefs, attitudes, and behaviors will affect the future entertainment marketplace for years to come. Teens are active consumers in terms of the money they spend and in terms of the influence they wield in their families and on societal trends. Being raised during a period of rapid change, teens understand the need for spontaneity and to be able to change quickly, because they live with short-term change and volatility on a day-to-day basis. Perhaps because of this, teens display remarkable self-confidence in their judgment. They do their research prior to making large purchases because they want to make informed decisions; in addition, they are particular about what they spend their money on. Teens trust advertising in magazines more than that on television, the radio, or the Internet. Teens tend to multitask less when they read magazines than they do with other media. Unlike previous generations, today's teens also live with ethical and moral paradox, and as a result, they realize that the choices they must make are a mixture of good and bad elements.[9]

A. C. Nielsen's work on Thai teen consumer behavior provides some illumination of teen consumer behavior, as does McCann Erickson's study on Malaysian teens in general and their Internet behavior in particular. Similarly, research reports from *Ogilvy* & Mather are confirming that Japan is seen as the fashion center for many

▪▪▪▪▪▪▪▪▪▪▪   **BOX 6-4**   ▪▪▪▪▪▪▪▪▪▪▪

Focus on Global Teens

MTV REACHES OUT

MTV's hit show *Laguna Beach: The Real OC* reaches teens worldwide.

Teens are growing up in a digitized and exciting ad world where U2 promotes their iPods, McDonald's gets them to see *Star Wars,* and an EverQuest II video game delivers their patronage to Pizza Hut. But with all these branded entertainment campaigns, what works and what's doomed to turn off the savvy teen? Entertainment marketers worldwide must determine how to craft youth-focused, buzz-worthy branded entertainment programs in order to successfully reach global teens. Here are ways to tap into this market.

1. Know what's hot.
   Teens are passionate about electronics and entertainment, and about products such as iPod accessories. Target is the place to be seen. Netflix is gaining momentum over Blockbuster in the race for teens' movie dollars. *Laguna Beach* is the only must-see TV show for teens.

2. Pick music over film any day.
   Music is something that has a shelf life of longer than three weeks. Looking at music versus films, films are great, but buzz about a film lasts for three weeks and then disappears. The buzz about a CD, however, can last for a year or more.

3. Turn off the TV.
   TV is background noise for teens as they IM friends or do other things. TV is "there" and is something teens pay attention to, but it doesn't define who they are.

4. Get into their social networks.
   In a recent survey, 89 percent of the teens polled said they were fine with friends sending them info about products through MySpace, but 92 percent of them were not fine about being advertised to directly on MySpace.

5. Integrate causes that matter.
   Cause marketing is very important to teens. They care about changing and improving the world for the better.

6. Let them explore and discover.
   Teens are the "Google Generation" because Google is more than a search engine to them—it's a window onto things that they may not have accessed so easily before.

7. Give them the tools to customize and document.
   Young people are big on owning their own universe and on being able to document it and share it with friends, which is why uploading photos or writing and sharing music are big trends.

8. Keep them communicating and connecting.
   Teens are creating their own communities. Instead of having a big group of trendy friends, young people exist, mix, and mingle in their own "pods."

9. Find them on their cell phones.
   Because teens are on their cell phones more than ever, traditional research practices should be cell-phone based.

(Continued)

10. Be funny, cool, and on the Internet. The company called "Jib-Jab" is a great example of why this is important. Teens who saw this company's site immediately sent the URL to their friends, because the site content was the funniest thing they had seen.

SOURCE: Tina Wells, Buzz Marketing Group, 2005.

Asian teenagers (those living in Thailand, Hong Kong, and Singapore, specifically) and that trends often start there. (Several worldwide trends have also originated in this part of the world, for example, the Pokemon and Hello Kitty rages.) In short, Asian teens are influenced by a complex mix of East Asian, Western, and their own cultures.

In addition to age (specifically, teens), four other important global demographic segments are profiled for the importance to entertainment marketing: gender, religion, economics, and ethnicity.

Gender Segmentation

The cultural definition of *gender* is behavior appropriate to the sexes in a given society and the cultural capital (i.e., possessions) associated with a set of gender roles.[10] Gender roles affect purchasing and consumption. Numerous studies over the years have shown that women and men process information differently, and these gender differences offer marketers an opportunity to reach audience members by appealing to gender-specific leisure, sports, and shopping needs. In travel marketing, for instance, focusing on the male role would emphasize the functional benefits of travel (self-orientation), while focusing on the female role would emphasize social aspects of travel (other-orientation).

In a study of male and female entertainment consumers, researchers found that married women select entertainment that can be enjoyed by the entire family, while married men most often chose activities for themselves.[11] And although gender roles differ from culture to culture and often country to country, gender-based meanings and symbols are often used to tailor entertainment genre messages regardless of the culture in which the messages are being used. In India, for instance, the $60 million traditional music cassette/CD industry remains gender-specific in terms of performers and audiences.

In the last decade or so, gay men and lesbian women have been recognized as ideal targets for leisure and entertainment marketing because of their economic clout and distinctive value orientation. Ikea was one of the first retailers to feature a gay couple in its furniture commercials. Cruise ships offer gay/lesbian cruises for singles and families, and music venues provide entertainers who reflect the preferences of their gay clientele. The leisure industry has recognized the potential revenue generation to be gained from addressing distinct sexual orientation- or gender-based groups with messages tailored to their needs and values.

Religious Segmentation

Useful in markets where religion is an important component of identity, segmentation by religion addresses consumers' spiritual value systems. Jewish people are noted for their philanthropy, Catholics for their consumption of holiday icons, and Buddhists for their abstinence from meat. Marketers use knowledge about the preferences of religious groups to craft media messages that will not offend a given segment. Conversely, religious sects use the media to deliver spiritual entertainment; Trinity Television Network provides 24 hours of programming per day, including game shows, talk shows, concerts, and soap operas, to viewers nationwide. Targeting worldwide Christians, TTN has capitalized on this huge segment to generate revenue and proselytize their theologically based messages through broadcast entertainment.

Economic Segmentation

Income levels often determine the kind of promotion and message content used to market entertainment to a given audience. It would be foolish to advertise an exotic African vacation to working students, and no millionaire is interested in learning about bargain rates at Holiday Inn. Marketers note that economics determine not only what, but also how people of varied income levels consume entertainment (e.g., a tux or T-shirt for the opera?).

To segment consumption across segments on the basis of how potential audience members compete for status, we look at an audience's **symbolic capital**.[12] Financial resources (economic capital); memberships and social connections (social capital); and aesthetics, status, and education (cultural capital) combine to form a person's symbolic capital.

People with symbolic capital can use it to cross social segments in which a particular cultural knowledge is valued. Film stars such as Chow Yun Fat from Hong Kong or Hrithik Roshan from India can trade their national fame in their own countries as symbolic capital to obtain Hollywood credibility. Arnold Schwarzenegger was able to translate his film star credibility into access to political networks and was elected governor of California. To some extent, the nature of entertainment activities is status-oriented consumption for the participant, laden with status symbols that indicate a person's position, class, or group. Operagoers who sit through three nights of Wagner's *Rings* cycle consume the activity not only for enjoyment, but also as a badge of elite consumption (and, in some cases, only as a badge of elitism). Marketers must position status symbols for different economic and social segments in different ways to accommodate differences in how people consume symbolic capital.

Ethnic Segmentation

Multicultural marketing programs differentiate the interests of one group from another. *Ethnicity* implies common origin, a self-perpetuating population, shared cultural values, a field of communication and interaction with a common language, and members who define themselves as a distinguishable category.[13] Successful ethnic marketing depends on appealing to the basic motivational drive through benefit- and values-based segmentation. In the U.S., entertainment marketers target Asian and Hispanic consumers differently because of their different attendance motivations. Asian families value education-based entertainment, whereas Hispanic families are more interested in shared emotional experiences. Venues that advertise in Spanish are more apt to attract Hispanic audiences than those that do not; 53 percent of Hispanic consumers say they pay more attention to brands that are advertised in Spanish.[14]

Ethnic segmentation.

Global migration has resulted in groups of ethnic cultures living in every country. By addressing these groups individually and using distinct promotional messages, entertainment marketers can establish valuable relationships and build brand loyalty.

Global Psychographics

Worldwide, marketers are using lifestyle segmentation to develop promotional communications. The Japanese VALS system identifies four important dimensions: exploration, self-expression, achievement, and tradition. Other highly developed schemes include France's COFREMCA Sociostyles and Denmark's Minerva scheme, which uses color to identify segments. A study by the D'Arcy Masius Benton & Bowles ad agency identified four lifestyle groups of European consumers: successful idealists, affluent materialists, comfortable belongers, and disaffected survivors. It is important to understand cultural differences because they affect how promotional messages are developed.

The design shown in Exhibit 6.3 permits Japan-VALS to clarify the processes of social change and innovation diffusion (the spread of trends and technology) in Japanese society. It also identifies the consumer segments at the core of most consumer markets:

- **Integrators** (4 percent of population) are highest on the Japan-VALS measure of Innovation. These consumers are active, inquisitive, trend-leading, informed, and affluent. They travel frequently and consume a wide range of media—print, broadcast, niche, and foreign.

- **Self-Innovators** and **Self-Adapters** (7 percent and 11 percent of population, respectively) score high on Self-Expression. These consumers desire personal experience, fashionable display, social activities, daring ideas, and exciting, graphic entertainment.

▪ ▪ ▪ **EXHIBIT 6.3   VALS for Japan**

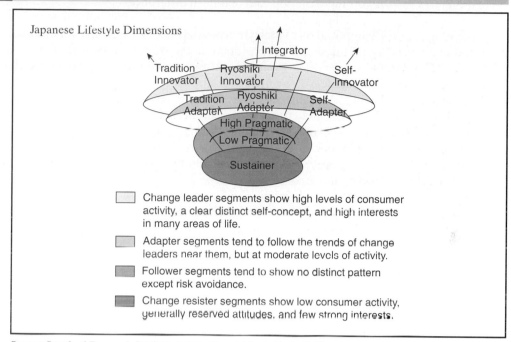

Japanese Lifestyle Dimensions

☐ Change leader segments show high levels of consumer activity, a clear distinct self-concept, and high interests in many areas of life.

☐ Adapter segments tend to follow the trends of change leaders near them, but at moderate levels of activity.

☐ Follower segments tend to show no distinct pattern except risk avoidance.

☐ Change resister segments show low consumer activity, generally reserved attitudes, and few strong interests.

Source: Stanford Research Institute International, Menlo Park, Calif.

- **Ryoshiki Innovators** and **Ryoshiki Adapters** (6 percent and 10 percent of population, respectively) score highest on Occupations. Education, career achievement, and professional knowledge are their personal focus, but home, family, and social status are their guiding concerns.

- **Tradition Innovators** and **Tradition Adapters** (6 percent and 10 percent of population, respectively) score highest on the measure of Traditional Ways. These consumers adhere to traditional religions and customs, prefer long-familiar home furnishings and dress, and hold conservative social opinions.

- **High Pragmatics** and **Low Pragmatics** (14 percent and 17 percent of population, respectively) do not score high on any life-orientation dimension. They are not very active and not well informed; they have few interests and seem flexible or even uncommitted in their lifestyle choices.

- **Sustainers** (15 percent of population) score lowest on the Innovation and Self-Expression dimensions. Lacking money, youth, and high education, these consumers dislike innovation and are typically oriented to sustaining the past.

Global Scan, a more universal and comprehensive lifestyle measurement scheme, was created by Backer Spielvogel Bates Worldwide (now Bates Worldwide). Global Scan measures a wide variety of consumer attitudes and values, media use, and buying patterns by conducting annual surveys in more than 18 countries. From its research, BSB concluded that five global segments describe the combined population: adapters, traditionals, pressureds, achievers, and strivers. As their names imply, these groups are categorized by their primary motivating behavior: adapting, maintaining tradition, trying to keep up, getting to the top, and making a difference.

Another scheme, Global MOSAIC, classifies more than 800 million of the world's consumers and is composed of 13 lifestyle types that can be found in every modernized country. It is based on the simple proposition that the world's cities share common patterns of residential segregation. Each has its low-income inner city area, upscale suburbs, and rural communities. Using highly localized statistics across eighteen countries, Experian has identified 13 types of residential neighborhoods, each with a distinctive set of values, motivations, and consumer preferences. The *global* version of MOSAIC serves as the common analytical currency among and between *country* MOSAIC typologies. MOSAIC types in every country can be cross-referenced to one of the global types on the basis of four primary attributes: age structure, family structure, extent of urbanization, and income structure.

Using one or more of the local or global typologies enables marketers to craft and deliver motivation-specific messages to their desired audiences. Audience research that ground these groups continues to be developed in countries new to capitalism.

Lifestyle Segmentation in Emerging Capitalist Nations

Within the past seven years, two countries developed their first consumer segments in response to global marketing demands. Turkey's scheme included both males and females, but males still dominate purchase decisions. In China, women are a strong force in the consumer marketplace, as indicated by the female-oriented segmentation scheme presented here.

Turkish research conducted in 1999 identified three lifestyles:[15]

- Liberals/trend-setters—college educated and high-income earners
- Moderates/survivors—predominantly male wage earners
- Traditionalists/conservatives—those concerned with price over prestige and style

In China, females' lifestyles were reported in 1998 as falling into one of four segments:[16]

- Conventional women—family is a priority
- Contemporary females—combine work and family as main priority
- Searching singles—career and image-oriented, postpone marriage
- Followers—low involvement in social, cultural, and physical activities

Problems with Global Lifestyle Profiling

Marketing research across borders and cultures is beset with problems. Lifestyles changes, natural disasters, and economic fluctuation create instability that underlies dramatic swings in circumstances for consumer groups. Another problem is that central concepts in this type of research are not universally defined, and it is not always clear why particular segments express certain consumer preferences. Additionally, current lifestyle measures are not very good at capturing the fluidity of lifestyle segment membership, especially in emerging free markets such as Turkey and China. Finally, there is a low level of correlation between lifestyle segments and particular behaviors such as brand or product preference, which vary widely across global geodemographics.

Some improvements to segmentation measures, however, can be made to address these problems, including strengthening the link between micro-motives and macro-behavior, that is, between lifestyle segmentation and macroeconomic data; extending data coverage on ongoing lifestyle changes, both voluntary and unintended; and analyzing the emergence of a global consumer culture using case and comparative studies.[17] Only with continuing efforts can global research remain current and address cultural nuances; marketing is held hostage to available data and must rely on academics and scientists to improve the accuracy and currency of that information. Without lifestyle information, the effectiveness of marketing would diminish dramatically.

▪▪▪ Generic Segmentation Factors

Regardless of where audiences are located geographically, demographically, or psycho-graphically, they can also be segmented according to usage behavior, price, benefits, and aesthetics. Niche marketing, which targets small groups of like audience members, is utilized to reach global audiences on a narrow-cast, or pinpointed, basis based on these additional, generic segmentations. The following discussion helps marketers identify which segmentation strategy is best for their clients and for developing appropriate audience messages.

Usage Segmentation

Audience members are divided into groups on the basis of differences in their knowledge, attitude, and use of or response to an experience. This type of segmentation focuses on how often people buy tickets or use entertainment genres, when they use them, and their usage patterns. Although usage behavior varies among global audiences, we can generalize based on usage in most world locations by rate, occasion, and loyalty.

• *Usage rate segments.* Usage rate segmentation sorts audiences by the amount of entertainment they consume. Very often, the best predictor of future behavior is past behavior. Using the 80–20 rule (80 percent of ticket purchases are made by 20 percent of a potential audience base), we call the 20 percent group *frequent* or *heavy users;* the remaining 80 percent are *light* or *nonusers.* Marketers know that it is much easier to stimulate increased attendance by current patrons than to attract people who never attend performances. A study by the Cleveland Foundation and the Pew Charitable Trust[18] found that *frequent users* placed a high value on leisure-time activities that spark the imagination or are new and different. At the other extreme, *light users* were defined as those who attended at least one activity of a particular genre during the year. Central to users' decision-making processes were cost, comfort, and convenience, as well as social interaction. *Nonusers* reported that their activities must be fun and entertaining, informal, involve friends, convenient, and inexpensive. According to Sidney Levy, *nonparticipants* "harbor many inhibiting images of the arts as relatively austere, effeminate, esoteric, inaccessible, and too demanding of study and concentration."[19] These folks are targeted at a *point of entry* that is familiar and accessible to potential audience members. Educational messages are an important consideration when attempting to recruit nonusers.

• *Occasion-based segments.* Occasion segmentation divides audiences according to when they attend a performance, travel to a destination, or visit a venue. Buyers can be distinguished according to the occasions when they develop a need, purchase a ticket, or encounter the experience. Performing arts centers increase demand by promoting season tickets as birthday and holiday gifts; movie theaters also provide coupons for gifting. Holiday performances, evening concerts, and society fund-raisers are among the occasions marketers use to segment audiences. New occasions may be created, such as hour-long rush-hour performances to attract commuters. Marketers should consider the many possible occasions when audiences might attend performances, parks, and attractions and create messages and incentives to promote attendance at those times.

• *Loyalty status segments.* A market can be segmented by consumer loyalty status. Strategy to promote a special concert to loyal season subscribers differs significantly from the strategy to promote the same concert to those who have only attended once before. This segmentation method functions with the aid of computerized databases, which allow marketers to direct their promotions to the appropriately loyal users.

Segmentation by Price

In general, buyer behavior in entertainment activities in all countries appears to be highly price sensitive, and many venue marketers (such as spas, casinos, and resort hotels) still act on the assumption that price is the key segmentation variable. In the resort industry, high-priced band venues (i.e., concert halls and stadiums) require feasibility studies to identify the ability and willingness of sufficient customers to pay the prices necessary to generate the level of revenue required to pay back investment, cover fixed costs, and create targeted profits. Segment-targeted tactical pricing is important, although limits are set by the strategic marketing mix decisions, costs of operation, and consumer satisfaction. Although pricing is not as important as the other variables discussed in this chapter, it continues to motivate large numbers of entertainment consumers.

Benefit Segmentation

This segmenting method addresses the additional value consumers seek from purchase decisions. The benefits one attendee seeks from an experience may differ substantially from those sought by another. Benefits take a variety of forms, from social and functional to health and safety, and have global application. For instance, attending a free performance of *Rigoletto* in Central Park provides benefits that might look like those listed in Exhibit 6.4.

Each benefit can be marketed to entice an audience segment to attend the concert. Benefits are derived through audience research to determine the nature of why people attend a variety of entertainment activities and performances.

Aesthetics Segmentation

Aesthetics play an important role in all of our lives, and audiences often choose their form of entertainment based on their aesthetic interests. Northwestern University proessor Sid Levy's audience resarch identified six factor adjectives used by audience members to describe what the important objects in their lives should be like.[20]

BOX 6-5

A Closer Look at Performing Arts Venues

SEGMENTING PERFORMANCE AUDIENCES

Segmentation is the engine that drives audience building for the performing arts. Recognizing that the audience is not a homogeneous mass, marketers treat them as a collection of distinct and discrete segments each with different needs, attitudes, and expectations. One approach[21] advocates engaging with and addressing the needs of all attendees, not just the reliable core audience, by segmenting the current audience into groups of attendees with similar needs. As with traditional segmentation, as described above, such approaches are most useful when prospecting for new customers or when little is known about current purchasers.

Most arts venues, however, know a great deal about their audiences: how long members have been a attending performances, what type of shows they like and which they avoid, how often they come, how many people they normally attend with, whether any of them are children or senior citizens, where they like to sit, how much they are prepared to pay, and how far in advance they will book. From this information, a venue marketer can track an audience's past behavior, predict the audience's future behavior, and tailor its communications to meet audience members' very different needs.

Venue analysis identifies the two primary defining variables as *frequency* (number of bookings over time) and *degree of difficulty attempted* (based on a classification of the accessibility of each show). These variables are based on behavioral data routinely collected by the box office system. This means that the development of each booker/audience

Lord of the Rings is both a family movie and a potential future play.

(Continued)

member (i.e., the increase in frequency and/or degree of difficulty attempted) can be easily measured and tracked. The degree of difficulty is closely correlated to psychographic or attitudinal data, which is widely used in other marketing sectors. By combining behavioral data with psychographic profiling, a comprehensive picture begins to emerge of each audience, making it easier to target it with an effective marketing campaign.

Here are typical definitions of existing live performance genre types broken into five categories according to *difficulty to market*. They are in order from most to least difficult.

1. *new writing:* work by unknown or obscure playwrights; work that is outside the mainstream
2. *serious drama:* Ibsen, Chekhov, Shakespeare's tragedies and histories, for example
3. *mainstream work:* plays that many people know (such as Tennessee Williams's *A Streetcar Named Desire*); or productions featuring well-known actors
4. *accessible work:* musicals such as *Chicago* that have catchy tunes and appealing story lines
5. *family shows:* major, immensely popular productions, such as *The Lion King* and *Cats.*

Frequency of attendance is broken into four categories of audience members by number of performances they attended:

1. once in the past 12 months
2. two or three times in the past 12 months
3. four or five times in the past 12 months
4. six times or more in the past 12 months

The Audience Climbing Frame[22] makes the frequency/degree of difficulty strategy practical and possible to implement using the two primary defining variables set against each other on the axes of a matrix. The combination of the two variables produces a number of discrete segments, each of which includes members who hold different attitudes from those in other segments. This framework helps to effectively target prospective audiences according to their past behavior. Those who have attended in the past are more likely to attend in the future than those who have not. Databases are built on behavioral measures for most performance audiences marketing functions. More details on this audience-building typology are discussed in later chapters.

What do you think?

1. Why is segmenting by frequency of attendance preferred for arts venues?
2. Which segment, first-time audiences or occasional attendees, is the most difficult to reach? Which one is the hardest to persuade to buy tickets? Why?

SOURCE: Morris & McIntyre, paper presented at the annual Arts Marketing Association Conference, 2005.

- *Factor 1* suggests that people in general want stimulation, movement, and excitement. Men chose *thrilling* and *awesome* more than women to describe their favorite experiences; stimulation adjectives were most pronounced among younger adults and middle-class indviduals.
- *Factor 2* concerns realism and is most strongly preferred by working-class and disadvantaged people; they use words such as *special* and *expensive* when describing pereformance experiences.

▪ ▪ ▪ ▪ **EXHIBIT 6.4** **Targeting Messages by Benefit Segment**

Message-Based Communication Based on Audience Benefits

Audience Segment	Benefit
Non-operagoers	Introduction to the opera genre
Opera lovers	An opportunity to experience the opera again
Students	A cost-free form of entertainment
Office workers	A chance to be outdoors
Teenagers	Socialization without parents
Tourists	A unique way to be part of New York City
Families	Occasion for a family activity
Tourists	Unique cultural exposure

• *Factor 3* suggests a conventional sexual identity dimension with traditional masculine (military metaphors such as *wipe out*) as opposed to traditional feminine (relationship metaphors such as *loving*) terminology; predominant among high-income groups.

• *Factor 4* yields references to shapes, such as *round, flowing,* and *curved,* indicating preference for visual stimulation; occurred among all demographics.

• *Factor 5* is oriented toward social status; high-income respondents preferred *comfortable* and *luxurious,* while disadvantaged and working-class respondents were more focused on *sentimental* and *customary.*

• *Factor 6* deals with seriousness and frivolity; women and young adults tended to prefer *funny, pretty, crowded, soft,* and *musical;* men, older adults, and male and female high-income earners were inclined in the opposite direction.

Adjectives yielded by such research were used to develop promotional messages that would relate directly back to actual audience descriptors.

Experience location, design, and appeal are reasons why aesthetics play an important role in marketing entertainment. Open to creative interpretation by performance marketers, these factors are strong indicators of the relevance of aesthetics for venue interior design, collateral material design, and message strategy.

Action Segmentation

One group of entertainment consumers, believed by some people in the industry to be the most powerful consumer segment of all, is called the **prosumers**. Several definitions of *prosumer* exist:[23] (1) A consumer who is an amateur in a particular field, but who is knowledgeable enough to require equipment that has some professional features ("professional" + "consumer"). (2) A person who helps to design or customize the products they purchase ("producer" + "consumer"). (3) A person who creates goods for their own use and also possibly to sell ("producing" + "consumer"). (4) A person who takes steps to correct difficulties with consumer companies or markets and to anticipate future problems ("proactive" + "consumer"). The text usage is occasion-specific, but always implies a step beyond the notion of a traditional consumer.

Regardless of how they are defined, prosumers are turning the heads of marketers worldwide. Euro RSCG, a large international ad agency, completed a nine-country study of prosumers that showed prosumers can represent 20 percent or so of any particular group or marketing segment. They can be found everywhere, are at the vanguard of consumerism, and what they say to their friends and colleagues about brands and experiences tends to become mainstream 6 to 18 months later. They also vary by category: a wine prosumer, for instance, will not necessarily be a prosumer of cars.

Prosumers often reject traditional ads and invariably use the Internet to research what they are going to buy and how much they are going to pay for it. Half of prosumers distrust companies and products they cannot find on the Internet. Thus, if a company wants to influence prosumers, it must be extremely open about providing information.

Further, marketing to the prosumer has taken on conflicting spins: the business sector sees the prosumer as a means of offering a wider range of products and services, whereas activists see the prosumer as having greater independence from the mainstream economy. Either way, prosumers present a challenge for marketers of entertainment and experiences.

The *cluetrain manifesto* (a futurist publication) noted that "markets are conversations," with the new economy "moving from passive consumers . . . to active prosumers." For instance, Amazon.com emerged as an e-commerce leader, partially due to its ability to construct customer relations as conversations rather than simple, one-time sales.[24] The emergence of producer consumers (prosumers) and the rise of the consumer-to-consumer (C2C) economy has been enabled by easier access to the Internet (open source software, blogs, message boards, and so on) and the availability of selling forums (eBay, for example).[25] To accommodate prosumers, entertainment marketers must establish and maintain a dialogue with audiences that provides more than a simple schedule of coming attractions.

Persona Segmentation[26]

Consumer models called **personas** are a set of fictional, representative archetypes based on the behaviors, attitudes, and goals of the people interviewed for a specific research phase. Personas have names, personalities, pictures, personal backgrounds, families, and, most importantly, goals; they are not "average" users but specific characters. A persona is a stand-in for a unique group of people who share common goals; at the same time, persona characteristics encompass those of people in widely different demographic groups who may have similar goals.

For example, people across all demographic boundaries have similar goals when using airline travel: to get from one place to the other with as little hassle as possible. These goals can guide a design team responsible for developing an airline marketing campaign to prioritize the feature list, design the interface, refine the scope of the target audience, and even uncover new market niches for a specific travel route. Personas bridge the gap between market segments and experience definition.

How do marketers select the right personas for a particular marketing effort? At the beginning of every project, researchers use qualitative methods to review the client's market segmentation and demographic data. Stakeholders, customers, and users are interviewed in order to gain insight into the experience domain and user population. This information feeds directly into the types and characteristics of the personas.

Personas and market segments provide different kinds of information. Market segmentation provides a quantitative breakdown of the market, while personas provide a qualitative analysis of user behavior. These two techniques serve different purposes. Market segmentation identifies *attitudes and potential buying habits,* such as those illustrated in the following example:

> In a survey of 150 people, participants were asked about Rear Seat Entertainment (RSE) systems. It was found that most respondents believed it was a "lifestyle" purchase for parents trying to entertain or distract their kids while driving. Most felt that the system was appropriate for children between the ages of 4–15yrs, as children needed to be old enough to use headsets as well as some form of remote control. Among the high quality brand names mentioned were Sony, Hitachi, Magnavox and Nintendo. High system prices were cited as a barrier to purchase in the next two years. However, many expected prices to fall significantly over the next five years.

Personas, on the other hand, reveal *motivations and potential usage patterns.* A consumer's motivation is what interests them in using a product. For example:

> Kathleen is 33yrs old and lives in Seattle. She's a stay at home mom with two children: Katie, 7, and Andrew, 4. She drives the kids to school (usually carpooling with 2–3 other kids) in her Volvo wagon. Kathleen is thinking about buying the Sony rear-seat entertainment system she saw last weekend at Best Buy to keep the children occupied on the upcoming trip to see family in Canada.
>
> She doesn't want to be distracted by the noise from the videos or games so wants to make sure she can set the sound to be heard only in the back seat. Kathleen also wants to make sure her kids are watching appropriate programs; therefore she wants some channel controls close at hand, but she thinks Katie should be able to control the system most of the time so she won't be distracted.

From this example, marketers can ascertain that Kathleen does not necessarily want her kids to be wearing headphones for an entire journey, as she likes to talk with them on their trips, and that she may want Katie to have some control of the entertainment system from the back seat. This information is used for concept development to promote the entertainment product.

Both market segmentation and personas provide useful information; one informs the other. Using the appropriate tool for the task at hand without bending, adding, or removing from either can provide a rich, complementary set of user and consumer models, which together can ultimately create a useful and more successful product definition than either could in isolation.

Niche Markets

People worldwide with special interests are considered niche markets. Best serviced first by magazine publishing, today's niche markets are great targets for Internet promotion. Directed Internet messages can reach larger worldwide audiences with lower initial cost than satellite channels. These specialized offerings may appeal to a small number of people, but cumulatively they represent a large market that can be easily aggregated on the Internet. Producers whose programming would never make it into prime time but who have very dedicated small audiences are using what might be called *silvercasting*.[27]

Sail.tv (a boating site), for instance, attracted 70,000 viewers in its first month of Web casts. OutZone.com features gay and lesbian programming created in conjunction with PlanetOut, a media and entertainment company focused on communicating with that audience. HGTVPro offers programming aimed at contractors and builders, and Discovery Communications offers 30,000 video clips excerpted from its library of documentaries and other educational programs to help grade school and high school students with their homework. Instructional videos also are available on the Web by TotalVid, which offers 2,300 programs for download, many of them videos teaching everything from how to play a guitar to the best techniques in tae kwon do.

Among the niche audiences that are considered both large and attractive to Internet broadcasters are immigrants and expatriates seeking news and entertainment from their home countries. JumpTV, a Toronto-based company, offers live Internet transmission of television station broadcasts from more than 60 countries to expatriates around the world.

As the global population increases, so does the trend toward niche marketing. No longer a world of mass-mediated viewers, niche audiences dominate the landscape with special needs, wants, and motivations. Successful marketing identifies niche segments to receive promotional communications focused on their specific interests.

FINALLY: LET'S SUM UP ▪▪▪▪▪▪▪

Although there is no single right way to segment a market, the implications for segmentating audience characteristics, before, during, and after attending entertainment events are great. Segmentation is a dynamic process; new segments emerge as older ones disappear or are no longer viable because of market changes. For this reason, segmentation justifies a considerable and continuous commitment to audience research, as explained in the next chapter.

GOT IT? LET'S REVIEW ▪▪▪▪▪▪▪

- There are many ways to segment entertainment audiences, but all segmentation sechemes should possess the same criteria: mutual exclusivity, exhaustiveness, measurability, sustainability, and actionability.
- Performance differentiation allows marketers to concentrate promotional strategies on a single segment or niche market to maximize impact and stimulate ticket purchase.
- VALS 2 is an important marketing tool that segments the U.S. population into financial-resource-based lifestyle segments that focus on principle, status, and action orientations.
- Prizm software clusters U.S. audiences by zip code according to buying habits and media patterns; MOSIAC's U.S. neighborhood classifications enable marketers to target buyers and households with greater precision. Global Scan and Global MOSIAC are based on lifestyle types appropriate for most world metropolitan areas.
- Gender, religion, economic, and ethnic demographic segments are important for

developing global entertainment marketing strategies.

- Segmenting by price, usage behavior, and benefits help entertainment promoters craft communication messages to the needs of these audience groups.

NOW TRY THIS: LET'S APPLY WHAT WE'VE LEARNED

1. Go to the Claritas Web site at www.yawyl.claritas.com and look up your own zip code. Do the PRIZM clusters for your code make sense? Why or why not?
2. Visit MatureMarketInstitute@metlife.com and revisit the American baby boomer market. What geographic locations are best suited to marketing leisure and entertainment activities? What does the group's racial and ethnic composition contribute to marketing strategy?
3. Select and compare an advertisement that portrays gender stereotypes with one that does not. Would the target audiences for these ads be similar or different? Why?

QUESTIONS: LET'S REVIEW

1. As the manager of the Bolshoi Ballet, your job is to develop a marketing strategy for their upcoming world tour. What global segments would you target for promotional messages? Provide a rationale for your decision.
2. Discuss the value of cohort segmentation for targeting mature consumers for a vacation destination.
3. Which system, PRIZM, MOSIAC, or MONITOR, would be best for promoting season subscriptions to an outdoor music venue for summer concerts in Massachusetts? Why?
4. What new market segments may emerge for global audiences in the future?

MORE TO READ

Brent Green. *Marketing to Leading-Edge Baby Boomers.* New York: Writer's Advantage, 2003.

Joe Marconi. *Future Marketing: Targeting Seniors, Boomers, and Generations X and Y.* New York: NTC Business Books, 2001.

J. Walker Smith and Ann Clurman. *Rocking the Ages: The Yankelovich Report on Generational Marketing.* New York: Harper Business Books, 1997.

Michael Walker. *Marketing to Seniors,* 2nd ed. Bloomington, IN: 1st Books Library, 2005.

NOTES

1. P. Kotler and J. Scheff. *Standing Room Only: Strategies for Marketing the Performing Arts* (Cambridge, MA: Harvard Business School Press, 1998), pp. 108–9.
2. Michael Walker. *Marketing to Seniors,* 2nd ed. (1st Books Library, 2005), p. 52.
3. J. F. Engel, R. D. Blackwell, and P. W. Miniard. *Consumer Behavior,* 8th ed. (Dryden Press, 1995), chap. 3.
4. MetLife's Mature Market Institute, Westport, Conn., 2003.
5. 50Plus.com, online case studies.
6. Joe Marconi. *Future Marketing* (NTC Business Books, 2000), p. 107.
7. S. Plog. *Leisure Travel: Making It a Growth Market . . . Again!* (Wiley, 1991).
8. J. W. Smith and A. Clurman. *Rocking the Ages* (Harper Business Books, 1997).
9. Mediamark Research Inc., teen market profile, 2004.
10. K. M. Palan, "Gender Identity in Consumer Behavior Research," *Academy of Marketing Science Review* (2001), p. 10.

11. Study conducted by graduate students at California State University–Fullerton using the *Sunday Los Angeles Times Calendar* as selection criteria and $500 as an entertainment budget for 25 women and 25 men who were asked to plan a month's entertainment.

12. This discussion is taken from Arnould, Price, and Zinkhan, p. 578.

13. *Ibid.*, p. 595.

14. J. Fetto, "Targeted Media," *American Demographics,* July/August (2002).

15. O. Kucukemiorgllu, "Market Segmentation by Using Consumer Lifestyle Dimensions and Ethnocentrism: An Empirical Study," *European Journal of Marketing* 35 (1999) (5–6): 1–9.

16. J. Tam and S. Tai, "Research Note: The Psychographic Segmentation of the Female Market in Greater China," *International Marketing Review* 15 (1): 25–51.

17. Fritz Reusswig, Hermann Lotze-Campen, and Katrin Gerlinger, "Changing Global Lifestyle and Consumption Patterns," Potsdam Institute for Climate Impact Research (PIK) Global Change & Social Systems Department, 2005.

18. "Philadelphia Arts Market Study," Pew Charitable Trusts, 1989, and "Marketing the Arts in Cleveland," commissioned by the Cleveland Foundation, 1985.

19. Sidney Levy, "Arts Consumers and Aesthetic Attributes" in M. Mokwa, W. Dawson, and E. Prieve (eds.). *Marketing the Arts* (Westport, CT: Praeger, 1980).

20. Ibid.

21. Morris Hargreaves McIntyre's *Audience Builder* schema.

22. From the keynote address made by Gerri Morris and Morris Hargreaves McIntyre at the 2005 Arts Marketing Association conference in Belfast, Ireland, on July 22, 2005.

23. As defined by www.wordspy.com.

24. en.wikipedia.org/wiki/Prosumer.

25. www.futurematters.org.uk.

26. Elaine Buchen, report located at cooper.com/newsletter, Feb.–Mar. 2002.

27. Saul Hansell, "Much for the Few," *New York Times,* March 12, 2006.

Researching and Measuring Entertainment Audiences

If you can't measure it,
you can't manage it.
— ANONYMOUS

Chapter Objectives

After reading this chapter, you should be able to answer these questions:

- What is *applied research* and what types of studies fall into this category?
- How do *projective techniques* enable audience disclosure?
- How do *new audiences* differ from past audience members?
- What are the various methods of *audience measurement*?
- How is *advertising research* different from other forms of evaluation?
- Why is *methodological convergence* necessary in today's marketplace?
- How is audience research *analyzed*?

The people who promote entertainment are not always the same people who conduct the research, but marketers in the entertainment industry must understand the research process in order to effectively utilize the results. Applied research is conducted with all types of consumers and audiences of entertainment for planning and predicting functions. This chapter details the most relevant qualitative and quantitative research techniques and their value for use in entertainment research. We also review audience satisfaction measurements and the use of syndicated services.

▬▬▬ Why, What, and Who of Research

The purpose of applied entertainment research is *discovery*. Discovery consists of three aspects: it is a process of finding out and *describing* what is; it is a way of *explaining* why things are the way they are; and it is a method of *evaluating* performance satisfaction. This chapter is organized around these three approaches to discovery, which are carried out using two distinct research techniques. Quantitative audience research, the first technique, measures how many people attend, watch, listen, and visit performances and venues, and most of it is conducted to determine what to charge advertisers. In such a competitive industry, entertainment producers must understand not only how many, but *why* audiences attend concerts, visit resorts and casinos, and enter performance venues. To answer the why questions, qualitative research methods, the second technique, are employed.

Why We Conduct Research

Discovery is conducted for a variety of reasons, mostly to learn more about audience preferences and wishes. Both qualitative and quantitative methods of data collection are appropriate. Three aspects of discovery and their purposes for audience research are explained here.

Finding Out and Describing

Research conducted to find answers to audience-related questions is called **descriptive research**. Common in the leisure, entertainment, and tourism areas, descriptive research helps marketers keep up with a constantly changing landscape. Field research is used to track basic patterns of behavior as needed for market profiles or needs assessment. Statistics gathered by syndicated services are also used to describe market conditions.

Explaining

Explanatory research seeks to answer the how and why questions and use the answers for predicting future trends. Going beyond description, this form seeks to explain the patterns and trends observed: Why is a particular destination losing popularity? How do casino developments gain approval against the wishes of a local community? Why do some social groups and not others patronize the arts? What venue modifications will make the consumption experience more enjoyable? The focus is causality, and the knowledge gained is used to predict. Prediction is a key aim of much of the research that takes place in entertainment.

Evaluating

Evaluative research arises from the need to make judgments on the success or effectiveness of programs developed or in place—for example, whether a particular advertising campaign for a performance has been cost effective. Evaluative research measures success and failure. Because audiences have monetary value, promoters measure them using ticket receipts, exit polls, advance reservations, and past performance. To measure audience satisfaction, for instance, venue managers solicit feedback through exit surveys or service-evaluation postcards. Resulting numbers determine advertising

Planning activities among decision makers are based on primary research.

rates and predict revenues. Research giants such as Nielson compile and syndicate purchase and attendance statistics and supply them to manufacturers and advertising agencies for a monthly fee.

The Purpose of Research

Research plays a key role for all organizations in the entertainment industry that engage in policy making, planning, and resource management to achieve their goals. Outcomes and examples of research efforts include *policies,* such as those made by an arts center to encourage contemporary composers; *plans,* such as those made by a casino to increase visits by a particular audience demographic; and *management systems,* such as those used by a national park to implement user-pay programs.

Who Conducts Research

Three important groups that conduct research for entertainment organizations are government agencies and commercial organizations, consultants, and venue managers.

Using their own in-house researchers, government agencies conduct censuses, which tourism bureaus use to tally departures and visitations. Because of the magnitude of these studies, few independent organizations can undertake them, yet they are invaluable resources for entertainment researchers. Advertising agency in-house research teams and private research companies also collect data for entertainment providers.

Consultants establish specialized areas of research and are occasionally linked with academic institutions. They work on a project-by-project basis with industry clients and advertising agencies.

Managers of entertainment venues and attractions see research as a vital part of their responsibilities. Managers supervise research on customers, staff, performance, competitors, and products that is used to make strategic decisions. For example, resort managers routinely receive information on usage levels from sales figures or bookings, while an urban park district manager conducts specific data-gathering exercises to determine attendance levels.

Foundations and government agencies provide free resources for analyzing consumer data. Some of these organizations are:

- *Pew Internet & American Life,* which provides unbiased research that explores the impact of the Internet.
- *U.S. Census Bureau,* which contains an endless supply of information on people and businesses, including the Economic Census with industry information from many countries, including quarterly financial reports. The bureau's American FactFinder, a government census database, focuses on demographics and features a population counter; Statistical Abstracts Fact Sheet provides a summary of demographic data compiled by city, state, county, or zip code.
- *U.S. Department of Labor's Bureau of Labor Statistics,* which has a demographic section that slices data by age and gender. The department's Consumer Expenditures report categorizes how much was spent on what.

▪▪▪ Approaches to Entertainment-Focused Research

Similar to standard market research, entertainment researchers rely on empirical research for decision-making tasks. *Empirical* research can be *theoretical* or *applied.*

Theoretical research is conducted to draw general conclusions about a phenomenon under study. Most theoretical research is deductive, starting with the explanation or hypothesis, then gathering descriptive data to test a theory or explanation, and finally analyzing the data to test the hypothesis against it. Academics conduct theoretical research, which may ground future study for a variety of marketing and consumer research applications.

Applied research, commonly recommended for entertainment, makes use of existing knowledge to find solutions to particular problems. Applied research is inductive, beginning with observation and description and utilizing data analysis to explain what happens. The ability to induce explanations from observational data is most appropriate for entertainment research. Exhibit 7.1 summarizes the two branches of research.

Empirical studies, both theoretical and applied, are the building blocks of research and knowledge, because their conclusions are based on specifically collected information. Studies following a *positivist tradition* are most often used in the natural sciences

▪▪▪ **EXHIBIT 7.1** Two Branches of Empirical Research

Empirical Studies	
Theoretical	*Applied*
Deductive, positivist tradition	Inductive, interpretive model
Hypothesis testing	Descriptive studies, projective techniques
	Explanatory studies, evaluative studies

▪▪▪▪▪▪▪▪▪▪   BOX 7-1   ▪▪▪▪▪▪▪▪▪▪

A Closer Look at Museum Research

SYDNEY'S POWERHOUSE MUSEUM

PROBLEM: When attendance levels dropped by 20 percent in two years, the Powerhouse Museum in Sydney (Australia's largest museum) conducted an inductive study to determine what people wanted from a museum experience. During in-depth interviews, visitors and members described what they wanted in experiential concepts, learning opportunities, and exhibits. The information is summarized here.

Experiential concepts:

- Hands-on (active) experiences
- The ability to use all the senses
- Something to take away from the visit

Learning opportunities:

- To start from familiar concepts and things and move to unfamiliar
- To control their own experiences and amount and depth of information they access

- To cater for all levels of learning, for different age groups and for adults and children
- Exhibitions that help them to learn something

Exhibits:

- To touch objects and displays
- Not too much reading
- Computer interactives that enhance knowledge; beyond button-pushing
- To get up close to objects and displays
- Exhibits that are well maintained and working at all times
- Staff on the floor to answer questions and bring the exhibition alive
- Exhibits that are realistic
- Places in exhibitions where they can sit down and "take it in"
- Exhibitions that encourage sharing among a group

RESULTS: Depth-interviews yielded information that was used to reinvigorate the museum. Innovations and improvements raised attendance levels by 23 percent, showing a net 3 percent gain in the number of visitors the following year. Membership increased by 9 percent overall, a healthy sign of growth for the museum.

What do you think?

1. What other research might be conducted to supplement the museum's original study?

2. How often should organizations conduct preference research with its audiences?

to prove a hypothesis from observed data. For social science, an *interpretive model* is adopted for its reliance on the people who are studied to provide their own explanation of their situation or behavior. This flexible approach to data collection involves qualitative methods and uses an inductive approach to entertainment research. Our discussions of research methods are devoted to applied techniques appropriate for learning about *new audience* members.

What's a New Audience?

We conduct audience research because we can no longer depend on audiences' previous levels of continuing and devoted attention to a specific entertainment brand. Today's audiences are challenging. Not only do they have hundreds of entertainment forms and brands to choose from, they have access to endless performance and brand information through the Internet.

Current audiences are pressed for time, have short attention spans, and don't trust mass media to provide the most reliable information. New audiences value genuine experience, not simply a mere performance commodity. Compare this idea to the difference between a Broadway play and the film version of the same play; many people prefer the original delivery system. In their quest for experience, today's audiences are *individualistic* in their needs and wants, *involved* in their purchases, *independent* in choice selections, and *informed* about experiential performance options.

To understand new audiences, entertainment marketers commission or conduct applied research. The next three sections characterize the techniques used for collecting data from audience members: descriptive, explanatory, and evaluative. Descriptive studies are useful to portray situations and experiences, while explanatory studies reveal the whys and hows of those situations or experiences. Evaluative studies analyze effectiveness and allow marketers to reconfigure entertainment experiences based on consumer input.

▪▪▪ Descriptive Studies

Description involves direct observation, what can be seen on site and while the action is happening. Researchers must get out into the field, which means meeting and talking with audience members as they experience all forms of entertainment. Anthropologists have shown us methods that we can apply to conducting entertainment research where it happens, rather than in a controlled or laboratory situation.

For example, one of the most effective ways to describe and understand what happens in entertainment environments is to employ **ethnographic research** to describe consumer cultures. The ethnographic approach to entertainment research draws on a variety of qualitative techniques to understand the world through the eyes of your research subjects. In leisure studies the approach has become particularly associated with cultural studies. Researchers use observation and conversation to study people's behavior in everyday contexts—what we call field research. Being in the field means integrating oneself into a particular consumer entertainment culture. We use *unstructured* data collection to focus on a specific group or culture—say, a group of

Consumer ethnographer documents household brands.

seniors experiencing a museum, or music fans. Analysis involves interpreting the meanings and functions of human action.

Like anthropologists who enter different cultures to research those societies, ethnographic researchers go into entertainment environments to understand how audiences behave at play, in venues, and while shopping. For instance, Hilton Hotels gave business travelers cameras to capture their feelings about hotel rooms. They learned from the photographs that business guests want wireless Internet connections and a well-stocked bar. At LegoLand, researchers posed as park attendees to observe families as they experienced rides and activities. Children were observed straining to see animals over rails and barriers. This information caused park officials to replace barriers with floor-to-ceiling glass, providing young children with unobstructed views of wildlife. By putting themselves in the consumers' shoes, researchers learn important information that is useful for entertainment brand enhancement.

Ethnographic research focuses on an *emic* perspective. That is, this type of research seeks to present an insider's view by using a nonjudgmental orientation to cultural practices. The researcher "hangs out" in a particular location, relying on the observation of visual symbols and consumption rituals to gain insight. He or she works with an informant or "native speaker"—a member of the culture under study—to answer questions and validate assumptions. To better understand the hip-hop musical culture, a researcher merges with the group. Identifying a particular group of hip-hoppers and spending time watching them is a first step. Next, it is important to meet and talk with group members about their music. An informant helps the researcher understand the group's dress code, language, and musical rituals.

The Museum of Modern Art (MoMA) used the ethnographic technique of observation to learn about the special needs of older visitors (60+ market segment), as presented in our focus on the senior audience segment.

Descriptive research has enabled entertainment providers to pinpoint the needs and wants of its audiences. This first step in understanding consumer motivations should be expanded with another type of research that probes more deeply into the culture of entertainment consumption. To do that, we turn to explanatory research.

▪▪▪▪▪▪▪▪▪▪ BOX 7-2 ▪▪▪▪▪▪▪▪▪▪

Focus on Research Ethics

SENIOR SPIES

The Museum of Modern Art saw a decline in senior volunteers and visitors during a recent exhibition season. To ascertain reasons for the decline, museum management placed a research team posing as museum docents to observe senior visitors for three months. The information would be used to develop new programs and recruit volunteers to maximize the museum's relationship with this audience group.

The spies gained an understanding of the particular wants and needs of this audience segment while working at the museum with a veteran docent who acted as their informant. Presented below is a list of discoveries the docent-spies made, as well as their recommendations for addressing the needs of this special group. Using research results, museum officials implemented the recommendations that caused a 17% increase in visitor satisfaction over the next six months.

Discovery	*Recommendation*
Unfamiliarity with museum environments	Offer guided tours for new visitors
Disrupted by noisy children	Schedule visits for early mornings
Difficulty standing in ticket lines	Modify ticketing system
Frequent fatigue	Provide seating and catalogs to read
Inability to go with the flow	Limit numbers in gallery at one time
Interest in stories and material from the era 1910–1960	Focus exhibitions on early decades
Limited information access	Promote activities through age-specific channels
Hours of uncommitted time	Recruit and train docent volunteers; reward their efforts with service symbols

What do you think?

1. How ethical is spying on mature audiences without their knowledge or permission?

2. How should the privacy issue be handled by museum officials?

▪▪▪▪▪▪▪▪▪

Critical Incident Technique and Trailer Calls

Two of the most popular methods of evaluation important for determining the success or failure of an experience are the critical incident technique and trailer calls as characterized in Exhibit 7.2.

In **critical incident techniques (CIT)**, end users are asked to identify specific incidents that they experienced personally and that had an important effect on the final outcome of an interactive experience. The researcher's emphasis is on obtaining information about incidents rather than obtaining study participants' opinions, which can be vague. The context of the incident may also be elicited. Data from many users is collected and analyzed qualitatively.

Elements of an Effective Marketing Research Program on Experiences[1]

Type of Research	Research Objective	Method	Frequency
Complaint solicitation	Identify dissatisfactions Locate service failure points	Qualitative	Continuous
Critical incident studies	Identify "best practices" Identify audience requirements	Qualitative	Periodic
Requirements research	Inputs for qualitative research regarding audience requirements	Qualitative	Periodic
Relationship survey, SERVQUAL survey	Monitor & track service performance Access expectation/perception gaps	Quantitative	Annual
Trailer calls	Obtain immediate feedback on performance of transaction	Quantitative	Continuous
Service expectation meetings	To create dialogue with audiences Identify audience segment needs	Qualitative	Annual
Process checkpoint evaluations	Determine audience perceptions Identify and solve service problems	Quantitative	Periodic
Market-oriented ethnography	Research audiences in natural settings Study global audience cultures	Qualitative	Periodic
Mystery shopping	Measure employee performance	Quantitative	Quarterly
Audience panels	Monitor changing audience expectations Provide forum for audience input	Qualitative	Continuous
Future expectation research	Forecast audience expectations Develop & test new ideas	Qualitative	Periodic
Database marketing research	Identify audience requirements	Quantitative	Continuous

Study participants are requested to follow the three stages described below in the same order:

1. Focus on an incident that had a strong positive influence on the result of the interaction and describe the incident.
2. Describe what led to the incident.
3. Describe how the incident helped the successful completion of the interaction.

There will be some variation in the number of positive and negative incidents to which users respond. Begin with a positive incident in order to set a constructive tone with the user. Hotels, amusement parks, and public television stations use CIT to gather perspectives in the customer's own words.

Trailer calls capture information about key service encounters with a customer. In this method, customers are asked a short list of questions immediately after a particular transaction about their satisfaction with the transaction and contact personnel with whom they interacted. Hotels use this method because visitors presume the call is following up to ensure that they are satisfied, so it serves both as a research tool and a form of customer service.

▪▪▪ Explanatory Studies

Audiences may not be as forthcoming with information as researchers and marketers would like them to be. Privacy concerns mean that audiences are often reluctant to disclose details that may come back to haunt them. People worry that information they provide to researchers may be used in ways other than those intended by the research.

When conducting consumer research, challenge begets innovation. If we are to understand the whys and hows of entertainment brand or product perceptions, we must develop clever methods for probing the minds of our audience. So, we do the prudent thing—we borrow from past success. In this case, "past success" refers to the practice psychologists developed of using inkblots, known as Rorschach tests, to probe the innermost thoughts of their clients. In this process, therapists show clients a series of seemingly random patterns, and then listen while clients interpret what they see based on past experiences or familiar associations. In one sense, they *project* their feelings on to an unrelated task, rather than responding to directed questions, thus avoiding uncomfortable associations to them. Nonetheless, they have disclosed information about a topic.

Projective Techniques

Audience researchers use the same type of projective techniques as those developed by psychologists. We give respondents a task to perform that provides us with insights about the respondents' perspectives on a given subject without directly asking them to

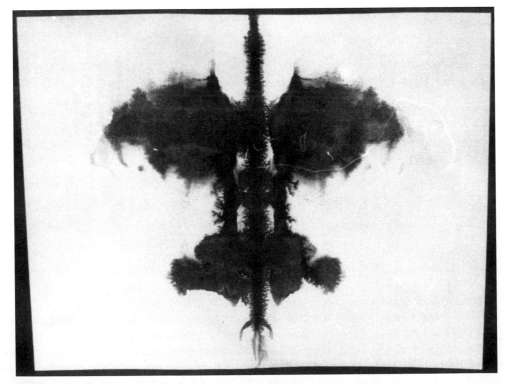

A Rorschach ink blot.

disclose their personal or private experiences. And we can make it fun. If ballet is the subject, bring out your respondents' "inner child" by asking them to draw and color their renditions of a ballerina, or to name the celebrity who might dance in that role. From respondents' drawings we gather information to use in promotional media that capture the humor and satire of the playful drawings.

Projective techniques uncover a person's innermost thoughts and feelings by allowing him to project his beliefs onto other people or objects. The notion is that unconscious desires and feelings can be explored by presenting participants with an unthreatening situation where they are free to interpret and respond to various stimuli.

This technique is especially useful for uncovering subtle differences in how consumers feel about brands in categories where no obvious differences exist. For instance, opera is a genre of performances where audience expectations are high, but opera as an experience may invoke a variety of associations that are based on specific consumer experiences or media promotions. Information about audiences' experiences, gathered through a series of projective techniques, may reveal that audiences choose to attend a specific opera based on the venue in which it is performed rather than on the quality of the performance. Armed with this information, promoters might present the *venue* as the star instead of the specific opera for the next performance. The new Disney Concert Hall in Los Angeles is such a venue, selling out seats a year in advance to audiences who are more curious about Frank Gehry's architectural creation than they are about the music.

Projective techniques differ from traditional research methods because they allow information to emerge from the research rather than from questions posed directly to audience members. Like all research techniques, however, projective methods require a problem that research can solve and a concise research question on which to focus. The only difference between traditional and projective research techniques is the way we go about getting answers to solve the problem.

As early as the nineteenth century, Rorschach tests were used to probe the minds of crime suspects for signs of guilt. Projective techniques were therapeutic in nature and consisted of five types: constitutive (modeling with clay), constructive (building blocks), interpretive (word association), cathartic (play), and refractive (expressive behavior). It was not until after World War II that psychotherapy was applied to market research. A famous study by Mason Haire used projective techniques to examine consumer attitudes toward Nescafe instant coffee by developing two shopping lists with a single ingredient difference. One list featured Nescafe instant coffee, while the other included Maxwell House drip coffee. Both lists' other items were identical.

Fifty women were asked to describe the woman who developed each list. The woman who listed Maxwell House coffee was characterized as a "good housewife" for buying fresh-roast coffee for her husband, but woman who listed Nescafe was called "lazy" for purchasing instant coffee for her family. Results of that study were used to develop an advertising campaign in which instant coffee was portrayed as being rewarding to a family and socially acceptable to serve guests.

Entertainment researchers, similarly, might compile two lists of entertainment preferences with a paired variable, such as the opera and musical theater, and ask two groups to describe the lists' developer. Such a study would produce results that provide information about the images that a specific demographic has of opera and musical theater, enabling marketing managers to develop promotions to either change or strengthen those images. The Haire list is shown in Exhibit 7.3.

▮▮▮ **EXHIBIT 7.3 Components of Haire Study That Create Projection**

Good Wife Shopping List	*Lazy Wife Shopping List*
Pound and a half of hamburger	Pound and a half of hamburger
2 loaves Wonder bread	2 loaves Wonder bread
Bunch of carrots	Bunch of carrots
1 can Rumford's Baking Power	1 can Rumford's Baking Powder
Maxwell House coffee (drip ground)	Nescafe instant coffee
2 cans Del Monte peaches	2 cans Del Monte peaches
6 lbs. potatoes	6 lbs. potatoes

Source: Zeithaml, Bitner, and Gremler, *Services Marketing,* McGraw-Hill 2006, p. 144.

One advantage of using projective techniques today is that they are cost efficient and compatible with other methods of market research, such as depth interviews and focus groups. With increased audience choices in the entertainment marketplace, researchers must find selling hooks to differentiate one brand from another. It is a researcher's job to uncover subtle differences between products or services that can be used to effectively promote those entities.

Exhibit 7.4 presents another situation. The answer choices given in the exhibit may seem competitors in a mere popularity contest, but a respondent's reasons for attending one party over another should reveal the motivations behind his or her choice and provide insight into the celebrity's image.

By comparing the celebrity's perceived image with the real image as reported by the dinner party respondents, marketers can develop appropriate strategies to close the gap between audiences' perception and reality.

▮▮▮ **EXHIBIT 7.4 Research Games**

The Great Dinner Party

In order to better understand the fan-worship response of audiences, celebrity industry researchers give interviewees these instructions:

"You have been invited to three dinner parties, all scheduled for the same night. For logistical reasons, you can attend only one. Of the hosts listed below, choose the one whose party you would attend and give the reasons for your decision."

1. Elton John: musician, performer
2. Madonna: entertainer
3. Mickey Mouse: Disney animated star
4. Dave Letterman: talk-show host
5. Sean Penn: film star

Source: Rein, Kotler, Hamlin, and Stoller, *High Visibility,* 1998.

Projective Techniques Are Used to Research Audience Motivation

By asking consumers to talk about other people or solve other people's problems, researchers have obtained insightful information that could not be obtained through other methods. Other-directed research can successfully elicit self-disclosure, rather than mere description, from participants. Four of the most common techniques used in projective research are word association, symbolic association, thematic apperception, and object sorting. Here are some situational examples of how these psychological tools can work to help researchers understand audience motivations.

• Let's say the Kennedy Center, in Washington, D.C., wants to develop a creative concept for advertising the upcoming opera season. Using *word association,* researchers ask study participants what types of performances come to mind when they hear words such as *foreign language* and *old-fashioned.* Or, researchers ask what words best describe performance genres such as *ballet* and *musical.* The results may help promoters position opera away from any negative connotations consumers have for such performances.

• *Symbolic associations* are made between an object and its meaning to a consumer. A casino may symbolize crime to one consumer and fun to another. Venue researchers may show respondents a party scene around a craps table to determine respondents' perceptions of gambling. This information is valuable for developing brand messages about their casino and its activities to a specific audience segment.

• Story scenarios are gathered from consumers as part of *thematic apperception* testing (TAT). Using a picture of people sitting in their cars in freeway traffic, we ask consumers to tell us a story about a time when they were in such a situation, or to develop a story about what the other drivers are thinking as they crawl along the freeway at five miles per hour. Participants' responses can be used in print advertising to show how commuting on Amtrak allows riders to relax rather than rage.

• Researchers may ask consumers to group items of like kind together—*object sorting*—to discover how audiences perceive different types of entertainment. In one object-sorting study, participants did not place Cirque de Soleil in either the circus or the dance categories, opting for a new category instead. From this research, Cirque decided to classify itself as a hybrid form of entertainment to avoid unfavorable associations with either of the other two alternatives.

These four standard approaches to uncovering layers of consumer thoughts have been improved to expand our understanding of the motivations and brand preferences of today's audience. You could visualize them as methods of peeling an onion—uncovering layer after layer of information about audience preferences.

Using Projective Techniques to Peel the Audience Onion

Sophistication and *discrimination* are adjectives used to describe the audiences that marketers must confront when peeling the information onion. To penetrate the layers of consumer thought, researchers must provide a stimulus to generate an understanding of the meanings consumers associate with that stimulus. Constructing an effective stimulus requires a great deal of creativity on the researcher's part.

Using open-ended formats, projective techniques are classified according to the type of information they yield—either diagnostic or descriptive. Whereas the use of projective techniques for psychotherapy is most often therapeutic, marketing and audience researchers use them to generate *rich description* and *self-disclosure.* Five types of projective techniques are available: free association, choice ordering (ranking), completion, construction, and expressive (role playing).

Free Association

Researchers use *free association* to understand consumer relationships with a brand or product by asking for participants' words, images, and thoughts in response to a specific stimulus. Word association has served as an effective elicitation technique for decades. *Neutral words* that have nothing to do with the brand—*theme park, performance, casino*— are used to mask the identity of the brand. *Key words* that directly relate to a venue brand—*comfortable, spacious, easy to access*—are useful for expanding neutral responses.

Brand-specific associations are best accomplished with *personification* techniques. Planners ask, "If Sea World were a celebrity, who would it be?" Visual personification, called *photo sorting,* requires participants to match pictures of people with a brand that reflects the brand's personality. This technique pairs facial expressions in photographs with brands in a single category to draw out a brand's personality. Brands that elicit smiling faces can be further grouped and sorted for distinctive characteristics.

The results of a photo-sorting study commissioned by the Laguna Art Museum showed that visitors matched the museum's brand with pictures of older audiences, enabling the museum to develop a trendsetting campaign that appealed to younger audiences, changing consumer perceptions about attending museum functions. Tattoo art, motorcycle artifacts, and surf culture exhibits replaced traditional offerings; percussion bands replaced string quartets at function openings; and the gift shop added jewelry and ceramics to its retail inventory. These audience-appropriate entertainment innovations enabled the museum to increase its membership and exhibit attendance.

A *photo-and-tale* technique used for Denny's Restaurants struck gold when consumer collages showed an association between the restaurant and overweight, old-fashioned men and women. Researchers used photo sorts to obtain self-image portrayals of mid-priced restaurant consumers. Subjects were given a group of 40 photographs featuring people of varying sizes and shapes, modes of dress, levels of occupation, and economic status. The participants were instructed to place the photos of people who were most likely to appreciate food preparation and appearance in one pile and photos of people who were unlikely to care about those features in another pile. By analyzing the similar responses of the folks in the likely-to-care piles, researchers found that their target audience cast themselves as intelligent, physically fit, and well-dressed. Research yielded the concept for a new campaign featuring stylish folks with discriminating taste in their ads with the tagline, "The meal that dictates the fashion." Word association generates adjectives usually associated with a brand, and personification helps researchers identify the images audiences and consumers hold of a brand and its competitors. Association techniques also are useful for determining the effects of brand slogans, logo designs, and sponsorships. Exhibit 7.5 shows word associations shoppers made for the Mall of America, located near Minneapolis.

Ranking

For this technique, consumers rank, or choice order, brand preferences and explain why certain aspects of a brand are more important than others in their entertainment

▮▮▮ **EXHIBIT 7.5   Associations Made for Mall of America**

Attributes

Product-Related Attributes	*User Imagery*	*Brand Personality*
Multiple shopping options Ample parking	Fashionable, trendy, stylish, unisex	Fun, adventuresome, outgoing, athletic, artsy

MALL OF AMERICA

Benefits

Functional Benefits	*Experiential Benefits*	*Symbolic Benefits*
Big names, wide range of prices, product variety	Greenery, escalators, kid activities, cafe smells	Feeling of self-expression and self-assurance

brand selections. When respondents rank brand benefits from most to least important, researchers can probe their reasons for choosing those benefits. Research done by Knott's Berry Farm theme park revealed that female consumers ranked LegoLand ahead of Knott's brand because of the tactical factor involved with building blocks. Marketers used these findings to focus a tactile-based advertising message ("Knott's will keep your feet moving and your hands busy") to women in gender-appropriate magazines. Ranking is a simple yet effective technique for understanding relationships among brands, benefit preferences, and other measurable characteristics.

BOX 7-3

Focus on Entertainment Brands

BRAND PERSONALITY PROFILES

Ratings are ideal for assessing brand personality traits. Professor Jennifer Aaker's research developed five factors of brand personality: sincerity (wholesome, cheerful), excitement (daring, up-to-date), competence (reliable, successful), sophistication (upper class, charming), and ruggedness (outdoorsy and tough). Consumers were asked to rate how descriptive each personality trait was for the brands according to a seven-point scale (1 = not at all descriptive; 7 = extremely

descriptive). Responses were averaged for summary measures. Here are a few of the 37 brand profiles Aaker collected.

Certain brands tended to be strong on one factor (e.g., MTV with excitement, CNN with competence), and other brands were high on several factors. For global destination brands, research reported that three of the five factors applied to Japan and Spain as country brands, but a "peacefulness" dimension emerged for Spain versus the "competency" dimension for Japan.

	Apple	*CNN*	*LEGO*	*Lexus*	*MTV*	*Sony*	*Visa*
Sincerity	0.92	0.99	1.11	0.87	0.70	0.87	0.90
Excitement	0.95	1.02	1.10	1.12	1.27	0.94	0.87
Competence	1.07	1.18	1.01	1.07	0.82	1.02	1.02
Sophistication	0.86	0.93	0.87	1.27	1.02	0.89	0.87
Ruggedness	0.92	1.01	1.10	1.03	0.93	0.90	0.87

SOURCES: Jennifer Aaker, "Dimensions of Brand Personality," *Journal of Marketing Research* 34 (8) (1997), 347–366; and Jennifer Aaker, Veronica Benet-Martinez, and Jordi Garolera, "Consumption Symbols as Carriers of Culture," *Journal of Personality and Social Psychology* 81 (3) (2001), 492–608.

Completion Devices

Audience needs and values surface by using *completions,* a technique that asks respondents to finish sentences, stories, conversations, or arguments.

Using a *first-person scenario,* planners ask participants to complete the phrase, "When I think of ballet, _____." Responses were stereotypical. When researchers used *third-person scenarios* ("When an average person thinks of ballet, _____."), respondents were more likely to reveal their innermost feelings. People are much more willing to talk about an average person or a friend rather than about themselves, because most people fear that negative connotations are associated with admissions about oneself.

Hotel and hospitality researchers often employ sentence completions to understand "whether or not" and "why" issues associated with visiting their venues. Look at the difference in responses the New York Hilton received by changing from first- to third-person scenarios. Asked in the first person, a respondent filled in the blanks like this:

- When in New York, I would stay at the Hilton *because* <u>I like the restaurant.</u>
- I'd stay at the New York Hilton *if* <u>it were across town</u>.

From this set of responses, researchers understand that the restaurant is better than the hotel, or that it is in the wrong location. If the hotel made changes based on this information, it could incur unnecessary expenses.

By asking questions in the third person, however, Hilton got these responses:

- When my neighbor is in New York, she stays at the Hilton because <u>she likes to show off.</u>
- My neighbor would stay at the New York Hilton if <u>she had the money</u>.

The second set of responses indicates that this consumer perceives the Hilton to be prestigious and expensive, answers not obtained when using the first-person orientation. This consumer is much more willing to be truthful when projecting her feelings onto the neighbor than when asked to admit her own feelings.

Completions work well in individual interviews and for group interaction. Focus-group leaders use completion techniques to begin discussions by asking participants to talk about what they were thinking as they finished the exercise. Because completions don't require extensive facilitation, they are easily developed and administered by researchers at all skill levels.

Construction Techniques

Requiring a more complex and controlled intellectual activity, *construction techniques* ask consumers to develop a story from a specific stimulus. One of the most effective of these techniques builds on consumer metaphors. The Zaltman Metaphor Elicitation Technique (ZMET) requires consumers to assemble a *collage* of magazine pictures to represent their feelings about a brand or a venue. On completion, the collage provides

Consumer collage.

a launching pad for consumers to discuss their feelings in detail with the researcher about the brand as portrayed by the metaphorical pictures they chose.

Cartoons also provide a creative mechanism for learning about consumer perceptions. Nicknamed *bubbles,* drawings of people in relevant branding situations are used to generate a response to a comment made in the cartoon. In the wake of a population explosion in Mexico, such cartoons were used to elicit information from Hispanic men about their attitudes toward practicing birth control. The fill-in-the-bubble, cartoonish nature of the pictured questions looked like a fictional story rather than an item whose purpose was to elicit incriminating personal admission from the respondents. Researchers learned from the cartoons that men, in order to retain their sense of machismo, refused to use contraception, a behavioral choice that resulted in large families that many of the men were unable to support financially. This revelation provided the input for a public education campaign using a macho cartoon penis character to extol the virtues of contraception.

Role Playing

Stories, myths, and legends are the stuff of consumer research. To generate consumer narratives, role-playing works well in situations where consumers cannot describe their actions or behaviors, but maybe can act them out. Assuming the role of flyer and flight attendant, Virgin Atlantic Airways passengers acted out a typical scenario between a rude attendant and a frequent flyer. Researchers learned that flyers prefer discretion to "being scolded for using the wrong toilet," yet they want attendants to keep passengers sober by refusing to serve them multiple alcoholic beverages on long trips. Virgin repositioned its attendants as "flight consultants" and trained their employees to respond to consumer requests rather than to initiate interaction.

Consumer *stories* are useful for gathering information based on specific situations. Virgin Atlantic also used a thematic apperception test (TAT), which, as we discussed earlier, presents an ambiguous situation in which the consumer assumes the role of a person in a photo or cartoon and constructs a story about what the person is thinking, saying, or doing. First-class flyers were asked to elaborate on what led to and what followed a scene depicting the inside of a cabin during a flight from London to Miami. As a result of flyer stories about aching backs and stiff necks from sleeping upright, VAA now features seats that become flat beds, a bar and bartender, and an opportunity to receive a massage. When passengers land, the airline provides them with a shower and a shave in a special "revival" lounge, then allows customers to use a free, airline-provided limousine service. Using participant interpretations from this study, themes were developed and used to name individual first-class flights: The Miami to London flight, for instance, is now known as The Trance Atlantic. "The transportation business has become the experience business," claims the VP of marketing for Virgin, "and we strive to provide our premium passengers with an experience they won't forget."

Brand Obituaries

By asking consumers to develop **brand obituaries**, researchers are presented with a holistic conceptualization of a brand's impact. Writing on Disneyland, consumers used phrases such as "cartoon stars," "animated ears," "American icon," and "mouse mania" to eulogize the park. One writer said, "Disneyland is survived by a mouse and a park full of kids standing in long lines!" Such "obituaries" are useful for helping marketers

---

▪▪▪▪▪▪▪▪▪   **BOX 7-4**   ▪▪▪▪▪▪▪▪▪

Focus on Brand Obituaries

EULOGIZING PLYMOUTH

On November 3, 1999, the president of the Chrysler side of DaimlerChrysler announced that the Plymouth brand would be discontinued at the end of the 2001 model year. Plymouth was introduced in 1928 as a direct competitor to Ford and Chevrolet, and in the 1960s, Chrysler began to reposition Dodge as a brand alternative to Plymouth. By 1982, Dodge was outselling Plymouth, whose sales continued to decline relative to Dodge and, by 1990, offered no unique products. Ultimately, Plymouths became re-badged as Dodges. The 1999 PT Cruiser retro-show car was initially

badged as a Plymouth, then reappeared with Chrysler badges, hinting that Plymouth's end was near. By 1999, Plymouth sales were less than 300,000 per year. Here is what three consumers had to say about the demise of their brand Plymouth.

- "No one loved their Plymouth more than I did, and I will mourn its demise forever."
- "Plymouth died a dignified death in the wake of a corporate invasion by Japanese cars."
- "Detroit can't understand that America wanted what Plymouth had. Plymouth was my ideal of a car for Americans."

SOURCE: The Rise, Fall and Death of an Automobile Brand, Nov 11, 1999, from www.joesherlock.com/riplogo.gif.

▪▪▪▪▪▪▪▪▪

---

generate messages to communicate an entertainment brand's equity and perceived value for collateral materials and advertisements.

Consumer brand tales help companies understand how its brand is perceived in the minds of consumers. The brand obituary of Plymouth featured in Box 7-4 serves as an example of how such research might be insightful for entertainment brand managers.

Although normally developed after the brand is dead (as in the above example), brand obituaries also can be conducted before a brand's demise to determine how consumers perceive its current image and its potential.

Cool Searching Techniques

The Look-Look Network, a Los Angeles marketing firm that focuses on youth culture, forges relationships with its target audience by monitoring audience dialogue and interpreting consumer trends and brand attitudes. Using its database of 35,000 14- to 35-year-olds, the company surveys can develop peer friendships among participants by using lifestyle images produced by amateur photographers.[2] In other words, people relate to other people who look like them.

The company also helped Latino Telemundo research its youth network, mun2, with ethnographic studies of 24 youths across the United States. It enlisted 24 others to create blogs, and both groups were then studied for marketing opportunities. Look-Look provided in-depth investigations into Latino youth culture that resulted in successful promotional campaigns for mun2.[3]

▪▪▪ Evaluative Research and Audience Measurement

Providers of entertainment rely heavily on quantitative measurement data to determine the relative success or failure of a performance or an activity. Box office receipts, or paid attendance, provide a baseline for calculating profits after promotional expenditures are deducted. Other common forms of entertainment measurement are rating services, behavioral research, the Q Factor, and incidental and convergent measures. This section looks at how and why marketers need to keep their fingers on syndicated and outsourced data for calculating the success of an entertainment venue, destination, or experience.

Media and the Ratings Game

Promotion success or failure is measured quantitatively at regular intervals in the entertainment industry. One of the most common measurement techniques is **audience analysis**. Managers who need to know whether their advertising campaign budget effectively promoted an event or performance rely heavily on audience analysis provided by a variety of measurement companies, such as Nielson and Arbitron. The information these companies collect is conceptually straightforward: It records people's exposure to media.

Ratings measure audience exposure to media for use in assessing audience viewing behaviors. Television and radio industries define *exposure* simply as program choice, rather than as attention or involvement with programming. These exposure databases reveal nothing about the effects of the exposure or viewers' choice motivations. If researchers know what determines exposure and can predict patterns of use likely to emerge under given circumstances, then they can interpret the data provided.

Exposure is measured in two distinct forms: with *gross measures,* which do not depend on tracking over time, and *cumulative measures,* which have a temporal quality in the data.

Gross Measures

Gross measures, or estimates of audience size and composition at a single point in time, include audience ratings, market shares, circulations, Web site hits, and sales (attendance, rentals). These measures provide a snapshot of a population without any definitive sense of repeat consumers. Gross measures of exposure are expressed in *gross rating points* (GRPs), which summarize ratings over a schedule, and simple cost calculations such as *cost per point* (CPP) and *cost per thousand* (CPM). The most common audience summaries reported by syndicated research companies, gross measures are best known and most widely used audience measurements. Their main drawback is a failure to capture information about how individual audience members behave over time. For such information, we turn to cumulative measures.

Cumulative Measures

Cumulative measures deal with *cume ratings* (a station's total audience), *reach* (how many viewers are targeted), *frequency* (how often the message is delivered), and *audience duplication* (channel loyalty, repeat viewing). Media planners work with these tracking measures to maximize audience exposure to a sponsor's message.

Producers who craft media content use these measures when monitoring popular culture trends to determine what viewers prefer in entertainment programming. Program preference research reveals a link between content and audience age and gender demographics: women prefer romance; teenage boys like action-adventure. Trend monitoring helped programmers anticipate the popularity of reality TV, for example, and allowed them to develop a variety of demographic-based program for the reality genre.

Behavioral Research

People's use of electronic media—audience behavior—has been the focus of audience research by advertising agencies, economists, and social psychologists. Both individual and structural factors are key determinants of audience behavior. As a collection of individuals, audience choice is of interest to communication studies and marketing; mass audience behavior is most used by sociologists, but has applications for marketing and advertising.

One model used to organize thinking about media audience behavior, shown in Exhibit 7.6, was designed to guide the analyst in considering all relevant factors for a study. Entertainment organizations can use the resulting analysis to make decisions on where to place advertisements.

▪▪▪ **EXHIBIT 7.6 Audience Behavior Model**

Long-Term Development of Technologies, Programming Services, Strategies		
Audience Factors	*Exposure*	*Media Factors*
Structural	*Group Measures*	*Structural*
Potential audiences	Audience ratings	Coverage
Available audiences	Market shares	Content options
	Circulation	
	Web site hits	
	Total sales	
Individual	*Cumulative*	*Individual*
Preferences	Cume ratings	Technologies owned
Group vs. solitary	Reach	Subscriptions
Awareness of options	Frequency	Repertoires
	Audience duplication	
Long-Term Cultivation of Tastes, Expectations, and Habits		

Source: Webster, Phalen, and Lichty, *Media and Audiences,* Open University Press, 2003, p. 191.

Techniques used for advertising research allow researchers to perform these functions. Researchers can:

- measure who sees ads through *audits of circulation or audiences* and *Web cookies,* which yield quantitative data on a representative sample and users' choices.

- determine how audiences respond to broadcast commercials and/or print advertising through *consumer surveys, depth interviews,* and *focus groups.* Response narratives provide and understanding of how audiences react to print and broadcast advertising.

- evaluate whether the ad sold the product using *mail orders, coupons* and *responses, retail surveys,* and *bar code scanner* data to measure success; such data link consumer responses directly to advertising promotions.

Two of the most common data collection methods are focus groups and surveys. Protocols are lists of questions or instruments for gathering information using these methods, which are briefly described in this section. For more information, refer to the suggested reading section at the end of this chapter.

Focus Group Protocols

Conducting a focus group requires a skilled moderator and a question protocol that addresses a client's needs. Comprised of five to twelve participants, focus groups are usually chosen from a panel of people who make themselves available to researchers because of their interest in a particular experience or use of a brand. The usual procedure is to visually record the discussion and for the researcher to produce a summary from the recording. The moderator's role is to guide the discussion, ensuring that everyone has her say and that the discussion is not dominated by one or two members of the group. Advertisers use groups to develop concepts or to evaluate commercials; behaviorists use groups to collect reactions to content. Focus group protocols include all the information needed to address the client's research questions. Points are not necessarily covered in a specific order, but are use to stimulate discussion and draw out participants opinions and attitudes. This qualitative method is often used as exploratory research on which surveys are developed to expand the sample size. Quantitative data collection is best achieved through surveys.

Survey Development

Questionnaire surveys developed for advertising, tourism, and entertainment research can be completed by interviewers or respondents, although there are some advantages to having an interviewer conduct the survey. Interviewer-completed surveys are more accurate, get a higher response rate, and obtain more complete answers; drawbacks to using it, however, are higher cost for the client and less anonymity for the participants. The most common types of surveys are household, street, telephone, mail, site/user, and captive group. Exhibit 7.7 provides a summary of types and characteristics.

An effective survey consists of four parts: introduction, instructions, questions, and respondent demographics. The brand is *never* mentioned at the beginning of the survey, only the brand category is noted. By keeping the survey short (10 questions), researchers can obtain higher numbers of responses. Incentives are usually a part of

▪▪▪ **EXHIBIT 7.7** Types of Questionnaire/Survey Characteristics

Type	Completion	Cost	Sample	Length	Response Rate
Household	self/interviewer	expensive	whole pop.	long	high
Street	interviewer	medium	most of pop.	short	medium
Telephone	interviewer	medium	most of pop.	short	high
Mail	respondent	cheap	general/specific	varies	low
On-site	either	medium	users only	medium	high
Captive group	respondent	cheap	group only	medium	high
Internet	respondent	cheap	most of pop.	varies	high

Source: A. J. Veal, *Research Methods for Leisure & Tourism,* 2nd ed., Prentice Hall, 1998, p. 149.

the completion process if response rates are important. These are the essential survey protocol components:

• *Introduction* includes the purpose of the survey and identifies the interviewer or organization conducting the research.

• *Completion instructions* must be included for every question or set of questions using the same format to avoid confusion or marking answers incorrectly.

• *Questions* best address information necessary for attitude surveys by using scaling methods that allow respondents to quickly mark the degree to which they agree or disagree with statements made. Open-ended questions are more difficult to analyze, but are most useful for eliciting in-depth responses.

• *Demographic information* is requested at the end of the survey, and only variables necessary for the topic under study should be asked; respondents are usually reluctant to answer income-related questions.

The survey protocol presented in Exhibit 7.8 is typical of those used for entertainment research. Note that demographic information is collected at the end of the survey.

The Q Factor

In order to measure how much a performer or celebrity is liked or disliked by the public, and how familiar the public is with a celebrity, the **Q Factor**,[4] or Q rating system, allows audiences to grade celebrities with a six-point scale. In Exhibit 7.9, a Q factor question elicits a specific opinion on a performer's "Q"uality.

Using the Q Factor method, researchers provide audience members with a questionnaire listing a sample of personalities. The scale yields dimensions of *familiarity* and *appeal*. Every year since 1964, more than 1,600 personalities have been evaluated by a national sample and categorized into 17 groups, such as comedians, fashion designers, sportscasters, film stars, and so on; this information is then syndicated to marketers. The report tells what kind of impression the celebrity makes on an audience.

▪ ▪ ▪ **EXHIBIT 7.8** Survey Protocol

This is an example of a survey developed to determine the Internet's role in making travel plans and to identify the most popular sites.

Introduction

This survey, sponsored by the city's travel council, is designed to find out how you plan your travel vacations. When you return your completed survey, you will receive a $10 coupon good for redemption for ticket purchases on any domestic airline traveling to this city.

Questions

For each of the questions below, write in the number that best represents your level of agreement with the statement using this raking system:

1 agree completely	4 disagree somewhat
2 agree somewhat	5 completely disagree
3 no opinion	

1. _____ I usually make travel plans months in advance.
2. _____ I consult Internet sources to plan my travel.
3. _____ Price is my first criteria for selecting an airline or hotel.
4. _____ Customer comments play an important role in my destination considerations.

Fill in the blank:

5. When I think of an Internet travel web sites, the brand that comes to mind is _____.

Check all the words that apply:

6. Adjectives that best describe my experiences with Internet travel services are:

___ convenient   ___ time-saving   ___ confusing   ___ invasive of my privacy

___ lengthy   ___ time-consuming   ___ simple   ___ better than a travel agent

Rank your preferences from 1 to 5, 1 being your favorite:

7. Which agencies are your favorites?

___ Travelocity   ___ ORBITZ   ___ hotwire.com

___ Expedia   ___ Cheaptickets.com

Check the appropriate answer:

8. How likely are you to log on to one of the above travel web sites in the next 3 months?

__ very likely   __ likely   __ unsure   __ unlikely   __ very unlikely

Demographics

Tell me about yourself by checking the appropriate answer:

9. I am   ___ female   ___ male

10. I am age   __ 20–35 __ 36–50 __ 51–65 __ over 65

Thanks for taking the time to complete this survey.

> *In your opinion, the performer is . . .*
>
> 1. one of my favorites
> 2. very good
> 3. good
> 4. fair
> 5. poor
> 6. someone you've never seen or heard

Polling and Incidental Measures

Polling research provides popularity measures regarding audience perceptions about celebrities and their image. Athletes, musicians, destinations, and venues are measured using pre-testing and post-testing designs to scan public attitudes about believability, compatibility with products, and potential to change public attitudes. Polls help match celebrities with products, events, and organizations for sponsorships, endorsements, and advertising. Audience sector polls conducted by Audience Studies Inc. can report an audience pull for a specific celebrity in a specific role, but it cannot predict the vehicle or role in which that celebrity would be successful.

Incidental measures are vast numbers of subjective data in the form of a celebrity's popularity indicators that include size of fan base, speaking invitations, videos or DVDs sold, mentions in gossip columns, number of magazine covers, and number of log-ins to celebrity home Web pages. Marketers use these data for image management and visibility indicators.

Measuring Convergence

Measurement standards are still being developed to determine the return on branded entertainment investments where advertising and entertainment converge. While there is not as yet an agreed-upon currency (dollar valuation) system for branded entertainment, there have been several attempts to attach value to such convergence deals, at least in the television industry. Nielsen Media Research, for instance, introduced a program in 2004 to track product placement ratings for broadcast networks. IAG's In-Program Performance service uses a panel of consumers who respond to online surveys designed to measure their recall of and reaction to product placements and sponsored program. Hopefully, a measurement system can be standardized to help both advertisers and entertainment producers calculate their return on investment (ROI).

A recent measurement tool introduced by research company Audible Inc. tallies podcast audiences.[4] (As we know, podcasts are Internet-based audio shows that are downloaded to listeners' computers.) This technology puts measurement capability in iPods and other MP3 players. Using a tracking service available to outside podcasters, Audible charges clients three cents per downloaded podcast to report whether a downloader listened, and if so, for how long. These tools provide a bona fide rate card for advertising on podcasts, enabling advertisers to determine how many people are really listening to shows, not just how many times a show is downloaded. These data give podcasters some audience information based on the same technology used for distributing newspapers, books, and other printed material into audio format.

Best Bang for the Research Buck: Combining Quantitative Data with Qualitative Research Methods

Although the quantitative data provide market researchers with a wealth of useful information, qualitative research provide the most efficient method for discovering and explaining audience behavior. Regardless of the techniques selected, qualitative research enhances our ability to understand entertainment consumers and the consumption process. The success of qualitative techniques, however, depends on the information-gathering process. Unlike questionnaires, structured interviews, and directed focus groups, ethnographic techniques are appropriate only for situations where elaboration is possible. Projective techniques can be incorporated into individual and group situations, paired with technology, or as a stand-alone methodology. Developing focused yet entertaining data collection techniques is a challenge every researcher faces. By incorporating popular culture with innovation, researchers are in a unique position to produce projection devices that result in *Ah-ha* discoveries.

Because of the complexity of the task, entertainment promoters often outsource qualitative research to private companies. Although the expense may be substantial, research costs are validated by the profits generated when research results are used to make the entertainment venue, brand, or experience more desirable to consumers.

Although researchers have learned a great deal about traditional media audiences, there is much more to discover about the behavior of Internet audiences. The latter are typically characterized as individuals seeking information and amusement, as being active, and as having unlimited potential for purchasing entertainment programming. By studying long-term relationships between the Web and its users, we may be able to develop a useful framework for collecting and evaluating ratings data.

Analyzing Audience Research

Researchers usually analyze consumer stories collected during interviews, but in the case of projective techniques, consumers play a significant part of the analysis process. With the researcher's guidance, participants interpret their own responses. Researchers then make connections that will uncover marketplace opportunities.

Methods

Both quantitative and qualitative analysis methods are appropriate for analyzing projective data. Consumer interpretations are *categorized* qualitatively to identify emerging themes. Alternatively, content may be classified into categories that are given a numeric value. Categories are counted for frequency of responses. Here is an example.

Results of research conducted on luxury cruises will yield dining (food quality and variety) and activity (types and difficulty level) aspects of cruise brand preferences. All references to activity aspects are grouped into one category, while another group is created for dining features. By counting consumer references to each aspect of the cruise, researchers can identify important features consumers use for making their selections. If

▪▪▪▪▪▪▪▪▪▪ **BOX 7-5** ▪▪▪▪▪▪▪▪▪

A Closer Look at Tourism Research

HAWAII AS A VACATION DESTINATION

PROBLEM: The Hawaiian tourism board statistics reveal that tourists are choosing destinations other than Hawaii for their vacations.

RESEARCH OBJECTIVE: To learn about visitor perceptions of Hawaii to see if the islands' image is part of the reason for reduced traffic

RESEARCH QUESTION: What comes to mind when travelers think about taking a Hawaiian vacation?

TECHNIQUE: Photo sorts to generate visual consumer perceptions about Hawaii

METHOD: Ten groups of ten people who were planning a vacation within the next year were asked to participate in selecting photographs taken of the Hawaiian Islands to produce brochures advertising the destination. None of the participants had ever been to Hawaii.

FINDINGS: As participants selected photos for their brochures, they explained to researchers the reasons for their choices.

Brochures from each group contained photographs of

- 146 beach scenes
- 99 palm trees
- 34 luaus
- 18 sailboats
- 13 pineapples
- 06 sunsets

Conversations validated what the brochures revealed:

People think the only thing to do in Hawaii is go to the beach.

USE: An advertising campaign called *"1,001 things to do in Hawaii when you're not at the beach"* was developed to change consumer perceptions about the destination.

RESULT: Tourism increased by 22 percent during the first year of the campaign.

What do you think?

1. If research also showed that people want the beach to be a good part of their vacation agenda, would you include beach activities in the next advertising campaign? Why?

2. How would you test the campaign to see how it might be updated?

---

comfort is mentioned many times in conjunction with stateroom aspects of ship life, we know our target segment values cabins with amenities. Few mentions of swimming pools indicate that this feature is unimportant for selecting cruise options for our segment. This method is useful for uncovering response frequency, looking at "top of mind" preferences, or plotting conceptual maps. This technique, however, helps you understand only that consumers have certain preferences; it does not help you understand *why* consumers have them. It is to explain the latter issue where the participant comes in. Probing consumers' reasons for making the choices they did helps expand their answers.

Projective technique results can also be analyzed through interpretation of *patterns* that reveal meanings behind the projections. Again, researchers achieve the most insightful results by asking participants what their answers mean. Similarities and differences that emerge between respondents' comments show inherent patterns indicating how a particular market segment really feels about the brand or service.

Triangulation

To validate or reinforce findings, researchers often use an additional technique to see whether similar patterns emerge from a second or third round of projective research. The use of different methods to check results is called **triangulation**. One way to accomplish triangulation is by using three groups from a single target segment and using a different method for each group. Results from all three groups should generate similar patterns, which then verify your conclusions and give you confidence that your research yielded consumer truths.

Using three different researchers to gather the data also can triangulate research. Hopefully, similar patterns will emerge regardless of the person administering the projective technique. Triangulation is like insurance in that it offers a protection device against response aberration. If wide differences are detected, research can be repeated until dominant themes prevail (if differences continue to be revealed, that may signal faulty study construction). The only research constant must be the consumer segment. Creative treatments are developed specifically for a particular consumer group and are rarely applied to the public at large.

Using the Internet to Conduct Audience Research

In order to minimize costs and travel, entertainment researchers are beginning to utilize technology to collect interviews. There are two main ways of doing qualitative research on the Internet: synchronous and asynchronous. *Synchronous* is "all at the same time," or the online equivalent of a focus group. *Asynchronous* software (e-mail, instant messaging) lets people respond whenever it is convenient for them. The main use of synchronous Internet research is through chat groups, listservs, threaded discussions, groupware, and forms with open-ended text areas. Here is what you can expect from the various modes of online inquiry.

Chat Groups

People use chat groups to meet online at a specific Internet location. A moderator asks chat room participants to discuss a particular issue and later studies the transcript for common themes. Web sites available for free chat groups are:

- Parachat (www.parachat.com)
- Anexa (www.anexa.com)
- Talk City (www.talkcity.com)

Some researchers find that chat room conversation is more stilted and does not flow as well as in-person focus groups. Others swear by the efficiency of obtaining results using the Internet.

Listservs

Researchers can send email to a group of people with listserv software. Anybody can reply, either to everybody else or to the organizer. Some providers of free listservs are:

- Yahoo groups (groups.yahoo.com)
- Tight Circle (www.tightcircle.com)
- Topica (www.topica.com).

Listservs without advertising that charge usage fees are: www.listhost.com, www.sparklist.com, and lyris.net. Many ISPs also have such software available for their clients; Majordomo is widely used, but it is not user friendly. Listservs are best used for participatory interactive research where it's an advantage for people to see each other's responses. Listserv discussions can run for up to a week, giving motivated respondents time to provide thoughtful their answers.

Groupware

Groupware is software that a group of people can use to communicate between themselves. Research can be conducted through bulletin boards, guestbooks, forums (newsgroups), threaded discussions, ICQ (which stands for "I seek you"), and conferencing software.

Threaded Discussions

First developed in Internet Newsgroups as a form of hypertext, these forums are discussions on a particular theme or thread. Each thread is made up of a number of contributions. Some of the best packages for threaded-discussion software are:

- Discus (www.discusware.com)
- Webboard (webboard.oreilly.com)
- Wimba (www.wimba.com)—based on spoken messages and requiring speakers and microphones on computers

Threaded discussion systems work well for answering specific questions, but the sheer number of threads makes reading a whole set of contributions very difficult. This discussion vehicle is best suited to a large number of participants—100 or more—mostly making occasional contributions.

Guestbooks

A guestbook is the computer equivalent of a hotel or bed-and-breakfast book that invites guests to sign in and write their comments. Researchers use this format to get visitors' reaction to a venue using questions such as, "Of the venues in your city, which do you like to attend most for musical concerts and why?" Here everyone can see everybody else's responses, resembling a group discussion in that respondents will influence one another. Many ISPs provide guestbook software for their clients, but numerous sites offer free or low-cost software. Some popular providers are:

- Bravenet (www.bravenet.com)
- Guestpage (www.guestpage.com)
- Site Gadgets (www.sitegadgets.com).

■■■■■■■■■ **BOX 7-6** ■■■■■■■■■

Focus on Research Tools

FREE SURVEY WEB SITE

One of the easiest ways of doing qualitative research on the Internet is to adapt a normal Web survey for obtaining open-ended responses. Most participants who use the HTML form respond coherently and in detail to open-ended questions if the population is right, the questions are well worded, and the subject is of interest to the sample. Try the free www.surveymonkey.com for your next open-ended format survey.

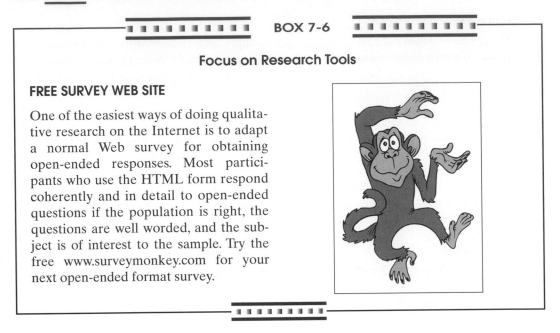

A German program called Zeno, described as group meditation software, includes facilities for rating variables and may be appropriate for qualitative research. Details can be found at zeno.fhg.de.

Social Networks

Two sites that provide users with blogs collected hourly from the Internet also allow users to rate the blogs and bookmark their favorites.

- Delicious (www.del.icio.us)
- Digg (www.digg.com)

Researching Online Compared with Face-to-Face Discussions

A big advantage of online discussions is that it is always possible to comment on what somebody else has said. Normal focus groups can be fairly expensive to execute and require that people meet at a specific location. By using the Internet, researchers can access a broad population—and one that often does not need to be paid. Online participants have more time to consider their responses than live-group participants, who are forced to respond within the structure of 90-minute sessions. A major disadvantage of using online groups is that researchers are not privy to the emotional and nonverbal content of discussions. Also, respondents' meanings are not as clear as they are when tone of voice and facial expressions are part of the dialogue. Emoticons or *smileys,* keyboard-created pictures, can be used to some extent, but only if respondents agree on their usage beforehand.

Online Measurement

In an attempt to reconcile discrepancies that exist between panel- and census-based online audience measurement solutions, Nielsen/NetRatings created a vehicle that combines the two. An integrated methodology called Data Integration brings together results from a NetView panel and its SiteCensus Web analytics approach. By linking the panel with its site-centric solution, the Data Integration method comes up with what NetRatings calls an "integrated audience number" that delivers reach and frequency metrics, audience demographic profiles, and other metrics for pre- and post-campaign analysis tools.

There has been a long debate about the precision of each approach to audience measurement. A panel-based method gives more detailed demographic and behavioral data, but opponents believe panels count too narrow a subsection of visitors. An analytics-based approach provides information across a broader section of a site's audience, but has the drawback of relying on cookies for information packets. The cookie approach could lead to overestimating visitor counts and underestimating visitor frequency metrics when more users delete or block cookies.[5]

FINALLY: LET'S SUM UP ▪▪▪▪▪▪▪

So, after studying this chapter about applied audience research, you should now see how discovery, explanatory, and evaluative research methods are used to understand entertainment audiences and consumers. Qualitative methods are ideal for collecting stories about branded entertainment experiences. Innovative projective techniques stimulate discussion and generate large amounts of rich information. To evaluate media audiences, managers use syndicated measures to gauge exposure and predict attendance trends. Once collected in person or on the Internet, data are analyzed for themes and patterns that help us to understand the relationship between the consumer and the entertainment brand.

GOT IT? LET'S REVIEW ▪▪▪▪▪▪▪

- Entertainment research can be descriptive, explanatory, or evaluative; it is designed to measure satisfaction with the entertainment experience and to understand audience motivations for attending.
- Empirical research using inductive methods is most appropriate for conducting entertainment studies.
- Projective techniques are developed to gather consumer stories about their entertainment experiences; limits are set only by the creativity of the researcher.
- Results from projective techniques can be analyzed quantitatively and qualitatively and used for developing creative marketing concepts.

- Gate receipts, media audience ratings, Q Factor, and incidental measures are used to determine profits, attendance numbers, viewing patterns, celebrity popularity, and performer image.
- Audience analysis provides useful measures for developing entertainment programming and predicting audience behavior.
- Triangulation of methods or researchers ensures result reliability.
- The Internet is a valuable data collection resource for entertainment research.

NOW TRY THIS: LET'S APPLY WHAT WE'VE LEARNED ▪▪▪▪▪▪▪

1. Develop a bubble cartoon for a client who owns a chain of hotels to help him understand how consumers feel about national-brand lodging as opposed to boutique accommodations.
2. Create an online projective method for generating self-disclosure from female consumers with children about how they use theme parks.
3. Design an audience satisfaction survey for an entertainment event of your choice. Compare it with those designed by classmates. What did you miss? What did they miss? Would you administer the survey in person or over the Internet? Why?
4. Have a group of five theme park visitors select pictures of people from those you provide who most likely patronizes each of three specific park brands. Then, group the pictures by park brand and identify patterns of similarities and differences across the pictures. From the patterns, come up with a description of the type of person who prefers each brand theme park.

QUESTIONS: LET'S REVIEW ▪▪▪▪▪▪▪

1. What is the best method for researching declining attendance at a local performance venue? How would you design the data collection and analysis?
2. How would you use the Internet to gather information on satisfaction with service at a specific spa resort?
3. What ethical issues are involved in gathering personal information from attendees or participants of events? How can they be overcome?
4. How can technology contribute to developing new research techniques? What advances in research methodology can you predict for the future?

MORE TO READ ▪▪▪▪▪▪▪

P. Alreck and R. Settle. *Survey Research Handbook,* 4th ed. Chicago: Irwin Publishing, 2004.

D. Lewis and D. Bridger. *The Soul of the New Consumer.* New York: Nicholas Brealey Publishing, 2000.

D. Rook (ed.). *Brands, Consumer, Symbols and Research: Sidney J. Levy on Marketing.* Thousand Oaks, CA: Sage Publications, 1999.

S. Sayre. *Using Qualitative Methods for Marketplace Research.* Thousand Oaks, CA: Sage Publications, 2001.

A. J. Veal. *Research Methods for Leisure and Tourism: A Practical Guide,* 2nd ed. New York: Prentice Hall, 1997.

G. Zaltman and R. Coulter. "Using Projective Methods in ZMET to Elicit Deep Meanings," *Journal of Advertising Research* 36 (1996), 36–61.

W. G. Zickmund. *Exploring Marketing Research.* Dryden, 1997.

NOTES ▪▪▪▪▪▪▪

1. Reproduced from V.A. Zeithaml, M.J. Bitner & D.D. Gremler, *Services Marketing,* New York: Mc Graw-Hill, 2006, pp. 144–46.
2. Gina Piccalo, *New York Times,* Oct. 9, 2005.
3. *Ibid.*
4. Syndicated Performer Q Stydy, 1996, Marketing Evaluations, Inc.
5. Kevin Newcomb, www.clickz.com, Sept. 9, 2006.

CHAPTER

8

Mixing, Branding, and Communicating

*The term science should not be given to anything
but the aggregate of recipes that are always successful.
All the rest is literature.*
—PAUL VALERY

Chapter Objectives

After reading this chapter, you should be able to answer the following questions:

- What modifications must be made to convert marketing's *4Ps* for use in the entertainment marketing mix?
- What role does the *audience* play in the marketing mix?
- What are the significant elements of *audience-based brand equity*?
- How do communication *objectives* frame the marketing message?
- What three *message types* are used to serve delivery functions?
- Which integrated marketing communications (IMC) *strategies* help you reach audiences, develop creative, position the brand, and buy media?
- How can you best *compete and communicate* in a global marketplace?

The marketing mix has long been the standard approach to delivering products and services. The brand, a crucial element of the product component, gives the parent company or entertainment franchise its identity and power. This chapter focuses on these two important entertainment marketing considerations: the mix and the brand. We investigate some revised mix typologies as they apply to experiences, and look into the key role of branding in audience relationship building.

Taken together, the marketing mix and brand concepts provide a recipe for successful entertainment marketing. To review briefly, the **marketing mix** is the optimal combination of marketing variables an enterprise can use to generate the most revenue from its target market. To determine the weight or emphasis placed on each variable in the mix, the marketing manager takes into account the actions of competitors, reworking the balance of variables according to prevailing marketing conditions. Since the first days of radio and television, brand concepts and theories have been incorporated into marketing strategy. **Branding** is a way to identify, guarantee, structure, and stabilize an entertainment property, entity, or company. Because the primary capital of many entertainment businesses is its brand, marketers realize the importance of developing a branded "landmark" for their audience members.

▪▪▪ Mixing and Matching: Updating Old Standards

Most university business schools embrace the teachings of early marketing pioneer, E. J. McCarthy and marketing management guru Philip Kotler. Let's quickly look at how we got from their initial work to today's perspectives on marketing.

McCarthy to Kotler

In 1960, McCarthy[1] developed the classic four-variable system—the "4Ps"—on which marketing management decisions should be based: *product, price, place,* and *promotion.* This system was standard practice for almost three decades. As the economy changed to a service economy, however, it became clear that McCarthy's model virtually ignored the consumer. So, in 1999, Kotler[2] restated the mix's variables, adding a component for the consumer that reflected the consumer orientation necessary for marketing in a service economy.

Today's Experience-Based Marketing Mix

The principles of the entertainment marketing mix are similar to those in McCarthy's model. Entertainment terminology and applications differ from those of traditional marketing, however. Exhibit 8.1 defines the entertainment marketing mix, showing how consumer buying and paying take on new meanings when applied to entertainment audiences. In the next section, we characterize the transition from a P-product-based orientation to C-consumer-based orientation.

Target Market as Audience Usage Segment

Traditional marketing theory segments consumers by demographics, psychographics, and loyalty dimensions. Usually, however, an entertainment experience crosses gender,

▪▪▪ **EXHIBIT 8.1** The Experience Marketing Mix

The 4Ps Reconfigured for Entertainment Services		
Marketing Element	*What It Means*	*How It Applies to Entertainment*
Target Market	who buys	audience usage segment
Product	what they buy	audience experience
Price	what they pay	audience investment
Place	where they buy	venue, destination, Internet
Promotion	why they buy	information, persuasion, and incentives

age, and lifestyle segments, because entertainment is available to anyone who wants it. Entertainment marketing, therefore, must address the needs of audiences. To reach an audience, marketers focus on the users, or consumers, of the activity, performance, or destination, rather than on the activity, performance, or destination itself, i.e., the product.

Product as Value of Audience Brand Experience

A consumer product's value lies in its consistency and brand association. An entertainment product's value, on the other hand, is the form the experience takes; it's what audience members get when they attend or play. **Audience value** is the audience's assessment of their experience as weighed against the ticket price or investment and compared to other entertainment options. For entertainment, experiential components include component design, venue style or ambience, service element, and identity through branding.

- *Component design* is how the experience (the components) is assembled for consumers, such as a four-day spa package that includes meals, treatments, and lodging.
- *Venue style or ambience* is the character of the place where the entertainment or activity is performed, which aligns with brand image and price. The ambiance of the Golden Door Spa in Escondido, California, for example, is minimalist, food is vegetarian gourmet, and treatments are professional. Price is the highest in the spa resort category. In this and every case, guests must determine whether the venue is worth the price charged.
- The *service element* of the staff includes the work and attitudes of all persons engaged in delivering the experience to audiences. Front-desk receptionists, servers, ushers, hot dog vendors, massage therapists, reservation takers, and so forth are all part of the service element of an entertainment experience.
- *Brand identity,* the primary focus of communications, identifies an experience by making known a particular set of values, a logo, an image, and an expectation of the entertainment to be delivered.

Price as Cost to the Audience for Entertainment Brand Purchase

Price in a formal sense is the negotiated value (translated into money) that an audience member is willing to pay for experiential content provided by the producer, who, in turn, takes into considerations sales volume and revenue objectives. Price simply is what we pay to experience something. In marketing some experiences, travel for instance, price is sometimes considered a personal investment rather than an expenditure. **Promotional pricing** of entertainment is common. This approach responds to the requirements of a particular audience segment or the need to stimulate demands that fluctuate by season or the competition's overcapacity. Disneyland, for instance, offers discount coupons to residents during the winter season to offset tourism decline during that time. During peak season, however, many venues typically raise prices in anticipation of high demand.

Place as Convenience and Comfort of Venue or Distribution Access

A location or attraction venue includes all points of sale that provide prospective audiences with access to entertainment experiences. This expanded idea of place, a

servicescape (see Chapter 4), is a physical space where audiences come together to enjoy and experience a consumption activity. **Convenience of access** is how easily audience members may access the venue, what hotels are available to make their stay more pleasant, and how simply can they make reservations. The Internet is a convenient way for audiences to acquire tickets and make reservations for performances, parks, and travel destinations.

Promotion as Information, Persuasion, and Incentives

For communicators, promotion is the primary variable—it includes everything the entertainment marketer needs in her bag of tricks: advertising, direct mail, sales promotion, merchandising, sales force activities, brochure production, Internet communication, and PR activity. Promotional communications can make consumers aware of products, stimulate demand, and provide incentives for purchase. (These actions or

---

▪▪▪ **EXHIBIT 8.2   The Marketing Mix for Entertainment Venues**

	Spa	*Museum*	*Concert*	*Casino*	*Park*
Experience as Product					
Content	Treatment/food	exhibit	group/style	game variety	rides
Packaging and design	location/buildings/ facilities/décor/ food/ambiance/ light	building/design/ lighting/space/ café/shop/ display	venue/lighting/ sound/seats/ lobby/lounges/ refreshments	building/ glitz/rooms/ ambience/ theme	location/ rides/food/ rest areas/ theme
Service	staff/masseuse/ attendants/	docents/ director/staff	ushers/servers/ ticket window	dealers/ waiters/staff	characters/ security
Branding	Golden Door	MOMA	Lincoln Center	Monte Carlo	Six Flags
Image/position	luxury/budget	global/local	state-of-the-art	high/low roller	friendly
Investment or Expenditure as Price					
Normal	rack/corporate	adult/senior	orchestra/loge/ balcony	minimum bet	adult/kid
Promotional	online discount/ package price	group/children/ member rate	group/ subscriber	regular client	group/ partner
Venue or Destination Sales as Price					
Reservation systems CRS/ third-party retailers/ Web sites	CRS/Internet	Internet/hotels/ tourist offices	CRS/box office/ retailers	Internet/phone	CRS
Promotion					
Ad media/ Merchandising/ PR/brochures	brochure/print ads/ feature stories/ soaps/towels	print ads/PR/ event calendar/ tote bags/books	brochure/print/ radio ads	outdoor/print/ Web ads/ t-shirts	radio/tv ads clothing

results are explained more completely in Chapter 9.) Reinforcing awareness and building a positive attitude helps potential customers make purchasing decisions and stimulates repeat purchases.

Every element in the marketing mix is an organizational expenditure that has direct implications for pricing and sales revenues. Exhibit 8.2 illustrates how the marketing mix works for specific entertainment venues.

In the exhibit, you can see that the mix is adaptable to a variety of entertainment experiences. For instance, the *spa experience* is dependent on each component: content is judged on the quality of treatments and food; packaging manifests itself in the way food is presented and the design of the treatment rooms; service is measured through personal attention to individual needs; branding is the spa's logo or mark; the positioning places it in the consumer's mind as luxury, affordable, rural, urban, and so forth. A visitor's expenditure is dependent on both normal and promotional offerings, such as day packages or weekend specials. Spa sales are accomplished through the Internet and reservation systems. Promotion takes the form of glossy brochures and products sold at the spa as well as feature stories and spa reviewers. The trick is making the most effective selection for your client. And as the next section details, the mix is *always* audience dependent and must be viewed within the context of specific audience needs and characteristics.

▪▪▪ Mix in Context

At the core of all marketing mix decisions is the audience member, the ultimate consumer. Think of the consumer as the core of an onion, as was suggested in Chapter 7. The first layer surrounding the consumer contains the *mix decisions* (which elements to use); the next layer consists of the *organizational resources* (financial, personnel, operations, branding, location, and all physical assets); and the outer layer consists of the *external factors* that make up the entertainment environment and influence all the other components. The external factors are technology, distribution channels, competition, political, social and environmental attitudes, the legal and regulatory framework, and any trends that motivate consumer actions. Each element of the mix circles around the core, the audience, which is called a *locus of control*. This concept indicates a marketer's gradually decreasing degree of control: Marketers have complete control over the mix decisions; less control over the organizational resources; and no control over the external factors. Thus, marketers must work "backward," in a sense, to anticipate external factors that may affect decisions, and use the organizational resources that they can control to develop an appropriate mix. Using the layers of the marketing mix "onion" helps you plan entertainment experiences. The process begins with a situation analysis of *external factors*—those conditions over which managers have no control—against *internal resources*—factors that can influence management decisions and fall under the organization's direct control. Both external and internal factors are needed in planning marketing strategies.

The Missing P

As we noted earlier in this chapter, McCarthy's traditional model is, for today's entertainment marketing needs, missing a P: *people*. As identified by Kotler, the most important component of the marketing mix is the people directly involved in the production and presentation of the entertainment event. Three groups of participants are most important to marketing functions:

• *Audiences* are groups of individual consumers of entertainment content; audience interactions are an inseparable part of the satisfaction the experience provides. You *market directly to audiences,* who then use the power of word-of-mouth to determine an experience's fate. Happy audiences keep the lights on and the curtain rising; unhappy audiences shut the place down.

• *Employees and staff* include both frontline workers who deal directly with audience members and non-contact workers who provide support. Third-party suppliers also are represented in this group.

• *Community* consists of the residents of neighborhoods where large venues, such as amusement parks, outdoor concert theaters, or casinos, are located; they often interact with audiences informally.

Mix Extenders

Marketing management can extend the mix in three important areas. First, because *frontline employees* so closely interact with audiences during their entertainment experience, their attitudes are vital to audience satisfaction and ultimately the success of the event. In fact, it has been said that managers must operate with the belief that employees are "walking billboards from a promotional standpoint."[3] Second, *internal marketing* is an important way to effectively address employee concerns and promote value. Finally, *physical settings* are crucial to both audience enjoyment and employee satisfaction. Let's and examine these areas in more detail and provide a few examples.

• *Frontline or contact employees* must reconcile the internal operational requirements of an organization with the expectations and demands of audiences. This is a difficult task. Not only must contact employees show empathy with visitors, they must do so within the organization's rules and regulations. A museum docent may be torn between adults' interests and those of noisy parties of children. Dealing with conflicts between visitors is often stressful, so training employees in developing strong interpersonal skills is essential.

• *Internal marketing* (promoting to those within the company or organization) is an often-neglected extension of the marketing mix, yet has value for harnessing employee potential. As organizational stakeholders, employee needs must be addressed, and this process starts with assessing levels of job satisfaction, identifying problem areas, and recognizing their ideas for product improvement.

• For entertainment, the *physical setting* or venue can be the *raison d'etre* (or "reason for being"—one's whole purpose) for audience attendance. As we saw in Chapter 4, a venue acts as the experience's packaging; it communicates messages about quality, positioning, and differentiation that help determine and reach audience expectations.

C Words Proliferated: Lieberman's View

Al Lieberman, a veteran of entertainment marketing, characterizes the entertainment industry with an entirely different set of words from McCarthy and Kotler's

▪▪▪▪▪▪▪▪▪   BOX 8-1   ▪▪▪▪▪▪▪▪▪

Focus on Careers

PROFILE OF A PEOPLE FINDER

As a "people finder" for Young & Rubicam (Y&R) Brands, James Rosetto handles recruiting responsibilities for the agency's Irvine, California, office. Screening and interviewing applicants for temporary and permanent hires, Rosetto negotiates contracts with temporary employee agencies, headhunters, talent agents, and production companies.

Much of Rosetto's time is spent identifying key candidates for positions in account and project management, IT, and creative (writers and artists). Identifying "talent" for television commercials and appropriate experts to produce them is a large part of this activity. "Finding the right candidate for the job makes a hiring manager happy," says Rosetto.

After graduating with a B.A. degree in advertising from the University of Central Florida, Rosetto worked in broadcast production, graphic design, and advertising sales before joining Y&R in 2004.

In His Words . . .

Recruiting is a great way to get a full 360-degree view of the advertising industry. Seeing people across different disciplines grow into their jobs is very rewarding—you get to know all the winners and scammers. I act as a matchmaker, trying to fit the perfect person into the perfect position. When it works, it's fantastic—when it doesn't, it's a disaster!

A Pitfall to Forget

One of our large automotive clients was under a deadline to deliver dealership promotions, which coincided with the untimely departure of our account manager. I scrambled around to locate someone with similar expertise who could fill the bill. A colleague at another agency recommended a promotion guy who had interviewed with them a month before, so I called him in for an interview the next day. Because we were in a rush, I hired him on the spot, assuming my colleague's agency had checked out his references. Unfortunately, it wasn't the case. Instead of taking over, he took off after two weeks, leaving us in the lurch. And I was to blame. After the fact, I learned that the guy had a terrible reputation among his former employers—and there were many—for being a flake. People tend to move around quite a bit in this business, but his resume read like a phone book. Wish I'd let my fingers do the walking!

Advice

To lean about job openings in the advertising field, consult the job opportunity postings, in print and online, in trade publications *AdWeek* and *Advertising Age*.

▪▪▪▪▪▪▪

"P-words"—the "C-words."[4] He describes the industry structure as consisting of these elements: *content, conduit, consumption,* and *convergence.*

Content

Content is the entertainment product delivered to the consumer. Part of the creative process involves copyright protection, a legal transaction that gives content creators and their assignees exclusive rights to reproduce, distribute, and make the most of their original works.

Conduit

Conduit refers to the where and how the performance is delivered—the venue.

Consumption

Consumption is the result of advertising and promotional activities that result in the purchase of tickets and performance attendance.

Convergence

Convergence is the experience created when live performance is converted to a digital format. Convergence is very much a part of the present as well as the wave of the future, especially where advertising and entertainment are fused to deliver both an enjoyable experience and brand awareness as a simultaneous activity.

▪▪▪ Branding Experiences and Places

To many audience members, brands are not just *in* the culture, they *are* the culture.[5] Brands have become the tools with which people construct their personal and social identities. Our postmodern culture is thrusting people and brands together at warp speed. A new ethos of brand participation is emerging; people see brands as shared cultural property, where familiarity breeds ownership.

Bikers who choose to be buried in Harley-Davidson–branded caskets are just one example of the results of the collision between brands and fans. When people think they own brands, they do funny things—such as wear brand tattoos, form Internet brand tribes, and use brands to characterize themselves in personal ads. Brands as a type of cultural infusion are here to stay, and, as a result, entertainment franchises *must* adopt an unusual but relevant view of what their brands are and what they mean.

Branded Everything

Branding involves creating mental structures for a product and helping audiences organize their knowledge about entertainment experiences in a way that clarifies their decision making and provides value to the producer. With products, brand distinctions are related to specific attributes or features and to product benefits. With entertainment, although venues have specific features, the benefit of all experiences should be an enjoyable emotional association. Brand symbols help make intangible or abstract experiences more concrete. Here are some of the ways entertainment is branded.

- *Venue brands,* e.g., Hilton Hotels, Disneyland, Museum of Modern Art
- *People and organizations,* such as Madonna and MGM. Some celebrities even become product brands in their own right (Newman's Own salad dressing; Glow by J Lo).
- *Sports teams* where marketing is a highly sophisticated combination of creative advertising, promotions, sponsorship, direct mail, and other forms of communication.
- *Bands and films,* such as the Grateful Dead and *Star Wars.*
- *Geographic locations,* such as Paris, whose strong images have drawing power.

By tying brands to an entertainment-driven experience, marketers can create brands as personalities, not just products, and connect the brand with consumers as such. Experiential branding takes core values of the brand and introduces them into an actual environment; good branding is the conversion of entertainment and marketing.

Audience-Based Brand Equity

Brands gain their equity from audiences. The **customer-based brand equity model (CBBE)**[6] approaches brand equity from the perspective of the consumer or audience member. Its premise is that the power of the brand lies in what audiences have learned, felt, seen, and heard about the brand as a result of their experiences over time. Best applied to products, this model is nonetheless a valuable approach to building knowledge about entertainment genres with potential audiences. To illustrate how audience-based brand equity works in practice, you can compare customer expectations with the actual entertainment experience.

Brand Awareness

Repeated exposure through personal association with a performance experience creates familiarity with a brand. *Brand recognition*—the ability to identify a particular mark as belonging to a performance category—is the most basic form of awareness. If you see *Bolshoi* and know that it is a ballet brand, you have just experienced brand recognition.

Brand recall, on the other hand, is more difficult to attain because it requires an audience member to come up with the brand without prompting. If you ask a person what ballet company is her favorite and she replies, "Bolshoi," you are witnessing brand recall. Visual and verbal reinforcement through communication avenues such as advertising and promotion, sponsorship and event marketing, publicity and public relations, and outdoor advertising contribute to improving brand recall.

Brand Image

Marketing programs create a brand's image with a strong creative message that links favorable associations of the brand with a person's memory. Brand associations are created directly through experience, commercial and nonpartisan sources (e.g., reviews), and word of mouth, and indirectly through identification with a company, a country, or an event. Image development grows primarily from *brand benefits,* which are the characteristics of value and meaning that audience members attach to the entertainment form. Venue image results from descriptive features or *brand attributes* that characterize a location of entertainment performances.

Integrated marketing communication programs contribute to brand equity by encouraging favorable brand associations. To make an association favorable and create desire for a target audience, marketers depend on a brand association's *relevancy, distinctiveness,* and *believability.* A brand's image must be unique and distinguished from competitive brands with meaningful *points of difference* that cause audiences to choose it over other brands. Brand associations can also be equal in favorability with competing brands and function as *points of parity,* which are jumping-off places for negotiating points of difference. Points of parity are easier to achieve than points of difference, which are needed when the brand must demonstrate clear superiority. Not all

■ ■ ■ **EXHIBIT 8.3** Brand Associations

Location	Points of Parity	Points of Difference
Theme park	Rides, food	Largest roller coaster in the world
Hotel	Rooms, pool	Five-star luxury with spa
City	Buildings, shopping	Winding canals and gondolas
Concert venue	Seats, crowds	Outdoor amphitheater
Theater	Rows face front	Seating in the round
Casino	Wheels, tables	500 quarter slot machines

brand associations are considered important or viewed favorably by audience members, and not all brand associations will be relevant for a consumption decision. Points of parity and difference for a variety of entertainment locations are presented in Exhibit 8.3.

Entertainment genres often are communicated as brands. Continuing the ballet example, let's consider ballet and modern dance brands of dance and compare them. The parity between the two brands is that all dance involves people performing to music on a stage; a difference between them is that female ballet dancers often dance on their toes, while modern dancers never do. An individual dance troupe may also be a brand. The Bolshoi is, like other troupes, a touring dance company—a point of parity with other companies. But, unlike other troupes it features traditional dance with a Russian heritage—a point of difference.

A distinct *brand identity* distinguishes the Bolshoi and attaches *meaning* to it: The troupe's Russian dancers (identity) have a history of intrigue from its dancers who fled the Iron Curtain for sanctuary in America (meaning). How an audience member feels about that brand is the *emotional response* generated by the association. Finally, a connection between that brand and the audience creates a *relationship* between them.

Creating relationships between audience members and various forms of dance may begin with the familiar and accessible: local presentations of *The Nutcracker* ballet during the holiday season. If the experience, a ballet that is easy to share with children and other family members, is favorable, marketers can extend that feeling to another ballet story and educate audiences to understand and appreciate more ballet performances.

Brand imagery can also be developed through associations with the type of person who uses the brand. If audiences think ballet goers are stuffy and boring, ballet's brand image is unfavorable. Marketers must demonstrate that ballet has universal appeal and is exciting and beautiful. To create a favorable association, ads may feature ballet lovers as young and vibrant families.

Brand Loyalty

Branded products work toward developing a habit of repeat purchasing. With branded entertainment, loyalty may not be an important factor because of the temporal nature of the product—here today, gone tomorrow. How many times can we expect one person to purchase tickets for the same play?

The exception is building a fan base to create loyalty to a sports team or music brand. Like sports stars and teams, musicians work to develop loyal fans who attend the artists' concerts and purchase their music. In the book *Brands that Rock,* authors Roger Blackwell and Tina Stephan focus on how bands create loyalty and devotion in their fans. Converting consumers into fans requires an understanding of human behavior. The devotion of longtime fans to their favorite performers, from Frank Sinatra to 50 Cent, illustrates that getting audiences to incorporate a brand into their lives requires that a deep connection be developed between that brand and an audience. To make this deep emotional connection, marketers must figure out what makes audiences tick. Successful bands break through the clutter to become long-term industry leaders by creating awareness and targeting a single market segment to generate high profits.

The Internet plays a crucial role in cementing fan status through interactivity. Fans come together to support bands, create new songs for them, and build relationships with other fans through their common love of a particular group, vocalist, or musical type. Fans act as "spotters," keeping other fans abreast of news about group appearances and star gossip.

Music Marketing

Blackwell and Stephan present prime examples of how performers blend music and marketing. Elton John turns brand equity into sales, whether he is promoting his latest CD, concert, Broadway show, or commercial endorsement. KISS broke the record industry's traditional mindset with pyrotechnics and fireworks. The Rolling Stones created a unique experience built on the personality of Mick Jagger that people paid big bucks to see. Aerosmith involved fans in rejuvenating their band and transforming it into a stronger brand than its predecessor. Lessons for branding bands include:

- Stay fresh
- Focus on the entire experience
- Package talent well
- Create realistic expectations
- Match the message with the mission and the audience
- Exude energy and passion
- Define the band with functional and emotional attributes
- Monitor brand adoption
- Play for cultural adoption
- Resist the temptation of overexposure
- Empower your fans

Exhibit 8.4 shows the distinctions that music marketers make among various audience members.

▪▪▪ Brand Positioning and Equity

As an entertainment marketing manager, once you have segmented and selected your audience, you must promote the experience's most appealing aspects. Developing a focused positioning strategy means *designing an image to occupy a distinct place* in the audience member's mind. Imagine that all the entertainment options in a particular genre or category are set on a step ladder, each occupying its own rung. Audiences can

Rock Band Audiences

Customers	*Friends (Repeaters)*	*Fans*
Price driven	Value driven	Experience driven
Shop opportunistically	Shop purposefully	Shop for pleasure
Need a reason to buy tickets for band	Prefer to buy from band	Devoted to band
Surprised by good experience	Had some good experiences	Expect good experiences
Drop band if disappointed	Give band a second chance	Express disappointment, will forgive and forget
Indifferent to band	Feel rational/emotional connection	Actively invest in relationship—and $$
Don't talk about band	Casually recommend band	Praise band

Source: Blackwell and Stephan, *Brands that Rock* (2002), p. 5.

easily distinguish one rung from another and make choices among them. That is the role of positioning, which involves creating a real differentiation and making it known.

To successfully position a brand, you first establish the *category membership* of the performance, or simply the genre or the type of entertainment: dance, opera, music, and so on. Category membership is communicated through benefits, by comparing exemplars (the best of what is available) and by relying on experience descriptors. Positioning is established and maintained over time using a means–end chain.[7] In this chain, attributes lead to benefits, which, in turn, lead to values. Audience members select a performance that delivers an attribute that provides benefits that satisfy values. Using a laddering progression, we see how the progression flows in the means–end chain:

$$\textit{Brand} \qquad \textit{Attribute} \qquad >>> \qquad \textit{Benefit} \qquad >>> \qquad \textit{Value}$$

Let's say an audience member selects to attend a performance at a venue because of its marvelous acoustics (attribute) that provide fantastic sound (benefit), which she values because it designates her as an aficionado of music, making her feel great— enhanced self-esteem is the result. Marketers use this chain to appeal to the desired value, in this case self-esteem, when promoting the venue's orchestral performances. Another example is Disneyland, which provides life-size cartoon characters (attribute) that delight children (benefit) and satisfies the parent's family values of sharing experiences. Disney promotes family fun in its advertising. Exhibit 8.5 illustrates the means–end chain concept.

Brand-Positioning Strategies

Every entertainment brand needs a focused positioning strategy so that its intended place in the total market—and the audience member's mind—is clearly reflected in its communications. The strategy requires coordinating all the attributes of the marketing

▪▪▪ **EXHIBIT 8.5**   **Means-End Chain for Theme Parks**

Brand	Attribute	Benefit	End Benefit (Value)
Disneyland	Mickey Mouse	Delight	Sharing
SixFlags	Roller coasters	Thrill	Adventure
LegoLand	Legos	Activity	Education
Universal Studios	Movie sets	Fantasy	Esteem
Sandiego Wild Animal Park	Wild animals	Wonder	Nature

mix to support the brand's position. The most common strategies are shown in Exhibit 8.6.

Brand Equity Strategies

Promoting entertainment events requires developing a strategy to either *push* tickets to the consumer through a retailer or middleman or *pull* bookings directly from audience members. The Internet has made both strategies popular; you can go to a ticket broker (Ticketmaster) or directly to the venue to purchase tickets.

With a push strategy, venues rely on the retailer to deliver a full house. With a push strategy, venues promote their own distribution center. Using both strategies, however, yields the highest return. Push strategy commonly requires indirect channel use of retail segmentation and cooperative advertising; pull strategy uses direct channels, such as venue ticket sales. Both strategies take advantage of the Web to integrate and maximize selling power.

Brand Contacts

Messages about the brand must reach the audience at each point of contact—thinking about buying, locating a place to buy, actually buying tickets, and attending the performance. At each stage of promotion, a positive brand image must be communicated to the

▪▪▪ **EXHIBIT 8.6**   **Positioning Strategies**

Seven alternatives for constructing a positioning strategy are:

1. *Specific feature*—the Venetian Hotel's canal or a theater's reclining seats
2. *Benefit*—the excitement of visiting a foreign destination or the self-esteem received from attending an opening night performance
3. *Usage occasion*—summer concerts in the park or special matinee performances
4. *User category*—senior and single vacation cruises or family nights at the circus
5. *Against another brand, performance, venue, or destination*—a television network claiming it has better news coverage than another network
6. *As number one*—an assertion by an orchestra that it is the best in the country
7. *Exclusivity*—a spa that claims to restrict membership to the most upscale guests

target audience in promotional materials, staff, reviewers, media, and personal contact. By managing the consumer's total impression of the brand, you control the contacts you can, influence the ones you cannot, and allocate dollars to the most important contacts available. Chapter 10 presents a detailed plan for developing an integrated marketing communications approach to building brand equity through contact management.

Brand and Line Extensions

The most powerful tool for maintaining brand equity is through **brand extensions** and **line extensions**. To extend a *brand,* entertainment producers enter another category. For instance, a film studio goes into the recording business, or Donald Trump adds condominiums to his hotel brand; these are brand extensions. When extending a *line,* producers offer the same brand in a different way within the category; when Hilton adds a new location to its hotel chain, it makes a line extension. MTV has extended its line of television music programming globally, while Disney has extended its brand to include films, recordings, and hotels.

Brand extension is part of entertainment product synergy—morphing one product into others. The Harry Potter brand was extended from books into the film genre, while *The Lion King* film was made into a stage play. Both extensions were merchandised by translating the brand into thousands of spin-off retail items.

Licensing

Another form of brand extension, **licensing**, allows a brand to use its image and logo to change genres. *National Lampoon* magazine had a million subscribers in its heyday during the 1970s.[8] Lampoon Inc.'s first film, *Animal House,* was the highest-grossing comedy of its time. Taking its writers, performers, and attitude from Lampoon's example, late-night TV spoof program *Saturday Night Live* was touted for changing the world of comedy. Few people knew that *National Lampoon* deserved much of the credit. The magazine's organization was effectively responsible for launching the careers of actors John Belushi, Bill Murray, and Chevy Chase. After working in magazine and movie genres, Lampoon moved on to a radio show and recorded a musical parody of *Moby Dick* in the style of a Maine community theater.

Brand Characters

Many characters have been successfully developed to bring heightened awareness and brand association to products and services. One of the most famous characters of all time, Mickey Mouse, has symbolized Disney and family fun for decades. Ronald McDonald and the MGM roaring lion also are associated with fun and entertainment, as well as with their respective companies, McDonald's and the MGM movie studio.

In keeping with this tradition, the characters representing GEICO and Aflac insurance company brands have become advertising icons. GEICO's gecko is a wise-cracking amphibian who uses humor to help audiences remember the company's difficult brand (the character corrects people's mispronunciation of "GEICO" as "gecko"). Video and print messages motivate potential customers to call or go to the Web for more information. In Aflac's commercials, the company's vocal duck screams "Aflac!" to consumers who are having difficulty solving their insurance problems. This began as a mnemonic device to help viewers simply connect the duck's honk with the company name. As the campaign progressed, however, the duck took to synchronized swimming and other

▪▪▪▪▪▪▪▪▪ **BOX 8-2** ▪▪▪▪▪▪▪▪▪

Focus on Licensing

CREATING CHARACTERS FOR SALE

California artist Debby Carman, president of Faux Paw Productions, creates characters and product concepts for licensing in niche markets to a variety of goods manufacturers. Russ Berrie and Company Inc., a U.S. gift corporation, licensed more than 50 products from its Bowzers & Meowzers™ character series. These same characters are supported by published children's books, and their stories have been animated into short digital films for presentation in Cannes, France, for introduction into the vast entertainment and digital markets.

A license works as follows: Characters, or another unique product or property collection, are developed and a license is negotiated with a manufacturer, depending on the property collection's variety of applications in varying markets, e.g., gift, tabletop, home décor, textile, paper goods, stationery, or accessories. A manufacturer secures a license to produce, market, and distribute that collection in the form of

Bowzers book characters were licensed to a plush toy manufacturer.

(Continued)

finished goods, and pays the licensor a royalty based on sales. Royalty fees differ depending on the type of product and the market. Plush animals and ceramic products generally command a 5–10 percent royalty on wholesale sales. Fabric and textile licenses may range from 3 to 15 percent. Typically, an advance against royalties is negotiated in good faith and in advance of the goods being sold.

Books may translate into licensing opportunities as the characters achieve brand recognition with readers and as they cross into entertainment and toy product licensing. Other entertainment media opportunities exist for characters building brand recognition in their potential for digital content, interactive games, DVD, cartoon series, animated film shorts, or TV network programs. Consider the SpongeBob SquarePants property, which is licensed for TV and appears on hundreds of varying manufactured products. SpongeBob Square-Pants is expected to generate in excess of $3.5 *billion* in licensing revenues in 2006.

antics. Once the campaign was successfully established, synergy infused all aspects of the brand.

Brand Synergy

The payoff of brand synergy evolves from licensing, merchandise retailing, and sponsorship. Effective marketing strategy results in revenue streams that enhance the bottom line. Licensing is a $100 billion industry[9] in the U.S. alone. Revenues from licensed-based merchandise retailing generate funds for future performances and

Gecko and duck as brand characters.

maintain shareholder value in this competitive segment of the world economy. Fashion is well integrated into the growth of sponsorship sales for the entertainment industry—Armani-sponsored events, including a retrospective of his design at the Museum of Modern Art in New York, are just one example of fashion as entertainment. Runway shows are themselves entertainment performed for producers of the fashion industry and consumers of branded designs. Product placements and product tie-ins link fashion and food with entertainment products and brands. Branding as a long-term strategy is a huge commercial support system that creates synergy. We discuss branding strategies and synergies in more detail in later chapters.

Brand Slogans

In its heyday, advertising jingles and slogans ruled the airwaves. Today, slogans still help position a product or service. Take MasterCard's "Priceless" campaign. Thanks to the popularity of retro ad campaigns, many old slogans are still recognizable. See if you can identify these experience-based slogans from the past:

1. When you care enough to send the very best
2. Reach out and touch someone
3. Ho, ho, ho!
4. We'll leave the light on for you
5. Something special in the air
6. Diamonds are forever
7. Leave the driving to us

Check the end of the chapter to see how many you guessed correctly!

Interactive Branding

Brands adapt to new selling environments in different ways. By assessing the potential of interactive platforms to assist in ticket sales, branded entertainment can improve its volume and increase its usefulness to audience members.

Creating interactive messages takes a different set of writing skills than developing a script for a television commercial or copy for a brochure. Interactive scripts for CDs, DVDs, and Web sites require the marriage of the identity crafting talents of traditional agency creative directors, direct marketing skills, and knowledge of appropriate content development disciplines.

When producing convergent communications, brand messages must be coordinated among the various interactive platforms to develop a consistent stream of strategically compelling content. Concentrating on how a brand's overall identity is presented to individual consumers within the framework of their needs is the best strategy for integrating approaches. The next section continues to explore and develop the topic of convergent communications.

▪▪▪ Communication Objectives and Message Development

Business schools preach that marketing strategies are incomplete without proper message development. Branding is about communicating the brand to audiences, and promoting entertainment is about developing informational, persuasive, and reminder messages for current and emerging audiences.

Once the marketing mix elements are in place, you must develop objectives for the promotional effort. Communication objectives, unlike marketing objectives, cannot be measured by sales, market share, or profit. Instead, pre-tests given prior to and post-tests given after an advertising or public relations campaign serve to measure objectives for awareness and attitude. Now is the time for action. To achieve the communication objectives that have value for the advertiser, you must execute your creative concepts. This section outlines the principles that drive message development, looks at message strategies that apply to experiences, and defines management strategies for developing a well-executed message delivery system. Also, because we live in a global marketplace, we will look at competitive communication strategies that are appropriate for international audiences.

Audience Aggregates

Aggregate-directed messages are essential for effective marketing communication. **Audience aggregates** are groups of consumers expressed in terms of usage or visitations by a group of like kind. Classifications of *current audience members* are divided into heavy, medium, and light users of entertainment venues, performances, and destinations. *New* or *nonaudience members* are potential users who have not yet experienced a performance genre or others who can be developed into users through education or incentives. *Users of competitive entertainment* genres also are potential users who must receive specialized messages. Promotional messages are tailored to each aggregate according to designated communication and action objectives, and then user aggregates are subdivided for more focused targeting. Exhibit 8.7 illustrates the message types used to target each audience aggregate.

Communication Objectives

Necessary components of objectives require that they are measurable, time sensitive, target audience directed, and behavior specific. Measurable determinants of communication objectives are category need, awareness, attitude, and purchase intention.

Category Need

Before audiences can be convinced to buy tickets, they must have some understanding or desire for the specific experience genre. For instance, nonusers of ballet performance likely will not respond to ticket promotions because ballet is not in their *evoked*

▪ ▪ ▪ **EXHIBIT 8.7** Tailoring Messages about LegoLand to Each Aggregate

Audience Aggregate	Message Themes
Current users	We appreciate your patronage; Try our off-season bargains.
New/nonusers	Why not try an alternative to standard theme park experiences? Mom gets in free on your first visit.
Competitive users	You owe it to yourself to experience a new kind of park. LegoLand offers father-son workshops on weekends.

set (brands familiar to a consumer) of entertainment criteria. In order to put ballet into this evoked set, communications must deliver generic information about ballet and the benefits of watching it. Like the "Got Milk?" milk campaign designed to put milk onto a shopper's list of things to buy, a generic campaign about ballet (got tutu?) introduces the notion of attending to people unfamiliar with this kind of dance. Only after audience members agree to consider attending do you switch from a generic message to messages with brand-specific objectives.

Awareness

After an audience member is familiar with a performance type, communication must make him aware of specific entertainment brands, which can be movies, musical groups, dance performers, and so on. Awareness has two levels—recognition and recall.

Recognition is the easiest awareness behavior to achieve. By placing impressions of the brand in front of the public, marketers establish visual or aural recognition. If you are shopping movies on the Internet and you recognize a director's name (brand) or film title (brand), you might find out where the movie is showing and even purchase tickets. Recognition occurs at the time of purchase and is usually delivered through mass media.

Recall is more difficult to achieve because it requires that a person bring up the brand in advance of purchase. For instance, when shopping a movie, you would hunt for one directed by Oliver Stone because you remembered his name. Recall occurs before purchase and requires more directly targeted repetition of the marketing message.

Attitude

The attitude objective is to develop, maintain, or change attitudes about an entertainment experience, venue, person, or destination. Introducing a new entertainment

brand requires marketers to create a specific and positive attitude in consumers' minds toward that brand. If research determines that brand attitudes are already positive, messages must maintain that momentum. Messages also can change a negative attitude to a positive one, or dispel attitudes that are based on misinformation. Important for public relations as well as advertising campaign, this objective is key to achieving purchase behavior.

Purchase Intention

Although communication objectives cannot be measured by actual purchases, they can help marketers determine whether the campaign has stimulated the intention to buy

Converting shoppers to purchasers is an action objective.

tickets or make reservations. Promotional messages help activate purchase behavior, and special pricing acts to stimulate immediate response.

Writing Objectives

Measurable, time-sensitive, usage-based, target audience-directed, and behavior-specific components of a *written objective* enable marketers to focus on exactly what must be achieved and by when. Here is a handy formula for writing an awareness objective:

Communication will _____ among _____ percent of _____
                        objective   *measure*   *target audience/usage based*

within _____ that _____ will do something.
        time limit   *brand*

Example: Communication will <u>create awareness</u> among <u>60 percent</u> of <u>regular theatergoers</u> within <u>the two weeks</u> that <u>*MaMa Mia*</u> will appear at their local theater.

An objective created to change attitudes may be phrased like this:

Communication will <u>improve negative attitudes</u> about <u>Six Flags Park</u> among <u>40 percent</u>
                          objective   *brand*   *measure*

of <u>theme park visitors</u> within <u>two months</u>.
   target audience   *time limit*

Unless objectives are specific, they cannot be measured; all four components are necessary for formulating written objectives prior to campaign development. Communication objectives drive IMC campaigns for entertainment content and destinations before creative concepts are developed or media and delivery vehicles are selected.

Action Objectives

Communication objectives determine the success or failure of message delivery; action (or behavioral) objectives determine the success or failure of marketing efforts. Actions are behaviors that result in buying tickets or redeeming promotion incentives that result in usage. As with communication objectives, action objectives are developed for each audience aggregate and are measured by box office receipts.

Entertainment industries are interested in getting consumers and audiences to take these actions:

- Buy a ticket
- Subscribe to a season
- Travel to a destination
- Book reservations to a resort

- Visit a park or attraction
- Play in a casino

Action objectives propel the bottom line. Most actions require behavior modification, which involves persuasive messages with purchase incentives. Message development is crucial for achieving action objectives.

▪▪▪▪ Message Development

Audience-based messages serve three functions: *to inform, to persuade,* and *to remind.* The messages delivered through media, by buzz, via the Internet, and in person must be directed by action objectives. Informational messages are designed to stimulate curiosity and increase understanding about the experience among nonusers or light users; similar informative messages are developed to drive ticket sales among medium and heavy users. Persuasive messages use sales promotions to provide incentives that drive buying behavior for all audience collectives. Reminder messages trigger buying behaviors in audience members who are regular experience visitors.

Informing (and Educational) Messages

If you want young adults to understand the nuances of opera so they may consider purchasing tickets, you inform them with messages that create excitement about the genre and encourage self-enlightenment through education. These messages also act as educational tools for new or nonaudience members who may not know that crawling subtitles and librettos are provided to simplify their ability to understand operas presented in other languages.

Persuasive Messages

When incentives are needed to stimulate timely ticket sales, persuasive messages can provide light and medium users with a reason to purchase immediately. Promotion-driven messages can be combined with informational messages for cases in which both action components—selecting venues and buying tickets—are necessary, such as in subscription drives and group sales. Incentives are important components of persuasive messages and are designed to entice new or nonaudience members to try a performance genre, visit a venue, or travel to a particular destination.

Reminder (or Informational) Messages

To communicate schedules and information about artists to heavy users of opera so they will purchase tickets, you use informational reminder messages to communicate subscription renewals, season opening performances, and loyalty program information (awards or point totals) to user aggregates. Best delivered on the Internet or by mail, informative reminders are used to provoke action.

There are two questions to ask when developing all forms of communication messages.

1. *Is the message actionable?* Unless you ask people to do something, they will mentally file your message and possibly never refer to it again. Audiences must be able to take action—buy tickets, make reservations, subscribe—or your message is not of use for marketing purposes.

▮▮▮ **EXHIBIT 8.8** Objective/Strategy Grid for Live Performance Audience Aggregates

	Audience Aggregate:		
	Current	*New/Non*	*Competitive*
Communication objective	Maintain positive attitude	Create recall awareness Develop positive attitude	Change attitude
Action objective	Buy more tickets	Try one performance	Compare options
Message strategy	Inform, remind; Loyalty rewards	Education, inform; Incentives	Inform, persuade: Incentives

2. *Is the message easy to understand?* People are able to grasp only one idea at a time. The more simple the message, the more apt the audience is to respond to it. Use visuals when ever possible and adhere to the old "KISS" principle: keep it simple, stupid.

Exhibit 8.8 indicates the difference between objectives and strategies recommended for current, new, and competitive audience groups.

Message Strategy

Consisting of objectives and visual techniques, message strategy defines advertising goals and how they will be achieved. Methods involve the mode of delivery and form the message takes. Unlike product ads, entertainment promotion relies less on brand recall, scare tactics, and brand image for audience persuasion than on product promotion. Awareness, attitude, and purchase intention objectives can be achieved by using advertising that creates *emotional resonance* with audiences. *Affective advertising* is the most effective strategy for venues and performance companies, as well as tourist bureaus and some media, because it incorporates celebrities, music, costumes, and visual delights to make emotional connections with audiences. Sharp editing in movie trailers and video performance previews, regional music for travel ads, and close-ups of sensational costuming presented in plays and opera performances are techniques used to tease audiences into purchasing tickets.

▮▮▮ Managing Communication Strategies and Tactics

To be successful, marketers absolutely must develop appropriate management strategies to ensure that their messages are properly created and directed. Managing the audience, the creative, the brand's image and extensions, and the media are important aspects of developing and executing a successful entertainment marketing campaign.

Manage the Audience

Audience relationship management involves conducting ongoing research and using the results to communicate and update. To track audience activity, venue and performance marketers use data-based mechanisms that pinpoint where a consumer is in the buying cycle. Customer interactions are managed with regular contacts that attempt to educate, inform, remind, and persuade. Providing regular contact without inundating aggregate members is effective audience management.

Performing arts centers and concert venues mail out regular subscription and special performance notices to audience members who have attended previous performances or who are present or past subscribers, as well as to potential audiences who have visited the center's Web site. Tourist bureaus use the Internet to send notices of special attractions to consumers who have requested information online, or who have downloaded travel brochures. Museum and theme park and attraction visitors also receive direct mail and Internet messages; past and current ticket buyers are informed about new exhibits, new rides, and seasonal promotions. Unless a relationship can be maintained, audience members will drift to other sources of entertainment that value their patronage. Because it is more efficient to maintain current patrons than to recruit new ones, managing these vital audience relationships is a first priority of every marketing program.

Manage the Creative

Creative strategy drives advertising by delivering a memorable concept to audiences. Creative development centers around three factors, information, emotion, and motivation. *Informational* strategies are appropriate for all audience aggregates; *emotional* strategies are designed to excite and involve potential audience aggregates; and *motivational* strategies provide promotional incentives to drive ticket purchases by infrequent or new audience aggregates.

Regardless of the nature of the creative strategy, all communication must be linked by a single concept through unusual and exciting executions. "Creative for creative's sake" may win awards for ad agencies, but it does nothing for entertainment's bottom line. Creative concepts and executions must achieve the campaign's communication goals in order to be effective.

To market its 45 regional theme parks, Six Flags developed a creative strategy that unified the brand's image and strengthened brand awareness. Six Flags' ad campaign featured a dancing senior who became the park's brand, helping to position the

regional parks against national competitors. Moving to the beat of "We Love to Party," the brand character helped deliver the brand's emotional message—Six Flags is the "ultimate release" from schedules and pressures of work and home. This emotional creative strategy that used humor and music drove park attendance way up, surpassing both the communication and action objectives developed for the advertising campaign.

Six Flags creative included a brand character.

Manage the Brand

Brand management is usually associated with product brands, but entertainment brands also require attention to aspects of branding. Let's look at positioning, image, and extensions.

Brand Positioning

Effective entertainment brand management requires creative and relevant positioning. An effective position:

- Leverages existing brand strengths.
- Focuses on perceived consumer benefits.
- Goes where the competitors are not.
- Establishes a credible fit between expectations and receipts.
- Updates the position to fit growth strategy.[10]

Brand positioning is audience driven. All the theme parks featured offer thrills, chills, and food; we call these *points of parity* (POP). To stand out in consumers' minds, each park must distinguish itself from the others with a position determined by audience feedback and message management; we call these *points of difference* (POD). Exhibit 8.9 shows the ways in which amusement park brands differentiate themselves.

To develop advertising that reflects positioning strategy, advertising themes must highlight points of difference. Advertisers may select from benefit, user, and competitive positioning themes for their promotional messages.

"Excitement you can count on" is an example of a *benefit* positioning theme; what the audience gets is the ad's single focus. Benefits are functional, emotional, and self-esteem oriented. Spas and resorts may declare relaxing and restoration as a functional benefit of their location. Audiences derive both emotional and self-esteem benefits from performance and destination-based entertainment.

User positioning themes revolve around the target audience. Disneyland always features families in its advertising because the parks are positioned as family entertainment. Carnival Cruise Lines often casts mature travelers in its vacation promotions to attract affluent seniors.

Competitive positioning can benefit casinos, resorts, and destinations, but is rarely selected by performance venues, parks, or attractions because gaining audience loyalty is not a factor for the latter types of entertainment brands. Because tourism promotes

▬▬▬ **EXHIBIT 8.9**   Positioning a Theme Park

Theme Park	*Position/Point of Difference*
Cedar Point	Roller coaster capital
Disneyland	Fantasy and family fun
LegoLand	Hands on learning
Six Flags	Regional excitement
Sea World	Animal habitats
Universal Studios	Hollywood backstage

all theme parks, it would be counterproductive for parks to position themselves against competitors. Visitors to California may combine their trips to Disneyland with stops at Knott's Berry Farm or LegoLand. Messages presenting the subtle advantages of casinos, resorts, and destination imply superiority rather than directly referencing the competition. Mandalay Bay competes with Wynn casinos in theory, but it rarely uses that strategy in its advertising.

Manage the Media

Media selection and buying (see Chapter 9) are important for creating awareness through advertising, but there are other important ways for entertainment marketers to manage the media. Public relations is a key factor in managing brand image. Audiences respond to editorial information, and they may be likely to buy tickets as a result of buzz of word of mouth rather than pure advertising. Networking with arts and entertainment writers, reviewers, and editors is important to generating publicity and exposure. Good managers understand how to use the tools outlined below to their advantage.

Zagat

Marketers must not underestimate the role Zagat ratings play in entertainment success. Since 1910, the **Zagat Survey** has been the restaurant, hotel, resort, spa, entertainment, shopping movie, music, theater, golf, and travel bible for many consumers. A best-selling publisher of guides, Zagat uses an approach that separately rates the distinct qualities of restaurants (food, decor, service, and cost), hotels (rooms, service, dining, and public facilities), and other leisure categories based on a 30-point scale. This format allows people to search for and find the best places to meet their individual needs based on a variety of criteria.

Zagat also has developed business relationships with more than 3,000 companies, including entertainment entities such as AOL, MGM, Microsoft, News Corp, and Verizon. Because Zagat relies on online voting, it offers a subscription-based site with all Zagat Survey's ratings and reviews, as well as maps, driving instructions, a monthly e newsletter, and the ability to vote and shop online. Now the world's leading provider of consumer survey-based date, Zagat has more than 250,000 voters participating worldwide.[11] Not all is written in stone, however. Like all quantifiable data, results may be manipulated to serve specific interests.[12]

Media Reviews

Media critics comment on every form of media in an attempt to influence audience selection. Critics are routinely in opposition to one another, so no one review should act as criteria for buying tickets to a performance. Several sources combine reviews to present a well-rounded approach to criticism.

In spite of the fact that journalistic reviewers see any given film only once and have only a day or two to formulate opinions (if that long), they have an important impact on the success of films. The exceptions are mass-marketed action, horror, and comedy movies that are not greatly affected by a critic's overall judgment. For prestige films such as most dramas, however, reviews are extremely influential. Poor reviews often consign a film to obscurity and financial loss.

With so much riding on reviews, studios woo film critics with press kits or small gifts. Studios also offer to fly groups of critics from cities across the U.S. to New York or Los Angeles for a weekend that includes a screening of the studio's new film. Following the screening, critics are asked to write short reviews. It is from these reviews that advertising blurbs are drawn. Some of the most renowned critics are Roger Ebert of the *Chicago Sun-Times,* Richard Roeper of TV's *Ebert & Roeper,* A. O. Scott of the *New York Times,* and Peter Travers of *Rolling Stone.*

Web sites that seek to improve the usefulness of reviews by compiling them to ascertain general opinions are Rotten Tomatoes and Metacritic. Log on to www.rottentomatoes.com/ for reviews of entertainment products categorized by source, critic, date, or rating. The site's reviewers hail from the *New York Times,* the *Los Angeles Daily News,* the *Boston Herald, Cinema Em Cena, Filmfocus,* the *Christian Science Monitor,* and *Rolling Stone,* among many other publications and Web sites. Rotten Tomatoes' approved Tomatometer critics meet the standards of accredited media outlets and online film societies for consistent and unbiased reviewing. A recent academic study,[13] however, claimed that buzz, regardless of good or bad reviews, determines box office revenue more than any other factor. According to researcher Dr. Liu, word of mouth influences people by affecting their awareness, not their attitude.

Smaller film releases, however, are more closely tied to a circle of reviewers who influence the success or failure of independent offerings. One such group is Rogue Reviewers, a select group of B-movie review Web sites dedicated to bringing reviews to and by members on their "movies under the bed" roundtable. Schlock Audio Theater dedicates a Web site to producing "madcap audio productions of the world's cheesiest B-Movies."[14] Schlock takes its format from the traditional cablevision show that features an eccentric host who provides colorful commentary as the program progresses. One of the recent episodes is "Attack of the Giant Leeches," a Web article in a zine covering the world of independent and cult cinema.

Performing arts, books, video games, and destinations are all reviewed by a particular set of critics, guidebooks, and Web sites that give power to audience members for selecting entertainment.

▪▪▪ Communicating across Borders

Most entertainment content is designed for global distribution. Only a few Middle Eastern countries ban imported content, and, volume for volume, this is more than compensated for by China's and India's thirst for Western entertainment vehicles. In order to market content to a variety of destinations, you must understand the challenges and restrictions involved in distributing content across borders. This section addresses some of those concerns.

Strategies for Competing in Global Markets

The United States exports more entertainment product than any other nation. U.S. organizations and franchise corporations must, therefore, decide how to market across national, international, and cultural boundaries to maximize ticket sales and profits. Four general strategies prevail.

All Disney's theatrical productions of *The Lion King* contained the same costuming, music, and promotional communications aimed at a global audience.

Same Product/Same Communication

When Broadway shows, such as *The Lion King,* and musical concerts, such as Jimmy Buffet's, go on tour, their products are essentially the same each time they are presented. *The Lion King* features the same actors, costuming, set design, and language. Promotional materials follow the same format away as at home, using English as the primary language. Controlled promotional tactics may vary slightly by city for Buffet, but generally audiences receive the same advance hype, syndicated ticket sales, and media advertising. Margaritaville, Buffet's official Web site, provides radio, online chatting, café locations, and recipes for his tequila concoctions. Both play and performer have extended their brand with licensed products.

Same Product/Different Communication

Destinations such as the Grand Canyon and Paris, France, are permanent experiences, but different promotional messages for them are directed to specific audience demographics. When promoted to Europeans, Grand Canyon brochures feature spectacular vistas and Western-style lodging; promotions to Australians focus on hiking, camping, and visits to Native American Indian sites. Paris is touted as a romantic destination to Americans, while marketing it to Europeans takes into account the city's proximity and Euro-based economy. Promotional materials are produced in the language of the audience and produced with cultural considerations in mind.

Different Product/Same Communication

Each Hilton Hotel is a different experience, but all are promoted under the same brand. Graphics for the chain depict a variety of locations featured on Web sites and newspaper ads. Communications direct audiences to Web sites and travel packagers. The Blue Man Group, which began in New York and Chicago with three guys and

The name's the same, but Blue Man Group performances and actors vary by concert location and audience.

some drums, changes its show to suit the location and the audience. They use vaudeville techniques—such as catching thrown gumballs in their mouths—with tribal rhythms hammered out on contorted PVC pipe for matinees and families. Evening performances from their Las Vegas location include more sophisticated musical interpretations.

Different Product/Different Communication

If you like soul, blues, rock and roll, or jazz, you have probably purchased a CD from Ace Records. Boasting the largest and most active back catalogs of any record concern, Ace produces high-quality reissues. Its promotions are targeted toward aficionados of each music genre. In most cases, album cover designs act as the primary promotional graphic. Boasting 25 labels, Ace's Web site provides an introduction to the music the company releases, as well as background on the artists and a list of top 10 recordings. Music by Ace artists is played on BBC2 and MTV, reviewed in 26 magazines, and played on radio stations in Great Britain, Ireland, Scotland, and the United States. The NFL also uses this strategy: one league and sixteen teams means promotion to fans with different tastes and reasons for attending football games. Team advertising, public relations, and merchandising are tailored to home and visiting cities according to fan preferences.

Global Communication Strategies

Strategies for both the delivery system and the message content must be set prior to developing creative concepts. Audience reception is predicated on an understanding of the audience's needs, wants, perceptions, and expectations—in each location where the entertainment experience takes place.

Promotional communication can be produced in a central location, in several locations, or in a combination depending on audience diversity and corporate policies. We look at three options.

Standard/Central

The Australian Tourist Board has produced a standard message ("A Different Light") from their headquarters in Sydney. Their Web site features 10 language selections and offers 410 locations from which to choose your viewing point. Yet the site's logo, graphics, jumping kangaroo, and message presentation are standardized. This is a typical case of standardized messages emanating from a single location to a global audience.

MTV maintains a consistent identity on Web sites developed for Japan, Asia, and Italy, but does not interfere in local programming decisions.

Decentralized/Autocratic

Music and programming developed for MTV is produced autocratically at each of its 24 locations around the world. Only the logo and graphics unite the stations, which connect youth to music in a variety of sounds and content. The music is promoted to its targeted audience and controlled by each affiliate independently of the home office.

Central/Locally Produced

In the case of Disneyland, all communications are developed at corporate headquarters but are produced with local actors and targeted to local audiences. Hong Kong, Tokyo, and Paris locations, however, must have approval from Disney for all of their message development and delivery. Central control enables Disney to maximize the quality of the experience for all of its visitors worldwide.

Cultural Considerations

Communicating across cultures and borders is a necessity for global entertainment companies. Structuring messages that persuade audiences to buy tickets, attend performances, and travel to destinations is predicated on acknowledging specific differences among cultures. Here are some of the considerations marketing communications must address in global promotion.

Language

Americans like to believe that the world is learning to speak English, but the truth is global audiences prefer to be communicated to in their own language. Literal translations have caused embarrassments for advertisers in the past, so native speakers craft messages for local offices of global agencies. Web sites with global entertainment products provide visitors with language options to enhance their usability.

Collective or Individual Perspective

Japanese prefer to travel in groups; Australians like lone adventures. The way you promote depends on your audience's mindset and preference for engaging in experiential entertainment. You market to collective societies by extolling the benefits of engaging with family and friends. For societies where individual preferences rule, you highlight activities for singles or the virtues of going it alone. Individualistic cultures such as the

U.S. generally use a direct mode of communication in which intentions and meanings are displayed clearly and expressed explicitly. Audiences in collective cultures prefer less direct communication based on a trust-generating orientation and nonverbal acts that are not threatening or unsettling to their sense of self.

Expression

Communication is inextricably bound with meaning. Cultures in which people have extensive information networks among family and friends are considered high-context. In high-context cultures, people collect information from their networks. These cultures are recognized by their indirect communication using less copy and more symbols. In low-context cultures, people without information networks require a great deal of detailed information from other sources. Low-context–culture audiences tend to need more copy, augmentation, facts, and data than their high-context counterparts. To communicate effectively across cultures, you must ascertain the correct level of context for each audience you address.

Social Norms and Cultural Values

Social norms are standards that define what is considered an appropriate or normal way for a society's citizens to be and act. A *value* is a single belief that guides and determines actions, attitudes, and judgments. Norms are related to a culture's *instrumental values,* which are the basic values that motivate members of the society to reach desired ways of being, called end-states of existence. *End states* also are known as *terminal* or *core values;* these are simply values that bring the state of existence that everyone in the society wants to achieve, whether that state is enlightenment, financially security, success, or incredible intelligence.

The notion of a value system implies a rank ordering of terminal or instrumental values along a single continuum and can be used to compare people along different measurement systems.

Values are learned and are enduring. For instance, Americans share values of freedom, equality, fairness, achievement, patriotism, democracy, and luck. Japanese share values of group unity, education, and loyalty. Cross-cultural communication requires an understanding of the audience values for each segment targeted. Rather than featuring symbols of independence as American advertisers do, Japanese communications feature symbols that express their preference for group collectiveness.

Gender Roles

In addition to the ways in which sex determines individual roles, gender differentiations can be country-specific. A strong role differentiation exists in so-called masculine cultures, while a subtler role differentiation is present in cultures where women have dominant social roles. Gender stereotypes are more pronounced in countries that score high on the masculinity index (Japan) and less pronounced in countries labeled as feminine (Thailand). Cultures can be matriarchal (some African-American cultures) or patriarchal (some Hispanic cultures). Men and women in feminine cultures are seen as more responsible and caring than in masculine cultures, in which decisiveness and ambition are more visible. Communications must be gender-sensitive to be effective.

FINALLY: LET'S SUM UP ▪▪▪▪▪▪▪

Marketing mix elements and branding principles from product and service marketing are a departure point for those who promote experiential content, venues, and destinations. These principles provide a foundation for the strategy development and campaign planning that are necessary for structuring effective entertainment promotions. When the creative product succeeds, models and theories cannot be far behind.

For years, marketers have coordinated graphic and message elements for campaigns; only recently has convergence made more sense than simple integration. By focusing on audience benefits, entertainment promotion efforts can utilize all elements of the marketing mix for effective message delivery before, during, and after campaign implementation.

Each element of the marketing integration process—objectives, message strategy, management support, and global considerations—is necessary to ensure an effective marketing communication message. The challenge is determining which element to emphasize and which to minimize; when determined correctly, the results yield a solid bottom line and client satisfaction.

GOT IT? LET'S REVIEW ▪▪▪▪▪▪▪

- McCarthy's 4Ps are reconfigured for entertainment as 5Ps: audience usage segment, audience experience, audience investment, performance venue or destination, and communication and incentives
- A marketing mix locus of control is the consumer or audience member; management controls mix decisions and influences organizational resources, but it has no control over external factors that can affect ticket sales.
- Audience-based brand equity ensures that expectations of performance and venue are met; brand awareness, image, and loyalty are important factors for developing brand equity.
- Communication objectives—category need, awareness, attitude, and purchase intention—are used to measure advertising effectiveness. Objectives must be measurable

and include a behavior, specific audience segment, and time limit. They are measured with pre- and post campaign testing.
- Promotion-oriented messages inform, persuade with incentives, or remind; they must be actionable and easy to understand. Action objectives are developed to stimulate ticket sales and are measured with box office receipts.
- To develop advertising that reflects a positioning strategy, advertising communication themes must emphasize points of difference. Advertisers may select from benefit, user, and competitive aggregate positioning themes for their promotional messages.
- Global marketing requires an understanding of cultural differences and gender roles across borders and ethnicities.

NOW TRY THIS ▪▪▪▪▪▪▪

1. Go to the Web site of your favorite musical group. How does the group distinguish itself through logo, type style, and graphics? How does the site contribute to or detract from the band's brand image?
2. Check out the brand blogs on http://web. mit.edu/cms/bcc/2005_04_01_brandculture _archive.html, especially the archives such as "Babies recognize brands," or other branding reports. What does the site

contribute to your understanding of entertainment and branding?
3. Now try using http://brandnoise.typepad. com/ to see what's new in branding strategy. What role does advertising play?
4. Comparing two museums of your choice, enumerate their points of parity and points of difference. What do these points suggest for positioning strategies for each of the museums?

5. Compare the promotional messages used to market two destinations from either their Web sites or travel brochures. What structures do the messages take—informative or incentive? What action objectives are communicated by these messages?

QUESTIONS: LET'S REVIEW ▪▪▪▪▪▪▪

1. Which typology would you choose, McCarthy's recrafted 4Ps or Liebermann's 4Cs, to characterize the entertainment industry? Why?

2. When is point of parity a better strategy for positioning than point of difference? Give an example.

3. How would you explain the difference between integrated and convergent communication strategies to a client who asks?

4. Awareness is generated through recognition and recall. What are the key components of each type of awareness generation?

5. How would you state a communication objective for promoting travel to Mumbai, India to active seniors who like to travel?

6. Why are communication objectives rather than marketing objectives used to measure advertising effectiveness?
   Answers to brand slogan quiz: Hallmark, ATT, Green Giant, Motel 7, United Airlines, DeBeers, Avis.

MORE TO READ ▪▪▪▪▪▪▪

Roger Blackwell and Tina Stephan. *Brands That Rock.* Hoboken, NJ: Wiley, 2004.

Morica DeMooij. *Global Marketing and Advertising.* London: Sage Publications, 2003.

Thomas Gad. *4-D Branding.* New York: Financial Times/Prentice Hall, 2001.

Kevin Lane Keller. *Strategic Brand Management,* 2nd ed. Upper Saddle River, NJ: Prentice Hall, 2003.

Thomas McPhail. *Global Communication: Theories, Stakeholders and Trends.* San Francisco: Allyn & Bacon, 2002.

J. R. Rossiter and S. Bellman. *Marketing Communications.* Australia: Pearson Education/Prentice Hall, 2005.

P. R. Smith and J. Taylor. *Marketing Communications: An Integrated Approach.* London: Kogan Page, 2004.

Lynn Upshaw. *Building Brand Identity: A Strategy for Success in a Hostile Marketplace.* New York: Wiley, 1995.

NOTES ▪▪▪▪▪▪▪

1. E. McCarthy, *Basic Marketing: A Managerial Approach,* 7th ed. (Boston: Irwin Publishing, 1981).

2. P. Kotler and G. Armstrong, *Principles of Marketing,* 8th ed. (New York: Prentice Hall, 1999).

3. V. Zeithaml and M. Bitner, *Services Marketing* (New York: McGraw-Hill, 1997), p. 304.

4. A. Liebman, the *Entertainment Marketing Revolution* (New York: Prentice Hall, 2002).

5. Andrew Zoli, "Brands, Consumer Behavior, Trends," *American Demographics* 27 (9) (2004), p. 44.

6. Based on K. L. Keller, *Strategic Brand Management,* 2nd ed. (New York: Prentice Hall, 2003), chap. 2.

7. M. Vriens and F. T. Hofstede, "Linking Attributes, Benefits and Consumer Values," *Marketing Research,* Fall (2000), pp. 3–8.

8. Jake Tapper, "National Lampoon Grows Up by Dumbing Down," *New York Times,* July 3, 2005.

9. Licensing Institute of America report for June 2004.

10. Scott Davis, *Brand Asset Management* (Jossey Bass, 2000), p. 117.

11. zagat.com/about/about.aspx.

12. fairness.com/resources/.

13. Alex Mindlin, "What Counts at the Box Office is the Buzz," *New York Times,* July 24, 2006.

14. rouguereviewers.com/, Aug. 6, 2005.

CHAPTER 9

Promotional Communications

Promise, large promise, is the soul of an advertisement.
—SAMUEL JOHNSON

Chapter Objectives

After reading this chapter, you should be able to answer the following questions:

■ How are *advertising media* used in integrated and converged communications?

■ How has the *Internet* changed the way entertainment is promoted?

■ Why has *product placement* become such big business for the entertainment industry?

■ How do *promotion, merchandising and licensing, and personal selling* factor into the entertainment marketing mix?

■ What role do *public and media relations* play in promoting experiences?

■ How are *events and sponsorships* integrated into an entertainment brand or corporation's overall marketing strategy?

As you know, the original promotion mix had four components: advertising, public relations, sales promotion, and direct sales. Today, the list of promotional mechanisms for delivering persuasive messages is endless. The formula for mixing the perfect communications creation is dynamic—it changes with social trends, audience preferences, and budgetary concerns. Because your entertainment product is experiential, you must deliver the message to audiences in unique formats that can achieve specific action-oriented behaviors. For every entertainment organization or franchise, perhaps the most important yet challenging part of managing brand image involves coordinating all the communication vehicles that provide information to audiences and consumers. This chapter presents an overview of all the promotional tools available to entertainment marketers for sending those messages.

▪▪▪ Advertising

Advertising is any paid form of nonpersonal promotion by an identified sponsor. In today's mediated world, however, the *identification* part may be elusive, as many advertisements are disguised as print editorial and electronic content. As you know, television, radio, newspapers, magazines, outdoor signage, movie theaters, and the Internet are dominant advertising vehicles. Product placement is catching up in a major way. It is the most current innovation now capturing the imagination and dollars of advertisers.

In years past, a company spent a major portion of its promotional budget buying media. Today, advertising has extended beyond traditional media channels to become *place based. Place advertising*—ads that appear where the buying takes place—allows consumers to purchase insurance at airports, see demonstrations of tools in hardware sections, and even order made-to-measure jeans in retail outlets. This chapter reviews and updates the basics of advertising as it coordinates with and converges with entertainment. The downside of convergence is the movement toward increasingly fragmented advertising venues, so marketers must make innovative use of all avenues to make sure their messages reach target audiences.

The traditional tools of print and broadcast advertising are purchased to reach a specific target audience over a specific period of time with measurable results. Entertainment companies and advertising agencies choose media to create a buzz and to deliver scheduled messages in a timely fashion. Media are invaluable sources of mass communication and achieve broad reach and frequency objectives for advertisers.

Media are never purchased in a vacuum—reach (number of audience members targeted) and frequency (number of times message is delivered to a target audience) measures extend to global audiences. Regulation and accessibility are two factors advertisers consider when purchasing both national and international media time and space. Media target both mass audiences and niche markets, where audience members have a distinct commonality. Let's quickly review print and broadcast media with an eye toward how they can direct promotional communications to current and potential entertainment audiences. Chapter 10 addresses message content.

Developing Persuasive Messages

The **AIDA model**—*a*ttention, *i*nterest, *d*esire, *a*ction—to creating advertising messages in every media continues to hold true for configuring ads. However, the process of getting attention, creating interest, fostering desire, and stimulating action (buying tickets, going to a Web site) must be tailored to the sophistication level of the target audience.

As discussed in Chapter 8, advertising messages delivered by any mass or personal medium are broadly classified into three types:

- *Informative*—conveys information to raise awareness; educates with news and performance updates
- *Persuasive*—creates desire and stimulates purchase; often used in conjunction with ticket promotions, special offers, and discounts
- *Reminder*—reinforces existing knowledge and benefits; appropriate for long-running performances and annual or subscription-based events; includes entertaining ads that reinforce brand image.

Print Advertising

Print media include newspapers, magazines, mail brochures, packaging, and all forms of printed message delivery systems that carry theme park and resort brand names, for example, or museum exhibition and movie logos. Print advertising is especially useful for entertainment because of its timeliness and wide availability.

Newspapers

Regardless of readership decline, newspapers can play a vital role in announcing performances to local audiences and posting schedules and locations. Short lead time and low production cost maximize the potential of newspaper advertising for most entertainment experiences. Coverage can appear as part of a special calendar or entertainment section of metropolitan newspapers.

Newspapers with full-sized pages, such as the *New York Times,* are called **broadsheets. Tabloids** are half the size with a more sensational focus. Entertainment reviews, features, and biographies are treated more favorably in tabloids, but editors of the entertainment sections of both types of papers rely on news releases provided by public relations firms representing entertainment-oriented companies.

Of the basic types of advertising—classified, display, and supplements—only two are appropriate for experience marketers; **display ads** are used most frequently. Sold by column inch (2″ × number of columns), the standard advertising unit (SAU) for display ads is 40 column inches. Occasionally, theater or blockbuster movie advertising takes advantage of free-standing inserts to promote an upcoming spectacular event.

Newspaper advertising is bought on a market-by-market basis, anticipating a metro penetration of around 35 percent and community penetration as high as 85 percent of households. Standard Rate and Data Services (SRDS) provides media buyers with profiles, production requirements, and advertising rates. With daily circulations, most metro newspapers are a source of timely information for loyal subscribers and pass-along readers. Even with a life span of one day, newspapers play an invaluable role in of publicity and promotion. Newspapers are the most personal and localized media.

Consumer Publications

Classified by publication frequency (weekly, monthly, bimonthly, quarterly) and by audience type (consumer, business, trade, and professional), magazines are distributed by paid circulation or by controlled circulation (distributed free to readers of a given profession or organization). Magazines focus their coverage on a specific subject area, and advertising can be tailored to reach interested readers in niche markets.

Several entertainment trade publications (*Entertainment Weekly* and *Variety*) bring news and features about films, stars, and revenues to members of the industry. *Fade In, Interview, Rolling Stone, Talk,* and *Wired* are among a variety of consumer-oriented magazines. Advertising is purchased by page (or page part) and location—covers cost more. Branded entertainment messages can appear in gatefolds, tip-ins, and pop-op advertising designed to grab readers' attention. Major metro areas also have city magazines that include calendars of events.

Standard Rate and Data Systems (SRDS) publishes two magazine directories (consumer and business) for media buying. Space is sold in portions of a page—quarter-, half-, and full-page, as well as double-page spreads—by salespeople working directly for the publication.

▪▪▪▪▪▪▪▪▪▪▪ **BOX 9-1** ▪▪▪▪▪▪▪▪▪▪▪

Focus on Tie-In Advertising

PRODUCT PROMOTES FILM IN PRINT AD

Bombay Sapphire, a dry gin spirit, bought a two-page advertisement in *New Yorker Magazine* to present its INSPIRED VISIONS promotion, which highlights visionary filmmakers. *The Constant Gardener,* starring Ralph Fiennes, was profiled in the magazine prior to its August release in theaters. This advertisement is an exam-ple of pairing a product with entertainment to share costs and create interest in both. Purchased by interested readers, magazines are directed toward a specific audience willing to accept advertising from their lifestyle providers. Color and graphics make magazines ideal vehicles for impressionable entertainment messages.

▪▪▪▪▪▪▪▪▪

Trade Publications

The entertainment and advertising industries have a variety of trade publications where service providers place *business-to-business* advertising. Some of the best-known of these trade publications are:

- *Advertising Age*
- *AdWeek*
- *Amusement Business*
- *Billboard*
- *BrandWeek*
- *Broadcasting & Cable*
- *Emedia*
- *Hollywood Reporter*
- *Variety*

Broadcast Advertising

Broadcast commercials are more intrusive than print ads, and they can be quickly passed by changing channels or TiVo. Creative approaches to broadcast advertising are critical. Broadcast time is sold in units (30-second [:30] and 60-second [:60] spots) based on the daypart (prime time, drive time, and so on) and the audience size. Ad rates are more negotiable than rates for print, because commercial time is both fixed and perishable—there are only 24 hours in the day, and once the spot airs, it is gone forever. (You may want to review Chapter 5 on broadcast audience measurement.)

Television

No other medium has the visual impact of television, especially for capturing the excitement of a performance or the glamour of a resort. With the broadest exposure of any medium, television reaches a large audience and can deliver messages with dramatic effects. Networks offer fragmented audiences, while cable or satellite providers offer more selective viewers with specific interests. For instance, blockbuster movie trailers are featured on networks, while independent films find their audiences

Weeds star Mary Louise Parker at a Showtime premiere.

on cable channels. Not surprisingly, the biggest users of television advertising are the networks themselves; they heavily promote their own season line-ups and returning series.

Television advertising is no longer about advertising on television. Instead of just buying ads, sponsor PepsiCo joined with MTV's show *Laguna Beach* to jazz up the message format. Pepsi paid for Pepsi Lime's logo to appear on the wrapping of a DVD release of the show's first season, and sponsored text alerts about the show sent to selected cell phone users and a special Web site that features exclusive content from the show.[1]

With traditional 30- and 60-second spots under assault by TiVo and other recording services that allow *zapping* (i.e., enable the viewer to edit out ads), television networks are scrambling for new ways to lure marketing dollars. Potential customers are reached through interaction. Advertisers take advantage of program DVDs, the Internet, and mobile phones to promote their shows. E-mail lists, Web chat rooms, and contests are sold on all these technological venues.

Many shows offer a cable or network-organized Web stream or message board, conversations carried out on the Web through updates by fans. For example, ad deals by Disney's ABC allow *Alias* fans to watch video clips on various Internet sites and purchase show memorabilia online. Lifetime TV offers viewers of the *Beach Girls* summer drama a chance to download ring tones heard on the show from their Web site. Such alliances put advertisers in touch with consumers in ways that may not be as disruptive to audiences as traditional commercials.

The next step might be giving a computer and video camera to a participant in a network reality show so the person could operate a blog. This would provide product placement opportunities for both the computer manufacturer and the camera maker on the Web and TV. The more contacts are used in concert with products, the stronger the impact on viewers.

Television time is sold to advertisers by **dayparts**, which include early morning, daytime, early fringe, early news, prime access, prime time, late news, and late fringe. Prime time and late news are the most expensive commercial dayparts. The high cost of production is not a detriment for entertainment advertisers who often use performance segments or edited trailers as opposed to specially scripted and produced commercials. Cable station time is purchased locally, and network media buys can be local, regional, or national in scope. Subscription channels have a range of purchasing location options.

Radio

Radio provides a soundtrack for your daily activities. It is the most reasonably priced cost-per-thousand broadcast medium in advertising. The good news is that it is always

▪▪▪ EXHIBIT 9.1 Comparing Media Advertising for Entertainment Brands

Media Selection Criteria

Medium	Reach	Frequency	CPM	Production Time	Coverage
Newspaper	limited	limited	high	short	local/national
Cons. mags.	niche	unlimited	high	long	regional/national
Trade pubs.	specific	unlimited	medium	long	regional/national
Network TV	broad	unlimited	medium	long	national
Cable TV	niche	unlimited	low	medium	local/regional/ national/global
Radio	broad	unlimited	low	short	local/national

on; the bad news is that often no one is paying attention. One advantage is that each radio station has a specific kind of programming or format, such as country, Top 40, jazz, or talk, which improves targeting capabilities. Also, on-air personalities can be brands in their own right; some are quite attractive, live promotional tools for entertainment events.

Another advantage of advertising on radio is its ability to broadcast from remote locations where sponsored events provide live audiences. Disc jockeys broadcast live from community fairs, festivals, and street exhibits, urging listeners to "come on down" to the event. Contests and giveaways can promote movies, concerts, and live performances in conjunction with radio stations. Entertainment providers offer free tickets to stations in exchange for on-air promotion, which simultaneously benefits the station, its listeners, and the entertainment provider. Exhibit 9.1 compares media advertising available to entertainment branding.

Many entertainment marketers prefer radio when they need to deliver a localized and cost-effective ad, because programming, with either a music- or talk-show program format, can easily target specific audiences. With short lead times and minimal production, radio is ideal for announcing events and promoting performances. Announcements to audiences whose entertainment preferences are synonymous with station content can be made on time and with accuracy.

Humor can contribute to successful message delivery. Musical and humorous commercials fare best; soundtracks from movies and musical events are ideal sources commercials for radio advertising. Morning drive-time, which boasts the largest listening audience, is the most expensive daypart on which to purchase radio advertising.

Subscription radio permits listeners to select musical genres without commercial breaks, as well as commercial stations in a variety of geographic markets. Without censorship, program content can stretch the boundaries of control by the Federal Communication Commission in the same way cable and satellite television does. The growing popularity of subscription radio indicates that listeners are willing to pay for greater selection and programming choice. In 2006, only Sirius and XM provided subscription services for listeners, and in 2007 their merger was awaiting FCC approval. Car dealers often provide it for their new customers as part of a purchase package.

▪▪▪▪▪▪▪▪▪▪ **BOX 9-2** ▪▪▪▪▪▪▪▪▪▪

Focus on Advertising Ethics

CHOOSE CLIENT OR CONTENT?

As a member of a popular radio station management committee, you are caught between the conflicting demands of your most popular consumer program and your sales representative. Your station's *Consumer Watch* program has been following a series of critical reports on defects of one automaker's brand and on court cases against a particular car model. Your sales rep is concerned because a dealership who sells this car is a major sponsor of the station.

The client told the rep to stop the continuous exposure or lose its advertising. If the station keeps running the programs, it risks losing substantial sums of badly needed income to sustain the broad range of other station activities.

During a meeting on the dilemma, the program team said that the car's problem is important consumer information, that the station should not be promoting a dangerous car, and that no commercial operator should be able to dictate station policy.

The sales team insisted that if the station is to reach revenue target goals, this advertiser must be mollified and *Consumer Watch* must drop this particular story. The team isn't saying that the program has to shut down altogether, just that it cover other issues, instead.

What do you think?

1. Should you ask the sales team to find alternative advertisers? Why?

2. Should you ask the program team to switch to other equally important topics? Why?

▪▪▪▪▪▪▪▪

Direct Response Advertising

Communicating directly with audience members brings a personal dimension to promoting entertainment products. It directly connects the marketer and the audience, bypassing sales reps and retail outlets. In direct response, audiences respond to infomercials and interactive marketing vehicles via phone or Internet. Responses are most often fulfilled using toll-free, 1-800 numbers or through Web addresses.

The most crucial component of direct marketing is reaching the right audience. Success for direct mail pieces is based on the effectiveness of the *mailing list,* the group of names and contact information that defines the target audience. Member names, addresses, and relevant information must be captured and organized in a company's database in order to deliver appropriate messages. Unfortunately, however, direct response marketing is synonymous with the pejorative term *junk mail.*

Direct marketing's primary objective is to elicit a response to an offer, hence the term *direct response.* Blogs, cell phones, and e-mail alerts are useful for increasing ticket solicitation and performance reminders. Performing arts venues, amusement parks, and travel companies advertise ways for consumers to purchase tickets and book reservations by direct response. Internet ticketing programs require attention making an offer to targeted prospects, order fulfillment, and customer service.

On-Screen Advertising

Advertising on the big screen has been standard procedure in European theaters for year, but it is relatively new to American movie houses. According to the Cinema Advertising Council, on-screen advertising revenues grew 20 percent in 2004 to $384 million, and off-screen promotions—including revenue from in-lobby promotions—rose to $64 million.[2] Providing an attractive alternative to television advertising, theaters are an ideal canvas for quantifiable ad messages. Theaters can demonstrate reach, frequency, and recall, all of which lead to a very good return on investment.

More than 28,000 of the total 38,000 movie screens in the U.S. run cinema advertising. The film audience's educational levels and spending power are attractive to marketers. Vonage, a broadband phone company, ran a special 30-second on-screen animated spot on a trial basis, and executives were so pleased with the results they signed up for a month's worth of advertising. A special presentation called "The Twenty" presents 20 minutes of advertising prior to the feature presentation in many California cinemas. Not always welcomed by moviegoers, cinema advertising nonetheless has gained in popularity. As long as box office receipts are up, it is worthwhile for makers of branded products and services.

Place-Based Advertising

Reaching people where they eat, shop, and exercise has become the preference of entertainment promoters who have not succeeded with media—even when the product is mediated! *Out-of-home media*—purchased signage on taxis, busses, trucks, and trains—include outdoor advertising (billboards) and posters that work well for advertising long-run performances, theme parks, and resorts. Digitized running messages capture pedestrian attention in large cities. Designed to reach mass audiences, out-of-home media extends both reach and frequency of an entertainment branded message. An increasing array of outdoor alternatives make up the more than 200 out-of-home formats in use today.[3] Brands are built on our roadways, where billboards telegraph their messages to America. They act as guides, directing us to hotels, eateries, and amusements. They help us find businesses and services and help businesses find

Taxis carry place-based advertising for many brands and products.

Full bus-wrap entertainment ad.

customers. Nike's interactive display on a 23-story digital billboard in Times Square allows passersby to temporarily control the billboard and design their own shoes on the huge screen by using their cell phones.

Outdoor advertising is growing faster than most other media segments. Spending for this form of advertising is expanding at the rate of 5.5 percent a year, faster than newspapers, network TV, and radio combined. In 2005, ads reached New York City's newsstands, bus shelters, and public toilets in a deal that generated $1 billion in advertising revenue.

Advertising as *street furniture*[4] (such as bus shelters) offers protection from the rain to transit riders, acting as a consumer magnet. Big, bold, and night-illuminated, the ads are magazine pages come to life. Whether providing broad-based coverage in many markets or targeted to a single neighborhood, street furniture is perfect for entertainment marketing.

Advertisers who go directly to the places where audiences buy related services and products maximize message impact. Here are some ways in which place-based advertising targets consumers.

- *Airports* carry advertisements for products related to travel as well as destinations and hotels that serve travelers.
- *Point of purchase* displays help tourists choose destinations by providing travel brochures and attraction promotions.
- *Cell phones* have become a new music-buying venue: Samsung's "Anymotion," a musical ad produced to promote its $600 Anycall telephone, sold more than three million copies (at $2 each)[5] as a cell phone-only download. In other words, people will pay to hear an ad for a cell phone delivered to them via cell phone!

Outdoor Signage Goes Global

Out-of-home advertising, long considered a backwater on Madison Ave., is getting tougher to ignore as it branches out beyond national borders to gain a global presence.

These gigantic building billboards (here featuring a magazine promotion on a hotel) are simply "Wallpaper without the WOW factor," according to a creative director in the Russia office of Saatchi & Saatchi.

In India, which produces the largest number of films of any country in the world, movies are prominently advertised on large silhouetted cutout figures that rise into the air above their billboard frames.

Even Moscow is becoming a city of billboards, as building-size ads transform the Russian capital into its own version of Times Square. In the city's downtown area, advertisers from around the world vie for consumer attention with size and color. The country's $3.8 billion ad market is the world's fastest growing, and it is expected to continue expanding by 30 percent a year (compared with 4 percent in the U.S. and Europe).

Aerial Advertising

Airplanes pulling signs, skywriting, and branded blimps direct gazes upward to entertainment messages. Virgin Lightships rents small blimps to advertisers for around $200,000 per month. The Family Channel and NASCAR are frequent blimp users, receiving high brand recall for their advertising dollars.

Specialty Advertising

A huge business, specialty advertising uses clothing and all sorts of other products to display logos, brands, and company names. Useful products targeted at a specific audience create loyalty and stimulate recall for potential purchasers. Golf resorts, for instance,

Specialty advertising as a Chevrolet-logo watch.

▪▪▪▪▪▪▪▪▪▪▪   BOX 9-3   ▪▪▪▪▪▪▪▪▪

Focus on Nontraditional Advertising

ATTENTION-GETTING PROMOTIONS

Here are just a few examples of the many nontraditional forms of taking the message to the masses that have worked for experience marketers.

• To promote their new series, the History Channel gave diners at Greek restaurants brochures along with free salads on premiere day of *Alexander the Great.* Screenings in Atlanta, screenings at the Boston Greek Festival, and spot radio ads helped secure a 2.8 rating for the channel.

• The Mexican Tourism Board lured travelers to Mexico by putting a beach (complete with swim-suited models) inside Plexiglas trucks and placing them at chilly corners in New York, Chicago, Montreal, and Toronto, yielding 410,000 interactions.

• Verizon went into the take-out business by covering the exterior of boldly colored Chinese take-out cartons and handing them out to consumers at restaurants in dozens of markets across the U.S. Hundreds of thousands of containers were distributed at Chinese restaurants for their takeout food.

• Toy maker Hasbro sponsored an unconventional series of make-believe newspaper classified ads to promote a new version of Monopoly board game. For a few thousand dollars, Hasbro's agency, Arnold Worldwide, bought space in publications including *Deals on Wheels* and *Yacht Trader* that featured photographs of tokens from the new game that imitated the real houses, boats, and cars featured in corresponding classified ad sections. One ad read, "1935 classic. Just upgraded. Low mileage. Mint condition. Chrome finish. Runs like a dream in Monopoly 70th Anniversary Edition, the best board game money can buy. Go to monopoly70th.com."

SOURCE: Promomagazine.com, Sept. 9, 2005, and Stuart Elliott's advertising column in the *New York Times*, Nov. 25, 2005.

▪▪▪▪▪▪▪▪▪

inscribe balls, hats, shirts, and towels with the resort logo. Guests literally take the brand home and wear it as advertising for the place as well as for themselves (as evidence of having been in a special place).

Nontraditional Advertising

Balloons, restroom art, sidewalk messages, mouse pads, and roving characters are but a few of the attention-getting media designed to carry advertising messages to people in unconventional forms. Examples of such promotions include Jim Carrey's face on peel-off stickers attached to California apples promoting *Liar Liar,* entertainment brands embossed on the sails of *feluccas* (traditional sailboats) as they travel up the Nile River in Egypt, and actors dressed as butterflies who skate around New York to promote MSN.com. In Chicago, ads were attached to manhole covers to promote the Museum of Science and Industry's U-505 German submarine exhibit.

▪▪▪ Internet Advertising

Online advertising is on the rise due to consumers' changing preferences in media. A full 80 percent of Internet users are there because of the entertainment factor. Today's Internet advertising is *search-based,* eliminating the banner ads that used to clutter users' computer screens and be measured in click-through rates. ADWords, a pay-per-click advertising service provided by Google, allows advertisers to buy the "search" rights to words and terms related to their business. When consumers type in one of the keywords, the advertiser's URL appears beside the search results. Payment occurs when a user clicks on the ad. For only about 5 cents a click, advertisers are linked with prospective buyers.

Pop-ups, banner ads, interstitials, and browser placements promote global entertainment, venues, and attractions to the masses over the Internet. Because many forms of Web advertising have become irritating to consumers, new formats such as *advergaming* and *addressable media* are more user friendly. *Advergames,* brought to the Web by Orbitz to advertise its Internet travel service, are pop-ups with charm. Their first game, Pluck the Chicken, yielded a golden egg for expert feather pluckers and garnered Orbitz three times as many responses as their pop-ups without the game. Orbitz's rationale for advergames: Today, travel is a game, and Orbitz wants people to know that it is the way to win that game.[6]

Addressable media serve as communication vehicles for offers to consumers by e-mail. With the correct messages, this medium develops a more intimate relationship between entertainment providers and audiences. E-mail campaigns are most successful with permission—consumers who request communication are much more likely to pay attention to ads they have agreed to receive than to unsolicited or spam messages, which are often filtered out by junk-filtering software. Sent as ads and publicity, e-mail advertising is effective for specific communication objectives such as recognition or recall. Ads with streaming video provide audiences with previews of performances, movies, and special events, and are effective for getting audiences to the brand's Web site. E-mailed news releases distributed online to editors encourage immediate publicity.

Another form of Internet advertising, **rich media**, combines flash animations and streaming video and is predicted to grow faster than the search market. Similar to television advertising, rich media is easily coordinated with its video counterpart.[7] One example of rich media bundles television, film, and the Web. In conjunction with its "Be Cool" movie co-promotion and product integration, Cadillac launched a five-second-film contest that ultimately drew an amazing 2,648 entries and boosted Cadillac.com traffic 458 percent over a six-week period.[8]

A virtual version of the weekly local circulars usually found in newspapers gives national advertisers a way to reach online readers in local markets with promotions tied to neighborhood stores. PaperBoy, devised by a unit of Gannett called PointRoll,[9] is accessed through newspaper Web sites by using a mouse to roll over a branded message. The ad expands on the screen to become a miniature, animated version of a newspaper circular. Readers may check prices or products at other locations by entering another zip code.

Book publishers are using Internet and TV to draw buyers under 35. Aimed exclusively at the 18–34 crowd, Viacom Inc.'s Simon Spotlight Entertainment used cross-promotions with TV shows and bookstores as well as ads in college newspapers and radio stations giveaways to promote novels, books on poker, and Japanese *manga* titles.

Entertainment marketers add online advertising and Internet TV to their mixture because they recognize that managing their media strategy as a whole maximizes campaign effectiveness. If revenues are any indication of profits, Internet advertising will continue to be a key factor of integrated communications. For Internet advertising standards, check out the Interactive Advertising Bureau, iab.net, the organization that provides industry information for ad agencies, entertainment companies, and media buyers.

Viral Advertising

Viral advertising is a way to distribute commercial messages over the Internet by circulating individual e-mails through a desired audience—like a virus. By producing an entertaining and compelling commercial or spot, advertisers not only get viewers to watch, they get them to send the ad on to friends, who, in turn, send it to other friends. These pass along ads are spread by word of mouse: the goal is to make ads so funny, charming, sexy, or controversial that viewers e-mail or post them to Web sites.

Burger King has caught the virus. Using a Web site that hardly mentions the chain, BK's www.subservientchicken.com got an average of 10 hits a second in the first 18 months of its debut. How?

A person in a chicken costume standing in a dingy living room responds to typed commands like "tap dance," "take a bow," or "do push-ups." And the show keeps on going. According to the Interactive Advertising Bureau, the stealthy nature of viral ads on the Web appeals to young people and enthusiastic groups (such as car buffs) who don't mind killing a little time with ads they find compelling.[10]

New Line Cinema, Anheuser-Busch, and the Gap are creating commercials that live only on the Web. By invoking frogs that sing and dance about beer, a strip poker game for Victoria's Secret, and "confessions of a self-admitted pooper" for dog food, these advertisers find that entertainment is the best way to create attention for their products. The more crude and less like traditional ads these Web-only ads are, the more the audience seems to like them. To promote movies online, film trailers allow people to upload headshots and replace the movie stars' faces with their own.

Gap deployed a viral online promotion in 2005[11] called watchmechange.com that let viewers create characters who boogey to music as they take off and put on Gap clothes. What is different about Gap's approach was its lack of obvious advertising for the site and the inability for viewers to purchase clothes. Visitors could create an animated character and e-mail it to a friend, however, and that was the viral part. Hoping to stimulate pass-alongs, Gap used saucy Web characters that set a different tone from the retailer's traditional advertising campaigns, which featured musicians in TV commercials or celebrities in print ads.

Marketers like viral videos because of their low cost—advertisers pay only to produce the videos, not to buy airtime. Although there are no accurate measures in place, Web hits and interactions indicate that there are millions of watchers and participants for Internet advertising. Content traits outlawed elsewhere—sexual innuendo, juvenile humor, and crass language—may be the reasons viewers send the ads to others.

Despite the frowns some traditionalists may make, giving viewers advertising that is interesting is what works.

For instance, transmitters mounted on billboards are beaming out text messages asking people to watch video clips on their Bluetooth-equipped cell phones in UK train stations and shopping malls.[12] By asking first, advertisers avoid annoying consumers. One promotion introduced a new album from rock band Coldplay with 30-second spots of interviews and clips from their music videos, adding new clips to phone screens daily.

Blog Advertising

Using the Internet to generate awareness for a specific audience segment was particularly successful for Budget Rent-a-Car. Impax Marketing Group in Philadelphia created a $20,000 campaign for Budget using ads on 177 Web logs, or **blogs**. The ads directed readers to visit a Web site and enter a treasure hunt held for four weeks in 16 cities; cash prizes of $160,000 were awarded. Appropriate for Budget's young, tech-savvy audiences, these blogs featured cartoon characters urging readers to enter the contest. Ads appeared on popular sites such as Blurbomat, BoingBoing, CityRag, Daily Heights, DCist, Gothamist, IndieWier, and That Is Broken. Blogs were screened to cull inappropriate content and were successful enough for Budget to sign up for another blog campaign and contest in spring 2006. Preliminary counts indicated that blog pages where Budget ads appeared had 19.9 million impressions, which generated about 60,000 click-throughs to the Budget blog.[13] Read about how one movie studio used blogs to promote an upcoming film in the *Focus on* column below.

Social Networking

Social networking sites, such as MySpace, are part of marketing efforts to promote movies. Disney, for instance, publicized a contest on its own MySpace page as well as advertising on MySpace's front page. With more than 85 million users, MySpace draws advertising by offering "safe" content in official areas. Acquired by News Corp in 2005, MySpace is the most heavily trafficked sites on the Internet, and its teenage membership is very attractive to advertisers. In sections highlighted on the front page, the site offers articles books, movies, games, comedy, horoscopes, and links to related blogs elsewhere on MySpace. Advertisers spend tens of thousands of dollars to build "profile" pages to promote brands and entertainment experiences.[14]

In addition to advertising, social networks allow companies to learn from fans about what they like and what they are interested in. Social networks such as dig.com and del.icio.us allow visitors to search and rate blogs collected instantly from Internet-generated information. Agencies use these sites for advertising to thousands of visitors who receive and send information from the privacy of their virtual spaces.

Web Site Marketing

The Internet, especially Web sites, is a brand-message expander. Ads, publicity releases, and events can direct audiences to an entertainment brand's Web site for more information and possible ticket purchase. Creative, interactive, and fun Web sites enjoy frequent hits and extended stays. Interactivity is crucial; by using games and feedback vehicles, sites can be entertaining as well as informative and persuasive. By registering

▪▪▪▪▪▪▪▪▪▪   **BOX 9-4**   ▪▪▪▪▪▪▪▪▪▪

Focus on Blog Buzz

IS SPREADING THE WORD ENOUGH TO SELL A MOVIE?

In mid 2005, a running joke among Hollywood insiders said that New Line Cinema was making a movie called *Snakes on a Plane,* arguably the worst title in movie history. Entertainment blogger Jeremy Smith loved the name, however, and praised the studio for not being afraid to advertise "essential trashiness" with their title.

When the studio tried to change the title to *Pacific Air 121,* the film's star, Samuel L. Jackson, had a fit. "We're totally changing it back," he said in an e-mail, which Smith posted on media Web site Collider.com.

Called the "Everlasting Gobstopper of movie titles" by the film's screenwriter Josh Friedman, "snakes on a plane" became a Net buzz phrase, even taking on a meaning of its own. A full year before the $35 million (production cost) horror flick was released on Aug. 18, 2006, Web sites, video parodies, and proposed sequels (*Snakes on a Bus, Bears on a Train*) sprouted like mushrooms.

When New Line's vice president of new media marketing figured out the title had a bizarre zeitgeist effect with the Internet crowd, he decided to give fans what they wanted. In March, the studio spent five days re-shooting scenes to cater to the fortuitously erupting Internet fan base. To fuel the online mania, the company pitted fanatic against fanatic in a series of contests, including a song competition for a coveted spot on the film soundtrack, a chance to win a video-chat with Jackson, and a private screening for the winner and 100 friends.

New Line also added viral content to the Web, often masking clips on YouTube, a video-sharing site, and dedicating sites so they would appear fan-generated. On Aug. 3, the studio launched a Web campaign with digital audio company VaniTalk that allowed people to send friends personalized phone messages in Jackson's voice, which surpassed the 2 million message mark within two weeks.

Snakes on a Plane went from nearly discarded movie title to potentially industry-changing paradigm (in spite of mediocre box office sales). Here is how the year's Internet phenomenon progressed:

Aug. 14, 2005	Blogger Smith loves the title.
Aug. 17	Blogging in response, screenwriter Friedman coins an R-rated catchphrase the producers wrote into the script.
Aug. 23	*Snakes on a Plane* added to Urban Dictionary, an online slang dictionary compiled by users.
Oct. 3	First entry for *Snakes on a Plane* put up on Wikipedia.
Jan. 13, 2006	Wikipedia page edited 100 times (up to 1,600 revisions as of Aug. 16).
Feb. 19	First movie trailer spoof is posted on YouTube.com.
March 17	Film featured on Best Week Ever, VH1's pop-culture show.
June 22	New Line Cinema and social networking site TagWorld announce song contest winners. Of 500 entries, two songs are chosen for the soundtrack, one of which is added into the movie.

(Continued)

July 31	*Entertainment Weekly* hits newsstands with movie cover story.
Aug. 3	Samuel L. Jackson personalized message campaign launched. More than 100,000 messages are sent in the first 24 hours, before any advertising is done.
Aug. 4	Traditional marketing campaign of $20 million spent on movie prints and television advertising; no critic screenings were held.
Aug. 17	Film was No. 1 draw at the box office with opening screenings, yielding $1.4 million.
Aug. 21	Reported weekend box office revenues were $15.2 million, lower than the predicted $20–$30 million.

The lesson learned here? Internet interest in a movie doesn't necessarily translate into good box office sales.

SOURCE: Amanda Schupak's Hollywood column for Forbes.com, Aug. 17, 2006; and Sharon Waxman for the *New York Times,* Aug. 21, p. B1.

the site with multiple search engines, industry franchises gain visibility and site visits. As with other media, marketers must create awareness of the site, then give visitors a reason to go there.

A company's Web site is its consumer communication vehicle. It should reflect the look, feel, and content of the company and be coordinated in theme and content. The company, of course, must match service delivery with promises.

Web sites give entertainment providers a cost-effective way to distribute brand information and provide online ticketing to worldwide audiences. Theaters, events, destinations, and theme parks use online ticketing because it is fast, convenient, and easy. Audience members can print out tickets from home, along with information such as schedules, maps, and updates.

Measuring Online Activity

Web sites traditionally measure their traffic using click-through and unique visitor measures. For an entertainment venue to determine how well its Web site is performing, some of the following measurements, fairly standard in the industry, are used. The factors here relate to a performing arts venue or a movie Web site.

- *Lift:* How many additional ticket purchases were made by season ticket holders who visited the venue's Web site? What is the ratio between trailer hits (number of times site visitors clicked on a movie preview, or trailer) and box office attendance?
- *Conversion rate:* What percentage of nonsubscribers signed up for season tickets after visiting the Web site? How many trailer viewers purchased online tickets after viewing?
- *Brand knowledge and perception:* What percentage of site visitors thought more positively about the venue compared to those who did not visit the site?
- *Number of visits:* How many viewers hit, either through a search or a click on a URL, to visit the Web site? This number is useful in determining the level of

interest in performance schedules and movie plots. Hits and click-throughs, while creating brand awareness, may generate misleading measures with regard to actual purchase.

- *Length of time on site:* How long did viewers remain to explore the Web site? The longer viewers stay, the more likely they are to learn about the brand and purchase tickets.
- *Number and types of inquiries:* How many and what kind of responses were collected? Interaction and dialogue engage visitors and stimulate purchase.

▪▪▪ Product Placement as Entertainment

The practice of placing products in every medium has become so widespread that it has fostered in industry of its own. Movies themselves have become advertisements; product placement has turned the movie screen into a moving billboard.

Annual retainer fees paid to specialty placement agencies range from tens of thousands of dollars a year for an emerging brand to a few million a year for major automaker.[15] The Entertainment Marketing Association acts as a trade association for groups that have a vested interest in the practice of product placement. Advertisers include:

1. corporations looking to get their brands placed into entertainment vehicles.

2. studios and production companies seeking to defray costs with products "comped," or placed in their projects.

3. placement agencies.

Brands (product and place) are placed in at least five different ways. As

- silent props or *creative placements* (Kellogg's cornflakes on a kitchen pantry shelf or on a table during a breakfast scene).
- props that provide dimension to a scene, called *on-set placements* (Marlboro cigarettes to signify American male freedom).
- props that advance the plot, or *embedded placements* (BMW chase car for James Bond).
- props that star or *feature placement* (Caesar's Palace from *Rocky III,* or a geographic location that figures in the central plot of a program of film).
- *virtual placements* (outdoor boards seen in NBC's *Law & Order*); permits visual manipulations and allows for intra-brand comparisons.
- *in-game* advertising on X-Box and PlayStation video games (Coke logo in *SWAT 4,* updatable graphics in networked games such as *Anarchy Online*) where racing game players can test-drive a Porsche or outfit their characters in Rocawear's new fall line.[16]

Studies have shown that the more likeable the product's user (film star), the more likely the viewer is to remember that product. According to consumer memory authorities, the less overt the placement the more likely it is to be retained. Placements occur on television, in print, in music, in movies, in games, and even at staged settings.

Someone at Alcatraz, the island museum in San Francisco Bay that once housed a maximum-security prison, placed an empty package of Marlboro cigarettes in a cell that was designed to replicate an actual incarceration cubicle to reflect authenticity. No

▪▪▪▪▪▪▪▪▪▪ BOX 9-5 ▪▪▪▪▪▪▪▪▪▪

Focus on Ethics

PRODUCTS FOR THE POPE

Marketers seeking pontifical product placements were encouraged when, in 2006, the pope was spotted wearing Serengeti-branded sunglasses, carrying an Apple iPod, and wearing red loafers rumored to be made by Prada.

How far can religion be exploited for hyping a product? Using Benedict XVI's snazzy profile as encouragement, marketers see a papal association worth at least 100 times more than an A-list celebrity because the pontiff has a more devoted following. But unlike movie stars who can command huge sums for product endorsements, the pope, as moral and spiritual leader of more than one billion Catholics, endorses holiness and chastity, but not products.

That means companies have to hope the pontiff uses a product they have donated to him, then capitalize on a photograph showing him using or wearing the brand. But pursuing the pope-and-product juxtaposition poses risks. Companies and their brands have to be careful not to appear opportunistic or they risk backlash from pope followers.

Placement on such figures as the pope raises an enormous number of questions in terms of the ethics of each company, according to the research director of an international advertising-research firm. Ethical issues have not reduced the interest in papal brand placement, however.

Companies like to be associated with the pope because he is so lightly accessorized. The founder of Geox Spa, an Italian shoe company, was a friend of a papal spokesman, so following Benedict XVI's election in April 2005, Geox gave the spokesman several pairs of Uomo Light loafers as a present for the new pope. Although Geox didn't publicize the event, it was delighted when word got out. Apple's gift of a pencil-thin Nano engraved with "To His Holiness" and packed with Vatican Radio programming was considered a real coup. Natuzzi leather created the internal upholstery for a golf cart that GE gave the pope last year, and issued a joint news release to let people know about the vehicle, which is used only inside the Vatican gardens.

Volkswagen and BMW both jockeyed to replace the Mercedes as the next maker of the Pope Mobile, arguably the world's most visible sport-utility vehicle. Because, like the pope, BMW is "Bavarian made," the automaker hopes the pope will use the bulletproof X5 it donated to the Vatican in October 2005 for his next vehicle.

Mercedes Pope Mobile.

(Continued)

one will divulge whether the tobacco company paid for the placement, or whether park providers dressed the set using their own idea of what was an appropriate prop.

The next step in product placement, *product integration,* occurs when advertisers move from being clients to becoming partners and subsidizing program development and production costs. Integration is closer to *sponsorship,* where financial backers or sponsors get involved in tuning content to the goals of their brands, while making commitments to provide advertising support. Television programming is often a result of product integration.

A talent management agency in Beverly Hills merged with a brand-placement shop to facilitate access among their respective client bases. The talent agency clients include Leonardo DiCaprio, Cameron Diaz, Martin Scorsese, and Snoop Dogg. Citing "organic product integration efforts as the strategy to place clients" brands into films and TV programs, the firm helps talent firms break through the clutter of advertising with branded content. Other talent firms are merging their clients as well. Endeavor, which represents Adam Sandler, Matt Damon, and Drew Barrymore, works on behalf of American Express and AOL. William Morris agency, which represents Russell Crowe and Halle Berry, handles Anheuser-Busch, GM, and Saks Fifth Avenue. That merger involved getting Saks a key role in the movie *Shopgirl.* A partnership between ABC and MindShare (WPP Group) media was formed to develop content that offers WPP clients a deal to have their ad messages embedded into the programming.[17]

Digital technology has made it easy and inexpensive to dub product placements into overseas versions of the same movie.[18] Product dubbing is largely confined to still shots in which the brands are little more than props in the background. This technique was first used in 1993 action movie *Demolition Man.* PepsiCo bought a major role for its Taco Bell brand in the film's U.S. release, while its overseas version featured Pizza Hut, another PepsiCo brand. Refrigerator magnets were switched in *Spider-Man 2* from one touting Dr Pepper to another for Mirinda when the film moved beyond the U.S. Because foreign markets contribute as much as 60 percent of the box office take for most Hollywood pictures, the practice of tailoring product placements for international markets is a mainstay of a studio's global marketing campaign. By changing the can in someone's hand and from one brand to another, studios open up new avenues of revenue generation.

Most placement agreements are made 18 to 24 months before a film's release. Costing between $10,000 and $100,000 to dub a logo into a short scene, big-brand film promotion for Europe is one way to leverage films as promotional tools. To build international sales, a movie-marketing group, LA Office, hosted an international meeting of

---

▮ ▮ ▮ ▮ ▮ ▮ ▮ ▮ ▮ **BOX 9-6** ▮ ▮ ▮ ▮ ▮ ▮ ▮ ▮ ▮

Focus on Ethics

SELLING IN THE MOVIES

With advertising lamenting the difficulties of measuring the ROI of product placement, the film *Sideways* demonstrated impossible-to-ignore numbers on the powers of persuasion. Thanks to the main character's snobbish partialities, sales of pinot noir, traditionally an ignored varietal of wine, skyrocketed in the first month after the film's release, increasing 22 percent in the U.S. One wine brand, Blackstone Pinot Noir, saw sales increase by almost 150 percent after the film opened. The film's disparaging of merlot, on the other hand, had a negative effect on sales of that varietal. Additionally, the film increased tourism to California's wine region and drove business up 30 percent at The Hitching Post, a restaurant featured in the film. *Sideways,* a 2004 Oscar nominee, showed very measurable results for its placements.[19]

Stephen Spielberg's 2002 *Minority Report* is said to have compromised the merger of commerce and content.[20] More than 15 real-life sponsors reportedly paid more than $25 million— approximately a quarter of the futuristic film's budget—to attach themselves to the branded universe. *Minority's* star Tom Cruise was spoken to by a Lexus, used a Nokia phone, wore Reeboks, got splashed by an Aquafina billboard, and visited the Gap, and American Express revealed that he had been a member since 2037. Another example is footage from FedEx that covered approximately 80 percent of *Cast Away*'s budget in exchange for story-driving presence in the 2000 film.

So what is wrong with such blatant product placement? Opponents of advertising's "overbearing invasiveness" claim that we cannot escape the deep editorial influence brand sponsors foist on us. They assert that in the context of a commercial media landscape that demands higher profit margins with every merger, advertisers and studios, networks, publishers and music labels have too much control over what we watch, hear, and read.

What do you think?

1. Is your viewing experience compromised by the appearance of brands on the big screen? Why?
2. Should legislation be enacted to prohibit paid placement in fictional stories?
3. Can you make an argument for freedom of brand expression in all mediated content?

SOURCE: www.brandchannel.com/brandcameo_brands.asp, Sept. 12, 2005.

▮ ▮ ▮ ▮ ▮ ▮ ▮ ▮ ▮

---

brand marketers designed to help spur overseas product placement and promotion. You will find more examples of product placement in Chapter 14.

Sprint logos were replaced with Orange logos when the *Looney Tunes: Back in Action* film was sent to France. Likewise, when the character played by Lucy Liu in *Charlie's Angels: Full Throttle* shows her camera phone to U.S. audiences, Cingular's logo appears. When it is released overseas, however, viewers see a T-Mobil logo. In the same film, background billboards were changed to push picture-messaging. Radio promotions, contests, and DVD giveaways also accompanied the Angels film release in the UK.

▪▪▪ Sales Promotion, Merchandising, and Personal Selling

Sales promotion is a function that offers a tangible added value designed to motivate and accelerate a purchase response. Sales promotion is best used when sales are low, performances are nearing their completion, or new destinations are being introduced. Promotions can be directed at middlepeople (retailers and distributors) who *push* tickets on to their own customers, or directly to audience members themselves with a *pull* strategy. Performance, experience, and venue providers use both trade and consumer promotions to encourage purchase.

Trade Promotion

When targeting members of a distribution channel, marketers use a **push strategy** to motivate retailers—businesses that act as go-betweens among content providers and audiences—to promote branded entertainment products to their customers. Entertainment producers provide incentives to ticket distributors, such as Ticketmaster and Expedia, to promote their shows, venues, resorts, theme parks, performances, and concerts on retailers' Web sites.

Trade promotions are designed to encourage retailers to push entertainment products directly to audience members. These promotions include *bulk discounts* on tickets and *spiffs* as sales incentives for retailers. Other sales promotions for the trade include *incentive travel,* which rewards top producers with vacations. Carnival Cruise Lines, for example, conducted online sweeps entries for travel agents for each cruise booked using Visa, their advertising partner. Participating agencies sold 12 percent ($1.3 million) more than other agents.

Consumer Promotion

Marketers promote directly to audience members or ticket buyers with a **pull strategy**. Direct mail brochures announcing season performances is an example of a consumer promotion that pulls audience members into a venue. Multiple-ticket discounts and premier seating premiums function as incentives for audiences to subscribe or purchase tickets.

Coupons, two-for-ones, premiums, and contests are the primary vehicles of promotions for experiential brands. The Safeway grocery chain gave out discount tickets to Disney's California Adventure when it first opened to help stimulate traffic among locals. Subscribers and season ticket holders often receive bonuses (free parking or a special lounge area) as audience member promotions.

Sales promotion tools used in the entertainment industry are similar to consumer product promotional tools. Sweepstakes and games are especially popular for promoting experiences and often involve tie-ins with product brands with the same target audience. Here are some examples.

• *Premiums* are free items given with purchase to reward a buying behavior. Season subscribers to an outdoor concert series may receive a branded stadium seat, or frequent hotel guests are presented with logo-embossed robes as a thank-you for purchasing or booking. Movie figures, included in fast-food lunches reward your family trip through the drive-thru as they encourage you to see the film. Such premiums often

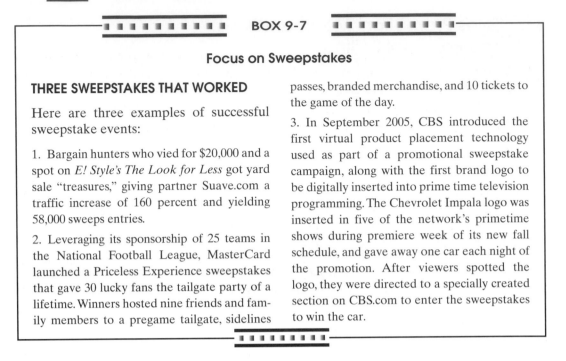

BOX 9-7

Focus on Sweepstakes

THREE SWEEPSTAKES THAT WORKED

Here are three examples of successful sweepstake events:

1. Bargain hunters who vied for $20,000 and a spot on *E! Style's The Look for Less* got yard sale "treasures," giving partner Suave.com a traffic increase of 160 percent and yielding 58,000 sweeps entries.

2. Leveraging its sponsorship of 25 teams in the National Football League, MasterCard launched a Priceless Experience sweepstakes that gave 30 lucky fans the tailgate party of a lifetime. Winners hosted nine friends and family members to a pregame tailgate, sidelines passes, branded merchandise, and 10 tickets to the game of the day.

3. In September 2005, CBS introduced the first virtual product placement technology used as part of a promotional sweepstake campaign, along with the first brand logo to be digitally inserted into prime time television programming. The Chevrolet Impala logo was inserted in five of the network's primetime shows during premiere week of its new fall schedule, and gave away one car each night of the promotion. After viewers spotted the logo, they were directed to a specially created section on CBS.com to enter the sweepstakes to win the car.

become collectables, encouraging multiple purchases. Premiums are successful if they (1) appeal to the target audience, (2) have perceived value, (3) are relevant to the brand image, and (4) create a buying response.

• *Specialties* are given free to the customer but not intended to stimulate immediate buying behavior. Typically, T-shirts, visors, pencils, and mugs are provided to audience members to keep the brand's name top-of-mind. Usually inexpensive and distributed to a mass audience, specialty items can also be higher priced gifts to valued customers.

• *Coupons* are certificates that offer a stated price reduction on a specific performance or attraction. Coupons can be paired with most consumer goods. With the purchase of $100 in groceries, supermarkets may give out coupons good for $3 when redeemed at a local theme park. Off-season hotel sales can be stimulated with coupons for breakfast with a room booking, or reduced admission at a nearby museum. Coupons are delivered in stores, newspapers, magazines, and electronically online.

• *Sweepstakes,* or drawings, are used by vacation packagers in conjunction with radio stations to to draw attention to the brand. Hotels, theme parks, and motion picture studios commonly use sweepstakes. For example, film promoters may offer the winner an evening with the film's star or a trip to Hollywood for the premiere showing.

• *Games* are popular for use with entertainment attractions because they are conducted over an extended period of time and keep the branded experience alive after the game ends. Usually played on the Internet, marketers use film characters to create games for promoting multiple-sequence films, such as *Harry Potter* and *Star Wars*. For a mystery game kudo, Hallmark Cards seeded clues on-air, online, and through cell phones and e-mail that let viewers solve film "crimes" for a weekly prize of $10,000.

The company's Web site ratings jumped 82 percent for the quarter after the game went online.

• *Contests* require skill and involve a brand. Guessing the weight of Shamu at Sea World encourages participants to become involved with ocean mammals, while promoting the park.

Price reductions, rebates, and sampling are product-specific, consumer-oriented promotions that have little value for experiential products. Cross-promotions and tie-in promotions are more applicable to entertainment marketing.

Cross-Promotion

Cross-promotion is the promotion of two or more brands together, such as a beverage and a movie, that allows the brands to share promotional costs while benefiting from each other's image. CBS and Campbell soup produced a joint print promotion that included the network's fall lineup schedule on the back of the piece and inside pages devoted to various shows and corresponding meal suggestions. Campbell aligned its soups with different shows, such as pairing the *NFL Today* show with its hearty line.

If action figures can help sell film to kids, then it follows that sake-infused oils would help promote a film to adults. At least that's what Sony Pictures Entertainment prepared for *Memoirs of a Geisha* to adults by partnering with Banana Republic, Bath & Body Works, and Fresh, Inc.'s beauty products.[21] Geisha themed items such as kimono-inspired dresses and oils, lotions, and body scrubs inspired by Japanese beauty rituals were developed especially for the partnership.

Such movie promotion deals offer two-way advantages. Consumer-good companies benefit from brand exposure without paying a licensing fee, and studios get a compelling chance to put the movie's name and image into heavily trafficked retail spaces.

Tie-In Promotion

Tie-in promotions link two products through advertising and in-store merchandising and typically occur between movies (the film's characters) and fast-food restaurants. Electronics marketer JVC acted as exclusive sponsor *Lord of the Rings*. Action figures were used as premiums in 10 thousand Burger King restaurants. Co-branded DVD players and VCR packages by JVC were packaged with movie trailers and behind-the-scenes footage. Tie-ins benefit both partners in different ways. Entertainment characters and stars provide glamour to otherwise bland packaging, and the wide product distribution heightens the awareness of the experience.

Partnerships developed between organizations are designed to promote both brands. Most tie-in promotions occur during summers and holiday seasons. Universal Pictures' *The Grinch Who Stole Christmas*, for instance, was partnered with Sprite, Nabisco, Hershey, and Wendy's on some $85 million in marketing support. In addition, the partners made an agreement with the U.S. Postal Service to mark more than 6 billion pieces of holiday mail with cancellation stamps from the Grinch's fictional town of Whoville.[22]

Loyalty Programs

Keeping audience members coming back is best achieved by rewarding them with more of what they purchased—in other words, more of the same experiences. Hotels

BOX 9-8

A Closer Look at Promotional Tie-Ins

DREAMWORKS' EXTRAVAGANZA

Some promotions use all available promotional tactics to create a blanket strategy that works with specific audience segments. The film-to-disk promotion described here is an example of one such marketing effort.

To kick off their campaign for launching the movie *Madagascar* on DVD and VHS, DreamWorks developed a five-month-long promotional campaign supported by a host of packaged good companies. The tie-ins worked for the brands and the home entertainment division because the animated feature targeted families with children. The film property gave the package goods companies a fresh face, while the companies' tie-in allowed DreamWorks to extend its marketing reach beyond a traditional media buy, to have a presence in a variety of locations, and to extend its brand.

Madagascar tells the tale of four animals living in New York's Central Park Zoo who are taken from their home to the exotic island of Madagascar. Once on the island, the city-dwelling New Yorkers must learn to survive. The *Madagascar* DVD includes bonus material with more than 100 interactive games and activities. Both DVD and VHS versions retailed for $19.95. Here is an overview of the tie-in products and brands that supported the effort.

• In the lead up to release, packaged goods makers Betty Crocker, Pringles, and Pringles Prints, Peter Pan peanut butter, Chef Boyardee, and Crunch 'n' Munch themed their packaging with *Madagascar* images. Some 150,000 cans of Chef Boyardee and 500,000 jars of Peter Pan peanut butter included *Madagascar* temporary tattoos. Crunch 'n' Munch featured mail-in offers for a *Madagascar* "adventure ball."

• Further driving awareness at the grocery store shelf, Hunts Ketchup added *Madagascar* bottleneck hangers to select products. The bottles included a mail-in premium offer for a *Madagascar* plate. The same month, *Madagascar*-themed stickers were added to some 900,000 packages of Hunt's Snack Pack pudding.

• Kid Cuisine entered the mix by theming five million packages of its frozen meals with *Madagascar* characters. Specially marked packages included a mail-in rebate for $4 off the purchase of the *Madagascar* DVD with the purchase of five Kid Cuisine meals.

• TV ads and Internet materials supported the promotion. Kids voted on their favorite *Madagascar* character, got free *Madagascar* downloads, and registered to win a free *Madagascar Animal Trivia* DVD game by logging on to Kidcuisine.com.

• Three million packages of Orville Redenbacher microwave popcorn offered a $4 rebate off the *Madagascar* DVD. Consumers who bought Kid Cuisine and Orville Redenbacher products and mailed in the rebates jointly received an $8 rebate.

• Applebee's themed four million cups and kids menu activity books at participating restaurants in the U.S. and Canada. In addition, select restaurants supported the promotion with in-restaurant point-of-purchase materials.

What do you think?

1. How were the promotional tactics coordinated to create an overall splash for the film's release?
2. Would similar tactics work with a film for adults? What changes would be necessary?
3. Was the tie-in mutually beneficial? Why?
4. Did they miss any avenue you can suggest?

SOURCE: Amy Johannes, PROMO Xtra, promotionmagazine.com, Aug 25, 2005.

reward their frequent guests with extra night stays or nights at another facility of the same brand to keep occupancy rates high with a minimum of promotional expense. Designed to build repeat usage, loyalty programs are the preferred promotions of theme parks, attractions, casinos, and resorts.

Merchandising and Licensing

Merchandising involves creating or licensing others to produce merchandise that is based on a movie, performance, destination, or character. Disney, master of merchandising, produced 186 items associated with *The Lion King* movie. Brands, such as Batman or Rugrats, are lumps of content that can be exploited through film, broadcast and cable television, publishing, theme parks, music, Internet, and merchandising. Movie soundtracks are another form of profitable merchandising. Most entertainment content and experience providers are heavy users of merchandising, which often makes up for box office losses. Merchandising and licensing are covered more extensively in Chapters 8 and 14.

Personal Selling

Face-to-face presentation by a company's representative builds customer relationships and completes sales. Group sales for performances and incentive travel companies make use of personal selling to optimize volume and guarantee box office or tour success. Employees of hotels and resorts also act as personal sales representatives by referring guests to house services and sponsored events. Performance subscriptions are commonly solicited by phone, a process that's also an aspect of personal sales. Personal interaction with audience members is a vital component of many promotional mix strategies. Discussed as a tourist service, personal selling is presented in Chapter 12.

▪▪▪ Public and Media Relations

For entertainment companies, public relations are invoked to create good and a positive image between the organization and its stakeholders. Public relations is one of the most important parts of the promotion mix for entertainment marketers. Serving as a source of information about the organization, *public relations,* or PR, is a system that uses a variety of media to bring news and attention to a product, service, or experience. Marketing PR and brand publicity are the functions most relevant to the entertainment industry. "The deliberate, planned and sustained effort to establish and maintain mutual understanding between and organization and its public" is the definition provided by the Institute of Public Relations. An entertainment company's *publics* include the following groups, among others:

- the community
- employees
- government
- financial community
- distributors
- audience members
- opinion leaders
- media

When connected to entertainment promotion, PR employs a variety of tactics to manage audience perceptions about an experience. These aspects of the public relations operate separately and in tandem to maintain positive communication about a specific celebrity, venue, performance, attraction, or destination. Here are the major components of public relations activities.

Media Relations

One of the most important activities of PR is to use non-paid media messages to deliver persuasive branded communications to potential and current audience members. No entertainment experience can survive on paid advertising alone. A well-placed editorial will catch the attention of potential and current audiences and provide objective reviews. News releases and feature stories delivered to newspaper editors and broadcast station producers can result in more positive exposure than advertising, and for far less cash.

A good publicist—one who has an inside track to media gatekeepers—is worth her weight in gold. Publicity supports brand communication and promotion directed at prospects. All experiences require some amount of buzz, a hard-to-define quality that essentially says, "people are hearing about your product," and buzz is developed and dispatched through constant publicity and media coverage. PR objectives seek to build awareness and visibility, create or change attitudes, create buzz, influence opinion leaders, and generate a sense of involvement for audiences and other publics.

The value of public relations is the perception that it provides branded entertainment with third-party endorsements. Audiences believe that communications presented by a media source that has no vested interest in the success or failure of the brand is more credible than paid advertising. The success of many performances comes from positive advance reviews, feature stories, and news segments prior to their debuts.

To receive timely and frequent coverage, entertainment PR professionals must maintain positive relationships with the media. Paid space and time guarantees advertising messages; not so with PR. The only way to ensure coverage of an event or news item is to deliver it personally to a reporter who covers the entertainment or travel beat, an editor of the features section of major newspapers or magazines, or a television producer of entertainment news.

Courting reporters, editors, and producers involves providing timely, credible, and interesting news. Media professionals don't want to hear a story they could have gleaned from an ad. Creative and innovative news ideas must be crafted for the audience of each medium and presented to the gatekeeper (reporter, etc.) in a way that demonstrates the benefit of delivering the story. Media relations work well when relationships are built on honest communications.

Publicity

Publicity is editorial written about a brand—it is being mentioned in print or over the airwaves. Publicity's strength is its ability to reach audiences that are difficult to reach with advertising, such as business professionals and groups with limited exposure to traditional commercial messages. Publicity, especially over the Internet, is very cost

- *News release*—print, visual, or broadcast news delivered by a franchise or corporation
- *News kit*—packet of information with photos, histories, biographies, feature stories, and a fact sheet about an attraction, event, or destination
- *Press conference*—event where corporate officials meet with media with a major news story
- *Media tour*—scheduled live appearances to promote a film, performance, or experience
- *Media event*—special event to generate coverage and involve company publics
- *Speeches*—ghostwritten statements provided for media use
- *Pitch*—story idea proposal for an editor or reporter
- *Fact sheet*—information to provide background data for media use in story preparation

effective and is perceived to work better than advertising in many cases. For instance, moviegoers are more likely to go to a reviewer's Web site than to respond to a pop-up ad on that film. Motion picture studios provide media with a steady flow of quotes, research data, photographs, trailers, interviews, and access to directors in order to generate positive coverage of a film in advance of the film's release. Tourism bureaus dispatch segments to travel channels, distribute feature articles to major newspapers, and offer free trips for editors to experience the city for themselves, which is standard practice in the industry. Publicity tools used by PR practitioners are listed in Exhibit 9.2.

Again, you will find that public relations are an essential element of all marketing plans for entertainment-based product promotion, *especially when your news has value.*

Creating Buzz

Buzz is the natural, authentic version of hype—the CNN of the street. Hype is intended to promote, whereas buzz often is truthful about an entertainment product and therefore higher in credibility. And while hype takes time, effort, and expense to circulate, buzz can move like wildfire through a community. A PR professional's role is to generate buzz, not create hype, surrounding a new entertainment innovation.

Corporate PR

PR is used to develop positive relationships between a brand (film, performance, destination, or attraction) and its audience. Typical corporate PR functions include:

- *Corporate communications,* which focus on identity, reputation management, and management counseling. Publicity functions include monitoring public opinion, addressing community concerns, informing public officials and regulatory agencies, and engaging in activities with the industry itself. Hotel chains, media conglomerates, and entertainment franchises consider this an important function for maintaining brand equity.

▪▪▪▪▪▪▪▪▪▪ **BOX 9-9** ▪▪▪▪▪▪▪▪▪▪

Focus on Philanthropy

SONY SUPPORTS LOCAL COMMUNITIES

Sony Pictures Entertainment is a major supporter of arts education and community involvement, and the spirit of philanthropy is imbedded in the culture of Sony in America. Every philanthropic activity provides countless opportunities for feature stories that work to maintain Sony's positive brand image.

Listed below are a few of the company's philanthropic associations with arts education, cultural organizations, film festivals, health and human services, and community outreach.

Arts educational program: New York University's Tisch School of the Arts, among others, has received generous support from Sony. The school is one of the nation's leading centers of undergraduate and graduate study in the performing and media arts.

Museums and other cultural organizations: American Film Institute, American Museum of Natural History, Holocaust Museum, John F. Kennedy Center for the Performing Arts, Metropolitan Museum of Art, Muhammad Ali Center, El Museo del Barrio, and Smithsonian Institution are a few organizations that have all benefited from Sony's support.

Film festivals and awards shows: Los Angeles Asian Pacific Film & Video Festival, Los Angeles Latino International Film Festival, and OUTFEST have received help from Sony.

Health and human services: Support from Sony has gone to Recording for the Blind and Dyslexic and the T. J. Martell Foundation, which is dedicated to raising funds for the initial and ongoing research into the treatments and cures of leukemia, cancer, and AIDS.

Civic and community outreach: The company has a program that matches the donation employees make to the nonprofit organizations of their choice.

SOURCE: sony.com/philanthropy.

▪▪▪▪▪▪▪▪▪

- *Employee relations,* which are internal communication programs to build morale, acculturate, and reward positive activities. Theme parks like Disneyland rely heavily on their employee community for delivering favorable experiences to park visitors.

- *Investor relations,* which provide information programs for investors and members of the industry's financial community. This function is especially important for the motion picture industry, which secures its funding through venture capitalists and private individuals.

- *Philanthropy,* which is comprised of corporate giving and nonprofit or cause sponsorship has become part of corporate brand identity. Giving back to the community is not only good business, it is an excellent marketing strategy. By becoming advocates for medical research, educational scholarships, public broadcasting, or curing disease, entertainment corporations bring attention to another side of their enterprise—a caring presence in the community at large. Marketers should never lose sight of the "greater good" philosophy when developing a promotional campaign.

■ ■ ■ ■ ■ ■ ■ ■ ■ ■ **BOX 9-10** ■ ■ ■ ■ ■ ■ ■ ■ ■ ■

A Closer Look at Publicity Stunts

GOLDENPALACE ONLINE CASINO

Bodacious brand-building is about performing crazy acts just to generate publicity. GoldenPalace online casino bought a haunted walking cane ($65,000), a collection of Michael Jackson puppets ($15,099), and the privilege of being able to officially name a new monkey species after the site—*caallicebus aureipalatii* ($650,000) The biggest and most recent purchase was a "Pope Mobile," a VW Golf formerly owned by Pope Benedict XVI on eBay for a mere $244,591.

An admittedly crass marketing strategy, bidding for bizarre items is effective in an industry where advertising is controversial. Because online gambling is considered illegal, GoldenPalace's $20 million budget still runs plenty of traditional and online ads, but PR stunts are a cheaper and better way to build name recognition. Press mentions regarding its eBay purchases are equivalent to at least $30 million in ads. Plus, middle-weight boxer Bernard Hopkins was paid to stamp the GoldenPalace brand on his

back for a Madison Square Garden bout, resulting in multiple lawsuits—which were covered by News Corp-owned media outlets such as *USA Today* and *The Howard Stern Show,* of course.

Promotion strategy for Golden-Palace, one of the world's top three gambling sites, has also include hiring people to streak at over one thousand sporting events, from Wimbledon to Pamplona's running of the bulls, all with the Web site's name on their bodies. After a man with the brand's URL streaked through half-time of the 2004 Super Bowl, visits to the site jumped by 380 percent. With 2.4 million U.S. visitors per month to the site, revenue—upward of $80 million—is growing at 5 percent a month.

What do you think?

1. When buying eBay's odd objects loses its luster, what can GoldenPalace do to trump itself?

2. What are the merits and pitfalls of using publicity stunts as the main marketing strategy?

SOURCE: Elizabeth Esfahani, *Business 2.0,* July, 2005, p. 60.

■ ■ ■ ■ ■ ■ ■ ■ ■

Crisis Management with PR

One function of PR that often goes unheralded is the important task of managing crises. It is vital, for instance, for theme parks to have and execute a crisis plan when a patron is injured or killed on a ride, or for venues to use in anticipation of uncontrollable crowd actions, or on a large scale for destination cities should they be struck by a natural disaster or terrorist attack. When Magic Mountain roller coaster injured a rider, Disney had a plan in place for interfacing with the media to report the status of the rider's health and the measures being taken to ensure the ride's safety.

Most recently, Nielson Media Research, the television ratings arbiter, spent hundreds of thousands of dollars fighting groups objecting to their ratings system, which they say has undercounted minority viewers and hindered the development of shows geared to those audiences. News Corporation, whose Fox television stations produce shows for special audiences, mounted a campaign to determine why people meters were failing to register the viewing preferences of many black and Hispanic homes. Nielson has paid lobbying firms to coordinate a campaign to reach out to blacks and Hispanics, including the sponsorship of the annual Real Men Cook, a charity devoted to encouraging African-American men to stay involved with their families.[23] This is a type of crisis that highlights the need for entertainment corporations and franchises to anticipate and arm themselves against negative publicity with a effective plan.

▮▮▮ Event Marketing and Sponsorship

Event management and sponsorship activities, sometimes the purview of public relations efforts, work because they are experiential rather than mediated. Both activities connect a brand with audience members. Because consumers prefer to purchase lifestyles, experience, and emotions rather than products, events and sponsorship opportunities provide a large component of the promotion mix for entertainment companies.

Event Marketing

Event marketing is a fast-growing, high-profile industry and a very successful marketing strategy. Events provide a promotional occasion that attracts and involves the brand's target audience. Billions of dollars pour into sponsorships of entertainment, sports, venues, and attractions annually. Events marketing integrates the corporate sponsorship of an event with a whole range of marketing elements such as advertising, sales promotion, and public relations for these reasons:[24]

• Companies can break through the advertising clutter by creating a brand image associated with an event.

• Both the event and the brand profit from the pairing a financial partnership with an advertising budget and added leverage to sell tickets.

• Sponsorship allows for profitable, "ownable" territories that can be leveraged, catering to audience members who purchase experiences. For instance, John Hancock Insurance "owns" the Boston Marathon sponsorship.

Event marketing offers companies the flexibility to reach specific geographic and demographic audiences for a depth of exposure. Important considerations are event selection, return on investment, terms of agreement, marketing integration, execution, and results. You must make certain that the expenses incurred in presenting an event will generate enough revenue to turn a profit.

Companies spent an estimated $166 billion on event marketing in 2004, up 9 percent from the previous year, and signs are strong that marketers are committed to events: Companies earmarked an average 25 percent of their 2005 budgets for event marketing, up from 10.8 percent last year, according to PROMO's survey of event marketing executives. Media and entertainment promotions lend themselves to local events for creating attention and media coverage.

Savvy product promoters say that the right combination of persistent public relations and event creativity can deliver national—even global—results from a local event. In August 2005, the New York-based Grand Central Marketing set up a temporary, or pop-up (prefabricated), store near the corner of 42nd Street and 5th Avenue in Manhattan to introduce Meow Mix Wet Food Pouches. The boutique and dining establishment for cats and their human friends spurred news reports in England, Japan, Brazil, South Africa, and Australia, to name a few. The story even got a mention from nationally syndicated shock-jock Howard Stern and video clips allegedly appeared on Al Jazeera, the Arab TV network. Not bad for a four-day event that was extended for an additional week and received 3,000 live visitors daily.

Media entertainment marketers also use local events in their mix. To promote its fall series *Three Wishes,* NBC played the role of fairy godmother to boost viewership. During the week of Sept. 12, the network traveled to 15 markets and granted three wishes—two at various retailers and one at a local charity in each market. NBC surprised shoppers and restaurant patrons by picking up the tab at select retailers, including grocery stores and restaurants. The campaign was part of NBC's newest grassroots effort to reach consumers in an engaging way and create buzz around a new series. As part of the campaign, NBC paid retailers with stickered $1 bills, which cashiers distributed to customers with their change. The sticker was intended to drive recipients to a *Three Wishes* section on the NBC Web site and encourage consumers to use the marked dollars to fulfill another person's wish to coincide with the show's theme. Following the campaign, NBC tracked how consumers used their *Three Wishes* dollars by asking consumers on its Web site how they received the dollars and how they used them to grant someone else's wish. Input could be used for another network promotion.

Across gender, age, and ethnicity, audience members indicate that experiential marketing is more likely to influence both consideration to purchase tickets and actual ticket purchase than other forms of marketing tested. Events engage audiences, and for that reason alone justify their existence.

Sponsorship

Sponsorships are always financially motivated: an organization or individual trades financial support for publicity and mutually beneficial association. Sponsorships add value and differentiate brands by developing unique associations. Events, sports teams, celebrities, entertainment venues, and causes lend themselves to sponsorship activities.

Entertainment brands that serve as event sponsors display their brand and logo, target a self-selected audience, create awareness, improve brand image, encourage purchase, and achieve product mentions in media coverage of the activity.

Obtaining financial support by providing branded placement has become the promotion of choice for both product and experience providers. Sporting events prominently display beverage logos, and special events provide a multitude of exposure opportunities. Auto racing and fan conventions provide the most lucrative venues for brand placement

NASCAR, the granddaddy of sponsorship opportunity, has soaring TV ratings, flowing corporate money, and exploding crowds—which is why entertainment companies are lining up to get logos placed on cars. With 84 television cameras on a 2.5-mile track, no aspect of the 43-car, 400-mile race escapes viewers. Beginning with a two-day tailgate party, the Indy 500 race draws a quarter of a million fans to the track of commerce.

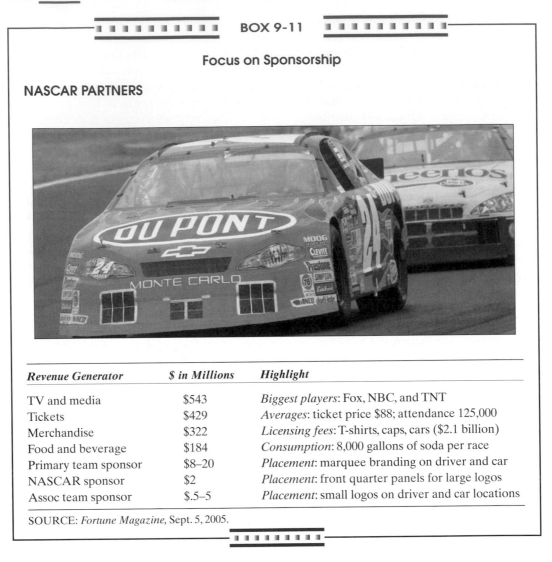

BOX 9-11

Focus on Sponsorship

NASCAR PARTNERS

Revenue Generator	$ in Millions	Highlight
TV and media	$543	*Biggest players*: Fox, NBC, and TNT
Tickets	$429	*Averages*: ticket price $88; attendance 125,000
Merchandise	$322	*Licensing fees*: T-shirts, caps, cars ($2.1 billion)
Food and beverage	$184	*Consumption*: 8,000 gallons of soda per race
Primary team sponsor	$8–20	*Placement*: marquee branding on driver and car
NASCAR sponsor	$2	*Placement*: front quarter panels for large logos
Assoc team sponsor	$.5–5	*Placement*: small logos on driver and car locations

SOURCE: *Fortune Magazine,* Sept. 5, 2005.

Racetracks have become profitable commercial venues and are the second most-watched sport on TV after pro football. The media-savvy, fan-friendly drivers are marketing machines, creating a total corporate sponsorship revenue of $1.5 billion in 2004.[25]

NASCAR's goal is one film a year with a stock-car related plot (*Herbie: Fully Loaded* and *Talladega Nights* are two examples) and TV placements (*West Wing* in 2004). Most fans appreciate this "post-modern automotive performance art" and reward sponsors with their product loyalty.

Special event sponsorship participations take place at many levels, as illustrated by a call for sponsors from the presenters of the Star Wars Celebration III, held in April 2005 at the Indiana Convention Center. This four-day fan event celebrated the release of *Revenge of the Sith.* Event presenters Lucasfilms Ltd. and the Official Star Wars Fan Club guarantee media coverage and offer sponsors the opportunity to increase brand

▮▮▮▮▮▮▮▮▮▮ **BOX 9-12** ▮▮▮▮▮▮▮▮▮▮

Focus on Careers

PROFILE OF AN ADVERTISING ACCOUNT EXECUTIVE

After receiving a scholarship from the Lifeguard Foundation toward his college education, Matt Smart surfed right into a job as account coordinator for Team One Advertising. Of course, he graduated first—from Cal Poly State University in San Louis Obispo, California—as a journalism major, knowing he wanted to write for a living. But instead of writing for a newspaper, Smart ended up writing advertising copy.

He first served as account coordinator for the Lexus Dealer Association, then as an assistant account executive for Lexus National and Lexus Collateral. As a key player in the development of "MY '05 Brand" television and print advertising for Lexus, Smart created and presented the campaign's advertising analysis, dealership displays, fliers, and special edition posters. Smart was also an account executive for the Ritz-Carlton, in charge of creative solutions for North East and South East properties.

To learn about the advertising business, Smart attended the Los Angeles Advertising Agencies Association's Advertising University, and a year later, completed a program at the Institute of Advanced Advertising Studies presented by the American Association of Advertising Agencies. Currently, he is working toward his M.A. degree in Communications. "The best part of my job is traveling and being able to see interesting places and meet fascinating people," says Smart.

IN HIS WORDS . . .

Planning for Disaster

Last year, in preparation for a big new client presentation in Maryland, our team planned out how we were going to get all the presentation materials to the hotel. We packaged it off and sent it UPS to the hotel our executives were staying at for next-day delivery. The executives boarded the plane, landed, and checked in to the hotel. No meeting materials had arrived. And they never arrived. The plane with our materials was grounded for mechanical issues. We asked our account coordinator, who was in her second day on the job, to fly to Washington, D.C., on a red-eye and carry the new materials to the director at her hotel near the Capitol. The entire day was used to create new materials. With 45 minutes to spare, every material had been recreated. Such moments of disaster are really opportunities for major success. Those hours at work from the moment we found out our materials were not going

(Continued)

to arrive to the moment they were delivered into the hands of our director were filled with tremendous team work and camaraderie. That was exciting.

Getting Ahead

Go the extra mile. Get the job done. Exceed expectations.

Many people in today's workforce are there to cover the expenses of life.

Find what you enjoy doing and you will have an easier time succeeding at it.

It is important to approach assignments with a lot of humility. You will be asked to do things that you know your supervisor can do. You are right. But that isn't the point. It is your turn to do it. And do it again. And again. That is why they call it work. That is why you get paid for it.

loyalty and create a high level of national awareness and visibility. Presenters were offered a variety of *sponsorship packages* from which to choose:

- Presenting Sponsor
- "Brought to You By" Sponsor
- Cosponsor
- Product Sponsor
- Service Sponsor
- Contributing Sponsor
- Special Event Sponsor—A sampling of opportunities including Costume Contest, Jedi Training Academy, Star Wars Collectibles, Panels & Auction
- Hotel
- Concessions
- Promotional Partner

Each level of sponsorship offered exposure, media coverage, brochure placement, banners, PR opportunities, and so forth. Solicitation began a year in advance and required months of planning and coordination.

FINALLY: LET'S SUM UP ▮▮▮▮▮▮▮

Promotional strategies are not simply a recipe for mixing and matching random tactics; they are carefully coordinated efforts to deliver timely and persuasive messages in a variety of strategically placed locations. While budgets may dictate the extent to which mass media and sponsorships are invoked, you can create effective yet economic campaigns with public relations and nontraditional or viral advertising. By understanding an audience's habits and desires, you can deliver behavior-changing messages that result in high box office receipts and profitable attendance.

GOT IT? LET'S REVIEW ▮▮▮▮▮▮▮

Here are the important points from this chapter on integrating promotional elements:

- Place-based and out-of-home media bring performance messages directly to consumers where they eat, shop, and travel. Nontraditional advertising puts messages where they are not expected to be, reaching audiences almost anywhere.
- Viral, online, and Web site marketing provide invaluable opportunities for marketing performance, venues, media, destinations, and resorts.

- Direct marketing takes advantage of customer lists to solicit subscription renewals and sell tickets to performance audiences.
- Product placement not only puts products into films, it also promotes venues and destinations that appear in movies.
- Sales promotions, including cross-promotions and tie-ins, link brand constellations or brand pairs to consumer needs and stimulate purchase.
- Public relations tactics use mass media to create buzz for entertainment experiences. Sponsorships and event marketing provide entertainment brands with numerous opportunities to reach audience niche markets.

NOW TRY THIS ▮▮▮▮▮▮▮

1. Locate a specialty promotions company on the Internet and identify creative ways in which they deliver nontraditional messages. Which ones are relevant for entertainment marketing?
2. Visit the NASCAR Web site as a potential advertiser and explore the variety of opportunities to expose a particular entertainment brand for under $100,000. What do the opportunities suggest with regard to budgeting and company size?
3. Peruse the calendar or entertainment section of your local newspaper. How much of what appears has been placed there by public relations efforts (features, reviews)? Advertising efforts (paid display)? Which element offers readers the most persuasive messages? Why?
4. Check out the *Wall Street Journal's* update on the most-placed products in media. Is Apple still in the top 10? What does this say about placement as a marketing tactic?

QUESTIONS: LET'S REVIEW ▮▮▮▮▮▮▮

1. Of the many product placement opportunities discussed in this and previous chapters, which method is the fastest growing and receives the least amount of consumer resistance? Why?
2. How do sales promotions differ from loyalty programs? Aside from hotels and airlines, what entertainment experiences might benefit from loyalty programs? How would they be administered?
3. If hotel guests at an upscale resort became infected with an airborne virus that made news headlines and resulted in hotel evacuation, how would you handle the crisis? What PR tactics would make most sense for recouping occupancy rates?
4. How do a sponsorship and an event differ in their approach to branding entertainment? Which provides the best opportunity for television or movie promotion?

MORE TO READ ▮▮▮▮▮▮▮

Scott Donaton. *Madison & Vine: Why Entertainment & Advertising Industries Must Converge to Survive.* New York: McGraw-Hill, 2004.

Mary-Lou Galican, ed. *Handbook of Product Placement in the Mass Media.* New York: Best Business Books, 2004.

T. O'Guinn, C. Allen, and R. Semenik. *Advertising & Integrated Brand Promotion,* 4th ed. Mason, OH: Thompson Southwestern, 2006.

O. Pickton and A. Broderick. *Integrated Marketing Communications.* New York: Financial Times/Prentice Hall, 2005.

B. H. Schmitt. *Customer Experience Management: A Revolutionary Approach to Connecting with Your Customer.* New York: Wiley, 2003.

NOTES ▪▪▪▪▪▪▪

1. Brian Steinberg, "TV Networks Find New Ways to Attract Ads," *Wall Street Journal,* June 28, 2005, p. B1.
2. Jane Levere, "Advertisers Pour More Money into the Big Screen," *New York Times,* June 22, 2005.
3. Mike Esterl, "Going Outside, Beyond the Billboard," *Wall Street Journal* July 24, 2005, p. B3.
4. "Street Furniture" is a term used by TDI Primetime Media, who also provide examples for this chapter as found on www.tdiworldwide.com.
5. A. O. Scott, "Post-Popism," *New York Times,* Aug. 8, 2005.
6. Stuart Elliott's "Advertising" column in the *New York Times,* Sept. 21, 2005.
7. V. Zeithaml, M. J. Bitner, and D. Gremler, "Technology Spotlight," *Services Marketing* 4th ed. (New York: McGraw-Hill, 2006), p. 498.
8. AdAge.com, case study brief, July 2005.
9. Bob Teedeschi, *New York Times,* Oct. 31, 2005.
10. Chris Gaither, "A Web Contagion," *Los Angeles Times,* August 28, 2005, p. B1.
11. Reported by Amy Merrik for the *Wall Street Journal,* Aug. 10, 2005.
12. Aaron O. Patrick, *Wall Street Journal,* Aug. 22, 2005.
13. Stuart Elliott, *New York Times,* Nov. 25, 2005.
14. Julia Angwin, "Advertising" column, *New York Times,* June 21, 2006, B1.
15. B. Klayman, "Driven to Stardom: Product Placement in TV and Film Extends to Cars and Trucks," *Toronto Star,* May 23, 1998.
16. John Gaudiosi, "Product Placement to Die For: The Rise of In-Game Advertising," *Wired,* April 2006, p. 136.
17. Ethan Smith and Suzanne Vranica, "Advertising" column, in the *Wall Street Journal,* July 6, 2005.
18. Charles Goldsmith, "Dubbing in Product Plugs," *Wall Street Journal,* Jan. 6, 2004, B1.
19.
20. Jennifer Pozner, "Triumph of He Shill," *Bitch Magazine,* Winter 2004, p. 51.
21. Kate Kelly and Stephanie Kang, "The Selling of a Geisha," *Wall Street Journal,* Oct. 10, 2005.
22. D. Finnigan, "Marketers of the Next Generation: Beth Goss," *BrandWeek* 42 (13) (2001), p. 32.
23. Lorne Manly and Raymond Hernandez, "Nielsen, Long a Gauge of Popularity, Fights to Preserve Its Own," *New York Times,* Aug. 8, 2005.
24. B. Avrich, *Selling the Sizzle* (Maxworks Publishing, 2002), p. 80.
25. Brian O'Keefe and Julie Schlosser, "America's Fastest Growing Sport," *Fortune,* Sept. 5, 2005, pp. 50–64.

CHAPTER 10

Producing an Integrated Marketing Communications Campaign

*When society requires to be rebuilt
there is no use in attempting to
rebuild it on the old plan.*
—JOHN STUART MILL

Chapter Objectives

After reading Chapter 10, you should be able to answer these questions:

- What choices and changes drive *integrated marketing communications* (IMC)?
- What role does *research* play in planning a campaign?
- What are the *10 steps* for planning a campaign?
- Why is *evaluation* of the IMC mix and campaign important for accessing campaign effectiveness?
- When does a campaign warrant a *globalized execution?*

Communicating Entertainment Brand Messages

The objective of all marketing communications efforts is to present a coordinated, cohesive, unified branded message to a specific target audience. **Integrated marketing communications**, or **IMC**, is the management of all brand contact points through an integrated, audience-driven strategy. The difference between consumers' expectations

▪▪▪ **EXHIBIT 10.1** Integrated vs. Convergent Communications

Traditional IMC		*Convergent Communications*
Marketer's need to synchronize programs	< Reason for being >	Create programs that address consumers' needs w/impact
Common strategy, look, theme	< Approach >	Common elements, but modified according to medium's capacity to communicate benefit(s)
Consistent advertising, PR, direct response, etc.	< Communications created >	Consistent advertising, PR, direct response, etc.
Well-coordinated marketing communications program	< End result >	Well-coordinated program with maximum benefit communication

Source: Lynn Upshaw, *Building Brand Identity,* Wiley (2005), p. 212.

and product or venue delivery—the gap discussed in Chapter 3—is what distinguishes a well-executed experience from a poorly executed one. Audience expectations are shaped by both uncontrolled and management-controlled factors, yet audience needs are the main factor for influencing expectations. Messages delivered through advertising, promotions, sponsorships, PR, and Internet communications are vital to the success of an experience. All these communication devices must be crafted to represent the entertainment genre as accurately and specifically as possible.

From Integration to Convergence

Hollywood has always been creative in the ways it reaches its audiences. What it has not always been good at is crafting a unified message across its communication vehicles. Message delivery is not simply sending out a piece of advertising, a press release, and a direct mail solicitation that have similar graphics. Integration ideally results in a metamorphosis of advertising, promotion, and merchandising that presents the same message and the same brand image throughout all audience contacts. Convergent communication adds the branding message to the mix.

Exhibit 10.1 shows the natural progression from a traditional IMC strategy to convergent communications. Both approaches are based on similar principles and goals, but by planning for convergence, brand benefits are maximized through specifically directed communication. Eventually, all marketing will make the transition to convergence.

▪▪▪ Campaign Planning, Strategies, and Tactics

Campaigns are developed to solve problems. Because marketing problems for the entertainment industry usually center around revenue generation, most campaigns are designed to promote new content, venues, and destinations. Some campaigns focus on bringing back prereleased content and properties, or on changing attitudes about an attraction or destination. The nature of the marketing problem determines the campaign's objectives. This section presents a step-by-step approach to planning and developing an integrated marketing communications (IMC) campaign for performance, experiential, and mediated entertainment and their venues.

Promotional tools are continually changing in response to technology's rapid advances. Marketers constantly monitor audience preferences in message delivery. Which media channels should be purchased to develop a relevant promotional campaign? Research is necessary to negotiate the plethora of delivery options. How are audiences learning about entertainment options and where are they buying their tickets? The Internet continues to play a major role in information distribution and purchase facilitation. What's the best way to pay attention to Web sites and online advertising?

Research Options

Primary research uncovers brand, consumer, or image problems that campaigns are designed to circumvent. Using qualitative techniques (focus groups and depth interviews), marketers determine the nature and extent of problems as well as the audiences consumption habits, preferences, and attitudes. Dollars spent on marketing research have increased, largely because marketers need to understand audience involvement in an experience against the backdrop of ever-expanding delivery and purchase channel options.

Secondary sources provide market, company, and audience statistics at no charge from research and business reporting services and tourist bureaus. Some of the most useful *free resources* are

- ESOMAR world research organization for global markets, consumers, and societies
- Greenbook (greenbook.org), a directory of worldwide marketing research and focus group companies
- Hoovers Research
- Internet World Statistics
- Market Research Association (mra-net.org)
- Market Research Library (export.gov)
- Market Research Portal (marketresearchworld.net)
- U.S. Government Bureau of Labor Statistics (bls.gov)

Syndicated Services

Audience usage data are available only through subscription affiliations. Most advertising agencies subscribe to syndicated services that supply such data to help them determine media buying expenditures. The best-known of these services are A. C. Nielson, Harris Interactive, and Simmons.

Designed to understand the market as a whole, syndicated research is often conducted on a national scale and involves hundreds, if not thousands, of participants. The idea behind syndicated research is to share the cost among a broad base of users. Prices for syndicated research can range from roughly $300 for a subscription to a newsletter-style report to more than $11,000 for the rights to get a peek at the data on, say, the online buying habits of Quake-playing retirees. Syndicated research is a good way to shape long-term strategies, and it can be an excellent jumping-off point. Two of the biggest data providers in the online arena are Forrester Research and Jupiter Communications.

▪▪▪▪▪▪▪▪▪▪ BOX 10-1 ▪▪▪▪▪▪▪▪▪▪

A Closer Look at Convergence

ORCHESTRATED EFFORTS, HARMONIOUS RESULTS

As marketers and academics dispute the merits of IMC, we provide reasons why the convergence of planning and implementing a campaign will drive twenty-first century entertainment marketing efforts.

Entertainment Marketing Has Gone from Marketing Oriented to Market Driven

The incredible explosion of technology of the last two decades has, for all practical purposes, shattered the mass market and made many of the traditional techniques of mass marketing obsolete. In the marketplace of the twenty-first century, the driving force is not "companies" with entertainment products to sell, but "customers" controlling what, where, and how they want to purchase tickets. Not only has technology changed the way consumers make their purchasing decisions, it has also revolutionized how companies market their entertainment products to consumers. The customer's role has become so dominant that companies are shifting their focus from being marketing oriented to being market driven. Consumer sophistication, media proliferation and fragmentation of mass markets has made it essential for marketers to establish and maintain a consistent voice across multiple media.

Marketers Must Use an Audience-Oriented Approach

For any marketing communication campaign to be able to produce effective results, it must solidly be anchored on a deep understanding of the consumer audience. To effectively direct messages to, and affect the behavior of, consumers, entertainment brand communications programs must incorporate segmentation/ aggregation, customer valuation, and database management.

Planning Is an Essential Element of Audience-Based Marketing

As a concept of marketing communications planning, IMC recognizes the added value of a comprehensive plan. Such a plan evaluates the strategic roles of a variety of communication disciplines— for example, general advertising, direct response, sales promotion, and public relations—and combines these disciplines to provide clarity, consistency, and maximum impact through seamless integration of discrete messages.

Convergence Requires a Collaborative Strategy

Effective convergence requires coordination on strategy as well as tactics. To be effective, collaboration embraces an understanding of the different roles that all communication techniques play in the marketing process (e.g., promotion might prompt trial, but only once public relations has raised awareness).

Each component of the marketing mix should work in unison with the others, leveraging the strengths of other components and presenting a consistent set of benefits and images to the audience member. The key to an IMC approach is to be able to select an appropriate combination of marketing communication tools that achieves the marketing communication objectives set out for an entertainment brand.

(Continued)

Convergence Is Not a Management Fad

This approach is a fundamental and marked shift in the thinking and practice of marketing communications by clients and advertising agencies. The critical issue concerning convergence is that of evaluation and measurement of integrated programs. Part of the difficulty is that traditionally advertising, sales promotion, direct marketing, and the public relations disciplines have developed separate and distinct measurement approaches. The measurement of integrated programs, which can estimate the synergy between elements, is a totally new field—one that remains relatively undeveloped.

Still an emerging discipline, IMC exists in a period of transition between the historical product-driven outbound marketing systems and the new information-driven, interactive, consumer-focused marketplace of the twenty-first century.

SOURCE: Manoj Khatri for strategicmarketing.com.

Ten Steps to Developing Your Campaign

There are many approaches to developing a comprehensive campaign to promote an entertainment brand, performance, or mediated property. This text recommends a 10-step approach to developing an integrated communications plan for entertainment companies. In addition to describing these steps, we provide an example of how they are applied to a campaign developed for the national Public Broadcasting Service (PBS).[1] This example, featured after the plan outline, shows you how to craft an appropriate campaign plan for an entertainment client.

Step 1: State the Problem and Campaign Objective

Why is the client conducting a campaign? State the reason as a problem clearly and succinctly.

Supporting Facts

Look at relevant data regarding the problem situation.

Campaign Objective and Duration

The reason the campaign is being conducted and length of implementation needs to be formulated.

Step 2: Conduct a Situation Analysis

An analysis of the current marketplace is the means for identifying the most important factors in campaign development. Situation analysis begins with an industry overview that includes a determination of its size, sales volume, growth trends, and attendance statistics. Company background, target market, and current marketing mix are included in this section. Once these data are determined, you must review significant and mitigating factors that impact the industry.

Industry Overview

Begin with a broad stroke of your client's entire industry segment and where it is today. Focus on developments and trends within the industry by enumerating the most important aspects, such as a saturated marketplace.

Corporate History

Include your client's most recent company or corporate data here. Rather than repeat what the client already knows about itself, elaborate on important events in the company's past and its current status in the marketplace.

Economic, Technological, Political, Social, and Legal Environments

Because technology, circumstances, and unforeseen events change today's entertainment marketplace, you use secondary research to determine what uncontrollable factors may impact the campaign.

Competitive Analysis

Analyze the major competitors to your client and their market shares. Look at the strengths and weaknesses of the competition, plus threats they may pose.

Step 3: Conduct a SWOT Analysis of the Property or Brand

Determine the brand's "SWOT"—its *s*trengths, *w*eaknesses, *o*pportunities, and *t*hreats. Identify internal and external threats to the client; internal threats are controllable, while external threats are not. Exhibit 10.2 illustrates how these variables are plotted for analysis.

▪▪▪ **EXHIBIT 10.2** Components of a SWOT Analysis

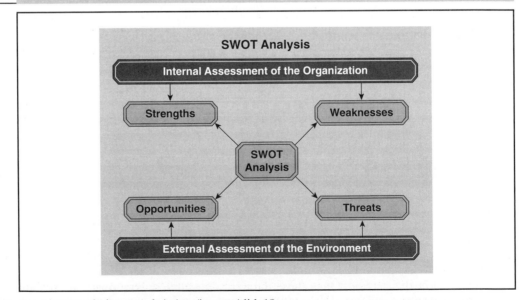

Source: www.admin.mtu.edu/.../nca/images/slide19.

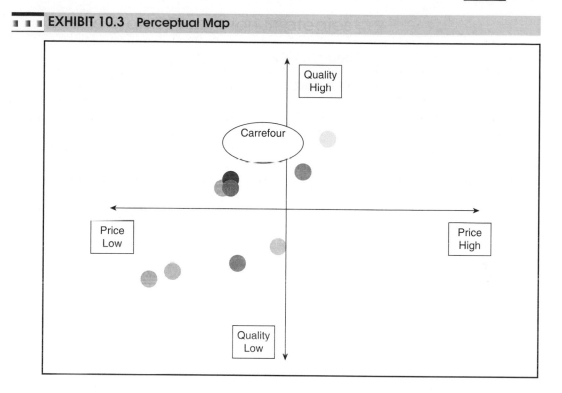

Step 4: Characterize the Target Audience

Describe the overall target market and profile the specific audience targeted by this campaign. Present as much information about them and their perceptions about the brand as possible. *Perceptual maps* can dramatize audience perceptions of the client's brand in relationship to competitive brands. Exhibit 10.3 is an example of the configurations used for perceptual mapping where each color represents a different entertainment brand.

Step 5: Determine the Brand Positioning Strategy

Use your competitive analysis and audience research to determine how to position your client's brand in the marketplace. The alternatives suggested in Chapter 7 for construction of a positioning strategy are to position

- on a *specific feature,* such as a Frank Gehry architectural venue, Cedar Point's highest roller coaster, or state-of-the-art staging technology.
- on *benefits,* such as Six Flags' excitement, thrills, adventure, and so forth.
- for specific *usage occasion,* such as Saturday afternoon concerts, Christmas showing of the *Nutcracker's Suite,* or Tanglewood's summer outdoor theater.
- for *user category,* such as gay and lesbian weekends on a Carnival Cruise.
- *against other brands* in the category, such as Golden Door touting itself as the "most expensive spa experience in the U.S."
- *as number one,* such as Paris' claim to be the most visited city in the world.
- as *exclusive,* such as PBS unique status as the only nonprofit broadcasting entity.

▪▪▪▪▪▪▪▪▪ **BOX 10-2** ▪▪▪▪▪▪▪▪▪

Focus on New Technology

DIGITAL UTOPIA FOR CONCEPT TESTING

The fastest-growing advertising medium, the Internet provides access to virtual worlds that allow marketers to tests products and concepts. Sites that meld elements of gaming, advertising, and entertainment, such as Second Life, also can be used as a corporate businesses test bed. BMG Music Entertainment, Sun Microsystems, Nissan, and Starwood Hotels are among the more than 30 companies holding "real estate" in Second Life's virtual world.

Conducting a promotional venture in a virtual world is relatively inexpensive compared with the millions spent on other media. Companies and ad agencies can buy a virtual "island" for a one-time fee of $1,250 and a monthly rate of $195. MTV, for instance, has launched a Virtual Laguna Beach where fans of the show *Laguna Beach: The Real O.C.* can fashion themselves after the show's characters and hang out in their faux settings. Performers promote new albums with virtual appearances and host opening parties at virtual resorts and virtual complexes, such as Sony BMG's Media Island.

Site owner Linden Labs leases "land" to tenants for around $20 a month per acre or $195 a month for a private "island." Second Life's land mass grows at about 8 percent a month, and as many as 10,000 people are in the virtual world at any given time spending Linden dollars (400 = $1). Linden's economy totals about $500,000 a day, and its growth rate is 15 percent a month in real U.S. dollars.

Projects such as the Aloft hotel (an offshoot of the W Hotels brand) provides feedback from prospective guests before the first real hotel opens in 2008. Sony BMG's building has rooms devoted to popular musicians that allow fans to listen to tunes or watch videos before purchasing them online. Online press conferences and corporate events further enable pre-release testing for entertainment companies.

A few problems—such as the Second Life Liberation Army that stages faux attacks on American apparel stores and copyright infringement—don't seem to deter virtual pleasure and promotion from marketers and users alike.

SOURCE: Richard Siklos for the *New York Times,* Oct. 19, 2006, C1; pc.joystick.com.

▪▪▪▪▪▪▪▪

Step 6: Structure Campaign Objectives

Remember that objectives drive strategies and tactics at all stages of IMC planning. This step helps you determine the amount of funds needed to achieve those objectives. Develop specific marketing, advertising, media, promotion, and action objectives here. Review Chapter 8 if you need help.

Marketing Objectives

Select objectives from sales, revenue, profits, or market share to provide an overall allocation of emphasis. Remember, these must be measurable.

Advertising/Communication Objectives

Choose from category need, awareness, attitude, or purchase intention. Objectives include a measurable component that is attainable by the campaign's conclusion.

Media Objectives

State media objectives based on reach (percent of demographic), frequency (number of impressions), and continuity (continuous, flights, or pulsed).

Promotion/Action Objectives

For each consumer aggregate your campaign will target, specify what action(s) you want from each audience aggregate.

Step 7: Allocate a Budget

Using the objective-task method, determine the resources needed to produce and deliver a promotional campaign for your client. This method is most appropriate for limited budget campaigns, because it determines the resources needed to accomplish media and promotional objectives. If the objective is to raise awareness by 5 percent, the budget reflects media costs and expenditures for promotional activities needed to accomplish that task.

Step 8: Select the IMC Mix Needed for Delivery Strategies and Tactics

Using all the options described in Chapter 8, decide on a promotion mix for your communications.

Media Advertising

Select media vehicles that are appropriate for reaching your campaign audience. Determine media selections through localized focus groups with target audience members. Nationally syndicated resources on demographic media usage (such as Simmons) can inform your media choices.

Product Placement

Determine places where the logo or property can be imbedded into a form of entertainment or activity.

Licensing

Use garments and products produced by other manufactures to feature brand logo. Licensing is both a profit-generating activity and method of spreading brand awareness.

Sponsorship/PR

Sponsoring an event generates media coverage and creates a favorable association with the audience's preferred activity or cause. Resulting exposure improves brand image and increases awareness.

Internet

Creating a Web site to induce audience interaction and build positive audience relationships is mandatory in today's global marketplace. Web site design and maintenance costs, although typically separate from the marketing budget, are necessary elements for the campaign's overall effectiveness.

Publicity

Editorial commentary in print and broadcast media must appear concurrently with advertising and promotion. To ensure adequate coverage, you must deliver publicity materials to editors and producers in advance of campaign activities.

Promotions/Incentives

Develop promotional incentives using both push and pull strategies. Dollars spent on incentives is insurance against non-participation and increases opportunities to reach revenue goals.

Direct Response

Design personal contact with audience members to induce responses that results in a positive relationships with the brand.

Step 9: Develop Message Strategies

Create appropriate messages for each consumer aggregate that will be targeted in the campaign. (See Chapter 8 for a review of message strategy development.)

Step 10: Set Evaluation Criteria

Campaign effectiveness can be determined only through research conducted by the client, the advertising agency, or an outside research firm. Evaluation methods include but are not limited to:

- pre- and post-tests to measure attitude changes
- post-campaign sales data and market share statistics
- contest and sweepstake entries
- exit polling from venues
- attendance measures
- Web site hits
- revenue indicators from box office sales, merchandise purchases, and subscriptions.

Once the plan is completed, the creative team, develops concepts for advertising execution, and the plan is implemented. At the campaign's conclusion, outcomes are measured to determine levels of success or failure. The plan can also serve as the basis of a new campaign or modifications to the previous effort.

▪▪▪ Example of a Campaign Plan for PBS

The following campaign follows the above outline and provides an example of what the bones of a campaign plan should look like. All plans should be embellished with visual illustrations of proposed creative when possible.

Integrated Campaign for Public Broadcasting System
Problem and Campaign Objective

Research determined that many PBS services go unnoticed and unused because of a lack of information about programs and performances. Many audience members think PBS is purely educational with no entertainment value for them.

Supporting Facts   There is high awareness among children regarding kids' programming and among seniors who watch BBC sitcoms. On the other hand, many parents, teachers, teens, and young adult audiences remain unaware of PBS entertainment offerings.

Campaign Objective and Duration   Develop awareness among teens and young adult audiences of PBS entertainment offerings and expand viewership among that age demographic by the end of the six-month campaign.

Situation Analysis

Industry Overview   Most broadcast companies are privately owned and provide programming on network TV stations funded by advertising or paid subscription services sold through cable and satellite companies. PBS operates as a nonprofit enterprise, funded solely by donations from members, individual donors, corporate sponsors, and foundation grants.

Corporate History   Founded in 1969, the Public Broadcasting Service is a private, nonprofit corporation PBS, headquartered in Alexandria, Virginia, whose members are America's public TV station affiliates. PBS oversees program acquisition, distribution, and promotion; educational services; new media ventures; fundraising support; engineering and technology development; and video marketing. There are 170 noncommercial educational licensees operating 349 PBS member stations. Licensees include 87 community organizations, 57 colleges or universities, 20 state authorities, and 6 local educational or municipal authorities. A trusted community resource, PBS uses the power of noncommercial television, the Internet, and other media to enrich the lives of all Americans through quality programs and education services that inform, inspire, and delight. Available to 99 percent of American homes with televisions and to an increasing number of digital multimedia households, PBS serves nearly 110 million people each week.

PBS's operating revenue in fiscal year 2004 was $333 million. Leading sources of revenue included: station assessments (47 percent); CPB and federal grants (24 percent); royalties, license fees, satellite services and investment income (14 percent); and educational product sales (12 percent). Leading expenditures for PBS in fiscal year 2004 included: programming and promotion (72 percent); member and educational services (15 percent); satellite interconnection and technical services (9 percent); general and administrative (4 percent).

Economic, Technological, Political, Social, and Legal Environments   Although the economy continues to grow in the U.S., contribution to arts and nonprofit organizations has declined over the past five years. Technology has enabled television viewers to receive programming over handheld devices as well as computers, DVDs, and large-screen plasma TVs. Governmental support is also declining, although regulations have not significantly effected programming selection. Mature adults actively participate in

PBS's *Teletubbies* is only one show of many that compete with network TV for viewers.

philanthropic campaigns and exhibit social responsibility for people who are less fortunate. Social trends vary by demographic group.

Competitive Analysis   Competition includes:

- Nature, news, history, and lifestyle channels
- Network television and broadcast programming delivered by cable and satellite

Competitive advantages:

- Paid advertisers to subsidize broadcast costs
- Ability to develop content and properties

Disadvantages:

- Advertiser control
- Viewing disruption by commercials

Share of television viewership:

- 30% Network TV
- 60% Subscription or pay channels
- 11% Public television

SWOT Analysis of the Brand
Strengths

1. Educational services

    • "Ready To Learn" helps to increase school readiness for all of America's children with programming and short educational video spots. These programs are enhanced through outreach services including workshops, free children's books, a magazine, and other learning resources to help parents, teachers, and childcare providers prepare young children to enter school ready to learn.

    • "TeacherSource" helps pre-K–12 educators learn effective ways to incorporate online tools in the classroom through nearly 5,000 free lesson plans, teachers' guides, homeschooling guidance, and other resourceful activities correlated to national and state curriculum standards.

    • "TeacherLine" provides professional teacher development through more than 90 online facilitated courses in reading, mathematics, science, curriculum and instruction, and technology integration.

    • "Adult Learning Service" provides college credit TV courses to nearly 500,000 students each academic year.

2. Programming activities

    • The National Programming Service is the major package of programs that PBS distributes to its member stations. It features television's best children's, cultural, educational, history, nature, news, public affairs, science, and skills programming.

    • Programs are obtained from PBS stations, independent producers, and sources around the world. PBS offers news, science and nature, life and culture, and history programming to its viewers.

3. Digital leadership

    • PBS.org is not only one of the most visited dot-org Web site in the world, it is also the home of comprehensive companion Web sites for more than 1,000 PBS television programs and specials, as well as original Web content and real-time learning adventures.

    • Member stations are digital television leaders, from groundbreaking work in interactive TV and a monthly schedule of original high-definition programming (on the PBS HD Channel) to the PBS YOU multicast services.

4. Brand equity

    • Award-winning news, documentary, and children's programming; Web site; educational activities; logo; membership loyalty.

Weaknesses

- Dependence on outside sources for funding and programming
- Stodgy image among teens and young adults
- Limited programming directed at teens and young adults

More than just TV.

Opportunities

- Add affiliates and college licenses
- Solicit more corporate sponsorships
- Attract a more solid teen and young adult audience base
- Increase sales through the Web store and other outlets

Threats

- Ever-increasing programming competition
- Decreasing government subsidies
- Economic downturn

Target Market   The current public TV audience reflects the social and economic makeup of the nation. PBS and its member stations reach nearly 90 million people each week through on-air and online content.

Target Audience   The campaign will target teens and young adults of all demographics in major urban metropolitan areas. Secondary targets are parents and teachers of the primary demographic.

Audience Perceptions   Primary research determined that the campaign audience's perceptions of the entertainment brand are not ideal. While the brand's image evoked adjectives such as educational and informational, they did not convey a sense of excitement or relevance for this demographic. Audience members characterized the brand's personality as being introverted, serious, and playful for kids.

▪▪▪▪ **EXHIBIT 10.4   Perceptual Grid for PBS**

Teens and TV Networks

	Entertaining	
MTV		*ESPN*

Fun ─────────────────────────────────┼───────────────────────── **Factual**

Discovery		*PBS*
	Educational	

Brand Position—Exclusive Strategy

The nation's only nonprofit broadcasting alternative that provides uncensored, original entertainment programming for all audience segments.

Positioning for Campaign Audience—Benefit Strategy

Information television that entertains

Marketing Objectives

- Increase Web site sales by 5 percent
- Increase revenue generated by corporate sponsors by 7 percent
- Increase television viewing market share by 1 percent

Advertising Objectives

- Increase awareness of PBS programs directed at teens and young adults by 20 percent
- Improve positive attitude toward PBS among teens and young adults by 25 percent
- Increase intention to purchase merchandise from PBS Web site by 11 percent

Media Objectives

- Reach 40 percent of teens and young adults five times using a pulsing strategy

Promotion/Action Objectives

- Current PBS viewers: maintain current financial loyalty and introduce teens to PBS programming
- Emerging PBS viewers: play games on the PBS Web site; become a member and compete in online games
- Competitive viewers: Incorporate PBS into viewing selections

Budget Allocation

National budget for promotional spending is generated from 5 percent of revenues from governmental subsidies and global corporate sponsors, and 3 percent of profits from sales of DVDs, tapes, and related formats featured and sold on Web site store. Once that number is determined, the campaign budget is to be used for media and promotions directed at teens and young adults.

IMC Mix for Message Delivery

Media Advertising National media buys for general PBS game contest and sweepstake promotion; does not include affiliate promotions.

- 30-second TV spots on "Nick at Night," ESPN, and MTV
- Full-page magazine ads in *Seventeen, Teen,* and *Skateboarder* magazines
- 2-column-inch newspaper ad in *New York Times, Wall Street Journal, Los Angeles Times, Chicago Tribune,* and *Boston Globe* calendar or entertainment sections

Product Placement Logo images are displayed on television screens turned on during sitcoms and reality shows on ABC, NBC, and CBS; PBS logo can be seen on Tony Hawk skateboard used in competitions.

Licensing Some toys and clothing feature Sesame Street characters.

Sponsorship/PR

- Cosponsor a contest with Tony Hawk skateboard manufacturer for teens to design an online game for the PBS Web site. The winner receives a skateboard.
- Participate in a skateboarding event where PBS logo decals are given away to competitors.

Sesame Street characters for sale on pbs.shop.com.

Internet

- Feature skateboard and teen reality games on the Web site.
- Promote the Web site using sponsored links on skateboard manufacturer Web sites.

Publicity

- Develop press kits for distribution to teen and young adult magazine editors to create a buzz about the skateboard game contest.
- Send news releases to print and broadcast media announcing skateboard-related programming.

Promotions/Incentives

- Provide funding incentives for affiliates who join sponsorship activities.
- Offer skateboard prizes as incentives for teens and young adults to enter contests and sweepstakes and play games on the PBS Web site.

Direct Response Using databases from skateboard and teen magazines, mail out PBS contest entry forms that direct entrants to the Web site.

Audience Message Strategies

- Current PBS viewers: Turn your friends on to PBS Web site
- Emerging PBS viewers: Find excitement on PBS; enter a game contest; visit the Web site
- Competitive viewers: Enter PBS sweepstakes online

Tony Hawk skateboard as event cosponsor.

▪▪▪▪▪▪▪▪▪▪▪ BOX 10-3 ▪▪▪▪▪▪▪▪▪▪▪

A Closer Look at the Role of Research

DEVELOPING A CAMPAIGN TO RAISE RATINGS

PROBLEM: CW (formerly WB) television network's children's (6–11) program lineup has slumping ratings; the company turns to research to see how they can improve the product.

OBJECTIVE: How can CW breathe new life into the animated Looney Tunes franchise?

Agency Research Proposal

Methodology—use focus groups and depth interviews to probe audience thoughts and feelings about the following:

- Plot: Loonatics series set in year 2772.

- Characters who retain personality quirks of the original. Featured character is Buzz Bunny who is a natural leader of the Loonatics' spaceship; the new Daffy remains confident that he is the one who should be in charge.

Report format—agency meeting, written results

Budget—includes research and redrafting cartoon images

Primary research results provided CW's advertising staff the direction for creating a new campaign, which is outlined below.

Campaign Plan

Campaign Problem. Traditional images and animation, story lines, and characters are not appealing to audiences in the age range; need to promote the new versions that testing selected

Current Market Analysis. Japanese animation techniques, video games, cartoon networks, Disney Channel, and techno-logical innovation has rendered CW cartoons obsolete and uninteresting to its audience; kids market is weak globally; Saturday morning viewership down 26 percent among children 5 to 9 since last year

Trends. Slicker characters, craftier plots, and continuing innovation will drive entertainment; Loonatics and Buzz Bunny will improve cartoon viewing on Saturday morning

SWOT Analysis

- Strengths: Cartoon history, recognizable characters

- Weaknesses: Outdated images and plots

- Opportunities: Find a fresh way to tap the funny bone of an audience raised on Bart Simpson and SpongeBob; expand CW line of characters

Threats: Competition; past bombs, in particular, *Looney Tunes: Back in Action,* the WB movie that failed last year.

Behavioral Objectives—stimulate children's audiences, who are finicky and get itchy for something new, to bond with WB characters

- Current viewers: Keep tuned to CW programming and make it a preferential viewing selection

- New viewers: Develop a relationship with the newly imaged characters and request CW channel

- Competitive viewers: Tune in and experience the new characters

Budget—Objective Based. Determine preferences in character style and plot structure through a series of focus groups and in-depth interviews with children

(Continued)

who watch television cartoons. Budget reflects cost of focus groups and analysis as determined by an outside research company.

Mix Needed to Promote New Characters

- PR: editorial about new configurations in WSJ and NYT
- Licensing: new images on clothing for sale at CW stores
- Home video: Loonatics DVDs
- Advertising: cartoon trailers on CW channel and other kid-based channels
- Print: coloring books distributed through restaurants and schools that feature new characters
- Product placement: New Bugs will appear in branded product ads

- Sponsorship: Run for cancer and other marathon races to feature sprinting bunny
- Internet: Interactive games featuring New Bugs

Evaluation Techniques

- Nielson ratings
- Recognition surveys
- Attitude surveys

What do you think?

1. How would you create a buzz about the new Bugs?
2. In addition to licensing, how would you merchandise the updated character?
3. What other promotional methods are appropriate for the new Bugs?

Loonatics unleashed.

Campaign Evaluation Criteria

Objectives will be evaluated using:

- number of Web hits as tabulated by eMarketer
- contest and sweepstake entry totals
- Internet-generated teen surveys to measure post-campaign attitude changes toward PBS.

▮▮▮ Taking Campaigns Global

Entertainment properties, franchises, performances, destinations, and attractions have global appeal and can demand global campaigns. The global mindset is a fundamentally different perspective from international, multinational, and panregional mindsets, because it encompasses all cultures or nationalities. Global and cross-regional considerations include delivery systems, market regulations, agency options, logics, and campaign scope.

Global Delivery Systems

Of all the challenges facing promoters of global entertainment, media advertising may be the greatest. Availability and usage complicates the problem of deciding which combination of media will achieve the desired coverage of a market.

Newspapers, the most localized worldwide medium, provide the best programming information; however, they require the greatest amount of local market knowledge. Global magazine coverage is expensive, and the cost of full coverage in publications in a variety of languages is often prohibitive for all but the most profitable entertainment genres.

Global television networks using cable and satellite technology provide the best media availability and coverage. One of the largest networks, Viacom's MTV, reaches more than 400 million households worldwide. MTV offers an efficient means of reaching Generations X, Y, and Z around the globe, facilitating international campaigns for many global brands. Direct broadcast by satellite is available through systems such as SkyPort, which sends transmissions through low-cost receiving dishes. Satellite Television Asian Region (STAR) sends BBC, U.S., Bollywood, and local programming to 53 countries across Asia; it is on its way to becoming one of the world's most influential broadcasting systems.

Global Market Regulations

Depending on the market, advertising regulations can impose limitations on the kinds of data that can be collected from consumers, the types of message appeals used, languages and talent, and national symbols and taxes. Some promotional tactics, such as couponing and loyalty rewards programs, may also be restricted or regulated, which directly affects the hospitality and tourism industries.

Global Advertising Agencies

Entertainment promotions can be directed by a global agency, an international affiliate, or a local agency. The big four global agency groups, Omnicom, Interpublic, WPP, and Publicis, have each assembled a network of diverse service providers to deliver global

▪▪▪▪▪▪▪▪▪▪ **BOX 10-4** ▪▪▪▪▪▪▪▪▪▪

A Closer Look at Travel Campaigns

KILROY TARGETS STUDENTS

Client

An enterprise with subsidiary companies in seven countries, Kilroy Travels International is a market leader with people under 33 and students under 26 in Finland, Denmark, Norway, Sweden, Holland, the Netherlands, and Spain. The company, which was founded in 1997 by student organizations, has a mission to provide students and other young people with affordable quality travel products.

Product

By focusing on "the young independent traveler," Kilroy sells airline tickets based on freedom and flexibility that can be changed at any time, even after travel has begun. The Kilroy ticket is valid for one year and can be reimbursed if not used during that period. Kilroy operates from its own retail shops in 130 service centers. All sales consultants are members of the target group with travel experience.

Target Audience

Kilroy's primary target group is students in higher education aged 19–26. Its secondary group includes first-time travelers ages 16–19. To reach its target Kilroy uses cinema advertising. Until 1997, the brand was managed by Ogilvy & Mather in Copenhagen, who designed a campaign based on the value of independence. When market stagnation and decreasing sales caused a decline in sales and the Kilroy brand image, the company decided to reconsider its marketing efforts. Target group research revealed that the concept of independence was confusing because it did not have a clear connection to travel, and this resulted in negative image generation.

Campaign Objectives

Kilroy's goals for its new campaign were to:

- Create a positive relationship between the target group's perception of the brand and its products over the long term
- Communicate the benefits of travel
- Produce untraditional creative advertising with a "crazy edge" theme.

What do you think?

1. For their new campaign, on which attributes should Kilroy focus to differentiate its brand from other travel brands?

2. How might creative use the interplay between verbal and visual elements to achieve a positive brand image?

3. Should the campaign strategy focus on changing attitudes about travel and the brand be direct or indirect? Why?

SOURCE: Solomon, Bamossy, and Askegaard, *Consumer Behavior: A European Perspective,* 2002.

▪▪▪▪▪▪▪▪▪

brand promotions. International affiliates in foreign markets provide local market expertise. Managed by foreign nationals, affiliates provide knowledge about local markets and help avoid resistance to foreign ownership. Local agencies have well-established contacts for market information, production, and media buying. They are knowledgeable about competitive brands, culture, and conditions in a particular market.

Advertising Agency Affiliations

The top two global corporations, Omnicom and Interpublic, have acquired the largest advertising agencies.

Omnicom Group	Interpublic Group
BBDO Worldwide	Foote, Cone & Belding Worldwide
DDB Worldwide Communications	Lowe + Draft Partnership
TBWA Worldwide	McCann-Erickson Worldwide

Global Logic

The entertainment industry faces global logic (set of strategy variables) in the form of competition, industry, size, and regulations that must guide marketing decisions. Here are some details.[2]

• *Competitor logic*—The entertainment industry consistently encounters many of the same competitors, resulting in a chess-game activity whose game board is the world. A country-by-country position is called for when marketing live performances, parks, and destination locations.

• *Industry logic*—Transferring an experience from one country to another means taking key entertainment industry success factors and applying them across the globe.

• *Size logic*—Critical mass can be achieved in global markets to drive profitability. In the motion picture industry, for instance, foreign sales are the only way to achieve true profitability.

• *Regulatory logic*—Government can significantly affect global marketing strategies. In several entertainment industries, recent trends toward deregulation have opened up markets to foreign competitors and encouraged globalization. The telecommunications industry has been most affected by recent deregulatory activity that has given them access to many new markets.

Global logic patterns are rarely symmetrical, and it is important to understand the global logic that dominates your particular entertainment problem. For each global logic force, a situational marketing strategy can be adopted.

Campaign Scope and Branding

Universal expectations for entertainment and travel enable experience marketers to globalize their messages and their promotions across borders and cultures more easily than marketers of products. Entertainment brand campaigns can be globalized to take advantage of cost savings and creative strategies. Conditions that support globalized campaigns include:

• Global communications—worldwide cable and satellite networks and the Internet

• Global youth market with commonalities of travel norms and entertainment values

• Universal demographic and lifestyle trends

• Americanization of entertainment content

Branding plays a subordinate role in promoting specific performance genres, film titles, or television programs because global audiences seek experiences that are not brand-dependent. Conversely, destination, venue, theme park, and resort promotions must focus on branding to entice global travelers and local visitors, and to develop brand loyalty.

FINALLY: LET'S SUM UP ▮▮▮▮▮▮▮

Campaign development is essential for marketers of entertainment experiences. But unlike flashy, original brand and product campaigns, entertainment advertising most often relies on editing produced content rather than original material. Nonetheless, research into audience needs, wants, and attitudes drives campaign messages and delivery systems. Whether global or locally focused, entertainment campaign planning requires an in-depth understanding of media, advertising, and consumer behavior.

GOT IT? LET'S REVIEW ▮▮▮▮▮▮▮

- Data gathered from quantitative and qualitative research ground campaign planning activities; syndicated services provide national research data by subscription.
- The marketing problem helps determine the campaign's overall objective; marketing, advertising, media, and promotional objectives drive the campaign budget.
- A situation analysis involves gathering corporate and industry data as well as determining the social, economic, technical, political, and legal environments in which the campaign is situated.
- A SWOT analysis acts as an accounting of the brand's marketplace equity.
- Campaign evaluation is the key to understanding how well objectives are achieved.
- Universal demographics and lifestyles, as well as the Americanization of entertainment content, facilitate the use of globalized campaigns.

NOW TRY THIS ▮▮▮▮▮▮▮

1. Log on to the site of Japanese agency Dentsu (www.dentsu.com) and note the specific services the firm offers its clients. Would you characterize Dentsu as a local, national, or global agency? Why?
2. Find examples of successful entertainment brand campaigns (films, theme parks) and see if you can identify the overall campaign objective. What media were used to deliver the campaign's main message?
3. Go online to www.Jib-Jab.com. How does the activity on this site reflect the teen demographic? What can marketers learn about message delivery to teens from this site?
4. Peruse www.pc.joystiq.com and read about how the Internet fuses marketing with entertainment opportunities. What ideas can you suggest for testing a theme park ride in Second Life's virtual universe?

QUESTIONS: LET'S REVIEW ▪▪▪▪▪▪▪

1. What are the major differences between marketing and communication objectives? Which are more important for promotional message delivery?

2. Name the elements of the situation analysis and give an example of how each element influences the final form of an entertainment campaign.

3. What forms of evaluation are important for determining the success or failure of a campaign for a destination such as Australia?

4. If you were creating a global campaign for Six Flags Parks, what emphasis would you put on newspapers in executing your strategy? What factors complicate their value for achieving broad market coverage?

5. What factors make consumers around the world similar to one another? What factors create diversity among consumers in different countries?

MORE TO READ ▪▪▪▪▪▪▪

Eric Arnould, Linda Price, and George Zinkhan. *Consumers.* New York: McGraw-Hill, 2004.

Kenneth Clow and Donald Baack. *Integrated Advertising, Promotion and Marketing Communication,* 2nd ed. Upper Saddle River, NJ: Prentice Hall, 2003.

Jeannet Hennessey. *Global Marketing Strategies,* 5th ed. Houghton Mifflin, 2001.

Donald Parente. *Advertising Campaign Strategy.* Fort Worth, TX: Dryden, 2003.

Shay Sayre. *Campaign Planner for Integrated Brand Communications,* 3rd ed. Mason, OH: Thompson/South-Western, 2005.

NOTES ▪▪▪▪▪▪▪

1. All PBS information retrieved from pbs.org, November 2005.

2. Jeannet Hennessey, *Global Marketing Strategies,* 5th ed. (New York: Houghton Mifflin, 2001), chap. 7.

CHAPTER 11

Live Performances and Events

It's an odd job, making people laugh.
— MOLIÈRE

Chapter Objectives

After reading Chapter 11, you should be able to answer these questions:

- What is the importance of *drama* to entertainment marketing?
- How do we market *theatrical performances?*
- How do we market *live performances* and *concerts?*
- Which marketing strategies have worked for *bands* and *recording artists?*
- Which practices maximize an organization's brand image through *public relations* and *planned events?*
- What *communication objectives* and *strategies* can best meet goals and reach performance audiences?

The performing arts are constantly challenged by low attendance, shrinking audience patronage, spiraling expenses, and reduced government support. Nonetheless, live performances provide audiences with exciting and vibrant experiences that cannot be duplicated by mediated entertainment. This chapter looks at marketing theater and live concerts, marketing bands and musicians, the economics of audience development, and the role of public relations and planned events for generating a positive organizational brand image.

Marketing Theater and Staged Performances

All the world is a stage, as evidenced by twenty-first–century presentations that circle the globe and become cultural manifestations. Whether on Broadway or on a street corner, theatrical performances have been entertaining audiences since the beginning of human history. Venue attendance data indicate that two-thirds of Broadway audiences are university-educated females averaging 42 years of age who attend 5 shows per year. Who else goes to theater, and how can we reach them? Let's take look at how performances in residence and on tour are marketed to local audiences.

What's on Stage

The business of theater requires one essential ingredient: a great product. Good scripts have become scarce resources, a fact that plagues many theatrical venues. Producers are trying to rebound from the lack of new product and improve their chances at success by mounting revivals of previous hit shows. They are cultivating audiences by appealing to new segments. Theaters' newest targets are kids and their parents. *The Lion King, Beauty and the Beast,* and *Cats* were overwhelming successes because of their family appeal. Whether on Broadway or in a local venue, live theater is the ultimate shared experience, representing a brilliant composite of promise, escape, survival, and satire.

Audiences seem to love live theater more than ever before. According to the League of American Theaters and Producers, paid attendance in 2005 was the highest in 20 years—just shy of 12 million people, an increase of almost 6 percent from the previous year. Those theatergoers paid an average of $68.86 a ticket, about $2.75 more than the previous year. Gross sales reached $825 million for Broadway's 39 theaters, a jump of more than 10 percent from 2004. The total number of performances, another indicator of the industry's health, increased by about 4 percent, and attendance per performance was up, too, by about 1.5 percent.[1]

That box office record was set due to three elements: targeted productions (e.g., *The Color Purple* to African American and female demographics), premium seat pricing, and the appearance of Hollywood stars in shows (e.g., Julia Roberts).

Like all marketing efforts, promoting stage performance involves influencing the behavior of a market segment. Creating, building, and maintaining communication and message exchanges are the foundation blocks of effective marketing.

What's on Tour

The touring business gives producers an opportunity to recoup their Broadway investment and make money by exploiting key markets. Touring often makes shows into international phenomena, and the road business has created a market for theater everywhere. Also, with changing Broadway economics, producers need the backup of a road tour to give investors assurance that there is a plan B.

Success means branding the experience of a first-class Broadway show across the United States and internationally. Some new theater centers rival the New York and London stages. Toronto is ranked third as producer and exporter of world-class theater.

When theater productions tour, 69 percent of the audience is female, the average age is 46, and patrons are affluent, white, and well educated. This group attends six productions a year, lives less than 50 miles from the venue, and generally responds to advertising and word-of-mouth recommendations. Knowing this, regional venue managers are eager to book touring performances for their loyal audience members of similar demographics.

The first step of taking a show on the road is **selling off**, which is the process of securing the dates with local promoters, who receive a royalty and a profit participation in exchange for mounting the production. Another option is self-presenting, known as **four walling**, which involves renting a theater in each market and assuming all the risks of mounting the show. In addition to theater, single acts also prefer touring to a stationary venue.

Bob Dylan, for instance, has left the big cities to perform in state fairs, corporate events, urban street fairs, and Native American Indian casinos. Since 1988, Dylan has performed 1,700 shows, reintroducing himself to fans using a keyboard instead of a guitar and turning his act into one of the most unusual road shows in rock.[2] Dylan seems almost anti-promotion; there are no themes, little publicity, and no tractor trailers—he just plays the shows in as many venues as possible, even playing successive nights in different theaters and clubs in larger cities. Unlike most highly choreographed rock concerts, which charge hundreds of dollars, the singer's small ensemble plays from among his huge repertoire in an unscripted format, and his tickets are moderately priced at under $50.

Other road shows include regional performances of Broadway flops and discards, shows that have lost money on Broadway and have little name recognition.[3] Crowds from Providence to Sacramento love revivals of shows such as *La Cage aux Folles*, which won a Tony but closed after a six-month run at two-thirds capacity. *Bombay Dreams*, which lost all of its $14 million investment on Broadway, played to a full house during its 20-week tour in regional theaters. Shows can be victims of harsh reviews by powerful critics or fail to connect with audiences in spite of good reviews. Nonetheless, regional markets provide a rousing second act.

Road shows do have their risks, however. First, they are expensive. Trucking costs alone run to $20,000 per move, or $1 million for a typical 50-city tour. It is still cheaper for regional theaters to import fully realized productions rather than mounting multimillion-dollar ones from scratch. A presenter who brings in a road show typically pays an upfront fee to the original producer, ranging from about $225,000 to $300,000 per week. In return, he gets a 10 percent to 40 percent cut of the gross—which can run as high as $1 million a week. For producers, this is better than busting down sets and going home. Ideal audiences are people tired of amateur revivals and willing to see big shows irrespective of their Broadway fate.

Summer tends to be a slow time for Broadway productions, both in New York and on the road. So, regional theaters use celebrities and recognizable titles from other media as draws for their own revivals. In the summer of 2005, for instance, the La Jolla Playhouse in California presented *Zhivago* as a musical to sellout crowds; Julie Andrews directed *The Boyfriend* in East Haddam, Connecticut; Olympia Dukakis starred in her original Broadway role of a performance of *Rose* in Hartford; and *Dangerous Liaisons* was successful in Madison, New Jersey.

Promoting Stage Performances

The best philosophy is to get audiences to move beyond the reviews and into the theater—and advertising, promotions, and direct mail are the strategies of choice. Marketers typically work with budgets of about 10 percent of the productions' potential weekly gross. Producers can spend up to $1 million for a dramatic performance's preopening publicity and up to $75,000 each week on advertising and promotion. Musicals

▮▮▮▮▮▮▮▮▮▮ **BOX 11-1** ▮▮▮▮▮▮▮▮▮▮

Focus on Marketing Theater

A TONY FOR *AVENUE Q*

Jeffrey Seller is a theater producer with an uncanny ability to market unconventional musicals, such as *Rent* and *Avenue Q,* with tactics that include offering a limited number of $20 front row tickets to attract young adults. For the adult puppet show called *Avenue Q,* he used e-mails and ads that said: "Warning: Full Puppet Nudity," as well as airline-style pricing of theater seats to ensure full houses. He even incorporates ads into the set, usually seen as heresy for serious theatrical production.

Unlike the standard approach to selling a play via radio spots, newspaper ads, and posters, Seller's marketing strategy involves Broadway's No. 1 sales tool— the Tony Awards. The Best Musical campaign was an aggressive push targeted at the 730 people who vote for the Tonys that included parties, advertising, and gifts. As part of the campaign, Seller and his partners targeted voters from outside New York, who normally vote as a block, by wooing them with an argument that could not ignore—selling the play in regional theaters. He positioned *Avenue Q* as a quirky little musical up against a glitzy Hollywood-backed production. *Avenue Q* won the Tony.

Seller's marketing strategy is drumming up media coverage—especially on TV, because, he says, "Nobody young

Actress Suzanne Somes with puppet from the Broadway musical *Avenue Q* at award ceremonies in New York in 2006.

(Continued)

reads newspaper ads." One stunt—a staged political event in Times Square—generated coverage by 14 television stations, including two in Japan. The crowd munched free popcorn while a CNN reporter covering the event chatted with "Rod," a closeted gay Republican puppet. Seller's strategy was to make news that got the play off the arts page and into mainstream exposure.

His other tactics include keeping theater seats filled during slow months by selling seats at lower prices close to show time, advertising on ethnic radio stations, and handing out fliers in bars and nightclubs. He even spent thousands of dollars distributing textbook covers featuring artwork of his shows to high school students.

Produced at a cost of $3.5 million, *Avenue Q* grossed $36 million in its first two years of production. After winning the Tony, Seller signed an exclusive agreement with the Wynn hotel in Las Vegas for a second production. And, a third production opened in London in 2006.

SOURCE: Brooks Barnes for the *Wall Street Journal,* March 10, 2005.

are the most popular form of entertainment in the world; they require far less of a marketing budget to get audiences to buy tickets than drama or comedy.

In theater, the creative elements always start with commanding artwork and poster design. Logos become the brand identification for the show. Great artwork results from studying scripts, listening to the music, and talking with the writer or director long before the show begins rehearsals. One- or two-line summaries provide direction for creative; themes are developed using fashion styles, advertising, or art from the time period of the performance.

Once developed, themes should take a variety of forms, so that newspaper advertising can change weekly to keep the show looking fresh. Two types of advertising—*review ads* and *quote ads*—make use of positive narrative from reviewers and audience members to position the show in print as a winner. Electronic advertising is essential for effectively launching a musical. Radio and TV spots promote the quality of production values of sets, costumes, and cast. Television and radio commercials are ultimately the show's communication. When good reviews appear, producers often increase the weekly advertising budget to convey the message in a big way.

Developing a Plan for Theater Promotion

After the demographics and on-sale date for your marketing plan are determined, it needs to integrate the following components:

- Press announcement—releases and press conference
- Group sales—begin when exact dates are determined
- Subscription or show sponsor campaign—precede public on-sale period
- On-sale period—exact date tickets go on sale to general public
- Promotions—tied to sponsors or media presenters; opening night galas, anniversaries, and holiday seasons
- Advertising—pre-opening, post-opening, and sustaining media schedules prepared

The role of advertising and publicity are crucial for introducing a new play. Media sponsorship, audience development, database marketing, and licensing are equally important components of marketing theater.

Advertising's Role

Advertising is directed to the primary audience, one that is most economically and easily reached. The pre-opening period builds and creates anticipation. Launching the campaign on a weekend drives Monday sales. Once reviews are generated, the post-opening period begins with media to scream victory and declare the show a hit. A sustaining campaign follows opening night to maintain awareness and stimulate sales. Newspaper ads should have a consistent presence; they should be placed at least once per week in the entertainments sections with the highest circulation. Short flights of radio and TV advertising allow a continuing presence in the market.

Media companies can align themselves with chosen theatrical productions in what are called *presents deals*. Three sponsors, each representing a separate medium, sign on to stretch marketing dollars. The most common tactics are:

- Broadcast or Internet contests with tickets as prizes; winner gets an opening night package with limo, dinner, and tickets
- Run of show tickets for daily call-in radio contests
- Media logo identification on playbill

Such promotions get airtime or space valued at two to three times media buying expenditures to drive the contests. Bonus airtime or space at a value equal to the face value of tickets, as well as editorial coverage in the form of opening night and feature stories, are among the benefits of presents deals.

Publicity's Role

The publicity machine begins with a call to local entertainment columnists to leak a rumor that the show is coming to town. By persuading journalists to write about the show, promoters gain hype that leads to box office or ticket sales. As free advertising, publicity plays a crucial part of promoting the production. Publicity arms audiences with information and provides them with information and compelling reasons to purchase tickets. *Press kits,* in turn, provide journalists with a wealth of information to convey to audiences and include photographs and marquee posters, playbills and production notes, actor and director biographies, and ticket sale information. Journalists are usually in the audience on opening night. Publicists create fun, media-driven promotions and opportunities for publicity that hopefully result in lots of editorial coverage. T-shirts, soundtrack giveaways and midnight box-office openings that accompany opening night backs up the publicity hype. Other tricks used to promote shows include:

- media events with local auditions and local casting (*The King and I*).
- contests and giveaways on cereal boxes (*Phantom,* Canada).
- trivia contests to generate entries and awareness (*Phantom*).
- television promotion asking viewers to guess the location in the city of an actor staring in the show, with prizes including tickets (*Fiddler on the Roof,* Tampa).

Audience Development

Performance venue marketers use a variety of pricing strategies to change audience perceptions that live performances are out of reach. These include:

- Internet pricing discounts
- student subscriptions
- pay-what-you-can pricing
- rush seating one hour prior to performances
- lottery seating in the first two rows for persons who cannot afford full-price tickets
- mini-subscriptions and special packaging

Any booking of more than 20 tickets is considered a group. Group sales to tour operators, booking agencies, schools, and private organizations are an essential part of selling tickets. Groups usually receive incentives such as discounts, preferred seating, promotional materials, and pre- or post-show events. Group sales brochures present the stars, schedules, and ticket prices and include a bold call to action and clear reservation deadlines.

Advertising to outlying areas is another essential audience builder. Theater education programs, special family performances, and co-branding with airlines and hotels can all bring audiences to the performance.

Unlike movies and television, there is no after market for theater. However, astute marketing can produce an event that allows audiences to share a live experience, regardless of how large or small the production.

Database Marketing

Live performance requires personal contact with audience members based on active contact information. An audience database is an information-intensive, long-term marketing tool that serves as the cornerstone of message delivery and audience management. More than a simple list of patrons, a database contains lifestyle, demographic, and financial information; purchase transaction records; and promotions and media response characteristics.

Using databases as the central tool for marketing communications includes several critical elements and functions:

- Loyal patron identification—frequency of attendance and subscription purchases
- New audience development—consumer profiles developed and used to recruit by common characteristics
- Message delivery—communications targeted to groups based on usage patterns and motivations for attending
- Program development—behavior patterns analyzed to identify musical or performance preferences that can be used to develop a new season's program

List creation results from collecting information on audience members who have expressed some level of prior interest. Coupon ads may offer a purchase discount, and respondents are added to the database. Radio broadcasts can make similar offers that result in new names; lead cards can be left at the box office or on a table in the lobby, placed in programs, or distributed at corporate sponsors' offices, area restaurants, and local libraries. Arts organizations should go beyond their own lists to maintain a full range of lists and update them on a regular basis.

House lists, external lists, and specifically created lists maximize database marketing. **House lists** are current patrons who can be segmented into categories of: single-ticket buyers, first-year subscribers, two-plus year subscribers, lapsed subscribers, group sales buyers, and special plan or event buyers. **External lists** are obtained from a variety of outside sources, such as exchanges with other organizations whose patrons match demographics, performance preferences, or attendance patterns. **Rental lists** can be purchased from commercial sources such as video rental stores, magazine subscribers, mail-order houses, and museums.

Lists must be prioritized according to likely response rate, and lists with lowest response rates should be eliminated on a regular basis. House lists can be rented to other organizations to generate revenue, charging 50 cents per name; a 50,000-name mailing list will gross between $12,000 and $25,000 per year. Professional list managers implement a selective list rental program, advertise its availability, collect revenues, and monitor use. A financial commitment from organization's management and continuous updating of the data and system in response to the dynamic environment are two essential factors.

Licensing Theater

Stage productions are taking advantage of licensing agreements that often yield more revenue than the performance itself. *Wicked,* a musical that flopped in 2003, was a money-making machine in 2005, thanks to a strategy that took it to the launch pad for a much broader brand. Backed by Universal Pictures, the musical tapped into a new mother lode for the theater business—worldwide touring and licensing. By using the initial production as a platform for building a global franchise, the musical about teen witches scored a hit with audiences from teens to grandparents.

Success evolved from a licensing deal between *Wicked*'s producer and Stila, a cosmetics company that developed a line of clothes to sell at theaters. Karaoke contests at malls offered people a chance to win tickets by "auditioning" for parts in the show. Revenues for the cast album and advance ticket sales for a 30-city national tour in 2007 allowed *Wicked* to license its way to achieving the status of a cultural phenomenon. Other revenue streams include a movie version and tie-ins with Sprint cell phones and green M&Ms; a 192-page coffee table book is also popular among fans.

When it opened in St. Louis, *Wicked* sold $1.5 million worth of tickets in the first 48 hours after they went on sale. Sales for future shows, based on the *Wizard of Oz,* stand at about $30 million. Weekly sales of products—everything from $20 "Wicked" golf balls to $35 themed necklaces—exceed $300,000, which is more than most Broadway plays gross in a week.[4]

Audience Economics

Performing arts operate under somewhat different economic assumptions than other types of entertainment. In the 1990s, syndicates owned chains of theaters and controlled bookings and fees. Today, producers select a play, raise funds, and hire a director and cast, while theater owners generally handle box-office personnel and stagehands, advertising and sales functions. Gross receipts from commercial theater presentations on the road have overshadowed gross receipts on Broadway. This shift in

▪▪▪ EXHIBIT 11.1 Typical Financial Participations in Theater Productions

Gross Participations (%)	
Playwright	10
Lead performer	05
Director	02
Theater manager	25
Profit Participation (%)	
Playwright	5–10
Director	05
Lead performer	5–10
Other performers & mgr.	10
Producer	15
Investors	50–60

Source: Entertainment Industry Economics, 2001.

economic balance has led to the development of publicly owned companies that specialize in the production and staging of off-Broadway performances.

Returns on investment in a major musical production are high and long lasting, even in comparison to potential returns on popular films. Touring reproductions of musical and restorations of past Broadway hits have accounted for more than 80 percent of total commercial ticket sales. Resident or repertory theaters around the country are supported by a combination of subscription fees, foundation grants, individual contributions, and ticket and merchandise sales, and often are the source of new productions. Exhibit 11.1 shows typical financial participations of major players in the production process.

Financing for new commercial theater productions closely resembles financing for films. The producer acquires the rights to a play or literary property for adaptation to the stage, and prospective investors are sought for financing. Broadway runs are more likely to be funded by large entertainment companies than by individual investors. Financing may be available in the form of sale of stock in a corporation organized for production of a play, or as a development investment granted by film studios in return for movie rights. Broadway theater owners often take profits through limited partnerships or limited liability company arrangements.

A major star in a small play can receive weekly guarantees plus increasing percentages of gross after receipts reach certain levels. Directors may receive upfront fees and smaller percentages of weekly grosses. Playwrights normally earn at least a minimum author's royalty of 10 percent weekly, and the general manager receives weekly salary and perhaps a small percentage of net profits. High fixed costs of operation mean a large leveraged effect on profits. This creates either a smashing hit or a crashing failure—few shows fall between these extremes.

▪▪▪ Marketing Live Performances and Concerts

Live performances come in a variety of forms other than theater. You'll need specialized marketing strategies and tactics to promote ballet and dance, opera, classical and popular music, and the circus.

Promoting Ballet and Modern Dance

New York City Ballet, the American Ballet Theater, and San Francisco Ballet dominate domestic ballet performances. At least six nationally important dance groups present modern dance, a format that is usually dependent on a single choreographer and small groups of financial benefactors.

Traditionally, marketing budgets for promoting dance have consisted of immeasurable educational and outreach programs along with media advertising. Studies have found, however, that this approach works only when the target audience does not require a reward of some kind.[5] Cooperative marketing efforts are an additional avenue for increasing return on investment of the company's marketing dollar.

Choreographer Michael Smuin learned from gigs in nightclubs and musicals that audiences don't have much patience. His recent effort, called *Fly Me to the Moon,* was an unembarrassed homage to Frank Sinatra, mixing Sinatra trademarks such as trench coats and high-crowned hats with ballet's traditional toe shoes. Smuin claimed that his old-fashioned ballet is new nostalgia, like a prom night for adults. And it sold out, even in Italy. What was his marketing strategy? Differentiation.

Promoting Opera

Four major opera companies operate in the U.S. today: the Metropolitan, San Francisco, Chicago Lyric, and New York City. Companies in Los Angeles and Houston have emerged as profitable in spite of inherent problems of sustaining payroll for singers, chorus, dancers, orchestra, conductor, and extras. With more than 200 professionals on a payroll sustained by 4,000 seats in most venues, it is not surprising that more cities do not have permanent grand opera companies.

San Francisco Opera's *Doctor Atomic* premiere in 2005 was a huge success. The creative team was headed by director Peter Sellars, who promoted the premiere throughout the city with lectures, panels, and exhibits; the event became a "must attend" for opera buffs in the Bay Area and from around the world, and it played to almost full houses during its run.

In its first advertising campaign since the 1970s, New York's Metropolitan Opera put promotion pieces in telephone kiosks, on lamp posts, in subway entrances, and on the sides of city buses to announce its 2006 season. Why now? The Met is finding it harder to fill 4,000 seats with people willing to purchase tickets that range from $15 to $320.[6] The $500,000 advertising campaign blanketed street-level New York with images from *Madame Butterfly,* the season opener. Aimed at younger people who may find opera intimidating, the campaign aimed to demystify opera by reaching commuters and pedestrians using mass transit. By bringing Lincoln Center performance awareness to the masses, the venue hoped to convince potential audiences that opera is also a vibrant form of entertainment. And next door to the Met at Lincoln Center, the New York City Opera sells every seat in the house for $25 on eight evenings during the

■■■■■■■■■■   BOX 11-2   ■■■■■■■■■■

A Closer Look at Opera

THE VICTORIA OPERA

Venue research provides valuable insight into who attends, how often, and why. Once the audience segments are characterized, appropriate media are bought to deliver relevant messages. This *Closer Look* focuses on an Australian investigation of 104,000 patrons, which revealed that Opera Australia audiences had these demographics:

- 61% were women
- 45% had a college degree
- 36% were aged 35–49
- 30% belonged to the Socially Aware Value segment*

* **The Socially Aware Value segment** of the Australian population, based on lifestyle, motivations, and attitudes, provides valuable insight into opera's most relevant segment, who are

- the most educated segment of the community.
- up-market professionals, often in areas where they can influence others.
- politically and socially active and environmentally aware.
- pursuing stimulating and progressive lifestyles.

These audience members are "information vacuum-cleaners," are attracted to the new and different, and seek opportunities for training, education, and knowledge. They take a thoughtful and strategic approach to life. Their attraction to innovation and passionate commitment to ideas can also lead to a relative disregard for price.

This is the segment most likely to perceive the arts as an integral part of their daily life, and their arts attendance is both regular and high. They have a strong orientation toward the interpretive and innovative in art, and are attracted to art that is genuinely new and different—not simply remakes and re-presentations. They have a preference for intellectual stimulation over entertainment or relaxation as such, and for form and structure.

Recommended media: Their desire for information makes them heavy consumers of newspapers, particularly national newspapers, and of magazines presenting information not available in the mainstream media.

Information source breakdown:

- Daily metropolitan or national newspaper (72%)
- Friend/relative (36%)
- Television (19%)
- Local/suburban newspaper (15%)
- Notice/brochure/pamphlet in mail (15%)
- Radio (10%)

Advertising: They respond to stylish, tasteful, and intelligent appeals, rather than hype and cliché, and prefer Internet reminders and informative Web sites to written communications.

Decision-making factors: Who mostly goes with:

- Spouse/partner (57%)
- Friends (52%)
- Children (13%)

Who mostly decides what to see:

- Self (84%)
  - Of which:
    57% are female
    43% are male

(Continued)

- Spouse/partner (37%)
- Friend (22%)

Motivation for attending opera:

- To see a particular performer/show/group (28%)
- Entertainment (25%)
- Part of a subscription (14%)
- It is an old favorite (11%)

Reasons for not attending more often:

- Cost
- Don't have time to go

- Competing leisure time activities
- Too far to travel
- Don't like what is currently available

What do you think?

1. Based on the information learned from audience research, what messages would you communicate and to whom about a special opera performance?
2. What form should advertising take to reach this segment?

SOURCE: www.arts.vic.gov.au/arts/general/archives/factsheet, Dec. 5, 2005.

season,[7] proving that lower prices attract larger audiences without expensive advertising campaigns.

For a model of how to open a new opera house, marketers might copy the Royal Danish Opera in Copenhagen. The strategy to dedicate that company's modern $441 million home was to open with an audacious new work. It drew mixed reactions but played to sold-out houses. As evidenced by past successes, promotional draws center on new work, new buildings, and new locations.[8] Taking opera out of the concert hall into other, more accessible venues is a strategy now embraced by the Houston opera, which sings at baseball games, and San Francisco Opera's free concerts of popular arias in Golden Gate Park.

New opera means omitting the word *opera* from promotion materials, according to high-art American composers who come from the world of music theater. Opera is trying to speak more clearly to a new generation. Some recent titles are San Francisco Opera's production of *Dead Man Walking* and the Michigan Opera Theater's production of *Margaret Garner.* If the momentum generated by these innovative performing and marketing efforts can be sustained by subscriptions and guest appearances throughout companies' annual seasons, opera should be able to hold its own against other classical forms of entertainment.

Promoting Classical Music

The American Symphony Orchestra League categorizes approximately 1,600 orchestras in the U.S. according to the size of their budgets. In addition to large concert hall productions, many local and regional performances are presented each year; their success depends on timely and effective promotion. Even the nation's oldest and wealthiest company, the Boston Symphony Orchestra, uses promotional strategies to recruit audiences. By offering half-price tickets for performances of new works and pairing composers from different centuries, the orchestra keeps classical music alive for Boston and for the world.

Audiences' motivations are supported by the desire to see and hear a particular performer, conductor, or orchestra, and to support the organization. Emotional appeals play into those motivations by featuring a star performer—the bigger the star, the larger the box office. Promotional materials may use "all-time favorite" messages. Brochures and advertising clue the audience in on something special or interesting about the performance, or position it as exclusive or distinctive from the competition.

Classical music is confronted by long-range challenges that will not solve themselves. Recording contracts for orchestras have dried up. Audiences resist what is loosely called contemporary music. Patrons no long purchase full-season subscriptions, and audiences are growing grayer. To cover rising costs, tickets keep becoming more expensive. In short, classical music is jeopardized and marginalized, and there is no easy fix.

One innovator, who manages Carnegie Hall in New York, has taken serious measures to generate revenue in new ways. Because recording companies are not offering to make CDs of classical music, he decided to do the recording himself by sharing the risk of financing them. Starting with the London Symphony Orchestra, he designed the self-produced series as an orchestra-controlled alternative to a studio recording system. The label, nicknamed LSO Clive, now offers 32 discs. By pricing CDs at slightly under $10 so they were accessible to everyone, orchestras that recorded with LSO sold 25,000 copies in the first year of release. The recordings have won prestigious prizes. The LSO made its entire catalog available for download online on iTunes in 2005. Though not as ambitious as LSO, the San Francisco Symphony released its first recording under its own label in 2002 as part of a Mahler series.

Another business-model strategy transforms unusual programs into events. One such event for which this strategy was used was a Shostakovich festival, featuring renowned cellist Mstislav Rostropovich conducting all 15 symphonies; it played to full houses. A discovery series was another event for which the orchestra illuminated the obscurities of modern music.

Education also is used to help audiences understand classical music. During a London Symphony Orchestra production intermission, the orchestra demonstrated how Stravinsky constructed the work in rhythmic chunks, then returned to perform the piece uninterrupted. Carnegie Hall developed a Sound Insights series for audience education. The Carnegie administration has ambitious orchestra residency program of eight-day visits from outstanding world philharmonic orchestras; the administration spends $8 million each year on education.

Finally, Carnegie Hall created an intermediate-sized basement space, Zankel Hall, which has 600 seats, to present innovative artists who are not mainstream enough to fill the 2,800-seat main auditorium. Following in their lead, regional performing arts centers are conducting capital campaigns to provide smaller, more intimate venues with lower prices and reduced overhead.

According to studies conducted by the Brooklyn and Fort Wayne philharmonics,[9] thematic and crossover programming brings in more first-timers. Results were unclear, however, about whether such concerts would lead to more regular subscriptions. In this study, education—such as more Web material, pre-concert lectures, and expanded program notes—did not increase ticket sales at all.

▪▪▪▪▪▪▪▪▪▪▪ BOX 11-3 ▪▪▪▪▪▪▪▪▪▪

Focus on Classical Music

NEW OVERTURES AT THE SYMPHONY

As existing audiences grow older and the public turns its attention away from concert-going, orchestras around the country are adopting a wide array of marketing strategies to bring more people into the concert hall—mainly audiences who are neophytes, dabblers, and the un-gray. Some of their innovations are presented here as indications of what can be done to invigorate lagging attendance.

Beethoven Bash T-shirts given free to audience members in their 30s who attend a Beethoven concert (Spokane).

A *Classical Connections* series during which the under-40 set can speed date, take salsa lessons, or exchange resumes before a performance, a shortened concert with onstage commentary and occasional videos (Milwaukee).

Friday night mixers that feature chamber music during the first half of the program, then provide a choice of chamber music or jazz in the lobby for the second half (St. Paul).

A S*even 18 Club* series for young professions with pre-concert drinks and post-concert socializing with young orchestra members (St. Louis).

A *Shorts* performance of four 20-minute concerts in one evening, each lasting one hour, from 7 to 10:00 p.m. (Miami Beach).

A *Beyond the Score* series that offers a live documentary on a major piece—film clips, an actor reading letters, comments from the conductor, and musical examples from the orchestra—followed by a performance of the piece in the second half of the program (Chicago).

A *Fun Factor Thursday* series that provides free buffet dinners in the hall's ballroom, and *College Nite* concerts that feature post-performance parties at which students nibble appetizers and listen to a local band (Cincinnati).

A *Symphony with a Twist* series of four concerts that are preceded by lobby gatherings featuring martini bars and jazz (Baltimore and Atlanta).

A *Fourth Ring Society* for the MTV crowd that features $10 balcony seats for ballet performances (New York City).

The use of media from *popular titles* such as *The Lone Ranger, 2001,* and *Star Wars* to package classical programs (San Diego).

SOURCE: David Waken for the *New York Times,* Aug. 21, 2005.

▪▪▪▪▪▪▪▪▪

Nonmusical methods to lure concertgoers have included producing shorter and earlier concerts, adding onstage commentary, and offering film-score programs for a broader appeal. More recent innovations include video screens in the concert hall, handheld electronic devices to provide running commentary, and musical programs built around pop culture themes.

When marketing any classical performance, splashy telemarketing, generous and flexible subscription packages, a mini-season of popular titles, reasonable prices, catchy print ads, and powerful radio ads are needed to guarantee ticket sales. Unique locations, such as the Denver Symphony Orchestra's performances in hip venues such as a basketball arena, are another innovation. Ultimately, orchestral delivery systems must provide an entertainment experience. As a marketer of classical music, you need to focus on what the audience wants, loosen the definition of classical music, offer lots of visual stimulation, and pay more attention to social functions to draw younger adults.[10]

The Music Business

Musical concerts geared to young adults are their own special case. Concert marketers have a direct link to the recording industry, and concerts are organized as seasonal line-ups of regular acts. Promotional players include a *promoter,* who is responsible for booking acts, paying for ads and venues, and setting performance details; the artist's *personal manager,* who selects tours, dates, venues, and markets; an *agent,* who works with the manager to book tours, hire promoters, and plot the tour route; and a *road manager,* who looks after the details. The genre comes with its unique problems—producers and marketers must anticipate and overcome crowd control, unruly fans, venue design, and ticket scalping.

The least expensive form of entertainment to market, concerts are usually limited to short engagements. Managers budget for three ticket-sales modules: the on-sale period, sustaining period, and panic period when goals have not been met. During the *on-sale* phase, print ads and a short flight of radio ads are used to promote the sales date one week prior to the performance. Radio promotions help to clean out the inventory left over from the on-sale period.

Timing is an important factor in marketing concerts. Ticket sales for smaller acts need a six- to eight-week advance along with a large advertising budget. When multiple concert dates are scheduled, each show should sell out before the next one is promoted. Booking should be matched with album release dates, and the use of "wild posting" heightens interest.

Publicity is crucial to box office success. Press releases must use a creative hook so media can promote the venue. Newspaper and radio entertainment calendars must be notified, and interviews are arranged with the press by phone or in person just prior to the concert. Merchandising giveaways in the form of T-shirts and stickers accelerate hype; retail exposure for albums, POPs, and joint promotion with record chains work well for promoting popular bands and individual performers.

Bands and Artists

Concert tours are typically the primary marketing vehicle of bands and artists. Tours provide the exposure that can leverage sales. Besides touring, marketing campaigns to promote music sales may involve cooperative advertising with local retailers, in-store merchandising aids (e.g., posters, T-shirts), radio and TV commercials, and promo press kits (free cuts are usually sent to radio stations). Marketing costs can often reach $100,000 for a standard release and in excess of $500,000 for a release by a major artist.

Promotional efforts focus on 200–300 radio stations nationwide. Tip sheets and trade papers, such a *Billboard* and *Radio & Records,* serve as measuring points. Music companies have their own staffs of trackers, whose job it is to know which songs and

▪▪▪▪▪▪▪▪▪▪ BOX 11-4 ▪▪▪▪▪▪▪▪▪▪

A Closer Look at Band Brands

KISS, THE STONES, AND AEROSMITH USE STRATEGIES THAT ROCK

In their book *Brands That Rock,* Roger Blackwell and Tina Stephan tell business leaders what they can learn from the world of rock-and-roll. This focus highlights three bands that reemerged after falling from grace by implementing unique promotional strategies that are relevance for entertainment marketing.

Kiss Elements that allowed the band to re-emerge successfully: Band members made personal connection with the audience and packaged themselves in Kabuki makeup for differentiation; sensory overload brought surprise to the stage.

Strategy:

- Induce trial in the right markets
- Roll out concert tours with performances in rural locations
- Court the press
- Merchandise makeup kits and games for fans

- Create an MTV special to remove Kabuki makeup
- Hold a Kiss convention starring the original band members
- Change musical content as fans change by using a migration strategy

Rolling Stones Elements of success and remaining relevant: Adhering to the business side of music revenue-generating areas such as album sales, royalties, and touring; creating a brand image with merchandising, tours, books, and corporate endorsements.

Strategy:

- Change and evolve style and music at a rate that doesn't alienate fans while keeping the band relevant to new fans
- Generate buzz with online ticket sales
- Develop corporate partnerships
- Feature new songs in commercials
- Use CDs as marketing tool rather than as revenue generators
- Invoke discriminatory pricing strategies

KISS, the band.

(Continued)

Rolling Stones.

- Alternate performance venues with a variety of prices and musical content to include stadiums, arenas, and theaters
- Generate revenue from sky boxes, bus tours, TV appearances, merchandising, and cross-promotions
- Co-brand with E*Trade on the Internet
- Adapt performances to baby boomer wants and needs

Aerosmith Elements of reinvention and marketplace reentry: getting clean and sober; perform with funky clothing, long hair, and painted nails; loyal male audience; combination that featured newness and familiarity. **Strategy:**

- Use grassroots marketing
- Implement a unique tour strategy by playing a concert and then returning in three weeks to play again
- Cater to fans of other band brands

Aerosmith.

(Continued)

- Create *angel fans* who discover bands before they become stars
- Invoke a trickle-up theory of cultural adoption
- Reverse audience intimacy by monitoring fans' behaviors during concerts and focusing on ways for fans to know the band better with *remote staging,* travel packages, and "meet and greet" backstage visits for fans

What do you think?

1. Which band strategy relied on an established fan base to make its comeback? Why was this an advantage?
2. What lessons can concert marketers learn from the brand successes?

SOURCE: Blackwell and Stephan, *Brands That Rock*, 2004.

CDs are being added to or deleted from play lists of stations and syndicated radio companies around the country. Competition is intense: each year an estimated 7,000 (nonclassical) albums are released.

The Internet and music downloads have changed the industry by providing an ideal distribution channel. Older forms of distribution are rapidly becoming less and less important, so marketing expertise will be needed to distinguish content and break through the clutter.

File Sharing

Although advocates believe that peer-to-peer (P2P) file sharing is the future of the music industry, not all lawyers agree.[11] The debate over the legality of Internet downloads and P2P sharing of music files has gone on for years. But one lawyer argues, "If you legalize P2P file-sharing, you decimate the legal download sales of the record companies and undermine hard-copy sales." Terry McBride of Nettwerk Music Group believes that, rather than suing file-sharers and using digital rights management (DRM) to protect the copyright, the industry should "give up control." McBride's new paradigm centers on "mobilizing the fans" by using a band's fans as a marketing team to spread the news about artists through word of mouth. In addition, downloads could be made freely available, either subsidized by pop-up ads or paid for by a minimal fee paid by subscribers to mobile phone or Internet services. "Let the market establish what the price is and the revenue litigation has never won. People who pirate music and make a profit should be sued out of existence," says McBride. "But file-sharing is our future."

The Music Marketing Mogul[12]

Jimmy Iovine, who runs Interscope/Geffen/A&M, is an executive with musical talent. Although he is a manager with Universal Music Group, the biggest music firm in the world (owned by French conglomerate Vivendi), artists regard him as much more than just another "suit": Iovine has street credibility. And—ironically enough—that may be the key to his success as a businessman.

The majors, as the big labels are known, used to have talent-spotting music executives at the helm, but things have changed. A television producer and a journalist head the second biggest music firm, Sony BMG. A group of private-equity firms own a big chunk of Warner Music Group. EMI's chairman used to run a biscuit company. Iovine is a different breed. He created the record label Interscope, which has consistently been on the cusp of some of the most profitable trends in American music.

Iovine got his first break from John Lennon, with whom he worked during his solo career. He then produced Bruce Springsteen, Tom Petty, and Patti Smith, among others. His techniques were innovative; he lent an air of Hollywood to the music with expensive videos and billboard advertisements. Iovine advanced the careers of artists from U2 to Eminem. Interscope ended up as part of Universal Music, which has 32 percent of the American recorded-music market, 26 percent worldwide, and its share is growing.

Iovine, recognized early that music marketing needed to be more sophisticated and that partnerships with the ad industry, done right, could benefit both sides. He saw marketing as a tool to combat piracy and overcome some of the built-in problems of the recording industry's business model.[13]

He has a reputation for giving artists more money than other record labels, and for making lots of 50/50 joint-venture agreements with musicians' own labels—so his artists tend to have more of a stake in their success than other labels' artists do. When Steve Jobs was developing iTunes, Iovine helped persuade the other labels to sell him their music alongside that of Universal Music. Jobs calls him "the future" of the music industry.

Iovine's latest idea for Universal Music is to earn money from sources beyond recorded music. In his vision, Interscope's artists can become multi-media entertainment brands. 50 Cent, for instance, starred in a film last year, *Get Rich or Die Tryin'* made under Iovine's film-production deal with Paramount, Viacom's film studio, and the rapper has also appeared in a video game. Universal Music takes a cut.

A 2006 example is the Pussycat Dolls. Universal Music has a deal with Hasbro, a toymaker, to sell dolls of the singers, as well as one for Pussycat Dolls makeup and a Las Vegas nightclub.

Planning Points for Concert Promotion

Using much the same planning process as for any performance, concert plans have four key functions:

1. Identifying what will make the product stand out and be noticed (unique selling proposition)
2. Positioning the event ahead of the competition
3. Staying current by reading trade magazines (*Billboard, Performance*) and consumer magazines (*Rolling Stone, Spin*)
4. Knowing the audience well

Planning is key for developing and implementing successful marketing strategies.

Message Development

Word-of-mouth is a big factor in popular music. Promotional messages directed at concertgoers are best delivered through friends, family, or anyone else who might influence targeted buyers. Unlike theatergoers, who wait for expert channels to review a performance before purchasing tickets, music fans are excited by the buzz created around a concert. Among young adults, opinion leaders—those whose opinion matters to a defined social group—have legitimate power by virtue of their social standing. Live concert performance marketers try to stimulate word-of-mouth exposure by providing opinion leaders with free tickets or special perks so they will spread the word and stimulate ticket purchases.

▬▬▬▬▬▬▬▬▬ **BOX 11-5** ▬▬▬▬▬▬▬▬▬▬

Focus on Band Promotion

CRAFTING A MYSPACE PAGE

Many music fans roam MySpace in search of good indie music. But with so many options, how do visitors choose whose music site to visit? MusicDish talent scout Anne Freeman checks two things:

1. Photo/graphic
2. Band name

The first thing consumers do when confronted with a list of potential bands is look at their photo or graphic. The second thing is to look at their name. The third thing is look at their photo/graphic again. That's it, period.

What that says to marketers of indie labels and band/artists is, Be very careful about your photo/graphic selections and, if you're just starting out, pay attention to the name you choose if you have a band. You must catch a potential fan or music industry professional in a few seconds.

Freeman's advice? Use a graphic or photograph that best communicates the band's *primary artistic sensibility.* Here are some examples:

The Pink Spiders used a photo of band members that is eye-catching with bold colors. The art conveys musical fun and creates a "must hear" from browsers to MySpace. Their site (www.myspace.com/thepinkspiders) is a perfect match for their pop/punkish music. Everything on the site contributes to their look and sound.

Creech Holler's band name confirms the intrigue and stimulates a click to their site. Their ominous graphic recons back to the old snake handlers of the deep South, so buffs know it is a Southern blues or folk band from both the name and the image. They have effectively married their music with their look and style. www.myspace.com/creechholler

Individual artists who are trying to stand out probably face a bigger challenge on a site such as MySpace, and this is especially true for artists in acoustic-based music. Individual artists have a

The Pink Spiders' page on MySpace.

(Continued)

much more difficult time trying to establish a Web presence.

Carie Pegeon is an example of an acoustic-based artist whose photograph created an eye-catching image of a strong female, acoustic-singer/songwriter with a hard, confessional edge. Her photo is well composed and interesting to look at, and should convince others to visit her site.

Networking sites are important for both new and established artists. Most consumers base their decisions whether or not to visit a site on the same two pieces of information: graphic and band name. What marketers, managers, and record labels must think through carefully is how to use those two portals to an artist's site, whether the browser is a fan or a music industry professional.

Band marketers should be very clear about primary artistic sensibility to ensure that every decision made for the site contributes to the band or artist's cause. If each choice does not actively contribute to the site, then it actively detracts from the artist. There is no neutral ground in this game.

Need a name for a band? Check out the Band Name Generator, a link with 10,000 names generated by MIT students and a computer.

SOURCE: MusicDish Network, August 5, 2006.

▪▪▪▪▪▪▪▪▪

Off to Market the Circus

Circuses are considered to be one of the major performing arts in Europe, where they commonly receive government subsidies. In the United States, circuses are operated by private, for-profit organizations. As such, they have become permanent traveling forms of commercial theater, operating with a blend of economic features seen in both theater and theme-park operations. Circuses are only marginally profitable, given the size and structure of the spectacle that must be assembled and disassembled every few days. Still, the 10 major domestic circuses enjoy attendance from more than 40 million people each year.

For the first time in its history, the once-classic three-ring Ringling Brothers and Barnum & Bailey Circus has presented a new show to its audiences—without any rings at all. When the 136th edition of the circus opened in 2006 at the St. Pete Times Forum in Tampa, the elephants, clowns, aerialists, and acrobats roamed an arena floor. In another huge departure from tradition, the show had a story line instead of being simply a cavalcade of acts.

Circus executives attributed the overhaul to market research. The circus's family audiences, primarily mothers of kids 2–11 years old, say their lives are already three-ring circuses, so they want something less distracting. They also wanted to connect with a story in an emotional way. Ringling expected 11 million people to watch their new show in one of 79 markets a year during the two-year tour. Internet sneaks hyped the new format, which was delivered with high anticipation from circus audiences.[14]

Audiences also respond to smaller circuses with extraordinary formats. The Dream Circus Theater in Los Angeles, founded by Teo Castro, offers a new kind of creative space for promoting parties that melds a club scene, rock scene, and arts scene as it creates a new venue for emerging performers.

Focus on the Circus

BRING ON THE POWER CLOWN

To boost their bottom line, circuses are turning to a new marketing tool: the celebrity clown. Circuses are paying branded clowns up to $600,000 a year to act foolish under the big top. Multimillion-dollar ad campaigns are focused on clowns such as Mr. Nock and "Grandma," of New York's Big Apple Circus. In addition to high salaries, clowns receive perks such as a staff, a custom RV, and up to 5 percent of the pre-tax gross of branded souvenirs such as rag dolls.

Headliner clown strategies date back to the late 1990s when animal acts were expensive to maintain, did not draw audiences, and were politically sensitive. After retaining Mr. Nock, Ringling sold 10 million tickets for a 10 percent gain over the previous year. Big Apple's ticket sales also improved after retaining star clowns. Here is what was offered in 2005:

Circus/City	Ticket Price	Star Clown(s)	Cool Souvenirs	Other
Big Apple	$15–$44	Grandma Goes Hollywood	Faux-slinky, $5	28th season, nonprofit
Carson & Barnes	$7–$21	Quina Brothers	Circus Girls' Cookbook $10	5 rings, 250-town tour
Cirque du Soleil	$30–$185	Corteo	Unisex tote bag, $99	17th production
Ringling/Barnum & Bailey	$13–$82	Bello Nock	Clown binoculars, $10	3 rings for 135 years
Zoppe Italian Family Circus	$9–$18	Nino	Nino plush clown doll, $12	U.S.-based

Source: Kelly Crow for *The New York Times,* Aug. 8, 2005.

Bello Nock, of Ringling Brothers, on the high wire.

Financing Live Performances

It is almost impossible to raise substantially the productivity of live performances, which are themselves end products. Productivity lag in the arts becomes more pronounced as productivity in other economic sectors increases and operating costs escalate. Ticket prices have risen at higher rates than the consumer price index, and indications are that higher prices reduce demand. Revenue sources that go beyond box office revenues, especially for nonprofit organizations, are desperately needed. The most prevalent funding source is donations from individuals and corporations.

Donations and Subsidies

Contributions to the arts by individuals and estates are the performing arts largest single source of voluntary funding. Orchestras and operas receive proportionately more regular contributions than theater or dance. Performing arts subsidies from state and local arts councils and through the National Endowment for the Arts are vital, but in the United States these subsidies are much less significant than in Europe. Private corporate support of cultural activities may stimulate local commercial activity as it may provide new business opportunities.

Because of the tremendous costs of establishing and continuing live performances, corporate philanthropy is an important source of revenue. Marketers establish liaisons with corporations by demonstrating to them a perceived benefit from associating with arts performances.

Support for the arts, regardless of the source, is normally dedicated to the development of specific facilities or to the patronage of fixed dance, orchestral, and opera groups. Usually no return on investment is expected. Always on a financial precipice, performing arts organizations are subject to audience size limitations and the expense of coordinating an effective production with venture capital from those willing to invest in risky ventures. With advances in technology, revenues derived from new media are becoming significant considerations in financing the arts. Cable television license fees or home video presentation formats may enhance profits and lower the risk of loss.

⚊⚊ Maximizing Public Relations to Promote Performances

Marketing is an integrated effort. One of the most significant components of integrated marketing is public relations, for many reasons. By integrating a program consisting of research, publicity, and lobbying, public relations efforts provide a coordinated effort for reaching the organization's publics. PR's merger with marketing functions enables the delivery of persuasive and influential unpaid promotions. By developing sound objectives, creating a positive image, and using event marketing, public relations becomes a star performer.

Synchronizing Objectives

Marketing's goal is to influence *behavior;* PR's task is to form, maintain, or change public *attitudes* toward the organization or performance genre. Publicity can make a profound impact on public awareness by placing stories in the media that bring attention to performances and performers. Publicity yields high rewards for improving an organization's image and visibility.

The benefits of public relations include high credibility, extending advertising's reach, and reinforcing messages sent by other delivery systems. Media coverage is an important component of image development.

PR requires a fraction of the cost of media advertising. In the face of shrinking arts coverage, PR managers can place features in alternative newspaper sections (food, travel, home, news), develop collaborative feature stories, and capitalize on holidays for image enhancement.

Event Marketing

A fast-growing, high-profile industry that began as an offshoot to PR, event marketing ties product brands with entertainment events to deliver a lifestyle experience to audiences. From world platforms such as the Olympic games to local programs such as marathon races, event marketing integrates the corporate sponsorship of an event with a whole range of marketing elements such as advertising, sales promotion and public relations. Events enjoy a growth rate of 20 percent each year, which points to their high level of success. Companies break through the advertising clutter with image association that drives awareness and sales. Sponsorship caters to audiences who have switched their allegiance from buying products to enjoying lifestyles, experiences, and emotions. Events can take many forms: international, such as the Olympics, or local and regional events that provide a captive audience both face-to-face and through live media coverage.

Why Develop an Event?

According to a recent IEG Sponsorship survey of 280 events,[15] sponsors' key objectives include establishing:

- corporate identification through displays of brand names or logos on event signage.
- target marketing to reach a select audience.
- promotional tie-ins to gain attention and drive purchase.
- entertainment for clients.
- sampling of a product or service through coupons or teasers distributed at the event.
- brand awareness from frequent impressions.
- usage stimulated by event promotions.
- PR for brand mentions in media coverage of the event.

Planning Events

Tactical and detailed plans ensure a positive return on investment. Following these six key elements helps to ensure success:

1. Select an event that meet business objectives and enhance the brand's image and try to lock in a long-term relationship to build high recall

2. Tightly define the target audience to ensure the development of a good match between them and the event

3. Leverage the sponsorship by integrating marketing programs to include product sampling, on-site signage, logo placement, and cross-promotions

4. Negotiate favorable terms and protect them in a contractual agreement that includes brand exclusivity, brand role in relation to other sponsors, brand protection measures, right of refusal for future events, and benefits such as complementary tickets and logo inclusion in advertising

5. Deliver relevance for your audience in order to build the brand's reputation

6. Use the Internet to promote the event, maintain continuous communication with the target audience, and follow up with the audience after the event

Events are best used to create an emotional tie with participants and spectators, and to increase brand awareness for an entertainment franchise or corporation. When the entertainment brand is the sponsor, selecting appropriate product brand partners is crucial for maximizing the audiences' lifestyle expectations. Brand constellations—brand groups valued by a specific target audience—must package brand images that are compatible with the event, the sponsors, and the audience.

The Sponsors Report, which tracks the number of times a sponsor's name is mentioned or viewed in a broadcast, adds up the exposure time and multiplies it by the cost of the advertising time to arrive at an overall figure. Broadcast time for elements such as logo, on-screen graphics, verbal mentions, uniform or clothing signage, and banners is valued, then totaled, to determine the equivalent value provided by the event.

For nonprofit organizations, special events in the form of benefits or galas are a popular fund-raising strategy. By selling an event at a premium price, organizations can link their mission and goals with coming events; a theater's dinner benefit may feature vignettes from an upcoming musical or comedy. Events are especially effective for attracting potential donors and new patrons to the organization, and improving an organization's image. Costly to run and highly labor-intensive, events nonetheless generate enthusiasm for a venue or organization that may outweigh individual fund-raising efforts.

⁗ Formulating a Communications Strategy for Performing Arts

As discussed in Chapter 10, the communication process is *who says what in what medium to whom with what effect.* To communicate effective marketing messages, the sender must successfully deliver a message using an understandable set of symbols to the audience so that it is understood and acted on. A process of coding and encoding takes place, concluding with a feedback loop that allows the sender to determine whether or not the message was successfully understood. This sounds simple enough, but marketers are not always able to achieve effective message development or feedback mechanisms. This explains how to set objectives and craft messages for performing arts. Delivering messages over the Internet and to editors and reviewers is also discussed here.

Setting Objectives

Our objectives for communicating to performing arts audiences are to achieve *purchase stimulation* and *performance satisfaction.* A long process of decision-making, purchase behavior begins with an understanding of how to move the audience to a higher state of purchase readiness. Buyer readiness has six levels:[16]

1. *Awareness*—let the audience know that a new opera will debut, a popular performance is back in town, or a new venue is opening.

2. *Knowledge*—convey the benefits of attending a particular performance to a specific audience segment.

3. *Liking*—the disposition toward a performance by the audience is either a point for emphasis or a problem to overcome.

4. *Preference*—given audiences' many stay-at-home viewing options, marketers must convince audiences that seeing live performance is the preferred choice.

5. *Conviction*—marketers often must convince audiences that attending is fun and exciting; incentives are often necessary to reach this level.

6. *Purchase*—advertising or e-mail reminders help deliver audiences to the box office.

Determining audience readiness states is critical in developing a communication program that will be cost-effective while inducing the desired response. Make them fall in love before you ask them to open their wallets.

Crafting and Delivering Messages

Like objectives, messages must gain *attention,* hold *interest,* arouse *desire,* and elicit *action.* Advertising creative teams use this **AIDA model** to develop effective communication appeals. Appeals should be unique to the organization or performance being promoted. The more direct the competition, the more necessary it is to develop a *unique selling point* (USP).

As with other entertainment activities or destinations, messages directed at audiences must be sent via channels frequently used and easily accessed by that audience. Because many performances are venue-dependent, the Internet is an excellent way to communicate with potential ticket purchasers. Advertising, PR, editorial comment, and performance reviews also should be part of the promotional mix for sending messages about live performances.

Internet

Web sites should stimulate visitors to explore a wide variety of information, including photographs of performers, historical information, milestones, upcoming events, and highlights with concert schedules and venue information. Seating charts with views of the stage, listing of nearby restaurants and lodging, and online links to other attractions also should be included. Special discount ticket offers for Web visitors and an order form that can be e-mailed or faxed to the box office also are essential components of a performance venue site. Pages containing information about the latest in performer news, excerpts of recordings, news items and press releases for media, educational programs, sponsorship, and volunteering opportunities should be easily locatable and accessible. Finally, contact information allows the visitor to send email directly to the directors of ticket service, marketing and PR, information services, education, volunteers, and development. The visitor also should be able to arrange to be added to the organization's mailing list.

Editorial and Reviews

Source credibility goes a long way in delivering positive, unbiased messages to current and potential audiences. With strategic management of feature stories and critical comments, public relations efforts can enhance marketing's impact.

Press kits, containing performance information, schedules, performer biographies, and suggestions for feature articles, should be delivered to editors of entertainment and calendar sections of local newspapers. Performance trailers placed with television news producers often provide welcome fillers that result in free coverage. Most editorial features are stimulated by paid publicists, and well-placed story ideas are worth their weight in gold.

Reviewers are important to producers of live performances because of their influence on attendance and box office sales. Providing reviewers with advance tickets, interviews with performers and anecdotal material improves your chances for positive commentary, or at least they may curtail negative remarks that can terminate a new show in an untimely fashion.

FINALLY: LET'S SUM UP ▪▪▪▪▪▪▪

Of all the entertainment genres discussed in this text, live performance is the least affected by technological advances. Digitization is no substitute for well-scripted productions, talented performers, and the dynamic energy generated by live performances. Yet, because of fierce competition from digitized entertainment, effective promotion is key for the success and survival of all types of theatrical, dance, and musical productions classified as performing arts.

Never underestimate the role of the Internet for promoting concerts and live performances. Fans always consult Web blogs, calendars, and reviews before purchasing tickets, so the design and implementation of an effective, attractive Web site is essential for a complete marketing communications effort.

GOT IT? LET'S REVIEW ▪▪▪▪▪▪▪

- Drama, the driving force of entertainment genres, produces conflict and resolution that enables audiences to experience the entire range of human conditions. Promotional efforts can be successful only when they connect audiences with the excitement of a particular genre.
- In order to get audiences to go beyond the reviews and into the theater, advertising, promotions, and direct mail are the strategies of choice for marketers.
- Concert managers budget for three ticket sales modules: the on-sale period, the sustaining period, and the panic period when goals have not been met.
- Corporate donations and government funding are necessary to finance live

performances that are part of the nonprofit sector.
- Because public relations forms, maintains, or changes public *attitudes* toward an organization or performance genre, events are best used to create an emotional tie between the genre and its participants and spectators, and to increase brand awareness for an entertainment franchise or corporation.
- Communication objectives for performing arts audiences are purchase stimulation and performance satisfaction; messages delivered over the Internet, in editorial coverage, and in positive reviews are most effective for reaching current and potential audiences.

NOW TRY THIS ▪▪▪▪▪▪▪

1. Consult the calendar or entertainment section of your local newspaper and count the number of ads for live performances. How do they compare with ads for mediated events? Sporting events? What do these numbers suggest about audience preferences?

2. Locate three sources on the Internet that provide scheduling information for live performances. How easy or difficult were they to find? What can you suggest for making this process easier?

3. Read three reviews of a single live performance and compare them. Which reviews

were most influential? Why? As a result of the reviews, would you attend or simply abide by the consensus of the reviewers?

4. Identify a regional theater in your area and obtain performance information about it.

From the messages and delivery system they use, what can you determine about their marketing effectiveness? What can you suggest for improvement?

QUESTIONS: LET'S REVIEW ▮▮▮▮▮▮▮

1. What elements are involved in planning a promotional campaign for theatrical productions? What type of research is necessary to determine promotional strategies?
2. Discuss the similarities and differences of marketing the five different types of concerts presented in this chapter.
3. Explain the types of funding appropriate for marketing and promoting a concert or live performance presented by a nonprofit organization.

4. How would you use public relations to enhance the marketing program for a circus? What role would the celebrity clown play, if any?
5. Why are editorial and reviewer commentary so important for the success of a live performance? How can use these sources to best serve your organizational client?

MORE TO READ ▮▮▮▮▮▮▮

www.thebuzzfactor.com.

www.aandronline.com.

Beat Wire (PR the for music industry).

Barry Avrich. *Selling the Sizzle: The Magic and Logic of Entertainment Marketing.* Canada: Maxworks Publishing Group, 2002.

Roger Blackwell and Tina Stephan. *Brands That Rock.* Hoboken, NJ: Wiley, 2004.

Philip Kotler and Joanne Scheff. *Standing Room Only: Strategies for Marketing the Performing Arts.* Cambridge, MA: HBS Press, 1997.

M. W. Krasilovsky, S. Shemel, and J. M. Gross. *The Business of Music: A Definitive Guide to the Music Industry,* 9th ed. New York: Billboard Books, 2003.

Bernard Schmitt, David Rogers, and Karen Vrotsos. *There's No Business That's Not Show Business: Marketing in an Experience Culture.* New York: Financial Times/Prentice Hall, 2004.

Harold Vogel. *Entertainment Industry Economics,* 5th ed. London: Cambridge University Press, 2001.

NOTES ▮▮▮▮▮▮▮

1. Andy Newman, *New York Times,* Dec. 29, 2005.
2. Bill Wyman, *New York Times,* June 12, 2005.
3. Robert Hughes, "Entertainment" column, *Wall Street Journal,* June 17, 2005.
4. Brook Barnes, *Wall Street Journal,* Oct. 23, 2005.
5. C. S. Huntington, *Marketing Professional Ballet* (Urbana], IL: University of Illinois, Institute for Entrepreneurial Studies, 2004).
6. Julie Bosman, "Advertising" column, *New York Times,* Aug. 29, 2006.
7. Robin Pogrebin, *New York Times,* Oct. 9, 2006, A1.
8. Anthony Tommasini, *New York Times,* Dec. 25, 2005.
9. Daniel Wakin, *New York Times,* Aug. 21, 2005.
10. Results of a 10-year research project of arts audiences in 15 American cities financed by the Knight Foundation.
11. Matt Byrne, *The Lawyer,* May 2006, p. 16.
12. www.economist.com, May 4, 2006.
13. Scott Donaton, *Advertising Age,* Aug. 1, 2005, Vol. 76 Issue 31, p. 12, 1p.
14. Glenn Collins, *New York Times,* Dec. 31, 2005.
15. Barry Avrich, *Selling the Sizzle: The Magic and Logic of Entertainment Marketing* (Canada: Maxworks Publishing Group, 2002), p. 82.
16. Based on similar steps cited in Philip Kotler and Joanne Scheff, *Standing Room Only* (Cambridge, MA: HBS Press, 1997), pp. 306–8.

CHAPTER 12

Destinations and Tourist Services

*Not bound to swear allegiance to any master,
wherever the wind takes me I travel as a visitor.*
—Horace

Chapter Objectives

After reading Chapter 12, you should be able to answer these questions:

- What are the elements of the *travel cycle* and *tourism market?*
- How does marketing *places* differ from other types of travel and tourism marketing?
- How are *destination brands* established, built, and maintained over time?
- What *promotion strategies* are appropriate for branding destinations and places?
- How do we market *tourism services?*

The tourism and travel industry employs more people worldwide than any other industry. Many local and regional economies are sustained through tourism-related revenues, including transportation, hospitality, food and beverage, recreation, and amusement-based attractions. This chapter begins with an introduction to the principles and dimensions of the travel and tourism market. Then, we focus on city and nation destination marketing and present promotional strategies appropriate for bringing attention to place brands. The final section presents the marketing of tourist services, including resort/hotel/spa, transport, and tour businesses.

▪▪▪ Industry Terminology and Dimensions

Like other leisure-based industries, the travel business has its own jargon. These classifications and measurements were standardized by the World Trade Organization (WTO):

- *Visitor*—any person out of his or her home
- *Tourist*—a person who stays over one night and collects mementos
- *Same-day visitor*—cruise passengers, border shoppers, or day trippers
- *Traveler*—commuters, diplomats, migrants, transport workers, and business people
- *Passengers*—nonrevenue travelers, such as infants or discount fares
- *Tourism*—visitor activities both international and domestic
- *Tourism industry*—provides services of hospitality (hotels and restaurants), transportation, tour operators, travel agents, and attractions

The three basic **tourism units** include *domestic travel* where residents visit their own country; *inbound tourism* when nonresidents travel in a given country; and *outbound tourism* when residents travel in another country. Units of tourism are combined in a variety of ways to form **tourism categories** of *internal tourism* (domestic and inbound), *national tourism* (domestic and outbound), and *international tourism* (inbound and outbound).

The travel or tourism market is defined by five criteria:

1. Purpose of the trip—business, leisure, and family emergencies are among the main reasons for travel; only leisure travelers are considered to be tourists
2. Distance of travel—100 miles or more is considered a tourist distance
3. Duration of trip—travelers who stay away from home for at least one night
4. Residence of traveler—where people live rather than their individual nationalities
5. Mode of transportation—how tourists and travelers get from home to their destination

Reasons for travel (the "purpose of trip" criterion above) fall into categories according to popularity and potential for revenue generation; they are (1) leisure, recreation, and holidays; (2) visiting friends and relatives; (3) business and professional; (4) health treatment; (5) religious or pilgrimages; and (6) homeland or cultural discovery. To successfully market tourism, messages must be directed at the appropriate market segment for each classification to acknowledge the reasons for that segment's travel and the benefits of particular destinations or hospitality selections.

Tourism marketing is similar to other forms of entertainment marketing in its challenges and problems:

- Intangibility—a trip cannot be seen or sampled before purchase
- Perishability—travel is fixed in time and cannot be stored for future use
- Heterogeneity—there is no standardization among destination offerings
- Inseparability—production and consumption are simultaneous

▪▪▪ Principles of Travel and Tourism

Travel is the process of getting from one place to another; **tourism** is the business of hosting guests and selling them things. The entertainment industry, while interested in both travel and tourism, focuses on tourism activities. The **travel cycle** plots a tourist's journey. For our purposes, a **tourist** is simply someone who travels for pleasure. The cycle begins at home with trip planning, takes tourists out of their homes and onto transportation, and ends with their arrival at destinations. Once there, tourists collect mementos and buy souvenirs, then use transport to return home, where they relive their trip through the mementos, souvenirs, and photographs. Marketing opportunities occur at each stage of the travel cycle. Marketing destinations to travelers and tourists requires a basic understanding of consumer demands and motivations, the units and categories of tourism, and market segmentation. Tailoring the development of the travel promotional message is also important.

Tourism Market Segments

Seven of the most important travel segments are: purpose of travel; needs, motivations and benefits sought; the characteristics of travel usage; demographic, economic, and geographic profiles; psychographics; geodemographics; and price. The major travel market segments and corresponding travel motivations can be generalized into six groups, as listed in Exhibit 12.1.

German researchers developed a criteria-based scheme that yielded a behavioral-intention measurement for deriving distinct travel market segments. The model can be

▪▪▪ **EXHIBIT 12.1   Major Travel Market Segments, Motivations, and Sales Messages**

Traveler Segment	Characteristics	Communication Message
Adventure	15% of the market; long trips with natural challenges; different perspectives; away from normal routine; experience foreign cultures; enjoy the outdoors; take physical challenges	Experience based
Budget	41% of all tourists; travel the most	Value and deals
Family	55% of market; take domestic trips; motivated to spend time together	"Something for everyone" message
Gay	2% of travel packaging; most growth potential; travel to be with friends, learn about culture; appreciate solitude	Unique experiences; quiet locations
Luxury	10% of market; spend most money; seek romance and feeling alive; enjoy being pampered	Special service emphasis
Baby boomer	51% of market; spend money but don't stay long; travel to relieve stress; schedule-free or retired; prefer being waited on	Discovery-oriented messages
Eco-travelers	Draw from all groups interested in sustainable tourism and natural phenomena; self-select wilderness tours in remote locations	Nature-oriented messages

Source: The Complete 21st Century Travel & Hospitality Marketing Handbook, Prentice-Hall, 2004.

used to identify customers who are most likely to make positive recommendations to others about a destination they previously visited. The research was conducted in 2000 with a population of 1,500 Virginia residents using a stratified sampling procedure delivered through a mail survey. The results provided a useful approach for identifying distinct actionable tourist market segments. Product satisfaction, pricing, and the need for assistance are the three critical factors that influence the recommendations the respondents made to others.[1]

The study yielded four unique tourist segments, two of which were characterized as *actionable*. Tourists in **actionable segments** (audience members ready to travel) are characterized as satisfied with products and services received. They are more likely to be female, older, more apt to spend money than other groups, and make their trip decisions early. The study found that product or service satisfaction was the most significant variable affecting this group's word-of-mouth communication. The study suggested that tourism marketers should treat the actionable segment as the most valuable target market to pursue. This actionable segment yielded useful information for identifying valuable markets. Consequently, in a challenging marketing environment that often leads to narrow profit margins, the discovery of ideal segments is a cost-effective vehicle.

Role of Government, Organizations, and Agencies

The WTO standardizes and coordinates global travel industry marketing efforts. On a regional basis, National Tourist Organizations (NTOs) cover a limited range of

Tourists visiting Red Square in Moscow.

segments. Most NTOs are outweighed by private-sector partnership marketing efforts and are relegated to a minor role in the industry. Still, marketers rely on NTOs for a number of services, including research data, representation in markets of origin, workshops and trade shows, familiarization trips, Internet sites, travel trade manuals, support of literature production and distribution, joint marketing ventures, information and reservation systems, consumer assistance and protection, and general industry advisory services. NTOs often provide the only research available for marketing campaign development.

A strategy of collaboration among travel professionals is necessary to coordinate all the elements of the travel cycle. Government promotional policies, low budgets, range of tourist products and locations, and joint promotions are all elements that tourism marketers must consider.

Travel Motivations and Markers

When making travel choices, today's tourists are selecting their activity first, destination second. That means marketers need to understand the key activity-based needs that motivate individuals, families, and groups. Travel researchers[2] have identified three groups of tourist needs:

- *Hedonism*—gifting oneself with good food, wine, sunshine, beaches, nightclubs, culture, and mounds of self-indulgence.
- *Self-improvement*—acquiring new skills or improving existing ones in sports and cultural pursuits or through artistic and culinary immersion.
- *Spiritual needs*—taking pilgrimages, visiting retreats and meditation centers, or simply getting away.

An important component of hedonistic travel is *collecting*—everything from pictures and mementoes to local art and indigenous products. Collected items are considered to be souvenirs or **travel markers**. Travel markers come in all forms, but can be classified into these categories:

- *Local arts, crafts, and products*—pottery, jewelry, wool, wine, and foodstuffs such as cheese or jam
- *Markers*—clothing and artifacts with the place name written on them
- *Miniatures*—replicas of an attraction or place icon, such as mini Eiffel Towers or cable cars
- *Pieces of the rock*—natural elements taken from the landscape
- *Treasures*—artifacts discovered at flea markets, garage sales, or antique shops
- *Visual representations*—photographs, postcards, home movies, and place-based picture books

Souvenirs generate revenue for local businesses and artisans and give tourists a shopping activity that helps define their overall experience of a particular place. Once you understand the needs and segments of tourists, you can begin developing promotional strategies to reach a particular segment and messages to stimulate trip and tour purchases.

Tourism marketing is about selling trips and tours; **destination marketing** is about selling places.

▪▪▪ Marketing Places

In the first chapters of this text we made distinctions among product, service, and experiential marketing. Marketing places blurs those distinctions, however, because it involves aspects of selling products (souvenirs), aspects of selling services (hotels), and aspects of selling experience (gaming and other activities). Because a **destination**, or place, is a total experience that encompasses all types of goods and services, it takes on a character of its own.

In principle, product and place marketing are the same. Both are about identifying, developing, and communicating the parts of place identity that are favorable to some specified target groups. In reality, however, analyzing target group perceptions and developing brand-building activities for places are much more complex tasks than those involved with products. Altering country brands is more difficult than changing even established product brands; obviously, a country cannot replace its beaches with mountains, or grow bananas if its climate produces snow. Although it may be possible for a nation to attract more foreign-directed investments or shift its economic base, there are always some constraints over which a country has little or no control. Manufacturers, on the other hand, are free to make product improvements or alter their physical appearance as needed.

The most important challenges currently facing place-marketing efforts are the lack of unity of purpose, difficulty in establishing actionable and measurable objectives, lack of authority over inputs and control over outputs, restricted flexibility, and relative lack of marketing know-how. Consider these challenges:[3]

• Place marketing involves multiple stakeholders, some with competing interests. Trying to market a country to tourists as a mountain hideaway inhabited by indigenous people may not serve the interests of those who wish to promote the country's budding industrial infrastructure to foreign investors.

• Measuring the effectiveness of place marketing is fraught with difficulties. The decision of a multinational firm to locate a plant on an island nation may have little or nothing to do with promotional activities by members of the host country (here, the island nation).

• Unlike product marketing, place marketing is seldom under the control of a central authority. Government or industry associations are rarely in a position to dictate policy to stakeholders. A typical business has more experience with marketing issues than do most countries. Many government officials who become involved in country branding are drawn to product marketing approaches because their countries are in desperate need of exports, tourism, or direct foreign investment. But few in government have the skill sets required to design major marketing campaigns.

• Marketers have far less control over place brands than over product brands. Besides country marketing campaigns, people may learn about a country in school; from media sources (including newspapers, books, TV, and movies); from purchases; and from trips abroad or from contact with citizens or former residents.

In spite of the obvious challenges, there are many paths to achieving a unique national identity. Spain has made tremendous strides in branding itself as a modern and developed country, while Denmark has successfully branded all of its government ministries and departments with graphic identities. In the past five years, Croatia has been working to reform its image in sports and tourism, and Poland has begun asserting itself in foreign policy. In other cases, promoting a country has involved identifying spokespeople, product brands, and events that can favorably influence public opinion in other countries about the destination.

One of the chief difficulties for many countries has been deciding who should run its national marketing campaigns, which are inspired at least partially by governments that want quick results. Because they may not remain in power for very long, governments are wise to work closely with the private sector when developing marketing strategies.

In spite of the challenges, global destinations continue to use sophisticated elements of marketing techniques. Competition between destination brands need not be a zero-sum game (in which one contestant can "win" only if the other loses); there is always room in the global marketplace for many brands, including niche brands and brands that compete on the basis of cultural excellence. The presence of multiple country brands in the marketplace almost certainly enhances overall interest in the offerings.

Destination Branding

Places are the world's biggest tourism brands, and branding is the most powerful marketing weapon available to destination marketers. Most destinations claim to have superb resorts, hotels, and attractions or a unique culture and heritage—and the world's friendliest people. Clearly, these amenities are relatively useless as differentiators. Instead, branding is about making lifestyle statements that communicate image to, and build emotional relationships with, audiences (tourists, in this case). Differentiation through loyalty and emotional appeal is more important for destination branding than tangible benefits.

To achieve successful destination branding, marketers must be in the business of delivering meaningful experiences rather than simply crafting clever identities with slogans and logos. Destination marketers must address political effects, conduct ongoing and comprehensive research to identify brand values, and build partnerships across stakeholder groups. A destination success is achieved through the strength of the brand's emotional relationship with the traveler.

Positioning Destination Brands

Many leading destination brands position themselves as place brands (Disneyland, Las Vegas), whereas countries, states, and regions focus on brand-building initiatives that include tourism and economic development. Positioning the brand often involves a relationship with events, such as the Olympics, held at the destination. Destination cities offer favorable economic conditions for businesses (i.e., no sales tax or affordable real estate). The Internet facilitates the creation of strong, highly branded sites and a much stronger presence for individual tourism suppliers. Positioning themes, branding, and images are keys to successful destination marketing.

The best taglines for tourist destinations are:

- Based on product values that can be delivered—"What happens in Las Vegas stays in Las Vegas"; "Make San Antonio your business address"
- Easily understood at the point of purchase—"Canada . . . the world next door"

▪▪▪▪▪▪▪▪▪▪▪▪ **BOX 12-1** ▪▪▪▪▪▪▪▪▪▪▪▪▪

A Closer Look at Destination Research

BRANDING WESTERN AUSTRALIA

Tourism to Australia's east-coast cities is flourishing—Sydney, the Gold Coast, and the Great Barrier Reef are popular tourist attractions. The west-coast cities, however, are relatively unknown to tourists in Europe and the U.S. In order to bring tourists to the less-populated region of the country, marketers conducted research to help them develop a relevant promotional campaign. This section is a closer look at problem-solving through tourism research.

Problem: Western Australia aims to differentiate itself from other Australian destinations by informing potential visitors of the range of experiences the region has to offer and promote itself as Australia's authentic, uncommercialized, and unspoiled holiday destination.

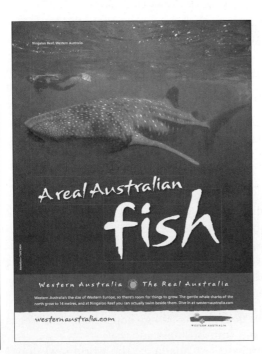

Research objectives:

• Identify a set of possible competitive advantages.
• Define a core personality of the Western Australia brand.

Research components:

1. Interview end users (past and present tourists) of brand Western Australia

2. Use market research to determine national and international markets and global tourism trends

3. Select appropriate travel consumer target markets and study their decision-making process

4. Determine the best message and media to reach each location-based target segment

Market segments: Using WTO and other migration data, five segments emerged as valuable targets for campaign development. They included:

• Australian national market—Sydney and Melbourne residents, adults 30–59 years who are high-income travelers that take long vacations

• Singapore—urban-based travelers ages 18–35 who take short holidays

• Indonesia—residential travelers ages 25–45 who take short breaks from work

• Malaysia—young families 18–29 who take annual vacations

• UK—upper-income tourists ages 30–59 who take long holidays

For each market segment, research was conducted to determine *access* (what airline, type of visa), *growth* (rate of outbound and visitation), *value* (market share of visitors), and *synergy* of online activity.

(Continued)

What the research found:

• Respondents were asked to describe Western Australia with relevant adjectives. Adjectives used to characterized the region's personality were "fresh," "natural," "free," and "spirited." These elements were used by the design team to develop logo and collateral materials.

• By choosing from among their reasons for travel, tourists revealed that Western Australia was perceived to be a holiday destination; this information was used in positioning.

• Respondents chose from a variety of the destination's strengths and weaknesses to reflect their travel experience; these helped marketers identify the message focus that would address both concerns.

4P strategy and IMC mix: The campaign strategy modified the 4Ps for campaign development:

> *Product*—is the *destination branding* centered on nature-based regional experiences

Price—is *value;* Western Australia was positioned as a value-for money destination.

Place—is *message delivery;* broadcast media were selected as communication channels.

Promotion—is *visit incentives;* celebrity endorsements were selected for advertising and event marketing programs.

Repositioning campaign objectives developed from research findings: Research allowed marketers to reposition the destination to better suit the identified segments and their perceptions. These steps were taken:

• Fix top-of-mind awareness of destination to position Western Australia as "nature-based fun"

• Create lifestyle broadcasts on travel channels featuring kayakers, surfers, and hikers

• Use tactical incentives to stimulate travel during slow periods using tie-ins with airlines for travel discounts and package deals

Co-op advertising (left) and tourism print ad for Western Australia.

(Continued)

- Establish a visiting journalist program to stimulate travel-based editorial for global newspaper and magazine exposure
- Design a consumer Web site for the segment database in each of the three market languages
- Build convention business among global corporations through liaisons with convention bureaus and conferences

Post-campaign research: In order to maintain the brand and to evaluate the success of the campaign, marketers conducted a survey to determine:

- Participants' perceived knowledge of Western Australia as a holiday destination
- The propensity for travelers to consider Western Australia for their holiday
- Visitor data, such as length of stay and spending levels

What do you think?

1. What kind of research would be necessary to determine American images and perceptions of Western Australia?
2. How would marketers use that information to position the brand to the U.S.?
3. How might this market be segmented?
4. What kind of promotions would be necessary to get Americans to travel across the Pacific to Western Australia?

- Easy to use in promotional efforts—"I love New York"
- Transferable onto souvenirs and clothing—"Experience Montana"

What does the destination mean to its tourist market segment? That is the question you need to answer to position a destination. Research tells you how to add value to any experience and find a unique selling opportunity for it. Good branding of a unique position must be sustainable, believable, and relevant. The "100% New Zealand" campaign conveyed the essence of the destination rather than any physical attributes of the country. Instead, the focus was on "pure romance," "pure spirit," and "pure adventure," connecting each emotion to the appropriate market segment.

Achieving Destination Celebrity

Image is the most important communication vehicle for a destination. Places rich in emotional meaning have great conversation value and hold high anticipation for potential tourists. These are the places that become brand celebrities. Celebrity destinations have high added value and high emotional pull, as shown in Exhibit 12.2.

Similar to a product's life cycle, brands, including destinations, migrate through a *fashion curve,* in other words, it shifts through stages of being fashionable to being famous, then familiar, and finally fatigued. The fatigued or mature phase of the life cycle necessitates that the brand be refreshed or reinvigorated if it is to survive in the competitive global marketplace. Whether a destination is a newly established one in fashion or one that has fallen from grace, the process of building or refreshing a destination brand is important for maintaining brand equity.

Building Destination Brands

A well-executed branding campaign requires an initial investment of public funds supported by private funds in both marketing and destination partnerships. This, in turn, enhances the destination experience, thanks to brand loyalty and world-of-mouth recommendations. Brands with emotional roots encourage local food, drinks, and craft

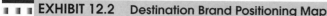

▪▪▪ **EXHIBIT 12.2   Destination Brand Positioning Map**

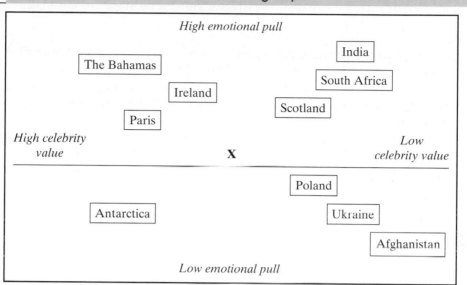

Source: Morgan, Pritchard, and Pride, *Destination Branding.* Butterworth Heinemann, 2002, p. 24.

brands to partner with the destination brand's values and emotions for their promotions. For instance, the key selling tool of Bushmills and Guinness is its Irishness—the values of authenticity, heartiness, and craftsmanship that imbue Ireland's brand. Guinness puts Ireland's brand mark on much of its international advertising.

▪▪▪▪▪▪▪▪▪▪▪ **BOX 12-2** ▪▪▪▪▪▪▪▪▪▪▪

Focus on Celebrity Real Estate as Destination

FOR RENT: STARS' MALIBU GETAWAYS

Villas of the World is a vacation rental property company that rents and manages real estate belonging to stars and celebrities. The market for celebrities offering their vacation homes and other getaways as private rentals is growing. Mick Jagger's four-bedroom, beachfront property in the West Indies rents for $13,000 a week. Bruce Willis offered his three-villa compound in the Caribbean's Turks and Caicos Islands near the Parrot Cay resort for $15,000 to $20,000 per night. Mel Brooks leases his 1927 Malibu beach cottage for $55,000 per month, and Pierce Brosnan's oceanfront Malibu home goes for $100,000 per month, as does Sting's Malibu getaway. These destinations do good business on the landlord's name; about 10 percent of the people who rent are attracted specifically to the idea of living among the star's personal effects.[4]

Marketing tip: If it takes a star to get travelers to a destination, all cities should capitalize on their famous residents and market the place as "Second home to (star's name goes here)."

▪▪▪▪▪▪▪▪▪

Brand building involves two distinct phases: research and identity development, as detailed in Chapter 7. Within each phase are several stages of destination brand development.

Market Investigation, Analysis, and Strategic Recommendations

The purpose of the first stage in building a brand, research, is to establish the core values (ideals most dear) of the destination that are durable, relevant, communicable, and salient to potential tourists. The key point with destinations is that positioning and values have to be rooted in the fundamental truths about the destination and its culture. Determining those values results from careful and systematic research on the brand's target audience. By surveying visitors, nonvisitors, business people, and regional economists, marketers can determine brand value with existing and potential visitors.

Brand Identity Development

In stage two, the brand identity (visualization) is developed. This graphic identity should communicate the brand values; logos and designs should reinforce these values. To create a successful emotional attachment, a destination brand has to be: credible, deliverable, and differentiating; it must convey powerful ideas, appeal to trade partners, and resonate with tourists. Destination benefits provide a brand with most of its identity. You can use the brand benefit pyramid to distill the essence of the brand's advertising position.

Exhibit 12.3 diagrams how a brand's character (personality, credibility) determines its brand value (economic worth), which, in turn, consists of psychological

▪▪▪ **EXHIBIT 12.3   Destination Brand Benefit Pyramid**

Level 5
Brand
character

Level 4
Brand value
for repeat visitors

Level 3
Psychological benefits
and emotional rewards
tourists receive by visiting the destination

Level 2
Benefits tourists get from destination features

Level 1
Tangible, verifiable, objectives, & measurable characteristics of the place

Source: www.brandchannel.com, June 27, 2005.

benefits and emotional rewards, benefits from destination features, and measurable place characteristics.

Branding Nations

Successful global product brands come from countries that have strong brand images of their own—the product brand is linked with the nation's brand image. Think of Ferrari, and you think of Italy—innovative design, speed, and style. Champagne gets its chic from its country of origin—who else but the French could produce the world's best bubbly?

A nation's brand behaves just like a product's brand when it acts as an umbrella of trust and guarantee of quality. A great deal of equity can be added to brands by leveraging the image of the country of origin. The movement of international capital is influenced by perceptions of countries as brands, and confidence comes along with investments. So, brand positioning and brand management have become critical for a country to attract global capital. A country's brand image profoundly shapes its economic, cultural, and political destiny. China is a good example of this fact, as explained in the discussion of rebranding below.

The Philippines rebranded itself many times over the past 30 years, with slogans ranging from "Pride of the Orient" to "Fiesta Islands" to "Philippines: The last bargain in Asia." Its 2006 slogan, "Wow Philippines!" was intended as much to instill national pride as to attract overseas visitors.

Coming back from its "Shrimp on the Barbie" campaign in 1984, Australia's newest slogan rocks: "So Where the Bloody Hell Are You?" The Australian Tourism Ministry's $135 million campaign promoted the tagline in commercials aimed at Western tourists. The old slogan, "See Australia in a Different Light," was not doing the trick, so Sydney agency M&C Saatchi spent $4.6 million conducting focus groups for six months. After testing the line on 47,000 people in seven countries, the agency found the tagline's response positive enough to adopt. Australia's new, creative tagline underscores the challenge that any tourist destination has in trying to distinguish itself among rivals targeting the same audience.[5]

The historical "rootedness" (or groundedness) of many global brands gives them their power—a strength of identity or character—not matched by many corporate constructs which aspire to become a new generation of global brands. The British consulate general foresees a day when the most important part of foreign policy is image, and when counties protect and promote their images through coordinated branding departments. The editor of the journal *Place Branding* predicted that the days when countries essentially open their own in-house marketing shops are right around the corner. To this end, governments try to achieve some kind of control over their images. They realize that image maintenance isn't just about reeling in tourists.

Branding Cities

In a study conducted on city branding, a market researcher found that successfully branded cities have the same qualities as strong product brands; they focus on reflecting the city's history, quality of place, lifestyle, culture, and diversity. City branding is proactive and forms cooperative partnerships between city municipalities and government.[6] Cities in need of a rebranding have confusing, nondistinctive images. Their

▪▪▪▪▪▪▪▪▪▪ BOX 12-3 ▪▪▪▪▪▪▪▪▪▪

A Closer Look at Rebranding

REPAIRING CHINA'S COUNTRY-OF-ORIGIN IMAGE

The increasing competition ongoing from China into global brand markets is the result of a deliberate two-pronged strategy—organically grown brands that are imbued with new meaning reflecting the changes in China itself, while acquiring the talent, credibility, and equity of established brands. It reflects a transition from a country viewed as a land of original-equipment manufacturers (one that remains in the background by supplying global brands with unbranded products) to one that creates and manages leading global brands.

China's objective is to acquire leading companies and brands. The People's Republic has executed a "go global" initiative of US$15 billion set aside for such acquisitions. Soon, Chinese investors could own dozens of the Fortune 500 companies.[7] A survey on Chinese branding was completed, using brandchannel.com, by 243 executive-level branding professionals during the first quarter of 2005. Respondents were from North America (41 percent), Europe (32 percent), Asia/Pacific (15 percent), Latin America (9 percent), and other countries (3 percent). A brief synopsis of that survey is presented here to reflect the importance of country of origin on brand image.

Q1. Do you believe the 'Made in China' label helps or hurts Chinese brands?

A1: 79% of respondents said the label hurts brands associated with China

Q2. Provide three words that represent your impression of Chinese brands today.

A2: Chinese brands suffer from negative perceptions, attributing these adjectives in order of importance: cheap, poor value, unreliable, unsophisticated, innovative, lack of track record, dated, unknown and aggressive.

Q3. Provide comments on Chinese brands and their future for competing internationally.

A3: Answers included:
- The need to overcome the lack of quality perception
- The need to enhance communications to grow awareness
- China is well-positioned for brand success
- The need to quickly become brand professionals and practice ethics in patent infringement (knockoffs)

The survey results provided these insights and conclusions:

- Chinese brands have the ability to threaten entrenched brands within specific industries
- China must move away from being low-cost originals to creating and managing dominant global brands.
- Attributes of prestige, trust and safety are not associated with Chinese brands, yet innovation and reliability fare well.

A recommended strategy for China involves traits of all good branding: emotion, uniqueness, adaptation, recognition and consistency. In other words, China must:

1. compete along *emotional* dimensions and symbolize a promise people can believe in.
2. brand products with a *unique position* to both internal and external audiences and across international markets.
3. *adapt* to the local marketplace while fulfilling a global mission.

(Continued)

4. gain strong brand *recognition* by industry leaders.

5. develop a *consistent identity* across borders.

Current commercial perceptions of China are clearly hurting Chinese enterprise, yet the opportunities to redefine the Brand China are endless. Chinese brands can leverage their dominance in their home market and they can benefit from the ingrained positioning as low-cost providers. Based on their business model and efforts to gain brand sophistication China's image can only improve.

What do you think?

1. How would you advise China to proceed with its rebranding to the U.S.? To Europe?

2. What media strategies would you recommend?

3. Can you suggest a tagline for a China image campaign?

SOURCE: J. Swystum, F. Burt, and A. Ly, "Strategies for Chinese Brands," *Interbrands*, 2005.

brands are not identifiable and lack awareness. This study identified a crucial group—the "Creative Class." These economically influential people—working in science, engineering, architecture, education, arts, music, and entertainment—can offer a city new ideas, new technology, and new creative content. City brands need to appeal to this group of people.

It is possible for a city to have a brand image that evolves into a "quality of place." This, in turn, establishes brand loyalty, which is essential to a city's survival. It is also possible for a poorly branded city, with the right strategy, to turn itself into a success. This cannot be done by branding alone, of course, as there are so many economic and social factors at play.

The way brands work for a city is how these qualities are projected: by word-of-mouth, public relations, and in some cases, advertising. These attributes must be based

BOX 12-4

Focus on Tourism Slogans

REVAMPING OLD TAGLINES

Country	Old Ad Slogan	New Ad Slogan
Bangladesh	Exotic Bangladesh	Bangladesh—Beautiful Surprise
India	None	Incredible India
Singapore	New Asia	Uniquely Singapore
South Korea	Dynamic Korea	Korea: Something More
Thailand	Happiness on Earth	Grand Invitation 2006
Uganda	Pearl of Africa	Gifted by Nature

Source: Wall Street Journal research.

on something substantial. The city must be "livable" and attractive to individuals. Much city branding is based on peoples' experience. Although we have the most technologically advanced ways of reaching people with advertising, most information is still communicated the old fashioned way: by word of mouth.

How a population is perceived is an important component of city branding. Take New York: When people think of New York, the normal associations are "cosmopolitan" and "rich." New York offers inhabitants and visitors everything one could ask of a city: finance, commerce, industry, colleges and universities, historical sites, and an enormous array of cultural and economic opportunities.

In order for a city to have a brand, it has to stand for something. San Francisco, the "City by the Bay," has stood for industry, technology, and culture. The rolling hills of California surrounding the city, and one of the world's most famous suspension bridges, the Golden Gate Bridge, are key attractions in San Francisco's tourist economy. Images that have defined San Francisco for the better part of the twentieth century have created a powerful city brand.

An important element of city branding is appearance. What a city actually looks like and the physical characteristics it possesses are extremely important. Cities now are largely defined by location, function, or cultural attainments. Rotterdam, Amsterdam, Barcelona, and San Francisco are known primarily for their harbors. Zurich and New York are famed as banking centers., Chicago has its Sears Tower and lakefront shopping, Atlanta boasts of an underground servicescape and former Olympics site, and Boston's brownstones reinforce its reputation as an "old" city by American standards. Boston will not allow its historical gems to be bulldozed in order to make room for commercial developers soliciting the highest price. This stability is a positive attribute for Boston, and an advantage for its promoters.

Branding on the Web

The Internet has been a boon to the travel industry in several ways. Despite the plethora of travel services that exist under one brand umbrella, formation of a unified brand identity can be achieved using images on the Internet to give national destinations a common marketing purpose and direction. Also, electronic commerce offers great flexibility for tourism suppliers operating in volatile markets. Promotional messages can be changed quickly, and perishable capacity (e.g., hotel rooms becoming unavailable as a result of hotel repair or a natural disaster) can be effectively managed.

The fundamental distribution channel of the travel industry consists of three primary players—principals, intermediaries, and consumers. *Principals* provide travel services to end users. *Intermediaries* pass on information about those services to consumers and try to influence niche markets to use their channel. The Internet has changed this middle part of the process, however, by facilitating direct access between principals (suppliers) and *consumers* (travelers), so consumers no longer need to resort to intermediaries (travel agents). The global distribution system (GDS) of information that once offered a closed, dedicated connection of terminals to travel agents has been replaced with global distribution networks (GDNs) on the Internet (such as Travelocity and airline sites) that provide consumers with direct access to the information once available only to travel agents. Distribution channels now facilitate the multidimensional flow of information and transactions.

▪▪▪▪▪▪▪▪▪▪ **BOX 12-5** ▪▪▪▪▪▪▪▪▪▪

Focus on Communicating Place

MARKETING THE CITY OF DUBAI

Dubai is one of the fastest growing city-brands among a select group of peer cities that include Barcelona, Auckland, and Shanghai. Dubai has historically earned its reputation as an international commercial center with an innovative, dynamic, and entrepreneurial business culture.

Strategically located at the cross-roads of trade and commerce between East and West, the city-state of Dubai (one of the seven sheikdoms within the United Arab Emirates) is an ideal gateway to access markets that span the Middle East, North and South Africa, and the Indian subcontinent. Today, Dubai has transitioned from a limited oil-resource-based economy to an investment-driven economy. Leveraging its strategic location, Dubai has developed a world-class infrastructure, air connections, and port facilities, making it the best-connected city in the region. Using its Gross Domestic Production as a measure, Dubai is a $24 billion brand. "Excitement" is the underlying brand personality factor, connoting daring, spirited, and competitive.

All enduring, influential brands periodically do a brand assessment and make mid-course corrections with a view to achieve their strategic brand intent. All brands—whether products, services, or cities—can be metaphorically compared to an iceberg. Structurally, any iceberg has two facets, the visible facet above the waterline and the invisible, larger facet below the waterline. The visible facets of a brand "iceberg" are its name, logo, advertising, communications, etc. The invisible aspects encompass quality, production,

R&D, service levels, supply chain, and so on.

Without doubt, the visible aspects of Brand Dubai are remarkable and have been painstakingly built over the years. An enviable brand image as a trading and shopping hub with brilliant infrastructure planning, excellent quality of life, a multicultural workforce, world-class shopping malls, clusters built around real estate, trade, and tourism are but a few of the visible aspects of the Brand Dubai iceberg.

Yet, the true measure of enduring brands often lie in the invisible aspects of the brand iceberg. It is often and accurately said that while a brand's visible aspects are easily replicated by competing brands, its invisible aspects are primarily responsible for its enduring competitive advantage. These intangible qualities transform a brand to stratospheric heights of esteem and reputation.

A quick assessment of Brand Dubai reveals that its intangible facets need to be developed quickly if it is to make a definitive transition to an innovation-based city brand. A few important intangible brand assets that Dubai needs to develop are discussed here.

Creating systems, processes, and institutions: It is axiomatic that excellent systems, processes, and institutions must coexist with, if not actually precede, infrastructure development. Dubai has world-class infrastructure, but does not have world-class systems, processes, and institutions. Very few homegrown private business entities in Dubai can replicate their business model on a global scale.

Developing human resource management: Dubai's peer city brand, Singapore,

(Continued)

which it seeks to emulate, has an enviable track record in human resource management across all business fronts. It boasts a merit-based economy in which qualifications and skills are the only passport for employment. Human resource management must be given its due importance in Dubai's march forward as a global city-brand seeking to accentuate its knowledge dimension.

Fortifying the educational backbone: Knowledge Village, an education cluster, was set up to develop Dubai into a destination for education for both regional and international learners. This new education and training hub also complements the unfettered Internet access enjoyed by Free Zone's other two clusters, Dubai Internet City and Dubai Media City, by providing the facilities to train the clusters' future knowledge workers. The underside of this mushrooming of these off-site educational establishments is the suboptimal manner in which many of these "teaching shops" are managed. Dubai's authorities must deal strictly with these errant management bodies before they undermine the infant educational edifice.

Streamlining the labor market: There are many reported instances of default on basic labor practice standards. Global

brands Nike and Gap have acknowledged the mistakes of producing low-cost goods in sweatshops and reinvented their supply-chain strategy. Customers have forgiven these brands for their moral and economic transgressions because the brands acknowledged their mistakes and are making sincere efforts to correct them. In building tomorrow's Dubai, unskilled and underprivileged workers must be treated with due respect and compensated adequately.

Doing a self-critical brand assessment and making genuine efforts to correct anomalies have been the driving forces of all great and enduring brands in history. It is extremely important that the touch-points (consumer perceptions) of Brand Dubai live up to the brand's promise. Dubai is still a young brand, but as an emerging global city-brand it must focus on building its critical intangible brand assets and make the world applaud Dubai as an "exciting and caring" city brand.

What do you think?

1. How and when should Dubai market itself to Western nations?

2. What strategy would you recommend to separate the city from the stigma that Americans attach to the Middle East?

SOURCE: Suni Varighese for brandchannel.com, June 27, 2005.

A destination's marketing position can be defined and reinforced on the Internet more effectively than traditional brochures, and destination databases can be developed and used for traveler targeting and request fulfillment. Destination databases include the BOSS system in Canada, CULLIVER in Ireland, SWISSLINE in Switzerland, and ATLAS in Australia. Merely having a Web site, however, is not sufficient for a tourist destination to enjoy continuing success—the destination's marketers must have a coherent strategy in place to develop, position, and promote the Web presence. And, repeat business is likely to develop only if tourists' expectations are met once they arrive at the destination itself.

▪▪▪ Place Brand Promotion Strategies

Promoting a destination or place requires creative ingenuity from, and partnership development by, marketers. Specific marketing strategies can extend place brands beyond the traditional media delivery systems. Using destinations as film and fashion locations, developing production partnerships between destination marketers and television series, and featuring destinations in special advertising sections are three strategies profiled in this section.

Film and Fashion Locations

Film locations are an excellent way for destinations to gain brand recognition. New Zealand is especially adept at attracting blockbusters to its two islands, and Eastern Europe has been luring studios with low production costs and historical locations for the last 10 years. By hosting film making, countries can enhance the destination's image and capitalize on the exposure enjoyed by hit movies.

In 2002, a report commissioned by the New Zealand's government found that a strong film and TV production industry would foster economic prosperity. That year, *The Lord of the Rings* and *Whale Rider* were filmed on location, resulting in a solidly profitable year for the country. As a result of the study, the government established the New Zealand Screen Council with a $280,000-a-year operating grant and set a goal to achieve sustainable foreign exchange earnings of $280 million a year by 2008.[8] To date, additional films successfully produced on location in New Zealand include *River Queen, The World's Fastest Indian, King Kong,* and *The Chronicles of Narnia.*

Another marketing tactic for branding destinations is using a location as a back-drop for fashion photography shoots. Saks Fifth Avenue set its fall fashion catalog in Morocco, integrating the country's scenery, costumes, and people with models in

Cappadocia, Turkey, where the first *Star Wars* was filmed.

designer gowns. The publication was produced in conjunction with Royal Air Maroc, Almeraie Golf Palace, La Mamounia Hotel, Imperial Morocco Tours, and the Moroccan National Office of Tourism. This partnership showcased the country and several attractions, and the association proved to be mutually beneficial to all parties involved in the destination promotion effort.

Media and Product Liaison Produce Branded Entertainment

Another place marketing tactic involves place as a virtual main character in film or television travel features. Kahlua coffee liqueur, for example, launched a branded entertainment television campaign: Kahlua and *Conde Nast Traveler* magazine teamed up to present *Bring Home the Exotic,* a television show that delves into the realm of exotic travel and home entertaining experiences. The first product to create, produce, and maintain full ownership of a show, Kahlua presented the five-part series on the Oxygen Network in 2005 with original episodes airing on Saturdays. The audience "travels" with a *Conde Nast Traveler* editor and a selected couple to exotic locations around the world where they explore the terrain, are treated to local foods and beverages, stay in unique accommodations, meet compelling real-life characters, and experience new cultures. When they return home, the couple hosts a themed party during which they recreate their exotic travel experiences for family and friends.

The television show created a platform to promote and communicate Kahlua's ongoing brand strategy, and to engage the target adult audience in a meaningful way that was relevant to their lifestyles. The program was fully integrated with on- and off-premise efforts, including a stand-alone insert in *Conde Nast Traveler* to reach 30+-year-old women across the country with a natural connection to travel.

Magazine Special Advertising Sections

Cooperative advertising is not new, but sponsored sections in upscale publications are becoming an economical way to market destinations, transportation, and travel accessories in a single effort.

One such section appeared in the April 2005 issue of the *New Yorker* magazine. It focused on journeys and travel, providing yielded destination advertising skillfully embedded into editorial content and feature articles. The section began with a retrospective of the Travel Channel series' journeys that were guided by heads of state in Jordan, New Zealand, Peru, and Jamaica. Other articles and their paid sponsors in the 24-page section are presented in Exhibit 12.4.

In addition to sponsor-based advertising, the section's full-page color ads featured these brands: Mexico, the Peninsula Hotels (two pages), Jaguar, Crystal Cruises, and St. Croix. Subscribers are likely to read the narratives and note the brands because the content is specifically directed at the up-market traveler. And, by advertising brand constellations—groups of products and brands clustered around a single experience—sponsors benefit from the image transfer produced by associating with other high-end brands.

▪▪▪ Marketing Tourism Services

The services industry is comprised of four major segments: hotels, tour operators, transport operators, and attractions, each with its own set of target audiences with specific needs, motivations, and spending patterns. *Hotels* target corporate clients,

▪ ▪ ▪ **EXHIBIT 12.4**   Advertising Editorial Sections and Sponsors

Article Title/Topic	Sponsor/Advertiser
"What to Know Before You Go"	Malarone pharmaceuticals
"Family Matters"	Embassy Suite Hotels
"Going with the Flow"	Tumi luggage
"La Dolce Getaway"	Silversea Cruises
"New Season on the Isles"	Brand Britain
"It's Like a Whole Other Country"	Travel Texas
"The Caribbean's Dutch Treat"	Curacao Tourism
"Natural Wonders"	Brand Colorado

groups on package tours, independent vacationers, and visitors taking weekend package breaks. *Tour operators* target singles and couples 18–30, families with children, retired people, seniors, empty-nesters, sports or activity participants, and culture seekers. Many alumni associations establish education-based tours as well. *Transport operators* target passengers in first-, club-, and standard classes, as well as charter groups. *Attractions* focus on local residents, day visitors from outside local areas, domestic and foreign tourists, and school parties.

Tourism services are affected by seasonal demand patterns. The services' high fixed costs of operation and fixed capacity must factor in rent, wages, marketing, equipment, salaries, and so forth. The interdependence of tourism products such as hotels, transportation, catering, and recreation also affect the tourism services industry. Because other texts cover hospitality marketing in much greater detail, we limit our focus to successful strategies in segments that provide examples relevant for entertainment marketing. This section overviews hospitality, specifically resort accommodations and their rating systems, cruise ships and their ports, and packaged tours. Attractions are covered in the next chapter.

Marketing Accommodations

The hospitality industry is dedicated to providing tourists with motels, hotels, resorts, and spas to ground their travel around a pleasant accommodation experience. Global resorts and spas engage in a constant quest for upscale visitors. Accommodations can be either serviced or nonserviced. Serviced hotels and resorts have a staff on the premises and target luxury travelers. Nonserviced facilities include furnished units and hostels that focus on the budget market as well as flathotels (furnished flats rented by the week or month), time-shares, parks, cottages, and apartments. A five-star rating is a marketer's most visible tool.

While prestigious ratings help lure upscale visitors, top-tier hotels don't need much of a boost from rating services. Amid a resurgence in business travel and a growing corps of leisure travelers who are willing to spend freely on luxury options, room rates at luxury hotels average $250 per night. In major cities such as New York, San

▪▪▪▪▪▪▪▪▪▪ BOX 12-6 ▪▪▪▪▪▪▪▪▪▪

A Closer Look at Destination

BRANDING THE CITY BY THE BAY

The San Francisco Bay area first began to develop as a city called Yerba Buena in 1822. Yerba Buena remained a small town until the Mexican-American war in 1846, when it taken over by a U.S. naval force and in the name of the United States was renamed "San Francisco" on January 30, 1847. The California Gold Rush began in 1848 and led to considerable immigration into San Francisco and the surrounding areas. During this time, San Francisco Bay became one of the world's greatest seaports, dominating shipping and transportation in the American West. Now, San Francisco is the fourth-largest city in the country, and the greater Bay Area population exceeds that of all other California cities.

The city's Chinatown district is still one of the country's largest, housing the biggest concentration of Chinese in any city outside of China. Many businesses started to service the city early in the 20th Century, such as Levi Strauss, Ghirardelli Chocolate, and Wells Fargo Bank, and still exist there today. Like many cities, the political situation in early San Francisco was chaotic. Military government was set in place to clean the city of crime and corruption, and soon San Francisco became the largest city west of the Mississippi River. The most recognized landmark in San Francisco, the Golden Gate Bridge, was completed in 1937and is one of the modern Wonders of the World. Progress and expansion were always priorities to San Francisco, and branding began early in its history.

Attractions

Among its many attractions, the city offers visitors special places such as the Golden Gate Bridge, Golden Gate Park, the Presidio, Sausalito, Treasure Island, Alcatraz, Chinatown, and Fisherman's Wharf, as well as numerous museums, art

(Continued)

galleries, restaurants, hotels, and architectural gems. The area also offers regional attractions such as Muir Woods, Half Moon Bay, Silicon Valley, Napa Valley, Monterey, and Carmel.

The creative community of San Francisco evolved similarly to the underground movements in Paris and New York, but San Francisco's counter-cultural movement evolved much later. San Francisco experienced her counter-culture renaissance in the 1960s as countless groups of nonconformist young people made the town their home. The already-liberal city turned exotic as "freaks," hippies, and "ethnics" created a hip social scene, especially in the Haight-Ashbury district east of Golden Gate Park. Street art flourished, and the city played a big part in the national cultural renaissance that occurred during this time. "The Haight," as the neighborhood is known, has become a major tourist attraction, but it retains a residual bohemian atmosphere—still attracts the homeless and teen runaways. Also during the 1960s, as well as the 1970s, large numbers of gay people moved to San Francisco. The gay population remains a crucial part of the city's diverse community and economy.

San Francisco faces numerous problems, despite its cultural and economic strengths. Homelessness, for instance, is a serious problem here, as it is for many large cities, and one that needs to be continually addressed. Efforts have been made to solve the homeless problem. For example, a "Care Not Cash" plan was set up by the city government, in which the welfare checks that homeless people previously received were replaced by housing vouchers for use at state and federal housing facilities.

Nickname
The City by the Bay

Branding Efforts
Destinations must be in the marketplace to remind busy consumers that they exist. They have to find new ways to maintain their brand awareness in the consumer population, and that is leading them to think more about promotional possibilities. San Francisco has a lot of branding advantages, but since its dot.com bust in 2000 and the added economic consequences of the terrorist attacks of September 11, 2001, San Francisco has suffered like many other cities. In June 2004, the San Francisco Convention and Visitors Bureau launched a new branding campaign developed by Eleven, an integrated brand marketing agency that came up with the tagline "Only in San Francisco" to try reestablish a new and improved brand identity. The main point was to enhance tourism's economic recovery.

Only in San Francisco do you have people from all over the world that are focused on their common humanity. San Francisco has many brand advantages. It is a place unique from the ground up because of its geography, landmarks, originality, traditions, cultures, tolerance, and diverse inhabitants.

Cities, however, are aiming for attracting more than just visitors. There has been a shift in how cities are thinking about themselves . . . they are more aware that they have certain assets and that if those assets are deployed in a strategic fashion, they stand to benefit more. In this way, it appears that the strategy behind branding a city is being handled in the same way agencies are branding commercial products.

Economics and Tourism
Tourism is one of San Francisco's largest industries and the largest employer of city residents. The Pacific Stock Exchange and many major American and

(Continued)

international banks and venture capital firms are located here. Companies headquartered in San Francisco include Anchor Brewing, SEGA, Bechtel, Charles Schwab, CNET, the Gap, Ghirardelli, Levi Strauss & Co., Macromedia, Pacific Gas & Electric, the Sharper Image, Viz Communications, Wells Fargo, and many others. Forty to fifty miles south of San Francisco lies the famous Silicon Valley, which is home to Apple Computer, Symantec, and many other electronic and digital companies.

The city is serviced by several public transit systems, including Muni, the city-owned public transit system, and the famous cable cars. BART (Bay Area Rapid Transit) connects San Francisco with the East Bay and San Mateo County communities on the San Francisco Peninsula. In addition, Caltrain, a commuter rail service, operates between the City and San Jose and Gilroy, making it fairly appealing and convenient to travel locally as well as regionally.

People: Residents and Visitors
San Francisco, like New York and Paris, is an extremely diverse urban center. Many

ethnic groups make up the city, and for the most part, visitors encounter friendly residents and locals. The climate is temperate, in part because it is strongly influenced by the cool currents of the Pacific. The air is dry and the weather is remarkably mild, with a so-called Mediterranean climate. San Francisco's charm is evident in its attractions, parks, coastline, and unique neighborhoods, such as Pacific Heights and Chinatown, whose restaurants, homes, streets, and architecture are famous. The history of Alcatraz (the once-infamous prison turned tourist attraction) attracts people from around the world.

What do you think?

1. How would you position San Francisco as a brand, given its unusual "small-town" feel with big-city attractions and its climate, people, diversity, history, and values, all of which offer many opportunities for branding success?

2. Which recognizable landmark would you select to appear prominently in promotional materials? Why?

3. What media and place-based materials would you use to market the San Francisco brand? Why?

SOURCE: Julie Winfield-Pfefferkom for brandchannel.com, Jan. 12, 2005.

Francisco, Washington, and Chicago, where rooms are filled all week and demand outweighs supply, the priciest hotels often ask for and get upward of $1000 per night.

Fine hotels are ideally suited to succeed in an experiential economy. More than 150 luxury hotels operate in the top 25 U.S. markets and have several hundred properties worldwide. But as traveler demands change, so does the definition of luxury. To determine luxury standards, travel magazines conduct annual reader polls, while travel guides and reviewers produce "best" lists and recommendations. Surveyed guests agree that comfort, style, service, and pampering are among their expectations in luxury hotels. Most crucial to those surveyed is the degree to which a hotel reflects its surroundings and delivers an experience that evokes the community.

Luxury has gone global; Four Seasons, for example, has 58 hotels and resorts in 27 countries. Premium brands targeting affluent global travelers need an effective sales

■ ■ ■ ■ ■ ■ ■ ■ ■ ■   BOX 12-7   ■ ■ ■ ■ ■ ■ ■ ■ ■ ■

Focus on Careers

PROFILE OF A TRAVEL PLANNER

For the past 10 years, Bridget Marnane has been the Director of Incentive Travel Planning for World Class Travel by Invitation, a San Diego-based incentive travel company. The incentive travel business serves corporations that reward their top performing employees or best clients with trips developed especially for them. World Class also helps plan and direct trips for corporate meetings. Working within clients' budgets, the company locates places, plans activities, and produces an ultimate experience for travel groups. To become knowledgeable about places to stay, staff are guests of resorts, cruise ships, and five-star hotels that vie for group bookings.

After graduating with a B.A. in Business with an emphasis in Marketing from the University of San Diego, Marnane worked as a bank loan processor and new accounts supervisor before assuming her current job. She was introduced to company president Nikki Nestor at a party, and followed up with a phone call to schedule an interview. "[Nestor] was looking for a person with marketing skills, and hired me on the spot," explains Marnane.

Marnane has a variety of responsibilities, including negotiating with hotels and other travel service suppliers, preparing budgets, and creating proposals for new and continuing clients. She attends educational seminars several times a year and conducts site inspections in locations where clients will travel. She also prepares contracts, organizes details of the

incentive programs, and ultimately travels with the groups as trip director.

"My favorite part of the job is traveling with the groups. It is most rewarding to see the incentive program come to fruition and to witness the excitement of the guests as they experience all that we have been planning for 12 to 18 months." The job's only downside, according to Marnane, is preparing the final accounting after programs are completed. "It's often a very long and tedious process."

IN HER WORDS . . .

Just Part of the Job

Last year, Prince Rainier of Monaco died while our group was in the air on the way to an incentive program in Monte Carlo, Monaco. The small principality was in a state of mourning, which included a moratorium on all entertainment and other forms of revelry in public areas. Within 24 hours, the on-site staff changed venues for two of the major events and greatly revised a third event. The gala

(Continued)

evening, specifically, required many modifications, which included moving the event from the Grand Casino in Monaco to a palace in [nearby] Nice, [France,] adding transportation for almost 300 guests (as the original venue was within walking distance of the hotel), moving and adding entertainment at the new venue, and modifying the décor to fit a different room size. It ended up being a very successful trip and many of the guests didn't even realize that the program had been changed because the revised itinerary ran so smoothly.

Advice for Newcomers

When you first enter a new industry or company, it is helpful to locate someone whose success and work ethic you admire. Ask this person to act as your mentor; over the next few months, watch and learn from this person. Learning "on the job" is the best way to become adept at your chosen profession, but it also helps to learn from others' accomplishments and failures, especially if they hold the position you eventually hope to assume yourself!

---

force to inform and support travel channels, and work with distribution partners in the meeting, incentive and wholesale segments of the travel industry. Marketing luxury hotels involves effective PR, image advertising, and branding. Magazine and newspaper editorials function as effective sources of information for luxury travelers. Image advertising can raise awareness levels and enhance a resort's reputation that result in an ability to generate premium pricing.

The Spa Market

Four types of spas predominate: club spas, day spas, resort and hotel spas, and other spas. According to PricewaterhouseCoopers, the average profit margin for all types is 17.3 percent, with the highest profits coming from day spas.[9] The International Spa Association reported industry revenues increasing at 75 percent a year since 2000. Hotels and resorts met increased demand by providing dedicated facilities for guests and day visitors. Cruise ships and hotel chains are adding independently run spas or partnering with established spa brands to attract guests who want both luxury accommodations and personal pampering. Growth in resort spa will be in square footage allocation and the number of qualified operators employed. In 2005, approximately 300,000 people were employed by spas across the United States.

Despite the fast growth, the spa industry remains surprisingly fragmented—the approximately 5,700 spas in the U.S. are operated by roughly 5,000 different organizations. Currently, two companies are poised as potential front-runners to become chain spas: Steiner Leisure of Nassau, Bahamas, and Miami-based Elizabeth Arden. Hotels continue to be a major destination for spas because hotels can finance spas and vacationers usually don't bat an eye at the spa's costly treatments. Many hotel spas are also open to the general public to attract a wider clientele. Some hotel chains, such as the Mandarin Oriental, are known as much for their spas as for their beautiful rooms.

Fairmont Hotels & Resorts, whose Willow Stream spas are located within its hotels, spent around $20 million on six spas in Scottsdale, Arizona; Bermuda; and Mexico, among other locations, and has plans to add nine more in the future. A top priority for the company is to lure more men to the spas, because 50 percent of the hotel guests are men. So, one part of the spa budget was spent to pay a cultural anthropologist who quizzed men and women about their bathing habits and least/most favorite body parts. The anthropologist learned that men feel uncomfortable parading around in bathrobes, so Willow Stream issued men boxer shorts in a program dubbed "Keep your shorts on."

According to the founder of Canyon Ranch Resorts, the purpose of its spas is to provide inspiration, guidance, education, and support to promote healthier living.[10] Rather than simply selling vacations, spas promote a direct, emotional connection experience devoted entirely to self-pampering. In their quest for a sense of control and authentic experiences, baby boomer consumers seek the sanctuary and camaraderie provided by the spa vacation community. Fitness facilities, healthy dining establishments, spa services and treatments, and lifestyle boutiques are necessary components for successful experience delivery.

Whether tied to an established hotel brand or positioned as a spa brand, spa promotion strategy is intricately associated with developing feature articles for travel and lifestyle magazines and providing video segments for broadcast on travel and entertainment channels. Exhibit 12.5 presents the top 10 spas in two categories: those that stand alone (no hotel affiliation) and those that are affiliated with a hotel brand.

▪▪▪▪ **EXHIBIT 12.5   The Ten Top Spas in the United States**

Stand Alone	*Hotel Affiliated*
1. Canyon Ranch, Tucson, Ariz.	1. Ritz-Carlton, Naples, Fla.
2. Golden Door, Escondido, Calif.	2. Four Seasons Resort, Maui, Hawaii
3. Canyon Ranch Berkshires, Lenox, Mass.	3. Lodge at Pebble Beach, Calif.
4. Miraval Life in Balance, Tucson, Ariz.	4. The Phoenician, Scottsdale, Ariz.
5. The Greenhouse Spa, Arlington, Texas	5. The Greenbrier, Hot Sulphur Springs, W. Va.
6. Nemacolin Woodlands, Farmington, Penn.	6. Arizona Biltmore Resort & Spa, Phoenix, Ariz.
7. Lake Austin Spa Resort, Austin, Texas	7. Grand Wailea Resort Hotel and Spa, Maui, Hawaii
8. The Ashram, Calabasas, Calif.	8. Hyatt Regency Kauai Resort and Spa, Hawaii
9. Cal-a-Vie, Vista, Calif.	9. Four Seasons Resort, Haulalai, Hawaii
10. Green Valley Spa, St. George, Utah	10. The Breakers, Palm Beach, Fla.

Source: Travel & Leisure Magazine Readers' Poll, 6th Annual Awards, 2006.

Kids Market Segment

Family travel rates have bee rising 8 percent a year for the past decade. Hoping to lure the littlest guests and their families, old-line resorts are adding million-dollar kids' centers and golf clinics for toddlers to their regular offerings. Once resorts had super-sized their spas, they had to woo guests in a new way—by focusing on families and providing million-dollar child entertainment programs that promise adults time off from parenting during family vacations. Going way beyond kiddie pools and teen clubs, resorts today offer everything from manicures for two-year-olds to hour-long Spanish classes for kids barely old enough to read. Similarly, the Kerzner International destination resorts spent more than $1 million at its Los Cabos, Mexico, location on its KidsOnly program, which includes golf clinics for four-year-olds and pool-sized sandboxes, in an effort to attract upscale families.

Some travel research firms set out to discover family vacations without theme parks or characters from *Sesame Street,* however. Their investigation of 12 resort properties' kids programs yielded some interesting marketing tactics.

The Ritz-Carlton in Puerto Rico was popular with kids for its free poolside hair braiding; kids at the Greenbrier in West Virginia liked bowling and air-hockey. Nemacolin Woodlands Resort took kids for Hummer rides; La Quinta Palm Spring Resort's kid visitors loved the strawberries that replaced fries in their dinners; Palm Beach Breakers challenged its kids with an outdoor maze; and the Hyatt Regency Kauai manages its kids' clubs on a point system (to the delight of vacationing parents).[11]

Club Med offers kids programs with age-appropriate activities—kite flying for young kids, horseback riding and martial arts for older ones. And for the whole family? Meringue lessons, of course. Resort marketing, like any innovative branding program, addresses the needs and wants of its most sought-after consumers.

Marketing Time-Shares

In the 1990s, Marriott and other resort property companies developed time-shares. "Time-share" refers to a vacation property (resort, etc.) that is owned by a hotel or other corporation that partners with travel marketers who sells memberships in the form of shares of time—usually a week's stay—at the property. The concept has been an economic boon for hoteliers, whose global properties are assured a certain degree of occupancy, and for marketers, who get up-front cash from the resort companies with which to draw in time-share members. The early days of time-shares had their share of problems, however, including members finding it difficult to schedule vacation time around their time-share's availability and encountering unsatisfactory lodging. In addition, the process originally was quite complicated. These issues became serious enough that membership sales diminished and the only activity was in re-sales.

In an attempt to address these problems, today's time-shares have been rebranded as destination clubs that are sold by private organizations to give members unlimited access to A-list vacation retreats around the world in exchange for club dues. These clubs deliver the kind of luxury home-away-from-home amenities that are similar to what is offered by luxury hotels, but without the client density. Time-shares are popular again because their initial downsides (such as scheduling conflicts) have been addressed and because vacation home maintenance and mortgages don't enter the experience.

With a limited member-to-property ratio, these new destination clubs allow year-long access to residences for, say, New York shopping, Outer Banks golf, or Colorado skiing. One-time membership deposits may rival the cost of a vacation home, but time-share memberships offer those with wanderlust the perfect travel option. Depending on membership level, Private Escapes Destination Club charges from $85,000 to $190,000; Abercrombie & Kent Destination Club fees start at $250,000; and Exclusive Resorts charge $375,000 to join. In addition, annual dues range from nearly $7,000 to $25,000.[12] Destination clubs advertise and plant feature articles in *Lexus Magazine,* the *Robb Report,* and *Executive Golfer.* It seems there is no shortage of luxury travelers willing to cash in their vacation real estate, preferring to live on their money rather than in it.

Internet Hotel and Resort Rating Systems[13]

Rating systems, used to be quantitatively ranked only by the *Mobil Travel Guide,* AAA, or Michelin internationally. These entities provide annual rankings that are derived from property inspectors who pose as guests to determine the quality of service in a number of different areas. Inspectors might call housekeeping, for example, to ask for extra toothbrushes, might request last-minute dry cleaning to determine whether it is available, or might order room service to see whether the bottled water is opened and poured by the staff.

These systems, however, have been joined by individual hotel booking Web sites that have their own systems. Thus, the same property can be assigned a different number of stars (or diamonds or other icon) by each rating service, making ratings-based positioning a potentially tenuous marketing strategy.

In spite of their inconsistencies, ratings are significant marketing tools. Considered to be among the toughest graders, for instance, Mobil has assigned its five-star designation to only 32 properties nationwide. In 2005, Mobil added nine hotels to its list of four-star hotels, including two Ritz-Carlton resorts in Florida and California, respectively, and the Venetian Hotel in Las Vegas.[14]

In down times (slow seasons), three-star hotels depend on tactical marketing promotional efforts to secure marginal sales. The most effective are: short-term price discounts, partnership deals, retail incentives, deep price discounts for tour operators, sales force, advertising, Internet deals, and loyalty program bonuses. In spite of rankings and reviews to the contrary, some properties even market themselves as five-star resorts to attract luxury travelers.

Most tourists either book or shop for destination accommodations online. There is no formal Internet standard for hotel rating systems, however. (Although several organizations are trying to impose some standardization on the rating systems used by each hotel booking vendor.) Given the shift from formal, standardized ranking systems to Internet systems that lack authority and standardization, it behooves the consumer to know how liberal or conservative a particular rating service tends to be. Below is a sampling of the *four-star hotel ranking criteria* used by the leading Internet travel sites:

- *Expedia:* First-class accommodations with an emphasis on hospitality and premium customer service. Highly reliable hotels offering a fine-dining restaurant, a range of amenities, and facilities for the sophisticated traveler; also appropriate for the business traveler.
- *Travelocity:* These superior properties distinguish themselves with a high level of service and hospitality, as well as a wide variety of amenities and upscale

facilities. A well-integrated design, stylized room décor, excellent restaurant facilities, and landscaped grounds are all present. The comfort and convenience of the guest is the staff's prevailing concern.

- *Orbitz:* Deluxe/upscale hotels: Find comfort, class, and quality that you can count on. These hotels will usually be in a prime location and other amenities may include: proximity to desirable shopping areas and restaurants, valet parking, concierge service, room service, well-equipped fitness centers, and state-of-the-art business centers. These properties may be newly constructed or recently renovated, and offer tasteful décor in each room or suite.

- *AAA:* These establishments are upscale in all areas. Accommodations are progressively more refined and stylish. The physical attributes reflect an obvious enhanced level of quality throughout. The fundamental hallmarks at this level include an extensive array of amenities combined with a high degree of hospitality, service, and attention to detail.

- *Priceline:* Four-star hotels will have the following amenities: Remote control TV with premium channels, telephone with voicemail, radio alarm clock, iron and ironing board, hairdryer, business services, 24-hour front desk, restaurant room service, bellman, concierge, and fitness center access. Four-star hotel examples: Hyatt Regency, Hilton, Sheraton, Marriott, Swissotel.

- *Hotels.com:* Mostly large, formal hotels with smart reception areas, front desk service, and bellhop service. The hotels are most often located near other hotels of the same caliber and are usually found near shopping, dining, and other major attractions. The level of service is well above average and the rooms are well lit and well furnished. Restaurant dining is usually available and may include more than one choice. Some properties offer continental breakfast and/or happy hour delicacies. Room service is usually available during most hours. Valet parking and/or garage service is also usually available. Concierge services, fitness centers, and one or more pools are often provided. Typical national chains: Hyatt, Marriott.

- *Hotwire:* These hotels are known for their attention to detail. Rooms are well-adorned with high-quality linens and furnishings. Upscale hotels are usually newly constructed properties or recently renovated, providing guests with the ultimate in updated facilities. Other amenities may include room service, concierge services, valet parking, and fitness centers. These hotels are usually located near popular shopping, fine restaurants and major attractions. Examples: Wyndham, Hilton, Westin.

To make matters even more confusing, many hotel Web sites use star ratings generated by someone else. For example, Travelocity.com uses AAA, and Travelweb.com often uses the ratings from one of its owners, Priceline.com. Sidestep.com displays the star rating from the Web site where it will eventually send you to book the hotel. So, what is a resort marketer to do? You need to position the property based on qualities not part of the Web booking/ranking system criteria to differentiate the property from the competition.

The Transport Industry

Getting tourists to their destinations include the transport industries of airlines, railroads, buses, and cruise ships. Each industry has special marketing considerations and makes efforts to position itself as distinct among a group of competitors that provide the same basic service—transportation. This section concentrates on the fastest growing mode of transportation of the North American travel industry for the past 30 years—the cruise industry. Consolidation has resulted in just 10 brands that control more than 90 percent of the market.

Cruise Ships and Cruise Markets

By combining the amenities of a hotel with the adventure of travel, cruising tries to offer an unusual vacation choice. As competition for the cruise vacation market intensified in 2000 because of the increasing demand, cruise lines took advantage of scale economies to build larger ships with more bells and whistles, and the distinction between mass-market and premium lines began to blur. Brands compete for the family, ethnic, and singles markets—a far cry from the cruise's narrow heritage of luxury older adult travelers.

According to some industry experts,[15] the cruise industry should focus its marketing on attracting noncruisers who are currently vacationing on land. This industry has identified its primary marketing goal: increasing trial among first-time users. Carnival Cruises's development of a first-timer base leads the industry with a ratio of 50 percent new-cruisers to repeat travelers. Converting customers from land competitors such as resorts and spas yields a larger market than other lines in the luxury segment. Ad agencies help to refresh Carnival's "fun" brand image to break through the clutter of other cruise liners seeking first-timers.

Also important are the repeat cruisers who make up 60 percent of the industry's passengers. Most premium and luxury cruise brands don't even track first-time cruisers, concentrating instead on tracking first-time-to-brand cruisers. Dedicating annual budgets to ongoing personnel training, making investments in quality food, and making service and entertainment upgrades allows cruise companies to meet the expectations of their repeat customers. Addressing how guests are treated onboard and once they return home is a natural extension of the brand promise for Celebrity Cruises marketing strategy. Loyalty marketing programs seek to create brand loyal consumers through outreach initiatives and special offers to encourage repeat visits.

Cruise *homeport packaging* is another important strategy for this industry. Travelers prefer spending three hours or less getting to the city from which their cruise embarks. Providing more choices of ports of embarkation makes it easier for prospective and past guests to enjoy cruising, so lines work to add new ports to their destination roster. Pricing, distribution, and promotional strategies also are important factors for reaching new and repeat cruisers.

Bottom-line, aggressive pricing coupled with product improvements makes cruising an accessible consumer vacation opportunity that is easily booked through Internet travel agents such as Expedia, Travelocity, and Orbitz. The development of outbound telemarketing and other direct initiatives enable cruise lines to pursue leads of qualified prospects. The core demographic of adults 25–54 has grown to include boomers who are reached through broadcast advertising on network and cable TV, spot TV, and radio; brand and tactical print advertising in consumer magazines and newspapers; and direct response mailings. Using infomercials as part of the media mix also facilitates direct response initiatives and helps cruise marketers access prospects who are interested in cruising.

Holland-America focuses exclusively on the 50+ market, which is expected to grow to more than 106 million by 2015, when it will account for 45 percent of the adult population and control spending power of $1.6 trillion.[16] According to census data, this market is the most affluent of any age segment; it spends more per capita on travel and leisure than any other age group. This segment travels more frequently and stays places longer, making it an ideal target for cruise liners.

Co-branding is the strategy used by Cunard's *Queen Mary 2* to draw luxury travelers. Cunard paired with exclusive Canyon Ranch Resorts and Chanel brands to communicate high quality and a distinct brand image. Other luxury brands featured on Cunard's lines are a Veuve Clicquot champagne bar for celebrating, Waterford crystal and Wedgwood china for dining, Microsoft X-Boxes for playing, and Simmons private label mattresses covered with Frette linens for resting. Co-branding is always a successful brand positioning strategy for attracting luxury travelers.

New ships and new ports also keep the cruise business alive. In 2006, six big new ships hit the waters. Royal Caribbean's *Freedom of the Seas* 3,634-passenger ship supplanted the *Queen Mary 2* as the largest ocean liner in the world. Equipped with the FlowRider surf park that combines a resistance swimming pool and Class V rapids, *Freedom* also offers fitness amenities such as a full-size boxing ring and a Pilates studio with eight machines. Another large launch was Princess Cruise's *Crown Princess,* which has mini-suites and interconnecting family suites that sleep up to eight people. And although the Mediterranean is the largest cruise draw, the Middle East has become an increasingly popular destination for cruise passengers: Dubai remains hot, and Libya has emerged as a destination. Ports in the Baltic, Northern Africa, and Black Sea are on itineraries as lines roll out shorter cruises. For the first time, Orient Lines' 826-passenger *Marco Polo* sailed around Iceland with stops in five ports.[17]

Packaging Niche Cruises   Travelers who seek a cruise experience but want to avoid conventional cruise vacations select a niche cruise line. Ships operated by niche lines are smaller, offer a more intimate cruise experience and concentrate on hands-on ports of call experiences. These lines market themselves by positioning themselves as being different from the competition and offer a variety of experience levels and trip durations. Some of the most unusually positioned are mentioned here.[18]

• American Cruise Lines offers voyages that travel along the inland waterways through the U.S., combined with an historical slant. The three-ship fleet offers cruises from Maine to Florida with nine itineraries to choose among for 7- to 13-day trips.

• The American West Steamboat Company has authentic sternwheeler ships offering a western cruise experience on the Snake and Willamette rivers in Oregon and Washington. Open-seating meals and casual ambiance are marketed to budget travelers.

• Cruise West provides close-up travel that focuses on the destination with personalized touches. Its itineraries include Alaska; Costa Rica; the Panama Canal; Baja, Mexico; California's wine country; and the Columbia and Snake rivers.

• Galapagos Explorer is a private organization dedicated to promoting Ecuador as a destination for tourism. Offering an ecological theme, the company's ship is equipped with a special sewage treatment system that minimizes environmental disturbance. During a 7-night cruise, visitors see 10 islands as they enjoy exceptional service amenities.

- Glacier Bay Cruises has three adventure-class small ships called sport-utility vessels. The company offers three levels of adventure: low-impact, for viewing wildlife; high-level, offering hikes, kayaking, and island exploration; and a medium level that combine the first two categories.

- RiverBarge Excursions offers a hotel barge experience that travels through America's rivers and inland waterways. They specialize in 4- to 10-day adventures to places off the beaten path with all-inclusive pricing.

- Star Clipper offers yacht-like experiences on tall ships. Clippers take guests to the Far East, Caribbean, and Mediterranean. International cuisine, pampered comfort, and lack of rigid schedule are part of the ambiance marketed to upscale tourists.

Luring Cruise Ships to a Destination Brand Port   The expanding cruise market often uses a *home-port growth* strategy to generate revenue. As cruising continues to grow in popularity, portage becomes a high-yield market for many coastal cities. Canadian coastal cities are embarking on campaigns to lure cruise ships to their ports.[19]

The Northern Territory, Australia, refreshed its tourism brand in 2005 by focusing on marketing and developing cruise shipping. The new brand was launched in March 2005, completing six months of intensive market and consumer research supported by a government committee. The research identified the Northern Territory's target market as "Spirited Travelers" and developed an alignment between the needs of potential domestic and international travelers.

Based on the opportunity to position the Northern Territory in key markets, a marketing communications strategy was designed to identify how best to reach and communicate with Spirited Travelers. The process included developing a suite of new visual and verbal tools and a campaign program. The strategy and core positioning of the destination is encapsulated in the Northern Territory's new tagline—*Share Our Story*. The successful development of the brand has resulted in the Northern Territory's use of a common platform for its domestic and international market positioning and associated marketing programs.

Not unlike cities who market to manufacturers and corporations, coastal cities lure prospective cruise lines by promoting benefits for their employees (schools, real estate, public transportation) and economic development.

Marketing Packaged Tours

The tour operator industry is far more fragmented than the cruise industry, but far less so than the hotel and resort industry. The dynamic packaging capability of online travel agencies presents a serious risk to tour operators without a niche product or differentiation. Consumers are willing to pay more for a known brand associated with expertise in destination or quality. Like cruise lines, the tour industry is focusing on the boomer generation to grow sales.

All-inclusive and escorted tours have grown in popularity because of their ability to serve niche markets and their no-hassle approach to travel. Tours are either standardized or all-inclusive. *Standardized packages* are manufactured by contractors who provide separate parts of a total tour, which include these basic elements:

- Price guarantees
- Convenience

- Accessibility to consumers
- Image and branding in brochures
- High standards and a sense of security

All-inclusive tours provide two or more service elements in these configurations:

- Transportation and accommodations packaged well in advance of delivery
- Accommodations with transport optional; hotels and visitor attractions are marketed together
- Hybrid or modular packages put together on short notice

Tour programs are retained on a central database and delivered to travelers in printed, glossy brochures or over the Internet. Providers receive bulk-rate airline fares. Tour packages, sold through computerized reservation systems, are developed to match competitor programs and maintain market share. Packagers must respond to the level of traveler sophistication, needs, and motivations.

Tours are subject to uncontrollable factors in the external environment that affect their ability to deliver the promised package. Economic events (exchange rates), political events, natural disasters, technology, and sustainable development requirements all affect the tourism industry and necessitate adaptation. Tactical tour promotions in economic downtimes include discounting, increased advertising, and consumer promotions featuring competitions, kids-go-free incentives, and booking date discounts.

One of the biggest growth trends in the touring industry is experience-based travel where tourists interact with environments. With special interest tours like car racing packages, for instance, participants are often so devoted to the theme that business is guaranteed through stable economic times as well as turbulent ones. From history-based travel packages that include elements of architecture and the arts to the merging of ocean cruise vacations with extended on-land hiking adventures, anything goes in today's packaged tour industry.

Big-Ticket Travels

Some high-cost travel agencies and concierge services pitch one-of-a-kind travel experiences, generally for members who have already paid initiation fees or annual dues. For a real marketing challenge, try developing a travel brochure for these three adventures.

- *After-hours at the Guggenheim Museum* in Venice offers a private tour and access to the museum after closing, plus champagne and hors d'oeuvres at sunset on the roof with the museum director. Cost: Part of a $200,000 two-week trip for a family of four (excluding airfare).

- *Astronaut training in Moscow* takes travelers to the Yuri Gagarin Cosmonaut Training Center where they don space suits and use flight simulations. The trip also includes dog-sledding in Sweden and racecar driving in France. Cost: Part of a $75,000 two-week European excursion.

- *Four-day cruise on a private yacht* includes a cruise along the French Riviera and dinner for 50 in Saint Tropez prepared by a celebrity chef. Cost: $1 million for the trip, including air transport and cruise for 50 of your closest friends.

Eco-Tourism and Sustainable Development

Eco-tourism is an industry that hosts visitors for the purposes of education and natural encounters with the environment. Economic benefits of eco-tourism include providing jobs for local residents and securing governmental funds for protecting natural areas. Environmental education and heritage preservation of parks, beaches, and underwater trails are among the industry's benefits for tourists and host regions.

Eco-tours are marketed to appeal to people who want to go beyond collecting souvenirs and markers. Watching whales in Alaska, snorkeling coral reefs in Belize, and photographing seals in the Galapagos Islands are a few of the options from which eco-travelers may choose.

Eco-tourism has helped to reposition the South African tourism brand to reap dividends for local business, residents, and the environment. The process was a cooperative approach between government and private eco-lodges. Kruger game reserve granted concessions to private game lodge owners who wanted to attract serious eco-tourists with deep pockets seeking five-star luxury and personalized service. South African tourism had identified four main brand audiences: luxury, backpacker and party crowd, business entertainment, and a family travel segment. To educate partners and interest local businesses in joining the branding effort, a sales team attended trade shows and workshops to set up one-on-one meetings. South African promotion efforts included print advertising, journalist visits, and consistency in communication materials to help create a strong and stable brand in the marketplace.

One of South Africa's flagship lodges, Singita (voted by *Conde Nast* readers as the best hotel in the world in 2001), is a perfect example of a successful eco-brand. Tourists pay top dollar for an all inclusive experience: professional game drives in luxury vehicles, gourmet meals, and opulent accommodation. Singita was careful to build brand value by providing excellence in all areas of the facility. The lodge promoted its brand by selecting the Born Free Foundation, an animal rights and conservation organization, as a strategic alliance partner, and by keeping its name in the paper with aggressive public relations and conservation activities.[20]

Sustainable development is a philosophy invoked to maintain a healthy balance between visitors and resources. Keeping global environments healthy for future travelers is the aim of sustainable tourism. Responsible entities are host communities, tourism firms, and tourists themselves. Every destination's host community is responsible for defining its philosophy and vision for tourism, and for establishing the social, physical, and cultural carrying capacity for the region. In other words they ask crucial questions such as: How many tourist can be accommodated before they out-number hotels and exhaust resources? What is a healthy balance of residents and visitors to insure the comfort and safety of both? Tourism firms must observe regulations set by regions and NTOs, as well as guidelines and practices established by each destination. Tourists need to accept responsibility for self-education about the customs and culture of regions before they visit. Responsible marketers work in conjunction with destination efforts toward promoting sustainability.

FINALLY: LET'S SUM UP

As the world's largest employer, tourism is an industry that deserves attention from experience marketers. Two aspects of the travel business involve marketing destinations and tourist services. Both functions demand attention to anticipating travelers' needs and motivations, and to maintaining positive consumer perceptions of a place or destination.

In the coming decade, marketing will become the primary driving force to motivate people to change their travel behavior. Just as lifestyles have changed, travel marketers must recognize behavior changes and adjust their product and strategy to accommodate consumers who have defined leisure time. Research will continue to be an important marketing tool to identify trends for formulating product development and marketing new programs. To embrace the value equation, travel marketers who can save consumers time and energy while customizing an experience will increase repeat business. With insight into tourist attitudes and behavior, effective marketing communication will lay the foundation for future success.

GOT IT? LET'S REVIEW

- The travel cycle involves leaving home, traveling by transport to a destination, collecting trip markers, returning home, and recalling travel through souvenirs.
- Tourist market segments include adventurers, the budget-minded, families, gay travelers, luxury travelers, baby boomers, and eco-tourists.
- Destination branding is accomplished with unique positioning, building the brand through constant market research, and identity development; marketing challenges include establishing actionable and measurable objectives, unifying marketing efforts and lack of authority, and control over marketing input.
- Countries are branded through the strength of their national identity; cities need specific economic, social, and climate-based conditions to be attractive destination for both workers and visitors; once identity is established and built, it must be maintained through active research and campaign adaptation.
- Promotion strategies for destinations include using them as film and fashion shoot locations, special advertising sections, and production partners for television series.
- Rating services are inconsistent and vary by Internet booking provider; nonetheless, they are an important function of the place marketing process.
- Packaged, all-inclusive tours and cruise ships provide marketers with guaranteed, reliable products for travelers.

NOW TRY THIS

1. Go online and find out what measures national parks take to ensure sustainability. From your investigation, how might parks better control access and use during peak seasons? How should parks promote themselves without impacting the environmental limitations of the park?
2. Select a resort you would like to visit. Check the ratings of that resort from four of the Internet sites listed in this chapter. What did you learn from the ratings? How likely would you be to base your decision on the ratings provided?
3. Take a look at Spain's tourism Web sites. How does this umbrella brand present specific regions to visitors? What collaboration is needed for a unified presentation of the country's various cities? Does the site provide links to specific locations? What recommendations can you make to improve Spain's destination image?
4. Inventory the items you collected from your last trip. How many of the categories discussed in this chapter are included in your collection? How did you use these items to recollect your trip? From this exercise, describe the role souvenirs play in providing a memorable experience.

QUESTIONS: LET'S REVIEW ▪▪▪▪▪▪▪

1. A travel agency's market area has a good potential to sell more eco-tours. How should the agency proceed to identify prospective buyers for these tours?
2. Describe the various resources available to a destination marketer to brand a place. What is the ideal combination of inputs and financial support to provide a successful marketing effort?
3. What is the image of Brand America? What aspects of the U.S. contribute to the global audiences perception of the country? How can the U.S. brand be redefined to improve its image?
4. For each travel segment outlined in Exhibit 12.1, suggest a destination to match their needs and craft a promotional message that will attract their attention to that destination.
5. Explain the similarities and differences between place marketing and tourist services marketing. What role do the 4Ps play in presenting travel places and services?

MORE TO READ ▪▪▪▪▪▪▪

www.atme.com, Association of Travel Marketing Executives.

www.centram.org, Center for Travel Marketing, online courses.

www.travelmarketingblog.com, industry newsletter.

www.tia.org/researchpubs, Travel Industry Association, market research.

Bob Dichenson and Andy Vladimir, *The Complete Travel & Hospitality Marketing Handbook*. French Forest, NSW: Pearson/Prentice Hall, 2004.

R. K. Dowling (ed.). *Cruise Ship Tourism*. Edith Cowan University, Australia, 2006.

Dennis Judd and Susan Fainstein (eds.). *The Tourist City*. New Haven, CT: Yale University Press, 1999.

N. Morgan, A. Pritchard, and R. Pride. *Destination Branding*. Oxford, UK: Butterworth Heinemann, 2002.

Dean MacCannell. *The Tourist: A New Theory of the Leisure Class*. Berkeley: University of California Press, 1999.

A. J. Veal. *Research Methods for Leisure and Tourism: A Practical Guide*, 2nd ed. New York: Financial Times/Prentice Hall, 1998.

NOTES ▪▪▪▪▪▪▪

1. Joseph Chen, "Market Segmentation by Tourists' Sentiments," *Annals of Tourism Research* 30 (1) (2003), 178–193.
2. Fiona Gilmore, "Branding for Success" in *Destination Branding* (2002), pp. 58–65.
3. Randall Frost, "Mapping a Country," brandchannel.com, April 19, 2004.
4. *Ibid.*
5. Bruce Stanley, "Advertising" column, *Wall Street Journal*, March 10, 2006.
6. Study conducted by Julia Winfield-Pfefferkorn; downloaded from brandchannel.com, Jan. 2, 2005.
7. J. Swystun, F. Burt, and A. Ly, "Strategies for Chinese Brands," *Interbrands* (2005).
8. Michaela Boland, *Variety*, Nov. 13–29, 2005, p. A4.
9. Christina Valhouli, "An Industry Tones Up."
10. Mel Zuckerman, "Capitalizing on the Canyon Ranch Difference," in B. Dickinson and A. Vladimir (eds.), *The Complete 21st Century Travel & Hospitality Marketing Handbook* (New York: Pearson/Prentice Hall, 2004), p. 570.
11. Nancy Keates, *Wall Street Journal*, April 1, 2005.
12. Ali Basye, *Lexis Magazine*, Fall 2005.
13. David Grossman, "Business Travels," *USA Today*, Aug. 3, 2004.
14. Peter Sanders, *Wall Street Journal*, Oct. 26, 2005.
15. Vicki Freed, "Carnival Cruise Lines' Winning Formula," in B. Dickinson and A. Vladimir (eds.), *The Complete 21st Century*

Travel & Hospitality Marketing Handbook (New York: Pearson/Prentice Hall, 2004), chap. 30.

16. A. Kirk Lanterman, "Adapting the Cruise Product to an Evolving Travel Market," in B. Dickinson and A. Vladimir, *The Complete 21st Century Travel & Hospitality Marketing Handbook* (New York: Pearson/Prentice Hall, 2004), chap. 33.

17. Amy Gunderson, *New York Times,* Feb. 26, 2006.

18. Cindy Bertram, Niche Cruise Marketing Alliance.

19. Northwest Territory Tourist Commission; downloaded from www.nttc.com.au/nt/nttc/industry/strategies/cruise.html, Jan. 2, 2005.

20. Ron Irwin, brandchannel.com, Oct. 28, 2002.

CHAPTER 13

Attractions and Themed Spaces

Mickey is the mouse that roared.

Chapter Objectives

After reading Chapter 13, you should be able to answer these questions:

- What are *attractions* and how are they promoted?
- How are *museums* marketed and how are they changing their focus?
- What key strategies underlie marketing of *shopping destinations*?
- What tourist groups do *casinos* attract and how can marketers address their cultural needs?
- How are *theming* and *branded venues* used to market attractions and servicescapes?

Now, we extend our discussion of tourism entertainment by focusing on attractions and theme-based experiences. First we look at marketing attractions such as museums, shopping malls, and casinos. Then we explore theming concepts and how they apply to marketing restaurants, malls, parks, venues, and even religious programming.

▬ Marketing Attractions

Attractions are location-based entertainment experiences that have a symbiotic relationship with tourism. Without tourist attractions there would be no tourism, and without tourism there would be no attractions. Attractions draw from local environments, and thus market themselves in their own right. They are diverse and include landscapes to see, activities to do, and experiences to remember. We explore marketing three of the most popular attractions: museums, retail locations, and casinos. First, however, we define *attraction* and discuss three research perspectives on attractions.

What's an Attraction?

According to one travel scholar,[1] a phenomenon must have three components to be considered an attraction: a tourist, a site to be viewed, and a marker or image that makes the site significant. Historic sites, amusement parks, and natural spectacles such as Niagara Falls are all attractions.

Three Perspectives

Research conducted on tourist attractions has three broad perspectives: definitions and description of attraction types, organization and development of attractions, and the cognitive perception and experience of attractions by different groups of tourists.[2] Aspects of each perspective have relevance for developing marketing strategies.

The *descriptive perspective,* the most frequent form of attraction typology in tourism research, describes the uniqueness of a site. Attractions are classified using the Standard Industrial Codes (SIC) into similar types, according to industry. This information is published in tourist guidebooks. The World Trade Organization (WTO) uses classifications that include natural beauty and climate, culture and social characteristics, sport, recreation, and educational facilities, shopping and commercial facilities, infrastructure, price levels, attitudes toward tourists, and accessibility. Research surveys incorporate these elements to ascertain their importance to tourists. Results allow an objective comparison between one destination and another.

The *organizational perspective* focuses on the spatial aspects (building and site), capacity (high and low), and temporal nature (visit duration) of attractions. Simple scale continuums are based on the size of the area that the attraction encompasses. Scale considerations provide insight into the organization of tourist attractions, their relationship to other attractions, and the relationship of attraction images to attractions themselves. Tourism marketers promote the images of specific, small-scale attractions to create identifiers for larger attraction complexes. Touring attractions are aimed at travelers who are in transit and characterized by short visits. Destination attractions are major centers of tourism characterized by numerous tourist activities integrated around a central point. For a planner, the primary considerations for smaller sites are mobility and access, while larger site planning focuses on providing a mix of variety and stimulation.

The *cognitive perspective* centers around safety and is based in tourists' natural curiosity to see "what's really behind things." The safest attractions occur in a staged, highly structured environment where tourists relate to the promoted or advertised *image* rather than to "reality," or a direct experience of the site. Research in this perspective has determined that an attraction's staging and level of renown are related to market scale. Globally branded attractions offer less risk to tourists than smaller market attractions. For local venues, safety is the marketing message.

Three less significant measures of attraction research are historical, locational, and valuational variables. *Historical measures* monitor a place over time to determine trends and changes in audience preference. Changes do not necessarily mean negative perceptions. The Coliseum in Rome, for example, has suffered damage from decades of traffic pollution and tourism, yet is still a favorite attraction for visitors to Italy. *Locational measures* compare the same attraction categories across different locations, such as the ancient ruins located at Ephesus near Izmir, Turkey, compared to those at Antica Attica outside Rome. *Valuational measures* (numeric ratings) are obtained through visitor preference surveys, tourist attendance and usage rates, guidebook analysis, surveys of experts or professionals, and economic expenditures and income. Marketers then use much of this research to develop campaigns for the attraction.

▪▪▪ Marketing Museums

The U.S. has more than 15,000 museums that host 865 million visitors each year. Half of these institutions charge only voluntary admission fees. The Smithsonian is the nation's largest museum, with 6,000 employees and 140 million items on display or archived. Traditionally, museums have contained dead things—artifacts from the past, art from old masters, or priceless collections from exotic lands. In the past decade, however, many museums have undergone serious transformations. Museums don't just compete with other museums, they compete with all other forms of entertainment and attractions. They are complete experiences that integrate art, artifact, and replica.

Museum Types

Museums are classified by their offerings. Exhibit 13.1 shows museum types by percentage of the total number.

Culture based museums have to do with satisfying curiosity about other groups and societies; they are places where audiences can experience something authentic. Museum curators mix constructed surroundings with authentic items to produce a realistic scene for viewing and discussion. The Congo Museum in Brussels mixes recreated scenes from tribal life with authentic artifacts to provide a realistic portrayal of African life.

Celebrity museums allow visitors to appreciate a virtual encounter with a star or offer fun "discoveries." At Madame Tussauds Wax Museum in Las Vegas, visitors might snuggle up to Marilyn Monroe or marry George Clooney in a wedding-party stage set—wedding gowns provided. The Museum of Jurassic Technology in Los Angeles and the American Sanitary Plumbing museum in Worcester, Massachusetts, rely imagination and audience involvement to present pseudo-inventions and whimsical experiences.

Science and learning museums, on the other hand, provide the real thing through hands-on interaction with exhibits and displays. San Francisco's Exploratorium is one example of a museum that offers actual and virtual location activities that entertain through education. Growing in popularity with family audiences, learning museums

▪▪▪ **EXHIBIT 13.1   Museum Classifications**

Type of Museum	Percentage of Whole
Historic	29
Historic site	24.5
Art	14.8
General	8.6
Natural history or nature center	6.7
Specialized	5.7
Arboretum/botanical garden	3.9
Science and learning	2.2
Other	3.2

Focus on Learning Attractions

ONTARIO SCIENCE CENTER

The Ontario Science Center in Ontario, Canada, has more than 600 exhibits in ten exhibition halls. In 2005, the center reached 3 million visitors through on-site experiences and traveling exhibitions, and generated 900,000 online visitors. The center competes with other national attractions by providing an entertaining and innovative space for family interaction and innovation. The center includes Family Innovation Experience Areas where visitors help real scientists with real research, use the latest technology to explore the connections between art and science, and work with a variety of new and familiar materials in innovative ways. These experience areas include:

• a *Challenge Zone,* which features a "Challenge of the Day," in which participant teams are encouraged to design and build practical solutions using a variety of common and unusual materials within an allotted time.

• *Citizen Science,* where visitors can meet scientists and get involved with real research projects. Visitors learn how to hone research questions, collect data, and analyze and visualize results. Visitors may create music with the stroke of a brush or a wave of the hands, design jewelry that monitors the level of pollutants in the air, or make robots dance and clothing talk.

• *Media Studios* that feature a variety of media tools for discovering what happens when the boundaries among music, fashion, art, technology, and science start to blur. Whether it is a new game interface, a stop-motion animation, or a video installation, each project created is archived and accessible for inspiration and use by future participants.

• *Material World,* which encourages visitors to look at the "stuff of life" in different ways.

Some of the challenges include experimenting with produced materials, such as sports equipment and toys, to improve performance, or dreaming up new materials that can solve real-world problems. Visitors also may work with artisans to explore the creative side of materials science.

• *KidSpark,* which was designed as a stimulating learn-through-play space for children eight and under; it focuses on experimentation and discovery. It is packed with more than 40 experiences that offer much more than hands-on fun. Encompassing six themes—Play, Build, Flow, Sing, Shop, and Move—*KidSpark's* open-ended, inquiry-based experiences are designed to foster creativity, problem-solving abilities, and innovation skills. The space also features an enclosed Primary Workshop for weekday school programs and kid-size family washroom facilities.

Marketers promoted sleepovers at the center for school groups, summer day camp for kids of all ages, and group meetings for organizations and businesses to expand on the normal facility activities. Other marketing strategies used in 2005 included:

• partnership collaboration with other major attractions to stimulate tourist vacations.

• twenty-five major promotions and increased channels of distribution to drive attendance.

• enhanced community access programs.

• visits by regional school board members.

Successful marketing efforts increased two-year memberships by 65 percent and generated 51 percent of the Center's expenditures; the Canadian government contributed the balance of financial support.

SOURCE: www.ontariosciencecenter.org, Jan. 4, 2006.

have substantial online collections with rich content offerings. They offer many kinds of learning activities suited to different age levels and learning styles. Their Web sites provide virtual visits that increase desire for a "real-time" visit to the museum building.

Specialty museums offer unique environments. The Frick in New York City is housed in one of Fifth Avenue's only remaining mansions. The architecture of San Francisco's Museum of Modern Art takes audiences through a catwalk that simulates being in a giant eye. Houston's Menil Collection combines modern art with ancient and tribal art in an urban neighborhood of art sites. New York's Museum of Modern Art is considered to have the best shopping,[3] but the Metropolitan Museum is the most intriguing, with its vast collections, tomb rooms containing Egyptian pyramids, and fascinating array of gifts shop items. Most museums have their own retail shops on location, as well as extensions of these stores in shopping malls, to sell collection reproductions and miniatures. Whether displaying Armani collections, Impressionist paintings, or tattoo art, museums compete for visitors with all other types of other attractions.

Museum Research and Marketing Tactics

The single promotion strategy of museums a few decades ago was "*Collect it,* and they will come." Today, audience needs and wants has become a primary focus for attracting visitors, and the strategy for marketing museums is "*Know them,* and they will come." The process of understanding audience needs and using that knowledge to promote museum brands involves a series of steps, as outlined here.

1. *Involve staff members in research efforts.* You cannot equate the term *audience* solely with visitors. Members, donors, staff, and volunteers are audiences too. Looking at these people as customers paves the way for marketing to become a museum-wide function. Questions and comments that museum front-line staffers receive from visitors can tell you what:

   - impresses people most about your institution.
   - they wish it had more of.
   - services are not being providing that should be provided.
   - the museum may think is working that actually *is not* working.

   Marketing efforts offer staff members a major role in creating the changes that will affect their departments. Don't be afraid to let them participate; chances are they have already given a lot of thought to workable solutions.

2. *Use comment cards to generate feedback.* One of the best ways to generate feedback on museum performance is with this simple listening tool. Comment cards should have two components—space in which visitors can tell their story and a mechanism for responding to visitors. Not only do these cards provide new ideas to museum staffs, but they also provide a method for museums to identify and reply to customers who have had a negative service experience and may be considering taking their patronage elsewhere. Comment cards are a powerful tool for service recovery, which can affect the bottom line by:[4]

   - keeping at-risk customers from leaving.
   - minimizing negative word-of-mouth advertising that would undermine marketing efforts.
   - increasing positive word-of-mouth advertising (visitors who have had a problem become vocal advocates of a company).

3. *Promote memberships.* Members are the lifeline of museum organizations and require consistent recruitment and maintenance efforts. Membership development involves two types of solicitations: (1) placing solicitations on site with signs at the admissions desk and gift shop cash registers, offering a premium with on-site membership purchases, using tent cards in the restaurant or cafe promoting membership, proclaiming a Members Month to double promotion efforts, and offering staff and docents incentives and commissions for selling memberships; (2) Conducting *direct mailings* with available in-house lists and by compiling lists of visitors from "free membership" raffle drawings.

    Membership offerings can be structured by promoting renewals and offering special benefits such as: gift memberships for trustees, boards, staff, and members; renewal promotions using special offers in each renewal notice; and a "Renew Online!" message on printed pieces. Enacting membership programming and benefits such as "double-discount days" in the gift shop for members during the holidays are also tactics for membership building.

4. *Establish a speaker's bureau.* Presentations and talks to local clubs, churches, service organizations, and professional groups take a museum's message directly to local audiences and provide opportunities for institutions to begin building relationships with those audiences. This tactic has more of a public relations and marketing research base than an educational one. Set up and promote the speakers bureau as a special event, with press releases, Web site promotions, and community liaisons. Recruit engaging speakers: Toastmasters International is an invaluable speaker resource with 8,500 chapters worldwide.

5. *Maximize hotel concierge services.* Building good relationships with hotel and corporate concierges can result in increased ticket sales, more facility rentals, and additional members, donors, and volunteers. Locate concierges by contacting hotels directly or through their area professional associations. National Concierge Association chapters can be located through the organization's Web site. Appoint a staff member to act as a liaison, and contact concierges on a regular basis to make sure that they are aware of what is happening at the museum. Or assemble a concierge's museum book containing staff names and addresses, museum information, and exhibit schedules. Concierge-referred incentives are not always necessary, but ticket discounts are a win-win situation for the museum, the concierge, and the visitor.

The San Francisco Museum of Modern Art offers both spatial and exhibit-based experiences.

6. *Affiliate with business databases.* The GuideStar database (GuideStar.org) contains information about more than 850,000 U.S. nonprofit organizations. Each week, tens of thousands of donors, funders, and members of the media use it to find and compare charities, monitor performance, and give with greater confidence. GuideStar draws its basic listing information from the IRS Business Master File and Forms. Listings can be updated and expanded at no charge. A number of nonprofits have received sizable donations from people who found them through the GuideStar search engine.

7. *Conduct regular tours.* Tours are excellent mechanism for attracting new visitors and retaining current members. For example, the Silver City Museum, a regional history museum in Silver City, New Mexico, gives half-hour tours focusing on the city's historic architecture and landmarks. The Delaware History Museum offers 60-minute tours of Wilmington's historic areas that act as a popular add-on to senior tours that include the museum's interactive exhibits. Both of these institutions began their guide service in response to visitor requests. To increase the marketability of a group tour program, announce the service in press releases, add a promotional page to the Web site, and get the word out to tourism promotion organizations. Don't forget group sales departments at nearby restaurants and hotels.

8. *Make the museum a movie star.* To create valuable audience awareness, feature the museum in a motion picture. Remember *Rocky*'s triumphant run up the exterior stairs of the Philadelphia Museum of Art? Did you notice the Metropolitan Museum featuring *Batman* running wild, or the break-in featured in *The Thomas Crown Affair*? If you saw *A League of Their Own*, you may recall the women's team visiting the Baseball Hall of Fame in Cooperstown, New York. In an attempt to bring celebrity to museums, movies are tying themselves to various venues—Imax Theaters, for instance, has screens in 55 museums. The Henry Ford Museum and Imax Theater in Dearborn, Michigan, have shown Disney and *Star Wars* films to packed houses. This kind of cooperation between private and nonprofit organizations also allows museums to receive educational materials and speakers. For example, Imax offered a study guide to accompany a museum showing of *Apollo 13* for school groups.

9. *Hold special receptions for new exhibits.* Well-publicized events, such as new exhibition celebrations, give members advance previews and generate a sense of excitement. The Laguna Beach Museum of Art, for instance, partners with local restaurants to provide food and beverages for invited members prior to artist receptions for the opening of new installations. A 2005 exhibition on surfing art generated great young adult attendance by appealing to an audience not previously associated with art openings and museum visits.

10. *Lease space to corporations and organizations for special events.* The Metropolitan Museum of Art leased space to a large investment firm in conjunction with a Lichtenstein exhibit that brought artist Christo, news reporter Diane Sawyer, and financial investors together for a special event. Held in the museum's Egyptian tomb room, the evening featured chamber music, a variety of wines, and a six-course meal with a Lichtenstein-based theme. Financial compensation was not the only benefit: the activity yielded media coverage and a generous gift from the

▪▪▪▪▪▪▪▪▪▪ **BOX 13-2** ▪▪▪▪▪▪▪▪▪▪

A Closer Look at Museum Marketing

DRIVING MEMBER LOYALTY AND REVENUE THROUGH E-MAIL AND WEB SITE COMMUNICATION

The Organization

Carnegie Museums of Pittsburgh is a collection of four properties, including the Museum of Art, Museum of Natural History, Science Center, and Andy Warhol Museum. Reaching more than 1.5 million visitors a year through its four museums, the organization serves 400,000 people through on-site and off-site educational and outreach programs and global traveling exhibitions.

The Challenge

With 90 percent of its membership marketing budget spent on replacing lost members, Carnegie Museums needed a strategic plan for membership retention. The organization understood that the Internet offered a cost-effective opportunity to reach its members more frequently and encourage them to renew, but it faced several obstacles:

- No consistent online relationship with the constituents
- Impersonal text-only messages were sent using a personal e-mail tool without tracking capabilities, and the site lacked member-only content.
- Site had no transaction capability for members to renew online

Site Objectives

1. Develop a strategic plan to develop ongoing relationships through e-mail and Web communication to improve membership retention.
2. Create an online solution to create more effective emails and site content and to provide built-in tracking and reporting capabilities for analyzing online results.
3. Streamline the transaction process and provide an easy way to renew online.

Implementation

- Online member was center created in 2002 with an e-mail marketing system that allow constituents to receive email newsletters and event alerts.
- Online surveys were developed to gather visitor information for targeting online communications.
- Online membership renewal/upgrade campaigns installed to alert donors of upcoming mailings.

Results

Better outreach and member services

- Increased quality and frequency of member communications
- Increased membership renewals
- Increased e-mail list from 5,000 to 12,000
- Survey data revealed that 78 percent of online members felt more connected with the museum and 89 percent intended to renew their memberships

Increased membership renewals and revenue

- E-mail newsletters renewed at a rate of 88 percent compared to the previous rate of 62 percent
- First-year members renewed at a rate of 58 percent compared with 40 percent the previous year
- Multiyear memberships renewed at a rate of 78 percent versus 73 percent previously

(Continued)

- Average online transactions on Member Center increased to $131 from $111 offline
- Organization raised $121,000 online after taking membership sales to the Web

Improved efficiency

- Marketing staff communications with members an additional 15 to 20 times per year
- Online cost effectiveness allows the organization to produce and promote more member-only events

- Easy site management by non-technical staff members

What do you think?

1. Take a look at carnegiemuseums.org and engage in their Web site. Discuss your experience with ease of use, attractiveness and entertainment value.

2. What additional steps might the organization take to further develop their Web site?

SOURCE: www.convio.com/site/DocServer?docID=2600035, Jan. 4, 2006.

---

meeting's sponsor. In a similar lease agreement, Armani paid dearly to put his fashion collection in the MoMA. As an alternative for leasing out space, some museums lease their assets to other locations. The Boston Museum of Art, for instance, rented 21 Monets to the Bellagio Casino in Las Vegas and continually leases art to shows held in London.

11. *Take the museum brand show on the road.* Once a museum has developed a national brand image, it can move beyond its walls. The Guggenheim, for instance, has global locations, including Las Vegas. London's Madame Tussauds left New York for the Vegas Strip to house a trendier version of itself in the Venetian Hotel. Exhibitions travel from museum to museum; now, museums can travel to audiences as well.

▪▪▪ Shopping Attractions

Beyond retail, shopping is now marketed as a global attraction set within a variety of themed and crafted spaces designed to lure both traveling and local customers. Shopping centers have become destinations for Asian, European, and North American tourists seeking brands and bargains. South Coast Plaza in Orange County, California, provides a visitors' tour complete with location maps, instant credit, and concierge service. Shopping vacations to Hong Kong are favorites of U.S. consumers who travel to Asia. Mall of American, partnering with Northwest Airline, offers shoppers a $50 fare discount if they choose to stop over in Minneapolis for shopping on their way to other destinations.

In New Jersey, the Meadowlands Xanadu "shoppertainment" center expects 45 million visitors a year to ride a mile-long roller coaster with views of Manhattan, hit the slopes in the first indoor ski dome in the U.S., take in a concert at House of Blues, and—eventually—shop. Slated for opening in 2008, Xanadu's initial tenants include Cabela's outdoor outfitter (it is installing an indoor trout pond), Borders, Virgin

Megastore, Balducci's gourmet food, and a 26-screen cineplex, including one 60-foot outdoor screen.[5]

Positioning

Positioning differentiates shopping venues. Department store positioning typically involves targeting specific audiences. The two largest department stores in Paris, Le Bon Marche and Les Galeries Lafayette, use three domains of cultural manifestations to differentiate themselves: the surrounding area, social aspects such as store window dressings and style, and the stores themselves. Located in a modern building on the Left Bank, Le Bon Marche fashions itself as an upscale shop for local and Parisian shoppers. Les Galeries Lafayette, on the other hand, markets to tourists and mass shoppers by providing an historical setting that is by itself an attraction in the fashionable area adjacent to l'Arc de Triomphe.

Window Shopping

Window displays are a favorite marketing strategy for retail locations seeking both local and global shoppers. Club scenes and models in animal costumes have adorned Selfridge's flagship store in London. Along with trendy brands and in-store restaurants, such tactics have helped turn the store into a more profitable one than most of its American rivals. Embracing shopping as a form of entertainment not necessarily linked to buying, London's Harrods also has turned itself into a leisure and tourist destination with lavish food halls, eateries, bars, and frequent exhibits.[6]

Loyalty Programs

According to retailers and mall managers, customer loyalty drives most specialty promotion programs. Here are a few examples:[7]

- *Mall credit cards:* In association with Visa and Master Card, special mall cards allow consumers to buy products easily. This helps track purchases and spending patterns.

- *Prize drawings:* Drawing programs require shoppers to save their receipts: For every $100 in mall receipts, shoppers receive one entry in an annual drawing for, say, a new car. The winner must be present to win, so drawing day brings a lot of shoppers to the mall.

- *Parking premiums:* Big spenders can receive a free valet service. By taking their receipts to the information desk in the mall to be validated, consumers who maintain a certain spending level receive a valet sticker entitling them to free parking services.

- *Wheels:* Making free strollers and wheelchairs available to moms and the elderly is an appreciated convenience.

- *Education rebates:* These programs partner malls with local schools to offer rebates in which a fraction of a percentage of proceeds from parent shoppers goes back to their children's schools.

- *Points programs:* Based on purchases in the shopping mall, customers acquire points for discounts or coupons. The program can be outlet or category specific and apply to all stores in the mall. Prizes also can be status symbols, such as club memberships, short holiday resort vacations, or concert tickets.

- *Frequent spender lounges:* For adult shoppers who use their mall charge cards or accrue spending points, mall lounges provide rest rooms, couches, and soft drinks.

============================ BOX 13-3 ============================

Focus on Shopping

INDIA'S MALLS LURE FOREIGN RETAILERS

Shoppertainment has come to India. A sharp rise in the number of malls across the country has changed the way Indian natives and tourists shop for retail goods. Air-conditioned malls are replacing stuffy mom-and-pop stores located amid cluttered streets and crowded outdoor markets. More than 240 malls existed in 2006, yet foreign retail giants cannot cash in on the trend unless they are willing to entrust their business to a local franchise.

India's burgeoning middle class has more disposable income than ever and an appetite for world-class shopping. Smaller than European malls, Indian retailers organize around cities where global manufacturers are located. The Saharan Mall, for instance, receives 150,000 visitors each week thanks to companies such as General Electric, Coca-Cola, and IBM, all of which are housed in the mall's Gurgaon location.

Management consultants rank India fifth on a list of the 30 best emerging destinations for foreign investment in the retail sector in spite of the country's heavy regulation. Retail giants such as Britain's Marks & Spencer manage to sell products in India by operating through local franchises. International players in India's retail market also include Landmark Group (Dubai); Metro (Germany); Shoprite (South Africa); Nanz (Germany); Mango (Spain); and McDonalds, Dominos, and Tricon Restaurants (U.S.).

Mall in Mumbai.

(Continued)

However, the mall is not only about shopping. It has a movie multiplex and amusement stores for hanging out on weekends. The mall also features designer clothes and accessories from Gucci, Arron, Rado, and Opal, as well as the Home Store and the Furniture Store. Shoppers Stop supermarket chain, Pantaloons clothing store, and Waterside clothing are the most prominent local retail chains. Other brands cashing in on available retail space are Adidas and Sony.

SOURCE: Sangeeta Singh, www.inhome.rediff.com/money, Jan. 7, 2006.

▮▮▮ Casinos and Gaming Attractions

We previously covered casinos as venues and travel destinations. Here, we look at casinos as attraction centers for gaming, live shows, and other engaging activities. Since gambling was legalized in some states and renamed *gaming,* it has come closer and closer to favorite pastime status. Casino billboards advertise entertainment shows as the "world's most daring" "most sensual," or "most exciting." A favorite attraction of tourists, casinos are the most popular form of gaming worldwide. More money is spent on gaming and wagering activities than on movies and recorded music combined. People play not only for the thrill of winning, but also because gambling is entertaining.

The U.S is the leading provider of gambling venues, with 1,624 casinos, and France has the second highest number, with 448. Other European leaders are Germany (125), Russia (170), and the UK (212). Japan's 37 casinos and Kazakhstan's 25 lead the Asian nations. Macau (China), with 19 casinos, anticipates adding 10 more in 2006. Las Vegas entrepreneur Steve Wynn is building an entire waterfront resort in Macau that is expected to rival all global facilities. In South America, Argentina leads the region's other countries with 79 casinos. Australia has 370 casinos, and South Africa has the most venues on the African continent, with 45 casinos.

A popular casino in the United State's Southeast is in Tunica, Mississippi; this is now the country's third largest gambling destination. Other locations are racing to catch up. Together, Detroit and Windsor, Ontario, which face each other across the Detroit River, are expected to become a significant gambling market as several megacasinos are being built along river. Casino operator Park Place Entertainment is buying up locally owned riverboat and land-based casinos in the Southeast and Midwest.

Connecticut is home to the most profitable casino in the U.S. and currently the nation's top Native American Indian tribal gambling market. Foxwood Resort Casino, operated by the Mashantucket Pequot Tribal Nation, averages more than 55,000 patrons each day and more than 20 million visitors each year. The nation's largest tribal casino, Foxwood employs more than 10,000 people. In the West, Harrah's Entertainment and Trump Hotels have each cut deals to develop and operate tribal casinos in California. Elsewhere, tribes in New York, Florida, and Minnesota reap hundreds of millions a year from gaming operations.

The casino business is retailing opportunities for betting and other gaming experiences that are stimulating, exciting, and entertaining. In spite of the fact that they receive nothing tangible in return for the money they spend, gamers return for repeated visits. The marketing challenge is to use advertising and publicity to get customers into casinos, then to keep them playing for as long as possible with service and frills. Casinos have found it necessary to create marketing images that appeal to the core players they most want to attract. Research determines which incentives are the most profitable to implement for each category of player.

Mandalay Bay (Las Vegas) casino hotel, for example, caters to low- and mid-budget players who don't require extensive credit-granting facilities or lavish meal and entertainment services. In contrast, Mirage Resorts and the MGM Grand profitably exploit the high-roller niche. Casino management is generally willing to "comp" (no charge) these guests up to 50 percent of the amount it expects to win from the players. Players are ranked by (1) buy-in amount to the game, (2) average bet, (3) largest bet, and (4) duration of play.

As players' tastes and demands shift, casinos must alter the mix of games. New slot machines are so popular, they now account for a steadily rising share of overall industry revenues. Tour promoters bring busloads of retired adults to casinos specifically for playing the slots.

Global Gaming

One aspect of casino marketing is determining objectives for attracting a variety of players. For example, a goal may be to increase international or domestic ethnic market share. The first order of business, then, is to determine how both existing and potentially new international customers perceive the casino. Research should reveal whether or not the casino is currently seen as capable of satisfying a mixed customer base of both domestic players and international players.[8]

Perceptions are normally related to visuals. To gain an international image, public signage must in different languages to indicate readiness to serve an international clientele. Brochures and printed materials must be available in different or multiple languages, and restaurants or menus should offer a variety of foods to satisfy a variety of domestic, ethnic, and international tastes. Another factor for increasing international market share is location. In most instances, location dictates increasing domestic or ethnic business first. Marketing efforts then create a springboard to target the more costly international or overseas business.

Gaming resorts offer a complex entertainment experience. The entertainment experience is delivered through several elements, both tangible (such as quality of food, type of slot machines) and intangible (such as employee courtesy, ambience of the building). Casino visitors determines their satisfaction and desire to return based not on wining or losing at the gambling tables, but on the experience's entertainment value relative to their expenditures. The value of the gaming experience perceived by each customer varies because of his or her individual background, variable expectations and valuation criteria, and perception of what happens during the time he or she spends at the casino. It is extremely important, therefore, for casino managers to understand how to create and add value to each guest's experience.

To succeed in overseas locations such as Macau, U.S. operators must adapt to a different way of doing business. The vast majority of Macau's gamblers, for instance, wager in private VIP rooms rather than on the wide-open floors in huge Vegas-style casinos. Table games such as baccarat generate the biggest profit in Asia; in Vegas, slot machines are the moneymakers.[9]

Customer satisfaction factors, as well as aspects that positively or negatively impact a visitor's experience in the casino, have been the object of many studies. Research suggests that repeated visits to a casino are a function of the casino location, casino physical attributes, games offered, extra amenities of the casino, hospitality attributes, and the skill and attitudes of the casino staff.

Because casino staff attitude is so important to business, training programs are developed to increase staff awareness of various groups' cultural values and particularities as well as communication methods so that the interaction between staff and customer can be as smooth as possible. For example, in the U.S., calling somebody by his or her first name may represent friendliness, but the Chinese interpret this practice as disrespectful communication.

Attracting Gamblers from Asia

Las Vegas is a favorite destination for Asians, from groups of budget travelers to high-stake gamblers who can individually affect a casino's bottom line. Gaming is part of the Asian culture. Eighty-five percent of the high rollers that play in Las Vegas visit from China, Taiwan, and Japan.[10]

Asians are well known for being among the high-end gaming customers. Sales increases at places such as the Forum Shops at Caesars Palace are directly attributable to Asian visitors, who are focused on the quality and brand name of products they purchase. The gaming industry is aware of the needs of Asian customers and the potential for the profits to be made by these customers if their needs are accommodated. Understanding Asian travelers' culture, needs, and expectations can lead to an increase in customer service and therefore customer satisfaction, which is a key factor in generating repeat visits to the same casino.

A study published by market analysis firm Bear Stearns estimates that three-fourths of the Las Vegas Strip's baccarat players come from Asia, indicating that the health of Asian economies has a direct bearing on the bottom line of several Las Vegas casinos.[11] To increase these numbers, some gambling companies have strategically placed executives in potential Asian markets, such as Hong Kong, Singapore, and Tokyo, in order to establish partnerships with local travel agents to send visitors to Las Vegas. But these efforts will be worthwhile only if properly prepared staff is ready to serve these customers when they arrive at the casinos. Getting to the casino is one thing. Having a positive experience while there is another.

Statistics show that in Las Vegas, losses by Chinese visitors have been extraordinary.[12] Even though the volume of Japanese people visiting Las Vegas is greater than the volume of Chinese visitors, the amount of money the Chinese gamers are willing to gamble is very large. For example, some reports indicate that individual losses by Chinese players at one casino reached US$10 million over eight months. Casinos consider Chinese New Year the best gambling weekend of the year, because thousands of Chinese revelers come to Las Vegas to celebrate and gamble.

All these factors have caught the attention of gaming companies for this emerging market. Considering the potential difference that Chinese customers can make to casinos' bottom lines, casino marketers should be extremely interested in better understanding this customer segment.

▬▬▬ Marketing Themed Environments

Synonymous with entertainment, themed environments pervade global landscapes. A *themed environment* is the ultimate in manufactured experiences: It markets authenticity to travelers and visitors within a single space. **Theming** is prevalent in parks, restaurants, malls, hotels, branded spaces, and religious venues. Themes have become a way for all businesses and destinations to differentiate themselves from like businesses in the hope of attracting and entertaining customers who consume goods and services. The increasing reliance on motifs and themes by businesses serves marketers well. In such environments, consumption is fused with fantasy and amusement. Not surprisingly, Las Vegas is the ultimate themed space.

Staging Reality

The process of theming connects the advertising, media, celebrity, fashion, and status markers that elevate symbols over substance. What do visitors expect from a themed experience? Theming characteristics include:

1. being *set apart* by specific boundaries, such as in theme parks or in enclosed structures for a restaurant or hotel.

2. being a *predictable* environment; visitors to the Mall of America know they can expect entertainment, shopping, food, and activities.

3. being an environment that is *safe and protected from harm;* Disney provides a security staff and well-maintained rides to ensure visitor safety.

4. focusing on a *single motif* with relevant artifacts, costumes, and architecture; visitors to Ruby's Diners sit on red-leather-and-chrome bar stools or in booths, eat hamburgers and fries, and sip sodas served by waiters in 1950s diner attire. The Venetian Hotel uses gondolas, canals, and ceramics to theme its hotel with an Italian motif.

5. enabling *licensing;* Hard Rock Café licenses its themed venues, menus, and T-shirt designs to establishments worldwide.

The Venetian Hotel brings Venice to Las Vegas by creating a theme based on the famed Italian city.

The theming strategy works. By incorporating recognizable symbols into everyday environments, marketers provide a way for visitors to experience the feeling of a historical era, faraway place, or exotic culture. The presence of symbols enhances audience enjoyment of almost every activity and attraction.

Theme developers base their marketing on research conducted to determine public preferences and to understand the theme itself. In order to duplicate the historical time period or location settings, information must be gathered. Music, talent, event marketing, and public relations jobs are part of this large and profitable industry.

Themed Restaurants

In order to enhance mealtime, roadside diners adorned themselves with symbols of nostalgia, and themed restaurants were conceived. Today, almost all eating establishments use thematic devices or become entirely themed environments. Most themed restaurants are synonymous with the image of their franchise chain in both exterior and interior design. Restaurant themes draw from popular genres such as film, sports, contemporary music, and ethnic cultures. Narrative is communicated nonverbally through the use of props, artifacts, sound, menu, and merchandise. Eating is not the central focus—diners are there to consume the theme as well as the food.

Ruby's Diner boasts a nostalgia theme.

New themed establishments use a variety of innovative strategies to differentiate themselves from the pack. At the chic Casa La Femme in New York's Soho, diners sit on the floor in designer tents, are served by waiters on their knees who explain the menu, and can visit a palm reader in her tent between courses. At Red Square in the Mandalay Bay Resort, people dine in the cold train-station atmosphere of a Moscow restaurant. At the restaurant's tiny vodka bar, drinks contain ice cubes in the shape of Lenin's head, and guests huddle in thick coats because they and the vodka bottles are chilled to Siberian temperatures.

Theming strategies for restaurants vary widely; the most common are reliquary, parodic, ethnic, and reflexive.[13]

Reliquary theming involves the use of relics and artifacts connected to a heroic figure or notable era or event that introduce a sense of pilgrimage to the experience. Diners visit to pay homage to the objects as much as to eat. This strategy makes a direct link to the famous. For example, Hard Rock Café's link to the music and film industries gives diners a sense of being in the presence of something special or even sacred in those industries.

Parodic theming (think parody) uses ambiance created through artifacts and decorative devices to create a magical (but knowingly fake) environment based on a strong motif. The jungle-themed Rainforest Café is the best example of this type of parodic theming. No customer really believes she is in a rainforest, but the experience is fun, just the same.

Ethnic themes provide somewhat stereotypical signals, such as art, décor, and music, to recognizably reflect a culture. North of the border, for example, sombreros and mariachi music say "Mexico."

Reflexive theming focuses on a brand that becomes a theme. McDonalds, Round Table Pizza, and KFC are examples of branded themes.

Themed restaurants are managed using a business model with these characteristics:

- Rational, standardized, and efficient operations that can be easily replicated

- Chains and franchising that are built on a successful theming formula

- Merchandising to boost sales and help advertise the restaurant. Hard Rock Café T-shirts make consumers into walking billboards for the brand. Merchandise also serves as markers or souvenirs of tourist visits to exotic locations.

Trade journals reporting on themed restaurants identified four problems that contribute to a decline in success: the inability to attract repeat visits; mediocre food and service and high prices; overexpansion; and lack of management focus on the core concept.[14] The biggest marketing challenge is getting customers to repeat their dining experiences. Special promotions, occasion parties, and tour packages are a few strategies available to drive repeat visits. Another strategy involves taking themed franchises out of urban areas and into shopping malls. City-center locations are highly competitive and an unreliable market frequented by tourists, but suburban enclosed locations get more repeat visitors. Thus, the themed shopping mall moves into center stage.

Themed Shopping Malls

Overarching motifs and coordinated symbolic schemes in total environments are typical of suburban U.S. malls that market themselves as places to be. As destinations, malls require some means of identification and differentiation. Malls are private commercial spaces that are expressly designed to make money and realize capital, yet they may disguise their purpose with motifs built around themes such as kitsch or high-tech urban space.

Suburban malls changed the nature of retail competition by adding the dimension of a dedicated entertainment space to the marketing equation. The grand themed environments of malls function as the host to a variety of commercial enterprises and is also attractive as a destination itself.

The newest retail environments structured around theming are "downtown walking areas" adjacent to popular attractions. Downtown Disney in Anaheim is one example of a location built around themed eating experiences. As with malls, the process of reliance on theming as a consequence of increased choice and spatial competition is seen in many types of tourist attractions around the globe.

Theme Parks

The Americana themed amusement park industry has evolved into a multibillion-dollar entertainment segment that draws visitors from around the world and spawns many imitations. Attendance at the top 50 theme parks worldwide increased in 2004 by 2.2 percent to 252.4 million visitors.[15] Visitors to the 10 most popular parks in Europe increased 2.8 percent to 41.2 million, 10 in Asia increased 1.1 percent to 68.1, and Latin America decreased slightly to 15.3 million. The most attended theme park in the world in 2004 was Magic Kingdom at Orlando's Walt Disney World, with 15.1 million visitors; second was Disney Tokyo. Company information, annual reports, and park sources are used to calculate estimates of park attendance.

Theme parks are brand magnets in any country because they create a brand halo across a wider geographic area than the theme park itself inhabits. Theme parks serve as splashy introductions to new markets and kick open the door to other ventures. This is why the Chinese government underwrote Disney's Hong Kong project, putting up $419 million for a 57 percent equity stake and providing $780 million in debt financing.

Disney began promoting the Magic World of Disneyland in Hong Kong with a television show designed to educate the Chinese about Disney's world and lure them to the $3.2 billion park that opened in September 2005. Hosted by a pop star, the show featured black-and-white

Romanians protested government plans to build a Dracula theme park in Transylvania.[16]

clips of Walt Disney explaining his California masterpiece, and modern-day images of the Hong Kong park, which is a replica of the original in Anaheim.

China posed marketing challenges Disney had not faced before—translating what are called "family values." To translate this corner of America to Hong Kong, park management retained white actors who speak English for their face characters, which is part of a global strategy that aims to best present the characters from the original animated motion pictures. Bringing the American Dream to China, however, was not the objective of WPP Group's JWT advertising agency, which promotes the park for Disney. Because most of what Chinese listen to on MTV is made in China, dreams, JWT says, must be built around the host country.[17]

Despite JWT's perspective, making a Magic Kingdom-style park was part of Disney's agreement with the Chinese government, which largely financed the venue. Thus, to determine what Chinese audiences wanted, Disney conducted research using focus groups. The study's participants said they wanted an authentic Disney experience. Hoping to avoid accusations of cultural imperialism, Disney conceded to government wishes in some areas: the park features Chinese and other Southeast Asian foods, and its grounds have correct feng shui design elements. Some rides, such as Jungle Cruise, set amid Cambodian ruins, were tweaked for local tastes.

Because Disney marketing is constrained by strict state media controls, promotional efforts were focused on a new Web site and advertising on Coca Cola cans. To build what Disney calls branded story education, Disney toured south China's malls, wooed travel agents, and teamed up with the Communist Youth League to sell stories in community centers. Theme parks are a cornerstone of Disney's international growth strategy, as they are coveted by local officials around the world who seek revenue-generating attractions. The company reportedly has its eye on Shanghai and South Korea[18] for the next park locations.

Usually dependent on an unskilled, seasonal workforce with high turnover rates, amusement parks have operating profits that are sensitive to visitor-days (attendance equivalent to the number of separate visitors times the number of days in operation) and average per-capita spending. Park performance depends on region, weather patterns, number of season days, local demographic and income characteristics, and the amount of capital recently invested. New motion simulator rides and other computer-controlled experiences, such as those developed in the framework of virtual reality and interactive video games, are the frontiers in the evolution of theme-park concepts. Quality of design, efficiency of service, and public fancy will continue to determine the degree of theme park success.

Branded Theme Retail Venues

Like respectively themed restaurants, branded themes rely on the brand to produce the theme and the theme to reinforce the brand. Introduced in 1991, NikeTown is a retail menagerie of themes, styles, and images revolving around sports. Shoppers become visitors in an atmosphere built around the "just do it" slogan that resembles a spiritual gymnasium or cathedral of consumption. NikeTown is a combination of amusement-centered themed environment and a mega-boutique.

Sony's Metreon, a 350,000-square-foot center in downtown San Francisco, is billed as four floors of ultimate entertainment experience. Located in the city's South of Market district, the Metreon's multiple levels provide shopping for Sony music,

Visitors to Hong Kong Disney are not as familiar with Mickey's role, so the park provides hats that feature him as both an introduction and a keepsake.

electronics, and brand extensions of products from the branded attractions. Products from sponsors Citibank, Pepsi, Levis, Intel, Mercury, and others are sprinkled among the shop offerings. Five themed restaurants feed visitors to the Metreon and its theaters. Like Nike, the Sony brand is the hero of this venue. Rather than thinking about Sony as a product, consumers are expected to experience Sony as a pleasant diversion, as a brand that belongs in their lives. Metreon's primary purpose is to provide entertainment for potential consumers within the context of a brand that becomes synonymous with enjoyment, fun, and wonder. The Guinness Factory in Dublin is Ireland's most visited attraction. Here, the beer's history, advertising campaigns, and brewing process are presented to visitors who pay to experience and sample the legendary beer that is synonymous with Irish culture. Munich's Hofbräuhaus is another beer-branded venue catering to tourists. Marketing branded venues entails transferring the brand image onto a space where visitors can experience the brand in real time.

Religious Theming

Theming has come even to religion. Trinity Broadcasting Network (TBN), the largest Christian religion-based television network, is headquartered in Costa Mesa, California. The network's facility entertains visitors with religious souvenirs and reenactments of milestones in Christianity's history. TBN features all types of programming—talk shows, quiz shows, kids shows, and reality shows—all based on religious themes. The station's most recent film, *Six: The Mark Unleashed,* starring Steven Baldwin, premiered on TBN in 2004.[19]

Trinity's Music City is Nashville's newest tourist attraction. The former estate of country music legend Conway Twitty features a complex with a 2,000-seat auditorium that hosts concerts, dramas, seminars, and special events. On the cutting edge of technology, TBN's virtual reality theaters are operated in Nashville, Dallas, and Costa

Trinity Broadcast Network founders Paul and Jan Crouch appear on their own national television station.

Mesa. Two more theaters are planned for Hawaii and Jerusalem to present visitors with an experience combining high definition digital video technology and a 48-channel digital audio system. The theaters showcase four original productions from TBN Films. Satellite technology has opened up opportunities for the gospel to reach global audiences over 33 international satellites. TBN's themed venues and programming are marketed through churches, print advertising, and tourism bureaus, making the business a profitable nonprofit.

Crystal Cathedral, an architectural marvel also located in California, is marketed to tourists of all denominations and hosts regular tours through the facility. Religious theming is used to market celebrity clergy, ideology, and venues of worship that attract visitors who partake in a variety of entertainment-based experiences. The Christianity brand has become so big, in fact, that PR professional Larry Ross claimed he "took a bungee jump for God and helped turn religious public relations into big business."[20] Representing multiple religious genres—the film *The Passion of the Christ*, Billy Graham, and the men's ministry Promise Keepers among them—Ross's ministry has been publicity, marketing, and branding since 1994. Ross characterizes his job as finding the sweet spot where faith and the culture intersect, because religion on its own often is not enough to generate mainstream press.

Theming Las Vegas

A composite of themed attractions, hotels, casinos and restaurants, Las Vegas is the ultimate staged environment. The world capital of show business, every square foot of

The Luxor Hotel's theme centers around replicas of Egypt's ancient artifacts.

the city is devoted to entertainment. Neon superlatives such as "best," "largest," and "biggest" dominate the landscape that dwarfs people and cars and evokes the materialization and megalomania of the town.

Las Vegas is a mega-resort that has repositioned itself from gambling enterprise to comprehensive entertainment capital where slot machines and roulette wheels take their places among top acts in music, comedy, art, and magic. Las Vegas radiates hope, humor, and extravagance, endlessly repeating the myth of instant wealth available to anyone who will play. Exploring marquees preach mantras of the Strip: Shop, shop, shop, win, win, win. Composed of vastly incongruous architectural styles and themes that are forced into senseless proximity, medieval Excalibur is a few blocks from Caesar's Palace of ancient Rome, which is not far from modern New York. Centuries and continents are jumbled together as the ultimate faux-travel experience. By immersing visitors in an imaginary world, Las Vegas is completely focused on its one-dimensional essence—razzle-dazzle.

So what can marketers learn from this expertly fabricated entertainment experience? One set of authors writing about Las Vegas offers these tips:[21]

• Interactivity is key to consumer enjoyment; always package and market shared experiences.

• Show business thrives on legends and lore—successful marketers create a new mythology for their clients.

• The customer service is king; make certain everyone in the business is informed and inclined to immerse the consumer in service.

• Efficiency and planning yield a successful operation that can be marketed with confidence.

- Try to own some show-business category that showcases the brand. MGM Grand Hotel aspires to "own" the luxury hospitality segment with its size and grandeur.

- Having a special jargon helps make the brand or experience immersionary; always try to use show-business talk to advertise and promote entertainment.

- If you cannot stimulate business where the consumers and audiences are, make the entertainment brand experience a destination Mecca of its own.

- Learn how to implement free show business experiences to bring audiences to your venue or attraction.

If, as the slogan says, "What goes on in Las Vegas stays in Las Vegas," hospitality and casino marketers can capitalize on the "forbidden fun" aspect of the destination's entertainment value. After all, what's more exciting than doing what doesn't come naturally?

FINALLY: LET'S SUM UP ▪▪▪▪▪▪▪

As tourism grows, so will attraction development and improvement. Marketing skills are needed to identify trends, reach audience segments, and differentiate offerings for audiences of all types. Theming is one strategy that helps set location-based entertainment apart from the competition.

However, authenticity has become a scarce commodity in simulated, fake environments. Whether this trend will continue or yield to realism is yet to be determined. For now, "fabulous fakes" seem to be the preferred entertainment strategy that marketers must understand and embrace.

GOT IT? LET'S REVIEW ▪▪▪▪▪▪▪

- Attractions provide tourists and residents with place-based experiences that are marketed by the hosting venue.
- Museums are marketed using research to determine the needs of visitors; staff members are used to implement new programs, and Web sites are used to recruit, maintain, and service members.
- With all forms of service marketing, customer service is a key element for gaining repeat customers and generating positive world-of-mouth promotion.

- Casinos attract ethic groups and Asians by understanding and addressing their cultural nuances through language-based signage and menu development.
- Theming is a motif-based marketing strategy to immerse visitors and differentiate eating, shopping, gaming, and playing experiences.
- Marketing branded tourist attractions, restaurants, malls, parks, and venues involves providing a safe environment, familiar symbols, an enhanced narrative, and providing incentives to stimulate repeat visits.

NOW TRY THIS ▪▪▪▪▪▪▪

1. While viewing your city's tourism bureau online, count and categorize the number and type of attractions promoted. What links are provided to connect visitors with each attraction? How do attractions partner with each other to provide tourist packages? What packaging improvements can you suggest?

2. Visit the Web site of a two local museums and compare their membership benefits. Which organization's membership is more appealing to you? Why? What could you suggest to the other museum to help it be more competitive with your age and lifestyle demographic?

3. Visit an ethnic-themed restaurant and make a list of the icons, artifacts, and symbols that support the theme. Then ask 10 friends which icons, artifacts, and symbols they would choose from that theme. Compare the two lists. What conclusions can you draw from this comparison that are valuable for marketing ethnic themes?

4. Develop a new themed space idea with the potential for global franchise. Describe the space, retail venue, and artifacts you would incorporate into this attraction. What audience would you target? What locations would you recommend? In your answer, consider (1) investment potential, (2) available labor force, and (3) sociocultural transferability.

QUESTIONS: LET'S REVIEW ▗▖▖▖▖▖▖

1. What marketing strategies do attractions use to connect with tourism boards? To reach local audiences? Which are most effective? Why?
2. How do museums structure their membership programs to capitalize on exhibit-based experiences? What other business-model methods might they use to generate revenue?
3. Why has theming become so pervasive for marketing location-based entertainment?

Which themes are most effective for repeat customers? Why?
4. When marketing casinos, what ethical issues should promoters consider when developing repeat-based incentives? How pervasive is gambling addiction?
5. What marketing measures can you suggest for theme-based restaurants to promote repeat visits? How will franchising expansion impact food-based entertainment revenues?

MORE TO READ ▗▖▖▖▖▖▖

Jean Baudrillard. "Disneyworld Company," *Liberation,* March 4, 1996.

Mark Gottdiener. *The Theming of America: American Dreams, Media Fantasies and Themed Environments,* 2nd ed. Boulder, CO: Westview, 2001.

Neil Kotler and Philip Kotler. *Museum Strategy and Marketing: Designing Missions, Building*

Audiences, Generating Revenue and Resources. San Francisco: Jossey-Bass, 1998.

Christian Mikunda. *Brand Lands, Hot Spots & Cool Spaces: Welcome to the Third Place and the Total Marketing Experience.* London: Kogan Page, 2004.

John Sherry Jr. (ed.). *ServiceScapes.* Chicago, IL: NTC Books, 1998.

NOTES ▗▖▖▖▖▖▖

1. James MacCannell, *The Tourist* (Berkeley, CA: University of California Press, 1976), p. 109.
2. Alan Lew, "A Framework of Tourist Attraction Research," *Annals of Tourism Research* 14 (4) (1987).
3. L. Delp, C. Ryan, and L. Sanders for *Travel Holiday,* November 2000.
4. Kathleen Khalife, museummarketingtips.com, Jan. 4. 2006.
5. Ryan Chittum and Jennifer Forsyth for "Property Report" in the *Wall Street Journal,* March 15, 2006.
6. Cecilie Rohwedder, *Wall Street Journal,* May 5, 2003.
7. www.marketingprofs.com/ea/ qst_question.asp?qstID=3074, Jan. 7, 2006.
8. Stephen Karoul, "Casino Marketing—Perception or Reality," March 3, 2002.
9. Peter Sanders, "Heard on the Street," *Wall Street Journal,* March 9, 2006.
10. Sandara Galletti, "Chinese Culture and Casino Customer Service." Unpublished paper, Loyola Marymount University, Los Angeles, CA, 2002.

11. D. Biers, "Bright Lights, High Rollers," *Far Eastern Economic Review,* March 22, 2001.
12. J. Pomfret, "China's High Rollers Find a Seat at the Table," *Washington Post,* March 26, 2002.
13. A. Bearadsworth and A. Bryman, "Late Modernity and the Dynamics of Quasification: The Case of Themed Restaurants," *Sociological Review* 47 (2) (1999), 228–257.
14. *Nation's Restaurant News,* Dec. 7, 1998, p. 29.
15. *Amusement Business,* December 2004.
16. cnn.com, Sept. 30, 2002.
17. Geoffrey Fowler and Merissa Marr, *Wall Street Journal,* June 16, 2005.
18. *Ibid.*
19. tbn.org.
20. Strawberry Saroyan, Sunday *New York Times Magazine,* April 16, 2006.
21. B. Schmitt, D. Rogers, and K. Vrotsos, *There's No Business That's Not Show Business* (New York: Prentice-Hall, 2004), chap. 14.

CHAPTER 14

Mediated Entertainment

Television?
The word is half Latin and half Greek.
No good can come of it.
— C. P. SCOTT

Chapter Objectives

After reading Chapter 14, you should be able to answer these questions:

- How are *films* positioned, promoted, and distributed?
- What are the macro and microeconomic *financial factors* affecting film marketing?
- What is the primary strategy used to market *television* shows?
- How is *product placement* used in movie and television marketing?

The cultural industries are defined not only by the nature of their cultural products, but also by the industry system in which they are produced and consumed. What is our national fascination with the cult of celebrity?[1] You need to study popular culture to understand the impact of the cultural industries on society. Marketing to an invisible, mass audience is a huge challenge for media marketers, who depend on advertising revenues, ratings, and seasonal fluctuations to judge the success or failure of their efforts.

Film and television marketing consists of three distinct phases: the *production stage,* during which a script is developed, capital is raised, and the movie or show is produced; the *distribution stage,* during which movies go to theaters and shows are broadcast on network or cable TV; and finally, the *after-market stage,* during which films go to DVD and television, and TV shows are syndicated to other channels and global markets. This chapter looks at how marketing for mediated entertainment— movies and television— is developed and executed with these stages in mind.

▐▐▐ The Business of Marketing Movies

Far from the glamorous side of the movie business, behind-the-scenes financing and mass marketing control the success or failure of a film property. Strategic gain for media properties has two stages: (1) first-time success with revenue and acclaim, and (2) the use of success to generate more sales. Moving a character to another genre, putting the film plot in another form, or using the film as an anchor to launch a movie of the same type are all forms of extending a property. To begin, we examine who watches and what audiences want, then how to reach them using a variety of promotional tools. Finally, we explore the basics of finance budgeting as it relates to taking movies to film audiences.

Who Goes to the Movies and What Do They Want to See?

Today's audiences want to be transported away from the gloom of 24-hour news; they want happy endings, but they won't buy a fake one. Audiences are very fickle, and film appreciation varies by segment and genre. So to lure and hold audiences, marketers direct their attention to niche markets. Among the many options, these segments receive special attention from promoters:

• **Gender:** *Women* generally go to movies about characters, so character development is crucial for attracting and keeping women in the audience. *Men,* on the other hand, prefer action, and today's studios direct most of their attention at shooting up the screen in an effort to attract male viewers.

• **Ethnicity:** *Hispanic and African-American audiences* frequent films 30 to 40 percent more often than the general population; universal themes, such as family loyalty, appeal to these markets.

• **Age:** Box office draws are aimed at *teenage audiences,* especially girls, and address topics of family, youthful rebellion, and teen pregnancy. *Baby boomers* react most favorably to nostalgia and are targeted for period pieces, biographies, and historical fiction.

• **Special circumstances:** *Military groups* and their families and military personnel stationed overseas have become audiences for movies that deal with anxieties and dilemmas of war and separation.

• **Genre:** Film genres appeal to specific audiences. *War movie* audiences, for example, want films with good guys and bad guys and black-and-white moral distinctions. To market a war movie successfully, the film story must be about having something at stake: honor or pride or personal dignity. That is why audiences like films about WWII: there is no gray in them. *Fantasy films*—many digitally animated—have wide appeal, allowing parents and children to view the same film for different reasons: the adults enjoy the special effects, while the kids delight in the super-heroic action.

• **Special interest:** *Independent filmgoers* are usually urban, at a median age of 33, with above-average household income, and more educated than blockbuster film audiences. These audiences want to be stimulated and challenged by film and are as focused on being facilely entertained. Unlike the happy-ending crowd, these audiences don't respond to in-your-face marketing, preferring instead to rely on word-of-mouth, critical reviews, Internet and film Web sites and posters hung at various locations around a city.

newest genre to captivate movie audiences is the Hollywood-style documen-
sed with fanfare and receiving huge revenues in 2005, *March of the Penguins*
the emotional and narrative satisfaction associated with popular commercial
ema. Earning more than $75 million at the American box office, *Penguins* became
the second-highest-grossing nonfiction movie ever. Why? This film gave audiences
everything they wanted—an epic journey; a family in peril; moments of humor, tender-
ness, and suspense; and a sonorous voice-over by Morgan Freeman—without using
stars or special effects.[2]

Positioning and Selling a Film

Marketers traditionally position films by genre, relying on the audiences' selective
perception to see movies like those that have previously entertained them. Directors
sometimes confuse marketability with playability, however—a movie can preview like
gangbusters with a recruited audience, but that does not mean it has marketable
elements. Several factors play a role in a film's marketing success, including trailers,
tie-ins, Oscar nominations, stars, previews and reviews, film festivals, the Internet, and
viewing venues. Each of these elements contributes to positioning a film (or the
viewing experience) apart from others in the marketplace. These distinctions are
discussed here.

The Role of Trailers

Since the first Internet trailer (for *Stargate*) was shown in 1994, trailers have become
the most important marketing tool for movie promotion. Teaser trailers, shown months
in advance of release, peak audience interest about a forthcoming film and begin
creating awareness of the title. Full-length trailers, shown prior to the film's release, are
produced for theaters and television commercials. When shown as part of a rolling
series of previews or at the beginning of a home video, trailers may run as long as five
or six minutes.

Trailers can be tailored to specific audience segments by focusing on certain
elements of a film. Often, two or three trailers are developed for different audience
segments. Shots are typically edited out of the film for use in a buzz-building trailer.
Because stars bring their own brand to a film, movie trailers must blend the star's traits
with the movie's strengths.

Budgets for trailers run between $500,000 and $2 million. Trailers are adapted for
television commercials and used in electronic press kits and as point-of-sale materials
in video stores and on DVDs. In style, they are moving away from straight narration to
include more music and less voice-over. The best trailers have a beginning and a
middle, but no end—audiences must see the movie to find out how the story ends.

The Role of Tie-Ins and Merchandising

Movie industry synergy is often created with what is called a *tent-pole film,* which is a
hit whose profits often hold up everything else at the studio. By branding movies as
lumps of content (merchandise and tie-in promotions), marketers can create a winning
synergy between products and the viewing experience. Once the brand becomes an
icon, it can be further exploited through merchandising and promotional tie-ins. Added
exposure for family films comes from a close association with toy makers, apparel

Memoirs of a Geisha star.

companies, and fast-food franchises. Movie tie-ins work most effectively with teens, who wear specialty brands and eat at McDonald's and Taco Bell.

As mentioned in an earlier chapter, tie-in partnerships have prompted retailers to go into new product lines with the film *Memoirs of a Geisha*. Assembled by DZP Marketing Communications, most of the products are, predictably, aimed at women. Based on the 1997 book of the same name, which described lavish tea ceremonies, fashions, and beauty rituals, the *Geisha* products are at the heart of the retail partnerships with Sony Pictures Entertainment. The most distinguishable tie-ins included these corporate partnerships:[3]

• Banana Republic launched a limited-edition line of Asian-influenced apparel and accessories, including a kimono-inspired dress, as well as tops, shoes, handbags, and a jacket.

• The Republic of Tea produced Spring Cherry Green Tea, a Japanese sencha green tea blended with cherries, rose petals, and white tea buds. Its packaging featured the film's star, Ziyi Zhang.

• Tonner Dolls introduced a Geisha doll collection; the dolls' outfits were based on the movie's costumes and included a kimono and 1940s street attire.

• Fresh, a beauty-products company partnering with Bath & Body Works, offered a *Memoirs of a Geisha* collection that included Rice Face Wash, Flower Petal Mask, and Shimmer Powder with Crushed Pearls. The cherry blossom packaging was inspired by a kimono in the movie.

Mel Gibson chose to partner his film *The Passion of Christ* with Christian organizations when marketing it. Enlisting 2,000 Christian retailers to build the buzz for the

BOX 14-1

Focus on Merchandising

TYING-IN WITH HARRY

For kids, Harry Potter tie-ins are the crown jewels in a far-reaching empire of merchandise and tie-ins. *Harry Potter and the Goblet of Fire,* the darkest of the four films in the series, doesn't mean dark times ahead for retailers, who had countless *Goblet*-related items in time for the film's holiday release. Here is a small sample of what one movie can conjure:

Wristwatches: Seiko's watch is designed to represent the story of the Hogwarts students in their fourth year and the Triwizard Tournament, including special-edition timepieces in collectible tins.

Calendars: Take your pick. Andrews McMeel Publishing offers a range of HP time-keepers, including a literary 2006 wall calendar with artwork by Mary GrandPre, illustrator of the U.S. editions of the books. Mini-calendars and desk calendars also are available.

Music—Soundtrack: Harry Potter & the Goblet of Fire: Original Soundtrack, features the score by Academy Award-nominated composer Patrick Doyle and three songs written by rocker Jarvis Crocker, which are performed by Crocker, Jonny Greenwood, Phil Selway, Steve Claydon, and Jason Buckle (all seen in the film, too).

Toys: Mattel's *Scene It?* Harry Potter DVD Game, designed for players ages eight to adult, has hundreds of images and movie clips and 1,000-plus questions from the four films. Mattel's many products also include action figures, dolls, play sets, and other games. With Lego play sets, youngsters can recreate key scenes from the movie, including a graveyard duel in which Harry sees the face of evil. Video gamers can enjoy "Goblet of Fire" by Electronic Arts for Windows XP, PlayStation2, X-Box, Game Cube or Sony PSP, GameBoy Advance, and Nintendo DS.

Clothing—T-shirts and trinkets: The burgundy-and-yellow Harry Potter Chenille Scarf, with or without Gryffindor patch, is a WBShop.com exclusive. Hot Topic stores or www.hottopic.com sells four dozen-plus items, ranging from a black Death Eaters Wrist Cuff to a Ron Weasley Yule Ball T-shirt.

Collectibles: A limited edition, 8-inch-tall pewter replica of the goblet in the movie is available from WBShop.com. That site has pages of bedding, posters, prints, novelty items, and other gifts.

Jewelry: "Flower" earrings, made of sterling silver and set with pink crystals, are similar to the ones worn by student witch Hermione for her transformation from bookworm to glam girl in the film.

SOURCE: B. Vancheri and S. Eberson, *Pittsburgh Post-Gazette,* Nov. 18, 2005.

---

film's release (on Ash Wednesday, an annual Christian holy day), Gibson and New-market Films promoted the movie through churches to 120 million parishioners using printed materials and by supplying online sermons to preachers. Retail outlets sold packs of witness cards (cards bearing messages from Christ) containing spiritual messages on one side and a promotion on the other for $5.95 a pack. Pendants of large and small pewter nails on leather thongs retailed at $13 and $25—100,000 were sold. Three thousand behind-the-scenes coffee table books about making the movie sold for $25 in

Mel Gibson on the set of *The Passion of the Christ.*

a single week. Framed paintings and prints based on the movie, selling for between $30 and $100, generated sales of 20,000 units in three weeks. *Passion*'s logo was prominent in NASCAR's Daytona 500. Ten-second television trailers were developed featuring specific churches for a cost of $795 to Newmarket and $1,000 to the cosponsor. So, despite the film's low box office take, licensed goods provided enough revenue for Gibson and Icon Distribution to cover the costs of production—and then some.[4]

The Role of Stars

A general assumption is that stars are absolutely essential to mainstream film production, both in Hollywood and at cinemas across the globe. Without a doubt, stars are a key element in the overall film package. A weapon in the film financier's armory, stars are essential for creating a promotable film package. The popularity of a star-driven film, however, depends on the marketing process connected with it.[5]

Stars must "work" the picture with publicity junkets and media interviews. Shortly before a film is released, appearance schedules are developed with producers of network and cable programs such as *The Today Show, Oprah, David Letterman,* and *Larry King.* Most stars rely on their publicist or the studio's publicist to develop junket schedules. Others determine their own availability for appearances. Tom Cruise has final approval over all marketing materials on his films and does a smart job of selling his own movies. For the film *Collateral,* for instance, he insisted on an ensemble junket (a junket for which co-stars appear together) because he knew Jamie Foxx would attract a different audience than he would.[6]

But marketing does not always create stars; the public often makes those determinations. Look at Johnny Depp: He is now a gigantic star, but he has been a great actor for many years. In spite of his tremendous talent, interesting roles, and good marketing, it took *Pirates of the Caribbean* to make him a big movie star—the audience spoke.[7] More star-powered strategy celebrity marketing is found in Chapter 16.

Gene Siskel often gives films a "thumbs up" rating.

The Role of Screenings, Sneaks, and Reviews

Test screenings presented at local movie theaters or mall locations measure target audience reaction to movies. Respondents see an unfinished version of a film, then complete a survey with detailed questions regarding plot, characters, and scenes. Producers use these comments to edit the film accordingly. Screenings are valuable pre-release tools.

To get favorable word-of-mouth promotion before a film is released, studios schedule sneak previews and capture audience comments as filmgoers emerge from the theater. Sneak comments are featured in news clips and video releases to correspond with the film's opening. Well-edited responses become positive testimonials to audience enjoyment and can be used to stimulate interest in the film within a specific audience segment. Sneaks are important for generating enthusiasm for a new film.

Professional reviews matter, but they are not enough to sell a blockbuster film. Roger Ebert, for instance, gives thumbs up to many of the films he reviews, and his comments usually headline print film ads. So, no one really pays attention to the "two thumbs up" designation. For independent or foreign films, however, reviews are significant determinants of box office revenues. These audiences may peruse three or four critics' columns before determining whether or not to see a film.

The Role of Ratings

Ratings affect audience make up and, ultimately, box office revenues. Achieving the ideal audience balance that includes both teens and adults is tricky; producers need the teens, but don't want to deter adults with a PG rating. R ratings, however, severely narrow the viewing field because they exclude the teen audience.

Ratings are determined by the Motion Picture Association of America (MPAA) board majority vote. A PG-13 rating is issued when *one* sexually derived word is used as an expletive; more than one requires an R rating. Trailers also require approval prior to release, and must be accompanied by information that tells the audience which rating the trailer and the movie being advertised are assigned. "All audience" rated trailers have a green designation, and "restricted" designations have a red background to prevent accidental substitution of one for the other. Ratings can be appealed, but appeals require a two-thirds majority vote to overturn a previously assigned rating.

The Role of the Internet

The Internet has brought a dimension to film promotion that exceeds what has been possible through all the other promotional devices combined. By bringing fans together, soliciting comments, and creating buzz, the Internet now has a primary role in movie marketing. As a result, substantial portions of a film's budget are allocated to developing and maintaining an appropriate Web site.

▪▪▪▪▪▪▪▪▪▪ BOX 14-2 ▪▪▪▪▪▪▪▪▪▪

A Closer Look at Promotion

MARKETING THE FANTASTIC FOUR

Remaining in the shadow of other comic superheroes such as Spiderman and X-Men, the Fantastic Four have stood by while other characters from the Marvel Comics lineup got the full Hollywood treatment. The first Marvel superheroes of the Stan Lee era, the Fantastic Four established the Marvel trademark of sympathetic heroes. When 20th Century Fox released its $100 million adaptation of the *Fantastic Four* (2005), it hoped this would be its best chance to turn the last superstars in the Marvel pantheon into a global franchise of video games, action figures, and assorted billions in ancillary revenue that follows—in other words, into a tent-pole film.

One advantage for promoters was the fans who had been waiting decades for the movie; with conventions and Web sites devoted to their beloved comic books, fans were potent tools for spreading buzz. After decades of development hell, Fox needed an outstanding screenplay to position itself among other releases in the competitive summer release season.

To stand out from the crowd, Fox and Marvel build the Fantastic Four release around a simple refrain: *Take the number "4" and repeat it.* Production chief Avi Arad spent weeks pressing the flesh with comic book-nerd elites at festivals such as Comic-Con in San Diego and Wizard World in Los Angeles. Given an audience unhealthily obsessed with what Hollywood would make of their childhood heroes, Arad faced the marketing challenge head on.

Using Web sites to act as superconductors for movie rumors and news, some sites generated Internet ads and as many as 3 million hits a month. But the fans who visited these sites came loaded with high expectations and hypersensitivity to any perceived misstep. Before the movie's release, the *Ain't It Cool News* Web site published a blistering critique of a script rewrite—which had been long-since discarded—that began a bad buzz.

Fox gave fan sites a level of access rarely granted, offering them "everything first" and enough unique content to build and expand their interest in the film. Fan sites were fed scraps of news and concept art at strategic intervals. The cast was sent to comic book conventions where publicists distributed plastic vials of "cosmic dust." And the studio held a junket for "genre media" (fan site developers), flying correspondents to the set in Vancouver with complimentary rooms at the Four Seasons (remember the number four strategy)? Media were allowed to interview the director and cast and were given exclusive images from the film to post on their sites.

As the months passed, bitching from studio dweebs inferred that the movie needed to be hipped up and sexed up. Still, trailers were shipped to 3,200 theaters with *Elektra*, another Marvel movie that seemed like a great way to introduce *Fantastic Four* to its target audience. Unfortunately, *Elektra* was Marvel's biggest flop ever. The next association to grab the fans was with *Revenge of the Sith*. Arad learned from these tactics that courting comic book fans is only part of the game—the general public needed to be introduced to these films, as well.

So the movie was promoted in TV, print, and radio ads; Burger King aired its

(Continued)

own *Fantastic Four* commercials for both adults and kids. Kraft hawked *Fantastic Four* Lunchables. Star Michael Chiklis (as Ben Grimm) appeared as The Thing in TV spots for Samsung phones, delivering the tagline, "It's fantastic!" The pushing included wooing theater owners at the ShoWest industry convention in Las Vegas with an hour-long, celebrity-heavy presentation emceed by studio chairs. A splashy highlight reel previewed the upcoming Fox lineup complete with a plume of smoke and music from "Fantastic Voyage" as Chiklis and costars strode to the podium.

Ultimately, it was the franchise that generated the profits. The first weekend box office was $56 million, and total gross revenue came to $155 million after six months. *Fantastic Four* pleased some fans, but dismayed others—and most reviewers. Roger Ebert gave the PG-rated, 110-minute film a thumbs down, moaning that the picture was "All set-up and demonstrations without any character development."[8]

What do you think?

1. How else might Marvel have used its fans to help promote the film?

2. How should they have educated the public about the comic book characters?

3. What could the studio have done to control high expectations for the film before it was released so fans were not disappointed?

4. What kind of research might have added to the film's script revision?

SOURCE: Jonathan Bing, *Wired*, July 2005.

▪▪▪▪▪▪▪▪▪

Film Web sites give audiences an opportunity to experience the brand before and after its release. Most of these sites use games and gimmicks to entertain and involve potential audiences. Fan blogs and sites also are important for stimulating interest in, creating buzz around, and generating box office revenues for films.

The Role of the Oscars

The leverage of an Oscar nomination is well known; the ceremony is one of the most-watched broadcasts in the world. In terms of box office and DVD sales, a Best Picture Oscar has lasting value, while Best Actor and Best Actress awards matter only to the actor and actress who win them. What really helps a film at the box office is numerous nominations. In our volume-conscious society, 10 nominations is very impressive.[9]

Even more significantly, nominations for independent and foreign films create new audiences from the recognition and publicity the Oscars generate. Other awards, such as recognition from Sundance and other film festivals, as well as the Golden Globes (which precede the Oscars), add equity to a film brand and also usually result in enhanced box office sales.

The Role of Niche Audiences

In 2005, Disney took grassroots marketing to a new level by providing activities for juvenile detention centers in Los Angeles as a tie-in to the movie *The Chronicles of Narnia: The Lion, the Witch and the Wardrobe*. A class of teenagers enacted a mock trial of Edmund, a character in the movie; made crumpets in a cooking class; and recreated movie sets in construction classes as part of a buildup to see in the film when it was released.[10]

Disney and its partner Walden Media have reached out to a panoply of special-interest groups, from the Coast Guard Youth Academy to Ronald McDonald House, wooing them with invitations to glitzy presentations on the studio lot and lavishing them with posters, snow globes, and other promotional gear. The team's marketing strategy included pulling a variety of themes from the storyline to build their campaign around. The themes included a World War II historical backdrop; the religious references of the characters; the fantasy element of the story; and such traits as loyalty, courage, good-vs.-evil, and the importance of family.

Disney and HarperCollins, the publisher of the book written by C. S. Lewis, provided books to schools for in-class reading. The publication of 19 new editions of the novel, as well as activity books with glitter pens and magnets, coincided with the movie's release. *Narnia* materials were sent to every elementary and middle school in America, including posters, educational guides, and more than 90,000 copies of the novel and accompanying teaching lesson plans.

To back up these grassroots campaigns, a slew of promotional partners were recruited. Together, they brought in marketing efforts valued at $15 million that targeted kids and families at shopping malls with everything from elaborate exhibits to fake snow. Walden has the rights to adapt six other Lewis books in the series and an 18-year franchise deal, so this was only the tip of the impending promotional iceberg.

The Role of Venues

Movie venues can be in-theater or out-of-theater. New in-theater experiences are being created to lure audiences to movie houses. Out-of-theater locations include airline viewing and outdoor locations.

In-flight movies offer marketing value through licensing fees and features in airline magazines. Summer attendance at outdoor movie locations is soaring. Audiences are watching movies among sculptures at the North Carolina Museum of Art in Raleigh, amid the skyscrapers in New York City's Bryant Park, in a parking lot across from a Seattle pub, and from a marble mausoleum in Hollywood's Forever Cemetery.[11] Because *temporary venues* are so flexible—they can be almost anywhere—the practice is not likely to disappear soon. What the temporary venue really speaks to is how much the idea of novelty is central to the entire viewing experience. Audiences insist on it. Perhaps that has been true all along, but lately it seems that viewers set the pace, and distributors struggle to keep up. The temporary venue is a response to that shift, one that will work until something else comes along and makes it seem obsolete.

Traditional viewing venues also are upping the novelty ante. Theaters located in malls, in an effort to set up the movie-going experience as a special event, are combining adult-only screenings with dinner before the film or with desert following the feature. Such packaged marketing efforts help studios promote movies to specific market segments. Cineplexes also foster multiple viewing options for families with different preferences.

Some movie viewers, however, complain that pre-film advertisements are ruining the movie-going experience. To address this complaint, Screenvision, one of two companies that package on-screen advertising for exhibitors, invested $50 million in a digital projection system to improve the viewing quality of advertising. The other company, National CineMedia, is introducing 20-minute packages, which include, along with the ads, behind-the-scenes segments from the sets of movies such as *King Kong.* With many audiences preferring home viewing, venues are taking measures to bring them back to theaters, including previewing experiences and in-theater entertainment (dining, interviews with stars) prior to the movie.

The Role of Aftermarket Sales

In 2004, about half of the revenue made by studios on feature films was generated by DVD sales; 23 percent from theatrical releases, 12 percent from video rentals, and 17 percent from other sources such as merchandising and licensing.[12]

To ensure continuing sales of aftermarket products, film studios must make their initial marketing efforts strong enough to carry audience momentum to the next stage—buying or renting the DVD or video. Because DVDs are a larger part of Hollywood's revenue stream than any other source, concern over slowing sales runs high.

The Role of Film Festivals

Much media hype centers on film festivals. The most popular currently is Utah's Sundance Festival, where major and minor players come looking for hits. In 2006, Fox Searchlight set a Sundance record by paying $10.5 million for *Little Miss Sunshine,* a quirky road-trip comedy; Warner spent $6 million on *Science of Sleep.* Such pricey festival acquisitions indicate a realignment from low- to higher-budget films within the independent film marketplace. According to agents, producers, and buyers, a new class division has been created in the independent market—the so-called *mini-majors.* Most of these "bigger" **indies** (independent films) are actually owned by giant studios, who pursue independent movies with the potential to earn substantial money at the box office. Smaller "micro-distributors" are left with the many titles that could turn a profit at much lower prices. According to a representative of William Morris Independent, the independent-film arm of the famed talent agency, studios are moving out of the low-budget art-house business and are looking for home runs such as *Sideways,* a 2005 *sleeper,* or surprise low-budget hit.[13]

Films that gross under $5 million are most interesting to smaller studios, such as Lions Gate, which paid nearly $3 million for worldwide rights to *Right at Your Door,* a low-budget thriller about a terrorist attack that paralyzes Los Angeles. The studio offered the production company a percentage of the box office gross and of region/territory opening takes. Roadside Attractions is another successful player in the new lower-priced indie landscape; it paid more than $600,000 for domestic rights to *Stay,* an offbeat comedy with a bestiality angle.

The Role of the Global Film Market

The expanding foreign box office has helped rejuvenate a number of films that have suffered in the U.S. market, especially epics set in ancient times, such as *Kingdom of Heaven, King Arthur,* and *Alexander.* Animated films are also getting a boost from foreign interest, and many studios are now focusing more on international releases for both epics and animations.

Creative campaigns for U.S. films don't always translate across borders. For *War of the Worlds* (2006), for instance, a separate creative campaign was designed for Japan to play up the link between the daughter and her father protecting the family—a

▮▮▮▮▮▮▮▮▮▮   **BOX 14-3**   ▮▮▮▮▮▮▮▮▮▮

Focus on Studio Mergers

THE CAST OF CHARACTERS NEGOTIATING HOLLYWOOD IN 2006

Name	*Title*	*Role*
Brad Gray	Paramount Chair, CEO	Ex-talent manager trying to revive Paramount
Stacey Snider	Universal Pictures Chair	Runs Universal's movie business; might join DreamWorks
Tom Freston	Viacom CEO	Banking on Paramount turnaround
Ron Meyer	Universal Studios Pres.	Trying to calm unhappiness at movie division
Steven Spielberg	DreamWorks cofounder	Paramount's new star director
Jeffrey Katzenberg	DreamWorks cofounder and Animation CEO	Influential player in the integration of DreamWorks
David Geffen	DreamWorks co-founder	Negotiated the DreamWorks sale to Paramount

Source: Wall Street Journal, Feb. 25, 2006.

▮▮▮▮▮▮▮▮▮

response to the importance of females in the overall Japanese audience. According to a Warner Brothers marketer, Europeans prefer more character-driven films, while Asia and Latin Americans prefer action movies.[14] Marketing with customized trailers helps bring a cultural focus to ensure a movie's success abroad.

In just five years, China has become what Hollywood considers the world's most important producer of foreign-language blockbusters, catapulting beyond France, Spain, or India in global box office receipts. Why? Chinese filmmakers have mixed high-quality productions, exotic settings, gorgeously choreographed action, and universal themes that sell equally well in Boston and Beijing.[15]

By marrying low-cost, high-quality projects with U.S. distribution, Chinese producer Bill Kong has made hits grossing a total of $500 million. Yet he has never produced a picture in Los Angeles or in English. His first film, *Crouching Tiger, Hidden Dragon,* was a result of wooing Hollywood to front half of the movie's $15 million budget. Kong also succeeds because he films in Shanghai, shoots six days a week, and completes a film in four months for $30 million—half the cost of shooting in the U.S.

Filmmakers from Hollywood, Hong Kong, and China have teamed up to duplicate Hollywood's long-successful formula: earn enough money domestically to cover the costs of making a film and then generate big profits through global distribution. In 2005, more than 200 films were in production on the mainland. China now offers Hollywood studios a growing audience, and the buzz on Chinese films has sparked a gold rush among investors. The Hengdian Group, a Chinese pharmaceutical company, built a film studio that is equivalent to Universal Studios—both the movie lot and the theme park. Revenues are generated from the 3 million tourists who pay to watch filming in China each year.

Focus on the UK

PITCHING *NATURAL BORN KILLERS* TO A UK AUDIENCE

Rather than pitching the Oliver Stone film *Natural Born Killers* (1994) to the huge audience aggregation it had identified in the U.S., Warner Brothers' marketers pitched it to a relatively narrow audience of young adult males in Britain. The film combined elements of both a cult movie and a mainstream hit and was positioned in the market as something of an outlaw film. But the promotion was not without its problems.

The circulation strategy of *Natural Born Killers* in Britain was based on the film's industrial setting, the film's classification delay, and the presses' response. The film had become surrounded by discourses of outrage in the period leading to its British release. Press commentators and reviewers generated enough anxiety about the effects of the film's violence to mobilize audience concerns about the film. Then, reports of "copycat" killings reportedly inspired by the film caused the British Board of Film Classification (BBFC) to postpone awarding a ratings certificate for two months, giving marketers eight weeks to runs their advertising campaign.

The target market comprised two main groups: working-class males enthusiastic about violent films and a more discerning, middle-class cinemagoer group who were already fans of the Tarantino-style cult hits *Reservoir Dogs* and *Pulp Fiction*.

Warner Brothers dedicated a more extensive advertising campaign to hook the "downmarket" audience group, which consisted of "unthinking males" and "new violence" audiences. Cutting across these two groups was a third faction—rock music fans. Copying the recording industry's advertising technique of flier posting, movie posters were distributed to independent record stores and big name chains. Promotions were held at selected universities with posters, T-shirts, competitions, and coverage in student publications.

Ultimately, the beneficial commercial advertising effects of the media hysteria put audience awareness of the film at 77 percent two weeks before its opening and 83 percent by the week of its release; among males under 25, an impressive 94 percent awareness was realized. Once awareness of the film was achieved, marketing efforts were directed at clearing up lingering confusion about whether or not it was banned and stressing its imminent release. Two advertisements were assembled featuring the film's stars: an ad featuring Woody Harrelson was aimed at men, while one featuring Juliette Lewis was aimed at women. The ads were placed in television programs with guaranteed male audiences—a boxing match and as a trailer preceding a James Bond film.

The press advertising campaign was aimed largely "downmarket," featuring Harrelson with a tagline, "The controversy starts when you see the film." Heavy publicity schedules were arranged for director Stone and producer Jan Hamsher. In the end, moral panic in the media and the delay in rating classification differentiated the film from other releases and positioned it as an outrageous and attractive product. *Natural Born Killers* opened in Britain on 203 screens in a moderately successful release.

SOURCE: Thomas Austin, *Hollywood, Hype & Audiences,* 2002.

Creating a Promotion Budget

There is no formula for creating a marketing budget for a film, but when creating a budget, studios consider these variables:

- The film's potential gross
- Audience makeup
- The gross achieved in similar genres
- The anticipated revenues from foreign or video sales
- The number of screens used for release
- The number of markets included in the release.

In a traditional budget, 65 to 70 percent of the funds are slated for TV ads, and the balance is spent on print and outdoor ads, with about 3 percent designated for the poster. Once the target audience is identified, a budget can be determined based on size. Major studios allocate advertising budges as follows:

Newspapers—15%
Network TV—24%
Trailers—6%
Internet—9%
Spot TV—18%
Non-media (tie-ins, publicity)—16%
Other media (radio, outdoor, magazine)—20%

According to 2005 data, movie studios are reassessing TV ads because audiences have caught on to studios' tactics for making an event out of every new movie. In a push to cut TV costs, some studios are aligning themselves with different types of advertisers. To market *The Wedding Crashers,* New Line Cinema joined forces with Anheuser-Busch, brewer of Budweiser beer. Budweiser sponsored the movie's New York City premiere, retail promotions, and local screenings and offered *The Wedding Crashers* content on its Web site. *Crashers* figured prominently in two Bud TV spots and in an online movie ad called "Crash This Trailer," which allowed users to substitute images of their faces on the bodies of *Crashers'* stars, Owen Wilson and Vince Vaughn. In another money-saving move, Fox spread the same funds it would have spent on network prime-time spots over a handful of cable channels, and purchased prime-time ads via local stations rather than through national networks.[16]

Budgeting for Independent and Short Films

Independent and specialty art films require minimal budgets for newspaper advertising, festival participation, and screenings aimed at opinion leaders. To avoid summer or holiday releases—the favorite times for blockbuster and other major studio releases— indies must consider and work around feature release schedules. Sites such as boxofficeguru.com or showbizdata.com publicize release dates around which indies should be scheduled to avoid the fiercest competition. It is wise to budget an allowance for reviewer tickets, as well. Marketers need to have films mentioned on reviewing sites such as indieclub.com and indietalk.com to begin creating buzz. Budget for the PR of sending news releases to magazines such as *Independent Filmmaker, Millimeter,* and *Markee,* and to cable shows that feature short films for public airing.

The most famous buzz-generating indie is the "mockumentary" *The Blair Witch.* Its producers, Central Florida Film School pals, developed an Internet site one year before the movie hit the screens in 1999. The site, which included messages posted about the film by the developers before it was released, generated 75 million hits and gained enough investors for the producers to see a profit on the film. Six months following the release, thousands of other sites appeared, and the hype continued to gain momentum. Editors who had not even seen the film posted rave reviews on the Internet, and after its presentation at the Sundance Film Festival, there was no stopping it. Based on the hype, Artisan Entertainment bought the film for $1 million and redeveloped the Web site into an interactive experience that convinced teens the footage was real.

Witch writers made the cover of *Time* and *Newsweek* and took every interview that came along; if none came, they were not ashamed to beg for one. Based on their success, the filmmakers offered these buzz rules for other independent filmmakers:

- It's not always important that people understand you.
- It's how things seem, not how they really are, that's important to the suits in Hollywood; pretend you have a film.
- Don't worry about the script, just start a Web site about your movie idea and talk about it as if it's in production.
- Get busy writing a script and hope it works.

Promoting short films on a small budget begins with the Internet, using sites such as undergroundfilm.com, ifilm.com, and brownfish.com, or producing a self-developed site. Promoting self-developed sites is accomplished with blogs that get the attention of *Ain't It Cool News* as well as *Film Threat,* shortfilminsider.com, and *Internet Video Magazine.* Sending formal press releases via fax or e-mail and placing short films on TV and cable shows that feature them also are prudent (inexpensive) strategies for marketing indies. Good publicity does not have to be expensive, just creative.

▮▮▮ Movie Economics

In no other business is a single example of product fully created at an investment of millions of dollars with no assurance that the public will buy it. In no other business does the public use the product and then take away with them merely the memory of it.[17]

In spite of numbers that report total domestic box office revenue through December 2005 at $8 billion and projected worldwide revenue for movie studios in 2005 at $50 billion,[18] Hollywood worries about where the money will come from for new feature films. Many of the factors that affect other industries—economic cycles, foreign exchange rates, technological advances, and interest rates—also affect profits and valuations for the film industry. A macroeconomic view suggests the following film industry givens:

- Seasonal demand patterns are more easily discerned and interpreted than *long-wave* (future) admission cycles.

- Ticket sales for new film releases normally are not responsive to changes in box office prices per se, but consumers may be sensitive to the total cost of movie-going, which can include fees for sitters, meals, and parking.

- Market share data have limited application and relevance for film because consumers have little brand identification with movie distributors and because market share tends to fluctuate considerably from year to year for every distributor.

- Trade effects or "cultural discounts" are low for U.S. films because the basic global language is English.

- Total fees from the licensing of films for use in ancillary markets have collectively far overshadowed revenues derived from theatrical releases.

Doing the Hollywood math involves more than just calculating box office sales; it reflects revenue generated from home viewing on DVD or video, TV, and merchandise licensing as well. In 2005, box office was down, but overall revenue was booming, thanks to the home market, sales to television, and rapid growth overseas. Record revenues of more than $50 billion also are boosted by mega-blockbusters that bring in between $100 and $200 million at the U.S. box office.

Convention-Generated Revenue

At the Indiana Convention Center in Indianapolis, the Star Wars Fan Club held a convention to celebrate Episode III of *Star Wars*. Film celebrities, archive exhibits of film props and costumes, contests—plus exclusive merchandise sanctioned by George Lucas—were all featured. Sponsorship packages came in a variety of forms and prices:

- "Brought to you by" for $130,000
- Co-sponsorship for $100,000
- Contributing sponsorship for $70,000
- Product or service sponsorship for $40,000
- Special events sponsor for costume contest, auction, Jedi training, a kids' room, concessions, hotels for a range of investment dollars
- Promotional partner sponsorship for $15,000

Sponsorship included two levels of benefits: media and site-based. *Media benefits* included e-mail blasts, online and print collateral materials, on-site exposure and signage, press kit mention, logo on publications and newspaper, online flyers, and ads in the programs. *Site benefits* included a booth, public address announcement, volunteer shirts, press room use, convention badges and hotel discounts, and collectible merchandising.

Fan Web sites, meanwhile, offered the sponsors substations, communications centers, recreation rooms, and docking bays to promote their brands at the convention.

Financial Foundations; Microeconomic Factors

The movie business is contract driven. Film studios simultaneously engage in four distinct business functions: financing, producing, distributing, and marketing/advertising. We now look briefly at these financing aspects.

Some of the most creative work in the industry is reflected in the financial offering prospectuses that are circulated in attempts to find film projects. Financing sources come from the *industry* (distributors, talent agencies, and so on), *lenders* (banks, insurance companies), and *investors* (public and private pools of funds). The most common financing variations available from investors and lenders are common stock offerings, combination deals with other securities, limited partnerships and tax shelters, and bank loans.

Labor unions have an important influence on the economics of filmmaking for their below-the-line production costs, which can be easily estimated. The major Hollywood unions include:

- American Federation of Television and Radio Artists (AFTRA)
- Directors Guild of America
- International Alliance of Theatrical and Stage Employees (IATSE)
- Producers Guild of America
- Screen Actors Guild (SAG)
- Writers Guild of America

For membership fees, unions negotiate contract terms with a studio's bargaining organization, the Alliance of Motion Picture and Television Producers (AMPTP).

Distributors

Films are first distributed to the market that generates the highest marginal revenue over the least amount of time. The usual sequence has historically been theatrical release, licensing to pay cable distributors, home video, network TV, and local television syndicators. With larger and larger amounts of capital being invested in features, the pressure on studios to generate faster recoupment for investors is moving the market toward the earlier opening of all windows. In fact, some studios are simultaneously releasing products to all channels of distribution.

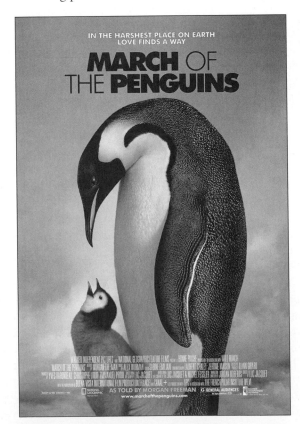

Distributors normally design their marketing campaigns with specific target audiences in mind. Some send bid letters several months in advance of a release to theaters located in regions where they expect to find audiences most responsive to a specific film's theme and genre. Theaters that accept bid letter terms receive a sliding percentage of box office gross after allowance for house (theater) expenses. For many theater owners, box office receipts are secondary to concession stand revenues, over whose proceeds they have total control. Film exhibitors are subject to capacity and competition as well as rentals percentages for which they bid. Volatile over the short run, theatrical exhibition is remarkably consistent over the long haul.

Revenue Recognition Factors

Revenues from theatrical exhibition is straightforward, consisting of either percentage or flat-rent contracts. The American Institute of Certified Public Accountants guide indicates that television license revenues for feature films should not be recognized until the following conditions are met:

1. Film license fee is disclosed
2. Film costs are determined
3. License fee is collectable
4. Licensee accepts film in accordance with license agreement conditions
5. Film is available (distributor retains discretion on availability date)

For inventoried (on the books) films, costs allocated to secondary markets and that are not expected to be realized within 12 months are classified as *noncurrent* in the following categories of film production: released, completed but not released, in process, and story rights/scenarios.

Big-Picture Accounting

The legal heart of most film projects is the production-financing-distribution (PFD) agreement, which includes step deals, packages, presales, and private funding. Each of these financial options provides the producer with different trade-offs in terms of creative control and profits. Most important is the distribution-agreement section for allocation of revenue streams.

Looking at what happens to a dollar when it flows from the box office helps explain the revenue process. Assuming that house expenses are 10 percent, the remaining 90 cents is a 90:10 split for the first two weeks in favor of the distributor, who realizes an 81-cent gross (90 cents minus 9 cents, or the 10 percent house expenses). A 30 percent distribution fee of 24 cents is subtracted, leaving 57 cents. Advertising and publicity costs (20–25 percent of rentals) deduct another 20 cents. From the remaining 37 cents, 6 cents is required for miscellaneous distribution expenses (prints, taxes, transportation). Thirty-one cents of the original dollar remains before negative costs of the picture are calculated. When gross participation to a major actor is factored in (usually 10 percent), that means 8 cents less with which to recoup negative costs (money spent to produce and market the film). If the movie is studio financed, half of any profit after recoupment is owed to the studios; the other half is split among other participants. Despite this risk, many investors find filmmaking financially attractive and worth the risk.

Movie studios engage in three distinct television-related activities: licensing features to networks, syndicating features to local stations, and producing made-for-television movies. Feature licensing is the most lucrative of the three; it may generate a profit margin of between 40 and 65 percent for the studio distributor.

The essential strength of major film studios is in their ability to control distribution from the early financing stages to the timing of theatrical releases. The enormous amount of capital required to operate film production and distribution facilities on a global basis presents a significant barrier to entry and reinforces the trend toward vertical integration of the industry. Production costs, or *sunk costs,* include most of the expenditures, so exposure to a variety of exhibition windows is essential for realizing a profit.

Threats to the Movie Industry

Two significant obstacles confront studios before they can see substantial incomes from making movies available to watch anytime on a big-screen TV or tiny iPod: piracy

---

BOX 14-5

Focus on Second-Tier Revenue

BOOSTING THE GRINCH

A year after the film *The Grinch Who Stole Christmas* hit theaters, Universal Studios Home Video had to recreate excitement about the film when it was released on DVD. By tapping into MSN's reach to help turn the movie into a must-own DVD or videotape, marketers developed an integrated online campaign that helped the film become one of the top-selling DVDs.

Brand goals:

- Regenerate awareness of *Grinch* months after theatrical release
- Create a dominating presence to rise above other home videos and DVDs released around the same time
- Turn the reenergized *Grinch* brand awareness into sales of home video and DVD

Campaign elements:

- Exclusive home page presence the day of the film's home release with an image of the *Grinch* built into the background and pointing to a special co-branded site
- MSN features included "blooper" content taken from the DVD and an interactive trivia game
- Movie image featured as the Blender puzzle game on MSN Games channel
- Co-branded site with access to all *Grinch* content
- Sweepstakes with prizes, including a theme-park vacation
- Downloadable *Grinch* wallpaper for Windows Media Player

Results:

- MSN drove more than 23,000 potential buyers to Amazon.com the first day of the DVD's release.
- The *Grinch* became the best-selling holiday movie to date in 2002 and the top video revenue generator of 2001, pulling in more than $330 million.

SOURCE: Microsoft Corporation MSN-05022.

---

and pricing. According to the U.S. movie industry's trade body (the Motion Picture Association of America), one in four people on the Internet have illegally downloaded a film and the problem is set to get worse.

Major film studio representatives say piracy on the Net has cost them billions of dollars, even though box office takings rose by 5 percent last year. The MPAA has put the increase down to rising ticket prices, while the number of total tickets sold dropped by 5 percent internationally and by 12 percent in Europe.

A study conducted by the MPAA questioned 3,600 Internet users around the world who regularly went to the cinema. The study found that a quarter of the participants admitted to having downloaded a film from the Internet. In Korea, six out of ten Internet users download movies.

Motion picture piracy in China costs U.S. studios nearly $300 million a year, according to industry estimates. Though the Chinese may allow as many as 20 U.S. theatrical releases into the country each year, the average number of U.S. films admitted is 14.[19]

More worrying for the film industry, many downloaders said they had cut back on trips to the cinema and were buying fewer DVDs. Thus, is seems that the extent of film piracy online will only increase as more and more people switch to broadband Internet access. In a bid to combat piracy, the MPAA has launched a global campaign to hammer home the message that piracy is a crime. But its attempt to change attitudes may be an uphill battle. The MPAA survey also found that 20 percent of downloaders had no qualms about getting a movie before it was released in the cinema. And, a majority said it was O.K. to download a film once it was available on DVD or video.

▪▪▪ Marketing Television Programs

Unlike movie marketing, promoting television is much more focused on specific audiences and time slots: It is all about the ratings game—getting a big share of the viewing audience. Rather than being controlled by studios, television production occurs through networks and cable stations (although network and cable station ownership often is held by a major motion picture studio). This section presents an overview of television promotion, including who watches, what they watch, which promotion strategies work, and discussion of continuing threats to the industry.

Who Watches TV?

The easy answer to the question "Who watches TV?" is, of course, "everyone." But audiences must be understood in terms of specific segments and viewing preferences. Ethnic groups and age or lifestyle segments make a difference in marketing television properties.

Ethnic Groups

Television advertisers are recognizing the power of ethnic audiences by adding programming and integrating ethnic actors into popular dramas and situation comedies. African Americans view more than 76 hours of television each week, as compared to the 53 hours averaged by the rest of the viewing public.[20]

Adding themed programming to their lineups, ABC presented *My Wife and Kids* and Fox brought out *The Bernie Mac Show*. A recent study, however, showed that themed shows are not fulfilling the needs of their audience.[21] Recent numbers showed that African Americans' viewing choices have become more like those of white viewers.[22] So, producers responded by adding African American characters and co-stars to hits such as *Law and Order, CSI,* and *Without a Trace.* In 2006, for instance, 67 series had multi-ethnic casts on the networks.

Another growing segment of viewers is the Latino audience, the largest minority group in the U.S. Hispanics retain a strong sense of ethnic identity and use media to help with the process of assimilation and for cultural maintenance. Consistent with past research, a 2005 study reported that Latinos don't see themselves as one homogenous group, and often travel between two cultures.[23] As with African American viewers, Latino audiences agree that media programming and formats are not meeting their needs, although they are encouraged by the inclusion of Hispanics into network television programs.

Age and Lifestyle Cohorts

Kid, teen, gay, and baby boomer shows continue to attract viewers and advertisers; this programming is profiled here.

SpongeBob SquarePants at a toy fair in London.

A booming market, *tot's* TV shows are being produced for the youngest viewers and the smallest eyeballs. Some of the most popular preschool shows in the U.S. are British, including *Bob the Builder* and *Thomas and Friends*. TV networks are chasing youngsters because unlike their older siblings, they have not abandoned TV for the Internet or video games, and they are home a lot. Preschoolers have their own channels, including Viacom's Noggin and PBS's Kids Sprout, launched jointly in 2005 by Comcast, Sesame Workshop, and PBS. Profits are driven by merchandising, so the commercial and creative sides of children's television are fusing to the extent that they are becoming indistinguishable from one another. Kids shows cannot rely on advertising revenue because commercials aimed at the very young seldom work. So, networks pay low fees to studios and turn to sales of toys and DVDs to make up the difference. Resembling a giant toy ad, Nickelodeon's *Dora the Explorer* generated about $1.4 billion in sales of toys, backpacks, clothing, and other products in 2005.

When Nickelodeon's popular *Kids' Choice Awards* program went to China in 2005, the producers were forced to make some serious modifications: There would be no voting on a favorite burp. Nor would children judge which movie character was the best at breaking wind. Viacom, which dominates youth-oriented programming in the United States and other parts of the world with its MTV and Nickelodeon networks, is aggressively courting Chinese youngsters, hoping to introduce them to its brand of playfully antiauthoritarian programming. After all, China has roughly 300 million people younger than 14, and Viacom executives warm to the idea of capturing even a sliver of a demographic that now exceeds the population of the entire United States. According to MTV, there is no such thing as a global strategy without China. Viacom already has a 24-hour MTV channel in southern Guangdong province. China

Central Television and the Shanghai Media Group broadcast Nickelodeon's *Wild Thornberries, CatDog* cartoon, and *SpongeBob SquarePants.*

Back in the U.S., shows for older kids also are booming. Teens are not only watching television, they are using all media simultaneously. With more media experience than any generation in history, these media-savvy adolescents watch less TV than any other age demographic. Yet, teens interact with program text in a variety of ways after the television is turned off. For example, after watching an episode of *Dawson's Creek,* teenagers are able to visit the show's Web site and read letters written by the characters. Teens buy the soundtracks to their favorite shows and read about their favorite television actors in magazines. But they don't watch network TV, preferring instead CW, MTV's *Laguna Beach,* the Disney Channel, and Nickelodeon.[24]

Other audience segments are going through a feature metamorphosis. Shows starring gay males and females, pioneered by *Soap, Ellen, Queer Eye for the Straight Guy,* and *The L Word,* have been phased out in favor of integrating gay characters into mainstream network and cable programming. Similar to what has occurred with ethnic groups (African Americans and Latinos), gay character prominence in major shows has quelled the necessity to produce gay-specific programming in favor of character integration into regular programming.

The most desirable segment for advertisers, baby boomer viewers tune into network shows that deliver news or reflect their values. Network shows that are hits with this large audience are:

- *60 Minutes* (CBS)
- *Mad Money* (CNN)
- *Wall Street Week* (PBS)
- *Law and Order* (NBC)
- *House* (Fox)
- *Weeds* (Showtime)
- *Sopranos* (HBO)

Advertisers love boomers because of their buying power, so they cultivate relationships with producers who determine brand placements, commercial buys, and sponsorships for the boomer audience.

What Do Audiences Watch?

Television programming has evolved or morphed into a plethora of reality shows and sitcoms of all forms. Because of their popularity with global audiences, we profile both formats. Then, we look at what is brand new in formatting.

Reality TV Shows

Why are there so many reality shows on television? Because they are economical, often interactive, and create an avenues to fame for viewers who audition. By keeping production costs low, using non-celebrities, and tying in with advertisers, reality television producers have less to lose and more to gain than producers of sitcoms or dramas that rely on established star-power and top-notch writers.

Accounting for 69 percent of television shows worldwide, television audiences are exposed to a plethora of characters, plots, and topics. Subcategories include:

- docu-soaps (*Real World, Big Brother*)
- celeb-reality (*Osborne's, Newlyweds, Simple Life*)

- game shows (*American Idol, Who Wants to Be a Millionaire?*)
- sports shows (*Contender, Ultimate Fighter*)
- multiple combinations of the subcategories (*Apprentice, Survivor, The Mole*)

Reality programs have invaded all aspects of television; lifestyle programs (*Wife Swap*) and dating shows (*The Bachelor*) are the most popular.

The genre has interchanged the role of audience member and audience subject by looking into the daily lives of ordinary people. According to a recent study, many reality viewers watch because of a personal desire for prestige and status.[25] Others are fascinated with status and prestige gained from auditioning or participating as contestants, which fulfills their need for 15 seconds of fame. Voyeuristic programs allow participants to gain a type of celebrity status.

Reality shows are economical and travel well across national boundaries because language is not as important as the action. One drawback to them, however, is that episodes cannot be rerun—doing so would defeat the notion of "real-time" action for viewers—so the networks that produce reality programming lose that potential revenue. But, because audience members are able to influence and determine program content, new episodes and programs are destined to be crowd pleasers.

Success for the reality show *Survivor* was the result of a variety of factors, but the most important include:

- co-branding with exotic travel destinations.
- creating excitement and hype through the contestant auditioning process.
- maintaining secrecy about coming seasons.
- promoting removed participants as celebrities to hype new episodes.
- using spot commercials to preview series events.
- maintaining an active Web presence.
- survivor finales and reunions at seasons' end.

Capitalizing on the genre's popularity, Fox broadcasts past shows 24 hours a day on its Reality Channel.

Going for innovation, China Central Television is launching a new kind of reality show that aims to pluck someone from the nation's 1.3 billion-strong population to become an Olympic athlete. China's Olympics rowing team is searching for coxswains: two diminutive people with big voices to steer the men's and women's teams of eight rowers in the 2008 Beijing Olympics. Drawing from parts of *Survivor, The Apprentice,* and *American Idol,* the network seeks to makes stars of China's rowers, whose sport does not have much of a following in that country. Sparked by the success of *Super Female Voice,* a singing contest that drew 400 million viewers to its 2005 finale (*American Idol* drew 36 million), China Central Television hopes that the show will draw millions of dollars in ad sponsorship for Olympic broadcasters.[26]

Sitcoms

A favorite genre since the onset of television in the 1950s, the sitcom, or situation comedy, has generated more fans over the years than any other type of programming. Loyal fans track sitcom characters and action over the decades, often viewing reruns of old episodes with several generations of their families. Para-social relationships—fans bonding with stars and treating them as real friends—are consistently formed between sitcom viewers and actors.

Taking fan loyalty to its logical heights, Fox asked fans of its beloved sitcom *Arrested Development* to make a formal declaration of their devotion. The loyalty oath was the brainchild of Fox executives who were increasingly leery about the show's future—*Development*'s ratings were sinking—and it offered fans an opportunity to speak out and take action against the show's potential hiatus. Viewers pledged never-ending loyalty and allegiance to the show and promised to tune in for every episode in the third season. Fox claimed to have 100,000 signatures on the oath, but the network may have used the tactic not as evidence that it should keep the show in production, but as a rationale for its impending demise because of fan disloyalty as evidenced by dwindling ratings.[27]

Marketers use gaming experiences to promote and retain sitcom audiences. Games often mimic sensibilities of the show that inspired them; *The OC* entwined players in an intricate social scene from the program. The experiences allow players to move freely through a simulated *OC* environment, said a Gameloft designer who developed the game. Producers like game promotion because it involves people with the show even when they are not watching it.[28]

GoTV enabled viewers use their video-capable cell phones to catch up on the complex plotlines of ABC's *Desperate Housewives* and *Lost* by providing short recap video clips. Major wireless carriers feature content inspired by many of the season's biggest shows, providing another promotional tactic for entertainment marketers.

Miniseries

Viewing among adults ages 18–49, the group that advertisers pay a premium to reach, was up 12 percent after the first season of the Sci Fi Channel's new group of miniseries. To promote the *Bermuda Triangle* miniseries, marketers dropped errant black socks into lockers and laundry baskets at gyms and Laundromats that contained a message reading "nothing stays lost forever" and the address for the show's Web site. On a bet that the mystery would appeal to a wide audience, the channel gave *Triangle* an advertising blitz to keep viewers tuned in: In one of the biggest promotional splashes ever undertaken by the channel, Sci Fi also lavished outdoor, print, radio ads on a campaign that featured a fake mayday distress call.

TV Audiences as Fans

Before the Internet, fans dedicated to television shows and characters were limited to conventions for connecting with other fans. Today, hundreds of sites and blogs bring fans together electronically. Fans are especially important to marketers for their purchasing power of licensed goods and for viewing, which, in turn, translates into audience ratings that dictate advertising rates and revenues.

Reality show fans anticipate season finales and log on to sites such as fansofrealitytv. com, which has 34,000 members, to follow show stars and plots. Created in 2003, nolookingback.org considered itself to be the official fan listing for *Newlyweds: Nick and Jessica,* with 3,000 fans in 71 countries. Among the many sites dedicated to sitcom fans, sitcomsonline.com provides fans of Fox's *Arrested Development* with news, message boards, photos, site links, reviews, theme songs, and games.

How Are TV Shows Placed and Promoted?

Placement is concerned with where and when and how a firm chooses to compete in the national television marketplace. Three positioning strategies predominate: stable, complementary, and competitive. *Stable* strategy places a show by time slot and length of time on the air; *complementary* strategy places the show immediately following a show of same type; *competitive* strategy is selected when there are few attractions or competing shows. Networks determine positions to retain audiences and to take audiences from other networks or cable stations by packaging their most popular series together.

Most television series are promoted using traditional methods: TV, print, radio, outdoor, Internet, and publicity. Commercials feature characters from the sitcom or weekly drama with laugh or music tracks that are familiar to the viewing audience. But what about the viewers who don't watch specific shows? If they have never seen the show, what is the incentive to begin watching it?

One solution is promotions that connect non-viewers to a show and get them to sample it. The plan is not to describe the show, but rather to draw viewers in on an emotional level. By building advertising platforms into the show itself, networks can multiply the pool of potential viewers. Internal promotion may connect a show with an enormous number of people who have not seen it so viewers are motivated to sample, and existing viewers are reminded to tune in again.[29] Strategies can promote the show and advertise the sponsoring product simultaneously. ABC's *Extreme Makeover: Home Edition,* for example, uses all Sears' Craftsman power tools, and host Ty Pennington frequently mentions that connection. The convergence of advertiser with program content is slowly invading network and cable programming. Is this the wave of the future? Our educated guess is, yes.

To generate buzz for 2005's fall season, networks went all out.[30] For the medical sitcom *Out of Practice,* CBS plastered ads on drugstore prescription bags and water coolers. NBC pushed reality series *Three Wishes* by slapping yellow stickers 100,000 real dollar bills. Head-shaving parties were part of Fox's marketing blitz for *Prison Break* dramatic series. Why such outrageous marketing? The growth of cable channels has eroded network share to less than 50 percent, down from 90 percent. On-demand cable, videogames, and the Internet also vie for viewers' leisure time. As a result, shows need a wider array of marketing ploys.

In 2005, UPN (now merged with WB to become a "new" network, the CW) ran promos on 1,500 movie screens, hired helicopters to pull aerial banners, distributed 1 million bumper stickers, and screened the first episode of *Everybody Hates Chris* on American Airlines flights for a month. In a stunt for Disney's *Lost,* ABC scattered 10,000 plastic bottles on beaches with a flier inside reading, "I'm Lost. Find me on ABC." By spending 80 percent of the fall marketing budget on *Lost* and *Desperate Housewives,* the network drew 20 million and 30 million viewers to those shows, respectively. For the shows' re-launches the following season, ABC partnered with *TV Guide* to attach a preview DVD of *Lost* to the magazine's front cover, and the network slapped stickers of the *Desperate Housewives* logo, bearing the tagline "New dirty laundry," on dry cleaner bags.

In 2006, new technology enabled more sophisticated promotional opportunities. Although marketing campaigns linking outdoor advertising with Bluetooth technology (point-to-point wireless connection that allows text, sound, pictures, and video to be sent to mobile devices) prevail in Europe, CBS was the first U.S. network to promote its new 2006 fall season with Bluetooth.[31] In a New York City promotion, the network brought to life five of Grand Central station's static billboards, which allowed

A large promotion budget for the TV show *Desperate Housewives* resulted in millions of additional viewers for the show.

people standing within 36 feet of the board to activate Bluetooth-enabled cell phones and download a 30-second clip. Clips of new prime-time programs and past hit shows, such as *CSI,* could be watched, saved, or passed along to friends. Bluetooth technology provides advertisers with a way to provide video clips directly to consumers, by bypassing the Internet and downloading content directly from appropriately wired subway stations, shopping malls, and athletic arenas.

Threats to the Television Industry

Technology is continually changing, so every industry that relies on technology also must continually change. And, with change comes a period of readjustment. Podcasting and Internet television are changing the way money is made in media.

Podcasting

After Steve Jobs announced Apple's release of the video iPod in 2005, podcasting became an Internet alternative to broadcasting through subscription Web sites that post audio and video programs. Video podcasts—made and published on the Web by both producers with large budgets and those with no budgets—enabled homegrown media makers to distribute their programming directly to global audiences. Given the thousands of blogs that now provide online news audiences with content, broadcasters worry that podcasting might eventually replace television broadcasts.[32]

One iPod user anchors a daily three-minute mock TV news report she shot with a camcorder. Edited on a laptop and posted on a blog called Rocketboom, the show reaches more than 100,000 fans a day. Providing consistently entertaining daily

Focus on Television

SELLING AN IDEA TO THE NETWORKS

Simon Cowell's *American Idol,* created for the benefit of his record label (BMG-UK), became an international hit—but only after being rejected by every American television network.

Entering the U.S. music reality show realm, *American Idol* followed Britain's *Pop Stars* and *Fame Academy.* After shooting *Pop Idol* in England with four judges, Cowell believed he could combine fun with candid criticism and fan voting to choose a winner in what would be almost a soap opera format. When Cowell tried to market the show in the U.S., however, ABC had already experienced a failed music show, *Making the Band,* and declined Cowell's offer. Then-WB network tried a similar format with a show called *Pop Stars* that found only a niche audience. Not surprisingly, WB said "no" to *Idol.* NBC's reality executives also passed, and CBS's reality division rejected the idea during an initial phone call.

That left Fox. Cowell's colleague fervently pitched the idea to the network, explaining that the format would be, essentially, all audition, complete with woeful early performances. In this show, the audience would rule. Needing fresh summer programming, Fox accepted the pitch. The network, however, agreed to air the program only if it could be a fully sponsored broadcast.

As talks with Fox dragged on, execs at News Corporation (Fox's owner) were witnessing the success of England's *Pop Idol*—and, crucially, the daughter of News Corp's founder, Rupert Murdoch, loved the show. With a call to the top decision-maker at the Fox network, Murdoch ordered a buy. In spite of faltering advertising sponsorship, Fox closed the deal by contracting a 15-episode series, like the British version. As part of the deal, Fox wanted Cowell's charismatic figure on the judging panel.

Cowell worried both about his lack of knowledge about American music and whether American television would insist that he water down his critiques of the contestants. Although the name was changed to *American Idol,* the British format was retained to the letter. Fox believed that American audiences were ready to rebel against what Cowell called "the terrible political correctness that invaded America and England."

The other judges were quickly selected. Randy Jackson, a former Journey band member, and Paula Abdul, who had her own solid musical and dance career, came on board. The judges were limited to three to avoid ties.

As the show progressed, Cowell unleashed his lash on every offending wannabe. He told one young woman to get a lawyer and sue her vocal coach. Others he labeled with terms such as *wretched, horrid,* and *pathetic.* As it turned out, *Idol* was an instant hit, with opening ratings of 10 million viewers, the most-watched show on American television on its first night. The second night it added a million viewers. Among coveted audience members in the 18–35 group, *Idol* finished first and second for the week.

Cowell embarked on a round of publicity, doing 50 interviews with American radio stations in one day alone. Within a matter of weeks, Fox was making arrangements to bring *Idol* back in the regular season. The show became more than fresh programming, it became a business-changer for all of network television.

SOURCE: Bill Carter for the *New York Times,* Sunday Business Section, April 30, 2006.

▪▪▪▪▪▪▪▪▪▪▪ BOX 14-7 ▪▪▪▪▪▪▪▪▪▪▪

Focus on Listening

RIP: IS RADIO DEAD?

Americans are no longer listening to radio as they had in the past. Between spring 1999 and spring 2006, the biggest losses were 12–34 year olds who tuned in three hours less (14 percent) over the last decade according to Arbitron ratings. Streaming audio, podcasting, iPods, and satellite radio have caused radio company stocks to fall between 30 and 60 percent, as investors wonder when the industry will bottom out. Clear Channel Communications, the nations largest radio operator; CBS; and Walt Disney are all trying to get out of the radio business by selling stations. Radio advertising is second only to newspapers in slow top-line growth. As XM and Sirius satellite companies amass more than 11 million subscribers in 2006, radio may be a loser in the battle to be "hip."

Change in Popularity of Top Radio Formats among Listeners, Fall 1998 to Spring 2006

Spanish +4.4	Country 0.0
Urban +1.9	Oldies −1.4
News/talk +0.9	Alternative −1.5
Religious +0.8	Rock −1.9
Contemporary hits +0.6	Adult contemporary −2.8

What to do? Radio companies are developing new formats, planning digital initiatives (HD radio), and moving into the Web businesses that incorporate video and other features to slow its fall from grace on Wall Street. Fighting back, Clear Channel signed a deal with BMW to provide real-time free traffic updates to navigation systems, and set another deal to beam radio signals to Cingular wireless phone users for on-demand content. Other remedies to keep radio listeners include reducing on-air clutter (advertising) by running shorter spots and aggressively moving online. Clear Channel has one of the most visited music sites on the Web, and CBS also has stepped up its Internet presence, streaming more than 70 stations live and starting KYOURadio.com, a YouTube for listener podcasts.

By pursuing Spanish language radio and flipping station formats, radio companies plan on generating cash for relatively little capital investment. But a more telling sign of the times is Google's sponsorship of the 2006 National Association of Broadcasters radio convention in Dallas in 2006.

SOURCE: Richard Siklos for the *New York Times,* Sept. 15, 2006, C1.

▪▪▪▪▪▪▪▪▪

episodes, the 14-month-old **vlog** (video log) type of podcast costs about $20 a day to produce. The rapid expansion in the number of vlogs offering podcasts strongly suggests how bored viewers are getting with standard commercial TV: out with networks, in with podcasts. Two of the best vlogs, Scratch Video and Minnesota Stories, can turn personal narrative about the tedious or mundane into micro-documentaries of wit, beauty, or intelligence. After signing a deal with TiVo, Rocketboom provides podcasters with all types of shows sent directly to computer, portable players, or the TiVo box for viewing at your leisure.[33]

Content

Virtually limitless content could revolutionize television viewing and cut cable companies completely out of the picture. Internet access to television means instant access to hard-to-find content and on-demand episodes of prime-time fare. Electronics hardware that brings Internet video to television screens includes Intel's Vivi, which facilitates hooking computers into TVs; Cisco's DP600 DVD player, which has a broadband connection for pulling content off the Web; Microsoft's X-Box 360, which routes video and other content from media center computers to TVs; AT&T/EchoStar's Homezone satellite TV service, which provides video on demand via the Internet; and Panasonic's PX500 line of TVs, which have computer inputs that can display any content off the Internet or a computer.

▪▪▪ Product Placement: On-Screen and In-Program Advertising

Branded entertainment, which embeds brands and products in the content of movies, TV shows, and Web programming, as well as on cell phones and in video games, has become increasingly important to marketers as they seek alternatives to commercials and other traditional forms of advertising.

Both film and television productions rely heavily on revenues from products placed in film and on TV. The practice has become so widespread that it has fostered an industry and trade association of its own. The Entertainment Marketing Association is made up of three constituent groups, each with a vested interest in the practice: corporations and manufacturers, that are looking to place their brands; studios and production companies that are seeking to defray costs with brand placements; and placement agencies. The impact and value of product placement is evident from quantifiable research data.

What has been euphemistically called "brand integration" by network television and Madison Avenue may be better characterized as steroid-enhanced product placement deals. Advertising companies—from Omnicom to MediaVest to Carat Americas—have started their own branded entertainment divisions to solidify their relationships with their corporate clients and the cash that comes with them.[34] This section shows how branded products are integrated into film and television.

Placing Products in Films

Product placement is now big business. Film studios have departments dedicated to sending out bids for products and negotiating contracts with corporations interested in placement opportunities. Likewise, brand managers assign the placement function to a negotiator. Media buyers allocate budgets for placement, and research companies monitor the brand awareness generated by film placements.

For films that are not tent-pole blockbusters, product placements serve to provide revenue for movie studios. Below are examples of brandchannel.com's third annual awards for Product Placement. Throughout 2006, Brandchannel tracked product and brand appearances in films, which are highlighted here.

▪▪▪ Brandchannel's 2006 Product Placement Awards

- Ford, which finished first with 41 appearances in 17 number one films, received the site's Brandcameo Award for Overall Product Placement.
- Everlast's product placement in the reality TV show *The Contender* and the films *Requiem for a Heavyweight, Raging Bull, Cinderella Man, The Hurricane,* and *Million Dollar Baby,* yielded it the Lifetime Achievement Award for most placements since 2001 when the awarding program began.
- Prada received the Coca-Cola Kid Award for Achievement in a Title: *The Devil Wears Prada,* which was not only a branded film title, but also a fully incorporated brand product in the plot.
- ET/Reese's Award for Achievement in Press Coverage went to *Casino Royal* for receiving most overall attention in the media (586,000 Google results to January 31, 2006), including a *New Yorker Magazine* mention. The film included 25 brand placements as well.
- An award for Brand Impact went to *Night at the Museum* for its immediate measurable impact. In the first ten days after its release, attendance at the American Museum of Natural History (the film's setting) increased by 20 percent.[35]

Placing Products on Television

During the 2004–2005 television season, more than 100,000 product placements appeared on the six broadcast networks. This was an increase of nearly 28 percent from the previous season, according to Nielsen Media Research. For television producers, these sophisticated plugs are a way to offset rising production costs. Advertisers end up buying more ordinary 30-second ads and paying a separate integration fee to the network, which splits the money with the studio. Or, instead of an integration fee, advertisers may include the show in their marketing efforts, such as mall promotions, magazine ads, and newspaper stuffers.

Some genres work better for placement than others. Reality shows, for instance, lend themselves to brand integration—thirsty, starving islanders gobble Doritos and guzzle Mountain Dew after vanquishing their opponents in a *Survivor* episode, and viewers usually accept the products' presence. But product placements in scripted shows are trickier some feel like commercials and offend audiences. Successful placements grow out of characterizations, such as a Campbell's Soup tie-in with NBC's *American Dreams* instituted to portray a character's wholesomeness. After a junior high student bribed schoolmates to send entries to an annual Campbell's Soup essay-writing contest, three times the number of entries were received from viewers of *American Dreams* than had been previously received from a typical show response.

During the same season, reality shows filled seven of the top 10 spots for product placements, according to Nielsen. Of those, a reality boxing show called *The Contender* carried the highest number. In just 16 telecasts, viewers saw products 7,477 times and

Seinfeld was one of the first television shows to use product placements in volume.

listened to 99 product mentions, Nielsen said. That was nearly double CBS's *King of Queens,* which took the top spot the year before with 3,691 total placements.[36]

Media giant Gannett sells product placement on local talk shows for about $2,500 a pop. The midmorning shows, which replace local news, talk programs, or syndicated fare, are a way for stations to underwrite local programming while milking a little more money from their daytime schedule. According to one station executive, these shows could increase the time period's revenue take between 50 and 100 percent. These broadcast *slotting fees* are the on-air equivalents of the slotting allowances that package goods pay retailers to get shelf space. Each station makes its own decision whether to launch the shows, but the introduction of the pay-to-appear shows is often corporate driven.

Local advertisers using placements have included cosmetic dentists, home builders, and auto dealer groups. More regional and national advertisers are beginning to take advantage of the shows through local *unwired buys*—buys made at the corporate ownership level. In an unwired buy with Gannett, the Richard Group, of Dallas, coordinated holiday appearances on two shows, *Colorado & Co.* and *Atlanta & Co.,* for its client Honey Baked Ham. This format helps advertisers integrate products into more of an editorial-style environment on a local level. The shows are the property of the sales and marketing department rather than the newsroom and, at the end of each segment and again at the end of the show, a host mentions that the segment was paid for by the advertiser. Denver's KUSA, the first Gannett-owned station to introduce the current format, has been moderately successful with slightly increased ratings.[37]

Some products help develop show set. Assuming an "also starring" role in NBC's *The Apprentice* was Poggenpohl, a German kitchen cabinet maker. The company sent out news releases to alert media that viewers could learn all about its pricey cabinets by visiting the TV show's Web site. Makers of furniture and appliances are getting in on the placement act—brands from Bosch appliances to Big John Toilet Seat—by wooing set designers and cozying up to TV and movie stars. Popular tool company Barbara K. Enterprises works with a product placement company to gets its female-friendly kits in movie and television scenes. Appeals to set designers and production companies landed the firm a bit part alongside Brad Pitt and Angelina Jolie in the 2005 film *Mr. & Mrs. Smith*. After placing pieces of furniture on *The Real World,* Blue Dot Design's sales of featured chairs and shelving units rose along with brand awareness.[38]

Plot Placement

Integrating a brand or product into a significant and engaging role in a storyline is *plot placement*. This technique is most prevalent in television programming. According to media buyers, becoming a central plot element is worth ten times the cost of running a commercial in the same television program for product brands. Plot placements in television and film include Revlon's corporate espionage plot line on soap opera *All My Children,* and Mini Cooper's central role in a heist featured in the movie *The Italian Job*.

Using Products to Promote Television

Guinness Draught teamed with ESPN for a holiday promo designed to drive consumers online to rank the dynasties of ESPN's new sports show *Pardon the Interruption*. In December 2005, national ads on ESPN, ESPN2, ESPN News, and ESPN Classic sent consumers to stores to purchase promotional packs of Guinness Draught. Consumers were directed to ESPN.com to rank sports dynasties. Those fans who ranked the dynasties in the same order as *Pardon the Interruption's* experts were automatically entered to win one of four weekly grand-prize trips to Washington, D.C., to meet the show's cast, have dinner at ESPN Zone restaurant, and have their photos displayed on the *Pardon the Interruption* set. On- and off-premise materials supported the effort.[39]

Placement Evaluation Methods and the Q-Ratio

Measuring a product placement's effectiveness is the domain of companies iTVX and IAG Research, among others. It is still an inexact science. But some results cannot be ignored, such as pre-selling 1,000 Pontiac Solstice cars in the 41 minutes following an episode of *The Apprentice* in which the car was plugged. Most networks believe that the benefits of branded integration outweigh any hypothetical downsides. After all, television is self-selecting; if audiences don't like product placements, they turn off the show.

In 2005, the industry examined the complexities of branded entertainment, deciphering who, what, why, and how much branding was involved. One source of examining branded entertainment's effectiveness is *ratings,* which don't take into consideration the quality of the placement. A second, stand-alone *quality component,* in addition to the ratings, helps measure the value of product integration.

iTVX developed a Q-Ratio™ that measures the quality of the product placement. The ratio represents a relative value, which is either expressed as a fraction of a 30-second commercial, or as the number of commercials it is equivalent to. For example, a placement with a .756 Q-Ratio signifies that the quality of that particular placement is valued at approximately 75 percent of a 30-second commercial.

▪▪▪▪▪▪▪▪▪▪ BOX 14-8 ▪▪▪▪▪▪▪▪▪▪

Focus on Ethics

REALITY TV LETS MARKETERS WRITE THE SCRIPTS

According to critics, the advertising industry is fighting back against TiVo and other ad-skip technology by altering preexisting content in ways that could threaten the visual and editorial integrity of television programming.[40] They claim that brand integration is largely responsible for the reality TV genre as we know it and not vice versa.

The trend was pioneered with *Survivor,* which CBS greenlighted only after its executive producer explained that instead of the network paying actors, advertisers would pay the network for a starring role. Envisioned as a commercial vehicle as much as a TV drama, *Survivor* is a pretext for contestants to interact with brands. According to *Advertising Age,* CBS thought it was one of the best bargains in TV history. Behind the program's long-term impact was the relentless promotion of the series by CBS's parent company, Viacom. To generate buzz, more than 100 affiliate radio stations ran segments, including dozens of drive-time interviews with Burnett, while 16 of CBS's TV stations and Viacom's MTV and VH1 covered *Survivor* as if its now-in and now-out contestants were news.

Other series, such as NBC's *The Restaurant* and ABC's *Who Wants to be a Millionaire?,* were produced by Magna Global Entertainment Company, a branded entertainment development wing of media giant Interpublic that is "dedicated to the creation of original television programming that is funded by and serves the needs of Interpublic's clients."[41]

By the time *American Idol* appeared, placing branded products gave way to placing branded wannabe pop stars themselves. Fox has reaped millions by making *Idol* contestants literally do back flips over corporate logos in mini-commercials disguised as music videos. The contestants who succeed are as much commodities as the product they hawk.

The argument against advertising-integrated program content is that the stronger the foothold, whether through ad buys or product placement, the more power advertisers have to define our collective values. Mike Darnell, Fox's reality guru, told *Entertainment Weekly* magazine that his dream project would be a beauty pageant featuring female prisoners: "You give them a chance to get a make-over and it's a 40-share special." So will Miss San Quentin sashay her way into prime time? Only viewers have the power to say.

What do you think?

1. Is the reality-show platform a natural context for branded products, or are corporations designing reality content around their brands?

2. Who should ultimately determine the amount and type of product placement appropriate for television audiences?

▪▪▪▪▪▪▪▪

The importance of having such a valuation is exemplified by the fact that the Q-Ratio does not change with the commercial cost. The Q-Ratio measures more than 50 variable factors pertaining to the quality of the product placement. Once tabulated, the Q-Ratio remains constant, allowing the marketer to multiply costs per 30 seconds by the Q-Ratio to get an estimated valuation of that integration. According to the company that provides this service, the methodology creates a logical standard of accountability.[42]

Evaluating the Effects of Using Branded Content

Raising the branded content bar, new methods to evaluate TV offerings are in place to determine how effective branded TV content offerings are at meeting advertisers' ROI goals. Ground rules, consisting of questions posed by advertisers to suppliers, may help evaluate whether or not to invest in a scripted series. Let's look at five criteria advertisers use for evaluating television placements.

1. *How will the show generate and maintain high ratings?* If the goal is to increase ROI, the sitcom or drama must generate high levels of sampling and maintain viewer loyalty so the brand will connect with a maximum number of people in a target audience.

2. *How likely is the show to be purchased by another network?* Once the season is over, cable channels may bid for the rights to broadcast. The better received the original series, the more likely it will be an attractive purchase for other distribution outlets.

3. *How will the show increase sales?* Placements that offer two-second product shots, banners, and name mentions only increase name recall. For a placement to be worth the money, the brand's benefits must be organically integrated into the show for sales to increase.

4. *How will the integration be a natural and logical element of each episode?* The brand must grow out of the story line so it is not an obvious commercial that suppresses results.

5. *How will the network's marketing extensions increase brand sales and show ratings?* Expect more than increased name awareness from promotional programs and Web sites.

Product Films

As commercials become TiVo-ed out, companies are looking to digital and other types of entertainment media to promote their brands more effectively than can now be accomplished with a 30-second spot. So, instead of placing their brands into other people's films, some companies are financing or producing their own branded movies.

The first brand to finance a film was a sneaker company who wanted to showcase its brand. A documentary about skateboarding, released in 2002, won several prestigious awards at major independent film festivals such as Sundance. Growing from a three-city release into a major phenomenon, *Dogtown and the Z-Boys* received extraordinary coverage from mainstream press, MTV, and National Public Radio. What makes this film unique is its financing—Vans sneaker company gave the director $65,000 to keep its shoes on the feet of everyone onscreen. By connecting teen fascination with skateboarding events with their movie-going habits, Vans' investment yielded revenues of $1.4 million before overseas distribution, DVD sales, and television licensing. And the company raised its profits 66 percent from increased U.S. sales.[43]

Automobile companies BMW, Ford, and Cadillac produced their own films for the Internet starring their products and brands that were hits among brand fans. Even magazines are getting into the film production business. *Glamour* magazine's Reel

Moments, a series of short films based on stories submitted by the monthly's readers, were featured on Glamour.com to extend *Glamour*'s brand to a new platform and also provide a dynamic environment for advertisers—both old and new—to reach young women. They get tremendous buzz around the brand by speaking to women through a different medium. *Glamour* culled movie ideas from a reader essay contest and adapted the winning submissions with help from Moxie Pictures and other Hollywood advisors.[44]

It's the Engagement, Stupid!

Inserting itself between traditional marketing activities and an increasing demand for ROI assessments, the metric of consumer engagement will soon become the Holy Grail for marketers and advertisers alike. *Engagement* can be defined as the outcome of advertising and marketing activities that substantively increases a brand's strength in the eyes of the consumers (and actually predicts sales and profitability). Engagement is being used more and more to allocate marketing budgets.[45]

Engagement comes in many forms. On-demand video content, for instance, is available for singles who are bored with the bar scene. Comcast, the country's largest cable provider, offers "Dating on Demand," which enables singles to use their remotes to view hundreds of potential dates' video profiles. Viewers contact their choices through online dating sites that work with Comcast, primarily the hurrydate.com site. On-demand technology stores video content on servers in central offices that can be accessed over cable lines anytime. Previously used to order movies, this on-demand service allows viewers to make their own mini-casts at home and upload them to the cable company over the Internet.[46]

Experiential marketing is another avenue to generate engagement. Research suggests that audiences believe that participating in experiential marketing increases their purchase consideration.[47] Marketers are responding to this notion by shifting experiential marketing into the heart of the marketing mix. PR and advertising campaigns have become extensions of brand experiences—not the other way around. For instance, the Pontiac Solstice was launched with a live concert by Jet in New York's Times Square, an event that was rebroadcast on the *Jimmy Kimmel Show*. Street teams went out in full force the following morning to keep the buzz alive and facilitate live national and local news spots featuring VH1 VJ Rachel Perry. Programs like these root their creative efforts in the live experience and its aftermath, recognizing its power to galvanize PR and inspire viral word-of-mouth advocacy. A trade group, the Live Brand Experience Association (LBEA), was created to help marketers understand and embrace experiential marketing's potential.

Coming next? Experiential movie trailers may be the next thing. Borrowing techniques from playgrounds, game play, and theme-park design, a new innovation in developing trailers drives emotional branding in entertainment marketing via Web streaming. Using a mixed-reality technique, boundaries between real and virtual content merge into a full spectrum of simulation in trailer development and presentation. The technique is currently in testing at the University of Central Florida's Media Convergence Laboratory with support from the Naval Research Laboratory and the Army Research Institute.[48]

Immersive Advertising

An evolutionary step forward in the traditional marketing practice of product placement, Neopets virtual animal kingdom has become a placement paradisc.[49] Neopia's Web site collapses the boundaries between content and commercials with corporate sponsored zones (Firefly Mobile Phone Zone) and branded games (Nestle Ice Cream Frozen Flights, Pepperidge Farms Goldfish Sandwich Snackers, and McDonald's Meal Hunt). Wins are rewarded with NeoPoints for purchasing Neopet toys.

This marketing strategy provides a link from Neopia Central, the site's shopping district, which takes members to a splash page for the Cereal Adventure zone. This home of breakfast mascots, including the Trix rabbit and the Cocoa Puffs cuckoo, leads to a game called Lucy Charms: Shooting Stars!, in which kids navigate a series of marshmallow treats to earn more NeoPoints. Visitors can also surf into the Disney Theater where they can buy their pets some popcorn and settle into to watch previews for *Lilo & Stitch 2*. They also can earn Neopoints by answering a market research survey linked from the homepage with questions like: "When was your last visit to Wal-Mart?" and "Are you aware of the new Power Rangers DVD?"

The roster of clients who have set up shop inside the land of Neopia runs from Atari and DreamWorks to Frito-Lay and Lego. While passive product placement has become standard in TV and film, the Neopets approach emphasizes interaction and integration. The seamless interweaving of marketing and entertainment is an advertiser's dream come true according to a Jupiter Research analyst. The only drawback is an ethical dilemma: should kids earn points for watching commercials for sugary cereals? For the time being at least, Neopia and its virtual economy (regulated by the Neodaq) thrive by pairing generations with a game they can play together—matching new users with old Neopets—while keeping the future of Neopia promising. This is marketing at a very sophisticated level.

Entertainment and Promotion on Cell Phones

In 2006, News Corporation created a mobile entertainment store called Mobizzo and a production studio to focus exclusively on developing cell phone entertainment. Capitalizing on the growing appetite for video, graphics, and music on cell phones, the store was the first virtual mobile shopping mall by a major media company. What makes it different from other offerings is its direct sales to consumers, bypassing the exclusive arrangements common with wireless phone companies. Its competitors—MTV and CBS—are vying for the same market.

Mobizzo acquired 2,000 pieces of content from a Hollywood tattoo designer, a Chinese art collective, and a Los Angeles street artist. Aspiring to make Mobizzo a global brand, Rupert Murdock's company is even pursuing products created by teenagers based on comic books for the 13–24 crowd. News Corp. committed tens of millions of dollars to a marketing campaign of TV, print, and online advertising, and hired a team to promote the service during spring break in Florida.[50] Media giants have devoted sizeable efforts to grow their own mobile businesses in order to capitalize on the exploding thirst for mobile phone entertainment such as games, film clips, and news flashes.

FINALLY: LET'S SUM UP ▮▮▮▮▮▮▮

This chapter has presented an overview of television and film audiences, budgets, and marketing strategies. Promoting movies involves millions of dollars dedicated to creating an opening weekend blitz; television promotion, on the other hand, focuses on keeping audiences interested enough to tune in for another season of network or cable programming. Ever-improving technology and venue consolidation allow us to view media in the palms of our hands wherever and whenever we choose. How to keep audiences visiting advertising-based broadcasts and box office venues is a challenge marketers of this generation must face and overcome.

GOT IT? LET'S REVIEW ▮▮▮▮▮▮▮

- Positioning films is best accomplished with trailers that can be used in TV commercials, in press kits, in point-of-sale materials, and on DVDs. Internet sites give audiences an opportunity to explore the movie brand before and after release; Oscar nominations enhance a films brand image and stimulate attention.
- Global distribution complements national film distribution and revenue generation by reaching international audiences through theaters and DVD sales.
- Promotional budgets for marketing films are determined by these factors: potential gross, audience makeup, gross of similar genres, anticipated revenues from foreign or video sales, number of screens used for release, and number of markets included in the release.

- The macroeconomic financial factors financial factors affecting film marketing are seasonal demand, movie-going costs, market fluctuations, and licensing fees; microeconomic factors include financing sources, labor unions, and distribution recoupment.
- Reality shows and sitcoms have the strongest appeal for global television audiences; their fans use the Internet to purchase licensed merchandise, support programming, and influence content. Marketers cultivate audiences from fans.
- Product placement in film and video is big business, involving brands, content, negotiation, and advertisers; ratings and quality measures are available to evaluate placement effectiveness.

NOW TRY THIS ▮▮▮▮▮▮▮

1. Visit the Web site of your favorite sitcom or reality show. What interactive tools are used to engage viewers? How are fans connected? How important is the site for viewers like you?
2. Google your favorite film star and visit several of the sites listed. What kinds of information are generated for the star? What sources provide this information? How reliable are they? What role does this star play in marketing his/her own films?
3. Assuming that you are an aspiring reality-show contestant, what avenues are available for you to get an audition? Where are auditions held? What steps are required for getting an interview? Are there any costs involved? Do you need an agent? What does this information tell you about the contestants who are finally selected for the show?
4. Locate four separate reviews for a mainstream Hollywood film of your choice. After reading them, how likely are you to go or not go based on their comments? Why? What does your attitude suggest about the importance of reviewers comments for audience generation?

QUESTIONS: LET'S REVIEW ▮▮▮▮▮▮▮

1. When marketing a film that has no top star billing, what strategies would you use to position and promote the movie to a national audience? A global audience?
2. What are the various ways marketers use the Internet to promote a television show or a movie? Which medium is most reliant on the Internet? Why?
3. Suggest a marketing plan for a small independent film about a jazz musician in post-hurricane New Orleans that combines documentary segments with fictional char-

acters and plot. Which festivals would you target? Would you develop a trailer as part of your strategy? Why?

4. What brands or products would you consider placing to help finance the film described in question 3? What criteria are necessary for making the most appropriate selections?
5. Make some predictions about movie attendance in the next five years and provide a rationale for your prediction. Do the same for television viewership.

MORE TO READ ▮▮▮▮▮▮▮

Thomas Austin. *Hollywood, Hype and Audiences: Selling and Watching Popular Film in the 1990s.* Manchester University Press, 2002.

EPM Entertainment Marketing Sourcebook, 2005 ed. EPM Communications Inc

Mary-Lou Galician. *Handbook of Product Placement in the Mass Media: New Strategies in Marketing Theory, Practice, Trends and Ethics.* New York: Hayworth Press, 2004.

Lisa Kernan. *Coming Attractions: Reading American Movie Trailers.* Austin: University of Texas Press, 2004.

Bernard Schmitt, David Rogers, and Karen Vrotsos. *There's No Business That's Not Show Business.* New York: Financial Times/Prentice Hall, 2004.

Michael Solomon. *Conquering Consumerspace: Marketing Strategies for a Branded World.* New York: AMACOM, 2003.

NOTES ▮▮▮▮▮▮▮

1. J. Wemple, J. Shamsie, and T. Lent, *The Business of Culture: Strategic Perspectives of Entertainment and Media* (San Francisco: Lawrence Erlbaum: 2005).
2. A. O. Scott, *New York Times Magazine,* Dec. 11, 2005.
3. Carol Memmott, "*Geisha* Tie-ins Are Some Real Beauts," *USA Today,* Nov. 2005.
4. Theresa Howard, *USA Today,* Feb. 24, 2004.
5. Justin Wyatt, *High Concept: Movies and Marketing in Hollywood* (University of Texas Press, 1994).
6. From an interview of Terry Press by Lynn Hirschberg for the *New York Times,* Nov. 14, 2005.
7. *Ibid.*
8. rogerebert.suntimes.com/reviews, Dec. 21, 2005.
9. *Ibid.*
10. *Wall Street Journal,* Nov. 25, 2005.
11. Charlotte Kaiser, *Wall Street Journal,* July 8, 2005.
12. As prepared by Adams Media Research and reported by the New York Times Company, July 10, 2005.
13. David Halbfinger, report on the Sundance Film Festival, *New York Times,* Jan 28, 2006.
14. Gabriel Snyder and Ian Mohr, "H'wood's New World Order," *Variety,* Sept. 26-Oct. 2, 2005.
15. Geoffrey Fowler and Karen Mazurkewich, *Wall Street Journal,* Sept. 14, 2005.
16. Kate Kelly and Brian Steinberg, *Wall Street Journal,* Aug. 19, 2005.
17. Quoted in Harold Vogel, *Entertainment Industry Economics* (Cambridge University Press, 2001), p. 99.
18. Lorne Manly, *New York Times,* Dec. 11, 2005.
19. BBC, newslbbc.co.uk/1/hi/technology, Dec. 16, 2005.

20. B. Evenkamp, "The Amazing Ratings Race," *Brandweek* 46 (2003), 3–6.

21. Study conducted by Falone Serna, graduate student at California State University–Fullerton, Dec. 2005.

22. G. Hernandez, "Blacks, Whites, Get to Like Same Shows," *Daily News*, Dec. 17, 2003, B1.

23. A study conducted by Maruth Figueroa, graduate student at California State University–Fullerton, Dec. 2005.

24. Aaron Patrick, *Wall Street Journal*, Jan. 27, 2006.

25. S. Reiss and J. Wiltz, "Why America Loves Reality TV," *Psychology Today* 34 (5) (2001), 52.

26. Mei Fong, *Wall Street Journal*, Aug. 29, 2006, B1.

27. Bryan Curtis, *New York Times Magazine*, Dec. 11, 2005.

28. Karen Idelson, "Hollywood Calling" in *Variety*, Sept. 26–Oct 2, 2005.

29. Developed by Ken Convoy of New Paradigm TV, Santa Barbara, Calif., April 5, 2005.

30. Brooks Barnes, *Wall Street Journal*, Sept. 2, 2005.

31. Emily Steel, "Advertising" column, *Wall Street Journal*, Aug. 24, 2006.

32. Robert Mackey, "TV Stardom on $20 a Day," *New York Times Magazine*, Dec. 11, 2005.

33. *Ibid.*

34. Lorne Manly, "On Television, Brands go from Props to Stars," *New York Times*, Oct. 2, 2005.

35. Abram Sauer, brandchannel.com/features_effect.asp?pf_id=355, Feb. 19, 2007.

36. Monica Soto Ouchi, *Seattle Times*, Nov. 30, 2005.

37. *AdAge*, Dec. 7, 2005.

38. Cheryl Lu-Lien Tan, *Wall Street Journal*, Sept. 22, 2005.

39. www.promomagazine.com, Dec. 27, 2005.

40. Jennifer Pozner, "Triumph of the Shill: Part II," *Bitch Magazine* 24 (2004), Spring, p. 56.

41. *Ibid.*, p. 59.

42. Frank Zazza, CEO of iTVX, in a Web site address featured on itvx.com, Dec. 2005.

43. Schmitt, Rogers, and Vrotsos (2004), chap. 3.

44. *MediaWeek*, Dec. 5, 2005.

45. *Wise Marketer*, Dec. 9, 2005.

46. Peter Grant, *Wall Street Journal*, Dec. 15, 2005.

47. Josh McCall, Jack Morton Worldwide newsletter, Dec. 17, 2005.

48. Christopher Stapleton and Charles Hughes, "Mixed Reality and Experiential Movie Trailers: Combining Emotions and Immersion to Innovate Entertainment Marketing," 2005. Downloaded from http://www.mci.ucf.edu/publications/SIMCHI-TrailerMR.pdf.

49. David Kushner, "The Neopets Addiction," *Wired*, Dec. 2005, 271.

50. Laura Holson, *New York Times*, Feb. 27, 2006.

CHAPTER 15

Stars and Celebrities

I am my own industry.
I am my own commodity.
—ELIZABETH TAYLOR

Chapter Objectives

After reading Chapter 15, you should be able to answer these questions:

- What is *stardom* and what are the components of a *star system?*
- What are the components of *celebrity* and *fame?*
- Who are the people making up star and celebrity *audiences?*
- How are celebrities and stars marketed as *brands?*

Hollywood stars, fame, fans, and media celebrities are the topics of this chapter. *Stardom* is an outgrowth of film and television image production, and it recently has been established as an area of academic study. James Monaco's taxonomy of fame includes three categories: (1) a *hero,* or someone who has actually done something spectacular (a firefighter on 9/11); (2) a *star,* or someone who achieves prominence through development of a public persona that is more important than his or her professional profile (Donald Trump); and (3) a *quasar,* or accidental celebrity, or someone who becomes a media darling inadvertently (Monica Lewinsky).

Our focus is on people who became **stars** through their roles in popular film, or became **celebrities** because of their television appearances or media hype. Both stars and celebrities become properties in their own right that can be sold to audiences and fans. The selling part is what we address in this chapter, focusing on the roles of movie stars and television celebrities for audience development and revenue generation. After exploring the nature of stars and celebrities and their audiences, we review branding for its relevance to marketing famous people.

▀▀▀ What Is Stardom?

Stars are the key elements in the overall film package. Stars are defined as a "group of people whose institutional power is very limited or non-existent, but whose doings and way of life arouse a considerable degree of interest."[1] The basic conditions for stardom are a (1) thriving economy in a (2) large-scale society that (3) enables social mobility. As an elite and privileged group, stars cannot know everyone, but everyone can know them; and anyone may become a star. While the development of the star turned the individual into a commodity to be marketed and traded by the industry, it also gave the star access to a new kind of power—a relationship with the audience that was independent of the vehicles in which they appeared. This section examines stars as production and consumption, the studio and star systems, stars as capital, and stars' images.

Stars as a Phenomenon of Production and Consumption

The audience/star relationship is market controlled. Stars are typically *produced,* that is, they arise out of what filmmakers promote. They are also consumption based, because they arise from what the audiences demand. Stars' physical appearances codify a type of beauty that first defines and then reflects norms of attractiveness. Many stars develop into nationally advertised trademarks.

Stars can be viewed in terms of their function in the economy of Hollywood, including their role in the manipulation of film audiences. Charisma has proven to be a marketable commodity, and as such adds an intrinsic property to stardom. Stars are a studio's capital. They represent a large financial investment and are used to sell films. The film industry spends an enormous amount of money, time, and energy building star images through publicity, promotion, fan clubs, and merchandising. Stars are challenged for top billing, however, by special effects and the star director.

The Studio System

In order to understand the role of stars in Hollywood, you have to know about the stars' controlling body, the studio. The situation in Hollywood in the 1920s through the 1950s was an *oligopoly,* an economic condition in which competition is limited because a market is completely dominated by a small number of companies. In 1930, eight studios dominated Hollywood:[2]

- The Big 5 (majors): MGM, Paramount, RKO, Fox, Warner Brothers
- The Little 3 (minors): Columbia, United Artists, Universal

The majors were *vertically integrated,* meaning they exercised control over production, distribution, and exhibition. The minors did not control exhibition, but had access to the major's distribution circuit.

The major studios made, released, and marketed their films; they even owned the cinemas in which they were shown. Exhibition was the most profitable sector of the film industry. Before TV and video, box office receipts were the source of income for recouping the money spent on making films. It made sense for the film studios to want all of those profits for themselves. They did not own all the cinemas in the U.S., but the ones that they did own were "first-run" cinemas and had exclusive access to the most popular films before their competitors' cinemas (as a result, the "first-run" venues delivered 75 percent of all theatrical revenues). The advantages of this system were that the major studios controlled the money and power within the film industry. They also controlled the stars, who were obligated to act for one studio until their contracts ran out. During the 20 years between 1930 and 1950, the studios made the stars. The former selected the latter's parts, prepared their promotion, and dictated when and where they appeared in public.

The Production System

In order to meet audience demand during this period, each of the studios produced, on average, one film per week. Studios modeled themselves on factories to achieve such vast production. Other than the producer, everybody involved with making the film (actors, cameramen, scriptwriters, prop-makers, and so on) was simply *salaried staff,* there to perform their functions in the overall process of making a film.

The only person who saw the film through the complete process would be the associate producer, who monitored the shooting schedule and budget for each film. The associate producers were answerable to the head of production, who was ultimately responsible for making sure the studio made money.

Stars are categorized as performance specialists: they are required to execute certain tasks. During pre-production, stars read scripts and learned lines; when in production, stars rehearsed and shot scenes; in post-production, stars dubbed or post-synchronized voice during sound rerecording. In addition, star labor involved participating in promotional tasks such as press interviews, premiere appearances, and television show interviews.

The Contract System

As part of this approach to filmmaking, all staff involved with producing a film were signed to long-term, permanent contracts with the studios. Stars were typically contracted to a studio for seven years. The contracts were such that the star had no choice in the films that they had to make or how many. Despite being crucial to the marketing of films, stars had very little power. If they refused to do a film, they would be suspended without pay and their contracts would then be extended. Frequently stars would be lent out to other studios.

The Star System

Today, star contracts are based on conditions of exclusivity. The work of stars is based on selling a distinctive identity, and contracts must determine the rights to the exploitation of a star's image. The rights to use a star's name, voice, and likeness are used to carry the star's image into other media, designed for commercial and promotional use. Stars' exposure is governed by the star system.

The **star system** refers to the institutional hierarchy established to regulate and control the employment and use of all actors. Stardom is a system of usage by three entities: (1) the film industry that tries to manage audience demands for films; (2) distributors that use stars to sell films to exhibitors in domestic and overseas markets; and (3) exhibitors who own and run theaters showing films that use stars to draw audiences. In this circuit of exchange, stars are a form of capital, a form of asset

Johnny Depp led fan popularity charts in 2006.

deployed with the intention of gaining advantage in the entertainment market and making profits.[3]

Stars as Capital

As a form of capital, stars are valuable assets for a production company; stars are a form of investment. Increasingly marketed through star differentiation, films have relied on star power for decades. During the studio era, stars stabilized demand, creating a consistent box office performance for a star's films. From an economic perspective, stars are thought of as a monopoly on personality.[4] Star monopolies are based on the belief in unique individuality—there is only one Johnny Depp.

As studios negative costs rise, stars become ever more central to the packaging of a project and securing production financing for it. Since moving to a package-unit system of production, in which stars are accompanied by financing promotional deals, the powers of talent agents to act as key mediators in the industry has achieved new importance. Studios no longer own a star, so it is the responsibility of the agent to negotiate for and secure the best deal possible for the client. The most powerful talent agencies are Creative Artists (Gwyneth Paltrow, Tom Cruise, Demi Moore), International Creative Management (Jodie Foster, Eddie Murphy, Julia Roberts), and the William Morris Agency (Clint Eastwood, Bruce Willis, Kate Winslet). Artists Management Group (Cameron Diaz, Leonard DiCaprio, Robin Williams) is a smaller agency managing powerful stars.

Agencies, their clients, and the studios remain in a situation of mutual dependence. Because stars are no longer bound by contract to studios, agency power is financially limited. It is the studios that hold the money, and agents are rich and powerful only to the extent that they can place clients in packages that receive financial backing.

Stars may choose to be paid based on a film's performance (*back-end deal*), with payment based on a star participating in a percentage of the profits. Participation deals vary depending on whether payments are made on the basis of gross receipts (based on the sale of the film in all markets) or net profits (what remains after gross receipts meet a break-even level). Compared to net points, gross points are of greater value, and the agents of top stars negotiate for these.

Box office performance has allowed stars economic and symbolic power in the film industry, yet even high-profile stars cannot always stabilize demand with their differentiation. Popularity does not always translate into profitability. Some stars become involved in film projects as joint producers through their own companies. Extra control acts as insurance against disaster—or so they hope.

Stars' Images

Stars need to appear in the right type of vehicle for their existing image or persona. The popularity of a star-driven film depends on its marketing.

Images are complex configurations of visual, verbal, and aural signs.[5] Stars' images come not only from their movies but also from forms of publicity and promotion, as well as from critical review and commentary. Images are also developed from the characters stars play and the style of performance they use to portray that role. Stars are categorized by social variables of age, gender, race, and nationality. Stars are mediated identities—audiences get images rather than a real person. As moviegoers form impressions of the star, the star becomes a collection of meanings.

Stars' images are inherently contradictory: The images make stars appear to be ordinary people, but stars also are shown to be exceptional and apart from society. Their images are interpreted in many different ways and can be historically transformed (Madonna, for instance, shows different images of herself as over time). Star images are circulated in various forms of media and in many different contexts.

Cinema audiences make choices based on stars' vehicles (films) as well as on stars' personalities. Some stars manage their image through associations with forms of performance other than film. Kenneth Branagh's association with classical Shakespearean theater draws on the cultural status of theater to distinguish himself from other popular film performers. Mick Jagger, on the other hand, has used his music-based celebrity to his advantage in landing a starring role with Angelica Huston that modified his rock image and established him as part of the Hollywood acting scene.

Star Vehicles

Films are promotional vehicles for a star. A star combines two methods of product differentiation: the personal monopoly of a star's image and the familiar conventions that establish generic expectations.[6] According to Richard Dyer,[7] a vehicle provides:

- a character of the type associated with the star (Reese Witherspoon's ditzy blonde roles; Clint Eastwood's tough-guy roles).
- a situation, setting, or generic context associated with a star (Hugh Grant in romantic comedies).
- an opportunity for a star to do his/her thing (Jim Carrey as a funny guy).

Mick Jagger with Jack Nicholson at the premiere of *The Departed,* which received the 2006 Academy Award for best picture.

BOX 15-1

Focus on Studio News

STUDIO ACQUISITIONS CHANGE HOLLYWOOD PLAYERS

• In December 2005, DreamWorks was purchased by Paramount Studios for $1.6 billion, effectively ending DreamWorks' 11-year run as an independent studio. DreamWorks was never able to produce enough films to cover the high cost of being its own distributor. The move allows Paramount to increase the number of films it releases each year. Spielberg remains director and producer, and Geffen will be chairman. The two agreed to produce up to six movies in 2007. In addition, Paramount has the right to distribute DreamWorks' future animated features. To pay for the purchase, Paramount plans to sell DreamWorks' library of movie titles for as much as $1 billion.

• Warner Brothers was acquired by AOL in 2005.

• In September 2004, MGM merged with the Sony Corporation. The purchase included the biggest library of color movies in the world, including franchises such as "James Bond," the "Pink Panther," and "Rocky." MGM continues to put out several films a year with Sony co-producing and co-financing the projects.

Film genres play an important role in defining star identities by setting limits on the contexts in which a star performs. These limits are not necessarily confining, however, given the industry's mixing of genres and the stars' traversing of genres to expand their acting range.

Special Effects as "Stars"

A recent rise in the emphasis of special effects as cinematic elements has given special effects a starring role. According to some motion picture analysts, special effects action/adventure movies with budgets of at least $100 million seem to be the only reliable moneymakers.[8] Startling special effects that are highlighted in commercials and trailers generate unstoppable momentum that even bad reviews cannot deter. One analyst stated that "Smart marketing shows that special effects can replace the traditional cornerstones of Hollywood films: *Star Wars* proved that a special effects film with no stars could still win big at the box office, and *Independence Day* proved that neither stars nor a story were essential. Special effects films are also popular in foreign markets where US films now derive half of their revenues."[9]

Directors as Stars

During the 1990s, marketers and publicists began to promote films on the name of their directors. Steven Spielberg's popular movies

Director/star Woody Allen.

mark him as a superstar; all questions of wealth, politics, and aesthetics became irrelevant to his star persona—he could do no wrong. In *vanity deals,* studios have helped some stars created their own production companies to pursue their personal projects. Clint Eastwood has been one of the most successful star-directors. Recently, however, a series of financial disasters caused by box-office flops and shareholder objections have caused studios to all but cease offering such deals to stars. Still, studio advertising incorporates expressions such as "From the Director of . . . ," director's cuts are now added to DVD movies along with director's commentary, and specials on directors appear in a plethora of film magazines.

Virtual Stars

From the big screen to the computer, all forms of animated and actual stars can be viewed and perused on the Internet. One of the most popular new forms of stars is a descendent of the Japanese printed cartoon (*manga*) and animated film (*anime*). Unlike American comic superheroes, anime characters grow and develop over time, and contain an underlying spiritual optimism. These virtual stars continue to gain popularity in games and feature-length films, and appeal to both children and adults.

Two performers from NBC's *Saturday Night Live* became recognized stars, not from their television appearances, but from the showing of their video *Lazy Sunday,* which was downloaded more than 1.2 million times from YouTube's video-sharing Web site. It cracked the video charts at NBC.com and iTunes Music Store, and even inspired a line of T-shirts. Video producer Andy Samberg claimed he was recognized more times after the video was aired on the Web than the entire first season he was on SNL.[10]

Hundreds of Hollywood stars enjoy Internet stardom generated by Web-browsing fans. Hundreds of sites dedicated to stargazing enable even the homebound to connect with their favorite screen star. Marketers use the Internet as a tactic to generate buzz and to maintain a positive image for client stars. Exhibit 15.1 shows ranking for top actors.

The Limits of Stardom

The notion of stardom has also been described as a discrete and recognizable episode in the life of a star. It is the period of inevitability where personality intersects with history. Every episode of stardom carries within it the seeds of its own demise. This

▮▮▮▮ **EXHIBIT 15.1** Top Ten Actors in 2005

STARmeter Reports

Selections are based on the search behavior of 30 million users of the IMDb.com movie database.

1. Johnny Depp
2. Angelina Jolie
3. Brad Pitt
4. Lindsay Lohan
5. Paris Hilton
6. Jessica Alba
7. Tom Cruise
8. Keira Knightley
9. Natalie Portman
10. Hilary Duff

"iron law" dictates that, because personalities can grip the general attention for only so long, stardom only lasts three years.[11] Is this notion a useful one for marketing professionals?

▪▪▪ What Is Celebrity?

Public figures become celebrities at the point at which media interest in their activities is transferred from reporting on their public role to investigating their private lives. We may describe **celebrity**, then, as a commodity traded by the promotions, publicity, and media industries that produces interest beyond a person's public role.[12] Celebrities are generated from the arenas of sports, politics, the arts, religion, business, science, the professions, academia, and, of course, entertainment.

Celebrities differ from *stars* in several ways: where film creates stars, television creates personalities; where stars play roles, personalities perform themselves. Stars are able to continually accrue meaning through successive appearances, while television personalities, by contrast, are in danger of exhausting the meanings they generate by continually drawing on them in order to perform at all. The film star is structured through the discourses of individualism—their performance roles and film narratives—while the television personality constructs his or her celebrity through perceptions of familiarity.

This section looks at the celebrity industry, fame and reality television, the celebrity economy, the manufacture of celebrities, and how celebrities are consumed.

Celebrity Industry

A celebrity's name has attention-getting, interest-catching, and profit-generating value. A mishmash of cultural and economic processes culminate in the wildly lucrative celebrity industry. The quest for celebrity, many critics say, indicates a shift toward a culture that privileges the momentary or sensational over the enduring.

Celebrities can be heroic, accidental, or public. We can type celebrity status according to how it's earned: *ascribed* (Prince Harry), *achieved* in competition (Lance Armstrong), or attributed by the media. But it is important to remember that what constitutes celebrity in one cultural domain may be quite different in another. Our focus here is on American culture and its media-generated iconic symbols.

In a world where everyone has access to a camera, a screen, or both, it is easier than ever to find fleeting fame. Whether, like Tiger Woods, a celebrity earns status through accomplishment, or like as George Lucas, through generating millions of dollars in ticket and merchandise sales for films, or like the one-and-only Oprah Winfrey, by being the nation's leading talk-show host for 21 years, the famous stand out. According to the *Celebrity Register*, a celebrity is a name that, once made by news, now makes news by itself. The best-paid celebrities (in descending order) are actors, athletes, authors, chefs, directors/producers, kid stars, magicians, models, musicians, and personalities from other areas, such as religion and politics.

A variety of services track the movements of celebrities in various sectors and sell access to celebrities. One such service, Celebrity Service International, charges subscribers $3,000 a year for bulletins. The modeling agency Celebrity Look-a-Likes by Elyse provides talent to advertising agencies for commercials. Home office and road

> According to a Forbes magazine poll, the top celebrities were:
>
> 1. Oprah Winfrey   6. Steven Spielberg
> 2. Tiger Woods   7. Johnny Depp
> 3. Mel Gibson   8. Madonna
> 4. George Lucas   9. Elton John
> 5. Shaquille O'Neal   10. Tom Cruise
>
> Compare this list of celebrities to the list of top ten-rated stars above. What do the combined lists say about our preoccupation with stars?

Source: Forbes.com, 2005.

staffers also serve the industry, as well as limousine drivers and bodyguards. *Forbes'* top 10 celebrities are listed in Exhibit 15.2.

Fame

As the saying goes, some are born famous, some work hard to achieve fame, and others have fame thrust on them.[13] People from politics and business were once successful and then famous, but now people in the entertainment industry are made famous by the media. Fame is now disconnected from achievement completely. The dream of fame has become inseparable from the idea of personal freedom.

Some of the factors of fame are exhibitionism, charisma, names, and drive. Demi Moore's nude appearance on the cover of *Vanity Fair* magazine during her pregnancy was an act of exhibitionism that certainly made her more famous. Charismatic figures reflect a self-assurance that is attractive to audiences. From the beginning, Hollywood stars changed their names because of the names' difficult pronunciation, country of origin reflection, or prior exposure in another field or capacity. Even stars a popular as Marilyn Monroe had to fight hard for recognition under her assumed name.[14]

Andy Warhol claimed that everyone gets his or her 15 minutes of fame. Like stars, people who possess political, economic, or religious power also can become famous. The establishment of personal Web sites offers the possibility of fame and public visibility to anyone with a computer and a camera. Certainly, the number of contestants auditioning for reality television attests to the truth of this statement. Which is why we turn our attention to the *ordinary celebrity,* as created and nurtured by reality television.

Reality Show Fame

According to the Nielsen Media Research, reality shows account for about 56 percent of all of American TV shows (both in cable and broadcast). They amount to about 69 percent of the world's TV shows (in cable and in broadcast).

The media's interest in manufacturing celebrities, especially on commercial reality television, has transformed media from being the end-user of celebrity to being the producers themselves. By using ordinary people with no special abilities and achievements as the talent in their programming, reality producers turn out each season a series of celebrities who are dependent on the program that made them visible — because they have no other platform from which to address their audience.

▮▮▮▮▮▮▮▮▮▮ **BOX 15-2** ▮▮▮▮▮▮▮▮▮

Focus on Naming

THE PARIS HILTON EFFECT

Dramatic surges in the use of names belonging to stars and celebrities occur as their popularity increases according to research by the Social Security Administration, which has tracked the top 1,000 most popular names for boys and girls since 1879. In 1956, for example, "Elvis" rose almost 60 percent after *Heartbreak Hotel* was released. And once Washington starred in *Mo' Better Blues* (2000), the name "Denzel" increased 55 percent from the previous year.

Although not all parents name their babies after stars, the repetition of a name causes familiarity, liking, and eventually adoption for personal use. To be popular, names must be compatible with the larger cultural moment to wield any influence. Perhaps that is why there were not thousands of little Madonnas running around playgrounds during the 1980s.

Other names on popularity charts that corresponded to star or celebrity fame are:

Prince, 1984 (rock star)

Tyra, 1998 (swimsuit model)

Cameron, 1999 (actress)

Serena, 2000 (tennis star)

Paris, 2004 (video queen)

Here are the most popular names for 2006. Can you find any celebrity-based names among them? Some names could be based on leading characters in TV dramas or movies, as suggested below.

Rank	Male Name	Female Name
1	Jacob	Emily
2	Michael	Madison
3	Joshua	Hannah (Star Daryl)
4	Matthew	Emma
5	Andrew	Ashley
6	Christopher	Abigail
7	Joseph	Alexis
8	Daniel	Olivia (*Law & Order* character)
9	Michael	Samantha (*Bewitched* character)
10	Ethan	Sarah

Go to ssa.gov and search for your own name to see what other names were popular the year you were born. Any matches with famous folks?

Sources: Forbes April 4, 2006, and ssa.gov.

▮▮▮▮▮▮▮▮▮

The publicity and promotion potential of the reality show format is varied: the program can be promoted as news, a cultural phenomenon, a launching pad for new celebrities, a contest, or just entertaining television. As each member of the *Survivor* team is ejected, for instance, he or she can be cycled through channel, network, or sponsors'

Carrie Underwood of *American Idol.*

promotions or act as a presenter in new programming ventures. When the season is over, the entire cast is processed through various program formats all over again, with retrospectives, reunions, and so on. Cross-promotions among networks, cable channels, newspapers, magazines, and radio are fundamental. *Survivor* participants are the epitome of the fabricated celebrity: Contestants want to be on television long enough to be famous, and fame becomes a personal justification of the participants' self-importance.

The growing importance of the camera as a means of validating everyday reality is implicit; reality TV offers to display our everyday identities as spectacle, as an experiment and as entertainment. Even the genre term *reality* sets out to eliminate the distance between television and everyday existence. The reality genre has cashed in on the promotional possibilities that fuel the production and consumption of celebrity with the promise of media validation for just being who you are, every day.

Reality show casting calls have become events in their own right. Web sites post calls, and books offer hints for getting auditions and pointers for being chosen for a part. So, who makes money on reality show fame? Almost everyone. Agents are paid to get their clients' work, brand managers pay winners to endorse products, show advertisers are exposed to millions of viewers, and producers sell their low-budget hits to global outlets.

The economies of reality shows help them proliferate. Both the low production costs and the payout to stars keep studios profitable; yet these shows have little value as aftermarket products for television. DVD sales of seasonal episodes account for some sales revenue, but the profit in reality shows comes mainly from product placement and sponsorships.

The Economy of Celebrity Endorsements

As valuable commodities for promoting products, celebrities are paid large sums to appear on infomercials, such as the star-studded, 30-minute version for Proactiv Solution, an acne-fighting product. P. Diddy, Jessica Simpson, and Alicia Keys joined host Vanessa Williams to testify for the pharmaceutical company that produced the drug. Considered shows rather than infomercials, the production mixed interviews with celebrities and average consumer types, lots of before-and-after photos, a smattering of scientific looking diagrams, and words such as *micronized*. What made the spots convincing was the notion that these stars hardly needed the money—implying that the reason for the star's involvement was that she or he used the product and that the product must work, else the star would not be hawking it on TV. Thus, the brand achieves a credibility attainable only via the involvement of these celebrities.[15]

U.S. celebrities also can make a lot of money abroad. Stars can net between $1 and $5 million for a single overseas ad campaign on the condition that no one will see the

---

▪▪▪▪▪▪▪▪▪▪ **BOX 15-3** ▪▪▪▪▪▪▪▪▪▪

Focus on Personal Brands

NICKNAMING

Nicknames have been around for centuries, certainly long before the digital age, but the process of acquiring a nickname changed significantly in the 1980s when computers and Internet use became more common and users had to create e-mail "handles." Unlike the names bestowed on us by our parents, nicknames can be awarded to each of us by ourselves. Nicknames can convey something about our demeanor that our birth names cannot.

According to Minya Oh, a writer and radio personality in New York, regular people can be stars in their own minds and in their own circle of friends. "It's all about the Everyman becoming the Superman," Oh says. Names have meaning and are imbued with varying degrees of potency. Movie stars often change their names to create a screen image, and singers often adopt short or single-word names (Ice-T, Cher). Internet users often create nicknames for themselves that express their alter-ego, or that convey a certain attitude. Internet sites such as MySpace and YouTube have enabled everyone to feel like a celebrity.

The Internet has several nickname generators, where one can acquire all manner of monikers, from Western-theme to porn-star-worthy. But the most popular are organic—they spring up from an event, a physical trait, or a hobby. As millions of people continue to express themselves with instant messaging, e-mail, blogs, forums, and Web sites, nicknames will create new digital genres.

What do you think?

1. What does your e-mail nickname say about your?

2. How might nicknames become personal brands?

SOURCE: Stephanie Rosenbloom for the *New York Times,* April 13, 2006.

▪▪▪▪▪▪▪▪▪

---

campaigns outside the country in which they were made. Britain is seen as a place where a celebrity's good name can be protected (for their eyes only!). Michael Madsen, Ed Harris, and Samuel L. Jackson are among the stars willing to make a buck abroad without compromising their image at home by endorsing uncharacteristic brands.[16]

In Japan, Hewlett-Packard released a digital camera designed by singer Gwen Stefani in a limited edition of 3,000 that sold for $249. Popular for her song "Harajuka Girls," Stefani is a *trend translator,* someone who translates to the mainstream a certain set of ideas about what's cool. HP figured it could be cool by associating with her and the Harajuka neighborhood in Tokyo she sings about, which is located next to the Shibuya shopping and entertainment district. Stefani showed off her new co-branded camera on the *Ellen DeGeneres Show,* a strategy that relies on the theory of consumer-celebrity relationship. What happened was not simply an endorsement but a pop star paying tribute to a consumer tribe—a specific breed of global hyper consumer. What was the value of the association to HP? Priceless.[17]

Manufacturing Celebrity

Celebrities are developed to make money. As property, they are financial assets to those who stand to gain from their commercialization. Celebrity is produced, traded, and marketed by the media and publicity industries. Its cultural function is purchased identity—a branding mechanism for media products.

Celebrity industries include:

- Entertainment—theaters, music and dance halls, sports arenas, and movies studios
- Communications—media
- Publicity—PR, advertising
- Representation—agents, managers
- Appearance—costumes, makeup, hair styling
- Coaching—music, dance, speech
- Endorsement—souvenirs, toys
- Legal and business services

Each of these entities contributes to the development, production, distribution, or maintenance of celebrities. After tourism, the industry is one of the world's largest, and it continues to thrive in step with the world population's need for stars, celebrities, and famous people to admire, emulate, and desire.

Consuming Celebrity

Audiences place individual celebrities somewhere along a continuum that ranges from seeing them as objects of desire or emulation to regarding them as spectacular freaks. As objects of desire, they create a process of audience bonding.

Publishers of celebrity magazines are experiencing surges in subscription and ad sales—*Us Weekly*'s ad page-count was up 25 percent in 2005; *Star Magazine* ads increased 17 percent over the previous year; *In Touch Weekly* ad volume rose nearly 22 percent in the same time period. Why? Star and celebrity focused magazines are advertising-friendly environments because readers cover the magazine from front to back. As advertisers become increasingly interested in reaching women, they select celebrity magazines where the bulk of readers are women.

Research conducted by TV Guide Publishing Group revealed that many readers buy two or three celebrity magazines because of the tremendous appetite for celebrity coverage. A sampling of readers on the street in New York City indicated that the attraction with celebrities has to do with escapism and a need to stay in the know on the latest gossip.[18]

The Internet is another medium through which stars and celebrities are consumed. In a list of the most googled celebrities in 2005, these names appeared at the top: Janet Jackson, Britney Spears, Angelina Jolie, Harry Potter, Martha Stewart, and Donald Trump.[19] Although publicists cannot control the search habits of audiences, they can create the type of spin that drives Internet users to google their clients. After all, without the audience, there are no stars.

▪▪▪ Star and Celebrity Audiences

Audiences accept stars and celebrities as a form of public personality with whom they identify, in whom they invest and maintain a personal interest, and to whom they ascribe a value that is cultural or social rather than merely economic. This section

▪▪▪▪▪▪▪▪▪ BOX 15-4 ▪▪▪▪▪▪▪▪▪

Focus on Ethics

DON'T CELEBRITIES HAVE PRIVACY RIGHTS?

Supermodel Naomi Campbell is an international celebrity. Discovered in London's Covent Garden when she was 15, Campbell became one of the best paid and most photographed supermodels, easily earning more than $1 million a year. Campbell often was irritable and manipulative, according to her reputation as a prima donna. She made the news after being arrested for assaulting her personal assistant and being dropped by her agency.

Campbell often sought the media spotlight. She was rumored to use cocaine. She publicly denied any drug addiction, even after being rushed to the hospital following a drug overdose. In February 2001, London's *Daily Mirror* tabloid published a photograph of Campbell leaving a Narcotics Anonymous (NA) meeting in a wealthy neighborhood outside London.

In response, Campbell sued the *Daily Mirror* in British courts for invasion of privacy and libel, saying the *Mirror* printed a very damaging article about her. In its March 2002 ruling, the British High Court awarded Campbell $6,000 in damages and ordered that the newspaper pay additional court costs equal to about $110,000. The judge noted that even celebrities were entitled to some privacy. Because the reported NA meeting and therapy related to her physical and mental health, it met the standards of being "sensitive personal data." The judge also noted, however, that the public clearly had an interest in knowing that Campbell had been misleading them with her denials of drug addiction. The *Mirror's* editor responded to the judgment by stating that the case was one "that should never have been brought. It is quite clear the judge thought we had every right to say she was a drug addict. What we shouldn't have said was that she was attending NA meetings."

What do you think?

1. If Campbell had admitted her drug addiction when first asked, would it have been ethical to publish the story?

2. Are celebrities ethically distinct from other categories of people when it come to privacy issues?

3. Can you predict whether this case might have been resolved any differently in the U.S. had Campbell chosen to sue there? Is your answer based in legal precedent or on ethical theory? Which is more appropriate in privacy cases?

SOURCE: P. Patterson and L. Wilkins, *Media Ethics* (2005).

▪▪▪▪▪▪▪▪▪

explores the psychological, playful, and fan relationships that occur between audiences and people who have gained fame in the movies and on television.

The Star-Celebrity Relationship

Psychologists have determined that people's favorite stars and celebrities are usually those of the same sex, a fact that indicates a relationship built predominantly on self-identification.[20] One model of star classification identifies four categories of star-celebrity/audience relationships.[21] They are:

- *emotional affinity*—a loose attachment of the audience member to the star; it is based on a star's charismatic attraction and the audience's motivation to care for and feel attached to figures on the screen.

- *self-identification*—a state in which the audience member puts himself or herself in the person or situation of the star.

- *imitation*—most common among young viewers, this condition occurs when a star serves as a role model for an audience member.

- *projection*—a state in which the audience member bonds psychologically with star, generating a para-social relationship.

Modeling theory[22] suggests that an audience member sees a star, imitates his or her actions, and receives a consequence from the new behavior. Among audience members of all types, imitation is a form of acquiring new ideas and behaviors from mediated people. As extremely visible role models, stars and celebrities often contribute to the formation of a viewer's identity. Self-identity has become increasingly interwoven with mediated symbolic forms, and in some cases leads beyond modeling to a para-social relationship. Here, stars can be regular and dependable companions to provide advice and support—they allow audience members to imagine alternatives of how they may create their own identities. Stars and celebrities enable viewers to experiment with their self-images. Experimentation yields opportunities for marketing—from star fashions and branded cosmetics to celebrity endorsed products bought by star-struck audiences, the fans.

Watchers and Gazers

Fans, readers, and viewers have their own menu of personalities in which they maintain interest, and some audiences are gullible regarding the truth of what they see, hear, or read about celebrities and stars. Celebrity and star watcher audience members have been categorized into a typology.[23]

1. *Traditional audiences* regard text about the celebrity from media sources as realistic. They believe that celebrity stories as arise naturally through the news media rather than through promotions and publicity. Their interaction with celebrity involves modeling, fantasy, and identification.

2. *Second-order traditional audiences* see a more complex narrative in which publicity plays a part, but does not pose an obstacle to esteeming celebrities. They believe in the deserving celebrity, and their interaction with the celebrity is more negotiated (i.e., mutual) than traditional audience members.

3.   *Postmodern audiences* see media coverage as fictional and know about celebrity manufacture. They often seek evidence and detail, rejecting or ignoring the story of the naturally rising celebrity as naïve and false. They have an active interest in the techniques of manufacturing celebrity.

4.   *Game players* regard the content of media as semi-fictional and are not bothered by where the stories come from of whether they are true. This audience type makes use of celebrity material for play and for its own cultural activities. It consists of two subgroups: detectives and gossipers. *Detectives* consider celebrity production a giant playground, and *gossipers* think of celebrity media as a rich social resource. The game-playing group is the dominant form of audience type integrated into mainstream media formats.

In all groups, those audience members who believe most in media truth about celebrity are those who know least about the production process. *Play* is an accurate description of audiences' mode of engagement with celebrity. Audiences see pleasure in the social exchange of gossip and stories the media develop about famous people. Fans are characterized by their enthusiastic mode of play-type engagement.

According to an audience involvement scale, levels of involvement with stars and celebrities determine their marketing priority. Audience scale levels include:

- Invisible—seek local celebrities, but don't travel to Hollywood
- Watchers—passive viewers
- Seekers—the largest group and the biggest spenders, seekers have a stronger attraction to celebrities; they go to performances and spend the most money on entertainment
- Collectors—buy souvenirs
- Fans—need personal interaction with stars
- Insiders—groupies who are celebrities by associating with them
- Entourage—the star's inner circle or network of close associates
- Ensnared—an obsessed fan

A celebrity marketer's objective is to move an audience member up the scale from being invisible to becoming a fan.

Fan Behavior

Fans are prime marketing targets for manufacturing celebrities and stars through mediated vehicles, and for cultivating audiences that ensure box office and advertising revenues. Because of their important role when developing marketing strategies, fans merit attention in any discussion of entertainment marketing.

Again, fans construct para-social, imagined connections to stars or celebrities who fulfill their needs for friendship; such interactions are substitutes for real relationships. "Fandom" is a surrogate relationship where audience members live vicariously through the lives of famous people.[24] This "intimacy" is mediated by television, movies, and the Internet; contact is continually available through one mass media conduit or another. Some associations even take on religious connotations, such as fan adoration for dead celebrities Elvis, Princess Diana, and James Dean; shrines, memorials, and gatherings signify religious dedication.[25]

▪▪▪ Promoting Stars and Celebrities

A visibility industry exists: its function is to design, create, and market celebrities as brands. Professionally managed and directed, celebrities receive power from media who give equal amounts of attention to a variety of famous types. A definable, publicizable personality can become a nationally advertised trademark. Sylvester Stallone was the first star to become a registered trademark. Arnold Schwarzenegger talked about his career as a brand name product and exploited it with the same dedication as would a fast-food chain. To create a star or celebrity brand, marketers use the same strategy as that used to brand products. A huge group of subindustries—from venue managers to the beauty industry to the legal world—provide services to produce and promote personal brands.[26]

Celebrity Branding

Celebrity brands are both homemade and licensed; when an individual produces a powerhouse company, a homemade Martha Stewart brand is created. When celebrities are hired to make a brand, such as Michael Jordan for Nike or Tiger Woods for Buick, they have become licensed brands themselves. The importance of the celebrity as a branding mechanism for media products has assisted their fluent translation across media formats and systems of delivery.

Three branding strategies are recommended for promoting celebrities:[27]

1. *Pure selling,* in which the agent presents a client's qualifications to an intermediary, such as when a singer's tapes are sent to a talent scout who solicits a record company. Here, the celebrity is sold to distributors, akin to getting shelf space in a supermarket for a cola.

2. *Product improvement,* in which an agent works with a client to modify certain characteristics to increase his or her market value. Madonna's transformation from East Village punk to a lacy virgin to a cowgirl and, yet again, to a kids' author, is an example of transforming a product in response to current trends.

3. *Market fulfillment,* in which an agent scans the market to identify unmet needs, finds a person that meets those needs, and develops a saleable product. Spice Girls and 'N Sync were created by assembling photos of young singers and developing a hybrid that would sell records.

Managing the Star-Celebrity Brand

If not managed properly, star brands can become a huge liability, even impacting Wall Street, as evidenced by Tom Cruise's cancelled production deal with Viacom's Paramount Pictures in August 2006. After watching a video of the actor manically bouncing on Oprah Winfrey's couch and hearing his outbursts about Scientology, Merrill Lynch & Co.'s head of structured finance asked, "How does one hedge that risk?"[28] He was referring to the impact of Cruise's actions on future film financing from hedge funds: the Cruise brand also supports stock prices. Viacom's stock, trading 18.5 times the forecast for 2006, is valued in line with rivals Walt Disney and News Corp.

Viacom's 14-year relationship with Cruise was terminated after a year of bizarre events that had been kept in check by Cruise's publicist, Pat Kingsley, whom Cruise fired in 2004. After hiring his sister, a fellow Scientologist, to act as his publicist,

▮▮▮▮▮▮▮▮▮▮ BOX 15-5 ▮▮▮▮▮▮▮▮▮▮

A Closer Look at Marketing Celebrities

MADONNA'S MARKETING MAGIC

Madonna has become in recent years the idiosyncratic female icon. Before looking at her marketing strategy, let's overview Madonna's images of herself during the course of her career, and what was going on outside, as well as inside, Madonna's work.

Physical Transformation Strategies

Material Virgin with a Boy Toy

Madonna offers a case history relevant to identity politics—she represents to her fans and critics a fantasy of what their own gendered or sexual identities might mean. The theoretical term "postmodernism" came into vogue in the '80s when Madonna was born on MTV with the release of her video "Lucky Star." "Into the Groove" is a song associated with the height of her "boy toy" phase, coming as it did soon after her first number one single, "Like a Virgin."

Body Builder

Madonna's next major image overhaul came when she completely resculpted her body through aerobics and weight training, dyed her hair Marilyn Monroe blonde, and began to wear self-designed lingerie that resembled body armor. While she had certainly been interested in self-consciously making herself a reference to American female retro-icons in her 1984 "Material Girl" video, "Express Yourself" gives its viewers a whole new series of image references to traditional American gendered and sexual icons—male and female—and a whole new level of irony.

One of Madonna's many images.

Dominatrix

During the early '90s, Madonna altered her image and identity once more. With the release of the documentary *Truth or Dare;* the book *Sex;* and the videos "Erotica," "Vogue," and even the recent "Deeper and Deeper," she became a self-conscious postmodern icon of gender and sexuality. Madonna understands her identity as a series of images which can be distinguished from each other mainly by understanding what they "refer" to. If we did not know her "real" identity, her personas might seem a little less like entertainment and a little more like schizophrenia.

Media Maven

The powerful seductiveness of Madonna's multiple identity-image, then, is precisely her ability to put identity-images on but remain uncontaminated by them. Madonna is now a part of history—her

(Continued)

identity-image has allowed her to strategically position herself as a famous marginalized person, in a time and place when certain marginalized identities have become powerful and recognizable enough to be famous in and of themselves. She has used images of sexual minorities and postmodernism in her work as a way of coping with her inevitable disappearance from the mass media limelight. By transforming her identity into the image of two famous subcultures bent on making history, Madonna borrows power from traditions not her own. Her revenge has gotten her right back to where she started from—tradition.

Image Maintenance

What is important to think about here is Madonna's relationship to the maintenance of her famous identity. When a product is profitable, it is most often the case that those who sell the product are interested in repeating the formula that fostered success in the first place—this, at any rate, is the safest route to go if you're in the business of marketing. Madonna is quite aware that she is in this business. But instead of simply *repeating* the product/image formula that gave her success, Madonna chose to repeat it ironically, "making fun" of her "boy toy" self, which so many juvenile women had come to emulate in their own style of dress. That is, she was offering her audience a slightly differentiated Madonna image to keep them coming back for more product. This, as anyone knows, is good business sense.

So after 20 years, Madonna consistently reaps profits. Reinventing herself in almost clockwork fashion, Madonna has transmogrified herself successfully into a virgin, material girl, boy toy, dominatrix, media maven, and working mom. The intricacies of Madonna's genius of reinvention and understanding of the inevitable end of the business cycle have kept her on top of revenue generation. Marketers can learn from this branding expert.

Madonna's outward reinvention is her most dramatic feature, but at the same time she's plugging away at her new spiritualism and lifestyle. Using the Madonna strategy, marketers have several avenues to magnify and reinvent their client's star-celebrity brand. The most important tactics are outlined here:

1. **Communication**—Trailers, Web sites, advertising with graphic uniformity, audience-focused messages, and continuity of message delivery

2. **Audience loyalty**—To maintain loyalty, reinvent and re-analyze the brand's image to address audience perceptions

3. **Failure analysis**—Analyzing and anticipate failure to optimize it and double the brand marketing success rate

4. **Reinvention**—The keys to reinvention are simple:
   a. Die a thousand deaths and come out on the other side.
   b. A star's brand image is money in the bank. Migrate it, don't ever change it.

What do you think?

1. What lessons can entertainment marketers learn from Madonna's transformative branding strategy?

2. What suggestions do you have for her brand maintenance for the next five years?

SOURCES: Unpublished article by Analee Nemitz, English Graduate Student, University of California–Berkeley; Sean De Souza for www.psychotactics.com/artmadona, Dec. 28, 2005.

Cruise's public image began to suffer. Viacom Chairman Sumner Redstone (who fired Cruise) anticipated that Cruise's behavior cost *Mission Impossible III* between $100 and $150 million in ticket sales.[29] Hollywood investors may be less willing to back sometimes-volatile producers like Cruise in the future if the stars' brands are not properly managed.

Brand asset management is one strategy for driving profitable growth from star brands. As developed by Scott Davis,[30] the management process has four phases and eleven steps. Here is a short adaptation of his asset management platform for managing star brands.

Phase One: Develop a Brand Vision

The ultimate vision for most stars and celebrities is to become a household name and to earn as much money as possible. But that's not always the case. Some personalities prefer to remain private (Kevin Spacey) or have as their goal to be recognized for their talent or ability as a performer (Sean Penn). Whatever the vision, agents, marketers, and stars must agree on a single vision that defines the best brand-based strategies to pursue. A brand's vision may determine whether to recreate the brand by repositioning, or to increase its value perception through brand extensions (merchandising, new endeavors).

Phase Two: Determine the Brand's Image

This step is research-driven, and it involves understanding audience perceptions of the star relative to the competition and opportunities for growth. To determine the star's brand image, audience members are asked about: the brands consistency across audience segments, the star's perceived strengths and weaknesses, and what audiences want from the star-brand in the future. By uncovering audience beliefs about a brand, marketers can work toward improving, changing, or maintaining the beliefs.

Phase Three: Develop an Asset Management Strategy

This phase includes determining the right brand-based strategies for achieving the goals set in phase one and from the audience perceptions discovered in phase two. There are four steps to the process.

1. *Establish a unique position.* Should the star be positioned by genre, as is an adventure star such as Sylvester Stallone? Or should the star be positioned as a comedian, such as Jim Carrey? The trick is not to limit the position, but to focus attention on that aspect of the star's abilities so audiences associate that quality with the star within the genre of film or television roles. Stars are sometimes positioned with taglines, such as "Oscar winner" or "Emmy nominee" to enhance the position.

2. *Extend the brand.* Most stars prefer to accept new challenges, such as changing genres, supporting philanthropic causes, or endorsing consumer products. Moving stars beyond their usual role extends both exposure and revenue generation potential for the brand. Brand extenders are discussed in more length in the next section.

3. *Communicate the brand's position.* Communication is about determining the right mix of media and place-based vehicles that will maximize the potential for achieving the image goals. Communication vehicles include advertising, Internet, public relations, and event marketing. All communication should achieve specific and measurable goals.

4.   *Determine the brand's worth.* Not quite a pricing strategy, determining worth involves setting fees for performing, guest appearances, and product endorsements. A factor of the star's popularity, the fees are predicated on the star's talent, the audience size, and the star's compatibility with branded products.

Phase Four: Measure the Return on Brand Investment

Because you cannot manage what you cannot measure, evaluation must be continual and appropriate. Common measures of branding success and star power include but are not limited to:

- Paid attendance as box office receipts
- Media coverage
- Google hits
- Fan base and club activity

▪ ▪ ▪ ▪ ▪ ▪ ▪ ▪ ▪ ▪   **BOX 15-6**   ▪ ▪ ▪ ▪ ▪ ▪ ▪ ▪ ▪ ▪

Focus on Superstar Economics

DO STARS EQUATE TO PROFITS?

A growing number of academics are studying how movies are made, financed, and distributed; most are finding that the studio's assumption that big stars will increase a movie's bottom line is simply wrong. According to a Rutgers economics professor, there is no statistical correlation between stars and success.

The term *superstar economics* was first used to explain the astonishing fees earned by top lawyers and star chief executives. When applied to movies, the dynamic means that improvements in technology that would make it easier for top performers in a field to serve a larger market would not only increase the revenue generated by stars, but would also reduce the revenue available to everybody else. For instance, concert revenue taken by the top 5 percent of artists increased to 84 percent from 62 percent between 1983 and 2003 when MTV, Napster, and iPod extended the reach of top acts.

The Hollywood star system is built on the premise that stars bring many different kinds of benefits: they are easier to market, they help sell more tickets, and they help drive home-video sales. But studio chiefs acknowledge that a star does not guarantee success.

A Harvard professor tried to measure the average effect of a star by analyzing casting announcements on the prices of stocks on the Hollywood Exchange where users trade stocks in movies based on their expected box office revenue. Good predictors of a film's financial success, exchange price analysis suggests that stars, on average, were worth $3 million in theatrical revenue, but have no real impact on the expected profitability of a studio.

The real benefit of using stars? They attract people to movie openings before the buzz of its merits are widely known, and they help launch a film. They also serve as insurance for executives who fear they could be fired for green-lighting a flop.

SOURCE: E. Porter and G. Fabrikant for the *New York Times,* Aug. 28, 2006, C1.

▪ ▪ ▪ ▪ ▪ ▪ ▪ ▪ ▪

- Award nominations
- Special appearances
- Endorsed product sales
- Polling research of audience perceptions of celebrities
- Arbitron, Nielson, and other rating services
- *Q Factor,* which measures the degree of like or dislike by audiences based on familiarity and appeal (see Chapter 7)
- *The Great Dinner Party* question, whose answer discloses which star's party fans prefer to attend (see Chapter 7)

Extending the Star or Celebrity Brand

Keeping the star-celebrity brand alive in a mediated world means constant exposure through as many means as marketing provides. In this section, we discuss media star stories, product endorsements, and political affiliations for their value as brand extensions.

Star Stories as Brand Extensions

Media vehicles are useful for bring stars and celebrities to audiences; biographies made for television broadcast and published as best-sellers give stars depth as "real people." Placement on talk shows, appearances on *Inside the Actors' Studio* (PBS, Bravo), and stints hosting game shows are other vehicles that give a client face time in front of audiences.

Featuring stars as models in magazine fashion layouts presents an opportunity for co-branding between star and fashion brand.

Politics and Brand Extension

Celebrities incorporate themselves into party politics, especially in the U.S. Stars and celebrities are involved with electioneering, fund-raising, lobbying, and so on. Such involvement contributes to the overall professional strategy of marketing celebrities and it gives stars political influence within their party. Some even, run for political office themselves—such as former President Ronald Reagan and California Governor Arnold Schwarzenegger.

Celebrities and stars take up political and philanthropic causes and are known to contribute time and money to emergency situations such as natural disaster, aid for small farmers, global overpopulation, health issues such as AIDS and cancer, and moral considerations such as a woman's right to choose. Celebrities' and stars' media presence in association with a cause brings attention to all forms of global strife and inequities. This is good for the cause and even better for the

Jane Fonda was one of the first actors to use stardom for political purposes.

BOX 15-7

Focus on Marketing Rights

THE LEGAL BATTLE OVER MARILYN

More than 40 years after her death, Marilyn Monroe's photos are used to hawk everything from T-shirts to wine. In 2006, a legal battle over who controls the rights to her profitable image involved more than $30 million in fees for two litigants. Anna Strasberg (wife of former actor and acting coach Lee Strasberg) and her business partner (a professional peddler of dead peoples' images) brought suit against the families of four photographers who had snapped Monroe's pictures, but who had earned far less in licensing fees. Confusion over Monroe's residency at her time of death is a central issue in the case.

Strasberg, majority owner of Monroe's rights of publicity (use of images for commercial purposes) insisted the star was a resident of California. The photographers, who own copyrighted images of the star, asked the courts to declare Monroe a resident of New York. Unlike copyrights, which are protected by federal law, publicity rights are creatures of state law. Monroe was born and grew up in California, but she moved to New York to study acting seven years before her death. In her will, the actress left much of her $800,000 estate to Strasberg and a smaller portion to her psychiatrist.

Strasberg launched her Monroe licensing business in 1982 and hired Los Angeles lawyer Roger Richman to harness publicity rights. Richman helped Strasberg to net more than $7.5 million over 13 years. In 1996, Strasberg dismissed Richman and hired Mark Roesler, owner of Indianapolis-based CMG Worldwide, to manage the Monroe publicity rights. Known as the "king of the dead celebrity business," Roesler also represents the publicity rights of James Dean, the second most valuable dead-star brand.

The greatest threat to Strasberg's control of the Monroe image is the children of the deceased photographers, who licensed her photos to makers of calendars, handbags, and a high-end winery. Strasberg is suing because she alleges some of the children's deals violated Monroe's publicity rights by excluding her from the licensing revenue. The photographers countersued, claiming Strasberg has no right to revenue because Monroe was a New Yorker where publicity rights expire at death. The photographers' children worry that the star's image is fading and manufacturers won't enter into licensing deals if they have to pay fees to two sets of rights holders.

Lawyers for the photographers' families attempted to prove that Monroe's Manhattan apartment, where she lived with Arthur Miller until their 1961 divorce, was her residence at the time of death. Strasberg's lawyers offer proof that Monroe's California residence bears an inscription that reads, "Here my journey ends." At this writing, the trial had not begun.

What do you think?

1. Should publicity rights cease at a star's death?
2. Should federal law supersede state law in this instance?

SOURCE: Nathan Koppel for the *Wall Street Journal,* April 10, 2006.

▮▮▮▮▮▮▮▮▮▮ **BOX 15-8** ▮▮▮▮▮▮▮▮▮▮

MANAGING DEAD CELEBRITY BRANDS

One of the most famous dead celebrity brands, Elvis Presley has, despite being dead, generated revenue from his 13.5-acre Memphis home for the past quarter century.[31] Graceland yielded about $40 million annually, until Robert Silverman, a billionaire media entrepreneur, bought the Elvis brand name and likeness for $100 million in 2005. Silverman's CKX Inc., which acquired 85 percent of Elvis Presley Enterprises, overhauled Graceland, transforming it from a rundown tourist attraction into a destination resort. After demolishing the original Heartbreak Hotel and visitor's center, Silverman built two 400-room hotels, convention space, an entertainment complex, restaurants, shops, an outdoor amphitheater, and a spa. And he will not stop there.

An interactive museum and Elvis theme show have been installed in Las Vegas, as well as a 15,000-square-foot exhibit that travels around the world. With 30 percent of Graceland's visitors coming from abroad, the Elvis franchise will go global by 2009, according to Silverman.

Revenues from Elvis Presley Enterprises in 2005 were generated from licensing and royalties from videos, DVDs, and photos, as well as from a Sirius Satellite Radio station (41 percent); tours and exhibits, including Graceland's 600,000 annual visitors (26 percent); retail operations at Graceland (24 percent); Heartbreak Hotel room revenues (5 percent); and other properties (4 percent). Silverman's investment is testimony to his faith in the Elvis brand's staying power.

▮▮▮▮▮▮▮▮▮

star's image. This marketing strategy is one that should not be ignored when promoting a star or celebrity.

Celebrity Endorsement

Brand producers clamor for the perfect celebrity to endorse their products. Celebrities project their image onto an advertised brand, transforming it from a simple product into an enhanced extension of a famous personality. Celebrities themselves are anxious to receive the exposure advertising provides, to say nothing of the millions of dollars in revenue. This section discusses the dynamics of celebrity endorsement for products, pharmaceuticals, nonprofit causes, and political affiliations.

Studies show that celebrity endorsers make advertisements more believable, enhance the recognition of a brand, create a positive attitude toward the brand, and create a distinct personality for the brand.[32] Evidence suggests that endorsement is most effective in sustaining ad recollection and brand name regardless of the product category.[33] According to advertising research, the economic worth of celebrity endorsers justifies the large costs they incur and makes them worthwhile investments. Research on the impact of celebrity endorsements proves that these contracts are positively associated with financial returns.[34] Consumer familiarity with the celebrity engages consumers at a deeper level; they aspire to be and live as the celebrities do with the products they use.

▪ ▪ ▪ ▪ ▪ ▪ ▪ ▪ ▪ ▪   **BOX 15-9**   ▪ ▪ ▪ ▪ ▪ ▪ ▪ ▪ ▪ ▪

Focus on Ethics

CELEBRITIES DEALING DRUGS

An epicenter of the celebrity endorsement phenomenon is pharmaceutical companies hiring celebrities to attract attention to the latest drugs and the diseases the drugs are produced to treat. The use of celebrities has become integral to a drug marketing strategy that includes paid advertising and aggressive public relations campaigns. Wyeth hired supermodel Lauren Hutton to hawk hormone replacement therapy for menopause. GlaxoSmithKline (GSK) contracted football star Ricky Williams to call attention to social anxiety disorder, helping make Paxil the world's top-selling antidepressant. Celebrities also plug drugs by appearing on programs such as *The Oprah Winfrey Show* and *The Today Show*. According to celebrity brokers, the stars' remuneration packages, though always confidential, can range from $20,000 to $2 million.[35]

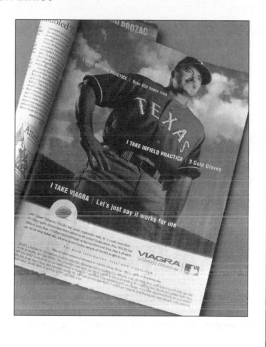

According to a senior marketing executive at Amgen, a Californian biotech firm, an Amgen study indicated that partnerships between a celebrity and a brand have an intangible magic.[36] Amgen hired *West Wing* star Rob Lowe to help market its anti-infection drug; Lowe was reportedly paid more than $1 million by the company. To be effective, pharmaceutical marketing must use an A-list celebrity, find a "news-hook" that links the celebrity and the product, develop simple messages, and ensure the celebrity delivers the message at every appearance.

On-air talk-show appearances on top-tier media venues such as *Oprah* can be better forums for celebrities than if they were hired to appear in straightforward advertisements, which are governed by regulations. The great advantage to celebrity endorsement over advertising is that the airtime is practically free, and there is no fair balance (equal time for candidates) to worry about. The downside of a media interview is that it is less controllable than a scripted ad. It can be tricky for the celebrity to ensure that all product messages are delivered during an interview.

When hiring celebrities to push products, advertisers are wise to rate prospective hires with a Q Score, which is related to the Q Factor and a measure of their likeability and recognizability with the public. (Apparently, Lowe's Q Score was high with women over 50, a key target of the Amgen campaign.[37]) Similarly, a recent report from within the industry indicates that drug marketers draw on

(Continued)

public opinion survey data to guide drug company marketers on the selection and "effective use" of celebrity spokespersons.[38] The survey was conducted by a Seattle firm called NexCura Inc., in partnership with the trade magazine that published the study. The survey's major findings echo the Amgen study's insights about credibility and underline the importance of a star being perceived as both generally trustworthy and specifically knowledgeable about the condition on which they are hired to speak. Perhaps not surprisingly, the survey found that people diagnosed as suffering chronic conditions were far more attentive to celebrity messages on health than were the general public.

NexCura researchers stress that the issue of credibility is important because the star's credibility rating is used as an indicator for buying behavior—an intermediate measure of whether the star can persuade people to request the target drug from their doctors. The survey found that Bob Dole was still the most recognizable celebrity marketer with the United States public at that time, but that figure skater Dorothy Hamill—who promoted Merck's arthritis medication Vioxx—took the lead in the credibility stakes. Significantly, though, almost 75 percent of those surveyed were correctly able to identify Dole with Pfizer's Viagra, despite the fact that the advertisements in which he appeared were unbranded ads for erectile dysfunction. The researchers concluded by recommending that drug companies choose a celebrity with personal experience of the target condition; who is trustworthy, perhaps a newsreader or sports figure; and who will promote a single cause or brand rather than multiple ones.

What do you think?

1. What ethical issues are present with celebrity endorsements of pharmaceuticals?

2. If you were a star's agent, how would you advise him or her regarding an appearance for a specific drug? Why?

Matching celebrities with brands is usually a function of the advertiser, but agents often solicit specific brands for their celebrity clients. The most important factor of successful endorsement is the celebrity-audience match-up. Boomers respond to stars such as Candice Bergen and Alan Alda, who had similar backgrounds, while younger adults are likely to emulate Tiger Woods or Mary Louise Parker, who represent attractive lifestyles. Kermit the Frog is perfect for endorsing milk when kids are targeted. Match-ups between celebrity and brand also are important; products must be something the star could be perceived as using for obvious self-benefit—Woods and TAG Heuer watches, for instance. Proper match-ups establish celebrity credibility with target audiences and maximize cross-promotional opportunities.

Celebrity-brand matches differ by level of consumer product involvement. Routinely selected products that are usually lower in cost—toothpaste, cosmetics—require little consumer involvement in the purchase process. Products that carry more risk (i.e., an incorrect choice means considerable loss of money or esteem)—cars, travel—require a high level of consumer involvement before making a purchase selection. As we learned in Chapter 10, some entertainment content is sold using a rational approach by providing information; other content relies on emotion to drive the purchase, and these are advertised using a transformational approach. The trick is matching the star to the correct approach.

	Informational Ads	*Transformational Ads*
Low involvement	Expertise	Likeability
High involvement	Objectivity	Similarity

Low-involvement products that require information are best suited to celebrities with product expertise; motor oil should be endorsed by a NASCAR driver. Low-involvement products sold with emotion need likable celebrities to be effective; Bill Cosby sold a lot of Jell-O. High-involvement products that need to be sold by providing information should seek objective celebrities; a travel show host is a good choice to recommend a hotel brand. Emotionally sold high-involvement products are best promoted by celebrities who are similar to the audience segment; an actor playing an attorney on *Law and Order* may be right to sell a life insurance brand.

The only real problem with product endorsement for celebrities and stars is overkill; redundancy can turn off the viewing public when a single personality is associated with too many products. Credibility levels drop for both the product and the endorser when a personality has multiple brand associations.

Valuing Celebrities

The arcane field of measuring celebrity appeal yields Q Scores that tell advertisers and media outlets how much the public likes actors, news anchors, and sports figures.[39] Q Scores are prepared by Marketing Evaluations of Manhasset, New York, which uses mail surveys to ask groups of people, selected from a 100,000-name database, about celebrities' likeability and familiarity.

A push from marketers for more-detailed research on the effectiveness of advertising resulted in a services offered through Omnicom's Davie-Brown entertainment marketing operation. Known as the Davie-Brown Index, the measure is based on regular surveys of people drawn from a 1.5 million-member research panel provided by i.think, a Dallas online market-research firm. The survey is presented four times a year and includes a list of more than 1,500 celebrities. Respondents are asked whether they view each famous person as being a trendsetter, trustworthy, and influential, and whether the celebrity's endorsement of a product would be believable. The Davie-Brown Index uses eight criteria for its evaluation: appeal, notice, trend setting, influence, trust, endorsement, aspiration, and awareness.

The index's resulting scores enable advertisers and ad agency personnel to determine whether a particular public figure will motivate consumers who see them in an ad to purchase the product advertised. As noted before, one of the risks of celebrity endorsement is overexposure, so number of previous endorsements is a prime consideration for valuing celebrity brands. Other measuring devices include e-polls and focus groups in which people react to actual commercials featuring celebrities.

Celebrities and Cause Marketing

Celebrities can bring visibility, credibility, and attract media attention to *cause marketing campaigns.* Successfully contacting, negotiating, and working with celebrities requires

▪▪▪▪▪▪▪▪▪ **BOX 15-10** ▪▪▪▪▪▪▪▪▪

Focus on Fashion

CELEBRITIES AND LUXURY FASHION BRANDS

The use of celebrity endorsement is especially valuable to brands in the luxury fashion sector, which have doubled in the past 10 years. Versace (Italy) has used Madonna, Demi Moore, and Halle Berry in its print ads; Gianfranco Ferre has hired Julia Roberts to appeared in its ads; and Vuitton ads have featured Jennifer Lopez, Scarlett Johansson, and Uma Thurman (pictured).

Celebrity endorsements are important to luxury brands for the following reasons:

• Brand awareness for new luxury brands
• Positioning and reposition existing brands
• Sustaining a brand's aura
• Revive and revitalize staid brands
• Generate PR leverage and opportunities for brands
• Create global brand awareness
• Promote a brand's products and appeal.

Although the most widely used method of using celebrities to endorse brands is paid-for media advertisements in fashion magazines and TV, additional ways include the following:

• Using products in movies and TV programs (*Legally Blond II* and *Sex and the City* for Jimmy Choo)
• Hosting fashion spreads at different events and locations

• Using products from a brand in promotion photographs
• Mentioning brands in music lyrics
• Inviting celebrities to be co-creators and partners in designing specific products
• Naming products after celebrities

Celebrity endorsement transfers the personality and status of the celebrity as successful, wealthy, and distinctive directly to the brand. To achieve maximum impact, matching a celebrity with the right brand should adhere to these five rules:

1. **Credibility**—high level of talent or expertise in a field (George Clooney and Tiger Woods)
2. **Global appeal**—known worldwide and appreciated by majority of people in the consumer and fashion society (Charlize Theron and Halle Berry)
3. **Personality**—celebrity and brand personalities must match in a positive way (Nicole Kidman for Chanel)
4. **Uniform power**—celebrity must not overshadow the brand
5. **Constancy**—celebrity must have lasting power, maintaining high appeal after the campaign is over

Public controversies and professional or personal circumstances that compromise the celebrity's image also compromise the brand. Marketers are urged to use caution and do their research before signing a celebrity to endorse an entertainment brand.

SOURCE: Uche Okonkwo for brandchannel.com, April 7, 2006.

▪▪▪▪▪▪▪▪▪

critical research and specialized rules of protocol, according to the president of The Celebrity Source, Inc. The firm has partnered Kareem Abdul-Jabbar with Energizer Batteries and the International Fire Chiefs Association, and Robert Guillaume was paired with Quaker Oatmeal and the American Heart Association, among many others.

Being Global

Although Hollywood is the most influential industry within the global film economy, the operation of stardom exists in other large markets, most notably in East and South Asia. Thanks to careful marketing, Jackie Chan became a global phenomenon in the late 1990s. Indian screen legend Amitabh Bachchan has starred in popular Hindi cinema since the 1970s. The large number of cinemagoers in India and distribution of Bachchan's vehicles in markets as diverse as Africa and Russia make him a globally recognizable star.

Stardom also has played an important part of the popular cinemas of Europe, although some European film still suffers from its equation with art-house productions.

Nowhere is the age of celebrity more apparent than in London, where celebrity faces and magazine titles take up most of the space in newspaper stalls. Celebrity sells everywhere, as reflected in London's rise as one of the main hubs of the international celebrity and marketeering circus.[40] Because English is the common language of the UK and U.S., major studios choose London for their international premieres and press junkets. However, the city's notorious tabloid press poses some dangers for visiting stars, making it just as hard to stay out of the tabloids as it is to get into them.

The tabloid business has become an entertainment industry in its own right. Its business model has two distinguishing features. First, celebrity has become the product—rather than just a device for marketing films. The talent owes its standing chiefly to the celebrity machine and not to any particular gift. It therefore depends on the attentions of the press to make money. Second, celebrities, agents, photographers and picture desks have found that the most efficient way to create an endless supply of celebrity news is to work together. A business that used to be based on intrusion has discovered a preference for collaboration.

The tabloid business is also expanding abroad. Northern & Shell, a British publishing conglomerate, launched an American edition of *OK!*, a celebrity magazine that already has Australian, Chinese, and Middle Eastern editions. The *National Enquirer,* a hard-nosed American scandal sheet famed for pushing back the boundaries of taste—and of free speech—was relaunched in 2005 stuffed with alumni of British tabloids and magazines.[41]

Media management is a global phenomenon. Developed in symbiosis with newly aggressive modes of reporting and newsgathering, *spin* is now so widespread across so

Bollywood star Aishwarya Rai is known throughout the world for her international films.

many national media systems that its power has become universal. Management of public personae has become a core activity not only for entertainment, but for contemporary politics as well. Strategies for both are derived from public relations models of crisis management or from the celebrity industry's methods for building the public identity of the celebrity commodity.

FINALLY: LET'S SUM UP ▪▪▪▪▪▪▪

Marketing celebrity and star brands involves the same skills and strategies needed to successfully market products. Audiences are fickle and must be constantly reminded of a personality's presence. Spin, gossip, and hype are the tools of the publicity trade for movie and television marketers. And, given the large amounts of capital invested in star-power, marketers' tactics must justify the bottom-line costs spent on manufacturing celebrity.

With a celebrity society in place, there is plenty of opportunity for alliance between that culture and all forms of celebrity marketing. Advertising, public relations, agentry, event promotion, and media relations are among the businesses most involved with celebrity management.

GOT IT? LET'S REVIEW ▪▪▪▪▪▪▪

- Stardom is a condition based on a thriving economy and social mobility; the star system includes audience demands on the industry, movie distributors, and exhibitors, all of whom rely on the selling power of stars for their success.
- Celebrities are commodities traded by media industries; mostly, they are television personalities who play themselves; factors of fame include exhibitionism, charisma, drive, and names.
- Most celebrity audience members are game players who get pleasure from social exchange of gossip and media-generated stories about famous people; fans construct para-social relationships with stars and celebrities.
- Celebrity branding strategies include pure selling, product improvement, and market fulfillment; brand asset management is a strategy that drives profitable growth for star and celebrity brands.
- Marketers coordinate celebrity endorsers with qualities of expertise, objectivity, likeability, and similarity with the audience's level of involvement with a product or brand.

NOW TRY THIS ▪▪▪▪▪▪▪

1. Visit a Borders or Barnes & Noble bookstore magazine section and inventory the periodicals focused on celebrities and stars. Peruse them to see what products are advertised in them. What do the products tell you about the readership of these magazines? What do the story titles tell you about what fans want to know?
2. Using your favorite movie star as a subject, use Google and star-based Web sites to trace his or her career. How much of what you read is generated by the star's publicist?

How much is reported by news media? What other sources provide star information? What can you conclude about marketing strategies for your star from this investigation?

3. Using your favorite television celebrity as an example, suggest several products that she or he might be likely to endorse. Poll 10 of your friends and see which product they would be most likely to purchase if endorsed by your celebrity choice. Which of the match-up criteria are most appropriate

to their selections: expertise, likeability, objectivity, or similarity?

4. Invoke your creativity to develop a reality show that is designed to bring members of a baby boomer audience segment into the public eye. What would the prizes be? Who would host the show? How might the winning contestants be manufactured into celebrities?

QUESTIONS: LET'S REVIEW ▐▐▐▐▐▐▐

1. Make the best match-up between stars/celebrities/personalities and products from the list below and provide a rationale for your choice. Answers follow.

   1. Musician P. Diddy
   2. Athlete Lance Armstrong
   3. TV show host Oprah Winfrey
   4. CNN reporter Anderson Cooper
   5. Former president Bill Clinton
   6. Author J. K. Rowling
   7. Actor Johnny Depp
   8. Radio show host Howard Stern
   9. Comedian Dave Chappelle
   10. Actor Kate Hudson

   a. Mont Blanc watch
   b. American Express
   c. L'Oreal hair color
   d. Nature Power Bar
   e. Sony electronics
   f. Motorola Razr mobile phone
   g. Oliver Peeples eyeglass frames
   h. Red Cross
   i. Bose speakers
   j. Xerox copy machines

   Answers to Question 1: 1–f, 2–d, 3–b, 4–g, 5–h, 6–j, 7–a, 8–e, 9–i, 10–c

2. How can the Internet be maximized to brand a star or celebrity? Which branding principles apply to this strategy?

3. How would you differentiate branding a film star or television celebrity from branding a sports or music personality? How are they different from mediated personalities?

4. Are stars better off without the studio system? What did they lose and gain from the demise of studio-based contracts?

5. Using criteria such as salary, endorsements, appearances, etc., calculate the approximate worth of a star or celebrity brand. How would you manage this asset over the next five years? What brand extensions would you consider?

MORE TO READ ▐▐▐▐▐▐▐

Thomas Austin and Martin Barker. *Contemporary Hollywood Stardom.* London: Hodder Arnold, 2003.

Richard Dyer. *Stars.* London: British Film Institute, 1998.

Andrew Evans and Dr. Glenn Wilson. *Fame: The Psychology of Stardom.* London: Satin Publications Ltd., 1999.

Joshua Gameson. *Claims to Fame: Celebrity in Contemporary America.* Berkeley CA: University of California Press, 1994.

Paul McDonald. *The Star System: Hollywood's Production of Popular Identities.* Thousand Oaks CA: Sage, 2004.

Irving Rein, Philip Kotler, Michael Hamlin, and Martin Stoller. *High Visibility: The Making and Marketing of Professionals into Celebrities,* 3rd ed. New York: McGraw-Hill, 2006.

Andy Willis (ed.). *Film Stars: Hollywood and Beyond.* London: Manchester University Press, 2004.

NOTES ▪▪▪▪▪▪▪

1. Francesco Alberoni, "The Powerless Elite" (University of Milan, Italy, 1963), p. 75.
2. www.studymedia.co.uk/hollywood_studio_system.htm, downloaded Dec. 27, 2005.
3. Paul McDonald, *The Star System* (Wallflower, 2000), p. 5.
4. J. Stacey, *Star Gazing: Hollywood Cinema and Female Spectatorship* (Routledge, 1994), pp. 85–153.
5. Richard Dyer, *Stars* (British Film Institute, London, 1998), p. 34.
6. McDonald, p. 93.
7. Dyer, p. 62.
8. Jonathan Burke, "Make Movies, Not War," *Red Herring,* January 1998.
9. *Ibid.*
10. Dave Itzkoff for the *New York Times,* Dec. 27, 2005.
11. Louis Menand, "The Iron Law of Stardom," *New Yorker Magazine,* March 24, 1997.
12. Graeme Turner, *Understanding Celebrity* (Sage, 2004), p. 9.
13. Andrew Evans and Glenn Wilson, *Fame: The Psychology of Stardom* (Satin Publication, 1999), p. 45.
14. *Ibid.,* p. 51.
15. Rob Walker for the *New York Times,* June 12, 2005.
16. Samuel Blake, "From Hollywood, For Our Eyes Only," *New Statesman* 133 (2004), issue 4709, 16.
17. Walker.
18. Louise Story for the *New York Times,* June 13, 2005.
19. Chris Noon for *Forbes Magazine,* Dec. 22, 2005.
20. Leo Handel, *Hollywood Looks at Its Audience: A Report of Film Audience Research* Urbana IL: University of Illinois Press, 1976).
21. Andrew Tudor, as presented in Richard Dyer's *Stars,* p. 18.
22. A. Bandura, *Social Learning Theory* (Prentice-Hall, 1977).
23. Developed by J. Gamson, *Claims to Fame: Celebrity in Contemporary America* (University of California Press, 1994), p. 147.
24. C. Rojek, *Celebrity.* (Reaktion, 2001).
25. J. Frow, "Is Elvis a God? Cult, Culture and Questions of Method," *International Journal of Cultural Studies* 1 (2) (1998), pp. 197–210.
26. Irving Rein, Philip Kotler, Michael Manlin, and Martin Stoller, *High Visibility: Transforming your Personal and Professional Brand,* 3rd ed. (McGraw-Hill, 2006), p. 46.
27. *Ibid.*
28. Merissa Marr and Kate Kelly for the *Wall Street Journal,* Aug. 24, 2006, p. 1.
29. Merissa Marr for the *Wall Street Journal,* Aug. 23, 2006, p. 1.
30. Scott Davis, *Brand Asset Management: Driving Profitable Growth Through Your Brands* (Jossey-Bass, 2000).
31. Julie Bosman, "The King's Legacy, All Shook Up," *New York Times,* March 5, 2006.
32. J. Agrawal and W. Kumakura, "The Economic Worth of Celebrity Endorsers," *Journal of Marketing* 59 (1995), 56–68.
33. H. Friedman and L. Friedman, "Endorser Effectiveness of Product Type," *Journal of Advertising Research* 19 (1979), 63–71.
34. Agrawal and Kumakura.
35. Ray Moynihan, "Intangible Magic of Celebrity Marketing," *POLS Medicine* 2 (Nov. 2004).
36. O. Benshoshan, "Celebrity Public Relations: An Alternative to DTC," *DTC Perspectives,* Nov. 2004.
37. D. Hamilton, "Celebrities Help 'Educate' Public on New Drugs," *Wall Street Journal,* April 22, 2002.
38. NexCura and DTC Perspectives, "Effective Use of Celebrities in DTC Promotions of Pharmaceutical Products," *DTC Perspectives* 2 (2003).
39. Brian Steinberg's "Advertising" column in the *Wall Street Journal,* Feb. 13, 2006.
40. Hatja Hoffman, reporting in "Inside London" for *Variety,* Sept. 26–Oct. 2, 2005.
41. *Economist,* Sept. 1, 2005.

■ ■ ■ ■ ■ ■ ■ ■ ■ C A S E S ■ ■ ■ ■ ■ ■ ■ ■ ■ ■

Case 1   Funding a Capital Campaign

Orange County Performing Arts Center

When the Orange County Performing Arts Center (OCPAC) opened in 1986, recent Pepperdine University graduate Todd Bentjen volunteered to be part of the new venue's staff. Twenty years later, during a second grand opening in September 2006, Bentjen was still with the center—but as Vice President of Marketing and Communications. Bentjen's most challenging task those years he has been with the center was directing the $200 million capital campaign in 2005 to fund two new auditoriums that completed the center's campus complex.

On a daily basis, the planning, building, and maintenance of a performing arts center is a formidable task. As with most other arts organizations, ticket sales never cover the costs of a venue and its performers. Inherent in the successful operation of an arts center is the ability to develop innovative and bold activities that generate funds to support performances. When a capital campaign is added to those duties, marketing must double its efforts to connect a vibrant organization with the community and its publics.

Celebrating its twentieth anniversary with the opening of new performance buildings, the Orange County, California, venue exemplified the struggles and successes of similar organizations throughout the country.

The efforts of Bentjen and his marketing staff are chronicled here to show how performing arts venues and capital campaigns are conducted.

History

The center began 45 years ago as the Orange County Philharmonic Society. A feasibility study conducted for the Society in 1972 determined that a successful Orange County (OC) arts center would have to be built on site near a confluence of freeways on donated land. In 1979, a board member contacted real estate mogul Henry Segerstrom to request that he donate the five-acre plot of land adjacent to South Coast Repertory's recently opened Fourth Step Theater.

To help the community establish a cultural identity, the Segerstrom family agreed to gift the land and pledged $1 million for the design and construction of a new hall. Site evaluation, market research studies, and fund-raising strategies were developed. Concurrently, the center's financial structure was put in place. The Guild, a system of volunteers who support the center, made up of 33 chapters through the county, raised operational funds. A Building Fund Campaign offered an additional $5 million gift as a challenge grant, and groundbreaking took place on July 7, 1983. Three years later, Segerstrom Hall, one of the nation's most acoustically innovative and advanced homes for the performing arts, opened with a gala extravaganza featuring soprano Leontyne Price and the Los Angeles Philharmonic Orchestra.

Mission and Organization

The organization's goals reflect the center's dedication to excellence in performance, education, and venue operation: The center's *mission* is to:

1. present best performances of symphony, dance, theater, and opera.
2. broaden the level of understanding, appreciation, and support for the arts through meaningful education initiatives and community partnerships.
3. operate, maintain, and endow the multipurpose facility in accordance with the highest professional standards for both audience and performing arts.

Brand equity resides in all three aspects of the center—performance, education, and venue.

Performances are rich, varied, and of world-class quality, as this abbreviated list of examples illustrates.

• *Dance companies*—American Ballet Theater, Bolshoi Ballet, Dance Theater of Harlem, Joffrey Ballet, Martha Graham Dance Company, Merce Cunningham Dance Company, New York City Ballet, Paris Opera Ballet, Paul Taylor Dance Company, Royal Ballet, and White Oak Dance Project

• *Broadway musicals*—42nd Street, A Chorus Line, Annie, Beauty and the Beast, Big, Cabaret, Camelot, CATS, Chicago, The Lion King, Evita, FAME, Footloose, Fosse, Grand Hotel, Grease, Jesus Christ Superstar, Kiss of the Spider Woman, Les Miserables, Little Shop of Horrors, Mamma Mia!, Miss Saigon,

Oliver!, RENT, Riverdance, Saturday Night Fever, and the Who's Tommy

• *Cabaret and Songbook Series*—Betty Buckley, David Campbell, Diahann Carroll, Cy Coleman Trio, Rita Coolidge, Forbidden Broadway, Jack Jones, Sally Kellerman, Eartha Kitt, Diana Krall, Michele Less, Hal Linden, Melissa Manchester, Leslie Uggams, and Tom Wopat

• *Concert Series*—Academy of Ancient Music, Australian Chamber Orchestra, Bartok Quartet, Debussy Trio, Emanuel Ax, L'Ensemble Pennetier, Mendelssohn String Quartet, Midori, Salzberg Chamber Soloists, Tokyo String Quartet, and Uncommon Ritual

• *Jazz Series*—Al Jarreau, Dianne Reeves, Billy Childs Quartet, Branford Marsalis Quartet, Count Bassie Quartet, Cyrus Chestnut, Dave Brubeck Quartet, Kiana Krall, Dizzy Gillespie Orchestra, Herbie Hancock, Mel Torme and George Shearing, Michael Brecker, Miles Davis, Ray Charles, Tito Puente, Tuck & Patti, Tony Bennett, and Wynton Marsalis

• *Special events*—Bill Cosby, Bobby Short, Bonnie Raitt, Boston Pops, Carl Reiner, Chicago, Chris Isaak, Dennis Miller, Jay Leno, Jerry Seinfeld, Julio Iglesias, k.d. lang, Lily Tomlin, Minnie Driver, Olivia Newton-John, Natalie Cole, Rosemary Clooney, Sesame Street Live, Tom Conway, and Harvey Korman

• *Spotlight Series*—Tony Bennett, Bill Cosby, Bebe Neuwirth, and Tommy Tune and the Manhattan Rhythm Kings

• *Up Close at the Center*—Carl Reiner and Julie Andrews

Arts research has continually proven that adults who received arts education as children were more likely to attend performances than adults who had no prior arts education. To ensure a continuing audience resource, educational programs became a key element of the center's mission. One of

OCPAC's most valuable products is its *educational program,* which provides educational activities for the entire community. A sampling of the programs include:

• *Family Series*—interactive performances for kids of all ages

• *Arts Teach*—arts-in-education program taking live performances from around the globe to local schools and community centers

• *Teacher Professional Development*—five-day intensive summer institute and seminars and workshops during the fall, winter, and spring.

• *ArtsConnect*—long-term partnership between five OC schools and the center that integrates the arts across all areas of curriculum and instruction

• *On Stage*—live performances for local students

• *Masters* classes that allow students to interact with artists

• *Tomorrow's Stars*—format for recognizing young artists for talent in dance, instrumental, jazz, voice, and musical theater

• *Summer Arts*—two-week musical theater program

• *Overture*—20-week musical theater course led by professional teaching artists for selected elementary school special education students

The *venue,* designed by the architectural firm of Caudill Rowlett Scott of Houston, Texas, integrates acoustics and architecture in a unified manner. Currently serving as center president, Terrence Dwyer previously directed the Tony Award-winning Alley Theater in Houston. With an MA degree from the Yale School of Drama, Dwyer's play development program resulted in the production of more than 31 world premieres, seven American premieres, and workshops showing 18 new plays for the La Jolla Playhouse in California. Dwyer oversees current and new venues, which include a 2,000-seat auditorium and a 500-seat space, each designed to reflect and reinforce the center's original structure. With more than 100 employees, the center operates year-round to serve the community.

The center's most valuable resource is a collection of active *support groups.* Financial support from community and business member groups is essential for the successful operation and capital improvement efforts of OCPAC. These are the center's key organizations:

• *The Guilds*—a network of individuals committed to encouraging appreciation of the arts to raise awareness of and financial support for the center; 31 chapters plus a youth chapter sponsor community events and fund-raisers

• *Bravo!*—a group of early to mid-career professionals who take an active role in OC's cultural scene, offering support through membership dues; members may volunteer, network, and host special events for the center

• *Docents*—volunteer who give guided public tours of the center; lead more than 3,000 children and adults each year on tours

• *Business partnerships*—business owners and key executives who support the center in exchange for special access, privileges, and recognition

• *Stars*—a group organized around shared interest in and commitment to the arts who entertain center members and friends; support through initiation fees and annual dues

• *Angels*—members who symbolize and promote performing arts through cultural and social activities, as well as initiation fees and dues

• *Founders Plus*—original supporters who provide experiences for the underserved through ticket distribution and educational programs; fund-raising efforts support the endowment fund

The Capital Campaign
Development of a Performing Arts Center Complex

The center's two venue halls are booked for performances, rehearsals, and maintenance nearly every day of the year. Plans for additional venues were needed and called for by the board of directors, who decided to explore the possibility of expansion. In 1999, the project was kicked off with a six-acre parcel across the street from the existing facility, which was donated to the center by the Segerstrom family to provide space for the expansion of the South Coast Repertory, new venues, and the eventual building of a visual arts campus using the Segerstrom name.

A year later, the Segerstrom family provided a $40 million lead gift to the capital campaign. The 2,000-seat concert hall and 500-seat multi-use theater and education center opened in the fall of 2006. An outdoor plaza also will join the existing 3,000-seat and 500-seat halls, making the center one of the nation's largest and most versatile complexes dedicated to the arts. The center's capital campaign, *Building on the Vision,* funded the $200 million expansion project. Designed by internationally respected architect Cesar Pelli, the plaza incorporates a major work of art by Richard Serra. In September 2006, a six-week festival of great artists, world premieres, and galas opened the new halls and celebrated the center's twentieth anniversary.

With a goal of $200 million, OCPAC's efforts extended across all community groups, businesses, and organizations. Large donations, however, were cultivated on a person-to-person basis by board members, who donated their time and effort to the campaign. To generate smaller donations, seat names could be purchased for $500 to $1,000, depending on their auditorium location.

Marketing Strategies

Unlike other venues, performing arts centers require a special breed of marketing strategies, specifically those focusing on fundraising, event promotion, and public relations activities. For OCPAC, Todd Bentjen focused on the venue itself—its past greatness that is extending into a new era. Because the center was a developed brand, the task at hand was expanding the brand's image.

The four Ps structured the marketing programs: *product* as performances; *place* as a retail and entertainment venue located adjacent to major freeways in Orange County, a 2,000-square-mile area with a population of 3 million; *price* as a range of charges from student and group discounts to luxury box seat tickets; *promotion* as a mix of internal and external communication, media advertising (radio, TV, print), Web site purchasing capabilities, and public relations.

Demographic Data

Orange County demographics, as reported by 2004 census data, suggest that the center has a viable audience population:

  64.8% white
  31% Latino
  14% other
  13.6 Asian
  1.7% African American
  0.7% Native American

Because the average home price in OC is in excess of $700,000, residents have the affluence and ability to attend and support arts programs. In addition, educational levels average college-level degrees, suggesting that performance arts are desirable entertainment options for OC residents.

Marketing Responsibilities

Bentjen concurrently marketed regular performances and promoted the capital campaign. "With 80 campaigns and 300 performances a year, we must maintain a synergy and excitement for all our subscribers and new audience members," he emphasized.

To attract new audiences, a new program called Opera in the Raw was created. It presents operatic arias in a casual setting that invites younger people to enjoy them with their friends. Symphony Outreach is a program that travels to nonvenue locations, and subscriptions are customized to suit every viewer's needs. One example of some of the other occasional highlights available is the *Dr. Doolittle Company,* an original review presented to a select audience of 250 people late on a Saturday night.

To maintain quality control, the center conducts regular program surveys and participates in the League of American Theaters' study for venues nationwide. To learn more about the center's potential and opportunities, 800 phone interviews and 40 one-hour depth interviews were conducted with both subscribers and occasional patrons to determine attitudes and perceptions, likes and dislikes.

What is the competition for the Orange County Performing Arts Center? As Bentjen says, it is "everything." All forms of entertainment, including computer games and sports, compete for entertainment dollars. The best way to recruit audiences is to get new audience members into the venue for a performance. And to that end, the center develops extensive communication vehicles.

Communication Strategies

According to Bentjen, messages are developed to resonate with community segments. Arts organizations must communicate with all of their publics—patrons, donors, subscribers, employees, community businesses, corporate sponsors, media, local governments, and the National Endowment for the Arts. Newsletters, annual reports, Web sites, subscription information, and publicity vehicles are needed to reach those publics with timely and pertinent information. Here are the primary vehicles produced by the center:

• *Revue*—a monthly magazine that previews upcoming events, profiles performers, spotlights donors, and provides a schedule of performances

• *Playbills*—produced in house and distributed to 30,000 visitors by the center for each performance

• *Web site* visitors were able to watch the new building materialize, book seats, and learn about volunteer opportunities

• *Advertising*—radio, television, and print ads are purchased for each new performance

• *Publicity/PR*—releases sent to entertainment editors; feature articles placed in business, arts, and community sections of local and regional newspapers (for example, articles on earthquake testing performed on new building's glass for a 10.0 quake and a category 5 hurricane)

• *Venue*—tours for school and college groups

Three months before the grand opening and the center's twentieth anniversary celebration, just over $130 million had been donated to the capital campaign. A musical program starring Placido Domingo was set, and the Gala Opening Weekend was planned; its 16 performances included a world premiere by composer Philip Glass, an American-Russian jazz festival, the Kirov Ballet's *Romeo & Juliet,* Wagner's *The Ring* opera, and rock artist Sheryl Crow.

2005 Financial Report

For the fiscal year that ended June 30, 2005, the report demonstrates the center's consistently solid financial performance. The 2006 statement also reflects progress of the *Building on the Vision* campaign for the expansion of the center, with $126 million in cash and pledge contributions recorded through June 30, 2005.

Total assets $418,299,656

Total liabilities $204,747,576

Program revenues less expenses ($10,509,570)

Net assets at end of year $213,552,080

Net cash provided by operating activities $26,570,851

Net cash used in investing activities ($80,375,609)

Net cash provided by financing activities $172,882,855

Net increase in cash and cash equivalents $119,078,097

Cash and cash equivalents, beginning of year $26,229,287

Cash and cash equivalents, end of year $145,307,384

Fixed assets at June 30, 2005, consist of the following:

Land $10,605,607
Building—Theater I $61,020,025
Equipment and furniture $15,745,200
Construction in progress—new performing arts venue $146,049,580
Fine arts $1,100,000
Total $234,520,412
Less: accumulated depreciation ($40,052,774) $194,467,638

Near the capital campaign's conclusion in 2007, Bentjen focused his attention on maintaining excitement for the upcoming programs and anticipated support of subscribers for the current performance season. Yet, another $70 million was needed to complete the capital campaign, and Bentjen had to devote some of his resources to promoting the Grand Opening festivities. In June 2006, Bentjen said, "I'm confident that we'll reach our goal, and that the community will ensure our success."

What do you think?

1. What new media could have been invoked to market the Orange County Performing Arts Center to prospective audiences?

2. Are the public relations efforts sufficient to generate public support for the center? What additions can you suggest?

3. What advertising efforts can be invoked outside traditional media to promote the center?

4. How can the center reward major donors and attract new ones?

Source: Todd Bentjen, VP Marketing & Communications, OCPAC, May 2006.

Case 2   Evolving The Ritz-Carlton Brand

Damien Smith had just been assigned as the account executive for The Ritz-Carlton Hotel Company, L.L.C., a client of his advertising agency, Foremost Inc. As account executive, Smith was responsible for managing The Ritz-Carlton Hotel production of print advertising for the Northeast and Southeast regions of the United States, and Caribbean. His assignment: to manage the alignment of the individual hotel property advertising with a new look for the brand's advertising.

The Situation

As a result of extensive research conducted by The Ritz-Carlton in 2005, the hotel company determined that its image, as portrayed through its advertising, was not in keeping with the company's desired positioning in the luxury category. Its customers had grown older, and younger business travelers and resort visitors were not responding to the image of what they perceived to be their parents' hotel. So, The Ritz-Carlton hired Foremost to develop a new national advertising strategy and produce creative executions to effectively change the image of the brand.

After reviewing the traditional print advertising for competitive luxury hotel corporations, Foremost decided to break away from the hotel advertising norm of *brick and mortar* imagery, which focuses on pictures of rooms, pools, and hotel architecture. With a relatively small global advertising budget, estimated at $10 million to $15 million by the *Wall Street Journal,* the new communication goal for the brand was to position The Ritz-Carlton as a luxury lifestyle leader offering experiences and values sought after by affluent consumers — regardless of age.

The hotel industry quickly reflects changes in economies because it is the type of business in which techniques, ideas, and modes of operation undergo continual alteration and evaluation. If a hotel remains static, it deteriorates. The famous New York Ritz, for instance, was a landmark building that housed a hallmark of service; yet because it did not keep up with the times, within 40 years it was obsolete and had to be torn down nearly 25 years ago. Foremost knew that not only must the physical space of a hotel be continually upgraded, but also that its brand image was vulnerable to deterioration and had to be updated as well.

In 2005, The Ritz-Carlton Hotel directed its efforts toward improving communication between the hotel and young, affluent consumers who perceived this luxury hotel brand as belonging to a mature demographic. Foremost's challenge was to change the perception of the brand and appeal to a younger demographic through a

relevant advertising campaign. Smith wondered how the revered brand could be repositioned to appeal to younger generations, especially considering the intense competition from other luxury hotel offerings in the marketplace. Because younger consumers have more wealth today than their counterparts in previous generations, they comprise a large target audience for luxury products. Many argue that similar products and services tend to be more or less equal, so consumers ultimately purchase what they believe is the brand to be seen with. Thus, in a high-fashion era, creativity and innovation are paramount for maintaining and fostering relationships with consumers.

The Industry

Tourism was once referred to as the largest peacetime movement of people. According to the World Travel & Tourism Council (WTTC) and Accenture (a global management consulting and technology services company), worldwide spending on travel and tourism in 2006 exceeded US$ 6 trillion. The WTTC issued positive forecasts including an industry growth of 4.3 percent an annual growth of 4.3 percent for the 10-year period of 2007–2016. The U.S. lodging industry attracted unparalleled investment interest in 2006. Jones Lang LaSalle Hotels research arm reported that in 2006, the transaction volume of hotels grew to an all-time high, which was 67 percent higher than the previous year's record-breaking level.

The Company

European hotelkeeper César Ritz and his lead chef, Auguste Escoffier, were among the first to make wealthy travelers feel comfortable dining out and entertaining while away from home. The pair's success allowed Ritz to merge the Paris Ritz with the London Carlton and to develop a name so valuable that U.S. investors moved to capitalize on this success by franchising the name Ritz-Carlton.

In Boston, in 1920, Albert Keller purchased the rights to the name from Ritz, who was celebrated at the time as "the king of hoteliers and hotelier to kings." In 1927, The Ritz-Carlton, Boston was opened, bringing Ritz's philosophy of service and innovations that had redefined the luxury hotel experience in Europe to the United States. Nine years after Keller died, the Boston hotel made history with numerous firsts in the American hotel experience: private baths in guest rooms, light-colored fabrics to ensure absolute cleanliness through easy inspection, a formally dressed waitstaff, fresh flowers throughout the hotel, and á la carte dining.

Tales of The Ritz-Carlton's elaborate service were legendary, making the society pages of the *New Yorker* magazine. Societal publicity gave The Ritz-Carlton an excellent name, because not only was proven to be true, but also free and freely grandiose. These stories carried the brand for decades, providing future brand managers of The Ritz-Carlton name with a focus for their communication.

The first and only hotel company to win the United States Department of Commerce's Malcolm Baldrige National Quality Award twice (1992 and 1999), many of The Ritz-Carlton hotel properties also have received awards, including: Mobil Five-Star Award, AAA Five Diamond Award, *Condé Nast Traveler* (Gold List), and *Travel + Leisure* (500 Greatest Hotels in the World). *Consumer Reports* ranked The Ritz-Carlton Hotel Company the top luxury hotel company in all areas, including value, service, problem resolution, and upkeep. With all these awards, why was the brand's performance lagging?

In 1995, Marriott International purchased 49 percent interest in The Ritz-Carlton. Three years later, that interest was increased to 99 percent. In 2001, The Ritz-Carlton Hotel Company partnered with the Italian Bulgari brand to operate a chain of hotels under the Bulgari brand. After the Bulgari hotels were built, a *Wall Street Journal* travel critic wrote in 2004, "The new chain's existence is a de facto admission that Ritz-Carlton can't garner the room prices equal to other top-luxury hotel chains such as Four Seasons and Peninsula Hotels Hong Kong." His words identified trouble for The Ritz-Carlton brand.

In 2006, the company managed 59 hotels worldwide in 20 countries (37 city hotels and 22 resorts) and had 28,000 employees. Marriott's purchase of The Ritz-Carlton did not encroach on its brand, but leveraged it by adding luxury hotels to the corporate brand portfolio in numerous locations throughout North America and abroad. A *Wall Street Journal* travel critic wrote in 2006, "By pressing for expansion, Ritz-Carlton put hotels in many places that weren't capable of supporting the kinds of prices they require. Service, amenities and eventually reputation suffered." Older hotels with traditional oil paintings were housed in the same brand as new resorts with modern grounds in exotic locales. This resulted in sending mixed messages to consumers, with the potential for consumer confusion and/or loss in brand equity.

The Competition

The luxury hotel business is a multibillion-dollar affair. The Ritz-Carlton operates at the top of the Marriott brand. Its main competitors in the luxury hotel business include Aman Resorts International, Fairmont, Four Seasons Hotels & Resorts, The Mandarin Oriental Hotel Group, The Peninsula Hotels, and St. Regis Hotels & Resorts. Challengers to the category include the W brand that was introduced by Starwood Hotels and Resorts Worldwide in 1998 to lower the entryway for consumers who desire a luxurious and stylish place to stay.

Likewise, countless independent luxury hotels exist in the marketplace and offer intensifying experiences for competitive rates while still promoting exclusivity. In a 2004 satisfaction ranking survey of the luxury marketing segment among 14,000 guests, Four Seasons ranked highest, just above the Ritz-Carlton Resorts; both were well above industry averages for guest satisfaction.

Hotel Advertising

The hotel print advertising category is one strewn with expected imagery of buildings, beaches, and smiling faces. Most brands have chosen to differentiate themselves from their competitors by the exterior and interior appearance of a specific hotel location. This approach features brilliant scenery but reduces the reader's ability to focus on the brand experience. When the only difference communicated to consumers is location, the hotel with the best location is more likely to be chosen. A location communication message marginalizes the important message of service and experience.

Furthermore, most hotel companies confine print advertising to newspapers and travel publications. Hotel advertising within newspapers tends to occur inside travel sections, with quarter page ads in highly cluttered environments. When ads for luxury brands appear next to major discounters, the messages can easily be missed by consumers. Quarter-page, or smaller hotel ads, in the back portion of travel magazines, are better suited to value messages than brand messages.

The Target Audience

Before new advertising could be created, the target audience needed to be precisely defined and characterized. Current consumers were aging along with the brand, and to invite next-generation affluent consumers to enjoy The Ritz-Carlton brand, research was conducted to determine how to evolve the brand and improve communications. To overcome the problems associated with the brand's rapid expansion and multiple conceptions, a new message and delivery strategy were required.

Labeled "discerning affluents" by Foremost, this audience segment represented the next-generation consumers who had an appreciation for the history associated with the luxury they consumed or aspired to consume. Discerning affluents perceive themselves as connoisseurs of finer things and avid collectors of unique life experiences. They aspire to live their lives confidently and look for ways to leave their mark. They tend to be leaders within their peer groups and share their knowledge in ways that influence others. Instead of adopting brands that defined the success of a previous generation, they search for brands that reflect their own place in the world. This consumer's definition of luxury is neither contemporary nor traditional. Instead, the kind of luxury that appeals to the discerning affluents comes from embracing a collection of category-defining brands and experiences that can help each individual realize his or her goals, dreams, and desires.

The New Advertising Strategy

The new advertising strategy changed both the creative execution and the media buys. In keeping with its new target audience, the fresh creative approach featured artistic photography in double-truck (two-page) spreads. Placement was to be at the publication's front end, reaching readers immediately with bold, stylistic photographic images that conveyed the emotional benefits of staying with The Ritz-Carlton, such as relaxation and rejuvenation. The ads were intended to have a strong connection between what happens at the hotel level and what the brand offers—service that goes beyond the expected to focus on anticipating every guest's needs.

Foremost's new advertising used stylish fashion-inspired photography to create a mood for the brand.

Prior to this campaign, The Ritz-Carlton confined its advertising to national and regional newspapers and travel magazines. The thought behind the original strategy was to affect consumers when they were thinking about destinations (when reading travel publications) or when they were looking for travel deals (when reading the newspaper). The new flight of ads included luxury lifestyle publications such as *Vanity Fair* to position The Ritz-Carlton among major luxury brands during the "pre-thinking about travel" process. Although newspaper ads were kept in the media plan to impact readers later in the purchase process, their placement was moved out of the cluttered pages in travel and repositioned in news sections. Positioning by publication choice and placement before the table of contents and with other influential luxury brands (Louis Vuitton, Ralph Lauren, Mercedes, etc.) was selected to create a "rub-off" effect for The Ritz-Carlton.

Foremost's new print campaign hit newsstands in late April 2005 for May inser-tions in *Condé Nast Traveler, Travel + Leisure, Town & Country Travel, Vanity Fair, W,* and *Wallpaper.*

Campaign Evaluation

Six months into the new campaign, *Travel + Leisure* hired Affinity Research to conduct a VISTA survey online to determine the effectiveness of advertisements in its June 2005 issue. The study measured total ad recall, brand association, and actions taken or intended as a result of seeing any national ad in *Travel + Leisure.* The results indicated that The Ritz-Carlton was the number one advertiser in *Travel + Leisure,* with readers having "formed a more favorable opinion" as a result of seeing the ad. According to Affinity's research, 63 percent of *T + L* readers recalled (the percentage of readers who remember seeing a specific advertisement) The Ritz-Carlton, which was above the issue average of 57 percent for travel ads and the magazine industry average for travel ads of 56 percent. The study reported that five percent of $T + L$ readers recalling The Ritz-Carlton ad had purchased or intended to purchase the service (visited the Web site, made a reservation, told a friend, etc.). The first round of feedback indicated that The Ritz-Carlton image resuscitation was headed in the right direction.

Vanity Fair took part in a similar VISTA study in June 2005, which also was conducted by Affinity Research. The study was held online and measured the same components. Out of 72 total ads, The Ritz-Carlton ranked #6 for ad recall. Out of five travel advertisements, The Ritz-Carlton ranked #1 for ad recall. Sixty-four percent of respondents who recalled seeing The Ritz-Carlton ad took some form of action. The average action taken for the 72 ads studied was 56 percent.

The Payoff

Brand repositioning is an arena strewn with miscommunication and failure. In order to find success, many steps needed to be taken to ensure that promises made were promises delivered. Although a campaign's reach and frequency are easy to track, it is difficult to identify precisely what precipitates success.

With multiple communication outlets, the effects of advertising, public relations, and public opinion all contribute to the social construct that exists within each consumer's mind. These mental constructs regarding brand strength and brand awareness create allure or distaste, and everything in between, for individual brands. For now, Foremost and The Ritz-Carlton have taken the first steps toward evolving The Ritz-Carlton brand and welcoming a new generation of consumers into its hotels.

What do you think?

1. What other research could Foremost have conducted to evaluate the effect of its advertising campaign?
2. What public relations activities could have accompanied the new campaign?
3. How could sales promotion tactics be used to reward The Ritz-Carlton staff? To provide incentives for discerning affluents?
4. Where would you take this advertising campaign from here forward? Why?

Source: Matt Smart, graduate student, California State University Fullerton, May 2006.

Case 3   Selling the Mouse

Marketing Disney's California Theme Parks

In 1955, the concept of the amusement park was defined by the opening of Walt Disney's Disneyland in Anaheim, California. Despite opening day glitches and early periods of uncertainty, the Disney Company's flagship amusement park has grown to include a second theme park, two hotels, and a shopping and entertainment district. The formula in Anaheim was translated, with varying degrees of success, to Orlando, Florida, in the United States and to Paris, Tokyo, and Hong Kong internationally. The Disney Company now operates or franchises eleven parks in five cities.

The Situation

With the introduction of Disney's California Adventure park, Downtown Disney, and the Grand Californian Hotel, the Disney Company sought to turn the Disneyland park into the centerpiece of a destination resort. This strategy that has been met with only qualified success. A shift in positioning of the Disneyland resort property, combined with a number of other factors, has posed some unique marketing challenges for the company.

• An economic slump resulting from high gasoline prices and fears of terrorism since 9/11 continued to limit international and long-distance domestic travel in 2005–06, hurting the entire tourism industry. This situation forced the Disney Company to refocus its marketing strategy by promoting its destination resort largely to a local population.

• Potential miscalculations in the design of the Disney's California Adventure (DCA) park may have resulted in an inability to capture visitor attention. The result has been a decrease in the resort's appeal as a multiday vacation attraction, as opposed to a day-trip to the park.

• Planning of the extensive 50th Anniversary celebration campaign that was held in 2005–06 redirected resources and refocused marketing objectives under the direction of Walt Disney's long-time agency, Leo Burnett Co.

• Ten people have died at the two Disney California parks since Disneyland (DL) opened in 1955; eight of these were the result of guests and or employees not following proper procedures, and of guest health issues. Since 1998, there have been 10 major accidents at DL and DCA; one involved a crash between two trains on the "California Screamin" roller coaster at DCA from which 15 people were sent to the hospital with minor injuries. An accidental death occurred in 2006, and the ride was up and running the following day. Fortunately, there was only one fatality attributed to an incident of equipment failure, and that occurred in 2003 at Disneyland. To counteract the series of setbacks that seemed to be accumulating, Disney recruited Donald Banks, a private consultant who had some successes marketing parks in Ohio and Georgia, to assist Leo Burnett with repositioning the California property.

The anticipated decrease in visitor traffic after the 2006 incident was a long-term concern for Banks. He projected, however, that proper planning could position the resort for a recovery from the effects of the other factors. The central strategy he proposed was the use of media to build public expectations and attract visitors to the resort in light of an accelerating economy, decreased fears of terrorism, and changes to the Disney's California Adventure park. To adequately develop a successful plan, Banks began with an overview of the leisure travel industry.

Market Overview

The market for leisure travel rebounded in 2005, especially for amusement parks. *Amusement Business* reported a 4 percent increase overall, with Disney's parks posted above average gains: 5 percent at Disneyland, 8 percent at the Florida's Magic Kingdom, and 9 percent at Epcot Center (2004 attendance). According to *Amusement Business* 2005, Walt Disney parks captured the top eight spots for theme parks worldwide, attributed largely to the 50th Anniversary Celebration. Attendance increased at all Disney parks worldwide in 2005.

As every visitor to Southern California knows, Disneyland is but one property in a crowded theme-park marketplace. Nonetheless, Disneyland remains the benchmark by which other parks are generally judged. As audiences evolve, however, other parks assume higher prominence among younger visitors seeking exciting rides that were noticeably absent at California Adventure.

Southern California is home to a variety of amusement choices. It has beaches, mountains, national parks, and other natural attractions; cities and public and private entertainment areas and venues, such as Hollywood Boulevard in Hollywood and

Colorado Boulevard in Pasadena; and a plethora of theaters, both for movies and for the performing arts. Local residents, who are generally media and technology savvy, are targets of a large and pervasive media market. The major theme parks, especially Disneyland, benefit from almost universal name recognition. Nonetheless, in an area so saturated with entertainment options, even as iconic a destination as Disneyland can benefit from careful assessment of the market.

Like that of any large amusement park, Disneyland's market can be segmented by geographic location—specifically by local visitors, domestic nonlocal visitors, and international visitors. Within these segments, Disneyland uniquely serves a large group of season ticket holders, its annual passholders. This segment is largely a subset of the local market, although some annual passholders do live outside of the Southern California area. Regardless of their location, these customers are commonly quite well versed in the history and mythology of the company, loyal, frequently vocal, usually well educated and technologically adept, and financially secure. Combined with the sheer size of this group, these traits can create a dramatic impact on park operations as well as public perception. As such, this group requires unique marketing and—especially—public relations activity.

Brand/Product History

Banks acknowledged that the Disney brand was rooted in a tradition of family-friendliness and quality, and it is positioned as a uniquely American institution. This global image was an important consideration to the ultimate repositioning strategy for the park's new strategy. The Disney theme parks are considered (accidents notwithstanding) safe, secure, and imaginative environments. Since opening in 1955, the Disneyland park has added (and removed) numerous rides and attractions, and has largely defined notions of the theme

Walt Disney and his mouse.

park. With the addition of DCA, the park has grown into a multiday destination, instead of a "simple" theme park.

The history of Disneyland and the Disney Company begins with the history of its founder, Walt Disney. Born in Chicago on December 5, 1901, Walter Elias was the fourth and youngest child of Elias and Flora Disney. He grew up in Missouri, Kansas, and Illinois, and served in Europe in the Ambulance Corp during World War I. After returning home from war, he continued the cartooning he had begun prior to his service, eventually becoming an animator. Moving to Los Angeles, Disney produced a number of animated and mixed-media films, but he eventually lost the chance to draw "Oswald the Lucky Rabbit," a character that was picked up by Universal Pictures. This professional blow motivated him to come up with a new star of his own: a mouse named Mickey.

Disney's first cartoon character soon turned into a stable of well-known characters, eventually financing the first feature-length animated film in 1937, *Snow White.*

▪ ▪ ▪ ▪ **EXHIBIT CASE 3.1** Year-End Attendance

Year-End Attendance Figures, Disneyland (DL) and Disney California Adventure (CDA)

Year	DL	DCA
2001	12,350,000	5,000,000*
2002	12,720,500	4,700,000
2003	12,720,000	5,283,000
2004	13,360,000	5,311,000
2005	14,550,000	5,830,000

* DCA opened on Feb. 8, 2001.

Source: Amusement Business.

Immensely successful, the film helped propel Disney's company to the forefront of Hollywood's film industry. Subsequent films met receptive audiences, some more so than others, but the popularity of Mickey Mouse and Disney in general ultimately led Disney to feel the time was right to build his "little park." Ground breaking occurred in June of 1954, and one year later, Disneyland opened to the public.

In the years that followed, Walt Disney (and the company he left behind after his death in 1966) made an indelible mark on the entertainment industry. The Disney Company has become a media powerhouse with ownership of broadcast and cable television properties, music, publishing, and travel subsidiaries.

Situation Analysis

Preliminary to proposing a marketing plan, Banks conducted a situation analysis of the product, and competition, to develop a SWOT (strengths, weaknesses, opportunities, and threats) analysis.

Product/Service Evaluation

Over the years Disneyland and its outcroppings have had their critics. The most common criticism may be that, through its flagship park the Disney organization promotes the perception of an idealized America and a homogenous and somewhat sterile culture, according to critics such as John Urry. Nevertheless, the park has remained a popular destination, even among periods of reduced tourism and travel. In getting a handle on the balance of positive and negative, Banks revisited previous research in the form of park visitor feedback, which consistently reinforced the notion that the Disneyland resort is a place many people visit to escape reality; many visitors specifically referenced the creative and interesting rides and environment.

Disney's California Adventure has presented a unique set of strengths and weaknesses with regard to visitor draw. Founded in 2001, this park was created with an overall theme of exploration of the state of California, showcasing the history and geography of the area. This concrete theme contrasts to the largely intangible concepts that underlie the four separate areas of Disneyland—the themes of fantasy, adventure, the future, and the past. CDA was tilted toward a slightly different audience; the intended market was a somewhat older demographic. It was designed with fewer rides for children and, in contrast with standing Disney tradition, the availability of alcohol in the park for adults. On paper, this different emphasis may have indicated that the resort as a whole would appeal to a wider range of visitors, but by 2003, reality had not borne that out. In fact, only after California Adventure became more like its neighbor by adding children's rides and the highly themed *Tower of Terror* attraction in 2004, did attendance begin to improve. Still, Adventure provides an on-property alternative to the traditional Disneyland experience, and the existence of this alternative may be a factor in decisions made by potential visitors. Exhibit Case 3.1 shows year-end attendance since 2001.

Competitive Analysis

In Southern California, the amusement park industry is highly competitive, with a number of large and small parks vying for visitors. Several of the parks are, like the Disney parks, owned by large companies with multiple properties. These include Knott's Berry Farm, Six Flags Magic Mountain, and Universal Studios. The competing parks likewise have mature marketing and public relations resources, and most operate with Disneyland specifically as their benchmark (and, by extension, their target). Banks's research data confirmed that the imaginative atmosphere and family-friendly nature of the Disney parks continued to provide a unique value to a large market segment.

The Target Market

Families and children of all ages are designated as potential and current visitors to Disney hotels, attractions, and parks. Markets are based on regional, national, and global geodemographic segments. Banks reviewed the promotional strategies that were developed separately for local area residents, regional visitors, U.S. tourists, and international guests.

SWOT Analysis

Taking into consideration the analysis he conducted, Banks outlined the resort's strengths, weaknesses, opportunities, and threats in order to determine the park's current position.

Strengths

• Disneyland is the generally considered the premier park of the premier company in the amusement park industry.

• The 50th Anniversary celebration brought increased media and consumer attention to the Disneyland resort.

• The Disney Company owns a wide variety of media outlets, including television, radio, and print; this permits cost-effective media buys and detailed demographic research to qualify marketing initiatives.

• The Disney brand (including Disneyland) has an extensive base of very loyal consumers in most (if not all) demographic categories.

Weaknesses

• Disneyland lacks the "thrill rides" many contemporary amusement park visitors seek.

• Disney's California Adventure has thus far failed to post significant attendance figures, resulting in poor word-of-mouth and additional operational costs, which are not offset by attendance revenue.

• High ticket prices may place a visit out of the reach of many potential customers.

Opportunities

• Rebounding economy and tourist industry means additional potential customers.

• New regional attractions (such as shopping malls and museum exhibits) increase the number of potential customers in the area.

• Corporate sponsorships with large companies (such as Vons and American Honda Motor Corporation) expand avenues for cross-promotion.

Threats

• New attractions and experiences at local amusement venues (including even Las Vegas) currently integrate their themes and adventure experiences with more "thrills" than Disney has, potentially drawing customers away from the resort.

• Significantly lower admission prices to local amusement parks may spark a "price war" during critical summer months.

• Other entertainment options, including movies, shopping, and outdoor sports may prove appealing to price-conscious consumers.

• Recurring accidents and the publicity surrounding them have been public relations nightmares.

Marketing Goals and Objectives

Recognizing the limitations of current conditions, Banks developed a set of objectives designed to position the resort as a primary tourist location for both national and international visitors.

Continued public awareness of ongoing park enhancements (such as new attractions and new entertainment) was important; even in the absence of changes to the property, potential visitors must continue to be made aware of the unique benefits the Disneyland Resort (which includes parks and hotels) can provide. Media buys would likely take the form of television, radio, and print advertisements. Possible promotions, tie-ins, and corporate cooperation to encourage resort visits would be structured. Keeping the park fresh was Banks' main consideration in developing an overall marketing strategy.

The California Adventure park required special attention, especially as its faltering starting years 2001–03 faded away and its attendance climbed. Continued monitoring of customer feedback would help Banks and the Burnett agency finalize the park's mission and goals. The California theme might have to recede to allow more opportunities for developing rides such as the upcoming Monsters, Inc. ride. New attractions could serve as the centerpiece of media events to promote the entire resort

in general, the California Adventure park more specifically, and the new attractions most specifically.

Banks surmised that added awareness and investments in the property would support higher attendance and revenue in the post-anniversary period. A higher improvement goal should be set for the California Adventure park, as the Disneyland park consistently drew crowds close to capacity. In the case of the California Adventure park, maintaining attendance figures consistent with those seen during the anniversary campaign was realistic.

The marketing communication objective, according to Banks, should be top-of-mind awareness of the entire Disneyland Resort brand, including Disneyland, Disney's California Adventure, Downtown Disney, and the resort hotels. By continuing to keep the park in the forefront, the current marketing investment could be leveraged to keep attendance figures high. Continued exposure in all media (especially Disney-owned outlets) would undoubtedly prove valuable. Attendance figures would serve as a useful barometer of the success the Disney Company experiences in the course of addressing this objective.

The Proposed Marketing Plan

A marketing plan designed to meet the goals outlined above would integrate the wide variety of local, domestic, and international media at the Disney Company's disposal with promotional strategies and enhancement of product offerings. The brand's promotional efforts would focus on the new or improved attractions and entertainment.

Banks's proposed marketing plan was designed to meet attendance and revenue goals for the Disneyland Resort in the post 50th Anniversary period. The primary elements of his plan included:

• A *publicity campaign* focusing on the success of the 50th Anniversary at the

Disneyland resort would be ready for implementation immediately following the completion of the current plan in 2006. This plan would focus on how Disneyland is still America's first and favorite theme park, how the park is ready to move into its next half century, and, perhaps, extending invitations to young park visitors to return for the park's 100th birthday.

• The current *crisis communication package* might be refined to better handle potential park accidents that differ from injuries and previous conditions.

• *Special events,* such as the current Halloween and Christmas events for annual passholders, should be continued. Additional, "invitation-only" events for both this special subset of the market and local regular ticket holders could leverage park resources after closing. Both special and additional events would be offered at added cost, although annual passholders would enjoy a discount on the fees. By including regular ticket holders in the audience for this promotion, awareness of these special park events could spread, and individuals could visit them without purchasing an annual pass.

• Disney-owned *media,* such as the ABC television stations, ABC radio stations, and Hyperion publishing media outlets, would outline the plans for the resort's future and provide feature stories on new or refurbished rides and attractions. Press events surrounding the special events previously mentioned would keep the Disney parks in the news, ensuring exposure on non-Disney-owned outlets.

• The Disney company has long maintained a high-profile *Internet* presence (including the purchasing of a major search engine, Go.com), and the company's new media strategy was largely sound. Tie-ins with ongoing publicity campaigns, special events, and changes to park attractions and entertainment offerings would provide additional exposure. Harvesting of e-mail addresses via online promotions and contests, creating mailing-list sign-ups, and bringing visitors to the Internet component of the new Buzz Lightyear attraction at Disneyland provide a valuable (and extensive) resource of customers with expressed interest in the park.

• *Segmenting* the market based on characteristics of affinity and loyalty to the parks will help better tailor marketing to those groups. Specifically, visitors to any Disney park worldwide will receive information on major changes at Disney, either through opted-in electronic or traditional communication, media outlets local to the park in question, and in-park cross-promotion. Annual passholders will continue to receive unique publications to encourage visits to the park and in-resort spending. Local residents will continue to be targeted by discounts and promotions specific to Southern California. Customers of peripherally related media products (movies, television shows, and so forth) will also receive offers of discounts or value-added enticements to visit the resort.

The Proposed Evaluation Plan

The success of Banks's IMC plan to retain sufficient attendance for the Disneyland Resort would be assessed by four specific accounting measures:

1. *Promotionally priced tickets* and other enticements coded for tracking

2. *Attendance figures* collected and evaluated and exit interviews with questions such as "Where are you visiting us from today?" asked randomly by ticketing agents

3. *Guest surveys* conducted to assess any specific marketing efforts that may have motivated visits to the park

4. *Attitude surveys* conducted at random among DCA visitors regarding perceived potential danger of rides

Additionally, Banks would commission market research surveys in nonlocal markets to evaluate the awareness and favorability of the Disney theme parks. Disneyland and

Disney's California Adventure would be specifically evaluated in different markets. Success of online marketing techniques could be assessed by evaluating click-throughs from Internet advertisements, particular online promotions that result in purchases, or in the collection of otherwise demographically pertinent data. The Burnett agency would use the sum of data collected via these means to evaluate the success of each element of the marketing plan.

Banks met with Disney marketing officials to present his plan, which was endorsed by the advertising agency as the most effective way to improve the resort's image and attendance.

What do you think?

1. Is the objective of keeping top-of-mind awareness appropriate for a recognizable global brand such as Disney? If not, what should be the primary campaign objective?

2. What additional publicity tactics might be used to maximize the Disney brand in mainstream news media?

3. Can you suggest other special events that would provide Disney with a tie-in brand that appeals to the same visitor demographic?

4. Price promotions and loyalty programs are in place at Disney parks on a seasonal basis. How else might Disney use incentives for new visitors and to reward loyal patrons?

5. Are the campaign evaluation measures provided adequate for determining the success or failure of this plan? What else is needed?

6. How might licensing be used to increase awareness and generate revenue for Disney during off-seasons?

7. Rate the proposed plan on a scale of 1–10, 10 being highest, and defend your score. What is missing? What could be added?

Sources: Written by David Brooks, graduate student at California State University, Dec. 2005.

Case 4   Revitalizing the Pink Panther Brand

Since his creation more than 40 years ago, the Pink Panther animated character has evolved in appearance, but his essence has remained the same. Whether it is the original, sophisticated panther from the opening credits of the multiple live-action movies or the sly, irreverent cat audiences know and love from the television cartoons, the Pink Panther has always epitomized style and relaxed confidence, which powers his enduring cross-generational appeal.

Brand History

Created in 1964 by animators Friz Freleng and David DePatie for the opening credits of the classic Peter Sellers comedy *The Pink Panther,* the Pink Panther won the hearts of millions and went on to enjoy a career that has spanned a variety of genres over the past four decades. He has appeared in the opening sequences of the popular Pink Panther live action movies, starred in cartoon shorts as well as several successful television movies, and received an Oscar for the 1964 animated short *The Pink Phink.* In nearly all his appearances, the Pink Panther has been musically brought to life by Henry Mancini's unforgettable, hummable, Grammy® Award-winning theme song.

While the Pink Panther built his reputation through his on-screen antics, the cool cat became the star of a long-running series of American comic books that eventually became international successes. Between 1971 and 1984, 87 comic book issues were published.

Furthermore, in 2005 a Sunday newspaper comic strip debuted in national syndication to honor the classic character's fortieth anniversary.

Pink Panther Prints

Since 1964, the Pink Panther has played many roles that were easily identifiable by audiences around the globe. In playfully named cartoon shorts, he has portrayed an optimist and a dreamer (*Pink-A-Rella,* 1969), invoked a bit of magic (*Genie With the Light Pink Fur,* 1966), and exhibited his artistic abilities (*Pink Da Vinci,* 1975). He also has served as an advocate for animals (*Bobolink Pink, Pink Elephant,* and *Salmon Pink,* all released in 1975), and acted in the television movie *Pink at First Sight* as an out-of-work messenger who falls in love. To this day, the Pink Panther has left his paw print on televisions across the world—the cartoons have been aired in the United Kingdom, France, Spain, Italy, The Netherlands, and Belgium.

Film History

One of the most successful film franchises of the 1960s and 1970s, director Blake Edwards's Pink Panther movies were a hit from the beginning. The original film introduced many of the series' hallmarks: Sellers's endearingly inept Inspector Clouseau, the cleverly animated Pink Panther of the credit sequences, and Mancini's instantly recognizable score.

The Pink Panther film titles include:

1963	*Pink Panther*
1964	*A Shot in the Dark*
1968	*Inspector Clouseau*
1975	*Return of the Pink Panther*
1976	*The Pink Panther Strikes Again*
1978	*Revenge of the Pink Panther*
1982	*Trail of the Pink Panther*
1983	*Curse of the Pink Panther*
1993	*Son of the Pink Panther*
2006	*The Pink Panther* (remake)

Pink Panther Advertising

An ideal icon to represent several major companies throughout the U.S., the Pink Panther has appeared in numerous commercials, in print ads, and on billboards over the past four decades. For the majority of consumers, the Pink Panther's image evokes a sense of trustworthiness, likeability, humor, and intelligence. As a result, corporations began licensing the character to capitalize on his positive attributes to sell their products.

"The Pink Panther's style and personality are traits that click with male and female audiences all over the world. His wordless antics translate well to any culture, which helps make him an international star that has stood the test of time," said Travis Rutherford, executive vice president of MGM Consumer Products and Location Based Entertainment. "Research shows that people remember the Pink Panther for his prankster comedy, which makes them feel carefree and cheerful—what more could you ask from a successful entertainment franchise?"

In the late 1970s, Safeco Insurance recruited the irreverent cat to assure potential customers that purchasing Safeco insurance was easier than working with competitors. Across the globe, Japanese-based electronics company TDK employed the Pink Panther for its holiday advertising campaign, portraying the Pink Panther and Inspector Clouseau enjoying Christmas dinner while watching a TDK video cassette.

But, perhaps the most famous partnership between the Pink Panther and a corporate entity began in August 1980, when the Pink Panther became Owens Corning's mascot, appearing in television commercials to promote the company's signature pink fiberglass insulation.

Pink Panther Food

To further capitalize on the brand's popularity, the Pink Panther was also used as a face for food-related companies. For example, during the 1960s, Pez™ designed a Pink Panther candy dispenser to attract fans of the cool cat and drive sales of Pez products.

In the mid-1970s, Post™ created *Pink Panther Flakes* cereal that, when put in milk, turned the milk "Pink Panther pink." In 1984, a Swedish company used the Pink Panther as part of the creative design to attract customers to purchase its soda. Burger King's *Kid's Club* meals featured the Pink Panther on their packaging and drinking cups as part of a unique partnership.

What began as an opportunity to put the Pink Panther's face on some of the world's most popular name-brand products has resulted in an abundance of timeless collector's items.

Brand Rejuvenation

The Pink Panther animated character has appeared in eight feature films and 172 seven-minute shorts since 1964 and has been the face for high-profile advertising campaigns and product launches. In the 1990s, however, the property became somewhat stagnant, due to a shrinking licensing program and no new theatrical releases or television cartoons to sustain buzz.

In 2003, MGM Consumer Products (the licensing-focused business unit taking the lead on behalf of the entertainment studio) began planning for the first stage of a four-year program that would reinvigorate the brand, thereby driving consumer awareness and demand for all things Pink Panther. Before the team began, it was imperative that they understood where Pink Panther stood in the mind of consumers, especially as the first year of the program revolved around the fortieth anniversary of the Pink Panther.

Pink Panther Research

MGM commissioned a research company to reevaluate the brand's characteristics as well as clarify the current target audience. Top findings from the consumer study included:

• Key attributes associated with the Pink Panther brand were "fun," "hip," "cool," and "sly."

- The brand's values were bold, charismatic, clever, confident, cool, funny, hip, memorable, mischievous, resourceful, sly, and suave.

- Awareness studies showed that the Pink Panther character was one of the most recognized cartoon characters in the world among:

  - Males 18–49: 91%
  - Females 18–49: 93%
  - Mothers with kids 2–5: 92%

- Consumers associated the Pink Panther brand essence more with luxury goods (such as diamonds, a Burberry trench coat, a Rolex watch, and cuff links) than downscale products such as sweatshirts.

- Many "core buyers" interested in buying Pink Panther products would be interested in purchasing merchandise with a new interpretation of the Pink Panther look.

These insights helped solidify MGM's short- and long-term plans for the franchise.

Pink Panther's Face Lift

To honor the fortieth anniversary year, MGM commissioned a new set of Pink Panther character designs from famed gallery artist SHAG (Josh Agle), which were licensed for the creation of higher-end consumer products in categories such as designer clothing, barware, jewelry, and automotive accessories. SHAG's hip retro/mod artwork was the embodiment of the Pink Panther brand message—the character is a timeless trendsetter.

MGM took the artwork and anniversary concept to potential partners and secured promotional partnerships in over 100 coun-

tries, including the Bellagio Hotel in Las Vegas, Italian scooter manufacturer Vespa, and Bliss Cosmetics in New York City.

As a tribute to the man who brought the Pink Panther to life through music, an honorary postage stamp was issued by the United States Postal Service. The stamp featured an image of Henry Mancini with the Pink Panther; and 80 million stamps were issued on April 13, 2004.

Furthermore, with the new artwork showcased on all fortieth anniversary products, the sales of these products were undeniably considered a success. For example, the Pink Panther DVD box set, which included four of the classic Pink Panther films, exceeded sales expectations by 63 percent and a Pink Panther Penthouse Party music CD, released by Virgin Records, exceeded sales expectations by 40 percent.

Pink Panther Today

The first theatrical release since 1993 hit the big screens in February 2006. To prepare for this momentous occasion, MGM developed a marketing strategy to complement the release of *The Pink Panther*.

Marketing Goals

The goals of the 2006 Pink Panther brand marketing were to:

1. extend the brand's reach with fresh, trend-forward creative and the introduction of new characters within the Pink Panther family.

2. become a formidable player in the contemporary, fashion-forward marketplace.

MGM employed several business facets to heighten the awareness of the Pink Panther, ultimately building the brand.

Marketing Strategies

- Leveraging heightened awareness of the brand via the successful release of the new film with retail buys, signage, and movie call-outs; licensing, PR, and movie premiere cross-marketing opportunities.

• Partnering with industry-leading companies for long-term (Owens Corning insulation) and short-term (Thomas Pink shirts) promotional opportunities.

• Leveraging new Pink Panther style guide artwork to position Pink Panther as a fashion brand.

• Launching *Pink Panther & Pals,* a TV show in development with Direct TV and TV production partners to extend the brand's reach.

Promotional Strategies

• Leveraging heightened awareness of 2006 movie and DVD release.

• Partnering with category leaders that elevated the awareness and visibility of the Pink Panther brand.

• Seeking quality long-term partnership opportunities.

• Keeping brand character visible worldwide.

• Partnering with companies that wanted to own the color pink in their respective categories, such as firms in women's fashions, flowers, high-end spirits, and cosmetics.

Public Relations Strategies

• Highlighting a new art program that included Vintage (a section in the official brand style guide) and Peter Sellers-branded artwork.

• Collaborating with MGM Home Entertainment and TV divisions on cross-marketing opportunities for licensed merchandise and promotions.

• Using celebrity seeding with pro golfer Paula Creamer, whose nickname of the professional golf tour is the Pink Panther.

The New Pink Panther Style Guide

MGM's creative department infused the history of the Pink Panther with a contemporary style and flair by creating a new Pink Panther style guide (official character artwork, icons, emblems, and patterns) for licensing purposes. The guide's new section,

"Vintage," brought back the look of the classic cat to resemble the artwork in the original Pink Panther short films. For the first time, the Peter Sellers estate released the licensing rights for Inspector Clouseau images. The style guide also included a "Pinkitude" section, which showcased retro-hip graphics and designs aimed at 'tween girls, and a "Toon" kids program, which embraced the mischievous nature of the cartoon cat. From this guide, products were designed and marketed to specific target audiences.

Global Licensing

As the business driver for MGM Consumer Products, the global Pink Panther licensing campaign has secured more than 300 licensees worldwide. From the establishment of Pink Panther boutiques in Kuala Lumpur and Singapore to a costarring role in a Japanese pop star's music video and tour, to a themed retail store at Universal Studios Japan and Pink Panther apparel in Zara stores throughout Europe, the Pink Panther has once again left his paw prints throughout the world.

The Brand Extension Strategy

The mission for MGM's brand extension was to leverage the brand's more than 40 years of equity by moving into the infant and toddler category of licensed products. As an incentive for parents to share the cool cat with their children, the target demographic for the Pink Panther & Pals products was parents with infants/toddlers, ages one to four years old. The target consumer was based on research that showed 92 percent of mothers with children ages two to five were familiar with Pink Panther and 90 percent of parents absolutely believed that Pink Panther & Pals would appeal to their child or children.

The New Face of Inspector Clouseau

In 2006, as a result of a strategic business acquisition, Sony and Columbia Pictures, along with MGM, released a new *Pink Panther* film starring Steve Martin, Kevin Kline, and Beyoncé Knowles, which went on

to become a top-grossing U.S. release. Worldwide box office sales as of April 2006 topped $150 million. The film ranked number one on opening weekend and number two for the second week, and box office dropped just 32 percent the third week. Internationally, the film was number one in foreign box office for three consecutive weeks in March. As a result of the overwhelming success, both domestically and abroad, a sequel was planned.

For most of the previous Pink Panther films, Peter Sellers had played the role of Inspector Clouseau. To pay homage to and bring to life the comedic genius of the Inspector in the 2006 version of *The Pink Panther*, renowned comic actor Steve Martin was cast. Not only did Martin bring a sense of humor to the role, but he also had a personal association with the brand.

"I grew up on the films so I had great affection for them. In my college days, Sellers' Clouseau got us through a lot of stuff because he was funny. Nice man. Never got to work with him," Martin said. (Martin did, however, meet Sellers in Hawaii while Martin was promoting his movie *The Jerk* in 1980.)

"Mine is a different Inspector, but his mannerisms remain the same—certainly overconfidence, and a little bit arrogant. And the way he likes to push around the small guy, he thinks he's some kind of mastermind, and has a great affection for women," said Martin in a February 1, 2006, interview by Paul Fischer in Los Angeles for darkhorizon.com.

In conjunction with *The Pink Panther's* 2006 release, tie-in promotions with key industry leaders were implemented across key licensing categories including: Sweet 'N Low, L'Oreal, Mercedes, Thomas Pink (a UK upscale clothier), and Best Buy electronics.

The Future

Darren Kyman, marketing director for MGM Consumer Products, stated "The Pink Panther's brand potential is unlimited. The existing library, as well as future Pink Panther films, will continue to build awareness for the brand. After 40 years of working with the Pink Panther character, we know he has his own distinct identity that is not strictly dependent upon any movies' commercial success."

What do you think?

1. Would the pink Cadillac used by Mary Kay Cosmetics make a good tie-in for the Pink Panther brand? Why or why not.

2. How does MGM distinguish between the Pink Panther brand and the Panther films?

3. What elements of the new campaign's promotion mix would you change or refine?

4. Log on to the Sony Pictures Pink Panther Web site and listen to the Mancini theme music. Watch the movie trailer. From these glimpses, how would you use Steve Martin and the Pink Panther to promote other products in addition to those previously endorsed?

5. In your opinion, was the marketing rejuvenation plan effective? What were its strengths and weaknesses?

6. Which medium (cartoon, film, comic) best suits the Pink Panther brand character? Why?

Sources: Based on a presentation developed by MGM Consumer Products and Jerry Beck's *Pink Panther: The Ultimate Guide to the Coolest Cat in Town* (DK Publishing, 2005).

Case 5   Marketing the Oprah Brand

Branding is marketing's most powerful tool. Brand equity gives value to a property that can be transformed into a valuable intangible asset—especially when the property is a celebrity.

Celebrity marketing assumes many forms. Some efforts are overt advertising campaigns; others are manipulated through public and press relations. Efforts can be behavioral, where celebrities appear at events or are seen with carefully selected people. Or, marketing may be a result of building on personal activity. So, how did a black woman with an eating disorder and from a dysfunctional family become an American icon?

For Oprah Winfrey and her team of advisors, brand equity resulted from a carefully planned brand manufacturing process. Highly protective of her image, Oprah has crafted and retained a positive image by restricting and controlling media exposure. She has been consistent, and often predictable, in how she has conducted herself for the past 20-plus years to achieve the highest level of celebrity status.

Conducting a professional life that has resulted in the enviable "Oprah brand," Winfrey has evolved to a plateau that few ever reach—"super brand" status. But her meteoric rise to American icon has not been without turmoil, and an over-saturation of the Oprah brand has brought some resentment. In spite of setbacks, Oprah's brand has retained its equity and image over time.

Oprah has been way more than a talk show host for some time. Oprah actually drives American commerce to a measurable degree. She has strong influence on what is considered *en vogue,* popular, acceptable,

moral, contemporary, readable, edible (or not), and cool. In a unique way, she has become America's conscience. The "Oprah Factor" is a barometer for what people read and how people think. Millions of fans use the "What Would Oprah Do?" filter for their decision-making process. This case presents the origin, creation, extension, and maintenance of a brand as developed for a famous personality. By examining each stage of this brand's development, we may better understand the strategic process necessary to produce celebrity brand equity.

Oprah Brand Origins

Oprah Gail Winfrey was born January 29, 1954, on a family farm in Kosciusko, Mississippi. Her father, Vernon, and her mother, Vernita Lee, were very young when Oprah was born, and they never married. Her father was a soldier stationed at a local Army base. Working as maid in Milwaukee,

Oprah's mother left her in the care of her grandmother, Hattie Mae Lee, for most of her formative years.

Winfrey's first speaking engagement occurred at age three during an Easter recital at the Buffalo United Methodist Church. Oprah, who could read and write before she was four, was frequently invited into recitals, poetry readings, and other programs sponsored by the church. In school, Oprah skipped kindergarten and after only a year was moved to third grade.

At age six, Oprah moved to Milwaukee to live with her mother, who had other priorities. Oprah, who neither understood nor appreciated being neglected, became disrespectful and disobedient at a relatively young age. When she was nine, her nineteen-year-old cousin raped her. Sexual abuse by her cousin, a family friend, her mother's live-in boyfriend, and her uncle continued until she was 14.

She left home to live with her father and stepmother, who mandated a twelve o'clock curfew, a book report every week, and memorizing five new words each day. Always articulate, Oprah found solace in books; the reports became her personal expression. Because food was withheld from her as punishment for rule infractions, eating became a psychological reward, her way of telling herself she was okay. As a result, she developed a lifelong battle with weight.

Oprah's career began during high school when she was elected school president and sent to the White House Conference on Youth. There, she met President Nixon and other school representatives from around the country. Drama classes gave her exposure and built confidence; she read the news for a local radio station and was offered a job that began her broadcasting career. Winning the grand prize in a public speaking contest provided a full scholarship to Tennessee State University where Winfrey studied Speech Communications and Performing Arts.

Oprah Brand Development

At age 19, while still at the university, Oprah took a job with the local CBS affiliate television station in Nashville as co-anchor. After college she accepted a job in Baltimore as a reporter. An emotional person, Oprah found it difficult to be objective and did not succeed as a reporter. When she became co-host of a local talk show called *People Are Talking*, Oprah knew interviewing was what she wanted as a career. The show was on the air for seven years, and in 1981, Oprah became host of *AM Chicago*. Four years later, the show's name was changed to *The Oprah Winfrey Show*, and quickly moved to a syndication deal with NATPE to appear in 113 markets.

The Brand Vision

Northwestern Professor Scott Davis's Brand Asset Management strategy provides a useful structure for analyzing celebrity brands in phases. During the first phase, agents, marketers, and Oprah agreed on a single vision for the celebrity's brand. One of the key factors to success for any brand is crafting the vision by defining the brand's mission and remaining true to its set of core values, competencies, and reason for being. After starting with a lowbrow, high-energy, surface story format typical of Sally Jessie Raphael or Jerry Springer's shows, the *Oprah Winfrey Show* found its true reason for being with a fundamental shift in the focus of story content. She and her producers re-engineered the show with a positive perspective, avoiding the trite and manipulative storylines of other talk shows.

During the positioning phase, the Oprah brand was crafted into what we know today. The show's positive approach found and exposed the smarter, more caring, more interesting sides of the show's guests. The optimistic format created differentiation from other daytime programming: soap operas had storylines with crimes of passion, infidelity, and murder; news programming headlined terrorism, crime, car chases, war, and death; other daytime talk shows were over the top with outlandishly intimate topics. Based on the strong ratings for Oprah show segments that featured "feel good" stories, there appeared to be an audience appetite for original programming with a more positive perspective than what was then available on television. The new format was a hit.

The Brand Image

Brand images involve research to identify audiences' perceptions of the star relative to the competition. Fan clubs, show ratings, and artistic endeavors revealed Oprah's strength in the marketplace and helped to identify what audiences wanted in the future—more of the same.

In 1987, her show was awarded three Daytime Emmys for Outstanding Direction, Outstanding Host, and Outstanding Talk/ Service Program. After celebrating its twentieth anniversary in 2005, the *Oprah Winfrey Show* still yielded $6 million per week, or $300 million per year. People who associated with Winfrey began to receive celebrity status just for being in her presence. Once her image was crafted, her managers needed to develop an asset management strategy for maintaining her vision and her image.

Managing the Oprah Brand

Positioned first as a daytime talk show host, Oprah accepted new challenges that afforded opportunities to extend the brand. In 1986, Oprah and her newly founded company, Harpo Productions, began to branch out, selecting media and properties that would extend her reach. The brand extended into the Oprah Book Club, magazine publishing, cable television ownership, movie production, development of a robust Web site, and even production of the show's twentieth anniversary DVD. Harpo, Inc. currently has $275 million in revenue and 250 employees.

Oprah's brand status created a powerful marketing referral opportunity for authors through a Book Club that turned more than one title into a bestseller. Barnes & Noble, Borders, and a number of other booksellers feature an Oprah Book Club display where followers can find a series of titles that Oprah recommended. Once on her reading list, authors and publishers have a near guarantee of success.

The Oprah brand has affected commerce in a significant way. Through 2004, 52 of her recommended titles became best sellers overnight. Publishers plan distribution and marketing campaigns around Oprah's Book Club schedule knowing that her thumbs up means instantaneous market demand. The "Oprah effect" lingered long after a book left the bestseller list.

As the Oprah brand continued to build, its reach extended into magazine publishing. A joint venture between Oprah and Hearst Magazines brought *O, The Oprah Winfrey Magazine* to life. Based on the successful model established by her television program, the brand visionaries crafted a magazine idea, and Hearst successfully sold advertising space in what was coined the "Oprah upfront." The upfront model of ad sales provides advertisers with premium spacing and better pricing if they commit to an annual ad budget before the magazine launch. Drawing equity from the Oprah brand, advertisers in the automotive, food, package goods, technology, finance, beauty, fashion, travel, and retail categories jumped on board. Stemming from Winfrey's personal devils—battles with weight, familial relationships, race relations, public perception—story categories reflected her desires to share personal experiences. The magazine remains popular *and* profitable in 2006, a difficult accomplishment in the hyper-competitive women's magazine field. Winfrey also edits another magazine, *O at Home*.

In January 2000, Winfrey partnered with America Online and ABC to launch the Oxygen cable network, a channel positioned to enable women to fully take advantage of their tremendous economic power. One of the primary business drivers in developing the network was the fact that women generally watch three more hours of television per day than men. Winfrey saw a business opportunity tied to her core brand attributes and her company's mission of providing tools for personal improvement. Part of the original programming included a midday block called "Working Lunch" targeted to working women. Also featured were an afternoon block targeting teenage girls and a prime-time block featuring shows such as *Roseanne* and *Grace Under Fire*—programs about slightly irregular families that figure out ways to make things work under difficult circumstances.

Film and theater also played a role in extending brand Oprah. Since long before her Oscar-nominated performance in the movie *The Color Purple*, Winfrey has been passionate about the need to play a role in telling the story of slavery in the United States. She financed the film production of *Beloved*, Toni Morrison's Pulitzer Prize-winning. And, in December 2005, she saw the opening of *The Color Purple* on Broadway.

After extending the brand from TV into magazines and film, Winfrey entered the world of subscription radio. In February 2006, she paid $55 million for a three-year deal with XM Satellite radio (6 million subscribers) to establish a new channel called Oprah & Friends that features programs on topics of health, fitness, and self-improvement, which are hosted by traditional Oprah personalities. She and Gayle King, her producer, host their own weekly show. Her nemesis, shock-jock Howard Stern, received $600 million to appear on Sirius Radio (3 million subscribers) for five years, hoping to capture some of the competition's audience with Stern's popularity among younger listeners.

Communicating the Brand's Position

Development and extensions help to establish the brand, but maintenance ensures its longevity. Periodic evaluation is used to determine the brand's strength and branding success. Keeping the brand in the public eye was a key communication strategy used to strengthen the Oprah brand. Little traditional advertising is used other than promotion of the media properties themselves, such as "tune in" messaging on ABC, local spot radio, and outdoor advertising.

Oprah's most powerful tool may be a Web site, www2.oprah.com, which attracts 2 million viewers a month and features a cacophony of choices for Oprah fans. Streaming video allows visitors to see select stories, mostly featured on the television show. Archived video allows you to see yesterday's show, information on today's show, and a preview of tomorrow's show. A "Tune in This Week" section allows for a menu of what is planned for future shows. Viewers can even share their stories with a chance of being featured on an upcoming episode. The site contains links to other areas of interest, such as "Spirit and Self," for ongoing self-improvement; books suggested for the book club; links with "Food and Home" tips; even a "Predator Watch List" featuring information on sexual predators throughout the United States. To retain good will for the brand, Winfrey supports a personal charity, Oprah's Angel Network, which provides grants for scholarships, schools, and homes for underprivileged children.

Oprah remains in tune with her audience and continues to make great efforts to provide information and entertainment that her loyal fans desire. According to Nielsen rating book for spring 2006, Winfrey's primary fan demographic is women ages 25–54, but she also has a male following, and it is on the rise. Her fans discuss the show and issues surrounding her on blogs such as technorati.com/tag/oprah and popwatch. ew.com.

Tarnishing the Image

With any famous person, public perception is swayed by factors sometimes outside of the control of the celebrity or the management team hired for advice and support. A dilemma occurs when momentum is established in a direction not foreseen by the celebrity's team. According to a close associate of Winfrey, Oprah has always made important decisions like "how to spin a crisis" herself.

Her brand suffered two setbacks: an untimely remark and a fictional nonfiction book recommendation. Oprah's April 1996 on-air comment about mad cow disease infuriated the meat industry, and she was sued by mad cattlemen. The ranchers claimed that remarks Winfrey made on her show negatively affected beef prices. One of the plaintiffs told Associated Press he lost $6.7 million after a guest on Winfrey's show said the practice of feeding ground-up animal parts to livestock could foster an epidemic of mad cow disease in the United States, which is still a serious possibility.

After her guest informed a TV audience about the dangers of getting "bovine spongiform encephalopathy," Winfrey exclaimed, to the audible delight of her studio audience, "It has just stopped me from eating another burger!" For cattlemen facing drought, high feed prices, and oversupply, Winfrey's comments were badly timed. In fact, the day the show aired, cattle prices began falling, and they continued to drop for another two weeks.

A not-liable verdict absolved the talk-show host, her show, and a third defendant of costing ranchers millions of dollars with perceived anti-beef remarks. "We did

absolutely nothing wrong," the TV personality said, calling the cattlemen's lawsuit an attempt to "muzzle" her voice, her opinions. "I refused to be muzzled," she declared.

In 2006, a flap ignited around James Frey's memoir, *A Million Little Pieces*—which was exposed as an embellishment, if not an outright fabrication, of the author's life—and was a news item for weeks. Winfrey defended her Book Club selection, insisting that the author's "underlying message" counted more than strict respect for the facts, and apologized to viewers for the error.

The controversy was an embarrassment for the publisher and Winfrey, who added a line to the book jacket, "With new notes from the publisher and from the author." A month later, on the *Larry King Live* show, Winfrey reversed her support for the author and explained that she felt duped by the situation. The apology to readers and listeners prevented the brand from losing any of its integrity. By acting responsibly in the face of compromising situations, the brand deflected both crises.

Measuring Brand Equity

In 2006, Winfrey was worth $1.4 billion, and *Forbes Magazine* ranked her as the 213th richest person in the United States. She has become the gold standard as it relates to advertisers' product placement efforts. Described by the *Washington Post* as "The product placement to end all product placements," the gifting of 276 Pontiacs to her audience yielded the automaker $20 million worth of unpaid exposure for an $8 million investment. Reaching beyond the traditional 30-second commercial, Pontiac also got to mix its brand DNA with a bit of Oprah magic.

How did it happen? Initially, Oprah turned down a proposal by General Motors' Pontiac division to showcase its new G6 sedan as one of "Oprah's Favorite Things."

Based on a notion of philanthropy, she decided to use the cars as giveaways in exchange for mentioning Pontiac's name 15 times during the program. The promotion strategy was brilliant.

Three weeks preceding the show's season premiere, Harpo's publicist began advising the press that a "major announcement" was in the offing. All journalists were required to abide by an embargo to prevent the news from leaking before the show aired the following Monday. Remarkably, everybody complied.

Ratings for the season premiere were the highest since the first show of the 1996 season, earning a national 10.1 rating, a 31 percent increase over the season-to-date Nielsen average of 7.7. Meanwhile, according to comScore Networks, which tracks Web-site traffic, visits to Winfrey's Web site jumped 800 percent the day after, with 600,000 logged on. Stories about Winfrey and the free Pontiacs were inescapable—not just in the U.S., but in all 112 countries where the show airs. Pontiac spent $7.8 million on the vehicles and used the program as the opening shot in a $50 million ad campaign. Pontiac's Web site traffic jumped 600 percent following the *Oprah* show.

Success of the Oprah brand can also be measured in the extent of her media coverage, Google hits, fan base, awards and nominations, special appearances, endorsed product sales, *Fortune* polls, Nielson ratings, and Q Factor. Her television show, which airs in every domestic market and reaches 30 million viewers weekly, has ranked number one for the past 18 seasons. No one will argue with the statement that this celebrity brand has achieved more equity than any other in history.

Achievements that contribute to the Oprah brand's equity include the George Foster Peabody Individual Achievement Award (1996), the IRTS (International Radio and Television Society) Gold Medal Award (1996), and the National Academy of Television Arts & Sciences' Lifetime Achievement Award (1998). She received *Newsweek*'s Woman of the Century (2001) award and the National Book Foundation's 50th Anniversary Gold Medal for her influential contribution to reading and books, and she was named one of the 100 most influential people of the twentieth century by *Time Magazine* (1998). Oprah also garnered *Newsweek*'s most important person in books and media, *TV Guide*'s "Television Performer of the Year" (1997), seven Emmy Awards® for Outstanding Talk Show Host, and nine Emmy Awards for Outstanding Talk Show.

The value of brand Oprah, apart from her financial holdings, is manifested in the influence she has on America's choices—what people read, what fashions are popular, and what topics are hot. According to *Time*, "Oprah has the market clout of a Pentagon procurement officer." Her effect on book sales saw the 1952 Steinbeck classic *East of Eden* with 80,000 copies in print soar to 1.8 million after her club selection as a "must read."

The Brand's Future

A celebrity brand often thrives and even increases in value after the celebrity's death. According to *Forbes Magazine,* the top 10 dead celebrities earn $167 million annually. When celebrities die, they leave behind items of value that can continue to generate earnings. Elvis, for instance, earned $45 million for his estate in 2005.

The Oprah brand will likely carry on beyond her living years, but because the brand is driven by Winfrey's personality, it will undoubtedly change in nature once she has passed away. Her properties—the book club, show syndications, Harpo holdings, *O* magazine, Oxygen Media, and the Angel Network—leave a legacy that most certainly will flourish and generate significant earnings. Without the brand's engine, however, Winfrey herself, there may be a significant void. Because people have attached themselves to Oprah the person, the brand minus the person is certain to lose some of its equity.

Lessons in Celebrity Branding

Parallels can be drawn between Winfrey and Howard Stern, a different but equally equitable celebrity brand. Both are hugely popular with their respective audiences. Both have risen against long odds to reach the pinnacle of their craft. Both would not be considered by most as overly physically attractive people. They are self-made and hugely successful, obtaining wealth beyond most peoples' wildest imaginations. But perhaps the biggest reason they have become icons with millions of fans is their honesty. This common trait suggests that a celebrity brands must maintain honest relationships with their audiences by exhibiting behavior that is consistent and innate to their personality.

The Oprah brand is testimony to the fact that the most critical element of a successful brand is identifying its vision and core values, then never wavering from them. Ad campaigns, taglines, logos, jingles, and spokespeople may change over time, but brands that are consistent and true to their mission endure to command the strongest brand loyalty in the marketplace. By sticking to her mission, Oprah Winfrey's rise to power and fame elevated her from a local talk show host to one of the richest Americans today and one of the richest women of all time.

What do you think?

The future of Oprah's brand image is speculative. As her advisor, propose answers to the following questions:

1. What strategy should Oprah use to maintain her dominance over daytime television?

2. What steps can her producers take to ensure successful brand equity over time?

3. How would you handle a tabloid expose of a Winfrey "private moment"?

4. What strategy would you use to get Winfrey back into the public's consciousness once she's no longer hot or in the daily limelight?

5. Should magazine-like television shows such as "Extra" or "The Insider" be used to promote Winfrey? In what cases should they be avoided altogether?

6. What would be the consequences of selling or franchising the brand once Winfrey retires? Would her brand ultimately rank high as a dead celebrity brand? Why?

7. What lessons can Winfrey learn from Martha Stewart?

Source: This case was developed by Ed Collins, graduate student, California State University–Fullerton in May 2006.

▮ ▮ ▮ ▮ ▮ ▮ ▮ ▮
Postscript

▪▪▪ Where Do We Go from Here?

No one can predict the future, especially authors, who work against a year's lead-time from writing to publishing. What we can do, however, is provide an overview of trends that indicate what the future might hold for entertainment marketing. Here are insights from experts who present their views on what trends you might encounter in the near future in advertising and media that will affect the entertainment industry.

▪▪▪ Widgets and Digits

Although the fast pace of technological development and breakthroughs makes foresight difficult, the technology revolution seems globally significant and quite likely to continue. Competition for leadership and participation in technology development will depend on regional economic arrangements, international intellectual property rights and protections, the character of future multinational corporations, and the role and amount of public and private sector research and development investments.

Independents Welcome

DVD technology will take film making back to its roots where the director has total control—a return to the auteur—and away from block-buster conglomerates. Evidence of this came in 2003 with the first feature film to have a worldwide commercial release on the Internet made its debut. *Nothing so Strange,* a mockumentary about the assassination of Bill Gates, could be downloaded for $3.00, free from copy protection or limited viewing disablers. More recently dubbed "fan film," a digital feature-length production of a *Star Trek* episode, featuring friends of the novice producer as actors, was posted on the Web in 2004. With the advent of the digital revolution, young artists no longer will be required to pass through film school to gain experience, nor will they need to live and work in Hollywood and cultivate relationships with industry "movers and shakers" to get their movies made. Audiences are already becoming content producers, and this trend will continue to escalate.

If you have always wanted to direct, **vlogging** allows the average non-geek to record, edit, and post videoclips to the Web for the world to see. In a recent VideoEgg study on eBay, used items that were sold using videoclips went for 70 percent more than similar items sold without videos.[1]

Mobile digital video will put TV in the pockets of hundreds of millions of more consumers by the end of the decade.[2] Now in South Korea, Japan, and Europe, mobile broadband digital video broadcast infrastructure and video-ready mobile phones will come to the United States in the next five years, depending on the amount of legal wrangling that takes place. Beamed from satellites, the mobile video signal can be viewed on laptop screens, dashboard-mounted LCD displays, handheld computers, and cell phones.

By the end of 2007, Verizon and AT&T will have services that broadcast several channels of live TV to specially equipped handsets. As of this writing, 5.3 million U.S. wireless subscribers pay for video—just 2.5 percent of all U.S. cell-phone users. But carriers think many more viewers will want to watch their favorite shows on a 2-inch screen. What do you think?[3]

Video on Demand

Video on demand (VOD) systems allow users to select and watch video content over a network as part of an interactive television system. VOD systems allow content to be purchased and downloaded to a set-top box or streamed (viewed during downloading). One example of VOD usage is having Super Bowl commercials available on demand following the annual broadcast of the game.

Near video on demand (NVOD) is a pay-per-view consumer video technique used by multichannel broadcasters using high-bandwidth distribution mechanisms such as satellite and cable television. Multiple copies of a program are conveniently broadcast at short time intervals (typically 10–20 minutes), enabling viewers to watch the program without having to tune in at a scheduled time. This form is bandwidth intensive and is generally provided only by large operators with a great deal of redundant capacity.

Proponents of VOD hope the medium will become as interactive as the Web itself, allowing viewers to get discount offers, enter contests, and even buy stuff. Burger King is considering running ads offering drive-through deals to late-night VOD viewers. Such ads could be priced based on the number of leads or sales they generate rather than the number of viewers they attract. "The intersection of video on demand and interactive TV is the next frontier," says Time Warner Cable (TWX) Executive Vice-President Peter C. Stern. "I look for it to emerge in 2007."

With more than 30,000 hours of feature-length entertainment and unlimited mass mediated programming available to the average consumer, audiences will learn to be more selective and premeditated about their choices of entertainment. Audience members will seek out loglines, synopses, and treatments to determine what to experience. Price points will play a key role in attracting audiences to VOD experiences.

Mobile Advertising

Mobile-phone marketing in 2007 is where Internet advertising was in 1996—it is about to take off. There are already more mobile phones in use worldwide than TVs and computers combined. Using location tracking, advertisers can send you a message with a coupon for a discount at a theme park as you approach its location. Asian markets already have "location aware" mobile-phone campaigns (Singapore) and phone-click payments via mobile phone for services (Japan).

And users downloading songs from peer-to-peer file-sharing services now receive pop-ups asking users to look at an ad in return for a free and legal copy of the music. Intent MediaWorks has figured out how to embed pop-ups in music and video files unobtrusively and claims that 60 percent of users are willing to endure the ads. In February 2007, Intent's digital media files were downloaded 1.7 million times, and they expect at least 10 million by December. According to Jun Group ad firm principal Mitchell Reichgut, "If you do something on peer-to-peer and do it well, it's marketing on steroids."[4]

Primetime Downloads

Futurists are warning that the explosion of distribution channels, which create practically unlimited viewing options, means the end of mass entertainment. Yet in 2006, News Corp. spent about $4.5 billion on the production and marketing of movies and TV shows, which seems to have paid off in operating profit for Fox and Warner Brothers, the biggest and best-run of the six major Hollywood studios.[5] In 2006, Fox made 30 percent of its primetime schedule available for downloads on a variety of platforms, from iTunes to fox.com to program sites such as americanidol.com to MySpace. It also produces one-minute "mobisodes" for cell phone users in Europe and Asia.

According to Fox chairman Tom Rothman, so called middle movies that appeal to everybody are getting harder to market, but movies that are either for a passionately devoted smaller audience or those that can be made into events for a larger audience are going to be of greater value through all forms of distribution. *Wired* editor Chris Anderson reported in his book *The Long Tail* that the future of entertainment is in the millions of niche markets at the shallow end of the bitstream.[6]

Fox's live television, described as user-generated content, helped draw a crowd to the studio and huge audiences who tuned in from home—about 30 million each week—to watch *American Idol*. Actually, *Idol* content is professionally produced so that every detail, from its aspirational appeal to intimate camera work that captures emotion to the way viewers get to vote for a stake in the outcome, works. *Idol* was a monster hit, even though it competed with programs on 300 other channels, Internet content, and every other way people spend their time. Now the cultural phenomenon, super-charged by a world of niches, is tracked by local newspapers, debated by bloggers, and showcased on iTune charts. Reminiscent of the 1950s gather-the-family-on-the-couch programs, *Idol* show no signs of going away.

Challenging Hollywood

Steve Jobs's movie downloads for PC, TV, or iPod-type devices sold for $9.99 to $14.99 in 2006, using a competitive squeeze strategy that made Hollywood nervous about future DVD sales. A device slated for release in 2007 will stream movies wirelessly from the PC in the den to the TV in the living room.

▬▬ Paid for By . . .

As audiences increasingly adopt interactive technology, they may use that power to turn away from advertising. The question then becomes, Will interactive audiences be enraged or engaged by advertisers? Spammers who persist on intruding into peoples'

▮▮▮▮▮▮▮▮▮▮ **BOX PS-1** ▮▮▮▮▮▮▮▮▮▮

Focus on Thought Leaders

HOW CONNECTIVITY IS CHANGING THE PLANET

Five corporate experts brainstormed on the impact of technology for *Fortune Magazine*. What follows is a summary of their discussions.

According to **Thomas Malone,** director of the Center for Collective Intelligence at MIT, organizational employees will rely on the Internet for information to make their own decisions instead of simply following orders from above. Such a "collective intelligence" lets people organize to solve problems. Google uses computational power; Wikipedia has produced the world's biggest encyclopedias in less than five years with entries written by people who are not getting paid; InnoCenter (Eli Lilly spin-off) uses the world as an R&D lab, harnessing scientists everywhere to solve problems without knowing in advance who will work on what.

MySpace CEO Chris DeWolfe thinks that advancements in mobile technology will have the biggest effect on individual empowerment because users get real-time representation of their lifestyles with unlimited mobile access.

Hung Huang, CEO of China Interactive Media Group, advocates using blogs because they allow people to group together by tastes and the way they think. She targets urban Chinese who have embraced this way of self-expression.

Multitasking is Martin Sorrell's approach to media consumption. As CEO of WPP Group, Sorrell says traditional media are yielding to individually created media where people create their own content on a variety of gadgets while simultaneously receiving content created by others.

Director of Microsoft's Live Labs, Gary Flake says that using community as an aggregate form of intelligence has significantly impacted the music industry. For example, any garage band can upload their MP3s to the web and become available to the world. And after uploading and mixing their play lists, community members make recommendations for each other that drive the industry.

SOURCE: *Fortune Magazine,* July 10, 2006, p. 103.

daily lives enrage users. What this means for entertainment marketing is unfriendliness toward viral marketing, and this sentiment applies across a range of technologies, including electronic games, cell phones, and more. Notably, digital-video recorders let people skip TV commercials, but audiences also take advantage of interactive technology to engage with commercial messages—as in the case of the popular BMW Films Web site. In reality, audiences will evade intrusive advertising and welcome interaction with friendly suppliers of entertainment services. But uncertainties remain about what attitudes toward advertising will prevail among future audiences and what steps the entertainment industry must take to engage audiences.

Advertising Metamorphosis

Ad agencies are making significant structural changes in an effort to incorporate a "holistic" approach to media choices for ad campaigns. Publicis USA developed a new position titled "Chief Holistic Officer," and it is her role to get agency staffers to think less about TV-centric campaigns and to devise campaigns that use whatever media suits the client's target audience. Other firms are making similar moves. For example, WPP Group's Ogilvy & Mather has combined the P&L statements of its ad agency with its marketing services unit, which includes direct marketing, PR, and in-store advertising.

According to discussions at the 2005 Association of National Advertisers conference,[7] the future of advertising is about customer engagement. Two hallmarks of the new marketing formula are collaboration and efficient production. Part of that equation must be mobility, personalization, control, and entertainment. Successful marketing will result from the brand being able to travel where the consumer is moving—especially as the average 18- to 24-year-old is typically managing 4.3 platforms simultaneously.

Media Buying Blues

Advertisers continue to shift money away from television and onto the Internet. Brad Adgate, research director for Horizon Media, says advertisers will have much longer upfront time to buy spots on shows. Advertisers are pushing to replace glitzy up-fronts with an online auction where they can bid for ad slots the same way eBay users compete for used golf clubs.

For the fall '06 season, networks held the first digital upfront, aggressively pushing ads for their newly developed broadband programming, cellular phone shows, and downloading services. CBS packaged its 30-second spots with ads on innertube, its broadband video site, and Fox cross-sold ads on shows such as *24* with promos on MySpace; such mixed buys prolong negotiations with media buyers. eMarketer predicts spending on broadband video advertising will climb to $640 million in 2007.[8] In the meantime, networks need to come up with more hit shows on the air and in digital arenas to lure advertisers for the seasons to come.

More Venues, Higher Costs

Compensation for actors in commercials is another area in need of an overhaul. The system's traditional methods paid actors a fee every time the ad airs. Because of cell-phone and iPod broadcasts, that system would render advertising prohibitively expensive, say the advertising industry. The Screen Actors Guild (SAG) doesn't agree. What they do agree on is the notion that an increasingly complicated media landscape needs to be addressed. Ad firms, hoping for a major overhaul, are working to keep talent fees down by using fewer actors in commercial spots. Exhibit PS.1 offers some projections that both sides of the issue must consider.

YouTube's Bet on Ad Revenue

As a vast repository of video taken without permission from television shows and movies constructed from commercial music and imagery, YouTube provides a daily fix of odd and interesting clips from White House speeches to frat house pranks. It also attracts mainstream advertisers such as Warner Music that might be a model for dealings

▪ ▪ ▪ **EXHIBIT PS.1** Statistics

PODCAST PROJECTIONS

Year	Podcasting Audiences	Ad Spending
2006	11.4 million audience members	$80 million
2010	56.8 million audience members	$300 million

MOBILE TV VIEWERS in 2006

Mobile subscribers watching video		$3 million
Watching broadcast TV		$300 million

MOBILE ADVERTISING AND MARKETING SPENDING PROJECTIONS

2006	$140 million
2009	$260 million

Source: Suzanne Vranica for *The Wall Street Journal,* April 17, 2006.

with Hollywood and record companies. A 2006 agreement has YouTube technology identifying Warner music used in uploaded videos that will allow sharing in its advertising revenue from copyrighted material.[9]

Accused of being a Napster-like pirate, YouTube now offers studios a share of ad revenues yielded from graphical banner and text ads. NBC has bought advertising and uploaded clips promoting shows for its upcoming season, but acknowledges that ad revenues from YouTube are low. Still, claiming the most content and largest audiences, YouTube expects many more entertainment advertisers to jump on board in the future. Google purchased YouTube in late 2006—we will see what happens.

Online Marketing

On the Internet, advertisers are finding more ways to intertwine marketing messages with entertainment. Orbitz online travel agency entices Web surfers by embedding ads in online pop-ups built around simple interactive sports-themed games such as "Sink the Putt." LiveVault (a mass data-recovery provider) produced and released a short comic online video about backing up data starring John Cleese (Monty Python). The $500,000 promotion was deemed a "bargain for a message that ended up all over the Internet," according the LiveVault CEO Bob Cramer.

A San Francisco company (pulse3d.com) has developed software that turns any image of a person or animal into a semi-animated talking head, complete with moving lips and a voice that delivers any lines typed in by a user. The resulting blabby cyber-creature can be e-mailed to friends. Royal Caribbean has made these online characters the centerpieces of successful Internet campaigns. One-third of the cruise line's 2006 visitors came because of the characters, according to the president of Celebrity Cruises Line.

━━━ ▪▪▪▪▪▪▪▪▪▪ **BOX PS-2** ▪▪▪▪▪▪▪▪▪▪ ━━━

Focus on the Future

NICHE CABLE BRANDS WIN

In the past decade, networks used on-screen logos to brand their stations. During the next decade, brands will become more important, not less, according to Rainbow Media chief Josh Sapan. The CEO's success with IFC (independent films), Fuse (music), and WE (women's entertainment) is testimony to the monumental importance of intangible branding. And, it's even more important as video transformation unfolds. With constraints on capacity disappearing, screens of various sizes proliferating, and linear programming being replaced by on-demand delivery, "we're going to see a reformation of the cable universe," said Sapan in a May 2006 interview published in *Business 2.0* magazine.

Earning brand allegiance is key in a time of technological advances, says Sapan. Trying to replicate the "nativeness" of Internet brands, such as eBay, that were born on the Web, Rainbow's credo is: brands rule, niches rock, and new formats require new forms of programming. Examples of the new programming Rainbow developed for on-demand and IID include four innovative genres:

Innovation	Format	Viewers
IFC in Theaters	On-demand service showing movies still playing on the big screen	11 million
SportSchool	Sports instructional videos using professional athletes	18 million
Mag Rack	Instructional content, cars to guitars to videogames and relationships	10 million
Vroom HD Networks	Specialty HD programs ranging from anime to fashion	600,000 subscribers

Positioned to deal with the advent of Internet TV, Sapan is ready to serve user-generated video niches on the Web. Niche (narrowcasting) program providers such as Rainbow Media may prove to be complementary, not competitive, thus ushering in the long-predicted niche-ification of TV.

SOURCE: John Heilmann, *Business 2.0*, May 2006.

Below are four companies bringing new-wave advertising techniques to America.

Company	Innovation
Claria.com	Behavioral targeting service tracks online habits of Web surfers and hits them with relevant advertising.
Enpocket.com	Sends ad messages, coupons, and branded video files to mobile phones, often tracking the phone's location.
Zebraimaging.com	Produces large promotional holograms of 3-D images.
Massiveincorporated.com	Inserts ads via an online connection into video games while they are being played.[10]

Crystal Balling

The top 10 online advertising and interactive marketing predictions include:

- Consumer-generated media will become increasingly attractive to advertisers

- Advertisers will continue shifting traditional ad spending to the Web due to an increase in Internet use and better targeting/reporting capabilities

- Advertisers, cable providers, and interactive marketing experts will collaborate to address "the TiVo effect" (ad skipping)

- Brand advertisers will drive the next wave of growth for the paid search market; best practices in localized mobile marketing will be perfected overseas

- Online advertisers will employ holistic targeting methods to deliver better results and reduce reliance on high-profile, high-CPM ad buys

- Technology and better data access will transform online advertising success to a formulaic equation

- Japan will be the next frontier for paid search and interactive marketing

- Mobile carriers will adopt new ad models to boost revenue beyond usage

- Performance-based pricing models will demonstrate the true value of search engine marketing as a lead-generation channel

▮▮▮▮ Profits for a Nonprofit

With dynamics similar to those of PBS, National Public Radio has become a trendsetter by embracing new technology. That was certainly the case in the 1990s, when it began to archive and provide streaming-audio Web casts of some of its programming, such as *All Things Considered.* And, that has also been the case with the network's embrace of high-definition radio. In 2005, NPR was a trendsetter in the podcasting realm—not because it provided downloadable MP3 files, but because it developed a proven way to make money with them.

NPR: The 800-Pound Podcaster[11]

According to VP Ken Stern, NPR has an existing sponsorship model on-air that's been transported to the podcasting world. Ten-second "Gateway" sponsorships and interior sponsorships within the podcasts are NPR's standard, on-air model. This model features one minute and 30 seconds of on-air sponsorships per hour.

Reach and frequency of the podcasts are aggregated into the podcast listenership, offering sponsors some real bulk in what is an audience with a great deal of disposable income. That tactic of aggregating podcast listeners has not escaped the notice of commercial broadcasters. Infinity Broadcasting, for example, now has its nine all-news AMs supplemented with individual podcast pages, and each station offers a selection of downloadable files. Podcast pioneer Adam Curry's own fledgling venture, PodShow, is attempting to aggregate podcast listeners, too. PodShow recently secured some venture-capital financing.

Ultimately, though, the reality is that NPR's brand presence on the Web is formidable when compared with the presence of single commercial radio stations—even one as important as Infinity news WINS-AM (1010 WINS) New York. According to Nielsen//NetRatings, WINS generated 5.6 million Web page views during September 2006.

That number represents the overall total for page views; it does not break out unique visitors or provide any other specific data.

By comparison, NPR's own Web site generated nearly seven times that total—20.3 million Web page views—during the same month, with help from its member stations. As of October 2005, 52 separate stations and networks provided a total of 174 different podcasts, all available at NPR's Web site. Bolstered by new growth, NPR has developed strong online sales activity, quadrupling revenues from online in 2006, which includes podcasting and all the other aspects of NPR's Internet presence.

An important aspect of the organizing process is culling content from the enormous number of individual podcasts that are available globally. In the commercial world, Infinity started this winnowing process with its own "KYOURadio," the all-podcast KYCY San Francisco. The AM now has the beginnings of a program grid, with some dayparts filled with recurring, weekly podcast shows. Stern says he expects NPR to start curating its own Web site podcasts and to allow listeners to comment on the content in some fashion.

▮▮▮ Movie Mapping

Drawn by China's fast-growing economy, inexpensive production sites, and popular martial arts and feature films, Western studios are stepping up their presence and hope to turn China into a major production base. American studios are investing more than $150 in China's burgeoning film industry.[12]

Homesteading, Asian Style

Disney Pictures is considering a live-action martial-arts remake of *Snow White* to be shot in China and replace the dwarves with Shaolin monks. The Chinese director and choreographer who worked on the *Kill Bill* series, *Kung Fu Hustle*, and the *Matrix* movies will participate. Sony's Columbia Tristar Pictures is producing and financing feature films in China, and Time-Warner's Warner Brothers studio formed joint ventures to make films in China. Merchant Ivory Productions filmed *The White Countess*, set in 1930s Shanghai and starring Ralph Fiennes, in Shanghai in 2004. Warner Brothers formed a partnership with the state-owned China Film Group of Beijing to coproduce mostly Chinese language movies, which are exempt from the country's quota of 20 foreign films a year. Hollywood studios expect to produce a mix of Chinese and English-language films in the next five years.

Time-Warner is also putting money into more than 70 cinemas around China in preparation for a potential theater-going boom. Wealthier citizens in Beijing, Guangzhou, and Shanghai are already avid moviegoers. Hollywood is also tapping into China's growing television, Internet, gaming, and mobile phones. Some of the most telling signs of the movie world's interest in China were the appearance of a Chinese language version of *Variety* magazine and the opening of a new Beijing bureau of *The Hollywood Reporter*.

▮▮▮ Media Makeover

The way people consume media has changed, but the way media companies make money has not. However, their traditional mass audiences are being replaced by niche audiences, and competition from content creators is coming from the audience themselves. Meaning, content is no longer king—the audience is. Erick Schonfeld, a writer for *Business 2.0,* came up with ways to fix the ailing media empire conglomerates. Here are five problems media companies have today and Schonfeld's solutions for them.[13]

> **Problem 1:** Distribution channels are proliferating, and the cost to deliver media to homes is plummeting, making capital-hungry distribution assets less important strategically.
>
> **Solution 1:** *Dump distribution.*
>
> Companies are unable to continue controlling both content and distribution because high-speed Internet, video-on-demand, TiVo, video iPods, and 3G cell phones are usurping control. By dumping capital-hungry distribution businesses, media companies can focus on pure content.
>
> **Problem 2:** Media companies are organized around their product lines (books, magazines, movies, Web sites) instead of their audience segments.
>
> **Solution 2:** *Structure the company around customers, not products.*
>
> Once distribution goes, the real work begins. Instead of selling products one at a time, companies should restructure themselves into businesses that try to meet the needs of specific target audiences—retiree news junkies, teen sports fans, suburban home decorators—across all forms of media.
>
> **Problem 3:** Blockbusters are becoming more expensive to produce, while drawing smaller audiences as media consumption continues to fragment.
>
> **Solution 3:** *Create nichebusters instead of blockbusters.*
>
> Once the businesses are organized around audience niches, creating blockbusters becomes less necessary. Media business that focus narrow audiences will naturally give rise to the more cost-effective "nichebuster," which is a hit with people in a target audience.
>
> **Problem 4:** As people spend more time creating their own digital media—on blogs, in podcasts, or simply sharing photos and Web links—it is becoming difficult to compete for their attention.
>
> **Solution 4:** *Let the audience play with content.*
>
> Big media execs must come to grips with the fact that the audience is now able to entertain itself. Increasingly, content alone will have less value than what people can do with it. Making content available in spliceable chunks will encourage consumers to do with it what they will. By understanding how people come together in self-defining groups around reconstituted forms of content, companies can then target those new niches with other media and ads.
>
> **Problem 5:** Once the audience gets ahold of the content and reuses it, companies cannot charge for it the way they used to.
>
> **Solution 5:** *Become a content rebuilder.*
>
> Companies cannot simply let consumers loose in their archives; instead, they must cane all the newly atomized content and rebundle it in ways that would be difficult for audiences to do on their own. The best providers attract the most attention, and in the media world the most attention will attract the most ad dollars and the most opportunities to upsell more content.

What should you make of this scenario? Get into a career that involves researching audience behaviors or rebuilding content for niche audiences.

▮▮▮ Blogcasting

We are fast becoming an "age of peer production."[14] Using democratized tools like blogging and video-sharing, we are an aggregate, creating a distributed labor force. What we cannot forecast, others can. From Hollywood to Wall Street, Blogs provide current updates and trends of the industries they serve. They give voice to millions. Here are a few we recommend.[15]

adrants.com—One of the best ways to keep up on Madison Avenue's ups and downs is with this blog published by a former ad agency employee.

slashdot.com—Excellent blog for technical issues and the social and political trends surrounding them.

lefsetz.com—Former artist-management executive Bob Lefsetz posts his opinions on everything to do with the music business.

mediabistro.com/tvnewser—Focused on TV news, the blog presents snippets from top stories of the day and is constantly updated with items ranging from major network decisions to gossip about behind-the-scenes fighting at morning news shows.

broadwaystars.com—Filled with an exhaustive list of daily theater news, the site also contains links to various discussion boards.

defamer.com—Compiles Hollywood entertainment news and adds a heavy dose of snarky opinions.

paidcontent.org—This blog tracks the latest developments from a range of businesses interested in delivering entertainment, news, and other services to consumers in new ways (cell phones, for example).

▮▮▮ Death of the Hit[16]

According to Chris Anderson of *Wired* (July 2006) magazine, "The era of blockbusters is over, the niche is king, and the entertainment industry will never be the same." A hit-driven mindset prevails in our national culture. Fixated on star power, we follow the absurd lives of A-listers with attention that exceeds our interest in their actual work. Americans see the world through a hit-colored lens. Signs of the hit's death are easily recognized, they include:

Decline of Rock Radio

Now at a 12-year low, listening to the radio is out of favor, and rock radio is among the formats suffering the most. Why? Competition. A plethora of FM stations fragmented the market and depressed the economics of incumbents. Syndicated radio, cell phone music, and iPods have rendered FM obsolete.

Movie Malady

In 2006, box office take fell six percent, and the average top 25 blockbusters in any given year in this decade have accounted for five percent less of the total box office gross than in the 1990s, even as they have cost 57 percent more to make.

Tumbling TV Ratings

As viewers scatter to cable channels, rating continue to fall; cable channels have now surpassed the networks in total viewership. Even TV mega-events have lost their allure. The 2005 World Series had its worst ratings of all time, 30 percent lower than the previous year. NBA playoffs were down 43 percent from the previous year for record lows. And the 2006 Winter Olympics had the lowest Olympic's ratings in 38 years.

Other Media Tales of Woe

The print industry is really in trouble. Only half of Americans read a daily newspaper, and in spite of expanding titles, magazine newsstand sales are at their lowest level since 1970.

Internet Unraveling

The Internet has changed the way we consume entertainment. Today's techno-savvy audiences are turning to distribution media that don't favor hits alone—we are abandoning the tyranny of the top and becoming a niche nation. The mass market is yielding to a million minimarkets. Hits have lost their monopoly, and they must compete with an infinite number of niche offerings. Read the entire story on the death of the hit in Chris Anderson's *The Long Tall: Why the Future of Business Is Selling Less of More* (Hyperion Press, 2006).

▖▗▘ Wagering Goes Mobile[17]

In March 2006 after months of legal deliberations, political maneuvering, and public hearings, the Nevada Gaming Control Board cleared the way for business to propose ways in which establishments can offer wireless gaming. Beginning in 2007, the state gambling board began conducting field tests of the devices used in casinos to become wireless.

Industry Changes

Mobile gambling has the potential to radically change how casinos do business by allowing players to free themselves from tables and slots to multitask while they wager. Wireless function would allow betters to wager on a variety of games at once while eating or watching a show elsewhere.

Here is how it is supposed to work: A gambler turns in a credit card to a cashier, who then provides a hand-held wireless device. The amount of money wagered is charged against the card, and winnings are collected when the device is returned.

R&D efforts by Cantor G&W have created Java-based software that can be used on virtually any Wi-Fi-enabled device. A leading online bookmaker in Britain, Cantor isn't the only major player developing software and devices. Shufflemaster entered into a partnership with Sony Wireless to create a service called Casino on Demand. Shufflemaster's marketing director said the company will offer table, slot, and sports services on their wireless platform so customers will be able to watch sports in real time on their devices and wager on them as well.

▪▪▪▪▪▪▪▪▪▪ BOX PS-3 ▪▪▪▪▪▪▪▪▪▪

Focus on Up-and-Comers

PEOPLE TO WATCH

Patricia Russo, CEO, Lucent Technologies

Already one of the most powerful women in corporate America, Russo is extending her powerful reach into Europe. Lucent and French telecom equipment giant Alcatel are planning to merge and become a next-generation telecom equipment powerhouse that will provide the cutting-edge gear needed to roll out advanced broadband services. And with sales of $25 billion and 88,000 employees, they will be the company to beat.

Chad Hurley & Steven Chen, Cofounders, YouTube

On track to becoming the Napster of online video, the YouTube site (founded in 2005) attracts 6 million users a day who watch, post, and comment on a selection of 40 million short videoclips—and the company is still in its first year of doing business. This pair of entrepreneurs made it easy to post, play from, and search through a vast library of clips, many created by do-it-yourself film makers. Their partnership with NBC in 2006 established a viral model that changed the video distribution game forever.

Jack Ma, CEO Alibaba.com

The most powerful Internet executive in China, Ma heads China's biggest company, alibaba.com, as well as Tobaco.com, an auction site that draws a 67 percent market share and left eBay in the dust in 2006. Ma controls Yahoo's Chinese portal and has launched a Chinese search engine to go head-to-head with Google. With 111 million Internet users, China is second only to the U.S. and it is still in its infancy. Watch out for this guy.

Emerging Global Middle Class

In the next decade, more than 800 million people in China, India, Russia, and Brazil will qualify as middle class, earning more than $3,000 per year, according to Goldman Sachs. These ambitious, well-educated workers represent both a threat to and an opportunity for corporate America. Global competition is bringing brutal cost pressure to bear on U.S. products for this consumer group that has more than $1 trillion a year to spend.

You!

You, or rather consumers as creators, continually create and filter new forms of content. You do it on Web sites, via podcasts, and SDMS polling, and on millions of self-published blogs. In every case, you have become an integral part of the action as a member of the aggregated, interactive, self-organizing, auto-entertaining audience. Even advertisers have entered the You Revolution, incorporating your ideas into their ad slogans and new products. You constructed open-source and are its customer and its caretaker. And somewhere out there, you are building Web 3.0. Whatever that is, one thing is for certain: it will matter.

SOURCE: "The 50 Who Matter Now," *Business 2.0*, July 2006.

▪▪▪▪▪▪▪▪▪

Risky Business

Some of the many problems associated with mobile gambling are potential hacking and security breaches, and underage gamblers who obtain devices from older players. Identification systems have been proposed to the Gambling Control Board, which is leaning toward a biometric scanner that can read the user's thumbprint. Another potential ID system uses gambling behavior to ensure that the same player is placing different bets.

This new element in gaming technology may revolutionize the way people play as well as the way casinos market. And, it is only a step away.

▮▮▮ Impact of Film Piracy

A report released in 2006 from the Institute for Policy Innovations in Texas found that motion-picture piracy hurts the industry and results in the loss of tens of thousands of jobs outside the industry and costs billions of dollars in lost wages, lost tax revenue, and diminished overall economic output. Revenues movies companies would have earned if pirated products had not been available amounted to a loss of $6.1 billion with domino effects for many other industries.[18]

How can piracy be contained in the upcoming decade of increased Internet access? This and other piracy problems will dominate the industry for years to come.

▮▮▮ Where Else to Look for Trends

Go online to these sites to update your understanding of what is new.

- *Insidebrandedentertainment.com*—best of brand promotion
- *Redherring.com*—the business of technology today
- *Siliconvalley.com*—hot topics in technology
- *TZM.com*—what is hot in show biz

What do you think?

These are but a few of the forecasts provided by a variety of interested parties from media, advertising, and entertainment marketing sources.

1. After reading these forecasts, what additions can you make?
2. Which items have become non-issues?
3. Which items have become realities?

Stand by—the best is yet to come!

NOTES ▮▮▮▮▮▮▮

1. Oliver Ryan, *Fortune,* Dec. 2005.
2. Peter Lewis, *Fortune,* Dec. 2005.
3. Michal Lev-Ram, *Business 2.0,* April 2007, p. 34.
4. Michael Myser, *Business 2.0*, April 2007, p. 30.
5. Marc Gunther, *Fortune,* May 16, 2006.
6. *Ibid.*
7. Teressa Lezzi, *Creativity,* Nov. 2005, p. 31.
8. Devon Leonard, *Fortune,* May 29, 2006.
9. Saul Hansell for the *New York Times,* Sept. 30, 2006, B1.
10. David Freedman, "The Future of Advertising Is Here," *Mass Media 07/08* (Dubuque, IA: McGraw-Hill Contemporary Learning Series, 2008), p. 171.

11. Tony Sanders, *Radio Monitor,* Oct. 28, 2005.
12. David Barboza, *New York Times,* July 4, 2005.
13. *Business 2.0,* "What Works," April 2006.
14. Chris Anderson, "Six Trends Driving the Global Economy, *Wired Magazine,* July 2006, p. 132.
15. "*Wall Street Journal's* Guide to Blogs Insiders Read to Stay Current," January 2006.
16. Chris Anderson, "The Rise and Fall of the Hit," *Wired Magazine,* July 2006, p. 127.
17. Marc Weingarten, *New York Times,* May 3, 2006.
18. Steven McElroy, *New York Times,* Sept. 30, 2006, A16.

Glossary

Actual audience   the ambiguous and highly contestable component of the audience product that is subject to questionable measurement sources.

Addressable media   serve as communication vehicles for offers to consumers by e-mail; used to develop a more intimate relationship between entertainment providers and audiences.

Advergaming   an Internet game developed that encourages consumers to engage in a branded experience by enabling them to spend time voluntarily with an ad.

Advertising   any paid form of media placement promoting a brand or product with a visible sponsor.

Aesthetics   appearance, design, and visual appeal.

Affective advertising   marketing message based on an emotional appeal, often using humor.

AIDA model   stands for *a*ttention, *i*nterest, *d*esire, and *a*ction; used to develop advertising appeals and messages.

Alignment fever   advertising agencies lining up their brands with just a few international agencies to consolidate the global industry.

Amusement   diversions such as games and the satisfaction derived from playing games.

Applied research   makes use of existing knowledge to find solutions to particular problems.

Attraction   consists of a tourist, a site to be viewed, and a marker or image that makes the site significant; historic sites, amusement parks, and natural spectacles such as Niagara Falls.

Audience aggregates   the most important means of audience segmentation to use for developing objectives and creating messages is by audience aggregates; expressed in terms of usage or visitations as: current audience members, non- or new audience members, and users of competitive genres.

Audience analysis   based on attendance and/or demographic breakdown of audience composition.

Audience-based messages   promotional messages developed to inform, persuade, or remind all audience aggregates based on their action or behavior objectives.

Audience expectations   standards or references brought to an experience from marketing, advertising and promotion, or word-of-mouth.

Audience perceptions   subjective assessments of the actual experience.

Audience product   predicted, measured, and actual audience delivered to advertisers in exchange for advertising dollars.

Audience value   the audience's evaluation of their experience as weighed against the ticket price or investment, and compared to other entertainment options.

Blogs   Internet commentary (from "Web logs") that allows audiences to communicate and to connect in ways that both inform and entertain.

Brand extension   taking the brand to another category.

Brand fashion curve   migrates a destination through stages of being fashionable or being famous, then familiar, and finally becoming fatigued.

Branded entertainment embeds brands and products in the contents of movies, TV shows, online, on cell phones, and in video games; is increasingly important to marketers as they seek alternatives to commercials and other traditional forms of advertising.

Branding a way to identify, guarantee, structure, and stabilize an entertainment property, entity, or company.

Broadsheets newspapers with full-sized pages, such as the *New York Times*.

Business-to-business advertising and promotion delivered from one business to another in trade publications.

Casinos legalized establishments where commercial gambling operators make their profits by regularly occupying advantage positions against players.

Cause marketing campaigns IMC campaigns promoting a political or health-related cause.

Celebrities people who are exposed by the media or who become well known through their outstanding accomplishments.

Celebrity a commodity traded by the promotions, publicity, and media industries that produces interest beyond a person's public role.

Celebrity endorsement marketing strategy that associates stars and celebrities with a particular product; highly remunerative for the endorser.

Cognitive dissonance a theory that involves post-decision regret about having made the wrong purchase choice.

Cohort analysis understanding an age cohort by examining the significant events that occurred during that cohort's lifespan.

Communication objectives must be measurable, time sensitive, target audience directed, and behavior specific. Measurable determinants of communication objectives are: category need, awareness, attitude, and purchase intention.

Competitive pricing strategy based on the going-rate or pricing that imitates that of similar venues or performances.

Convenience of access how easily audience members may access a theme park or entertainment venue, access hotel availability, and enjoy reservation simplicity.

Convergence a dynamic that is transforming the way in which media, music, and advertising industries merge to reach their markets; also called Madison and Vine.

Creative class people in science, engineering, architecture, education, arts, music, and entertainment, whose economic function is to create new ideas, new technology, and/or new creative content.

Critical incident techniques (CIT) a technique where end users are asked to identify specific incidents that they experienced personally and that had an important effect on the final outcome of an interactive experience.

Consumer-based brand equity model (CBBE) a method of evaluating a brand's equity based on consumer perceptions.

Customer orbit a Disney customer experience model that uses a progression scenario to improve visitor experiences and to identify opportunities for repurchase.

Daypart advertising rates based on the time of day in which the radio or television spot will appear (e.g., morning drive time and prime time).

Descriptive research research conducted to find answers to audience-related questions; involves direct observation, what can be seen "on site" while the action is happening; meeting and talking with audience members as they experience all forms of entertainment.

Destination the total experience of a place that encompasses all types of goods and services.

Diffused audiences people involved in everyday events who come to see themselves as performers as well as observers.

Direct response advertising a connection made between the marketer and the audience, bypassing sales reps and retail outlets; consumer responses are usually made by phone or Internet.

Discriminatory pricing occurs when an organization sells a performance at two or more prices that do not reflect a proportional difference in cost; goes a long way toward maximizing audience size and revenue.

Display ads newspaper advertising sold by column inch ($2'' \times$ number of columns); the standard advertising unit (SAU) for display ads is 40 column inches.

Eco-tourism   an industry that hosts visitors for the purposes of education and natural encounters with the environment.

Entertainment   consumption activities containing significant elements of amusements and diversions; live and mediated performances such as a concert, dance, or drama, including the pleasure received from comedy or magic. Includes four types: passive, educational, escapist, and aesthetic.

Entertainment marketing   techniques and strategies developed to sell tickets to activities that amuse or involve us.

Ethnographic research   used to describe consumer cultures drawing on a variety of qualitative techniques to understand the world through the eyes of those being researched.

Evaluative research   judges the success or effectiveness of programs developed or in place; for example, whether a particular advertising campaign for a performance has been cost-effective.

Evoked set   all the experiential brands and activities known to an individual audience member that are used when making purchase decisions.

Experiential marketing   messages designed to increase a purchase intention for a product or service through the fusion of activity with brands.

Explanatory research   seeks to answer the how and why questions, then to use the answers for predicting future trends.

External lists   promotional rosters obtained from a variety of outside sources, such as exchanges with other organizations whose patrons have matching demographics, performance preferences, or attendance patterns.

Fan intensity ladder   a tool illustrating the hierarchy of flow from one level of celebrity involvement to another; used to develop marketing strategy.

Fashion curve   a popularity cycle.

Fishbein and Rosenberg models   method of attitude measurement used to develop survey instruments.

Four walling   renting a theater in each market when touring a show, and assuming risks involved.

Franchising   paying for the brand's name and concept and running the business independently.

Free associations   projective technique where the respondent relates a thought or object to another object or a brand.

Gambling   games of chance; involve monetary wagers or bets.

Gaming   references both games of competition and games of chance; an entertainment industry.

GAPS model   developed to help experience providers assess their satisfaction strategy; based upon closing the gaps that exist between *audience expectations* and *audience perceptions.*

Global communication strategies   promotional communications produced in a central location, several locations, or a combination depending on audience diversity and corporate policies.

Hedonic needs   involve the pleasing and aesthetic aspects of entertainment experiences.

House lists   current patrons of a specific venue who can be segmented into categories of: single-ticket buyers, first-year subscribers, two-plus year subscribers, lapsed subscribers, group sales buyers, and special plan or event buyers.

Images   mediated constructions resulting from publicity and exposure.

Indies   independent films.

Individualism/Collectivism   a cultural dimension illuminating the degree to which a particular society reinforces individual or collective achievement and interpersonal relationships.

Intangibility   element of experience marketing; experiences of the moment with ever-changing content.

Integrated marketing communications (IMC)   a coordinated campaign that includes and combines the efforts of advertising, public relations, direct selling, Internet, and promotions.

Laddering   a research technique used as an effective method for developing motivational communication messages.

Leisure   time not spent at work in a profession or in an occupation in pursuit of compensation, or in taking care of children and the household.

Licensing   gives manufacturers the right to put your brand on their products.

Line extension   adding a product to a brand's existing product category.

Long-term orientation   a cultural dimension focusing on the degree the society embraces long-term devotion to traditional, forward-thinking values.

"Madison and Vine"   a dynamic that is transforming the way in which media, music, and advertising industries merge to reach their markets; most frequently referred to as convergence.

Mailing list   compilation of current customers or audience members contact information.

Market segmentation   a way to group audiences that adhere to five general categories: psycghographic, geodemographic, demographic and cohort, behavioral, and benefit segments.

Marketing mix   the optimal combination of marketing variables that an enterprise can use to generate the desired level of revenue from its target market.

Masculinity/Femininity   a cultural dimension indicating how much a society reinforces the traditional masculine role model of achievement, control, and power.

Mass audience   an invisible group, because its members are entertained at home or in movie houses.

Measured audience   measures the size and composition of the audience reached to determine how much an advertiser spent to reach a particular size and type of audience.

Mediated entertainment   radio, television, newspaper, magazines, movies, and the Internet; experiences delivered via some form of nonpersonal delivery.

Merchandising   reproducing logos, characters, and symbols related to films and live performances onto articles of clothing and other retail items.

Message strategy   objectives and visual techniques that define advertising goals and how they will be achieved.

Modeling theory   consumers or audience members often model their behavior after an opinion leader, celebrity, or star.

Moguls   people who have risen to power in the entertainment industry through both achievement and acquisition.

Movie trailers   primary marketing tool to promote films; customized for each audience demographic and delivered to audiences in theaters and online.

Operating statement   presents a summary of sales and expenses over a specific period of time and serves as a major tool for analyzing a company's financial performance.

Out-of-home media   promotional messages delivered to audiences and consumers at the location where purchase transactions occur.

Parasocial relationship   imagined connection between a fan and a celebrity or star; intimacy is mediated by TV, movies, and the Internet.

Perceptions   consumer beliefs toward a particular brand.

Perceptual grid   developed to dramatize audience perceptions of the client's brand in relationship to competitive brands.

Perishability   element of experiential marketing; time-bound; experience diminishes in importance as time passes.

Personal branding   identity developed by using text and graphic-based tools.

Personas   brand characterizations based on human traits.

Place advertising   promotional messages delivered in a particular area where a desired audience demographic will interact with the ad.

Play theory   suggests that work deals with reality and production, while play provides self-satisfaction and pleasure.

Plot placement   instances where a brand provides a key role in a movie or television show's story line.

Podcasting   practice of downloading and playing live and recorded video through an iPod or other MP3 player.

Postmodern audiences   members who identify with a *postmodern self,* a concept of identity that is continuously in flux; derived from a notion of postmodernism that is the confluence of past and present, new and old in the context of mass media and advanced technology.

Power distance   a cultural dimension determining the degree of equality between people in the country's society.

Predicted audience   segment most likely to view or addend a show or performance. Difficult to characterize because it is continually changing.

Price   the negotiated value (translated into money) that an audience member is willing to pay for the experiential content provided by the producer, who in turn takes into considerations sales volume and revenue objectives.

Price discrimination   a method of pricing tickets that allows for variations by age, season, economic status, etc.

Product integration   instances when a brand is integrated into a game or mediated performance.

Projective techniques   an explanatory research technique used to uncover a person's innermost thoughts and feelings by allowing them to project their beliefs onto other people or objects.

Promotional pricing   responds to the requirements of a particular audience segment or the need to stimulate demands that fluctuate by season or competition resulting from overcapacity.

Property   content of three types: *media-dependent* content created, sold to a studio, and produced for distribution; *performance content* developed around music, dance, and theater for presentation by bands, quartets, and orchestras or theatrical production companies; *experiential content* occurring in or at attractions, resorts, spas, casinos, theme parks, and travel destinations.

Prosumers   a powerful consumer segment with several definitions: (1) A consumer who is an amateur in a particular field, but who is knowledgeable enough to require equipment that has some professional features ("professional" + "consumer"). (2) A person who helps to design or customize the products they purchase ("producer" + "consumer"). (3) A person who creates goods for their own use and also possibly to sell ("producing" + "consumer"). (4) A person who takes steps to correct difficulties with consumer companies or markets and to anticipate future problems ("proactive" + "consumer").

Public relations   event sponsorship and publicity generated for media placement designed to give credibility to a brand, create favorable brand images, or communicate with a brand's publics.

Pull strategy   a promotional message or incentive sent directly to consumers or audience members by a producer or venue.

Push strategy   a promotional message or incentive aimed at the retailer or ticket wholesaler designed to help get the brand into the hands of consumers or audience members.

Q factor   rating system used to measure how much a performer or celebrity is liked or disliked by the public, and how familiar the public is with a celebrity.

Ratings   measure audience exposure to media for use in assessing audience viewing behavior and for determining advertising rates.

Recreation   activities or experiences carried on within leisure time, either for personal satisfaction or creative enrichment; an entertainment industry.

Rental lists   purchased from commercial sources such as video rental stores, magazine subscribers, mail-order houses, and museums for use in delivering promotional messages.

Return on investment (ROI)   the bottom-line profits generated after expenses are deducted.

Rich media   a form of Internet advertising easily coordinated with its video counterpart; bundles television, film, and the Web for flash animations and streaming video.

Segmentation   dividing a target market into groups based on demographics, psychographics, geographics, brand benefits, media use, and/or brand loyalty.

Selling off   secures performance dates with local promoters who receive a royalty and a profit participation in exchange for mounting the production.

Services   intangible activities customized to the individual request of known clients.

Servicescape   a physical space where audiences come together to enjoy and experience a consumption activity.

Simple audience   an audience group marketed locally through a particular venue or location who attend concerts, plays, festivals, carnivals, sports, and religious events.

Situation analysis   marketplace analysis of internal and external factors; conducted prior to developing a campaign.

Social norm an activity considered appropriate behavior in a particular culture or society.

Sponsorship paid association between a brand and an activity or experience.

Stars a group of people whose institutional power is very limited or nonexistent, but whose doings and way of life arouse a considerable degree of interest.

Star system the institutional hierarchy established to regulate and control the employment and use of all actors; a system of usage by three entities: (1) the film industry that tries to manage audience demands for films; (2) distributors that use stars to sell films to exhibitors in domestic and overseas markets; and (3) exhibitors who own and run theaters showing films that use stars to draw audiences.

Stealth marketing undercover marketing that is a subset of guerrilla marketing (a war or battle strategy) where consumers don't realize they are being marketed to.

Subscription radio permits listeners to select musical genres without commercial breaks, as well as commercial stations in a variety of geographic markets.

Sustainable development a philosophy invoked to maintain a healthy balance between visitors and resources in tourist destinations.

Symbolic capital value associated to a brand based upon its personal or social meaning.

Syndicated services national research conducted to understand the media and audiences and sold to manufacturers and advertising agencies; A. C. Nielson, Harris Interactive, and Simmons are the best-known syndicated services.

Tabloids small newspapers with a sensational focus and include entertainment reviews, features, and biographies.

Taste cultures audience members who are dependent upon entertainment products outcomes of form, style, presentation, or genre that match the lifestyle of an audience segment.

Temporary venues removable or transportable performance locations, such as a circus tent.

Themed environment a space designed to replicate the signs and symbols of a particular era, ethnicity, region, activity, style, or sport.

Theming a strategy that reduces a product to its image and the consumer experience to its symbolic content; used in resorts, restaurants, parks, malls, and venues.

Theoretical research conducted to draw general conclusions about a phenomenon under study.

Theory of reasoned action purports that consumers consciously evaluate the consequences of alternative behaviors then choose the one that will lead to the most favorable consequences.

Tie-ins a way to connect an event or product with another event and/or product, so that both brands benefit from the association.

Tourism business conducted by a host region to attract, entertain, and house visitors.

Tourism categories include *internal tourism* (domestic and inbound), *national tourism* (domestic and outbound), and *international tourism* (inbound and outbound).

Tourism units includes *domestic travel*, where residents visit their own country; *inbound tourism*, when nonresidents travel in a given country; and *outbound tourism*, when residents travel in another country.

Tourist people who travel for pleasure as opposed to business.

Trailer calls research method used to capture information about key service encounters with a customer by asking customers questions immediately after a particular transaction about their satisfaction with the transaction and contact personnel with whom they interacted.

Transnational media corporations (TNMC) nationally based media and entertainment companies with overseas operations in two or more countries.

Travel a trip taken for a specific purpose rather than for pleasure.

Travel cycle plots a tourist's journey; it begins at home with trip planning, then takes travelers out of their homes and onto transportation, and continues with their arrival at a destination, onto transportation back home, and ends with reflections of their trip as derived from souvenirs collected during the journey.

Travel markers souvenirs of local arts and crafts, clothing, miniatures, rocks, treasures, and visual representations collected while traveling.

Triangulation   validates qualitative research through the use of multiple data collection methods, theories, or number of researchers to ensure authenticity.

Uncertainty avoidance   a cultural dimension focusing on a society's level of tolerance for uncertainty and ambiguity in unstructured situations.

Value   the inherent worth of a brand, ideal, or activity to a particular person or group.

Venue   a structure or location that houses an activity or performance.

Video on demand (VOD)   a viewer's ability to choose a particular program or movie.

Viral advertising   a way to distribute commercial messages over the Internet using individual emails to circulate them through a desired audience; spreads like a virus.

Vlog   video log.

Index